Bruce N. Waller

CONSIDER ETHICS
Theory, Readings, and Contemporary Issues

Taken from:

Consider Ethics: Theory, Readings, and Contemporary Issues
by Bruce N. Waller

Custom Publishing

New York   Boston   San Francisco
London   Toronto   Sydney   Tokyo   Singapore   Madrid
Mexico City   Munich   Paris   Cape Town   Hong Kong   Montreal

10 9 8 7 6 V0356 09 10 11 12

2008660027

KW

**Pearson
Custom Publishing**
is a division of

PEARSON

www.pearsonhighered.com

ISBN 10: 0-555-00965-3
ISBN 13: 978-0-555-00965-9

CONTENTS

✦ PREFACE ✦

Consider Ethics: Theory, Readings, and Contemporary Issues is aimed at promoting careful thought about ethics. In the first 14 chapters it covers competing ethical theories and a variety of related ethical issues, including the role of free will and moral responsibility in ethics, the relation of scientific inquiry to ethics, the nature of virtue, the role of both feelings and reason in ethics, the relation between religion and ethics, and the scope of ethics (who qualifies as an ethical actor and who warrants ethical consideration). Though the focus of the book is ethical theory, the issues raised are illustrated and debated through discussions of such practical ethical questions as abortion, euthanasia, scarce medical resources, and justice in warfare in the final chapter. Primary sources support the theoretical discussions at the end of each chapter and frame the debates in the final section of the book.

    Consider Ethics is an open inquiry into intriguing and disputed issues, and readers are invited to consider a variety of perspectives and reach their own judgments. Ethics involves questions that are inherently fascinating, and *Consider Ethics* is a relaxed and conversational book that encourages readers to think more carefully and in greater depth about questions concerning the nature of ethics itself, how ethical principles can be known (if indeed they can be known at all), how ethical systems might be constructed, the nature and existence of free will, and the relation of free will to value questions. These questions obviously are interconnected, and the response to early questions will influence conclusions concerning later issues; and later conclusions may in turn prompt reexamination of earlier views. Drawing out those implications—encouraging readers to think carefully about how their earlier answers are related to later questions—is a major goal of the text.

STRUCTURE AND FEATURES OF THE TEXT

- Fourteen chapters, each followed by related classic readings, cover major ethical theories. Chapter 15, "Current Ethical Debates," presents paired readings in a "pro-con" format, covering six contemporary ethical issues, including the Ethics of War, the Death Penalty, Euthanasia, Just Distribution of Medical Resources, Abortion, and Affirmative Action.
- Shows the connection between ethics and other fields including science and social science, and among ethical theories and issues; compares ethical theories with one another throughout the text. Connects the new material presented with what has gone before, drawing connections between theories, readings, and issues throughout the entire text. The result is that students are encouraged to revisit, re-analyze, and perhaps even revise their opinions.

- Coverage of Free Will and Moral Responsibility and its ethical implication (Chapters 13 and 14) shows their connections to ethics. These chapters offer additional opportunity for students to consider how their views are connected, to consider the implications of various ethical theories for questions about free will, just deserts, and the nature of ethical behavior.
- Thought-provoking exercises at the end of the chapters present stimulating problems and can be adapted for use in class discussions or as short written assignments.
- Selections from primary sources from a variety of influential ethical perspectives— Plato, Aristotle, Hobbes, Hume, Kant, Bentham, Mill, Darwin, and Baier, among others—help students to explore the actual writings of important philosophical figures and gain a sense of their systems and distinctive styles. Readings range from familiar contemporary problems such as euthanasia and environmental ethics to ethical issues in war, the justice of inheritance, and priorities in distributing scarce transplant organs.
- Open and balanced presentation has no bias toward any one philosophical agenda. The author helps students develop and formulate their own judgments about controversial issues.
- Coverage of care ethics.
- Many examples, often humorous ones, illustrate abstract philosophical ideas, facilitate students' understanding, and keep their attention.

ACKNOWLEDGMENTS

I am indebted to many people who helped at every stage of this book. My colleagues in the Department of Philosophy and Religious Studies have been a constant source of ideas, energy, encouragement, and friendship; special thanks to Chris Bache, Walter Carvin, Stephanie Dost-Barnhizer, Brendan Minogue, Mustansir Mir, Gabriel Palmer-Fernandez, Charles Reid, Tom Shipka, Donna Sloan, J-C Smith, Linda "Tess" Tessier, and Victor Wan-Tatah. I am also grateful to many others. Mark Shutes, until his untimely death, was a rich source of information about political ethics as well as about issues in anthropology and politics and pretty much everything else. Nawal Ammar has stimulated and improved my thinking on cultural differences in ethics. John White has frequently given me articles and ideas that proved very helpful. Homer Warren has been a wise guide through the tangles of many difficult contemporary social and ethical debates. Robert Weaver has discussed many of these ideas with me at various times, and has been a very valuable resource in understanding issues in biomedical ethics. Lauren Schroeder has offered fascinating ideas on a wide range of subjects, particularly in the area of environmental ethics. Lia Ruttan has provided very helpful comments on rough drafts, and I have learned a great deal from her concerning ethical systems in other cultures, as well as the ethics of cultural research. Richard Double has been a wonderful source of encouragement, has informed me of much valuable material I should otherwise have missed, and has kindly shared with me his very deep insights into the tangle of questions involving free will and moral responsibility. George Graham has broadened my philosophical outlook on many issues, especially on questions related to abnormal psychology and philosophy of mind. Robert Kane's books and conversations have forced me to think much harder and more carefully about many questions related to free will. Stephen Flora has been a very valuable resource in the area of contemporary behavioral psychology. Fred Alexander has taught me a great deal about ethics, to my joy; and also a great deal about poker, to my sorrow. Jack Raver has been a great stimulus on many contemporary ethical issues, and his unadulterated joy in ethical and social debates both inspires and invigorates. Joan Bevan, who manages our department, is genuinely remarkable: she does a staggering amount of work, and with such joyful efficiency that it looks almost easy. Whatever the problem—from computer malfunctions to dealing with painfully slow permission request responses—Joan invariably fixes it, and the book would *never* have been completed without her help. She is assisted ably and cheerfully by our student worker, Justina Rachella. James Sacco, research assistant in Islamic Studies, is wonderfully wise concerning the fine details of editing.

My editor at Longman Publishing, Priscilla McGeehon, has offered a great variety of very valuable suggestions for improving the text, has been constantly encouraging and appropriately prodding, and has answered all questions and smoothed every rough spot in the bumpy process of finishing a book. Her excellent assistant, Stephanie Ricotta, managed to find a remarkably helpful range of reviewers at every stage of the manuscript development process. Special thanks for the excellent suggestions of the following persons who reviewed the work in progress: Edwin Aiman, University of Houston; Fritz Allhoff, University of California, Santa Barbara; Lisa Bellatoni, Quincy University; Sheryl Breen, St. Olaf College; Jeff Broome, Arapahoe Community College; Stephen R. Brown, University of Oklahoma; Andrei Buckareff, University of Rochester; Maria Carl, Seattle University; John Draeger, Syracuse University; Howard Ducharme, University of Akron; George Griffith, Chadron State College; Maurice Hamington, Lane Community College; Kenneth D. Hines, Penn State Worthington Scranton; Aaron Meskin, Texas Tech University; Chris Meyers, Southern Methodist University; Jeffrey Morgan, University College of the Fraser Valley; Lawrence Nelson, Santa Clara University; Dave Raymond, Northern Maine Technical College; Franklin E. Robinson, Murray State University; Phil Schneider, Coastal Carolina University; Daniel Silber, Florida Southern University; E. Ssekasozi, Lincoln University of Missouri; Les Sutter, International College; Martin Tracey, Benedictine University; John Wadhams, Eastfield College; Stevens F. Wandmacher, University of Michigan-Flint; David Whitford, Claflin University; and Diane Wilkinson, University of South Florida.

My wife, Mary Newell Waller, has not only discussed many of these questions with me, but also provided much help in the area of contemporary clinical psychology. My sons, Russell and Adam, have been a rich source of ideas and comments, a great source of joy and pride, and have often been a sounding board for trying out ideas—the book is much better for their suggestions, including their clear guidance on what sections and exercises did *not* work.

Finally, my students at Youngstown State University have tried out many sections of the book, and working with them over the past fourteen years provided the inspiration for writing this text. My students at Youngstown State are the children of immigrants from every corner of the globe, whose parents often arrived penniless to work in the steel mills. Their parents and grandparents struggled—and some died—to establish and protect the rights of working men and women in this country. Their children, my students, grew up through the hard times of mill closings in the Mahoning Valley. Those students, gathered from the widest range of ethnic backgrounds, now study together and learn from one another in mutual respect and friendship. And those students—frequently the first in their family to attend college—work full-time jobs, care for families (often including children as well as aging parents or grandparents), take substantial course loads, and still approach their studies with energy, enthusiasm, insight, and good cheer. Sometimes they are students who have devoted decades to difficult and dangerous industrial work, lost their jobs and their pensions and their health care, and are standing up and starting over and heading off to college. Their remarkable fortitude, warmth, intelligence, and enthusiasm has been a constant source of inspiration, and it is to the students of Youngstown State University that I dedicate this book.

Bruce N. Waller

CHAPTER 1

ETHICS AND CRITICAL THINKING

This is an invitation to think carefully about the nature of ethics and ethical inquiry. You've no doubt already thought carefully about a good many ethical issues, such as abortion, capital punishment, sexual ethics, affirmative action, animal rights. And we'll be looking at some of those issues, and others besides. But we'll also do something that's not quite so common: we'll be thinking about the nature of ethics itself, how we have knowledge of ethical principles, is knowledge of ethics similar to knowledge of physics, *can* we have knowledge of ethical principles, are ethical principles fixed or changing, are they absolute or circumstantial? These are sometimes called *meta*ethical questions; that is, questions about the nature and concepts of ethics. Thinking carefully about those questions may help in thinking more carefully about such issues as economic justice and abortion and treatment of animals. In any case, it may help us gain a clearer perspective.

Thinking carefully about ethics involves, rather obviously, thinking *carefully*. So it will be useful to start with some consideration of *how* to think carefully and critically and effectively, and how to avoid some common errors. Some people maintain that ethics is *not* based on reasoning, but is instead built on emotions and feelings, or on intuitions. In fact, some maintain that ethics is not a matter of finding truth at all: there are no objectively true ethical principles, and thus there are no true ethical principles to be discovered through reasoning (nor by any other means). Those are interesting positions, and you may ultimately conclude that ethics is *not* based on reasoning. But even if that is your conclusion, it is still useful to start with some considerations about critical thinking, since in order to reach such a conclusion you will have to use careful reasoning. We will examine several people who argue *against* reason-based ethics (and of course several who argue that reason is the foundation of ethics). But all of them give *arguments* for their views, and those arguments must be critically examined.

What's the Question?

Perhaps the first and most crucial step in critical thinking is the most obvious, but also the most neglected: be clear on exactly what is at issue. That is, when examining an argument, think first about *precisely* what the argument is supposed to be proving; get clear on the *conclusion* of the argument. "Ladies and gentlemen of the jury, this was the most vicious crime I have ever come across in all my years as district attorney. It was cruel, callous, heartless, and brutal," the district attorney insists in her argument to the jury. Is the district attorney's argument *relevant?*

That depends. It depends on what *conclusion* she is arguing for. Suppose she is arguing that the defendant is guilty of a brutal murder, but the question at issue is whether the defendant is the guilty party (the defense claims this is a case of mistaken identity). In that case, the district attorney's argument is *irrelevant* to that conclusion. Everyone agrees the crime was awful; the question is whether the defendant did it. (Incidentally, relevance is not determined by whether the claim is true or false, but by whether it *matters* if the claim is true or false. It may be true that the crime was brutal, but it remains irrelevant to the defendant's guilt. And on the other hand, a *false* claim may be relevant: if an unreliable eyewitness *falsely* claims to have seen the defendant commit the murder, that claim will certainly be *relevant* to the question of whether the defendant is guilty. It's *relevant* because *if* it were true it would be strong proof of the defendant's guilt: it's relevant because it *matters* whether it is true or false). Suppose now that the defendant has already been found guilty, and since this is a capital case the trial has moved on to the sentencing phase. In that case, exactly the same argument ("this was a brutal and heartless crime") will be *relevant* to the question of whether the person who did the crime should receive the death penalty. Of course the argument may be *relevant* without being completely convincing; the jury might decide that the crime was indeed brutal, but other mitigating factors (such as the age of the defendant) count more heavily *against* capital punishment.

When an arguer uses an *irrelevant* point in support of a conclusion, we say that the arguer has committed the *fallacy* (or argument error) of *irrelevant reason*. It is sometimes called the *red herring* fallacy. When fox hunters would send the hounds out to chase a fox, and then ride their horses across the fields in pursuit of the fox and hounds, they would eventually tire of the "sport," and wish to go back to the lodge for tea and scones. But the dogs would still be chasing the fox, and thus be difficult to collar. So the handler of the dogs would drag a bag of oily cooked herring (herring turns red and becomes very oily when cooked) across the trail of the fox. When the dogs ran into the smelly oil from the red herring, they would lose the scent of the fox, would mill around aimlessly, and thus be easy to catch. So that's where we get the name for the "red herring fallacy": the fallacy "drags a red herring," drags a distraction, across the trail of the argument, and thus takes listeners off the track. We get so worked up about the red herring of what a brutal murder it was, we forget that the real issue is whether the defendant is guilty.

Red herrings are a common argument trick. When the Bush administration was arguing for an attack on Iraq, they spent a lot of time talking about the importance of fighting terrorism. Of course everyone is legitimately concerned about terrorism, but the real question was not whether we should fight terrorism, but whether Iraq was engaged in terrorism. By dragging the terrorism red herring across the trail of the argument, it was easy to distract people from the more difficult issue, for which proof was very thin: the question of whether Iraq was supporting terrorist activities or providing weapons of mass destruction to terrorists.

So the first step in evaluating arguments is to be clear on *exactly* what's at issue, exactly what the conclusion is. If I'm the defendant in a burglary trial, the *prosecutor* must prove every element of the crime beyond a reasonable doubt. But my *defense* attorney does *not* have to prove that I *didn't* do it; instead, he only needs to show that there is a *reasonable doubt* of my guilt. If you evaluate the defense attorney's arguments as if they were designed to prove innocence, then you will evaluate them badly.

Ad Hominem Fallacy

There are many argument fallacies in addition to the red herring fallacy, but one of the most important in the study of ethics is the *ad hominem* fallacy. An ad hominem argument is an argument "to the person"; that is, an ad hominem argument is an attack on the person. And an ad hominem *fallacy* is an attack on the *source of an argument*. If someone gives an argument, we must evaluate the argument on its own merits, not on the merits of the person giving the argument. Suppose you come into your ethics classroom and discover an argument written on the blackboard; say, an argument against the death penalty. In order to evaluate that argument, you don't need to know anything at all about who wrote the argument there. Suppose you read the argument and decide it is a strong and convincing argument, and then you find it was written by Bill Clinton, the politician you most despise: that would not change the argument. Then you learn that a mistake had been made, and the argument was written by Mother Teresa, one of your moral heroes: that does not change one word of the argument. So if you are evaluating *arguments*, the *source* of the argument is irrelevant. And if you attack the source of the argument in order to discredit the argument, you have committed the *ad hominem fallacy*.

It is especially important to keep that in mind when discussing ethics, because ethics discussions can get intensely personal and downright hostile. If you don't believe me, have a nice discussion of the abortion question with someone who holds a view diametrically opposed to your own. Such "discussions" often generate more heat than light, and one reason is because they often degenerate into ad hominem abuse: the prochoice advocate is branded a "baby killer," and the prolife side is called a "neanderthal." Difficult as it may be to discuss such issues without sliding into fallacious ad hominem arguments, it is essential if there is to be serious ethical inquiry. One way to avoid such abusive arguments is to keep in mind that the character of the arguer is irrelevant to the quality of the argument. When arguing about ethics—or anything else—you can attack *arguments* as vigorously as you wish, but attacking *arguers* is fallacious. To see why, think of an example. Spring break is approaching, and at the end of class I give you an *argument* for why you should not drink and drive: drinking and driving can be easily avoided if you plan in advance, it places others at unfair risk, and the negative consequences for you—if you are in an accident, or get arrested—can be very severe, certainly out of all proportion to any benefits you might derive from drinking and driving. Is that a good argument against drinking and driving? Not a very original one, but it does give some legitimate reasons to avoid drinking and driving. Now suppose later this evening you see me stagger out of the tavern, fumble around for my keys, finally get my car started, and weave away down the street, taking out three side view mirrors and one fender in the process. If you now say, "Well, there goes Bruce, totally plastered, driving merrily away. And just this afternoon he was arguing against drinking and driving. Any argument that sleazy hypocrite makes against drinking and driving must be pure rubbish." That would be an ad hominem *fallacy*. True enough, I'm a sleazy hypocrite who argues for one thing and then does another. But that does not change my *argument*. It's still the same argument, whether I'm a sleazy hypocrite or a paragon of virtue. Suppose you learn that it was my evil twin brother you saw coming out of the tavern and driving away. Would that suddenly rehabilitate my argument? Of course not. It's the very same argument, and it must stand or fall on its own merits, and it doesn't matter whether the arguer is drunk or sober, hypocritical or sincere, vicious or virtuous.

Ad hominem attacks on arguers commit the ad hominem fallacy. But not all ad hominem arguments are fallacious. Some may be perfectly legitimate. Think back to the O.J. Simpson trial: one of the key witnesses for the prosecution was police officer Mark Fuhrman (he was the first officer to arrive at the Simpson residence, and he found the famous glove—

the one that didn't fit when Simpson tried it on). He testified under oath that he never used racial slurs, and that he held no prejudice against Blacks. But he lied. It turned out that the man could hardly open his mouth without spewing out racial hatred (he once said that he would like to round up all African Americans and burn them), and he particularly despised interracial couples (like O.J. and Nicole) and often harassed them. This key prosecution witness was a lying vicious racist. The defense made an *ad hominem* attack on Mark Fuhrman; but it was perfectly legitimate. Mark Fuhrman was giving testimony, not argument, and in order to evaluate his testimony you need to know if he is truthful, unbiased, and objective—or that he was *not*. If Mark Fuhrman were giving *argument* instead of testimony, then his vile character would be irrelevant: you would have to hold your nose and evaluate his arguments on their own merits. If I give *testimony* that I have seen extraterrestrials ("Take my word for it, I saw them with my own eyes, they're here") then you need to know about my drinking habits, my history of drug use, my mental stability, and my reputation for integrity. But if I give an *argument* for the existence of extraterrestrial intelligence ("Think of the billions and billions of stars in our galaxy, and all their planets and moons, and how many opportunities there would be for life to develop in other solar systems") then my character and my habits and my mental state are *irrelevant* to the quality of my argument. So when you are arguing about ethics, you can attack one another's arguments with all the energy and ingenuity you can muster; but to avoid committing the ad hominem fallacy you must resist attacking the arguer.

The Principle of Charity and the Strawman Fallacy

One other principle of critical thinking is especially important in thinking critically about ethics: the *principle of charity*. That is simply the principle of being *charitable* or *generous* toward the positions and arguments we oppose. In other words, you should interpret opposing views and arguments as generously and fairly and honestly as you can. That doesn't mean you can't attack opposing views; by all means, subject them to the closest scrutiny and the fiercest criticism—and be willing to have your own views subjected to the same criticism. After all, that's one of the best ways of separating the wheat from the chaff when we examine ethical issues. But resist the temptation to score cheap points and win false victories by misrepresenting opposing views. When someone distorts or misrepresents a position in order to make it easier to attack, that is called the *strawman* fallacy. It's easier to knock down a strawman than a real man, and it's easier to defeat a distorted version of a position than the real thing. In both cases, it's not much of a victory. Following the principle of charity—always represent opposing views in their strongest and most plausible form—is the best way of avoiding strawman fallacies, and it is also essential if you are to have any chance of convincing your opponents that your own view is more plausible. If you attack and defeat a distorted and inaccurate representation of my position, I am not likely to be convinced that your arguments are effective.

Strawman fallacies are depressingly common in ethical debate. Think again of the abortion controversy. If I am prolife, I may accuse my opponents of believing that it is morally acceptable to kill infants up to age 1. In fact, there *are* a few people who do hold that view. But obviously that is not the view of most prochoice advocates, who favor elective abortion but vigorously oppose infanticide. If I represent my opponents as favoring infanticide of 1-year-old children, then I am attacking a *strawman*. I may win that argument against the strawman position, but I'm not likely to convince those prochoicers whose views I have misrepresented. Likewise, suppose I am prochoice. I then accuse my prolife opponents of wanting to outlaw not only abortion but also all forms of artificial contraception: there would be no birth control pills or condoms. Again, some of the opponents of legal abortion *do* take that view; but it is an extreme view, and certainly not the view of most persons who are prolife. It is a much easier position to attack, and so I may easily defeat this strawman version of the prolife position; but again, such a strawman "victory" is not likely to convince many people.

Consistency

One last point concerning thinking critically about ethics. A key question in examining ethical views is whether they are internally *consistent*, and whether they are consistent with our other beliefs. Suppose I oppose elective abortion but support the death penalty, and you accuse me of being inconsistent in my principles. I will respond that my views are *not* inconsistent: I oppose abortion because it is the taking of an innocent life, but those who are executed are *not* innocent. Or suppose the argument goes the other way: I oppose capital punishment, but support the right to elective abortions, and you accuse me of inconsistency. I will respond that abortion kills a fetus, but a fetus is not a full person; capital punishment is carried out against persons. Or I might say that in the case of the fetus, the mother's right to control of her own body takes precedence, but the imprisoned person considered for execution is not interfering with a woman's control of her own body.

Those may or may not be adequate answers to the charge of inconsistency: that will be a much debated question. However, I cannot simply accept inconsistencies in my ethical views. That is, I cannot legitimately say: okay, so I have views that are in conflict, beliefs that contradict each other; so what? I can't legitimately make that response, because allowing contradictions within my views make it possible to prove *anything*, and thus make careful reasoning impossible. Think about it for a moment. Suppose that you allow me both of these contradictory premises: "The sky is blue," *and* "The sky is not blue." Then I can "prove" anything at all. What follows from "The sky is blue"? Well, it follows that *either* the sky is blue *or* anything you like. (It's true that I am a human; therefore, it is also true that *either* I am a human *or* I am the richest person on Earth, and it is also true that either I am a human *or* Oprah Winfrey is an extraterrestrial, and it is also true that I am a human *or* there is no corn in Iowa.) So it follows that the sky is blue *or* genocide is good. But remember, we also have the contradictory premise: The sky is *not* blue. So let's put them together: Either the sky is blue *or* genocide is good; *and* the sky is not blue. (That's like saying "Either Brendan is in the library or he's at the tavern; and he's not at the library.") It follows that genocide is good. We could use the same reasoning to "prove" that Miami is in Maine, or that the Pacific Ocean does not exist, or *anything else*. If you allow a contradiction, then you can "prove" anything. And that makes accurate reasoning impossible. If your views contain contradictions, you have to deal with those contradictions (either by rejecting one of the conflicting views or by finding a way to reconcile them): you can't just let them fester.

There is a well-known saying by the American transcendentalist philosopher, Ralph Waldo Emerson: "Consistency is the hobgoblin of little minds." People sometimes use that slogan to defend sloppy thinking, to defend thinking that includes contradictions and does not insist on consistency. But that's not what Emerson meant. Emerson knew the danger of internal contradictions. What he meant was simply that it is alright for your ideas and beliefs to *change*. Beliefs that you now hold don't have to be held forever: it's *okay* to change your mind. Maybe some of your beliefs, perhaps even some of your ethical beliefs, cannot survive careful scrutiny. If so, perhaps you should discard them and replace them with new ones. As Emerson suggested, it's nice to keep an open mind. But it shouldn't be so open that it allows internal contradictions.

STUDYING ETHICS

If you take a course in geography, you expect that the course will make you a better geographer. If you take a course in creative writing, you anticipate that the course will improve your creative writing. And it is reasonable to hope that a course in chemistry will make you a better chemist. So when you take a course in ethics, what should you expect? That you will learn more about ethics? That seems a minimum expectation. But should you also expect that you will become more ethical, more virtuous, a better person?

Before we go too far in exploring whether a course in ethics is likely to make you a morally better person, perhaps we should agree on what would count as moral improvement. And there's the rub. It's not so easy to decide what makes a morally superior person. That is the sort of thing we'll explore: how do we decide—and *can* we decide—what counts as moral virtue and as morally good behavior. There are many different views on that question, and the purpose of this book is *not* to tell you which view is correct. Rather, this book will help you explore a wide range of distinctive and often conflicting accounts of ethics, and the focus will be on helping you decide where your own views fit. Perhaps in the course of examining these views, and where your own ideas fit along this wide spectrum, you may decide that some of your ethical opinions should change. But that's not the purpose of the book. There are plenty of moral self-help books, and there are plenty of books that will tell you in no uncertain terms what you *ought* to believe about ethics. This is not one of them. This book is designed to give you an opportunity to think more carefully about some major issues in metaethics (that is, about the nature of ethics itself), and about some specific ethical questions, and about how your own views fit. Nothing more—but also nothing less, and those are substantial goals.

The Nature of Ethical Principles

Should you expect studying ethics to make you ethically better, the way you expect studying math to make you a better mathematician? Some people say yes, and others say no. That's one of the questions we'll examine. But there are lots of questions in ethics. After all, ethics is a vast subject, with a long and remarkable history. There are many good places to start an examination of ethics, but among the most basic (and disputed) questions in ethics is this one: Do ethical truths have to be eternal verities, not really part of this world of decay, known through some special power; or are they more mundane, ordinary facts, part of the standard furniture of our world, and known through ordinary means? (Of course there is another option: ethical truths don't exist at all, anywhere; we'll set that possibility aside for the moment, but we'll return to it.) When you seek ethical guidelines, what characteristics must they have? It's hard to know if you've found them unless you know what to look for. What would count as an ethical guide, an ethical principle? "If you want to be trusted and prosperous, practice honesty." Benjamin Franklin thought that was really all the justification needed—and perhaps all the justification possible—for honesty: it *pays*, long term. Contrast that with the starkly unconditional form of the Hebrew commandment: "Thou shalt not bear false witness." Of course you could read this as: If you don't want to get into trouble with God then don't bear false witness. But most people interpret it not as some arbitrary rule that you must follow to retain God's favor, but rather as a basic moral principle that God (in His moral wisdom) recognizes and puts in the form of a commandment.

"What counts as ethics?" is a question worth pondering. Think for a minute about what ethical principles would have to look like, on your own view. Not whether you think abortion is right or wrong, whether it is wrong to cheat on your taxes or your lover, whether you have an obligation to help the impoverished or prevent global warming or protest human rights abuses; and not the question of whether you believe there actually *are* objectively true moral principles. Instead, think about what you would be willing to *count* as a genuine moral principle. (If you deny that such principles exist, or that such principles are objectively *true*, you must have some sense of what it is that you are denying the existence of: you can't claim that a jabberwocky doesn't exist if you have no idea what a jabberwocky is.)

The first reason to consider what counts as a moral principle is to avoid talking past one another. Suppose I think that genuine moral principles must be absolutes like "Never lie," and I deny that there are any true moral absolutes of that sort. You believe that moral principles are much more modest: "If you want to promote trust and harmony, then you should be truthful in your dealings with others"; and you insist that we have good reason to believe that there are such moral principles. We may suppose that we are in basic conflict— "There are no genuine moral principles," I shout; "There certainly are," you reply—when perhaps we really agree. You might agree with me that there are no moral absolutes, and I might agree with you that more modest moral principles make perfectly good sense. Or maybe not. Perhaps we really do have a fundamental difference in our views. But we won't know that until we look carefully at exactly what each of us counts as a moral principle.

There is another important reason to look carefully at what you count as a moral principle. It may tell you a lot about yourself, and some of your basic beliefs and assumptions. Those assumptions and beliefs may be so deep and influential that you hardly know they are there. Like wearing tinted contact lenses through which you view everything you see, such assumptions color the way you see the world without you even being aware of them. Perhaps you think real moral principles exist; perhaps not. That is a question you have probably thought about already. But what do you count as real moral principles? (Not the question of whether real moral principles exist: I don't think unicorns exist, but I know what I would count as a unicorn.)

For many people genuine moral principles must be very special indeed. Plato, the ancient Greek philosopher, believed they are eternal truths known only through pure reason: reason that sees through the illusions of the senses and discovers the fixed and absolute and immutable truth. Moses found moral truths on a mountaintop, in the awesome presence of God, permanent moral truths carved into enduring stone. Descartes, a French philosopher of the seventeenth century, believed that God implants moral principles in our minds as innate ideas. And in the eighteenth century, the philosopher Immanuel Kant discovered the basic governing principle of morality through rigorous reason, an absolute and unconditional moral truth that filled him with awe: "Two things fill the mind with ever new and increasing admiration and awe, the oftener and more steadily they are reflected on: the starry heavens above me and the moral law within me."[1]

In contrast, others have considered moral principles much simpler and more mundane. Aristotle, one of Plato's students, regarded moral principles as basic guides to living the good life. Thomas Hobbes, a British philosopher who lived in the seventeenth century, thought moral principles were devised by humans to bring order and peace to society.

Jeremy Bentham, in late eighteenth- and early nineteenth-century Britain, asserted that the basic moral principle is simple and obvious: maximize pleasure and minimize suffering for everyone. David Hume, a British philosopher of the eighteenth century, insisted that morality is rooted in simple affection that human social animals feel for one another.

There are many more examples of this fundamental conflict between those who regard morality as consisting in special absolute principles, and those who see moral rules as a more ordinary phenomenon based in natural affections or devised rules of order. And obviously there is enormous variation among those on both sides. For example, Plato thinks absolute moral rules are discovered by Reason, while Moses thinks they are ordered by God. On the other side, Hume thinks moral rules are based in natural animal affections, while Hobbes traces them to social agreement. Those differences within the two camps notwithstanding, it is worth noting the basic contrast between the two perspectives—and worth thinking about where your own sympathies lie in this basic conflict. For this contrast involves considerably more than the nature of moral principle. If moral principles are universal, absolute, eternal principles—as Plato and Moses and Kant believe—then we can't discover them by taking surveys. Nor can we find them through psychological or biological study, no matter how carefully and thoroughly we try. And we cannot create them by social agreement. Instead, such universal principles will require special ways of knowing. They are discovered, but they are not discovered the way we discover new elements or a new species of beetle or the Loch Ness Monster.

Knowing Ethical Principles

If at last we drag some reclusive beast out of the depths of Loch Ness, then we will discover that some species we had thought long extinct still survives. Maybe such creatures exist; probably not. Unconditional, absolute moral principles are different. Those who believe in them believe that they *must* exist. They don't exist only if we like them, or happen to recognize them, or choose to adopt them. Rather, they are universal, eternal moral principles that are unconditionally true whether anyone recognizes them or not. There might have been a Loch Ness monster; it happens there is not. But eternal moral principles have no such contingency. They are absolute truths, not discovered by fishing in Loch Ness nor by any other form of observation or experiment. So not only are there special universal moral principles, but we also require special powers or capacities to recognize them. The sensory powers that reveal a new beetle species are not adequate for this task.

What powers must we have to recognize such absolute moral truths? That varies, depending on what the absolute moral truths are. Some claim the truths are dictated by God, and are given to us by special revelation. Others hold that each of us has a special innate moral capacity—a conscience, or a moral sense—that implants in us the basic moral truths. Philosophers such as Plato and Kant maintain that the special power that reveals such eternal moral truths is the power of Reason: not the ordinary reason that enables you to select a horse to wager on in the eighth race at Belmont, but a power of Reason that enables you to see beyond mere appearances and surface features and discern deep underlying moral truths. But whatever the means by which we discover absolute moral principles—whether by God's special revelation, or some remarkable innate intuitive power, or through sublime Reason—this is not a natural capacity like sight or hearing that we share with other animals. Rather, this is a special power that sets us apart from the natural world: a power that makes us almost godlike.

If you think of moral principles as more mundane, conditional matters, then you are likely to have a more modest account of how those moral principles are recognized.

Moral principles aren't written in the heavens, nor are they special absolute truths. Since they are not extraordinary, they require no extraordinary powers for their understanding, and they do not set moral humans apart as unique and special. If morality is based in feelings of sympathy and social concern, then morality requires no special powers or esoteric capacities. For example, Darwin believed that morality is simply a natural result of social sympathy:

> The following proposition seems to me in a high degree probable—namely, than any animal whatever, endowed with well-marked social instincts, the parental and filial affections being here included, would inevitably acquire a moral sense or conscience, as soon as its intellectual powers had become as well, or nearly as well developed, as in man.[2]

Natural Morality Versus Transcendent Morality

So, when you think of morality, what is your image of the subject? Is morality something that rises *above* the natural world, something that *transcends* the natural world? Or is morality a more natural process: based on our emotions, perhaps, or on rules we draw up for promoting social harmony? We might call it, for convenience, the contrast between *natural* morality and *transcendent* morality, or between contingent morality and absolute morality.

This is an issue people feel strongly about. Richard Halverson, the former chaplain of the U.S. Senate, insisted that there can be no morality other than absolute morality:

> Abandoning an absolute ethical moral standard leads irresistibly to the absence of ethics and morality. Each person determines his own ethical/moral code. That's anarchy. Humans become their own gods and decide, each in his own way, what is good and what is evil. Evil becomes good—good becomes evil. Upside down morality! Good is ridiculed! Evil is dignified![3]

So only absolute moral standards can keep us from anarchy. Give up absolute moral standards, and soon murder and mayhem will be celebrated as virtue, and we will have no moral guidance whatsoever. Those who oppose absolute ethics have little patience with the transcendent absolutism favored by Chaplain Halverson. Ethics requires no mysteries or miracles, they would insist, and denying transcendent moral absolutes does not lead to moral anarchy. After all, humans come equipped with social sympathies and common needs and interests, and we don't require absolute God-approved moral principles to recognize that some types of behavior undermine society and others enhance the social welfare for all. Whether bond traders in Manhattan or cattle traders in the Sudan or spice merchants in India, the value and benefits of cooperation and honesty are obvious enough, and require neither divine sanction nor special insight.

GOD'S COMMANDMENTS AND ETHICS

Let's start by looking at some views that champion *absolute* moral principles: moral principles are eternal, universal, fixed truths. Like the stars, they exist whether we discover them or not, and they offer steady points of light for reliable moral navigation. Among such absolutist views we obviously find some religious doctrines. One religious version of absolutism goes by the name *theological voluntarism*. That's just a classy name for a very common view: moral principles are set by God, God commands them; and God doesn't change and doesn't make exceptions, so God's commandments are fixed and eternal and absolute. What is right is *whatever God commands*, or *whatever God chooses*. God doesn't condemn murder because murder is wrong; rather, murder is wrong *because* God condemns murder.

> Theological voluntarism is so named because it makes ethical principles dependent on what *God wills*. Something is good because God *wills* that it be so, not because God recognizes it to be good. It is sometimes called the *Divine Command* theory of ethics: Good is whatever God commands, and *only* what God commands is good. On this view, God's will or God's command is the whole of ethics. A law or principle is right *if and only if* it is willed (commanded) by God.

Many people turn to religion for ethical guidance. Indeed, there are some who adamantly insist that their personal religious beliefs provide the only acceptable ethical standards: "The Bible says it, I believe it, that settles it," is an example of such an approach. But even for those who have unwavering faith in the pronouncements of their own religion or religious leaders or sacred texts, ethical issues can sometimes pose quandaries. For example, one may insist on the importance of the commandment that "Thou shalt not bear false witness," and then when faced with a difficult situation—you are hiding escaped slaves from slave catchers—your obligation to "Do unto others as you would have them do unto you" might lead you to protect these escapees from capture and torture and enslavement and thus lead you to "bear false witness": "No, I have not seen any escaped slaves."

And the problems can get even thornier. In the very same chapter in which God orders "Thou shalt not kill," God also commands the slaughter of whole cities—men, women, and children—who have the misfortune of living on the land that God assigns to the children of Israel. "Put to the sword every inhabitant, and spare not one" is hard to reconcile with "Thou shalt not kill"; so what should we do?

Ethical Principles as Divine Commandments

This raises serious questions concerning the relation between ethics and religion. Perhaps the most basic of these troubling questions is this: Is an ethical guideline (or law) right because God commands it? Or does God command it because it is right? That is, do ethical principles exist only because God affirms them? Or does God affirm these ethical principles because (in His or Her wisdom) God *recognizes* the truth of these ethical laws? If you are religious, you might wish to take a moment to think about your answer to that question, for your answer makes a big difference in the way you think of ethics.

Does God command us to be honest because honesty is good? Or is honesty good because God approves of honesty? This may seem a strange, perhaps even a disturbing question. The question exposes a tension between two fundamentally incompatible sources that the Western religious tradition has struggled to combine: the religious views of ancient Greek philosophy, particularly the views of Aristotle; and the religion of the ancient Hebrews, of Abraham and Moses. Aristotle's God is a God of reason. In fact, Aristotle's God is perfect, completely self-sufficient, and absolutely unchanging. He wants for nothing, and passes eternity thinking about thinking. Since He is omniscient, He can't try to discover new truths: He knows everything already. And since He is already perfect, He can't engage in any self-improvement projects. Obviously Aristotle had little sympathy with the popular Greek notions of the gods Zeus and Diana and Triton: Gods who plotted, lied, changed their minds and their appearances and their affections, and generally seemed to fall a good deal short of perfection. Since God (Aristotle's God) is perfect, God must be changeless: if a perfect God changed, then any change would have to be for the worse and would result in imperfection.

Contrast Aristotle's conception of God with the traditional Hebrew notion. The God of Abraham changes his mind more often than some undergraduates change majors. He creates humankind, then becomes disgusted and resolves to destroy them all; but He finds one good man, so He changes his mind and saves Noah and his family to make a new start. God works out a special deal with the children of Israel, then becomes angry at them and sends them into bondage in Egypt. He eventually rescues them and gives them a new set of rules to follow, but then discovers them worshiping a golden calf and His wrath is kindled and He resolves to destroy them all. Again He changes his mind, and instead kills several thousand. Trying to combine this hot-tempered Hebrew God with the perfect unchanging calm of Aristotle's God is no easy task, and one place the tension comes into play is in considering God's relation to the principles of ethics. Aristotle's God knows all and reasons perfectly and thus knows and understands the true ethical principles. Aristotle's God recognizes true ethical principles because He is infinitely wise, not because He makes them. The Hebrew God, by contrast, wills a set of moral laws: the children of Israel must follow those laws because they are God's commandments, and what makes them ethical principles is that God commands them. Whatever God commands is right, *because* it is God's commandment. God does not recognize what is morally good; rather, the commandments are moral principles *because* God commands them.

If you believe that ethical principles exist *only* because God commands them (the position we called theological voluntarism), then the study of ethics is for you a rather limited exercise. It consists entirely of trying to discover what ethical principles God wills, and there is no room whatsoever to reason about or critically examine ethical questions. There are people who hold such a view, but it obviously requires powerful faith. After all, on this view you cannot examine the ethical principles pronounced by God in terms of their reasonableness or justice or fairness. If God says that it is good to be kind to others, that is *not* because God recognizes that kindness is good; rather, it is strictly because God *pronounces* that kindness is good. Had God pronounced cruelty good, then cruelty would be good, and there would be nothing more to say about it.

> "I do not feel obliged to believe that the same God who has endowed us with sense, reason, and intellect has intended us to forgo their use." Galileo Galilei

Problems with Theological Voluntarism

Those who adopt such a view hold one absolute principle: if God says it then that settles it. If God commands being kind to children, then being kind to children is good. If God commands torturing children, then torturing children is good. Those who believe in an austere and majestic and incomprehensible God often find this view appealing. It is motivated by the fear that *if* there were a moral law independent of God, then God would be *constrained* (by His perfect goodness) to follow that moral law. But God should not be constrained by anything, not even goodness. So God makes morality by His will, rather than following a moral law that He recognizes as true. Adopting this theological voluntarist view (good is whatever God wills it to be) requires a rather reckless leap of faith, for there is no way to critically evaluate such moral principles. You cannot say—if you adopt this view of morality—that you believe in this religion or this account of God because it is morally attractive: such an evaluation would require a standard of morality independent of what God pronounces. It is certainly possible to hold such a theological voluntarist view, and some people seem quite content with it; but it leaves little space for the critical study of ethics.

When they consider it, most religious people favor the other answer. It is not God's pronouncement or commandment that makes murder wrong; rather, God condemns murder because God (in God's great wisdom) recognizes the wrongfulness of murder. Such an approach leaves considerably more room for careful thought about ethics. If you hold religious beliefs, think for a moment about *why* you hold those beliefs. Surely your reason for holding your particular religious views is not merely because "my parents were Muslims" or "I was raised as a Christian" or "all my friends are Jewish." Your religious beliefs are a serious part of your life, and you have thought carefully about them. (Of course you may regard your religion as just part of your culture: you attend services on the High Holy days, and you enjoy assembling with your friends and community to perform various rituals, but you don't take the doctrines of the religion very seriously. In that case, you probably don't turn to your religion for your moral principles. You may find yourself in agreement with the moral principles promoted by your religion, but that is not because they are taught by your religion, and certainly not because you believe they were pronounced true by God.)

So—if you are seriously religious—*why* do you hold the religious beliefs you hold? There may be lots of different reasons for holding your particular religious beliefs, but among the most prominent is this: the religion I follow promotes sound moral principles. (If you have converted from one religion to another, it is not unlikely that one of the main motives for your conversion was dissatisfaction with the moral teachings of your old religion.) That is, one of my reasons for believing in this religion is because its moral principles seem just and fair and reasonable. If you offer that as grounds for your belief, you must have *some* standard of what counts as just and fair that is independent of your religious belief. ("Why did you convert from religion X?" "Because religion X taught that women are inferior to men and should be subservient to men, and I simply cannot believe that a just God would approve of such vile moral principles." In order to draw such a conclusion, you must have a standard of justice that is independent of God's pronouncements. You believe justice requires equal treatment of women, and therefore you count any claim that God approves of unequal treatment as false, because you believe God adheres to what is just; not the other way around, that *whatever* God wills *is* just.) If you take this view, then your religion certainly is not irrelevant to your ethics, but your critical examination of ethics is not hamstrung by your religious beliefs.

God's Law and Punishment

There is another way God's laws might be relevant to ethics. In some religious traditions, God metes out very severe punishments to those who transgress against His laws, and substantial rewards to those who follow the rules. Such punishments and rewards might give one a strong *motive* for obeying God's commandments, but in themselves they provide no *justification* for believing that God's commandments are just and good. When the Fugitive Slave Act was passed in the United States, it became a criminal act to aid escaped slaves, and those who helped runaway slaves could be subjected to imprisonment. During the Nazi era, Germans and citizens in the occupied countries were forbidden to help Jews, and those hiding Jews were often punished by death. In both cases, one would certainly have a prudent motive for following the rules; but the fact that turning Jews over to the Gestapo and slaves to the slave catchers was the best way to escape punishment certainly did not establish that the laws requiring such behavior were ethically legitimate and morally just. Likewise, if God's rules are backed by powerful punishments and rewards, that in itself is no reason to think the rules are ethically sound.

This point is beautifully expressed by a wise Islamic teacher from the Sufi tradition, a woman named Rabi'a. One day Rabi'a rushed through the marketplace, carrying a flaming torch in one hand and a jug of water in the other. When people inquired why she was carrying the torch and the water, she replied that she was going to burn Paradise and quench the fires of Hell, so that people would do morally good acts from love of doing the good, and not from hope of gain or fear of punishment.[4] Rabi'a's point is clear: the rewards and punishments might motivate people to follow God's laws, but they do not give good reasons to suppose those laws are morally right. Even if the divine laws *are* right, when you follow the divine laws only from hope of reward or fear of punishment it is very doubtful you have acted morally.

RELIGION AND ETHICS

If we reject theological voluntarism, that by no means implies the rejection of religious considerations in our inquiries into ethics. Martin Luther King's campaign for civil rights had special power and broad appeal because it drew heavily on the language and symbols of God leading the children of Israel out of bondage: a powerful story that is common to the Jewish, Christian, and Muslim religious traditions. And religious parables and traditions have often stimulated reform movements, and sometimes encouraged us to look more closely at our lives and our habits and our assumptions. Furthermore, organized religions have often contained groups of people who devoted intense systematic study to questions of theology as well as questions of ethics, and the results of their careful deliberations will merit our attention in later chapters.

So if ethics is not based on God's will or God's punishments, then what is the basis of ethics? Supposing that ethical laws are simply willed by God is certainly one type of transcendent, absolutist ethics, but it is by no means the only one. Plato rejected theological voluntarism, but he firmly believed in transcendent, absolute ethical standards. And one of the strongest and most uncompromising advocates of absolutist ethics is Immanuel Kant, who believed that absolute, universal ethical principles could be discovered through the meticulous use of higher Reason. Kant's rationalist approach to ethics will be our next topic.

EUTHYPHRO

Plato

This dialogue was written almost 2,500 years ago by the ancient Greek philosopher Plato, whom many regard as the father of philosophy. Alfred North Whitehead once said that "all philosophy is a footnote to Plato"; and at least in the sense that much of the history of philosophy has been either a defense of or an attack on Plato's views, there is some truth in that claim. Socrates, the hero of the dialogue, was Plato's teacher in ancient Athens. Socrates is an almost mythic figure, the "philosophical gadfly" who wanders about Athens raising disturbing questions, confident only that he himself knows nothing, and cheerfully puncturing the arrogant certainty of those who, like Euthyphro, attempt to instruct him. While it is difficult to separate Socrates from Plato, most scholars believe that Plato's attribution of his major ideas to Socrates is simply a way of showing respect for his great teacher. Wherever the ideas originated, the dialogue in *Euthyphro* is not only a good example of Plato's philosophical style, but also a powerful critique of the view that God's will can establish what is good.

EUTHYPHRO

Euth.   Well, I should say that piety is what all the gods love, and that impiety is what they all hate.

Socr.   Are we to examine this definition, Euthyphro, and see if it is a good one? Or are we to be content to accept the bare statements of other men or of ourselves without asking any questions? Or must we examine the statements?

Euth.   We must examine them. But for my part I think that the definition is right this time.

Socr.   We shall know that better in a little while, my good friend. Now consider this question. Do the gods love piety because it is pious, or is it pious because they love it?

Euth.   I do not understand you, Socrates.

Socr.   I will try to explain myself: we speak of a thing being carried and carrying, and being led and leading, and being seen and seeing; and you understand that all such expressions mean different things, and what the difference is.

Euth.   Yes, I think I understand.

Socr.   And we talk of a thing being loved, of a thing loving, and the two are different?

Euth.   Of course.

Socr.   Now tell me, is a thing which is being carried in a state of being carried because it is carried, or for some other reason?

Euth.   No, because it is carried.

Socr.   And a thing is in a state of being led because it is led, and of being seen because it is seen?

Euth.   Certainly.

Socr.   Then a thing is not seen because it is in a state of being seen: it is in a state of being seen because it is seen; and a thing is not led because it is in a state of being led: it is in a state of being led because it is led; and a thing is not carried because it is in a state of being carried: it is in a state of being carried because it is carried. Is my meaning clear now, Euthyphro? I mean this: if anything becomes or is affected, it does not become because it is in a state of becoming: it is

in a state of becoming because it becomes; and it is not affected because it is in a state of being affected: it is in a state of being affected because it is affected. Do you not agree?

Euth.   I do.

Socr.   Is not that which is being loved in a state either of becoming or of being affected in some way by something?

Euth.   Certainly.

Socr.   Then the same is true here as in the former cases. A thing is not loved by those who love it because it is in a state of being loved; it is in a state of being loved because they love it.

Euth.   Necessarily.

Socr.   Well, then, Euthyphro, what do we say about piety? Is it not loved by all the gods, according to your definition?

Euth.   Yes.

Socr.   Because it is pious, or for some other reason?

Euth.   No, because it is pious.

Socr.   Then it is loved by the gods because it is pious; it is not pious because it is loved by them?

Euth.   It seems so.

Socr.   But, then, what is pleasing to the gods is pleasing to them, and is in a state of being loved by them, because they love it?

Euth.   Of course.

Socr.   Then piety is not what is pleasing to the gods, and what is pleasing to the gods is not pious, as you say, Euthyphro. They are different things.

Euth.   And why, Socrates?

Socr.   Because we are agreed that the gods love piety because it is pious, and that it is not pious because they love it. Is not this so?

Euth.   Yes.

Socr.   And that what is pleasing to the gods because they love it, is pleasing to them by reason of this same love, and that they do not love it because it is pleasing to them.

Euth.   True.

Socr.   Then, my dear Euthyphro, piety and what is pleasing to the gods are different things. If the gods had loved piety because it is pious, they would also have loved what is pleasing to them because it is pleasing to them; but if what is pleasing to them had been pleasing to them because they loved it, then piety, too, would have been piety because they loved it. But now you see that they are opposite things, and wholly different from each other. For the one is of a sort to be loved because it is loved, while the other is loved because it is of a sort to be loved. My question, Euthyphro, was, What is piety? But it turns out that you have not explained to me the essential character of piety; you have been content to mention an effect which belongs to it—namely, that all the gods love it. You have not yet told me what its essential character is. Do not, if you please, keep from me what piety is; begin again and tell me that. Never mind whether the gods love it, or whether it has other effects: we shall not differ on that point. Do your best to make clear to me what is piety and what is impiety.

Euth. But, Socrates, I really don't know how to explain to you what is in my mind. Whatever statement we put forward always somehow moves round in a circle, and will not stay where we put it.

EXERCISES

1. Do you expect this study of ethics—that you are now undertaking—to make you more virtuous, less virtuous, or to have no effect on your moral character?

2. John has been found guilty of academic dishonesty by the student-faculty review board. John plagiarized a history paper (he bought it off the Web), and he was caught with a cheat sheet during a chemistry exam. Assume that we all agree that such academic dishonesty is wrong. What would you recommend as the best way of reforming John's dishonest behavior and character? Would your proposed reform process include a course in ethics?

3. The university has decided to develop a special ethics course for students who have been found guilty of violations of the honor code. First-time offenders can take the class, and if they pass the class they will have the academic dishonesty conviction removed from their permanent record. Is that a good idea?

   Set aside your answer to that question: Don't worry about whether the course is a good idea or not. Whatever you think about such a course, you have been given the job of designing the course honor code violators will take. What would you include in such a course? Are there any novels you would assign? Movies you would show? Field trips you would make?

4. One of your high school friends has a deep-rooted prejudice against homosexuals. You would like to help your friend get over this prejudice. What would you do? Do you think it would help if your friend took a course in ethics? If you were designing the course, what would you include?

5. I have come into possession of a small but lovely drawing by Michelangelo. (Never mind how I came to possess this drawing. Let's just agree that I own it fair and square, and that I did not gain possession of it by theft or deceit or fraud. The drawing is legitimately my own.) I have decided to paste the drawing over my dartboard, and use it as a target. You may think this quite stupid (even if I don't care for the drawing it is obviously worth an enormous sum of money). That's not the issue. The question is this: Would I be doing anything *morally wrong* by destroying the drawing in this frivolous manner?

6. If a movie wins an Oscar, that obviously increases its box office appeal and results in greater profits for the producer. Not surprisingly, there have often been intense campaigns to persuade members of the Academy to vote for a particular picture. The Academy of Motion Picture Arts and Sciences (the folks who are in charge of the Academy Awards, or Oscars) have become disturbed about the amount of campaigning and lobbying for the awards. Producer Sid Ganis, who headed an Academy

committee to look into the issue, said, "In the last number of years, there has been verbose campaigning, along with the press' depiction of studies vying against each other for Oscars, leading to a sense that Oscars could be bought with a lot of money." As a result of their study, Ganis's committee developed a set of guidelines in an effort to curtail such campaigning for Academy Awards. The guidelines note that recently there have been "an unfortunate series of manipulative and excessive Academy Awards 'campaigns,'" and the guidelines "set out some standards for ethical conduct where Academy Awards are concerned." But is this an *ethical* issue? If a film producer throws lavish parties and pays a public relations firm to run a campaign to have his film win the Academy Award for "best picture," has the producer done something *unethical*? (Of course if the producer bribes some of the academy voters to vote for his picture, that raises ethical issues; but is campaigning for an Academy Award itself an *ethical* issue?)[5]

7. We can divide and subdivide ethical views along a number of different cuts. This may be thought of as a preview of some of the issues we'll examine. You might use it to locate your own ethical perspective (your perspective for the moment, at least; you may change—and you may find it useful to compare your ethical views at the end of the class with those you hold now).

   A. Do you think ethics is a matter of natural processes, or is it transcendent (divinely given, or perhaps enshrined in a transcendent realm)? You might believe that ethical truths are special truths, not derived by observation of this world—transcendent truths—even if you doubt or deny the existence of God.

   B. Are ethical principles *made* or *discovered*?

   C. Is ethics objective or nonobjective? (Are there actual objective facts in ethics, or is it all just a matter of opinion? Can I be dead wrong about one of my ethical beliefs, the same way I am simply wrong if I believe that Venus is the largest planet in our solar system?)

   D. Is ethics a matter of protecting the individual, or enhancing the welfare of all? That is, is ethics basically individualistic or in some way communitarian? Another way of thinking about this: if you were marooned on a small isolated tropical island, and would never see another sentient being (you will have to subsist on bananas and nuts and berries), would ethics still be important for you?

   E. Is ethics known more through reason or by experience of some sort (including intuitions)? Even those who *deny* there are objective ethical truths can split on this question ("*if* there were ethical facts, they would have to be known by pure reason").

   F. Is ethics universal or more local or even individual? (If people from a different culture have different ethical rules from our own, must at least one set of rules be *wrong*?)

8. Go back to your own answers to Question 7, and think about how they are connected. For example, if you changed your mind about your answer to the first question, would that also lead you to revise your answer to some of the other questions? Of the questions in Question 6, which one would you select as the most *basic* question in ethics?

9. In Plato's *Euthyphro*, Socrates puts the following question to Euthyphro:

   > We are agreed that the gods love piety because it is pious, and that it is not pious because they love it. Is this not so?

   To phrase a similar question in more contemporary terms, we might say: "We are agreed that God loves just acts because they are just, and they are not just simply because God loves them, right?" If you agree that God's love of justice is determined by the goodness of justice (rather than God's will determining what counts as just), does that in any way diminish the power or majesty of God?

ADDITIONAL READING

There are many excellent guides to critical thinking. Among them are S. Morris Engel, *With Good Reason*, 6ᵗʰ ed. (New York: St. Martin's, 2000); Theodore Schick, Jr., and Lewis Vaughn, *How To Think About Weird Things*, 3ʳᵈ ed. (Boston: McGraw Hill, 2002); and Bruce N. Waller, *Critical Thinking: Consider the Verdict*, 5ᵗʰ ed. (Upper Saddle River, N.J.: Prentice Hall, 2004).

On the subject of the relation between ethics and religion, Plato's *Euthyphro* (excerpted here, and available in a number of translations and editions) remains the classic source for the argument against theological voluntarism. Kai Nielsen, *Ethics Without God* (London: Pemberton Press; and Buffalo, N.Y.: Prometheus Books, 1973), is perhaps the best and clearest contemporary argument against basing ethics on religion. A very sophisticated and interesting opposing view—which argues for the importance of religious considerations in ethics—can be found in George N. Schlesinger, *New Perspectives on Old-Time Religion* (Oxford: Clarendon Press, 1988). A brief argument for how ethics might be based on religion is given by Jonathan Berg, "How Could Ethics Depend on Religion?" in Peter Singer, editor, *A Companion to Ethics* (Oxford: Blackwell, 1991). Philip L. Quinn develops a detailed and sophisticated defense of theological voluntarism in "Divine Command Theory," in Hugh LaFollette, editor, *The Blackwell Guide to Ethical Theory* (Oxford: Blackwell Publishers, 2000).

There are two excellent anthologies on the subject: P. Helm, editor, *Divine Commands and Morality* (Oxford: Oxford University Press, 1981); and G. Outka and J. P. Reeder, Jr., editors, *Religion and Morality: A Collection of Essays* (Garden City, N.Y.: Anchor/Double-day,1973).

Among general works, Peter Singer's edited work, *A Companion to Ethics* (Oxford: Blackwell Publishers, 1991), is a superb guide to many topics in ethical theory as well as applied ethics. An excellent collection of readings is edited by Hugh LaFollette: *The Blackwell Guide to Ethical Theory* (Oxford: Blackwell Publishers, 2000). Another collection of outstanding contemporary articles is Stephen Darwall, Allan Gibbard, and Peter Railton, editors, *Moral Discourse and Practice* (Oxford: Oxford University Press, 1997).

NOTES

[1] Immanuel Kant, *The Critique of Practical Reason and Other Writings in Moral Philosophy*, trans. L. W. Beck (Chicago: University of Chicago Press, 1949), p. 259. First published in 1788.

[2] Charles Darwin, *The Descent of Man*, 2nd ed. (London: John Murray, 1875), p. 99. First published in 1871.

[3] Quoted (with strong approval) on July 7, 2002, by Cal Thomas, syndicated columnist.

[4] For more on Rabi'a, see Margaret Smith, *Studies in Early Mysticism in the Near and Middle East* (Oxford: Oneworld Publications, 1995); and Margaret Smith, *Rabi'a: The Life and Work of Rabi'a and Other Women Mystics in Islam* (Oxford: Oneworld Publications, 1995).

[5] This case is based on a report by Gregg Kilday in *The Toronto Star*, September 5, 2003.

CHAPTER 2

REASONING ABOUT ETHICS

If you are seeking the surest path to sound moral behavior, you might well decide that *reason* is your best guide. If you favor reason as the right guide to ethics, you are in good company. Throughout the history of ethics, stretching back well over two millennia to Plato and Aristotle in ancient Athens, most philosophers have insisted that careful thought and judicious reasoning are the foundation of ethics. Plato believed we know moral truths through the powers of pure reason. Our sensory observations are subject to error and illusion, but the wisdom we acquire through rigorous exercise of reason gives us eternal, unchanging, indubitable truth. Plato compared our situation to that of people in a dark cave. We are trapped on the ledge of a deep cavern, and from our narrow ledge we see only the opposite wall of the cave. Below us there is a fire burning, and someone is holding objects in front of the fire, but all we observe are the flickering shadows on the cave wall. Because we are entrapped and have no other experiences, we take the flickering shadows to be true reality. But if we can escape this world of the senses, and climb out of the cave to the true sunlight of reason, we will recognize how limited and deceptive our early sensory experience was: we were only seeing shadows of objects reflected in firelight, not the true nature of things seen by the light of day. Plato counsels us to abandon the shadowy senses and flickering feelings, and seek instead the wisdom that is revealed only by the bright light of reason. But acquiring that wisdom requires great discipline. In particular, all our desires and passions must be held in tight check, and ruled by our reason.

Reason and Emotions

You may have some doubts about the perfect reliability of reason, but if you are choosing whether to entrust your ethical decisions to your reason or your emotions, most philosophers have believed that reason wins. There are just too many cases where our emotions have led us astray. That emotional decision to buy the flashy new car busted my budget, and the damned thing is always in the shop: I wish I had thought more carefully, and bought a less expensive and more reliable model. My emotions tempt me toward a lunch of chocolate chip cookies washed down with beer, but my reason tells me I'll gain weight, raise my cholesterol, move more slowly when I play tennis, and will be in lousy shape to study for my history exam—a green salad will be a healthier and happier choice. And my emotions send me careening into passionate love affairs that my reason—and my friends—recognize as perfectly disastrous. In his lovely seduction poem, e. e. cummings counsels that "Wholly to be a fool when spring is in the world my blood approves, and kisses are a better fate than wisdom." Sounds good. But reason wisely counsels to think twice before jumping at his offer. At the very least, don't be *wholly* a fool: make sure you have some condoms handy.

So our emotions don't have a great track record as a reliable guide. Besides, for ethical guidance we want something with a bit of constancy and steadiness, and our emotions don't meet that standard. You fall madly in love, and a week later, as the song says, "your perfect lover just looks like a perfect fool." Engineering looked like a fine major—you get to carry a calculator, and you'd look great in one of those hard hats—but reason would have reminded you that you hate math and flunked all your high school science courses. Our emotions don't hold a steady course. Worst of all, they don't set a *reliable* course. Reason seems a better choice for an ethical compass.

Reasoning About an Ethical Issue

Reason may seem a more reliable guide than emotions, but some object that reason simply doesn't apply to ethics. We can reason about math, and economic theory, and how to build a safe and sturdy bridge across the Hudson River, and how to find a cure for cancer, but ethics is not a subject where we can effectively use reason. That objection raises some large issues about ethics, and we'll be returning to them. But however you resolve those larger issues, it seems clear that we do *some* reasoning about ethical issues. Consider this ethical argument, adapted from a contemporary philosopher, Judith Jarvis Thomson. You awaken this morning, ready to leap from your bed and rush to your ethics class. But as you gain consciousness, everything seems wrong. Instead of the sheets you haven't washed in six weeks you awaken to starched clean white sheets. There are no dirty clothes decorating the room, and you can't find your teddy bear. Worst of all, you realize there is a thick double tube attached to your arm, and the tube runs across the room and is attached to the arm of an older woman, apparently fast asleep, lying in another hospital bed.

Just then the door opens, and in walks someone all dressed in white: "Oh, I'm glad you're finally awake," she says. "A terrible thing happened last night. Remember when you stopped by the tavern on your way home from the library? While you were there, someone slipped a delayed-action sleeping potion in your beer, and after you got home and went to bed it caused you to fall into a very deep sleep. The people who drugged you—a nefarious group called the Society of Music Lovers—then kidnapped you, brought you to this hospital, and hooked you up to the woman you see sleeping over there. That's Sarah Sloan, the fabulous violinist. Sarah has acute kidney failure. Her kidneys have completely shut down, and the buildup of impurities in her blood would have soon killed her. It turns out that Sarah Sloan has a very rare blood type, and dialysis machines don't work for her. The Society of Music Lovers discovered that you—and you alone—have a matching blood type. So now Sloan's blood is flowing through your body, and your healthy kidneys are purifying her blood as well as your own. Don't worry, it won't cause you any harm. Your kidneys are capable of purifying the blood of several people with no strain. Please understand, we think what the kidnappers did was terribly, egregiously wrong. They had no right to drug you and kidnap you and hook you up to Sarah Sloan, and we at the hospital had no part in that. The first we knew of it was when a nurse came into Sloan's room last night and found you here. But the situation is this: If you unhook yourself from Sarah Sloan, she will die. And so now that you are hooked up to Sloan, you have to *stay* hooked up to her. Not forever, of course. We're building a special dialysis machine that will work for Sarah Sloan's rare blood type, and as soon as that machine is ready we'll detach you and hook Sloan to the machine, and you can go on your merry way. The machine is rather complicated and it will take some time to build: probably about nine months. Until then, you have to stay hooked up to Sloan, because if you unhook yourself then she will die. We can't let her die, so I'm afraid you have no choice in the matter: you must stay hooked up to the violinist."

So what is your reaction to that? What would you say to the people at the hospital?

Most people will be outraged. "It's wrong for you to compel me to stay hooked up to the violinist. I know she will die if I unhook myself; but you have no right to force me to stay hooked up to her. If I decide to stay attached, and save her life, that's one thing. But no one should be able to force me to do that."

Then Thomson gets to the point of this elaborate analogy. If you believe you have a right to unhook yourself from Sarah Sloan, even though she will die, then you must also grant that a woman who is pregnant as a result of rape has a right to an abortion. Even if we grant that the fetus is a person, with all the rights of any other person, then the raped woman still has a right to an abortion, just as you have a right to unhook yourself from Sarah Sloan. The violinist will die when you unhook yourself, and the fetus will die when the woman unhooks herself through abortion. But if you believe you have a right to unhook yourself from the violinist, then that same right extends to the woman who is pregnant as a result of rape. (Thomson is making a very *limited* argument. It is not a case for a general right to elective abortion; rather, she is attempting to demonstrate that even if we grant that the fetus is a person with full rights, there are still circumstances in which a woman would have a right to an abortion.)

There are many ways you might respond to Thomson's analogical argument. Some people find it convincing. Others dispute it. They might claim the analogy is flawed in some way (you aren't related to the violinist, but you are related to the fetus, and that is a morally relevant difference). In any case, we aren't going to settle the question of abortion today— maybe tomorrow. But notice this. When you consider Thomson's argument, you are using reason to examine an *ethical* issue. So first off, it is clear you can use reason to examine ethical questions. And second, think about your response to Thomson's argument. You may agree or disagree, you may think it's a bad analogy, you may think the two cases aren't really comparable. But there is one response to the argument that would seem nonsensical to you. Suppose I say: "Look, I certainly do have a right to unhook myself from the violinist; and while the woman who is pregnant as a result of rape is in a situation that is exactly similar to mine in every relevant moral detail, she does *not* have a right to an abortion." You would respond: "That's crazy. If you agree the situations are the same, then you can't say it's right for you and wrong for her. That is self-contradictory, and it makes no sense at all."

So what does Thomson's argument give us? Something like this: *If* you believe you have a right to make decisions about your own body (whether to have surgery, or give blood, or detach yourself from a violinist) then you must believe that others (including a woman who is pregnant as a result of rape) also have that right. Using reason, we have arrived at an ethical conclusion. So it seems that reasoning does have an important role to play in ethics.

Reasoning About Conditional Principles

Actually, very few people would deny that we can reason about ethical issues, as in the previous case. But the issue gets trickier, and considerably more controversial, when we move a step further. What was the conclusion of Thomson's argument? If you believe you have a right to make decisions about your own body, then consistency requires you to believe that others (including a woman who is pregnant as a result of rape) also have that right. That is a *hypothetical* or *conditional* conclusion: *If* this, then that. Reason seems to be quite useful in helping us with *hypothetical* reasoning, *conditional* goods. *If* you want to build a dam across this river, this is the best point for a dam. *If* we are going to provide everyone in our society with medical care, this is the best means of doing that. *If* you want a really greasy high-fat hamburger, go to Fat Mack's Grill. *If* you want to avoid cheating on the test, then don't look at your neighbor's paper. *If* you have a right to control what happens to your own body, what does that imply about the rights of others to control their own bodies? But we get tougher questions about the role of reason when we consider *categorical* claims, *unconditional* claims, claims with no *ifs* about them.

Kant and Categorical Principles

"Everyone has a right to control what happens to his or her own body." "Cheating is wrong." "Treat all people with respect." "Do not steal." Those are *categorical* statements. It's one thing to say "*If* you want a good reputation, don't tell lies"; quite another to say, simply and without qualification, "It is wrong to lie." "*If* you value the honor code, you shouldn't cheat" is a much more modest claim than "cheating is wrong." Obviously reason can help us in dealing with conditionals ("*If* you value trust in your personal relationships, you shouldn't cheat on your lover, because cheating will result in lies and deception and loss of trust"). But can it help if we are seeking unconditional categorical ethical principles ("cheating is wrong")?

Immanuel Kant insisted reason can indeed supply such absolute categorical ethical principles: ethical principles that reason reveals to be universally true, just as reason reveals universal truths of mathematics. In fact, Kant argues that *only* pure reason could reveal the absolute universal truths of ethics. The facts that we learn from observation and experiment—the number of planets in our solar system, the number of electrons in a nitrogen atom, the speed of light, the cause of AIDS—are all *contingent* truths that might have been otherwise. But truths of ethics must be absolute and universal; that is, they must be *categorical* principles, not conditional. And thus they must come from reason alone.

Kant believes reason can accomplish much more than merely provide guidance in accomplishing our purposes. According to Kant, reason can actually discover eternal, absolute ethical principles, principles of universal ethical truth that can be known with rational certainty—much as reason can guide us to universal truths of mathematics and geometry. And these are truths we *discover* through reason, not ethical principles of our own making or choosing. Just as the truths of mathematics are equally true in Moscow, Mozambique, and Minneapolis, so also reason reveals ethical truths that are universal. The square root of 16 is 4, without exception: it's 4 whether skies are sunny or gray, and it's 4 whether I like it or not. If I believe the square root of 16 is 5, then I'm not just different: I'm wrong.

Is it possible for reason to supply absolute principles of morality, principles analogous to mathematical truths? Kant assures us that reason, and reason alone, is up to the challenge. Consider a situation you might face: You are the CEO of ABRA Corporation, and you own an enormous amount of ABRA stock. If you manipulate the books a bit—create some subsidiary companies and transfer all the debts to them, and sell some of your assets back and forth between several subsidiary companies and thus show that ABRA has a great cash flow and is turning huge paper profits—then ABRA will look very profitable, and the value of your stock will shoot up. Then you can unload your stock while the price is high and pocket a fortune, while telling your investors and employees that everything is going great. When the bubble bursts, you'll be rich. Of course your employees lost their pensions and your stockholders lost their investments, in some cases their entire life savings. Is it legitimate for you to cheat people in this manner to enrich yourself?

Well (Kant would say) *think* about it: Would you think it fair if someone else did this to you? If someone cheated you out of your life savings—or did this to your dear old Mom—would you think it was okay? Of course not. You can't really prefer to be cheated, and you don't approve of a world in which everyone cheats everyone else whenever they have the opportunity. Instead, you want people to deal with you honestly. But there is *no morally relevant difference* between you and the people you are cheating. You can't consistently say it's okay for *me* to cheat others, but it's not alright for others to cheat me. All of you are rational, have your own lives and plans and projects, and are vulnerable to harm. So if you cannot think it right that someone cheats you—if you cannot genuinely will to be cheated and treated disrespectfully—then simple consistency demands that like cases be treated in a like manner, and so you must conclude it is not right to cheat others. It is illogical, *irrational* to treat similar cases by different principles. That would be like saying *this* angle is a right angle, but this other identical angle is not; or like saying 2 plus 2 equals 4 for *you*, but for me it totals 5.

Kant's Categorical Imperative

So we arrive, on purely rational grounds, at a basic principle of ethics (Kant's *categorical imperative*): always act in such a way that you could will that your act should be a universal law. This is hardly a new and surprising ethical principle. It is quite similar to what is often called "the golden rule": Do unto others as you would have them do unto you. Or as it is stated in the Jewish tradition: That which is hateful to you, do not unto others. But the difference is that Kant claims the rule can be derived purely from reason, without the aid of either emotions or revelation. Kant's categorical imperative is categorical, not hypothetical or conditional. *Reason requires* that you treat others as you wish to be treated. Kant insists that principle is eternally true, applying equally to Kenyan bankers and Kansas farmers and Kyoto carpenters (as well as any rational extraterrestrials). It is true whether anyone knows or acknowledges it. And the truth of the principle can be known through pure reason, without the need of experience or observation, and known by any competent reasoner.

Of course not everyone will reason well, or even reason at all. But that does not expose a weakness in Kant's argument. After all, if Steve refuses to consider a mathematical proof, or is simply incapable of reasoning about mathematics, we don't conclude that the mathematical proof is invalidated; rather, we conclude that Steve is closed-minded or stupid or willfully obtuse. Likewise, if Martha refuses to follow the rationally derived principles of ethics, that reveals flaws in Martha, but *not* in the ethical principles.

Kant believes there is a second way of formulating the categorical imperative: always treat all persons as ends in themselves, and never merely as means to our ends. That is, all persons are entitled to be respected as rational beings who are capable of knowing the truths of morality and living by them; anyone who has that special capacity is a moral equal, a member of the kingdom of ends, and cannot legitimately be reduced to a mere means, merely a tool, for someone else's goals. (Of course you can hire a carpenter to build your house, and in so doing you are employing her to accomplish one of your goals. But you cannot legitimately treat her as if she were only a means to your ends. Thus you cannot cheat her, nor enslave her.) According to Kant, this is just a second way of expressing the same principle. "All persons must be treated as ends in themselves" is essentially the same principle as "always act in such a way that you can will that your act should be a universal law."

Kant's ethics is an example of a *deontological* theory of ethics. "Deontological" comes from the Greek *deon*, meaning that which is binding, in particular a binding duty. According to deontologists, the nature of ethical rules is to bind you to your duty; and that binding is not dependent on consequences. You are duty-bound to keep your promise, even if a better offer comes along. And you are duty-bound, whether the consequences are pleasant or painful. Duty is not based on what is pleasant or beneficial or advantageous, but rather upon the nature of the obligation itself. Though Kant's rationalist view of ethics is the best known deontological theory, it is not the only one: theological voluntarism (the divine command theory of ethics) is another deontological theory. On the divine command theory, a law is morally binding because God commands it. The consequences of following God's law—whether pleasant or painful—are irrelevant.

Absolute Ethical Principles

On the Kantian view ethics is universal and absolute, and its principles are discovered by the same pure reasoning process that discovers the universal truths of mathematics and geometry. The principles don't depend on observation, or experiment, or affections, or preferences. When straight lines intersect they create identical opposite angles. That is true even if there have never been two perfectly straight lines in the world, and it is a truth that cannot be demonstrated by experiments or observations but only by reason. It is true whether it makes you feel warm and fuzzy or cold and upset, and it is true whether you like it or not. Basic ethical principles have exactly the same status. Legend has it that Diogenes walked around the streets of Athens, day and night, carrying a lantern and searching for an honest person, without ever finding one. Perhaps there has never been an honest person in all human history. If so, that does not change the basic ethical fact that honesty is morally right. "Be honest in your dealings with others" is still a true ethical principle. Maybe in our imperfect world honesty is *not* the best policy, and it would create more harm than benefit. That's irrelevant, Kant would insist. The truth of ethical principles doesn't depend on their usefulness or their consequences, but on their rational foundation. Ethical principles are universally and absolutely true, consequences be damned.

Given the exalted status of the moral law, Kant will allow no compromises. The moral law is stern and universal, with no exceptions. It would be irrational to will that it is alright to lie when lying is convenient; instead, we must will a universal principle that shows respect for all persons, and that principle will be: tell the truth. So when I ask what you think of my expensive new hairstyle, of which I am quite proud but which in fact makes me look like an orangutan on a bad hair day, you cannot tell me it looks great. Respect for the moral law, and for me as a person, requires that you tell the truth. Of course such honesty may damage some of your social relationships, but that is irrelevant. The moral law is universal and absolute, and it requires our singular allegiance, whatever our inclinations and whatever the consequences.

> "Morality is not properly the doctrine of how we may make ourselves happy, but how we may make ourselves worthy of happiness." Immanuel Kant, *Critique of Practical Reason*, 1788

Kant certainly believes his austere rational morality *applies* to this world: you *must* follow it in your daily ethical life. But it is not *of* this world: it is not derived by observation or experience, but by pure reason. The truths of rationalist ethics do not depend on God for their justification (though of course a rational God would scrupulously follow ethical principles), but this is nonetheless a *transcendent* moral system. It sets up absolute moral principles that cannot be refuted by any worldly events or empirical experiments or sensory observations. Our affections are part of the natural world, affections that may be felt by other animals, feelings that are apparently variable and changing—witness the amazing speed with which we can fall in love, and how swiftly those feelings of affection can be lost. As part of the natural world, someday these apparently chaotic feelings may be explicable in natural terms (like the apparently lawless wanderings of comets, which Newton and Halley turned into part of a cosmic mechanical clockwork). Kant wants a moral realm that is distinctively human and set apart from the mechanistic natural world, a realm governed by reason and by principles discoverable through pure reason. If human ethics is to be part of that special world it must be driven by reason, not animal feelings.

ELEMENTS OF KANTIAN ETHICS

Reason and Will

Kant marks the apex of the rationalistic approach to ethics. There are two key elements in Kant's ethical system. First, ethics is based on pure reason: neither our feelings nor our empirical observations of the world play any part in ethics. Second, the capacity to *follow* the purely rational dictates of the rational moral law must come from the special capacity of the human will (and not from emotions or inclinations). Rationality and willpower are the special glory of humankind. They are the features that justify the claim that we are "made in God's image," and that humans have a special status that sets us apart from and above all other creatures.

Kant's enthusiasm for the purely rational moral law pushes him into a rare burst of poetic exuberance: "Two things fill the mind with ever new and increasing admiration and awe . . . : the starry heavens above me and the moral law within me."[1] Note that Kant is speaking of *two* things, both awe-inspiring, but from distinctly different realms. The moral law is based in pure reason, not derived from inclinations nor from observations nor from anything else in the natural world of stars and atoms and animals. And the capacity to follow the dictates of the moral law comes not from our natural capacities—our inclinations and sympathies and desires—but instead from our special capacity of free will that empowers us to follow the moral law even though all our natural inclinations may work against it. It is this capacity to know the pure moral law and follow its dictates through our power of free will that elevates humans above the world of sense and guarantees our freedom from the mechanism of nature. The mechanistic operations of the starry heavens are awe-inspiring, and properly so; but not more wonderful than the *non*mechanistic power we find within ourselves to know and will the moral law.

Nonnatural Ethics

For Kant, genuine moral acts must stem from our special nonnatural powers of reason and will, not from anything in nature. Thus if your generous behavior is prompted by your own natural inclinations, then your generous acts have no moral worth. Indeed, your natural inclinations toward kindness and generosity can be an impediment to genuine moral acts: reliance on agreeable and generous dispositions may prevent you from seeking rational principles of moral law and following them through the power of your will. Without such reason-based acts of willpower there is no genuine moral act. Instead there is only behavior from natural inclinations, which may prove beneficial and agreeable but which could just as easily have been vicious and harmful.

The poet Ogden Nash (in a somewhat whimsical poem entitled "Kind of an Ode to Duty") writes:

> O Duty,
> Why hast thou not the visage of a sweetie or a cutie?

And for most of us—as well as for Aristotle—it would be wonderful if our *duties* had the charms of our desires. If my duty to visit my sick friend were as attractive as my desire to spend the afternoon at the beach, then duty would be a delight. It would be like steamed broccoli having the delightful taste of a hot fudge sundae.

But Kant sees it differently. If duty always matched our desire—if duty had "the visage of a cutie or a sweetie," rather than the stern demeanor of moral demand—then we would merely do right by inclination, rather than through the force and dedication of our wills. And for Kant, acting from inclination has no moral worth at all. For Kant, our uniquely human willpower enables us to overcome desire and follow the demands of the rational moral law, and it is that power which sets humans apart from the mechanical world and gives us our special status.

Even if you do not agree with Kant that we would be morally better if we entirely banished feelings, you may still grant that strong feelings sometimes obscure our moral outlook. More than one politician wishes his reason had exerted more effective control over his feelings. And strong desires are not the only feelings that can cloud our better judgment. Feelings of kindness and benevolence can also cause problems. In medicine, one of the most severe dangers to patient autonomy is the physician who "feels deeply" that the proposed treatment is really in the best interests of the patient; and so, since she is only working "for the good of the patient," she feels justified in overriding patient choice. Thus *feeling* that one is striving to provide good care may lead to abuse of the patient's right to choose and control his or her own medical treatment. The harms of such a process are particularly clear in geriatric settings, when caregivers—acting from sincere feelings of kindness and generosity—do things for residents they could do for themselves, and thus shape a debilitating sense of helplessness in those they are trying to help. So whatever the benefits of compassion and care, and whatever the joy of feelings and passions, there is also an important role for reason in ethics. Exactly what is that role? Absolute ethical lawgiver, as Kant maintains? Or menial assistant to the passions, as Hume suggests in the next chapter? Or some other role entirely?

CRITICISMS OF KANTIAN ETHICS

Who Is Excluded from Kant's Kingdom of Ends?

The uncompromising severity of Kant's moral system has prompted criticism of the Kantian model. But there is another basic element of Kantian morality that also raises questions. Kant's ethical system counts all *persons* as moral equals, as members of the moral "kingdom of ends," and in that respect Kant's moral system is wonderfully egalitarian. But to count as a person you must be capable of rationally deliberating about universal moral principles, and must have the special power of will to adhere to those principles. If you are not a member of Kant's kingdom of ends—if you are rationally impaired, or your rational capacities are not sufficient for grasping universal principles—then morally you count for nothing. Thus for Kant someone suffering severe and irreversible dementia (someone in advanced Alzheimer's, for example) has no moral standing whatsoever. There would be nothing inherently wrong in torturing such an individual, or in inflicting cruelty on dogs or cats or gerbils. Kant thinks such cruelty is a bad idea, because it may cause those who inflict the torture to become callous, and might lead from abusing puppies to the abuse of rational humans. But apart from such consequences, Kant holds that there is nothing wrong with torturing or otherwise abusing those who are not rational members of the kingdom of ends.

Conflicts Among Principles

Some believe there is another problem in Kant's position. Kant's eye is on the awe-inspiring majesty of rational moral principles, and he is perhaps less concerned with the grubby details of moral behavior. But when we endeavor to "act so that our acts might be willed as universal law," we soon generate an abundance of universal laws, and it is difficult to fit them into a consistent whole. Almost any act we are considering can be described in many different ways, and thus can yield many different—and perhaps conflicting—universal laws. Suppose you have a secret basement room, in which you are hiding several Jewish friends from the Nazis. You hear a knock on the door, and you answer it to find storm troopers searching for Jews: "Are there any Jews living here?" What should you do? Kant seems to require that you give an honest answer, though that means the murder of the Jews and likely the murder of you and your family for hiding them. Terrible consequences, certainly; but the rightness or wrongness of an act is not influenced by its consequences. But the problem is, the act you are contemplating can be described in a variety of ways: telling the truth; betraying friends; exposing one's family to harm; cooperating with a brutally murderous regime. It may be difficult to universalize the principle that we should tell lies, but it is also difficult to universalize the principle that we should betray our friends. Elegant as Kant's system is, it does not always provide clear moral answers to serious moral quandaries.

CONCLUSION

Kant offers a severe and demanding, hard and uncompromising account of morality. Kant would consider that a virtue, rather than a problem. Our capacity to follow the stern dictates of moral principle is what sets us apart from the natural world. We should hardly expect such a model to produce results that are always pleasant and agreeable in the natural world in which we live.

Kant develops a moral system that places morality—and human moral agents—in a distinct and special realm set apart from the natural world. Kantian ethics exists in a realm where desires and feelings and inclinations are excluded, the special powers of reason and free will reign, and the discoveries of the natural sciences cannot encroach. If you feel your cherished sense of the special unique human status threatened by astronomy or biology or psychology, Kant has fashioned a place of refuge.

But if you reject Kant's effort to separate ethics from the natural world, is there anything in Kant you could still find plausible? One need not buy the entire Kantian package in order to appreciate some elements of Kantian ethics. Kant's categorical imperative is in many ways a worthy ideal, and he makes his case for that principle using exclusively the resources of reason. Perhaps Kant's most significant contribution is to show that ethics can effectively employ reason, just as other areas of inquiry do. (Whether Kant places too much emphasis on the role of reason in ethics, and whether reason can establish everything he claims for it in ethics, are vexed questions that will occupy us further.) Reasoning is important in ethics, and it seems obvious that we can reason about ethical issues. After all, whether you agree or disagree with the conclusion of Thomson's violinist analogy, you used *reason* to evaluate her argument. (If I said Thomson's argument must be strong because it feels good to me, you would find that a strange and useless evaluation.) But are there limits to the use of reason in ethics? Can reason supply us with basic categorical principles, as Kant believes? Are feelings also relevant to ethics, or are they—as Kant insists—a distraction and an impediment? In particular, when we get to basic ethical issues, are the justifications for our views based on reason? On feelings? On tradition? *Can* we adequately justify our most fundamental ethical commitments? These are questions we shall examine through the rest of the book, perhaps the rest of our lives.

In its Platonic or Kantian purity, rationalist ethics has no use for feelings and emotions. In stark contrast, many have held that feelings are the foundation of ethics, and that without feelings there would be no ethics at all.[2] Those opposing views will be the topic of our next chapter.

THE FOUNDATIONS OF THE METAPHYSICS OF MORALS, CRITIQUE OF PRACTICAL REASON

Immanuel Kant

Immanuel Kant lived from 1724 to 1804, never leaving East Prussia during his lifetime. For over two centuries his work has been and continues to be a major influence on almost every area of philosophy, particularly ethics, epistemology, and metaphysics. His great work, the *Critique of Pure Reason* (1781), was aimed at nothing less than establishing the powers as well as the limits of reason. It was followed by his major works in ethics, *The Foundations of the Metaphysics of Morals* (1785) and *Critique of Practical Reason* (1788), from which our selections are drawn.

TRANSITION FROM THE COMMON RATIONAL KNOWLEDGE OF MORALS TO THE PHILOSOPHICAL

Nothing in the world—indeed nothing even beyond the world—can possibly be conceived which could be called good without qualification except a *good will*. Intelligence, wit, judgment, and the other talents of the mind, however they may be named, or courage, resoluteness, and perseverance as qualities of temperament are doubtless in many respects good and desirable. But they can become extremely bad and harmful if the will, which is to make use of these gifts of nature and which in its special constitution is called character, is not good. It is the same with the gifts of fortune.

Power, riches, honor, even health, general well-being, and the contentment with one's condition which is called happiness make for pride and even arrogance if there is not a good will to correct their influence on the mind and on its principles of action, so as to make it universally conformable to its end. It need hardly be mentioned that the sight of a being adorned with no feature of a pure and good will yet enjoying uninterrupted prosperity can never give pleasure to a rational impartial observer. Thus the good will seems to constitute the indispensable condition even of worthiness to be happy.

Some qualities seem to be conducive to this good will and can facilitate its action, but, in spite of that, they have no intrinsic unconditional worth. They rather presuppose a good will, which limits the high esteem which one otherwise rightly has for them and prevents their being held to be absolutely good. Moderation in emotions and passions, self-control, and calm deliberation not only are good in many respects but even seem to constitute part of the inner worth of the person. But however unconditionally they were esteemed by the ancients, they are far from being good without qualification. For, without the principles of a good will, they can become extremely bad, and the coolness of a villain makes him not only far more dangerous but also more directly abominable in our eyes than he would have seemed without it.

The good will is not good because of what it effects or accomplishes or because of its adequacy to achieve some proposed end; it is good only because of its willing, i.e., it is good of itself. And regarded for itself, it is to be esteemed incomparably higher than anything which could be brought about by it in favor of any inclination or even of the sum total of all inclinations. Even if it should happen that, by a particularly unfortunate fate or by the niggardly provision of a stepmotherly nature, this will should be wholly lacking in power to accomplish its purpose, and if even the greatest effort should not avail it to achieve anything of its end, and if there remained only the good will (not as a mere wish but as the summoning of all the means in our power), it would sparkle like a jewel with its own light, as something that had its full worth in itself. Usefulness or fruitlessness can neither diminish nor augment this worth.

To be kind where one can is duty, and there are, moreover, many persons so sympathetically constituted that without any motive of vanity or selfishness they find an inner satisfaction in spreading joy and rejoice in the contentment of others which they have made possible. But I say that, however dutiful and amiable it may be, that kind of action has no true moral worth. It is on a level with other inclinations, such as the inclination to honor, which, if fortunately directed to what in fact accords with duty and is generally useful and thus honorable, deserve praise and encouragement but no esteem. For the maxim lacks the moral import of an action done not from inclination but from duty. But assume that the mind of that friend to mankind was clouded by a sorrow of his own which extinguished all sympathy with the lot of others and that he still had the power to benefit others in distress, but that their need left him untouched because he was preoccupied with his own need. And now suppose him to tear himself, unsolicited by inclination, out of this dead insensibility and to do this action only from duty and without any inclination—then for the first time his action has genuine moral worth. Furthermore, if nature has put little sympathy in the heart of a man, and if he, though an honest man, is by temperament cold and indifferent to the sufferings of others perhaps because he is provided with special gifts of patience and fortitude, and expects or even requires that others should have the same—and such a man would certainly not be the meanest product of nature—would not he find in himself a source from which to give himself a far higher worth than he could have got by having a good natured temperament? This is unquestionably true even though nature did not make him philanthropic, for it is just here that the worth of the character is brought out, which is morally and incomparably the highest of all: he is beneficent not from inclination but from duty.

Thus the moral worth of an action does not lie in the effect which is expected from it or in any principle of action which has to borrow its motive from this expected effect. For all these effects (agreeableness of condition, indeed even the promotion of the happiness of others) could be brought about through other causes and would not require the will of a rational being, while the highest and unconditional good can be found only in such a will. Therefore, the pre-eminent good can consist only in the conception of the law in itself (which can be present only in a rational being) so far as this conception and not the hoped-for effect is the determining ground of the will. This pre-eminent good, which we call moral, is already present in the person who acts according to this conception, and we do not have to expect it first in the result.

But what kind of a law can that be, the conception of which must determine the will without reference to the expected result? Under this condition alone the will can be called absolutely good without qualification. Since I have robbed the will of all impulses which could come to it from obedience to any law, nothing remains to serve as a principle of the will except universal conformity of its action to law as such. That is, I should never act in such a way that I could not will that my maxim should be a universal law.

Duty! Thou sublime and mighty name that dost embrace nothing charming or insinuating but requirest submission and yet seekest not to move the will by threatening aught that would arouse natural aversion or terror but only holdest forth a law which of itself finds entrance into the mind and yet gains reluctant reverence (though not always obedience)—a law before which all inclinations are dumb even though they secretly work against it: what origin is there worthy of thee, and where is to be found the root of thy noble descent which proudly rejects all kinship with the inclinations and from which to be descended is the indispensable condition of the only worth which men can give themselves?

It cannot be less than something which elevates man above himself as a part of the world of sense, something which connects him with an order of things which only the understanding can think and which has under it the entire world of sense, including the empirically determinable existence of man in time, and the whole system of all ends which is alone suitable to such unconditional practical laws as the moral. It is nothing else than personality, i.e., the freedom and independence from the mechanism of nature regarded as a capacity of a being which is subject to special laws (pure practical laws given by its own reason), so that the person as belonging to the world of sense is subject to his own personality so far

as he belongs to the intelligible world. For it is then not to be wondered at that man, as belonging to two worlds, must regard his own being in relation to his second and higher vocation with reverence and the laws of this vocation with the deepest respect.

CONCLUSION

Two things fill the mind with ever new and increasing admiration and awe, the oftener and more steadily they are reflected on: the starry heavens above me and the moral law within me. I do not merely conjecture them and seek them as though obscured in darkness or in the transcendent region beyond my horizon: I see them before me, and I associate them directly with the consciousness of my own existence. The former begins from the place I occupy in the external world of sense, and it broadens the connection in which I stand into an unbounded magnitude of worlds beyond worlds and systems of systems and into the limitless times of their periodic motion, their beginning and continuance. The latter begins from my invisible self, my personality, and exhibits me in a world which has true infinity but which is comprehensible only to the understanding— a world with which I recognize myself as existing in a universal and necessary (and not only, as in the first case, contingent) connection, and thereby also in connection with all those visible worlds. The former view of a countless multitude of worlds annihilates, as it were, my importance as an animal creature, which must give back to the planet (a mere speck in the universe) the matter from which it came, the matter which is for a little time provided with vital force, we know not how. The latter, on the contrary, infinitely raises my worth as that of an intelligence by my personality, in which the moral law reveals a life independent of all animality and even of the whole world of sense—at least so far as it may be inferred from the purposive destination assigned to my existence by this law, a destination which is not restricted to the conditions and limits of this life but reaches into the infinite.

EXERCISES

1. Children under age 10 are of course of great moral *importance*, and it is a grievous moral wrong to harm them. But can they be moral *actors*? That is, can small children actually commit morally wrong or morally virtuous acts?

2. University professors are usually fairly bright, and they typically hold reason in high regard. But sad to say, university professors are not widely acclaimed as moral models. In fact, academic departments are notorious for being dens of intrigue and betrayal, and squabbling among faculty is common. (Perhaps you are familiar with the saying that university politics is so nasty because the stakes are so low.) If that assessment of the moral status of university faculty is accurate (and it seems clear that university faculty are not morally *better* than average), does that count against the claim that rationality is the core of ethics?

3. Mr. Spock—of Star Trek fame—apparently feels no emotions. Would that make him (in your view) more or less capable of living a morally good life?

4. Kant claims that his categorical imperative is a moral principle that can be known purely by reason, without dependence on any observations or experience. It is a truth of reason that can be established in the same way we work out a proof in mathematics or geometry. If you were proposing a candidate for a moral principle known purely by reason, what do you think would be the best candidate? (You may think it is not possible to know moral truths purely by reason; perhaps you don't think moral truths can be known at all; maybe you doubt that any even exist. No matter. What sort of moral principle do you think would be most plausibly derived by pure reason?)

5. Kant formulates two versions of his categorical imperative, though he claims they are merely different formulations of the same principle. Would it be possible for someone to *consistently* hold the first imperative (always act in such a way that you could will that your act should be a universal law) but *deny* the second imperative (always treat others as ends in themselves, and never merely as means)?

ADDITIONAL READING

Among Kant's classic works on ethics are *Groundwork of the Metaphysic of Morals*, trans. H.J. Paton, as *The Moral Law* (London: Hutchinson, 1953); *Critique of Practical Reason*, trans. L. W. Beck (Indianapolis: Bobbs-Merrill, 1977); and *Religion Within the Limits of Reason Alone*, trans. T.M. Greene and H.H. Hudson (New York: Harper and Row, 1960).

Excellent works on Kant's ethics include Lewis White Beck's *A Commentary on Kant's Critique of Practical Reason* (Chicago: University of Chicago Press, 1960); and Onora O'Neill, *Constructions of Reason: Explorations of Kant's Practical Philosophy* (Cambridge: Cambridge University Press, 1989). A fascinating brief challenge to Kant's ethical system is Rae Langton's "Maria von Herbert's Challenge to Kant," which can be found in Peter Singer, editor, *Ethics* (Oxford: Oxford University Press, 1994).

Many outstanding contemporary philosophers follow—to at least some degree—the Kantian tradition in ethics. A small sample includes Kurt Baier, *The Moral Point of View* (Ithaca, N.Y.: Cornell University Press, 1958); Stephen Darwall, *Impartial Reason* (Ithaca, N.Y.: Cornell University Press, 1983); Alan Donagan, *The Theory of Morality* (Chicago: University of Chicago Press, 1977); and Thomas Nagel, *The View from Nowhere* (New York: Oxford University Press, 1986).

Kantian ethics can seem cold and austere. For a more engaging experience of Kantian ethics, try some essays by Thomas E. Hill, Jr., who is clearly a Kantian, but writes with grace, charm, and clarity on a variety of ethical issues. See his essays in *Respect, Pluralism, and Justice: Kantian Perspectives* (Oxford: Oxford University Press, 2000); and *Human Welfare and Moral Worth: Kantian Perspectives* (Oxford: Oxford University Press, 2002).

NOTES

[1]Immanuel Kant, *The Critique of Practical Reason and Other Writings in Moral Philosophy*, trans. L. W. Beck (Chicago: University of Chicago Press, 1949), p. 289. First published in 1788.

[2]Some neuropsychologists now believe that reason itself *requires* emotions. For an interesting account of this view, see Antonio R. Damasio, *Descartes' Error: Emotion, Reason, and the Human Brain* (New York: G. P. Putnam's Sons, 1994). It is now available in paperback, and is delightful to read.

CHAPTER 3

<hr />

❖ ETHICS AND EMOTIONS ❖

<hr />

FOLLOW YOUR REASON OR FOLLOW YOUR HEART?

Christina and Dekisha are juniors at Beverwyck College. They have been close friends since the spring semester of their freshman year, when they suffered together through Professor Stewart's terminally boring introduction to philosophy. They are also dedicated, effective, and tireless volunteers in a local homeless shelter. They work long hours at the shelter, provide care and comfort to the residents, and they are apparently equally effective in their work and equally popular with the residents. Dekisha and Christina have spent their spring break working night and day at the shelter, and on the last day of spring break they are taking a late-night coffee break and talking together. "This has been the most wonderful spring break I have ever had," Christina says. "I can't think of anything that would have brought me more satisfaction and joy than working with these people, giving them a bit of hope and encouragement, and seeing their sorrows turn into smiles." Dekisha shakes her head. "Not me. I can think of lots of things that would bring me more joy: Just to name one, sitting on a warm beach of sugary sand, soaking up sunshine and margaritas, and snuggling with my sweetie. In fact, I would rather be almost anywhere than here. But these people are suffering, and I'm good at helping them, and I have an opportunity to relieve their suffering—so I believe I have a duty to help. It's the right thing for me to do, it's what I should do, and what I must do. But it's certainly not what I would prefer to do." Leave aside for a moment the question of how effectively Dekisha and Christina work at the shelter. Suppose that both are equally effective, equally comforting, equally kind. The question is simply this: which of the two, dutiful Dekisha or joyful Christina, would you consider the most *morally* upstanding? (Dekisha and Christina are the two finalists for Morally Outstanding Junior at Beverwyck College, and you are on the selection committee; whom would you choose?)

The correct answer is: Dekisha. Christina was merely following her inclinations. Fortunately her inclinations are generous, but that's just a matter of good luck. Her acts of kindness were not really moral acts at all, since they were not done out of deliberate duty. Dekisha wins. It's not even close.

But on the other hand, maybe Christina should be our winner. She doesn't need rules or duties to do the right thing; instead, her acts of kindness come from deep within her,

<hr />

from her own deep sense of care and affection, and she doesn't have to stop and think before doing the right thing. Dekisha may follow moral rules, but the real moral acts stem from Christina's loving heart. Christina wins.

So which is the best path to morality, Dekisha's rationalist rule-governed and duty-driven approach, or Christina's heartfelt commitments?

This question has stirred debate for many centuries. The debate takes many shapes, but it basically turns on this question: to act ethically, is it essential to overcome one's feelings and suppress sentiments in order to follow true rational moral principles that transcend our grubby, earthly, animal natures? Or is ethics rooted in our sentiments, in our feelings of warmth and kindness and compassion and affection: feelings that are not derived from reason and that we share with other animals?

"The great secret of morals is love; or a going out of our own nature, and an identification of ourselves with the beautiful which exists in thought, action, or person not our own. . . . The great instrument of moral good is the imagination. . . ." Percy Bysshe Shelley, *A Defense of Poetry*, 1821

Reason or Feelings: History of the Conflict

This fundamental conflict can be traced through the great religious traditions. One strong element of Jewish tradition is adherence to the divine law in all its majesty and detail, with the path to virtue passing through careful scrutiny of texts and commentaries and the scrupulous keeping of every law. In contrast, in Micah 6:12, the Jewish prophet Micah counsels that living a good life does not require such rigorous rationalistic study, but instead comes easy: "What doth the Lord require of thee, but to do justly, and to love mercy, and to walk humbly with thy God?" In the Christian tradition, Jesus taught the virtues of living simply, with more emphasis on feeding the hungry and caring for the sick and loving your neighbor, and less worry about the law and rules and reason and riches. With St. Paul, the pendulum swings to the other side: Paul emphasizes a precise formula for gaining salvation, and the path is straight, narrow, and difficult. The same marked contrast can be seen between the stern rationalism of St. Thomas Aquinas and the warm natural feelings St. Frances of Assisi found in birds, beasts, and humans. In Islam, the Sufi tradition emphasizes following one's God-given inner feelings (though this requires a process of discipline and purification), while such great Muslim theologians as Ibn Rushd celebrate reason as a legitimate pathway to God and to a virtuous life. The ancient Chinese Confucian philosopher, Mencius, believed that humans are naturally good out of a deep innate sense of compassion. It is this deep natural feeling of compassion, rather than rational reflection or strict rules, that guides humans to act virtuously. In contrast, Thomas Hobbes, the seventeenth-century British philosopher, regarded the natural state of humanity as a "war of all against all" in which life is "nasty, brutish, and short." According to Hobbes, the dominating natural sentiments are greed and self-protection, sentiments that can be held in check only by a "great leviathan" who rules through force and fear.

So if you wish to carefully examine your own view of ethics, one good starting point is the tension between duty and sentiment. Is ethics rooted in natural sentiments of affection and generosity and sympathy? Or is ethics primarily a matter of following duty and reason, and combating our natural tendencies of selfishness and greed?

Affection and Duty: the Case of Huck Finn

Here's another case to consider.[1] Huck Finn is floating along the river on a raft, accompanied by his friend Jim, an escaped slave. Life is good, as the two friends while away the leisurely days talking and fishing. As the raft moves farther north, Jim becomes more and more excited: soon he will cross over into free territory, and be a free man. He intends to work hard and save his money, and eventually buy his wife and children out of slavery. If their owner refuses to sell them, Jim plans to steal them. Jim is deeply grateful to Huck: Huck is helping him escape, and Jim regards Huck as his best friend, indeed "the only friend old Jim's got now." But as they move closer to Jim's freedom, Huck becomes despondent. He is helping Jim escape, and Huck regards that as no better than stealing. He is stealing the rightful property of Miss Watson, who owns Jim, and who always treated Huck well. Huck's conscience starts to bother him: "What did that poor old woman do to you, that you could treat her so mean?" Eventually Huck resolves to do his duty: Huck's moral code requires turning Jim in to prevent his escape. So Huck sets off with that purpose, but his resolve fails him, and when he has the opportunity he can't bring himself to betray his friend. Huck believes that he has done wrong, and that he's no better than a thief, but he can't bring himself to do "his moral duty."

Of course we think that Huck did the *right* thing. It was right to help Jim escape from slavery, and it would have been egregiously wrong for Huck to betray his friend to the slave catchers. But Huck believes he has done wrong. His moral code demanded that he turn Jim in, but his sentiments—his affection for Jim—prevented him from doing his duty. Did Huck perform a morally good act when he acted against his moral code and helped Jim escape? If you perform an act that you believe is morally wrong, can you still be morally right in your behavior? Suppose Huck had feared that if he turned Jim in Jim might escape and kill him, and so he decides not to turn Jim in (though he still believes he *should*). Is he performing a morally good act? A morally bad act?

In Western philosophy, most ethicists have favored Dekisha. The best path to morality is through duty, through following moral principles, through ignoring or suppressing our feelings and seeking the guidance of reason and moral law and moral principle. Our feelings tempt us to go astray, distract us from our duty. (Of course reason and duty can also go wrong, as illustrated by Huck's belief in his duty to return an escaped slave. But even though our reason is not infallible, it is still our best guide to ethical principles.) In any case, our feelings are too variable and inconstant to serve as a reliable moral guide.

Hume Versus Kant

In contrast, some writers on ethics have advocated the primacy of feelings over reason as a guide to ethics. Among that group David Hume stands out. Hume was a Scottish philosopher, who spent most of his adult life in France. Though he was a contemporary of Kant (born in 1711, 13 years before Kant), they were millennia apart in philosophical views as well as in temperament, and much of what Kant writes is an effort to refute Hume's position. It was Hume's work, Kant said, that "awakened me from my dogmatic slumber" and revealed the profound challenge awaiting anyone who favors rational ethical objectivity.

Kant spent most of his life as a philosophy professor at the University of Konigsberg, in the city of his birth, and he never ventured outside East Prussia. A man of simple, even austere habits, legend has it that the locals set their clocks by his daily walk. Though he was a famous person in his later years—in eighteenth-century Europe, philosophers could gain a substantial measure of renown—Kant continued to live quietly, pursue his writing, and deliver his lectures. David Hume, in contrast, traveled extensively from his Edinburgh birthplace (he returned in his later years, and is buried there), and felt most at home in the exciting and fashionable world of Paris. Eighteenth-century Paris was abuzz with revolutionary ideas—ideas that stimulated the American and later the French Revolutions, radical ideas concerning religion, debates in biology concerning the LaMarckian account of evolution, endless discussion of the implications of Newtonian science. Hume delighted in such debates, and was a charming and welcome guest at the most fashionable parties; indeed, his French friends nicknamed him "Le bon David."

Both Kant and Hume were profoundly influenced by the Newtonian scientific revolution, but Newton's theory pushed them in opposite directions. Kant, impressed by the precision and power of Newtonian physics, resolved to forge an ethical system based on a few principles that can be known through pure reason: a system that will set rational beings apart from the deterministic physical world of Newtonian science. Hume, also impressed by Newton's system, had no wish to set humans apart from the natural determinist world. For Hume, that is the only world there is, and we are thoroughly part of it. Kant believed there was no way of establishing universal principles of ethics on the basis of scientific observations, and so ethics must be established through the powers of pure abstract reasoning. Hume agrees that empirical science cannot offer us ethical truths, but neither can pure reason. That leaves Hume's ethics in the realm of feelings and passions. But since for Hume the only genuine knowledge comes from pure mathematics or empirical science, that excludes ethics from the realm of knowledge altogether. Feelings are important, and they are the basis for ethics, but feelings cannot provide an objective foundation for ethics. If we want objective truth, we must look to the sciences, and to the truths of mathematics and geometry that we know through reason. But reason cannot give us ethical truths. Not because reason is flawed, but rather because basic ethical preferences are the proper realm of the feelings, and reason does not operate there. Hume states his position unequivocally:

> 'Tis not contrary to reason to prefer the destruction of the whole world to the scratching of my finger.[2]

Most of us would find this a strange preference indeed. But if it does not involve any false judgment—such as the belief that a scratch on my finger would doom my immortal soul, or the belief that scratching my finger would cause prolonged agony for millions of people, or the belief that I would die from a scratch on my finger but survive the destruction of the world—then (according to Hume) reason cannot refute it. If you believe that smoking contributes to good health and improves your athletic performance, or that you are immune from any health risks from smoking, then reason may be used to change your views. But if you know the severe risks of smoking, but you really consider the pleasures of smoking sufficiently valuable to outweigh the perils of cancer and emphysema, then reason cannot touch your preferences. Our basic preferences, values, and desires do not come from reason, but instead they *use* reason to find means of gaining satisfaction. According to Hume:

> Reason is, and ought only to be the slave of the passions, and can never pretend to any other office than to serve and obey them.[3]

When it comes to *basic* ethical views, there is no truth of the matter for Hume. If you want truth, look to science or mathematics. Ethics is ultimately based on our feelings, and that is not an area where truth and falsity apply.

OBJECTIVE AND SUBJECTIVE FEELINGS

Some people view feelings differently. Hume insists that ethics is based on feelings, and feelings aren't subject to reason. But others insist that feelings can be a source of truth, and so ethics can ultimately be based on feelings and still be objective truth. Not all truths come from reason and empirical scientific observation, and the truths of ethics are the prime example of such nonrational (not irrational) truths. This *objectivist* interpretation of our feelings agrees with a famous saying from Pascal: "The heart has its reasons that the reason knows not."

If we think of ethics as based on feelings, as Hume does, can we also believe that some ethical claims are actually true? Or is ethics more like our tastes: you like white wine and I prefer red, and there's no question of who is "objectively right." Suppose we ask Christina and Dekisha. You remember Christina and Dekisha, who spend many hours working at the homeless shelter: Christina because she takes great joy in helping those who need help, and Dekisha because she believes it to be her moral duty. Dekisha, being a good Kantian, has no doubts about the matter. There is indeed a moral right and wrong; it is known through pure reason, and it is perfectly objective. Suppose Dekisha is challenged by her friend, Neville. "You know, spending all this time at the homeless shelter is wrong; everyone should think only of themselves, and not worry about others who are less fortunate." Dekisha will have a clear answer: "You are profoundly mistaken. Since each of us needs help at times, we could not will that ignoring the needs of others should be a universal law. When I am in need of help, I think people should help me; after all, I'm a person, not just some object you can ignore or discard. And there is nothing morally special about me that does not apply to other people as well. So rational consistency demands that I acknowledge the universal principle that there is an obligation to help those in need."

Subjective Feelings

How would *Christina* answer George's challenge? That's a more complicated question. There are two very different sorts of answers Christina might give. *Subjective* Christina might say: "Wow, we really feel differently about this. I gain such joy and satisfaction from helping these desperately unfortunate people, it's almost hard for me to believe that you feel it's not worthwhile. But then, I also love Jackson Pollock's paintings, and I know some people who can't stand them. It's not that I'm right and you're wrong, but I do wish your feelings about this were more similar to mine, because this is very important to me. It bothers me more that you feel this way about the homeless than that you don't like Jackson Pollock." *Subjective* Christina cannot say that George is mistaken, and she cannot give rational arguments to refute George's opposing perspective. But she does have other resources. She might do various things to develop such feelings in her friend George: have him read John Steinbeck's *Grapes of Wrath*, or give George the opportunity to meet a warm and fascinating homeless person who has suffered a series of terrible misfortunes (because George may have the notion that all homeless people are lazy bums who are exploiting the system, and when George understands the facts of how some good hardworking people wind up in such misfortune, his feelings about them may change). But if George has no factual delusions—"I know that some of the homeless are good and decent people, whose misfortune is not their own fault; still, it's not my problem, and I don't really care what happens to them"—and his feelings cannot be modified by imagination or literature, then there is nothing more for Subjective Christina to say.

Objective Feelings

But Christina may have a very different view. *Objective* Christina has strong feelings about the value of helping the homeless, but she does not think such feelings are just a matter of taste or preference. Instead, Objective Christina maintains that her feelings—the distress she feels over the suffering of the homeless, and the warm satisfaction she feels when providing help—are a reliable guide to moral truth. She does not believe that George's callous view can be refuted by reason, but she does believe George is *morally* wrong, and *objectively* wrong, to feel that we should not help the homeless. Some people see the world of science and mathematics and reason as the world of objective facts, and the realm of poetry and music and art and tastes and feelings as a subjective nonfactual realm. Objective Christina regards that as a false dichotomy. Of course science is objective, and a taste for bordeaux is subjective. But our sentiments regarding ethical issues are not like mere taste preferences. They aren't ultimately based on reason, but why suppose that reason is the only way to know objective truths?

So Objective Christina believes there is wisdom in our feelings. That doesn't imply, of course, that every feeling is a path to truth. Some feelings may be rejected as leading us astray—just as some scientific theories may also be flawed. Objective Christina acknowledges that feelings are not an *infallible* guide to ethics. But she denies that feelings are merely distractions on the path to ethical truth, and she believes feelings can be the source of ethical insight.

INTUITIONISM

We'll return in later chapters to questions about feelings, and what they do or do not contribute to ethics. But there is another view about ethics that must be distinguished from the position favored by Objective Christina, with her emphasis on the wisdom of feelings. This other view, which may sound superficially similar to Objective Christina's position, is called *intuitionism*. Intuitionists believe that reason is not the source of basic ethical truths, but neither are feelings. Rather, we *know* the basic truths of ethics by a special power of *intuition*. It is not just a matter of how we *feel* about something, but of what we intuitively recognize. If I find a lost wallet containing several hundred dollars, my *feelings* might be joy at my good fortune, but my *intuition* that I must return the money is something quite different. My power of ethical intuition is not like reason, but neither is it a feeling. Instead it is analogous to my power of vision. When I am in the right place, and my vision is clear, I can *see* a mountain. And in the right circumstances, I can also *see* what is right and what is wrong.

Where does this intuitive power come from? Some intuitionists answer that it is implanted in us by God, a special power that distinguishes us from beasts. Other intuitionists suggest other sources. But however we come by this power it is a power we all have, and if we are receptive to it and honest about it we cannot deny its existence. "How can I be sure this is an intuition of wrongness, and not just the effects of the sauerkraut pizza I had for lunch?" Our intuitive ethical insights are of a special nature and power. When you have a genuine intuition of rightness or wrongness, you cannot help recognizing that it is an ethical truth. Having the ethical intuition without recognizing it as an ethical truth would be like seeing a circle without seeing that it is round. "But I don't have such powers of intuition. I don't get these powerful intuitive ethical insights." Most likely you really do, but you are deceiving yourself because you don't want to acknowledge them. "No, I really don't have them." In that case, you are a moral monster. You have lived such a morally depraved life, and ignored so consistently the ethical prompting from your ethical intuition, that you have finally become ethically blind. But your failure to recognize ethical intuitions shows only the depth of your wickedness, not that such intuitions do not exist.

What Do We Intuit?

That is a rough outline of intuitionism. But once we get beyond that general outline, we soon discover a variety of views marching under the intuitionist banner. Perhaps the most controversial question for intuitionists is the nature of what is intuited. When you consult your ethical intuitions, what do you discover? This question is not just a question of whether we all share the same ethical intuitions. At a deeper level, it is first of all a question of what *types* of intuitions we have. Do we intuit a single basic ethical principle, from which all other principles may be derived (perhaps something like "treat others as you would wish to be treated")? Or do we intuit a number of ethical principles ("tell the truth" and "return favors" and "do not kill")? Or do we perhaps intuit some property of *goodness*, that we recognize as an irreducible fact? Maybe instead we intuit the rightness or wrongness of specific acts ("it is wrong to deceive Brenda about the bad brakes on the car I am trying to sell her"). Or possibly we intuit a general property of goodness, as well as general principles, and also the rightness or wrongness of specific acts. But most intuitionists are reluctant to claim such a rich variety of intuitions. Instead, intuitionists usually insist that we have a specific type of intuition that guides our ethical behavior. At the most general level, we might intuit some principle that would form the single overarching rule for all our behavior, and the truth of that principle would be immediately and intuitively evident. In contrast, an intuitionist might insist that rather than a general principle, we intuit the rightness of a specific act. For example, Henry Prichard counsels that we must examine each act we are considering as carefully and fully as we can, and then we will intuit the rightness or the wrongness of the act we are considering. Of course we might still make mistakes. But if we consider carefully and keep our intuitions in good working order, that is the best guide we can have to right and wrong.

Somewhere between these two views falls the intuitionist approach of W.D. Ross, who holds that we intuitively know *several* principles. We know, intuitively and immediately and objectively, that it is wrong to break promises. Likewise, we intuitively know that it is right to relieve suffering. These are direct and undeniable moral truths, that "come to be self-evident to us just as mathematical axioms do".[4] The hard questions arise when those simple principles come into conflict. What should I do if I have promised to meet you at noon to take you to lunch, but on my way I encounter someone with a broken leg who needs a ride to the hospital? I have a duty to keep my promise, but also a duty to relieve suffering, and I can't do both. So what should I do? Ross would answer: that's a tough question. In such cases of conflict, it's often difficult to be sure what the stronger duty is. That's not surprising. After all, no one should suppose that making the right ethical decision is always easy. But though we face uncertainty in trying to determine what we should do in specific cases, that uncertainty does not infect the general principles. I *know* that I have a duty to keep my promises, and I *know* that I have a duty to relieve suffering. Depending on the situation, one of those duties may be stronger than the other, and knowing what I should do requires careful thought about all the duties I have and the details of my specific situation. But when I reflect carefully, my knowledge that I have a duty to keep my promises and a duty to relieve suffering is immediately and intuitively obvious.

Questions About Intuitionism

Suppose we push intuitionists to tell us more about these special intuitions. How do we know our intuitions are sources of truth? How do we distinguish intuitions from mere feelings? The answers we get are rather limited: You just *know* intuitions when you experience them, and the truth of the intuitions is self-evident. No further explanation is possible, but neither is further explanation needed. Reflect carefully, and you will recognize the intuitive truth that it is wrong to lie.

The intuitionism of W. D. Ross has a solid common-sense appeal. Don't get tangled up in ethical theory and confused by moral speculation: You *know* what's right and wrong. Still, on closer scrutiny, certain aspects of his rule-intuitionism may be troubling. After all, there are many cases of "obvious intuitions" we have come to reject. For example, that slavery is just, that women should have no rights, that persons who do not share our religious doctrines should be killed. Why should we regard our ethical intuitions as any more reliable than our immediate conviction that the Sun is traveling over our heads? There is no doubt that we have strong feelings about right and wrong, and that these feelings have a distinctive force. I feel disgusted when June pours chocolate sauce over her broccoli, but my disgust is of a different order when Liz tells a racist joke or steals money from a blind fruit vendor. But the question of whether our strong feelings—or our "ethical intuitions"—are sources of objective ethical truth remains a difficult issue.

Which Intuitions Should We Trust?

As a young boy growing up on a farm, Joe has a strong sense—some would call it a strong feeling, others might classify it as a moral intuition—that it is wrong to inflict suffering on farm animals in raising them for slaughter. Joe sees a young calf pulled from his mother, then placed in an isolated stall with little room to move and fattened to produce the delicacy of pale veal. Both the calf and his mother appear to suffer significant distress. Joe watches young calves and lambs castrated so they will be less troublesome and grow more rapidly; they certainly do not seem to enjoy the experience. These observations cause Joe significant distress. He *feels* that what is being done to the animals is wrong. Or some would say he *intuited* that treating animals in this manner is morally wrong.

As Joe grows older, he is taught that treating animals in this way is simply part of the way farming is done, and that the suffering of animals is not something he should worry about. When he sees farm animals suffer, it still bothers Joe, but gradually it bothers him less and less. Learning to ignore animal suffering is part of becoming an adult in Joe's farm culture. Since he wants to be accepted as an adult, he eventually learns to ignore the suffering. It no longer disturbs him, and he no longer considers it morally problematic. "We don't intentionally cause the animals to suffer," Joe now says, "but when you raise farm animals for slaughter, they do sometimes suffer. However, farm animals aren't really moral beings, and so their suffering is not a moral issue. Oh, sure, when I was a child I thought that causing the suffering of farm animals was morally wrong. But I'm more mature now, and I don't feel that way anymore. Those childish feelings were mistaken."

This example brings up the question of animal rights, and often people have *very* strong opinions on that issue. That's not the question here. We'll be discussing it, but not quite yet. For the moment, focus on what is happening to Joe. He has one sort of feeling (or intuition) early in his life, and very different feelings now. Those who believe raising animals for slaughter is morally wrong might say that Joe's early feelings (or intuitions) were correct, and that his culture corrupted or destroyed those moral feelings. Those who believe raising animals for slaughter is morally legitimate will say that Joe's childish feelings were just mistaken: like feeling you have been wronged when asked to share your toys with a playmate. The feeling is certainly strong, but growing older you realize that such a feeling is not a useful moral guide. Set aside for a moment your own view about who is right and who is wrong about treatment of farm animals. Focus instead on the question of *how* one would try to resolve that question. Clearly different people can have different feelings (or conflicting intuitions) about moral issues. Indeed, the same person may have conflicting feelings at different times. If feelings (or intuitions) are to serve as moral guides, *how* can we decide which feelings or intuitions we should trust, and which ones we should reject?

The intuitionist W. D. Ross has an answer.

> We have no more direct way of access to the facts about rightness and goodness and about what things are right or good, than by thinking about them; the moral convictions of thoughtful and well-educated people are the data of ethics just as sense perceptions are the data of a natural science. Just as some of the latter have to be rejected as illusory, so have some of the former; but as the latter are rejected only when they are in conflict with other more accurate sense perceptions, the former are rejected only when they are in conflict with other convictions which stand better the test of reflection. The existing body of moral convictions of the best people is the cumulative product of the moral reflection of many generations, which has developed an extremely delicate power of appreciation of moral distinctions; and this the theorist cannot afford to treat with anything other than the greatest respect. The verdicts of the moral consciousness of the best people are the foundation on which he must build. . . . [5]

But his solution raises almost as many issues as it settles. How do we recognize "the best people" whose moral verdicts form the foundation of ethics? If we asked that question in the antebellum South, most Whites would have pointed to the slave-holding owners of the great plantations. They were, after all, the leaders of the society and the best educated people of the region (many plantation owners sent their children to top New England universities). Now they strike us as prime examples of moral blindness. The well-educated leaders of our society—the lawyers and doctors, politicians and journalists, professors and accountants, CEOs and CFOs of major corporations—are probably not the people who leap to mind when you think of persons with deep moral wisdom. In fact, there is a long tradition that the best source of moral wisdom is small farmers, who live close to the soil, earn their bread by the honest sweat of their brows, and are uncorrupted by the artificial contrivances of fashion and fad. That was a very popular view in the eighteenth and nineteenth centuries—Thomas Jefferson was one of its champions—and is represented today by the writings of poet and essayist (and farmer) Wendell Berry. Philosophy professors tend to be well-educated and rather reflective, but in all truth, I would not put them at the top of my list of "morally best people." So recognizing the "best people" (whose intuitions are supposed to be most worthy of trust) is a daunting task. And notice that we cannot identify the "best people" as those who hold the right moral intuitions, for that would just spin us in a tight circle.

So *if* there are disputes concerning moral intuitions, the disputes may be difficult to settle. But intuitionists still insist on the ethical importance of intuitions. After all, you know, clearly and intuitively, that it is wrong to lie. That's all the proof you can have, but that's all the proof you need.

CONCLUSION

The proper role of the emotions is one of the most difficult and contentious questions in ethics (and it is an issue we shall return to in later chapters). Plato and Kant insist that acting ethically requires vigorously *suppressing* the emotions, relying instead on the dispassionate power of reason. In contrast, Hume believes ethics is rooted in our emotions: without emotions, ethics would not exist. Some think ethics is based on emotions, and so *cannot* be objective. Others believe our emotions *are* a source of objective moral truth. And intuitionists maintain we have special objective intuitive powers distinct from our emotional reactions. You will have to make your own decision about which view is most plausible. But you need not make that decision yet. There are more options and more arguments to come.

A TREATISE OF HUMAN NATURE

David Hume

David Hume was born in Edinburgh, Scotland, in 1711. He wrote several major philosophical works, but was also known during his lifetime for his writings on history, political theory, and economics. Greatly influenced by Isaac Newton's experimental method and by British empiricist philosophy, he endeavored to apply Newton's method to the study of the human mind. A gracious, sociable, and generous person, he had many friends both in Scotland and in France. After spending much of his adult life in Paris, Hume died in Edinburgh in 1776. The following passage was originally published in 1738.

SECTION III.

OF THE INFLUENCING MOTIVES OF THE WILL

Nothing is more usual in philosophy, and even in common life, than to talk of the combat of passion and reason, to give the preference to reason, and to assert that men are only so far virtuous as they conform themselves to its dictates. Every rational creature, 'tis said, is oblig'd to regulate his actions by reason; and if any other motive or principle challenge the direction of his conduct, he ought to oppose it, 'till it be entirely subdu'd, or at least brought to a conformity with that superior principle. On this method of thinking the greatest part of moral philosophy, antient and modern, seems to be founded; nor is there an ampler field, as well for metaphysical arguments, as popular declamations, than this suppos'd pre-eminence of reason above passion. The eternity, invariableness, and divine origin of the former have been display'd to the best advantage: The blindness, unconstancy, and deceitfulness of the latter have been as strongly insisted on. In order to shew the fallacy of all this phi-

losophy, I shall endeavour to prove *first*, that reason alone can never be a motive to any action of the will; and *secondly*, that it can never oppose passion in the direction of the will.

The understanding exerts itself after two different ways, as it judges from demonstration or probability; as it regards the abstract relations of our ideas, or those relations of objects, of which experience only gives us information. I believe it scarce will be asserted, that the first species of reasoning alone is ever the cause of any action. As it's proper province is the world of ideas, and as the will always places us in that of realities, demonstration and volition seem, upon that account, to be totally remov'd, from each other. Mathematics, indeed, are useful in all mechanical operations, and arithmetic in almost every art and profession: But 'tis not of themselves they have any influence. Mechanics are the art of regulating the motions of bodies *to some design'd end or purpose;* and the reason why we employ arithmetic in fixing the proportions of numbers, is only that we may discover the proportions of their influence and operation. A merchant is desirous of knowing the sum total of his accounts with any person: Why? but that he may learn what sum will have the same *effects* in paying his debt, and going to market, as all the particular articles taken together. Abstract or demonstrative reasoning, therefore, never influences any of our actions, but only as it directs our judgment concerning causes and effects; which leads us to the second operation of the understanding.

'Tis obvious, that when we have the prospect of pain or pleasure from any object, we feel a consequent emotion of aversion or propensity, and are carry'd to avoid or embrace what will give us this uneasiness or satisfaction. 'Tis also obvious, that this emotion rests not here, but making us cast our view on every side, comprehends whatever objects are connected with its original one by the relation of cause and effect. Here then reasoning takes place to discover this relation; and according as our reasoning varies, our actions receive a subsequent variation. But 'tis evident in this case, that the impulse arises not from reason, but is only directed by it. 'Tis from the prospect of pain or pleasure that the aversion or propensity arises towards any object: And these emotions extend themselves to the causes and effects of that object, as they are pointed out to us by reason and experience. It can never in the least concern us to know, that such objects are causes, and such others effects, if both the causes and effects be indifferent to us. Where the objects themselves do not affect us, their connexion can never give them any influence; and 'tis plain, that as reason is nothing but the discovery of this connexion, it cannot be by its means that the objects are able to affect us.

Since reason alone can never produce any action, or give rise to volition, I infer, that the same faculty is as incapable of preventing volition, or of disputing the preference with any passion or emotion. This consequence is necessary. 'Tis impossible reason cou'd have the latter effect of preventing volition, but by giving an impulse in a contrary direction to our passion; and that impulse, had it operated alone, wou'd have been able to produce volition. Nothing can oppose or retard the impulse of passion, but a contrary impulse; and if this contrary impulse ever arises from reason, that latter faculty must have an original influence on the will, and must be able to cause, as well as hinder any act of volition. But if reason has no original influence, 'tis impossible it can withstand any principle, which has such an efficacy, or ever keep the mind in suspence a moment.

Thus it appears, that the principle, which opposes our passion, cannot be the same with reason, and is only call'd so in an improper sense. We speak not strictly and philosophically when we talk of the combat of passion and of reason. Reason is, and ought only to be the slave of the passions, and can never pretend to any other office than to serve and obey them. As this opinion may appear somewhat extraordinary, it may not be improper to confirm it by some other considerations.

A passion is an original existence, or, if you will, modification of existence, and contains not any representative quality, which renders it a copy of any other existence or modification. When I am angry, I am actually possest with the passion, and in that emotion have no more a reference to any other object, than when I am thirsty, or sick, or more than five foot high. 'Tis impossible, therefore, that this passion can be oppos'd by, or be contradictory to truth and reason; since this contradiction consists in the disagreement of ideas, consider'd as copies, with those objects, which they represent.

What may at first occur on this head, is, that as nothing can be contrary to truth or reason, except what has a reference to it, and as the judgments of our understanding only have this reference, it must follow, that passions can be contrary to reason only so far as they are *accompany'd* with some judgment or opinion. According to this principle, which is so obvious and natural, 'tis only in two senses, that any affection can be call'd unreasonable. First, When a passion, such as hope or fear, grief or joy, despair or security, is founded on the supposition of the existence of objects, which really do not exist. Secondly, When in exerting any passion in action, we chuse means insufficient for the design'd end, and deceive ourselves in our judgment of causes and effects. Where a passion is neither founded on false suppositions, nor chuses means insufficient for the end, the understanding can neither justify nor condemn it. 'Tis not contrary to reason to prefer the destruction of the whole world to the scratching of my finger. 'Tis not contrary to reason for me to chuse my total ruin, to prevent the least uneasiness of an *Indian* or person wholly unknown to me. 'Tis as little contrary to reason to prefer even my own acknowledg'd lesser good to my greater, and have a more ardent affection for the former than the latter. A trivial good may, from certain circumstances, pro-

HUME / A TREATISE OF HUMAN NATURE ◦ 43

duce a desire superior to what arises from the greatest and most valuable enjoyment; nor is there any thing more extraordinary in this, than in mechanics to see one pound weight raise up a hundred by the advantage of its situation. In short, a passion must be accompany'd with some false judgment, in order to its being unreasonable; and even then 'tis not the passion, properly speaking, which is unreasonable, but the judgment.

The consequences are evident. Since a passion can never, in any sense, be call'd unreasonable, but when founded on a false supposition, or when it chuses means insufficient for the design'd end, 'tis impossible, that reason and passion can ever oppose each other, or dispute for the government of the will and actions. The moment we perceive the falshood of any supposition, or the insufficiency of any means our passions yield to our reason without any opposition. I may desire any fruit as of an excellent relish; but whenever you convince me of my mistake, my longing ceases. I may will the performance of certain actions as means of obtaining any desir'd good; but as my willing of these actions is only secondary, and founded on the supposition, that they are causes of the propos'd effect; as soon as I discover the falshood of that supposition, they must become indifferent to me.

Those who affirm that virtue is nothing but a conformity to reason; that there are eternal fitnesses and unfitnesses of things, which are the same to every rational being that considers them; that the immutable measures of right and wrong impose an obligation, not only on human creatures, but also on the Deity himself: All these systems concur in the opinion, that morality, like truth, is discern'd merely by ideas, and by their juxta-position and comparison. In order, therefore, to judge of these systems, we need only consider, whether it be possible, from reason alone, to distinguish betwixt moral good and evil, or whether there must concur some other principles to enable us to make that distinction.

If morality had naturally no influence on human passions and actions, 'twere in vain to take such pains to inculcate it; and nothing wou'd be more fruitless than that multitude of rules and precepts, with which all moralists abound. Philosophy is commonly divided into *speculative* and *practical*; and as morality is always comprehended under the latter division, 'tis supposed to influence our passions and actions, and to go beyond the calm and indolent judgments of the understanding. And this is confirm'd by common experience, which informs us, that men are often govern'd by their duties, and are deter'd from some actions by the opinion of injustice, and impell'd to others by that of obligation.

Since morals, therefore, have an influence on the actions and affections, it follows, that they cannot be deriv'd from reason; and that because reason alone, as we have already prov'd, can never have any such influence. Morals excite passions, and produce or prevent actions. Reason of itself is utterly impotent in this particular. The rules of morality, therefore, are not conclusions of our reason.

But can there be any difficulty in proving, that vice and virtue are not matters of fact, whose existence we can infer by reason? Take any action allow'd to be vicious: Wilful murder, for instance. Examine it in all lights, and see if you can find that matter of fact, or real existence, which you call *vice*. In which-ever way you take it, you find only certain passions, motives, volitions and thoughts. There is no other matter of fact in the case. The vice entirely escapes you, as long as you consider the object. You never can find it, till you turn your reflexion into your own breast, and find a sentiment of disapprobation, which arises in you, towards this action. Here is a matter of fact; but 'tis the object of feeling, not of reason. It lies in yourself, not in the object. So that when you pronounce any action or character to be vicious, you mean nothing, but that from the constitution of your nature you have a feeling or sentiment of blame from the contemplation of it. Vice and virtue, therefore, may be compar'd to sounds, colours, heat and cold, which, according to modern philosophy, are not qualities in objects, but perceptions in the mind: And this discovery in morals, like that other in physics, is to be regarded as a considerable advancement of the speculative sciences; tho', like that too, it has little or no influence on practice. Nothing can be more real, or concern us more, than our own sentiments of pleasure and uneasiness; and if these be favourable to virtue, and unfavourable to vice, no more can be requisite to the regulation of our conduct and behaviour.

I cannot forbear adding to these reasonings an observation, which may, perhaps, be found of some importance. In every system of morality, which I have hitherto met with, I have always remark'd, that the author proceeds for some time in the ordinary way of reasoning, and establishes the being of a God, or makes observations concerning human affairs; when of a sudden I am surpriz'd to find, that instead of the usual copulations of propositions, *is*, and *is not*, I meet with no proposition that is not connected with an *ought*, or an *ought not*. This change is imperceptible; but is, however, of the last consequence. For as this *ought*, or *ought not*, expresses some new relation or affirmation, 'tis necessary that it shou'd be observ'd and explain'd; and at the same time that a reason should be given, for what seems altogether inconceivable, how this new relation can be a deduction from others, which are entirely different from it. But as authors do not commonly use this precaution, I shall presume to recommend it to the readers; and am persuaded, that this small attention wou'd subvert all the vulgar systems of morality, and let us see, that the distinction of vice and virtue is not founded merely on the relations of objects, nor is perceiv'd by reason.

EXERCISES

1. Suppose we find that some of our most basic and common moral "intuitions" can be traced deep into our evolutionary history: our history as weak and vulnerable primates who must live in close social groups for protection from fierce predators. If we made such a discovery, would that *weaken* or *strengthen* (or have no effect on) the claim that our intuitions are sources of genuine objective knowledge about moral truths?

2. You are facing a moral quandary, and you want advice. You must choose either of two advisers, but not both. One is Brenda, who is a very clear and careful thinker, but whose feelings and affections seem limited (you sometimes have the impression that she really cares about no one except herself). The other possible source of advice is Brandon: warm and caring, but he quickly becomes muddled when trying to think carefully. Whom would you choose as your moral adviser? Why?

3. If we don't want to make ethical decisions by consulting our feelings of pleasure and pain, and you aren't sure that intuitive feelings are the gold standard of ethical truth, is there any role left for our feelings in ethics? Or should feelings be subjugated by reason, held in check, mistrusted as irrational and misleading distractions from the true moral path?

4. You are a hospital patient, and you have your choice of physicians, both of whom are superbly qualified medical professionals. One is dedicated Dekisha; the other is joyous Christina. Whom would you choose? Does your choice have any relevance for the question of which one is "morally better"?

5. As we discussed in the opening chapter, one basic difference in ethical views is between *transcendent* ethical theories (ethical principles are fixed and absolute and universal) and *contingent* theories (ethics is simply part of our changing natural lives). Intutionists (like Ross) are generally in the transcendent camp, while those (like Hume) who emphasize feelings usually favor contingent ethics. Does that basic difference in perspectives explain the difference between intuitionists and feelings theorists? That is, do intuitioninsts and feelings theorists have the *same* experience, but just *interpret* it differently?

6. You have very reliable information that a gang of terrorists is hiding in a small town in New Hampshire (don't worry about *how* you know this; you just know it). These terrorists are masters of secrecy and disguise, and you have no way of discovering who they are, and no way of isolating the town to make sure they do not leave. The gang is plan-

ning to release a poison gas that will kill thousands of people in a Midwestern city. The *only* way to prevent this attack is to carpet bomb the small New Hampshire town, killing everyone there including the terrorists, but also including several hundred innocent people who have no idea there are terrorists in their midst. Would you be morally justified in bombing the town?

Do you have your answer? Good. I don't want to know what your answer is: keep it to yourself. Instead, look carefully at *how* you reached your answer. Were you guided by reason? Feelings? Both? Or what?

7.   You are a member of the university chamber orchestra, which is on a weeklong spring concert tour through several Southern cities. One of your friends, J, is not along on the tour. J is not your dearest friend in the world, but is certainly a good friend. J's lover—K—*is* along on the tour. J and K have been lovers for over a year, and it seems to be a serious relationship; you wouldn't be surprised if they married next year after they graduate. You and K both play viola in the chamber orchestra, and you've spent a lot of time together on this trip. It's spring, the birds are singing, the bees are buzzing, and after a long cold winter it's great to be soaking up the warmth in the sunny South. As the week wears on, you realize you have become strongly attracted to K, and K apparently feels a reciprocal attraction. You have a private room at the hotel where you are staying, and if you ordered a bottle of champagne and invited K up to your room to watch a movie—well, the outcome is not difficult to imagine. Both you and K are very discreet, and it's unlikely J would learn about it. Would it be *wrong* to have a fling with K?

Got your answer? Again, I don't want to know what it is. Instead, think again about *how* you reached your answer: through reason, feelings, or what?

Now *compare* the *process* you followed for answering Questions 6 and 7. Did you follow the same process in both cases? Or did you use different methods? Did your feelings play a larger role in one case than in the other?

Suppose someone says: "The first type of case must be answered using reason; but the *second* case is better handled through feelings." Would that make sense? Or do all ethical decisions require the same *type* of process (if feelings are important for one ethical question, then must they be important for *all* ethical questions)?

ADDITIONAL READING

David Hume has two classic works on ethics and emotions (though both works also contain much more). The first is *A Treatise of Human Nature*, originally published in 1738. A good edition is by L. A. Selby-Bigge (Oxford: Clarendon Press, 1978). The second is *An Inquiry Concerning Human Understanding*, originally published in 1751. A good edition is L. A. Selby-Bigge's *Hume's Enquiries*, 2nd ed. (Oxford: Clarendon Press, 1902).

Kai Nielsen, *Why Be Moral?* (Buffalo, N.Y.: Prometheus Books, 1989) is a very readable defense of nonobjectivist ethics based in emotions.

Among the most important and influential intuitionist writings are G. E. Moore, *Principia Ethica* (New York: Cambridge University Press, 1959); H. A. Prichard, *Moral Obligation* (Oxford: Clarendon Press, 1949); W. D. Ross, *The Right and the Good* (Oxford: Clarendon Press, 1930); W. D. Ross, *Foundations of Ethics* (Oxford: Clarendon Press, 1939); and D. D. Raphael, *The Moral Sense* (London: Oxford University Press, 1957).

NOTES

[1]For more detailed discussion of this case, see Jonathan Bennett's superb article, "The Conscience of Huckleberry Finn," *Philosophy*, 49 (1974), 123–134.

[2]David Hume, *A Treatise on Human Nature*, L. A. Selby-Bigge, editor (Clarendon Press: Oxford, 1988), p. 416. First published in 1738.

[3]Hume, p. 414.

[4]W. D. Ross, *The Right and the Good* (Oxford: Clarendon Press, 1930), p. 33.

[5]Ross, pp. 46–47.

CHAPTER 4

✧ UTILITARIAN ETHICS ✧

Some base ethics on pure reason, while others ground ethics in feelings or intuitions. But from the nineteenth century onward, many have thought that ethics should rest on a different foundation. *Utilitarians* appeal to neither intuition nor abstract reason. Rejecting mysteries or special powers, utilitarians believe that the starting point of ethics is simple and obvious. When we strip away the mysteries and confusions, what do we really want? We want to enjoy pleasures and avoid suffering. This simple truth applies to kings and serfs, rich and poor, butchers and bakers and candlestick makers, humans and chimps and beagles. Starting from this simple principle, ethics becomes a matter of calculating how to produce the greatest balance of pleasure over suffering. For any act or policy, the question of whether it is ethically right comes down to this: will it produce the greatest possible balance of pleasure over pain? If so, then it is right. Period.

UTILITARIAN THEORY

Making Utilitarian Calculations

Of course calculating the right act is not always easy. Simple acts may have large and complicated consequences. Telling a lie may seem a small matter, avoiding some immediate problems and not really causing any harm. But you have perhaps discovered from your own experiences the truth of the old dictum: "Oh what a tangled web we weave, when first we practice to deceive." Think of a case that may seem simple. You are a physician, and you discover your patient has an incurable disease that will invariably kill him in one year, but will show few symptoms until near death. Should you tell your patient the awful truth? If you lie to your patient, he will enjoy his remaining year with little worry. If you tell him, he will pass his last year in dread of his approaching death. The utilitarian calculation seems obvious. A year of worry-free enjoyment is a better result than a year of dread and fear, so you should lie to your patient.

But the calculation is not that easy. Your patient may be deprived of the opportunity to do things he had always planned to do: quit work and try writing a novel, or visit Paris, or reconcile with his brother. Furthermore, when he finally discovers he has been deceived, he may be profoundly bitter, and feel he was treated like a child rather than an autonomous adult. And others who know the real diagnosis will become enmeshed in the deception, and this may cause them stress. The discomfort of constant deception may also lead them to distance themselves from the patient, and leave him isolated. And there are other consequences, perhaps remote but still serious. If you deceive this patient about his fatal illness, that will undermine the confidence we have in what our doctors tell us. When I go to you for my annual checkup, and you assure me I am perfectly healthy, I will wonder whether you're telling me the truth: "Dr. Jones said I was in good health. However, she told Bill the same thing, and he had a fatal disease and died within a year. I wonder what she's hiding from me."

Taking the Mystery out of Ethics

So making the calculations of pleasure and pain will not be an easy task, but utilitarians are undaunted. They never supposed that ethics would be *easy*, but they do insist ethics is not *mysterious*. Deciding what is right and wrong is not a matter of deep intuitions or special mystical insight or ancient rules. It is a difficult but straightforward task of measuring, as best we can, the balance of pleasure over pain that will be produced by a proposed act or policy. The calculations may be challenging, but so are the calculations in plotting the path of Halley's comet. And of course we can make mistakes, just as we do in other calculations. If Halley's comet encounters a passing asteroid we know nothing about, then our calculations will be mistaken. Likewise, if events occur that we could not have anticipated, then our ethical calculations of consequences may also be wrong. But our best chance of plotting the path of Halley's comet is to make the calculations, based on all the information we have. And our best chance of plotting the right ethical behavior is to make our best calculations, based on all the information we can secure. This won't give us ethical infallibility, but it will give us a sound method for pursuing ethics, with *no* appeal to mysteries or intuitions or miracles.

Misconceptions of Utilitarian Ethics

Utilitarian ethics is often reviled, and often misunderstood. Before examining it further, we should clear up a few common misconceptions. First, the utilitarian is not recommending a policy of gross, egoistic, self-centered, short-sighted hedonism. This is not an "eat, drink, and be merry, for tomorrow you die" sort of ethic. What shall I do this evening? Well, I could go out and have a huge steak, a gargantuan chocolate dessert, and then spend the rest of the evening drinking myself into a joyous stupor. Such gluttony has its undeniable charms. But as some of us know from sad experience, it also has its less charming consequences—hours of nausea being only the most immediately obvious. So a good utilitarian—intent on maximizing pleasure, but also concerned about minimizing suffering—would counsel moderation. And when we add in the pleasures one sacrifices while recovering (the joys of philosophy, for example, are strictly incompatible with the suffering of a hangover) then clearly moderation is a better course. Besides, there are also the interests of others to calculate: having had too much to drink, my impaired judgment may lead me to drive, and that might cause great suffering for others. And the utilitarian will insist that the joys and sorrows of others must be part of the calculation. *All* pleasures and pains count. My own pleasures and pains are part of the sum, but they count no more and no less than the pleasures and pains of others. (The utilitarian would argue that it is irrational to count my own pleasures as more important than the pleasures of others. After all, I could not possibly have any reasonable grounds for drawing such a distinction—the distinction would be arbitrary. I can of course point out that these pleasures are *mine*, but you can say exactly the same about your pleasures, so that does not justify special preference for my own pleasures.)

Utilitarian ethics is an example of a *teleological* theory of ethics. "Teleological" comes from the Greek word *télos*, meaning end or goal. Such theories are sometimes called *consequentialist* theories, since they base ethical rules and judgments on the *consequences*. Roughly, an act is judged good if it produces good consequences, if it has good results, if it is productive of worthwhile ends. Utilitarian ethics (the right act is the act that produces the greatest benefits for everyone) is the dominant consequentialist view; but egoism (the right act is the one that produces the greatest benefits for the individual egoist) is also consequentialist. The contrast between teleological and deontological (duty-based) theories is one of the most fundamental divides in ethical theory. Deontologists basically believe that consequences don't matter in ethics; teleologists believe the consequences are the *only* things that matter.

ACT-VERSUS RULE-UTILITARIANS

Act-Utilitarians

Utilitarians aim to maximize pleasure and minimize suffering for everyone. But there are some issues that divide utilitarians. One basic division among utilitarians is between act-utilitarians and rule-utilitarians. Act-utilitarians claim that in determining what we should do, we must consider what *specific act* would produce the best overall consequences. If telling a lie—in this individual instance—would yield the maximum balance of pleasure over pain, then telling a lie is *morally right*. It may well be that in *most* cases telling lies causes more harm than good, but that doesn't matter. We're not concerned with most cases, but with this particular case. In different circumstances, telling a lie would be wrong, because it would not maximize pleasure. But in these circumstances, telling a lie yields the greatest possible balance of pleasure over pain, and so in this situation you *ought* to tell a lie. When we have a new situation, we'll make new calculations.

Rule-Utilitarians

Rule-utilitarians believe that is a superficial way of calculating. In order to determine what really maximizes pleasure and minimizes suffering, we must look more deeply at societal *practices* and *institutions*.

You have promised to meet your philosophy professor for lunch. You know your professor is looking forward to the occasion: you are charming company, and your professor is socially inept and does not often have the pleasure of such a delightful luncheon companion. However, you are likely to find it a rather boring occasion, your professor being a bit of a windbag filled with long and tedious stories. On the way to the restaurant you encounter the very attractive and fascinating person who sits near you in stats class, who suggests the two of you share lunch. As a good utilitarian, you quickly total up the pleasures and pains. On the one hand, if you keep your promise and meet your professor, then your professor will gain the pleasure of your company. But that has to be balanced against the fact that you will experience suffering—the suffering of listening to your professor's long-winded stories, compounded by the suffering of regret at the delightful lunch date you are passing up, and to that total must be added the suffering your stats classmate will feel when you decline the luncheon invitation. On the other side, if you break your promise to your professor and accept the more attractive offer, then you will gain the pleasure of a more enjoyable lunch and your companion from your stats class will gain the great pleasure of your company. Besides, there's a decent chance that this luncheon engagement might lead to further social relations involving very significant pleasures for you both. Of course your professor will be disappointed at being stood up for your luncheon engagement. But your professor is probably used to such disappointments, and will soon get over it. Before finishing the appetizer, your philosophy professor will probably be lost in thought about some obscure question in medieval philosophy, and so won't suffer for long. Besides, tomorrow in class you can tell your professor you received an emergency call from home, and you are so sorry about missing the luncheon engagement ("I had been looking forward to it all week"), and offer to reschedule the lunch for later. Your professor is quite gullible, and will certainly believe you. When you total it up, it is quickly obvious that a much greater balance of pleasure will result if you break your promise. So it's morally legitimate for you to break your promise in this situation. In fact, for a faithful utilitarian it's morally *obligatory*.

The Rules of Practices

Many utilitarians will applaud your reasoning, and affirm your decision as morally correct. But some utilitarians will disagree. They will insist that your utilitarian calculations have been too narrow. You left out the importance of our *practice* of promise-keeping. If you *promise* to meet me, that doesn't mean you'll meet me unless something better comes along. Of course if you must be rushed to the hospital for emergency surgery, or take shelter from an approaching tornado, or save the life of a child who is in danger of falling off a cliff—in such cases you are excused from keeping your promise. That is part of the practice of making and keeping promises: in genuine emergency situations, you are excused from keeping your promise. But a more attractive offer from a charming classmate is *not* an emergency, and is *not* a legitimate excuse for breaking your promise. If people could break promises whenever a more appealing or pleasurable option comes along, then the whole purpose and practice of promising would be destroyed. The point of promising is to bind someone to an obligation. "I promise to be faithful to you" does not mean "I promise to be faithful to you unless I meet someone better looking." If you promise to meet me, that means—barring extraordinary events—you will in fact meet me.

Having the practice of promise-keeping is very valuable to us. It enables us to make plans, and it offers an important measure of security and confidence. If having made a promise, we then engaged in utilitarian calculations to determine whether to keep or break the promise, the "promise" would no longer serve its present useful function. If you promise to go to the opera with me, then I can buy the tickets and make dinner reservations and send my jacket to the cleaners. If you can back out should you have a more pleasurable opportunity, I would be foolish to go to such expense. If you are promised a job in Minneapolis—but that promise can be cancelled if a more attractive applicant appears—you cannot confidently sell your house in St. Louis, hire a mover, and make a down payment on a bungalow in the Twin Cities. It might well be that giving the job to the better applicant would result in a greater balance of pleasure over suffering, even when your suffering is figured in the balance. But the whole practice of promising would be lost if we made and kept 'promises' by that manner of calculation. Because we value the promise-keeping *practice*, we cannot subject individual promises to utilitarian calculations.

Thus rule-utilitarians call for a more complicated, double-tiered method of utilitarian calculation. Rather than calculate the aggregate pleasures and pains of a particular act of promise-keeping, rule-utilitarians insist we should *first* calculate the overall pleasures and pains of the practice of promise-keeping. That is, will our society—on an overall long-term utilitarian calculation—gain a greater balance of pleasure over pain by having or not having the practice of promise-keeping? If that utilitarian calculation concludes that the practice of promise-keeping maximizes the overall balance of pleasure, then we should adopt that practice (on utilitarian grounds). Having adopted that practice, when we are faced with a specific instance of the practice, then as *rule*-utilitarians we must follow the *rules* of the practice. (Of course if the act does not fall under the rules of any practice favored by utilitarian standards, then we should evaluate the specific act by utilitarian calculations.)

Promise-keeping is perhaps the most obvious candidate for a practice justified by rule-utilitarian calculations, but there may be others as well. Consider a principle that governs our medical research: We should not perform medical experiments on competent persons without their informed consent. That principle offers us important protection and security. When we enter the hospital, we know we can't be used as unwitting guinea pigs in medical experiments. Medical researchers can't go through our records and draft anyone they find particularly useful for medical experimentation. Without that rule we would be very nervous every time we entered the hospital for testing or treatment. But suppose researchers could make an exception and use us in their experiments should they conclude that in *this case* coercing us to be experimental subjects would yield more benefit than harm. Such a utilitarian exception would destroy our sense of security. If we conclude that the practice of requiring consent passes the rule-utilitarian test of producing the maximum balance of pleasure over suffering, we should adopt that practice. We cannot have that practice if we allow exceptions on act-utilitarian grounds.

Consider another candidate for a practice that might be justified by rule-utilitarian calculations: We should not suppress freedom of speech. In a specific instance, it may be that we could achieve a greater balance of pleasure over pain by suppressing speech. For example, pro-Nazi speeches may cause significant pain to many people in our society, and the pleasure taken by neo-Nazis in spewing out their hate-filled diatribes hardly seems to balance out the suffering. But if we find the practice of freedom of speech valuable, we can't decide to suppress that freedom because a specific exercise of free speech causes an overall negative balance of suffering over pleasure. "You have freedom to say whatever you wish, so long as what you say doesn't disturb significantly more people than it pleases": that is *not* freedom of speech.

Some utilitarians—*act*-utilitarians—believe that the rule-utilitarian approach weakens the utilitarian position. According to act-utilitarians, *every* act—from promise-keeping to poetry-writing—should be subjected to utilitarian calculations. Of course as a thorough and careful act-utilitarian you must consider (when deciding whether to break a promise) what impact that would have on future confidence in promises, and on trust between people. That is an important consideration to add to the calculation, but it's still just one more of the many factors to be considered when calculating what act will produce the greatest overall balance of pleasure over suffering. Which version of utilitarian theory is more plausible remains a vexed question.

UTILITARIANS AND THE QUALITY OF PLEASURES

A second and perhaps even more divisive issue among utilitarians concerns *qualities* of pleasures. Do all pleasures count the same? I derive great pleasure from listening to Britney Spears, while you take delight in Bach and Mozart. There is no doubt that your musical tastes are more sophisticated than mine, and you almost certainly have a deeper understanding and appreciation of music. Still, I derive pleasure from the music I enjoy, just as you do. Is there any difference in our pleasures? If we must choose between satisfying your taste for Bach and my preference for Britney, should we simply flip a coin? That is, should utilitarians further complicate their calculations by factoring in the *qualities* of different pleasures?

Bentham: All Pleasures Are Equal

Jeremy Bentham, who first developed utilitarian ethics, would say there is no difference. Pleasure is pleasure, Bentham asserted. If they give equal pleasure to the participants, then "Pushpin is as good as poetry." The fact that pushpin is a silly game (something like pickup sticks) and poetry is a sublime art makes no difference. There are, of course, some important differences in pleasures. The pleasure derived from overindulgence is a pleasure; but since it carries suffering in its wake, that may make other pleasures a better choice on balance. And my pleasure in the music of Britney Spears is likely to be short-lived, as I soon tire of the repetitive and shallow arrangements, while your pleasure in Mozart and Bach is likely to grow and deepen as your appreciation for the nuances of their music increases. And my pleasure in cheering for the Minnesota Vikings is genuine; but might there be other pleasures that would not also involve so much agony of defeat? Still, according to Bentham, if I get pleasure from playing pinball games, and you take pleasure in poetry, and neither of our pleasurable activities causes harm or suffering to ourselves or others, then my pleasure in pinball is the complete equal of your pleasure in poetry, and there is no reason to favor one over the other on grounds of *quality*.

If we look closely at Bentham's development of utilitarian ethics, it is not difficult to see why he is reluctant to admit differences in qualities of pleasure. Bentham is living in late eighteenth- to early nineteenth-century London, and he is appalled at the conditions he sees around him. A few live in great luxury, with huge homes in the city, country estates, and crowds of servants. Many live in desperate poverty, and are forced into theft (punishable by public hanging) or prostitution to survive. Disease is everywhere, and for the impoverished there is little opportunity for an education that might free them from a short, desperate life. When Bentham formulates his utilitarian ethics, he is crafting a tool that can be used for reform. It is obvious that pleasure is good and suffering bad, so we ought to maximize pleasure and minimize suffering for everyone. No doubt Lord Mustard derives great pleasure from taking his carriage up to his country estate for a long weekend. But does it really maximize pleasure for everyone if Lord Mustard has a city mansion and a country estate, while families with small children live in the streets and sleep under bridges? The 12-course feast prepared for Lord Mustard and his guests is a great delight, but does the pleasure of such gluttony outweigh the suffering that could be relieved by feeding several hungry families? If we allow for differences in qualities of pleasures, Lord Mustard has an easy answer: the high quality of pleasures fancied by the aristocracy are so superior to the pleasures pursued by the lower classes that the *quality* of pleasure cancels out the great difference in *quantity*.

Mill and the Qualities of Pleasure

The notion of "higher-quality" pleasures has always been difficult to justify. What it typically means in practice is "the pleasures enjoyed by those in positions of power and privilege." In contemporary society, going to a Shakespeare play is considered a much "higher-quality" pleasure than playing a game of cards; but in Elizabethan London, when Shakespeare was writing his plays, attending one of Shakespeare's plays was regarded as crude, vulgar, and perhaps immoral. The quality of Shakespeare's plays hasn't changed. The people who attend them have. Furthermore, it is difficult to believe that what are regarded as "higher-quality" activities actually provide higher-quality pleasures. Even if we grant that an evening of the Boston Symphony playing Mozart is of higher quality than a Britney Spears concert, it requires a leap of philosophical faith to suppose that the patrons at Symphony Hall are experiencing greater pleasure than are the wildly enthusiastic preteens screaming in ecstasy and singing along with Britney.

John Stuart Mill—a second generation utilitarian, whose father was a close friend of Jeremy Bentham—would answer that the rock concert no doubt produces greater quantity of pleasure, but the symphony patrons enjoy a much higher quality of pleasure; and for Mill, even small doses of high-quality pleasure easily outweigh mass quantities of lower pleasures. The person of educated and discerning musical tastes may less often find a concert completely satisfying: she detects tiny imperfections that my cruder sensitivities miss. But in Mill's words: "It is better to be a human being dissatisfied than a pig satisfied; better to be Socrates dissatisfied than a fool satisfied."

Mill's version of utilitarianism is certainly more sophisticated than Bentham's. Does it destroy a basic element of utilitarian ethics in exchange for that sophistication? Is push-pin as good as poetry, Britney as good as Bach? That's an issue that still divides utilitarians.

CRITICISMS OF UTILITARIAN ETHICS

Psychological Criticisms

There have been many criticisms of utilitarian ethics. One important challenge maintains that utilitarianism is psychologically false. No doubt it is true that we sometimes seek pleasure. But is maximizing pleasure and minimizing suffering *always* our primary goal?

Consider our friend Soraya, who is a dedicated mountain climber. She endures grueling training, sore muscles, oxygen deprivation, severe cold, countless bumps and bruises, all in her quest to scale a challenging mountain face. No doubt there are beautiful vistas to enjoy and the satisfaction of completing a difficult challenge. But to suppose that Soraya climbs mountains for pleasure, or to maximize pleasure over pain, seems clearly false. There are lots of delightful pleasures to be had with much less suffering, and it also seems false to the entire experience. If you suggest to Soraya that she climbs mountains for pleasure, she will reject that as ridiculous. She climbs for the challenge, or to test herself, or "because it's there." But not to maximize pleasure, and certainly not to minimize pain.

The dedicated utilitarian will reply that in reality, Soraya's mountain climbing is really all about maximizing pleasure: "Soraya gets her pleasures in ways that wouldn't appeal to me; but still, for her the mountain climbing is really just a matter of pleasure. It brings her great pleasure, and that's why she does it. If she could gain more pleasure from playing bridge, she would pursue that." And so it will go with any example we offer: the activity pursued may not be obviously pleasurable to us, but the person doing it must expect to find pleasure in it. Otherwise, why would she do it, rather than pursuing something more enjoyable?

NOZICK'S CHALLENGE TO UTILITARIAN ETHICS

But is it true that our goal, in all our activities, is maximizing pleasure and minimizing suffering? Robert Nozick[1] developed a powerful challenge to that utilitarian claim. Suppose scientists have contrived an amazing "pleasure machine." When you are placed in this machine you have vivid experiences that are complete fantasies, but you are unable to distinguish these fantasies from reality (with "virtual gaming" now available, perhaps this example does not seem so incredible). To make the illusion complete, the machine erases your memory of entering the machine, so that your machine experiences seem to you genuine reality. The machine programmers are generous and trustworthy people, and they offer to place you in the machine and set the machine to provide you with a rich and wonderful and immensely pleasurable life. All your dreams will come true—or at least it will seem to you that they've come true. You will have not a clue that you are living a fantasy, and your pleasure will be maximized. You will win four Olympic gold medals, and be honored with a parade through your hometown. You will win the Nobel Prize for physics, and maybe two years later in literature. You will spend sultry summer nights on the beach with—well, you get the idea. And there will be just enough difficulties to keep things interesting. You will occasionally lose an Olympic event, but then come back four years later with an underdog triumph. None of this will really be happening, of course. But since you won't know that, your pleasure will not be diminished. You can enter the machine, but with one condition: once you enter, you can never leave. (After you enter the machine you will not have a frustrated desire to escape, since you will not realize that you are in the machine at all.) Would you choose to spend the rest of your life in joyous fantasy inside the pleasure machine?

For an hour it would certainly be tempting. Maybe even for a long weekend. But the rest of your life? Very few people would choose a life of blissfully happy machine-induced fantasy over the often-frustrating realities of life in the real world. (Obviously some people choose short periods of drug-induced euphoria, as an "escape" from reality. But if the condition were inescapable euphoria for one's entire drugged life, that would be a very different situation.) But why would you not choose a full life of such fantasy pleasure? You can think of several immediate reasons. Going inside the pleasure machine would take you away from your family and friends, and would cause them unhappiness. Or perhaps you don't really trust the operators of this pleasure machine: maybe their real motive is to perform some ghastly experiment on you. But even if all those problems were solved—your family will not miss you, and the machine operator is absolutely trustworthy—most people still would be reluctant to choose a lifetime of pleasurable fantasy.

If you wouldn't agree to life inside the pleasure machine, then obviously there are things you value *other* than experiencing pleasure and avoiding pain. You take great pleasure in working on problems in physics, and your secret goal is to make a breakthrough discovery in physics and win the Nobel Prize. But if we offer you the pleasure you would gain from your work in physics—as the pleasure machine does—you would quickly decline: "I don't want merely to have the *feeling* of making a great discovery in physics. I want to *make* the discovery. It's true, working on physics problems gives me pleasure. Still, I don't do it for the pleasure, but because I love doing physics."

That brings us to the basic criticism of utilitarian ethics: It confuses (what psychologists call) the positive reinforcer with the behavior shaped by that reinforcer. You gain pleasure from playing chess, and if not you probably would never have become an enthusiastic chess player. You also experience a few frustrations: that stupid move when you lost your bishop and blew a game you should have won still makes you angry. But that is part of what shapes your deep commitment to playing chess: if you always had success, you would enjoy the game but your dedication to chess would not run very deep. If you experience some pleasant success, along with occasional failures, that variable interval schedule of positive reinforcement shapes a deep dedication to the game. You don't play the game for the pleasure, but the pleasure is part of what shapes you to love playing chess. A steady diet of frustrating losses might eventually extinguish your passion for chess. If we didn't gain pleasure and satisfaction from the activity, we probably wouldn't do it; but we aren't doing it *for* the pleasure.

That objection to utilitarian ethics is closely linked to a second. Aiming at pleasure seems a lousy plan for finding happiness. Those who aim at pleasure rarely seem to find it. If you think of people you know who are happy, it's unlikely that your list includes many who focus on the pursuit of pleasure. Instead, the happiest people seem to be those who are pursuing goals and projects they find worthwhile, and happiness comes to them as a bonus.

> "I don't know why we are here, but I'm pretty sure that it is not in order to enjoy ourselves." Ludwig Wittgenstein, 1889–1951

Dostoyevsky's Challenge to Utilitarian Ethics

Finally, few of us can fully embrace utilitarian calculations in making ethical judgments. The Russian novelist, Fyodor Dostoyevsky, poses this powerful challenge:

> Tell me honestly, I challenge you—answer me: imagine that you are charged with building the edifice of human destiny, the ultimate aim of which is to bring people happiness, to give them peace and contentment at last, but that in order to achieve this it is essential and unavoidable to torture just one little speck of creation, that . . . little child beating her chest with her little fists, and imagine that this edifice has to be erected on her unexpiated tears. Would you agree to be the architect under those conditions? Tell me honestly![2]

By utilitarian calculations, the purchase of so much pleasure at the cost of one small child's agony seems a bargain, but very few people could give their moral blessing to such a transaction.

THE USES OF UTILITARIAN ETHICS

Its problems notwithstanding, utilitarianism still has its uses. We might not think that pleasure is our primary goal, and we may have doubts about resolving ethical issues by entering the pleasures and pains and pushing the total button. Still, we *are* concerned with pleasures and pains. When you consider having minor surgery or a trip to the dentist, you may not think much about the development of effective anesthesia. But if it were not available for the relief of pain, you would certainly think about it a great deal. The pleasures of a good meal may not equal the joys of philosophy, but they are hardly insignificant, and the pain of gnawing hunger can be a sad source of suffering. So even if calculations of pleasures and pains cannot capture everything about ethics, they are still important considerations.

Ironically, for a doctrine that was supposed to yield precise mathematical calculations, utilitarian ethics often works better as a battle axe than a scalpel. Utilitarianism is a blunt instrument, but it has a strong impact, especially in the hands of a contemporary advocate like Peter Singer. As Singer notes, when we test the safety of a new shampoo, we drip the shampoo in concentrated form into the eyes of rabbits, causing them severe pain and probably terror. No doubt a new shampoo that leaves my hair lustrous and manageable has its charms, but are those charms sufficient to justify the infliction of so much suffering? The taste of a char-grilled steak, juicy and tender, is a genuine source of pleasure. But can this gourmet pleasure (which is obviously not essential to sustain our lives, and in fact probably shortens our lives by contributing to higher cholesterol levels) justify the infliction of suffering on cattle that are raised on crowded feedlots and then herded into slaughterhouses? It must be delightful to live in an elegant mansion, richly equipped with jacuzzi and sauna and a master bedroom suite large enough for arena football; but is it really right to spend that much on luxuries that add only a small increase to our pleasure when the same resources could be used to care for many impoverished persons living in hunger and homelessness? If I add a spiffy and expensive new suit to my extensive wardrobe, it will bring me pleasure. But is that small increment of pleasure even remotely comparable to the pleasure and relief of suffering that would result if the same money were used to buy warm winter clothes for a cold and threadbare family? A tummy tuck will certainly improve my sagging appearance, and make me feel better. But the same medical resources could save the lives of many impoverished children who lack adequate health care to prevent and combat their terrible diseases. It doesn't require a careful utilitarian accounting to recognize that spending on such luxuries is hardly the best way to maximize pleasure and minimize suffering.

Utilitarian Ethics and Public Policy

Even if we have doubts about some of the details of utilitarian ethics, we may still find it a helpful general guide when considering what we should do. Furthermore, it may prove quite useful in evaluating legitimate social policy. If we are trying to decide whether a new football stadium with luxury boxes for the very rich is a better investment than decent inner-city schools and health care for the very poor, utilitarian calculations might prove their worth. Certainly they are a better guide than whatever politicians are currently using.

OPPOSITION TO UTILITARIANISM

Utilitarian ethics has enduring charms, and many champions. Utilitarians banish mystery from the realm of ethics, and utilitarians are never baffled by an ethical quandary. For utilitarians, ethical questions become engineering problems: they may require difficult calculations, but we have the methods and means to resolve them.

Yet for all its plain charms, utilitarian ethics often inspires deep, visceral, passionate hostility. The great Russian novelist, Dostoyevsky, thought of utilitarianism as a mean-spirited and ignoble ethical counterfeit: ethics is what makes us godlike, and ethical quandaries, though often difficult and sometimes tragic, are the glory of humankind. Utilitarianism turns ethics into a cheap and trivial bookkeeping system. Utilitarianism brings ethics down from the heavens and anchors it squarely to Earth, links ethics closely to basic desires to avoid suffering and secure happiness, dispenses with exalted ethical absolutes, and offers a clear practical method of resolving ethical issues. But precisely the features that utilitarians find appealing are the features that absolutists find appalling.

Ethical absolutists (such as rationalists and intuitionists) typically find utilitarian theory even more objectionable than the complete denial of moral objectivity. After all, if I deny that there are moral absolutes, at least we're still talking the same language. But if I claim that there is moral objectivity, but insist it's not the objectivity of majestic, absolute, eternal, moral principles but instead the objectivity of contingent practical calculations about how to maximize happiness, that seems to absolutists like a cheapening and demeaning of ethical objectivity. The absolutist hatred of utilitarianism is thus likely to be greater than their hatred of those who deny moral objectivity altogether: it is the intense hatred of the traitor and despoiler, as opposed to the dislike of a clear enemy.

For ethical absolutists, ethics is not relative to a situation nor contingent upon consequences. Ethics is certainly not about what feels good, or happens to make people happy. Rather, ethics is about principles that are eternally true, principles that demand our unconditional allegiance whether they make us feel good or not. Following the stern dictates of the moral law is not a feel good enterprise.

William James and Ethical Temperaments

William James, the great American psychologist and pragmatic philosopher of the turn of the twentieth century, maintained that the most basic philosophical issues were decided not by argument or reason, but instead by temperament. According to James, you do not become an absolutist or a utilitarian (or adopt some other ethical stance) because you calmly and objectively evaluated the different views and selected the most reasonable alternative. Instead you favor absolutism (or utilitarianism, or whatever) because it just seems right to you: it fits your temperament, it matches the way you live and think, it fits your view of the world. You don't become a utilitarian because you are persuaded by good reasons to adopt utilitarian ethics; rather, you find the reasons for utilitarianism convincing because the utilitarian perspective fits you. The reasons that justify your utilitarian position are not what convince you to adopt the utilitarian view, but are instead an after-the-fact rationalization or justification of a theory you adopted for the much deeper reasons of temperament and outlook.

Of course most philosophers and ethical theorists would dispute James's account. But it may help make sense of why conflicts between different ethical perspectives—between absolutists and utilitarians, for example—are so enduring and so difficult to resolve. In any case, you might consider how it applies to your own thoughts about ethics. When you encountered utilitarian theory, did it seem to you immediately plausible, or did it seem to you somehow completely wrong? Was that reaction a reflection of your own ethical temperament?

AN INTRODUCTION TO THE PRINCIPLES OF MORALS AND LEGISLATION

Jeremy Bentham

Jeremy Bentham lived from 1748 to 1832. He was both a philosopher who set forth the basic principles of utilitarian ethics as well as a social reformer who worked tirelessly for improvements in British society, especially in the areas of legal, prison, and educational reform. Bentham used the principles of his utilitarian ethics as a blueprint for the reform programs he set in motion, and the political reform movement he helped develop continued long after his death. The following passage was originally published in 1823.

OF THE PRINCIPLE OF UTILITY

1. Nature has placed mankind under the governance of two sovereign masters, *pain* and *pleasure*. It is for them alone to point out what we ought to do, as well as to determine what we shall do. On the one hand the standard of right and wrong, on the other the chain of causes and effects, are fastened to their throne. They govern us in all we do, in all we say, in all we think: every effort we can make to throw off our subjection, will serve but to demonstrate and confirm it. In words a man may pretend to abjure their empire: but in reality he will remain subject to it all the while. The *principle of utility* recognises this subjection, and assumes it for the foundation of that system, the object of which is to rear the fabric of felicity by the hands of reason and of law. Systems which attempt to question it, deal in sounds instead of sense, in caprice instead of reason, in darkness instead of light.

But enough of metaphor and declamation: it is not by such means that moral science is to be improved.

2. The principle of utility is the foundation of the present work: it will be proper therefore at the outset to give an explicit and determinate account of what is meant by it. By the principle of utility is meant that principle which approves or disapproves of every action whatsoever, according to the tendency which it appears to have to augment or diminish the happiness of the party whose interest is in question: or, what is the same thing in other words, to promote or to oppose that happiness. I say of every action whatsoever; and therefore not only of every action of a private individual, but of every measure of government.

3. By utility is meant that property in any object, whereby it tends to produce benefit, advantage, pleasure, good, or happiness, (all this in the present case comes to the same thing) or (what comes again to the same thing) to prevent the happening of mischief, pain, evil, or unhappiness to the party whose interest is considered: if that party be the community in general, then the happiness of the community: if a particular individual, then the happiness of that individual.

4. The interest of the community is one of the most general expressions that can occur in the phraseology of morals: no wonder that the meaning of it is often lost. When it has a meaning, it is this. The community is a fictitious *body*, composed of the individual persons who are considered as constituting as it were its *members*. The interest of the community then is, what?—the sum of the interests of the several members who compose it.

5. It is in vain to talk of the interest of the community, without understanding what is the interest of the individual. A thing is said to promote the interest, or to be *for* the interest, of an individual, when it tends to add to the sum total of his pleasures: or, what comes to the same thing, to diminish the sum total of his pains.

6. An action then may be said to be conformable to the principle of utility, or, for shortness sake, to utility, (meaning with respect to the community at large) when the tendency it has to augment the happiness of the community is greater than any it has to diminish it.

7. A measure of government (which is but a particular kind of action, performed by a particular person or persons) may be said to be conformable to or dictated by the principle of utility, when in like manner the tendency which it has to augment the happiness of the community is greater than any which it has to diminish it.

8. When an action, or in particular a measure of government, is supposed by a man to be conformable to the principle of utility, it may be convenient, for the purposes of discourse, to imagine a kind of law or dictate, called a law or dictate of utility: and to speak of the action in question, as being conformable to such law or dictate.

9. A man may be said to be a partisan of the principle of utility, when the approbation or disapprobation he annexes to any action, or to any measure, is determined by, and proportioned to the tendency which he conceives it to have to augment or to diminish the happiness of the community: or in other words, to its conformity or unconformity to the laws or dictates of utility.

10. Of an action that is conformable to the principle of utility, one may always say either that it is one that ought to be done, or at least that it is not one that ought not to be done. One may say also, that it is right it should be done; at least that it is not wrong it should be done: that it is a right action; at least that it is not a wrong action. When thus interpreted, the words *ought*, and *right* and *wrong*, and others of that stamp, have a meaning: when otherwise, they have none.

11. Has the rectitude of this principle been ever formally contested? It should seem that it had, by those who have not known what they have been meaning. Is it susceptible of any direct proof? it should seem not: for that which is used to prove every thing else, cannot itself be proved: a chain of proofs must have their commencement somewhere. To give such proof is as impossible as it is needless.

12. Not that there is or ever has been that human creature breathing, however stupid or perverse, who has not on many, perhaps on most occasions of his life, deferred to it. By the natural constitution of the human frame, on most occasions of their lives men in general embrace this principle, without thinking of it: if not for the ordering of their own actions, yet for the trying of their own actions, as well as of those of other men. There have been, at the same time, not many, perhaps, even of the most intelligent, who have been disposed to embrace it purely and without reserve. There are even few who have not taken some occasion or other to quarrel with it, either on account of their not understanding always how to apply it, or on account of some prejudice or other which they were afraid to examine into, or could not bear to part with. For such is the stuff that man is made of: in principle and in practice, in a right track and in a wrong one, the rarest of all human qualities is consistency.

13. When a man attempts to combat the principle of utility, it is with reasons drawn, without his being aware of it, from that very principle itself. His arguments, if they prove any thing, prove not that the principle is *wrong*, but that, according to the applications he supposes to be made of it, it is *misapplied*. Is it possible for a man to move the earth? Yes; but he must first find out another earth to stand upon.

14. To disprove the propriety of it by arguments is impossible; but, from the causes that have been mentioned, or from some confused or partial view of it, a man may happen to be disposed not to relish it. Where this is the case, if he thinks the settling of his opinions on such a subject worth the trouble, let him take the following steps, and at length, perhaps, he may come to reconcile himself to it.

(1) Let him settle with himself, whether he would wish to discard this principle altogether; if so, let him consider what it is that all his reasonings (in matters of politics especially) can amount to?

(2) If he would, let him settle with himself, whether he would judge and act without any principle, or whether there is any other he would judge and act by?

(3) If there be, let him examine and satisfy himself whether the principle he thinks he has found is really any separate intelligible principle; or whether it be not a mere principle in words, a kind of phrase, which at bottom expresses neither more nor less than the mere averment of his own unfounded sentiments; that is, what in another person he might be apt to call *caprice*?

(4) If he is inclined to think that his own approbation or disapprobation, annexed to the idea of an act, without any regard to its consequences, is a sufficient foundation for him to judge and act upon, let him ask himself whether his sentiment is to be a standard of right and wrong, with respect to every other man, or whether every man's sentiment has the same privilege of being a standard to itself?

(5) In the first case, let him ask himself whether his principle is not despotical, and hostile to all the rest of human race?

(6) In the second case, whether it is not anarchical, and whether at this rate there are not as many different standards of right and wrong as there are men? and whether even to the same man, the same thing, which is right today, may not (without the least change in its nature) be wrong to-morrow? and whether the same thing is not right and wrong in the same place at the same time? and in either case, whether all argument is not at an end? and whether, when two men have said, 'I like this', and 'I don't like it', they can (upon such a principle) have any thing more to say?

(7) If he should have said to himself, No: for that the sentiment which he proposes as a standard must be grounded on reflection, let him say on what particulars the reflection is to turn? if on particulars having relation to the utility of the act, then let him say whether this is not deserting his own principle, and borrowing assistance from that very one in opposition to which he sets it up: or if not on those particulars, on what other particulars?

(8) If he should be for compounding the matter, and adopting his own principle in part, and the

principle of utility in part, let him say how far he will adopt it?

(9) When he has settled with himself where he will stop, then let him ask himself how he justifies to himself the adopting it so far? and why he will not adopt it any farther?

(10) Admitting any other principle than the principle of utility to be a right principle, a principle that it is right for a man to pursue; admitting (what is not true) that the word *right* can have a meaning without reference to utility, let him say whether there is any such thing as a *motive* that a man can have to pursue the dictates of it: if there is, let him say what that motive is, and how it is to be distinguished from those which enforce the dictates of utility: if not, then lastly let him say what it is this other principle can be good for?

EXERCISES

1. Suppose for a moment that William James is right, and that the ethical theory one adopts is largely a matter of temperament. If that is the case, how would you go about trying to change someone's views?

2. One objection to utilitarian ethics is that it turns everything into an ethical issue: if I spend an evening at a baseball game, but would have derived more pleasure from going to a concert, then I have committed a moral wrong. Nothing is exempt from moral evaluation. Is that a fair criticism?

3. One evening you get a call from the hospital. Your beloved old philosophy professor, Ruth Zeno, is near death, and wishes to talk with you. You rush to the hospital. The attending physician confirms that Professor Zeno is indeed in her last hours. When you enter the room, your professor is there alone. She grasps your hand warmly and whispers to you that she has a last request. From her bedside table she pulls out an old shoebox. She opens it, and you discover that it is stuffed with hundred-dollar bills. "There is almost half a million dollars in here," your professor says. "I have no relatives, no debts, no special obligations. The money is rightly mine, saved little by little during the course of my life. All the taxes have been paid. I want you to take this money and build a monument to my favorite racehorse, Run Dusty Run, in the infield at Pimlico racetrack. I'm certain the officials at Pimlico will give their permission. Run Dusty Run was my favorite racehorse. He wasn't a super horse, and few people remember him. But I cashed a nice bet on him once in Miami, and I loved that horse. He wasn't super fast, but he was always dead game, and he raced his heart out. I want you to take this money—no one else even knows the money exists—and spend every cent of it building a monument for Run Dusty Run. Hire a sculptor, and build a beautiful bronze monument in his honor. No tricks, okay? Don't put the money in a savings account, draw out the interest for 50 years, and then finally build the monument. And don't spend just 10 grand on the monument and use the rest for something else. Use *all* the money, as swiftly as possible, to build a monument to Run Dusty Run. I don't have long to live, and I need your answer quickly." Professor Zeno reaches over with her bony fingers and grasps your arm tightly, and her voice becomes raspy. "You were my favorite student, and I have always considered you a friend. Will you *promise* me, now, that you will spend the money and build the monument according to my wishes?"

   Well, it seems a rather silly request. But then your dear old philosophy professor was always a rather strange bird, and you know that she dearly loved playing the ponies. And though her body is swiftly failing, her mind still seems to be clear and sharp. "Okay," you reply. "I promise. I'll build the monument exactly as you wish." Your professor smiles and relaxes her grip on your arm, and after a short conversation about the nature of time—always her favorite philosophical question—she slips into a quiet sleep, and within a few minutes her breathing stops. The doctor comes in and pronounces her dead.

You take the shoebox, filled with half a million bucks, leave the hospital, and head back to your apartment. "Where am I going to find a sculptor who does monuments for racehorses?" you think to yourself. And then some other thoughts cross your mind. "Nobody else knows about this money. I'm the only one who knows it exists, and I'm the only one who knows about Professor Zeno's weird request. Of course I should keep my promise . . . Or I *guess* I should keep my promise . . . Or really, *should* I keep the promise?"

"Certainly it can't matter any more to Professor Zeno. She's dead. If there is an afterlife, and she's sitting in heaven, then she's already as happy as she can possibly be, and one monument more or less won't change that. If she's in hell, then she's got more to worry about than a stupid monument. And if there's no afterlife, and she's simply dead and gone, then nothing I nor anyone else does will matter to her in the least. It's highly unlikely that Run Dusty Run will be happy about having a monument built in his honor. And as for the horseplayers at Pimlico, all they care about is trying to pick the winner of the next race. You could build an exact replica of the Taj Mahal on the infield of the track, and most of them wouldn't even notice. On the other hand, there's lots of wonderful things that could be done with half a million dollars. It could endow several generous scholarships at Professor Zeno's university. Or maybe add a much needed burn unit at the city hospital. Or start a lead-screening program in the city, and save many children from lead poisoning. That would be nice. We could call it the Zeno Scholarship, or the Zeno Burn Center. Those would be wonderful ways to use the money, ways that would really help people. In fact, it's hard to think of a dumber, more useless way to spend the money than by building that stupid monument.

Of course, I did promise Professor Zeno, and I would be breaking my promise. But what's the harm in that? Professor Zeno certainly won't mind. And no one else will ever know about the promise (I can just say that Professor Zeno *instructed* the money be used for scholarships for needy philosophy students). So it's not like anyone will lose confidence in promising or the practice of promise-keeping. Of course *I* will know I broke my promise, but that won't make me feel guilty. Instead, I'll feel great about using Professor Zeno's money for a really good purpose. In fact, I would probably feel more guilty if I wasted the money on the stupid monument. So when I think about it carefully, it seems clear that I *ought* to break the deathbed promise I made to Professor Zeno."

Do you agree with that conclusion?

It seems likely the student promiser in this case is an act-utilitarian. But what about *your* answer. Is it based on act-utilitarian ethics? Rule-utilitarian ethics? Kantian ethics? None of the above?

4. Of the three ethical theories mentioned in the final paragraph of the previous question, which of those positions—perhaps none, perhaps more than one—would yield an answer *consistent* with your own answer?

5. What's the difference between a rule-utilitarian and a Kantian? *Is* there really a difference? Can you think of a case in which a rule-utilitarian and a Kantian would reach different conclusions about whether an act is right or wrong? If in *every* case the rule-utilitarian and the Kantian reached the same ethical conclusion, would that mean that there is no significant difference between the two accounts of ethics?

6. There is a spot open in Professor Ponder's film class. Your friends who have taken Professor Ponder's class all rave about it: "I really learned to appreciate the artistic potential of films by taking Professor Ponder's class. Before taking the class I liked almost every movie I saw. Now that I have learned from Professor Ponder how to understand and appreciate the fine nuances of the art of film-making, most of the movies I once enjoyed now strike me as stupid and amateurish. But because of my new appreciation of film, I now deeply enjoy a few great movies that otherwise I could never have appreciated. I have gained a depth of enjoyment from those few wonderful films I never dreamed you could get from watching a movie. Of course, it's very rare now that I enjoy going to the movies—most movies I see now strike me as dreadful, even painful to watch. But on the few occasions when I watch a really good movie—wow, that's a great experience. Take Professor Ponder's class: it will change forever your experience of going to the movies." If you think that is likely to be your own result from taking Professor Ponder's class, would you sign up?

7. In Fall 2003, the Canadian Bar Association was formulating a new code of ethics. One of the issues they were considering was whether lawyers should be barred from sleeping with their clients. The code of ethics for doctors and psychologists prohibits sexual contact between professional and client/patient; should lawyers adopt the same principle?

   The Canadian ethical code for lawyers requires that lawyers must always keep their clients' interests paramount. Also, lawyers acknowledge that at least sometimes clients are deeply dependent on their lawyers, and are very vulnerable, so there may exist a significant imbalance of power between lawyer and client. With those things in mind, the Canadian Bar Association considered four options. One, they could simply ignore the issue in the new code of ethics. Two, they could prohibit sexual relations in which the lawyer "takes advantage" of the client, by exploiting a difference in power. Three, they could prohibit sexual relations except when a consensual sexual relationship already exists *prior* to the lawyer/client relationship. Or four, they could prohibit *all* sexual relations between lawyer and client.

   The Canadian Bar Association asked for advice in dealing with this issue. So give them your advice: What rule should they adopt? One of the four? Some other rule?

   In making your recommendation, did you roughly follow one of the ethical models (utilitarian, rationalist, Humean) that we have discussed? Did you use a combination of those methods?[3]

ADDITIONAL READING

The classic utilitarian writings are Jeremy Bentham, *An Introduction to the Principles of Morals and Legislation* (London: 1823) and John Stuart Mill, *Utilitarianism* (London: 1863). Perhaps the most influential contemporary utilitarian, and certainly one of the most readable, is Peter Singer. His *Writings on an Ethical Life* (New York: HarperCollins, 2000) is the work of a philosopher thinking carefully about ethical obligations, and also striving to live his life by the right ethical standards. Whatever one thinks of Singer's views—he holds very controversial positions on abortion, animal rights, the obligations of the affluent toward those who are less fortunate, and euthanasia, and has been the target of more protests than any other contemporary philosopher—not even his fiercest critics deny that Singer is an outstanding example of someone who takes ethical issues and living ethically very seriously. Singer's *Writings on an Ethical Life* shows a dedicated utilitarian wrestling honestly with serious ethical issues. See also Singer's *Practical Ethics* (Cambridge: Cambridge University Press, 1979) for his views on a variety of ethical issues.

For a critique of utilitarian ethics, see Samuel Scheffler, *The Rejection of Consequentialism* (Oxford: Clarendon Press, 1982). An excellent debate on utilitarian ethics can be found in J. J. C. Smart and Bernard Williams, *Utilitarianism: For and Against* (Cambridge: Cambridge University Press, 1973).

NOTES

[1] Robert Nozick, *Anarchy, State and Utopia* (New York: Basic Books, 1974).

[2] *The Karamazov Brothers*, trans. Ignat Avsey (Oxford University Press: Oxford, 1994); first published in 1879–1880.

[3] Information for this case came from *The Gazette*, Montreal, Quebec, August 16, 2003.

CHAPTER 5

✧ SOCIAL CONTRACT ETHICS ✧

We have examined several ethical theories, ranging from Kantian rationalism through intuitionism to utilitarianism. Though they offer very different views of ethics, they have at least one thing in common: all insist they are explaining how to *find* ethical truth (with the exception of David Hume, who seems to doubt that ethical truth exists). Kant believes you find ethical truth through reason, others believe ethical truth reveals itself through feelings or intuitions, and the utilitarians propose we discover the right act by calculating the balance of pleasure over pain. Social contract theorists take a different approach: ethical principles are *made*, not found. Ethics is constructed by social groups, and exists for the benefit of those groups.

Framing the Social Contract

In the "state of nature" there are no rules. As Thomas Hobbes (one of the most famous social contract theorists) describes it, life in a state of nature is a "war of all against all," and in the state of nature life is "nasty, brutal, and short." You take what you can from me, and I do the same to those who are weaker. And though you are very strong, and thus seem to have great advantages in this war of all against all, you still have to sleep. I'm weak, but deadly if I catch you napping. So no one, however powerful, will ever rest easy. Rather than endure this terrible strife, we decide to *contract* together. And it's not too hard to think of some rules we would adopt. I might find it desirable to kill you and take all your possessions; but since I stand a good chance of being the killee rather than the killer (and if you don't get me, someone else certainly will) it makes more sense to give up my state-of-nature right to kill and steal if everyone agrees not to rob or kill me. And of course we'll need someone to enforce the rules, so a government will have to be formed, with police powers. But its powers are limited, since it would be silly for me to agree to a powerful government that murders me at its whim. I would be better off taking my chances in the state of nature, where at least everyone is roughly equal in strength. So if the government fails to abide by the contract, then we have a right to overthrow it (governments are not run by "divine right," but instead by the "consent of the governed"). And if I violate the rules it is legitimate for the government to punish me for breaking my contract.

Social contract theorists construct substantial ethical systems on this modest foundation. Obviously we will have rules against murder and theft, but they won't end there.

Would you want to live in a society in which everyone constantly lied to one another, or constantly cheated one another? Of course not. So it is reasonable for you to renounce lying and cheating, if everyone else also lives by that agreement. Perhaps I would prefer a society in which I am allowed to lie and cheat and you are held to high standards of integrity. But you would never agree to such a contract. So if I want to live in a society where honesty is the rule—and don't we all prefer that?—then I have to live up to the contract. And the social contract may give us much more. Today you are young and strong and healthy and prosperous, but misfortune may strike any of us, and the infirmities of old age loom in the future. So we might readily agree that those who suffer misfortunes or illness should be helped by the more fortunate. I may not particularly like giving some of my goods to the sick and infirm, but I'm willing to do so if I gain peace of mind from knowing that when old age weakens me or misfortune cripples me I will also receive help.

There are other rules our social contract should contain. For example, I want to be free to practice my religion and suppress all other religions (after all, my religion is the *true* religion, and all others are vile idolatry). But I realize others also have strongly held religious beliefs, and they might gain power, and then my own religion would be banned. I would like to be able to persecute you for practicing a false religion, but I don't want to take a chance of being on the receiving end of the persecution. So I will agree to a freedom of religion rule in our social contract.

Social Contracts and Human Strife

This has solid natural appeal. It constructs ethics with no aid from metaphysics or divinities, bases ethics on agreements requiring neither mysteries nor faith, and places ethics squarely within the natural world. Social contract theory does not depend on any religious sanction or divine human spark or profound rational powers or special intuitions. It makes no assumptions that humans are special beings. To the contrary, social contract theorists often paint a rather gruesome picture of human nature, and still manage to construct a substantial ethical system on that minimalist foundation.

It's no accident that the most rigorous social contract theories tend to develop in times of political and social upheaval. One of the most famous social contract theories was devised by Thomas Hobbes during a time when Europe was racked with war. Protestant armies fought Catholic armies, and the basic rule was simple: if you're not for us, you're against us. Suppose you were trying to live a quiet peaceful life as a baker in a European town under Protestant rule. The Catholic armies sweep in and capture your village—and since you were living there peacefully, that probably means you are a Protestant, and so deserve to die. If somehow you escape death, a few months later a Protestant army arrives on the scene and recaptures your village; and if you survived under Catholic rule, well, that means you must be a Catholic, and thus deserve death. And if you don't get caught in that Protestant-Catholic whipsaw, there is still a good chance that a fervor of witch burning might sweep through your village. With dozens of tortured victims screaming out any names they could think of, the name of the baker might well come to mind, and you could find yourself standing at the stake with a large pile of wood around you and your neighbors eager for your death. And if you somehow survived all those disasters, you are likely to fall victim to the ravages of the terrible Black Death: the Bubonic Plague, which regularly swept through Europe killing thousands. Faced with such turmoil, you might begin to wonder if there was any justice or ethics guiding the world's fortunes. God no doubt keeps good order among the angels, and the stars and planets regularly follow their heavenly routes, but if we're going to have peace on Earth we'd better do it ourselves. A social contract seems a good start toward a peaceful and at least minimally harmonious society. And since the contract must govern our vicious natural impulses, it is essential that the government have great power and authority to keep our brutal natural tendencies under control.

Rousseau's Social Contract

On Hobbes's view we need a strong social contract because our *natural* tendencies are toward murder and mayhem and "every man for himself." In our natural state life is nasty and brutish. Only by establishing a powerful governing force can these natural tendencies toward violence and greed be held in check. But not every social contract theorist has had such a negative view of human nature. Jean-Jacques Rousseau, an eighteenth-century philosopher and novelist, was born in Geneva but spent most of his life in France. Rousseau believed the natural state of humankind is basically good. We are all motivated by the emotion of pity:

> Pity is a natural sentiment moderating the action of self-love in each individual and contributing to the mutual preservation of the whole species. It is pity that sends us unreflecting to the aid of those we see suffering; it is pity that in the state of nature takes the place of laws, moral habits, and virtues, with the added benefit that there no one is tempted to disobey its gentle voice . . .[1]

Since Rousseau's state of nature is not so bad—pity holds our self-interests in check, and "will deter a robust savage from robbing a weak child or infirm old person"—we are not so desperate for a social contract that will hold vicious tendencies in check. Instead, we join together in an association in which we all share common goals and principles, and so no one relinquishes any freedom, and no one has greater power than another. John Locke, a British philosopher who lived shortly after Hobbes, also believed in a relatively peaceful and gentle state of nature—and relatively peaceful natural human tendencies—and thus the social contract he proposed was also more limited than that of Hobbes. In particular, Locke insisted on preserving the individual rights of citizens against the temptation of social rulers to become tyrants.

Social Contracts and Human Nature

Social contract theories are sometimes criticized because the notion of persons sitting down together in the "state of nature" and drawing up a careful contract is too implausible. But that's not really a fair criticism: it takes social contract theory much too literally. Social contract theory is not meant to be a historical or anthropological account of how political systems developed. Rather, social contract theory is an examination of the *justice* and *fairness* of political and social and ethical systems. The question is not whether you signed a contract to live under the rules of our society. Obviously you did not. Rather, the important question is whether you *would* sign such a contract if offered the opportunity. If you would, then the system of rules we live under is basically fair, a system we could voluntarily accept. That doesn't mean, of course, that you think every rule we have is a good one. Perhaps you think we should have tighter restrictions on firearms, or a lower legal drinking age, or no laws requiring seat belts. Our social contract is not precisely the one you would draw up if you could arrange all the details. No one thinks the social contract is perfect. The question is whether it is sufficiently fair and decent that we would choose to live under this social contract rather than in a state of nature. If so, then the social contract may not be perfectly fair, but may be fair enough.

Would you prefer to live under our social contract, or in a state of nature? That is how Hobbes framed the question. But that stacks the deck in favor of the social contract. After all, I might prefer a rather lousy society and a seriously unjust government rather than a state of nature in which there is a "war of all against all," and everyone around me is trying to stab me in the back, and life is indeed nasty, brutish, and short. Only a very bad social contract is worse than the state of nature. Of course, that's the way Hobbes wanted it. Having lived through wars and revolutions, Hobbes craved peace. Though he believed people have a right to overthrow their government, he wanted that right exercised only in the most extreme circumstances.

FAIRNESS AND SOCIAL CONTRACT THEORY: JOHN RAWLS

Different social contract theorists start from different views of human nature, and propose a variety of social contracts. One of the best ways of using social contract theory is to compare contract possibilities. Rather than asking whether we prefer our social contract to a war of all against all, we might ask whether we would agree to *this* social contract in preference to some other social contract alternative. If in making that judgment we decide some other social contract would be much fairer, then we might conclude that our social contract is not as fair and just as it could or should be. John Rawls, a contemporary political philosopher, uses social contract theory in just that way. But Rawls adds a special twist. Rather than starting from a state of nature, locked in mortal combat with all around you, instead imagine finding yourself in the midst of a large group of people who have not yet been placed in the world. You might think of this as a group of disembodied spirits, about to be sent to Earth. No one has a gender or a race; you can't tell how tall you will be, how intelligent or dull, how industrious or lethargic; whether you will be fabulously athletic or severely disabled; you don't know what religion you will favor, whether you will prefer Wolfgang Mozart or Willie Nelson, nor what political doctrines you will hold. That is, you find yourself behind what Rawls calls "the veil of ignorance." You know nothing about yourself or your abilities, what advantages or disadvantages you will be born with. You know only that you will have need of food and water and shelter, that you will be vulnerable to fire and disease and sharp objects, and that you will have a desire to live and prosper. In short, you know you will be a human, and all your fellow disembodied humans are now meeting to draw up the rules for the human society you are about to create. Under those circumstances, what rules would you adopt?

Behind the Veil of Ignorance

From behind such a veil of ignorance I would never accept a rule that says women should have less opportunity to become president, or that African Americans should have less chance of going to college or be restricted in the places they can live. I wouldn't accept such rules, because there's a chance that I might step out from behind the veil of ignorance and discover that I am an African-American woman. So I would favor setting up a society in which everyone has equal opportunity to compete for everything. And that means real opportunity: not some sham, in which I am sent to inferior schools, suffer lead poisoning in rundown housing and perhaps malnutrition besides, receive substandard or no health care, and then when I turn 18 you announce that now I have the opportunity to "compete equally" with persons who have enjoyed an 18-year head start.

What else would I want in this new society I (whoever "I" turns out to be) am about to enter? I would want a wide range of basic freedoms, such as freedom of speech and freedom of religion. For though it might be great fun to silence those whose views disagree with my own, it would be much more painful to be among those who are silenced—and that's exactly where I might find myself. Besides, from this detached perspective, I can see advantages to allowing the free exchange of ideas, even weird and unpopular ideas (which sometimes turn out to be true, and even if they are false such challenges stimulate us to think more carefully and critically about why we hold the views we favor). And perhaps I would want some sort of guarantee that if the society I am entering is quite prosperous, then the worst off in that society should have sufficient resources to live a decent life and have genuine opportunities to improve their positions. It's nice to fantasize that I might wake up in this new society and be embodied as a billionaire. But if our society has enormous disparities of wealth, then there's a much better chance of finding myself in poverty. The difference between having a mansion that is 10,000 square feet and one that is 11,000 is not a big deal. I could hardly tell the difference. But the difference between being homeless and having a snug little cottage is enormous. So if I don't know what economic situation I'll be in, I would favor making sure everyone gets at least a comfortable little cottage before anyone builds a ridiculously gargantuan mansion. Everyone must have one bedroom before anyone has 12.

Justice as Fairness

Obviously none of us started as disembodied spirits, floating around in ether drawing up a social contract. Nonetheless, Rawls's model provides a valuable perspective. In particular, it helps us look at our society without the various prejudices and preferences we accumulate because of gender, race, economic class, religion, or political allegiance. His trick of asking us to step behind the 'veil of ignorance' is ultimately just a very effective way of asking us to think hard about: How would you like it if *you* were in that position? If we look at a rule of law or a principle of ethics or a social policy in our society, and we can honestly say we would adopt that policy from behind the veil of ignorance, then it is reasonable to conclude that the policy in question is *fair*. If we wouldn't adopt it, then perhaps the policy should be modified.

GAUTHIER'S CONTRACTARIAN ETHICS

David Gauthier has developed a contemporary version of the social contract theory that is quite different from that of Rawls. Rawls's social contract theory is designed to test our basic moral principles and social rules and institutions: from behind the veil of ignorance, stripped of our special interests and biases and privileges, would we regard those rules and structures as *fair* and *just?* Gauthier's social contract theory is designed to provide a rational justification for at least a minimal set of moral principles. Gauthier wants to demonstrate that as rational self-interested beings, there are some moral rules that it makes good sense for us to adopt and follow; and indeed, there are moral rules we rationally *should* follow, even when the rules are not to our immediate advantage. While Rawls uses contract theory to discover or *test* moral systems, Gauthier employs contract theory to show that purely self-interested individuals could and should favor at least a minimally cooperative moral system.

The Prisoner's Dilemma

The basis for Gauthier's social contract system—what Gauthier calls a system of "morals by agreement"—is recent work on game theory, especially related to the famous "prisoner's dilemma." The prisoner's dilemma is an intriguing case that has drawn much attention from economists and sociologists as well as philosophers. Consider the dilemma in its basic form. Susan and Kate are partners in committing a crime, and both have been caught. They are interrogated separately. Both know the police have enough evidence to convict them of burglary, for which they will each receive sentences of five years in prison; but they also know the police do *not* have enough evidence to convict them of the bank robbery they also committed. If both continue to deny they were involved in the bank robbery, then neither will be convicted of the bank robbery, and both will serve five-year sentences for burglary. But if Susan is willing to testify that Kate is guilty of the bank robbery (while Kate continues to deny that either of them were involved in the bank robbery), then the police are willing to give Susan a special deal, and reduce Susan's total sentence to only two years. In that case, Kate will get full blame for the bank robbery, and receive a sentence of twelve years, while Susan gets only two years. But if *both* Susan and Kate "rat" on one another, then they will both get ten-year sentences. So thinking only of her own rational self-interest, what should Susan do? Of course if she and Kate could get together, they might agree to keep silent, and both serve their five-year sentences: not a great outcome, but much better than both going up for ten years, right? But Susan is being questioned separately, and she doesn't know what Kate is going to do, just as Kate doesn't know what Susan will do. As a self-interested rational person, what is Susan's best alternative? Obviously she should rat on Kate. Suppose that Susan rats on Kate, while Kate says nothing: in that case, Susan will get only a two-year sentence. (Kate will serve twelve years, but that's her tough luck. Of course we have to assume that Kate doesn't have violent friends who will do serious harm to Susan if Susan rats on her; but let's keep the story relatively simple.) On the other hand, if Kate is over in the other interrogation room ratting on Susan: well, in that case, Susan is still better off ratting on Kate, since Susan will get a ten-year rather than a twelve-year sentence. So whatever Kate is doing, Susan is better off ratting on her. Assuming both Susan and Kate are rational self-interested players (and Kate reasons just as Susan did), both will wind up with ten-year prison sentences. But that is a lousy result: though each avoids the twelve-year maximum sentence, had both of them kept quiet they would have had five-year sentences. It would be better for both if they could trust one another to forego immediate advantages in order to gain greater long-term cooperative benefits.

What's the moral of the story? If people always pursue their interests, they will wind up with results that are less desirable than if they had sacrificed some immediate advantages to cooperate for mutual gains. Thus a system of *morality* in which we honor agreements and cooperate with others is beneficial for each of us, and it is in my long-term self-interest to honor it. This has wide application. Suppose you and I are neighbors, and we are both building decks. The building projects will go much more efficiently if we work together as a two-person team, rather than individually. If we work individually, it will take each of us approximately fifteen hours to build our decks. If we work together, each deck can be completed in five hours, and both will be done in ten, and each of us will save five hours of labor. So it will be in both our long-term interests to cooperate. So I propose we start with my deck, and then when that's done we'll do yours. In order to make this work, you must trust me to honor my commitment, and I must be the sort of person who is trustworthy. Otherwise, you will fear that after you have contributed five hours to building my deck, I'll back out of the cooperative agreement and leave you with fifteen hours of single-handed deck building. Without a moral system in which promises are kept and cooperation is reciprocated there can be no mutually beneficial cooperative projects. Committing ourselves to act morally (by cooperating and keeping pledges) when others also act morally fosters the trust essential for mutually beneficial cooperation, and that is enough to establish "morals by agreement." Morality needs no divine or intuitive or mysterious foundation; as rational, self-interested persons we can calculate its advantages for ourselves.

The Social Contract Myth and Its Underlying Assumptions

Rawls doesn't suppose that we started out as disembodied spirits. And of course social contract theorists don't suppose that any group of people living in a brutal war of all against all one day sat down together and signed the social contract: one afternoon we all put down our clubs and spears, sat around the fire and drew up an elaborate social contract. No social contract theorist believes anything like that literally happened. The social contract is a *myth* that social contract theorists use to develop their position. It tells a story that helps us see important truths behind the story. Think of the Jewish creation *myth*. After God created the world, He had all the animals march by, and Adam assigned them names. It's an interesting myth, which signifies the dominion of humans over all animals. (You may not agree with the idea of human dominion expressed by the myth, but that's a different question.) But if you take it as a literal story, it soon becomes a bit silly. It's one thing to think of Adam happily whiling away a few hours naming the big photogenic species ("I think I'll call that a zebra; you with the long neck, you're a giraffe; and you are going to be named tyrannosaurus rex; and that bird over there will be named robin.") But by the time Adam finished with a few thousand beetle species, he might be getting a bit weary of the game, and he wouldn't even have started on the mollusks, much less the bacteria. Likewise, the social contract myth is not literally true, but the story it tells contains some very important ideas. Whether you agree with those ideas is a question you will have to consider for yourself.

What ideas are presupposed in the social contract myth? The Genesis creation story, in which Adam names all the animals, assumes that Adam is above and over the rest of the animal kingdom, and has control and "dominion" over it. That's important to note, since the assumptions made—but never stated—are often powerful and insidious. We may buy into those assumptions as we listen to the story, and it is sometimes difficult to bring them to the surface and subject them to critical examination. What assumptions are embedded in the social contract myth?

Think about how the social contract comes into being (according to the social contract myth). Each of us was fighting a war of all against all; growing tired of lives that were "nasty, brutish, and short," each of us agreed we would relinquish our state-of-nature rights to commit murder and mayhem in exchange for some peace and security. We each weighed the options, considered what was in our best interests, and signed the contract.

Radical Individualism

There are several underlying assumptions in that story, and perhaps the most basic is this: *Each of us, individually*, fought against every other individual in the state of nature; and then we each sat down and individually decided it would be in our best interests to sign the contract.

The social contract changes things, bringing order and security. But both as social contractors and state-of-nature warriors we function as distinct units, as atomic individuals fighting for our individual lives and contracting for our individual benefits. Thus the social contract myth includes a deeply embedded and quite radical assumption of *individuality*. In both the state of nature and under the social contract, the most basic rule appears to be: every woman and man for her or himself. I abide by the contract, but only because it satisfies *my* best interests.

The social contract myth is very powerful and pervasive, and its strong assumption of individualism has had a profound impact. Some of the individualistic emphasis is probably positive. For example, the emphasis on *individual rights* has given us important safeguards against both social and governmental intrusions into our lives. We could certainly make faster medical progress if medical researchers could "draft" a few dozen individuals, infect them with a deadly disease, and then test new drugs in an effort to cure that disease. Of course some of the drafted research subjects would die. But because we would move faster toward finding a cure, we would ultimately save more lives than are lost. We are morally repulsed at such a plan, the utilitarian benefits notwithstanding. We think it wrong to coercively *use* an individual for the benefit of society: it is a violation of *individual rights*. (Of course we draft people in times of national emergency, and require that they sacrifice their lives in battle for the interests—or the supposed interests—of the community. But that is regarded as a very special case.) Likewise, it might make the community happier if those who champion views we generally find repulsive—racists, religious bigots, neo-Nazis—were silenced. We tolerate their repulsive blather, basically because we strongly believe in the individual rights of free speech and free expression (and we fear that if their unpopular free speech is suppressed, our own individual right of free speech might be next: after all, if you can only espouse views that please the majority, that hardly counts as an individual right of free speech).

So there are clearly some good things in our notion of individual rights. But the radical individualism assumed in the social contract myth is another matter. In the first place, it is biological and anthropological nonsense. We are a profoundly *social* species, and we naturally live in families and societies, and our bonds with family and friends and community run very deep: much deeper than any social contract. We are a rather clever species, but we are neither swift nor strong, we lack sharp teeth for fighting and we have no bony exoskeleton for defense. Besides that, our young are born into years of extreme vulnerability, with few or no resources for protecting themselves. Had we been as radically and ruthlessly individualistic as the social contract myth suggests, we would have died out long before any social contract was drawn up.

While individual rights are very important, the "rugged individual" of social contract myth causes significant problems. It suggests we must each be totally self-sufficient (though we know that to be false). And it sometimes blinds us to how much we depend on our families and communities in order to live successfully, and thus we are also blinded to the needs of those who fail to receive such support ("*I* made it entirely on my own, so she can too.") As Virginia Held has noted, contract models characterize ethics as an agreement that is mutually advantageous to separated rational individuals of roughly equal strength; but much of life is better modeled in terms of building community and nurturing friendships rather than contractually resolving conflicts. If our model for ethical relationships were one of friendship, or perhaps the relation between mother and child—which is at least as central to our experience as are relations among purely self-interested contractors—then our conception of the good society might be quite different.[2]

Narrow Obligations

The second assumption underlying social contract theory is closely tied to the first. Since we are radically distinct individuals contracting together, the only obligations we incur are those we voluntarily and individually approve. Perhaps that's true. Some people think so. But it is important to note that the assumption is being made, for it is certainly an assumption that is open to question. You 'didn't choose to be born,' and you didn't choose your parents or your siblings. But most of us believe we have at least some obligations to them. (If you hear of a young man who makes a fortune, but leaves his parents and younger siblings in terrible poverty, most people will have a rather negative moral assessment of this person whom they will regard as selfish and unfeeling.) And a woman who makes a great fortune, but never "gives back" anything to the community that nurtured her, is regarded as selfish and ungrateful. Social contract theory pulls us in the opposite direction. If you help your aged parents, or contribute to your community, that's nice of you—but not a moral obligation.

Choosing Morality

The third assumption underlying social contract theory is somewhat similar to the second. Just as we "choose" our obligations to others, likewise all moral principles are a matter of "choosing" to accept that moral system. Ethics exists only as a contract among rational parties, each of whom approves the contract as the best deal he or she can get. Thus ethics is a system we make as a social agreement among reasonable self-interested contractors. If it's not in the contract, then it's not part of the ethical system. And the contract is designed by rational agreement, based on mutual self-interest. Feelings have nothing to do with it.

Outside the Social Contract

A fourth assumption of the social contract myth is perhaps the most subtle. If you can't join in the contract, and you can't live up to the demands of the contract, then you aren't part of the moral community. Those who are weak or infirm, including the very young and at least some of the very old, are not real members of the moral community. Those of us who are full signatories of the social contract may decide to grant them protection, but the protection is given only as a favor, not as a right. Those in that position are at best second-class citizens of the moral community, rather than genuine rights-holding members. Under this view, if you are insane, or so badly damaged in your character formation that you cannot meet the obligations of the social contract, then we may take pity on you and not punish you for the harms you cause. But the cost you must pay is the loss of your membership in the moral community: you become something less that a real moral person. That is why some who violate the law—who violate the social contract—prefer even harsh punishment to being "excused" as incompetent. We punish *members* of the moral community who violate the contract. To be excused or exempted from punishment is to be banished from that community. For profoundly social animals like ourselves, that is very harsh punishment indeed.

There are others who also did not sign on to our social contract. People from different cultures, who are not part of our society or our nation, are obviously "outsiders." Under social contract theory, they have no rights, and we have no obligations to them. The most brutal treatment of alien peoples might be regarded as "in bad taste," or "esthetically displeasing," but it is difficult to see how a social contract theorist could condemn it as morally wrong. And the same point applies to nonhuman animals. If they can't understand and accept and follow the rules, then they have no rights and are due no *moral* consideration.

Gauthier's contractarian "morals by agreement" raises disturbing questions of who gets left out of moral consideration. In Gauthier's view, rational self-interested persons will cooperate because they stand to gain more—at least long term—through cooperation. But in cases where we have little to gain through such cooperation (for example, where we have the power to coerce, or when dealing with persons so weak or disabled[3] that they have little to contribute to a cooperative arrangement) then Gauthier's purely self-interested individual would have little motive for making the scope of morality broad enough to encompass such persons. On the other hand, Rawls's theory can aid us in thinking more vividly about fair treatment for a wide range of persons: if I were behind the veil of ignorance, and *might* emerge as a severely disabled person, what would I insist upon as fair treatment for persons in my potential condition?

CONCLUSION

Social contract theory forges an ethical system with no help from God or "natural law" or transcendent truths or powers of intuition. It has some definite limits (though dedicated contract theorists may see those limits as legitimate and justifiable), and some of its basic assumptions may not square with what we know about the social nature of human animals. Still, in the hands of a theorist such as John Rawls, social contract theory can push us to think carefully and critically about the moral principles we favor, the society we live in, and the social structures and institutions we support.

LEVIATHAN

Thomas Hobbes

Thomas Hobbes was a seventeenth-century British philosopher. The following passage is taken from his most famous work, *Leviathan,* which he published in 1651, two years after the execution of King Charles I. Although Hobbes denied the divine right of kings, he argued that a powerful king is needed to prevent disorder and disaster. His views made him unpopular in England, and he found refuge in France for more than a decade. He was, however, an outspoken enemy of the Catholic church, and was suspected of atheism, which eventually left him somewhat isolated in France. He returned to England, and with the restoration of Charles II to the monarchy became a favorite at court. Hobbes wrote major works on a wide variety of subjects, including political theory, philosophy, mathematics, history, and optics.

Notice that Hobbes's example of people living in a "state of nature" is "the savage people in many places of *America* . . . [who] have no government at all; and live at this day in that brutish manner . . . ." This was a common belief among seventeenth-century Europeans; perhaps a self-serving belief, that served to justify the brutal treatment of native Americans. But at the time Hobbes wrote, the famous Iroquois Federation (the Five Nations) had been in existence for many years, with such an elaborate system of government that some have suggested the Articles of Confederation of the American colonies were modeled after their rules.

OF THE *NATURALL* CONDITION OF MANKIND, AS CONCERNING THEIR FELICITY, AND MISERY

Nature hath made men so equall, in the faculties of body, and mind; as that though there bee found one man sometimes manifestly stronger in body, or of quicker mind then another; yet when all is reckoned together, the difference between man, and man, is not so considerable, as that one man can thereupon claim to himselfe any benefit, to which another may not pretend, as well as he. For as to the strength of body, the weakest has strength enough to kill the strongest, either by secret machination, or by confederacy with others, that are in the same danger with himselfe.

And as to the faculties of the mind, (setting aside the arts grounded upon words, and especially that skill of proceeding upon generall, and infallible rules, called Science; which very few have, and but in few things; as being not a native faculty, born with us; nor attained, (as Prudence,) while we look after somewhat els,) I find yet a greater equality amongst men, than that of strength. For Prudence, is but Experience; which equall time, equally bestowes on all men, in those things they equally apply themselves unto. That which may perhaps make such equality incredible, is but a vain conceipt of ones owne wisdome, which almost all men think they have in a greater degree, than the Vulgar; that is, than all men but themselves, and a few others, whom by Fame, or for concurring with themselves, they approve. For such is the nature of men, that howsoever they may acknowledge many others to be more witty, or more eloquent, or more learned; Yet they will hardly believe there be many so wise as themselves: For they see their own wit at hand, and other mens at a distance. But this proveth rather that men are in that point equall, than unequall. For there is not ordinarily a greater signe of the equall distribution of any thing, than that every man is contented with his share.

From this equality of ability, ariseth equality of hope in the attaining of our Ends. And therefore if any two men desire the same thing, which neverthelesse they cannot both enjoy, they become enemies; and in the way to their End, (which is principally their owne conservation, and sometimes their delectation only) endeavour to destroy, or subdue one an other. And from hence it comes to passe, that where an Invader hath no more to feare, than an other mans single power; if one plant, sow, build, or possesse a convenient Seat, others may probably be expected to come prepared with forces united, to dispossesse, and deprive him, not only of the fruit of his labour, but also of his life, or liberty. And the Invader again is in the like danger of another.

And from this diffidence of one another, there is no way for any man to secure himselfe, so reasonable, as Anticipation; that is, by force, or wiles, to master the persons of all men he can, so long, till he see no other power great enough to endanger him: And this is no more than his own conservation requireth, and is generally allowed. Also because there be some, that taking pleasure in contemplating their own power in the acts of conquest, which they pursue farther than their security requires; if others, that otherwise would be glad to be at ease within modest bounds, should not by invasion increase their power, they would not be able, long time, by standing only on their defence, to subsist. And by consequence, such augmentation of dominion over men, being necessary to a mans conservation, it ought to be allowed him.

Againe, men have no pleasure, (but on the contrary a great deale of griefe) in keeping company, where there is no power able to over-awe them all. For every man looketh that his companion should value him, at the same rate he sets upon himselfe: And upon all signes of contempt, or undervaluing, naturally endeavours, as far as he dares (which amongst them that have no common power, to keep them in quiet, is far enough to make them destroy each other,) to extort a greater value from his contemners, by dommage; and from others, by the example.

So that in the nature of man, we find three principall causes of quarrell. First, Competition; Secondly, Diffidence, Thirdly, Glory.

The first, maketh men invade for Gain; the second, for Safety; and the third, for Reputation. The first use Violence, to make themselves Masters of other mens persons, wives, children, and cattell; the second, to defend them; the third, for trifles, as a word, a smile, a different opinion, and any other signe of undervalue, either direct in their Persons, or by reflexion in their Kindred, their Friends, their Nation, their Profession, or their Name.

Hereby it is manifest, that during the time men live without a common Power to keep them all in awe, they are in that condition which is called Warre; and such a warre, as is of every man, against every man. For WARRE, consisteth not in Battell onely, or the act of fighting; but in a tract of time, wherein the Will to contend by Battell is sufficiently known: and therefore the notion of *Time*, is to be considered in the nature of Warre; as it is in the nature of Weather. For as the nature of Foule weather, lyeth not in a showre or two of rain; but in an inclination thereto of many dayes together: So the nature of War, consisteth not in actuall fighting; but in the known disposition thereto, during all the time there is no assurance to the contrary. All other time is PEACE.

Whatsoever therefore is consequent to a time of Warre, where every man is Enemy to every man; the same is consequent to the time, wherein men live without other security, than what their own strength, and their own invention shall furnish them withall. In such condition, there is no place for Industry; because the fruit thereof is uncertain; and consequently no Culture of the Earth; no Navigation, nor use of the commodities that may be imported by Sea; no commodious Building; no Instruments of moving, and removing such things as require much force; no Knowledge of the face of the Earth; no account of Time; no Arts; no Letters; no Society; and which is worst of all, continuall feare, and danger of violent death; And the life of man, solitary, poore, nasty, brutish, and short.

It may seem strange to some man, that has not well weighed these things; that Nature should thus dissociate, and render men apt to invade, and destroy one another: and he may therefore, not trusting to this Inference, made from the Passions, desire perhaps to have the same confirmed by Experience. Let him therefore consider with himselfe, when taking a journey, he armes himselfe, and seeks to go well accompanied; when going to sleep, he locks his dores; when even in his house he locks his chests; and this when he knows there bee Lawes, and publike Officers, armed, to revenge all injuries shall bee done him; what opinion he has of his fellow subjects, when he rides armed; of his fellow Citizens, when he locks his dores; and of his children, and servants, when he locks his chests. Does he not there as much accuse mankind by his actions, as I do by my words? But neither of us accuse mans nature in it. The Desires, and other Passions of man, are in themselves no Sin. No more are the Actions, that proceed from those

Passions, till they know a Law that forbids them: which till Lawes be made they cannot know: nor can any Law be made, till they have agreed upon the Person that shall make it.

It may peradventure be thought, there was never such a time, nor condition of warre as this; and I believe it was never generally so, over all the world: but there are many places, where they live so now. For the savage people in many places of *America*, except the government of small Families, the concord whereof dependeth on naturall lust, have no government at all; and live at this day in that brutish manner, as I said before. Howsoever, it may be perceived what manner of life there would be, where there were no common Power to feare; by the manner of life, which men that have formerly lived under a peacefull government, use to degenerate into, in a civill Warre.

But though there had never been any time, wherein particular men were in a condition of warre one against another; yet in all times, Kings, and Persons of Soveraigne authority, because of their Independency, are in continuall jealousies, and in the state and posture of Gladiators; having their weapons pointing; and their eyes fixed on one another; that is, their Forts, Garrisons, and Guns upon the Frontiers of their Kingdomes; and continuall Spyes upon their neighbours; which is a posture of War. But because they uphold thereby, the Industry of their Subjects; there does not follow from it, that misery, which accompanies the Liberty of particular men.

To this warre of every man against every man, this also is consequent; that nothing can be Unjust. The notions of Right and Wrong, Justice and Injustice have there no place. Where there is no common Power, there is no Law: where no Law, no Injustice. Force, and Fraud, are in warre the two Cardinall vertues. Justice, and Injustice are none of the Faculties neither of the Body, not Mind. If they were, they might be in a man that were alone in the world, as well as his Senses, and Passions. They are Qualities, that relate to men in Society, not in Solitude. It is consequent also to the same condition, that there be no Propriety, no Dominion, no *Mine* and *Thine* distinct; but onely that to be every mans that he can get; and for so long, as he can keep it. And thus much for the ill condition, which man by meer Nature is actually placed in; though with a possiblity to come out of it, consisting partly in the Passions, partly in his Reason.

The Passions that encline men to Peace, are Feare of Death; Desire of such things as are necessary to commodious living, and a Hope by their Industry to obtain them. And Reason suggesteth convenient Articles of Peace, upon which men may be drawn to agreement. These Articles, are they, which otherwise are called the Lawes of Nature: whereof I shall speak more particularly, in the two following Chapters.

OF THE FIRST AND SECOND NATURALL LAWES, AND OF CONTRACTS

The Right of Nature, which Writers commonly call *Jus Naturale*, is the Liberty each man hath, to use his own power, as he will himselfe, for the preservation of his own Nature; that is to say, of his own Life; and consequently, of doing any thing, which in his own Judgement, and Reason, hee shall conceive to be the aptest means thereunto.

By LIBERTY, is understood, according to the proper signification of the word, the absence of externall Impediments: which Impediments, may oft take away part of a mans power to do what hee would; but cannot hinder him from using the power left him, according as his judgement, and reason shall dictate to him.

A LAW OF NATURE, (*Lex Naturalis*,) is a Precept, or generall Rule, found out by Reason, by which a man is forbidden to do, that, which is destructive of his life, or taketh away the means of preserving the same; and to omit, that, by which he thinketh it may be best preserved. For though they that speak of this subject, use to confound *Jus*, and *Lex*, *Right* and *Law*; yet they ought to be distinguished; because RIGHT, consisteth in liberty to do, or to forbeare; Whereas LAW, determineth, and bindeth to one of them: so that Law, and Right, differ as much, as Obligation, and Liberty; which in one and the same matter are inconsistent.

And because the condition of Man, (as hath been declared in the precedent Chapter) is a condition of Warre of every one against every one; in which case every one is governed by his own Reason; and there is nothing he can make use of, that may not be a help unto him, in preserving his life against his enemyes; It followeth, that in such a condition, every man has a Right to every thing; even to one anothers body. And therefore, as long as this naturall Right of

every man to every thing endureth, there can be no security to any man, (how strong or wise soever he be,) of living out the time, which Nature ordinarily alloweth men to live. And consequently it is a precept, or generall rule of Reason, *That every man, ought to endeavour Peace, as farre as he has hope of obtaining it; and when he cannot obtain it, that he may seek, and use, all helps, and advantages of Warre.* The first branch of which Rule, containeth the first, and Fundamentall Law of Nature; which is, *to seek Peace, and follow it.* The Second, the summe of the Right of Nature; which is, *By all means we can, to defend our selves.*

From this Fundamentall Law of Nature, by which men are commanded to endeavour Peace, is derived this second Law; *That a man be willing, when others are so too, as farre-forth, as for Peace, and defence of himselfe he shall think it necessary, to lay down this right to all things; and be contented with so much liberty against other men, as he would allow other men against himselfe.* For as long as every man holdeth this Right, of doing any thing he liketh; so long are all men in the condition of Warre. But if other men will not lay down their Right, as well as he; then there is no Reason for any one, to devest himselfe of his: For that were to expose himselfe to Prey, (which no man is bound to) rather than to dispose himselfe to Peace. This is that Law of the Gospell; *Whatsoever you require that others should do to you, that do ye to them.* And that Law of all men, *Quod tibi fieri non vis, alteri ne feceris.*

To *lay downe* a mans *Right* to any thing, is to *devest* himselfe of the *Liberty*, of hindring another of the benefit of his own Right to the same. For he that renounceth, or passeth away his Right, giveth not to any other man a Right which he had not before; because there is nothing to which every man had not Right by Nature: but onely standeth out of his way, that he may enjoy his own originall Right, without hindrance from him; not without hindrance from another. So that the effect which redoundeth to one man, by another mans defect of Right, is but so much diminution of impediments to the use of his own Right originall.

OF OTHER LAWES OF NATURE

From that law of Nature, by which we are obliged to transferre to another, such Rights, as being retained, hinder the peace of Mankind, there followeth a Third;

which is this, *That men performe their Covenants made:* without which, Covenants are in vain, and but Empty words; and the Right of all men to all things remaining, wee are still in the condition of Warre.

And in this law of Nature, consisteth the Fountain and Originall of JUSTICE. For where no Covenant hath preceded, there hath no Right been transferred, and every man has right to every thing; and consequently, no action can be Unjust. But when a Covenant is made, then to break it is *Unjust;* And the definition of INJUSTICE, is no other than *the not Performance of Covenant.* And whatsoever is not Unjust, is *Just.*

EXERCISES

1. Social contract theory is often used to justify punishing those who violate the law (they have accepted the benefits but have broken their agreement to abide by the social contract, and thus the other parties to the contract can legitimately penalize those violators). Jeffrie Murphy has argued that in our society—where there is enormous disparity in wealth, and also huge differences in opportunity (as evidenced by the contrast between urban ghetto schools and suburban schools)—the social contract cannot be used to justify punishment. At least the social contract cannot justify punishing property crimes committed by those in the lowest socioeconomic class, since persons in such circumstances would not likely agree to a contract that would leave them so severely disadvantaged. Of course there might be other arguments for the justice of punishment; but does Murphy's argument effectively undermine the *social contract* basis for punishment in societies like our own?

2. Though obviously many who commit criminal acts endeavor to escape blame, on some occasions prisoners insist they *should* be punished. In fact, some who seem to be as much victim as criminal are strongest in their insistence that their criminal acts resulted from their own choices and that they are deserving of punishment. John Spenkelink was the first person executed in Florida after that state resumed capital punishment. He had idolized his father, but at age 11 he was the first to find his father's body following his father's suicide. From that time he became involved in a series of petty crimes, drifted around the South, and ultimately murdered a fellow drifter in an argument. Shortly before he was executed he asserted that: "Man is what he chooses to be. He chooses that for himself." Under the social contract model, why might one who commits a crime *insist* he deserves punishment?

3. Social contract theorists generally believe our moral rules are made, rather than discovered. The rules are what we draw up or agree to in our social contract. Yet a number of social contract theorists—John Locke, for example—also believe there are objective moral truths, factually true moral principles that are just as true as the principles of math or physics. Are those beliefs fundamentally inconsistent, or can they be reconciled? In fact, the U.S. Declaration of Independence obviously contains a social contract view of government, but it starts with the famous pronouncement of *self-evident* ethical truths that do not wait upon social contracts: "We hold these truths to be self-evident: That all men are created equal, and are endowed by their Creator with certain inalienable rights." Is that a *consistent* or a *contradictory* position?

4. Under a strict social contract view of ethics, could we make sense of the notion of "rules of conduct" or "rules of war" between warring nations?

5. Is the United Nations charter an example of a 'social contract'?

6. Hobbes suggests that in the "state of nature," "Every man has a right to every thing; even to one another's body." Is it legitimate to speak of "rights" of any kind in the state of nature?

ADDITIONAL READING

The classic sources for social contract theory are Thomas Hobbes's *Leviathan*, John Locke's *Second Treatise on Government*, and Jean-Jacques Rousseau's *Social Contract (Du Contrat Social)*. Hobbes's *Leviathan* is available from Bobbs-Merrill (Indianapolis: 1958); it was originally published in 1651. Locke's *Second Treatise on Government* was originally published in 1690; an accessible edition is (Indianapolis: Bobbs-Merrill, Library of Liberal Arts, 1952). Rousseau's *Social Contract* was originally published in 1762; it can be found in an edition edited by R. Masters (New York: St. Martin's Press, 1978).

Discussions of social contract theory tradition include Jean Hampton, *Hobbes and the Social Contract Tradition* (Cambridge: Cambridge University Press, 1986); and P. Riley, *Will and Political Legitimacy: A Critical Exposition of Social Contract Theory in Hobbes, Locke, Rousseau, Kant, and Hegel* (Cambridge, Mass.: Harvard University Press, 1982).

David Gauthier's version of contractarian theory can be found in *Morals by Agreement* (Oxford: Oxford University Press, 1986) and *Moral Dealing* (Ithaca, N.Y.: Cornell University Press, 1990). For discussion and critique of Gauthier's theory, see Peter Vallentyne, editor, *Contractarianism and Rational Choice* (New York: Cambridge University Press, 1991).

Probably the best known philosophical book of the late twentieth century presented an updated version of social contract theory: John Rawls, *A Theory of Justice* (London: Oxford University Press, 1971).

NOTES

[1]Jean-Jacques Rousseau, *A Discourse on the Origin of Inequality*, trans. Franklin Philip (Oxford University Press: Oxford, 1994), 36.

[2]Virginia Held, "Feminism and Moral Theory," in Eva Kittay and Diana Meyers, editors, *Women and Moral Theory* (Savage, Md.: Rowman and Littlefield, 1987).

[3]Eva Feder Kittay has written an excellent book on the importance of care for those who are powerless and dependent; see *Love's Labor: Essays on Women, Equality, and Dependency* (New York: Routledge, 1999).

CHAPTER 6

✧ EGOISM, RELATIVISM, ✧ AND PRAGMATISM

Ethical egoism and cultural relativism are very different ethical theories, but it may be useful to consider them together (and it will be convenient to consider pragmatism at the end of this chapter, since many of its critics consider it a form of relativism). In some ways, cultural relativism is a bit like ethical egoism writ large. The ethical egoist maintains that whatever benefits *me* is the right thing to do. The cultural relativist says that whatever my *culture* approves is what I should do. Advocates of both views tend to represent themselves as tough-minded and scientifically oriented: the egoist claiming to start from stark psychological facts, and the cultural relativist from the hard facts of sociology and anthropology. Both tend to share a reductionist orientation: Whatever else you might romantically or idealistically imagine ethics to be, what *really* is involved in ethics is just seeking one's own good (the egoist says) or following the customs of one's culture (the cultural relativist claims). Both views are interesting, both views are admirable in their attempt to integrate scientific and empirical considerations into ethics, and both views are worth considering.

EGOISM

Egoism comes in two varieties. First is *psychological egoism:* the view that—as a matter of empirical psychological fact—all our behavior is selfish, or self-interested. Second is *ethical egoism,* which is the very different claim that we *ought* to always act in a way that is self-interested. Though often run together, they are very different positions. Sam could be a psychological egoist while fervently rejecting ethical egoism. That is, Sam could believe that we are psychologically constructed to always behave selfishly; but Sam might also believe that is an ethical disaster, since selfishness is bad. And Sandra could be an ethical egoist, who believes that we *ought* to act selfishly, but also believe that our psychological makeup is such that we often fail to act selfishly (according to ethical egoist Sandra, we sometimes behave altruistically rather than selfishly, and those altruistic acts are morally wrong). If one is both a psychological and an ethical egoist, then one is in the fortunate position of believing that everyone always and inevitably does right: selfishness is virtue, and we cannot avoid acting selfishly, and thus we cannot avoid acting virtuously.

Psychological Egoism

Psychological egoism has great appeal for many people, and psychological egoists are typically confident of the irrefutable wisdom and plain truth of the position they hold. From the right perspective, psychological egoism seems clear and unassailable truth. Why did you buy a cup of coffee? Because you want a cup of coffee, obviously; you have a selfish interest in enjoying a delicious rich cup of coffee. But why did you give money to a drought relief fund? Because I want to enjoy the reputation of a generous and public-spirited person; it's in my selfish interest to have such a reputation. But why did you make a secret anonymous donation last week? Because it made me feel good to think I was helping others: I received more satisfaction from spending the money that way than by any other use I could have found for the money. So even that "generous act" was actually selfish. But what about when your dear old mother rose from her bed and interrupted her own much needed rest, in order to hold a cool cloth to your fevered brow and bring you medicine and comfort? Was that a selfish act? Yes, that too was selfish. She gained greater pleasure from ministering to her child than she could have derived from resting. She did it, ultimately, for her own selfish pleasure.

Criticisms of Psychological Egoism

Psychological egoism begins to sound seductively convincing. No matter what case one proposes—the generous anonymous donor, the selfless loving mother—the psychological egoist easily shows it to have been a selfish act. But perhaps too easily. After all, psychological egoism is supposed to be an *empirical* claim. It is not based on logic, or pure reasoning, or definition, but based instead on empirical observation and testing. But if it is an empirical claim, then it must be possible to tell what sort of empirical evidence would count against the claim. Since psychological egoists believe that psychological egoism is empirically true, obviously they need not provide evidence that it is false. If it is to be an empirical truth, however, they must be able to tell us what *would* count as evidence that it is false. Suppose I claim that all moose are brown, and I assert that as an empirical truth based on long observation of moose. If it is an empirical truth, then I have to be able to say what would count *against* it. Easy enough. If you show me a purple moose, and I investigate to make sure the moose has not been dyed a different color, and this purple moose is a DNA match to brown moose, and its mother and father were perfectly respectable moose, then I will admit that I was empirically mistaken: it's not true that all moose are brown. (If I insist that this purple animal is not a moose, since all moose *must* be brown, I am proposing a new definition of moose, rather than making an empirical claim about the moose species.) So if psychological egoism is an empirically based claim that all behavior is selfishly motivated, what would count as proving the claim wrong?

That's the problem. Not even the most generous, selfless, noble act escapes the clutches of egoistic selfishness. You plunge into icy water, at great risk to your own life, to rescue a small child to whom you are not related. No one else is around, so there is no hope of reward or recognition. The child is a thoroughly obnoxious and ungrateful wretch, who is more likely to kick you in the shins than thank you for your heroic efforts. Even then, the egoist categorizes this as selfish, self-interested behavior: you take pleasure in the rescue, and you avoid the suffering of watching a small child perish. But this makes the claim empty: *nothing* could count as an unselfish act, since every purposeful act has some motivation, and the egoist is redefining all motivations as selfish. The claim is true, but it is reduced to a tautology: all selfishly motivated acts are selfishly motivated acts. But the psychological egoist is supposed to be giving us a genuine psychological claim, not a claim that is rendered true on the basis of a special definition.

The persuasiveness of psychological egoism rests on a special and all-inclusive meaning of "selfishness." If we are short of food, and you make a greedy secret raid on our limited food supply, then that is a selfish act. If you offer to take the smallest share, but you know that we are only minutes from being rescued and supplied with abundant food, and your only motive is to win honor and praise for your pretended generosity, then your behavior hardly counts as a shining example of generosity. But if you offer a portion of your food simply because you are concerned about the welfare of another member of your party, and you have no ulterior motives other than the benefit of that person, then that is a genuinely generous and unselfish act. If the act brings you satisfaction, that does *not* transform it into a selfish act. After all, finding genuine satisfaction and joy in the good of others is the hallmark of a generous person, one who is *not* acting for his or her own selfish goals. Furthermore, even when we do act for self-interested motives, those motives need not squeeze out all generous motivation. You want to do well in your calculus class, for self-interested reasons. You also want your friend to do well in calculus, and you unselfishly provide tutoring to help him reach that goal. By tutoring your friend, you may learn the material better yourself; but that doesn't transform your motivation into something selfish. When in high school you did volunteer work at an extended care facility for the elderly, you may have had a selfish interest in how attractive such volunteer work would appear on your college application; but that does not mean that you could not also have a genuine and unselfish motive as well: the motive of bringing comfort and joy to the people with whom you worked.

Far from selfish egoism being a universal truth, the fact is that we can find examples of unselfish generosity not only among humans but in other species as well. Charles Darwin cites examples of blind helpless birds that were fed by their companions. Whatever one thinks of unselfish behavior in other species, there seems to be abundant evidence of it in our own. Mixed in, of course, with a substantial amount of cruelty, selfishness, and callousness. But the presence of *some* level of unselfish behavior is sufficient to undercut the claims of psychological egoism.

Ethical Egoism

If we do sometimes act unselfishly, then the next question emerges: *should* we act unselfishly? Or should we instead, as the ethical egoist insists, always act for our own benefit?

Individual Ethical Egoism   Actually, there are at least two different versions of ethical egoism: *individual* ethical egoism, and *universal* ethical egoism. The individual ethical egoist maintains that everyone ought to do what benefits *me*. If Susan is an individual ethical egoist, then Susan believes that everyone, Susan included, ought to aim at the benefit of Susan. *Universal* ethical egoism is the position of extreme rugged individualism: everyone ought to aim exclusively at his or her own benefit, and should neither give, ask, nor receive help from others.

By its very nature, individual ethical egoism has few advocates. That is not to say that individual ethical egoism is a rare position. To the contrary, judging by the behavior of some corporate executive officers who enrich themselves at the expense of employees and investors and stockholders, one suspects that individual ethical egoism is alive and flourishing. But individual ethical egoists are unlikely to publicly promote their views. If Ken is a dedicated individual ethical egoist, who firmly believes that everyone should be working for the benefit of Ken (and that no other ethical rules apply), then Ken may attempt to create the impression that he is dedicated to the welfare of all and eager to help others. After all, if everyone else *should* be striving for *my* benefit, then the best way to accomplish that is to convince them that their work will benefit everyone, including themselves. That being the case (and since an individual ethical egoist will have no moral reluctance to tell lies, though he will of course think it wrong for *you* to lie to *him*), it is very difficult to tell how many individual ethical egoists there really are.

It is sometimes suggested that individual ethical egoism is self-contradictory, because advocating such a system is self-defeating: by openly asserting that you are only interested in yourself, and you believe that others should sacrifice everything for your benefit, you are likely to become an outcast. People will be reluctant to associate with you, much less devote themselves to promoting your welfare. But what this shows is not that individual ethical egoism is inherently contradictory, but only that the individual ethical egoist would be wise not to publicize her ethical views; or to speak plainly, the individual ethical egoist would be wise to lie about her ethical views (a policy she can adopt with no ethical qualms).

Is there any way to convince the individual ethical egoist to change her views? That's a difficult question. If it's possible, it won't be easy. After all, the genuine individual ethical egoist thinks no one else really matters. If we point out that other people are hurt by her actions, that will be a matter of indifference to her. We might point out to her how profoundly isolated she is: she can never really reveal herself to anyone, can never be open with others, cannot have any friends for whom she feels real affection and deep bonds of shared honesty. Individual ethical egoism begins to look like a rather lonely, loveless, and uneasy life. But if that is the sort of life one wants—a life lived with narrow and exclusive concern for oneself—then perhaps that will not be disturbing. In short, if you regard a totally self-centered life as a real and attractive possibility, then it is difficult to offer you good reasons not to adopt individual ethical egoism. Of course we can give good reasons for *appearing* to take a larger view, in order to gain the social benefits that accrue to that appearance; but it is much more difficult to give reasons why you should genuinely pursue a moral life, rather than a fraud that takes every possible exploitative advantage. Noting the implications of individual ethical egoism, however, is likely to severely limit its appeal. Few would wish to live a life of constant deception, a life cut off from genuine intimacy and friendship and concern for others and mutual affection. Individual ethical egoism looks more like a path to psychopathology than to happiness.

Why Care for Others?   If we seek self-interested reasons that can answer "Why be concerned for others?" we encounter other problems. There are traditional attempts to prove that a calculating egoist would not be happy: your conscience will bother you, your life will require constant deception, you will cut yourself off from any genuine relations (you hide your real motives, so no one can care for you as you actually are). But if you are the sort of person who can genuinely consider a life of systemic selfishness as an attractive "lifestyle," then probably such concerns will not weigh heavily on you.

Individual ethical egoism is a difficult position to refute. Some people take that as evidence of its strength. But it may instead be because the position starts from such an alien perspective—a perspective of absolutely no concern for others—that it is difficult to find any common ground for discussion. It is perfectly reasonable and morally legitimate to have a healthy regard for one's own interests. In fact, without at least some degree of self-respect, it is difficult to imagine having satisfactory relations with others. But exclusive concern for oneself, coupled with indifference to the needs and interests of others, is not likely to strike many people as a desirable or fulfilling perspective on the world.

Universal Ethical Egoism   Universal ethical egoism—*everyone* should pursue what is to his or her individual self-interested advantage—does at least have the advantage of being a position one can openly advocate. And it has had some champions. Some people argue that universal ethical egoism is simply nature's way: we all struggle for our own selfish purposes, the strong survive, the weak and unfit are eliminated, and thus we evolve and get better. It's harsh, but that's just the way it is. And if we want to be successful, we have to follow nature's plan.

Universal ethical egoism is red-blooded, two-fisted ethics. Unfortunately, it is based on a crude and distorted view of evolutionary science. Natural evolution doesn't have a plan, and it certainly has no goal or purpose. The evolutionary survivors aren't superior, morally or otherwise; rather, they are simply better suited for the particular environment in which they happen to land. In any case, the paved ground, polluted air, and shopping malls in which we now function, the bioengineered and heavily processed foods we eat, and the high-tech medical treatments we receive make talk of "natural" processes a bit strained. Even if we set all that aside, the old "every man for himself" stuff is more suited to Hollywood action movies than our own evolutionary history. Rather than rugged individualists we are a profoundly social species. Due to our extraordinarily long and vulnerable infancy, humans form strong family and social bonds. This has great advantages for our species, otherwise it would not have been a successful evolutionary strategy. Mutual affection and concern and cooperation are essential to making that strategy work. The notion of humans as rugged individuals is an artificial contrivance, while cooperation and affection comes naturally to members of our deeply social species.

A second version of universal ethical egoism is based in economic considerations: we will all prosper if everyone seeks his or her individual benefit, without worrying about others. Unfettered laissez-faire capitalism (as opposed to regulated capitalism with an extensive social welfare component) will promote everyone's ultimate good. But while that is often voiced as a timeless truth, the evidence for it is very weak. Of all the industrialized nations, the United States comes closest to that ideal of unfettered capitalism (having the least regulation, the lowest taxes, and the most meager social welfare support), and the U.S. economy has been successful in enriching a large number of people (though whether that is a result of an effective economic system or the power to exploit the workers and resources of other countries might be a debated point). But in any case, whatever the success of such a universal egoist economic system in producing wealth for a small segment of society, it is hard to say that it has benefitted everyone. After all, the United States leads the industrialized world in number of homeless, homicide rate, atmospheric pollution, number of people without health care, number of people in prison, number of children living in poverty, infant mortality rate; and—though I'm not sure anyone is keeping a careful count—probably enjoys a substantial lead in criminal enterprises by chief executive and chief financial officers. Whatever its virtues, it is difficult to maintain that unfettered capitalism (based on "every man for himself") has resulted in the maximum possible benefit for everyone. In sum, if the claim is that everyone pursuing their own selfish interests will result in the greatest possible benefit for everyone, it is difficult to find any empirical grounds—biological, economic, or otherwise—for that universal egoistic article of faith.

Relativism

Relativism. It's a term used in a variety of ways and disciplines, ranging from physics to anthropology to ethics. So it's important to be clear on what we're talking about. "Ethical relativism" is the thesis that what is right is *relative* to each culture. That is, there are no absolute or fixed principles of ethics, but only the ethical systems of various cultures. What is right in Canada is not the same as what is right in Indonesia. And what was right in ancient Rome is not what is right in contemporary Rome.

Sociological Relativism and Cultural Relativism

If relativism is simply the claim that different cultures have different ethical systems, that is an interesting claim but not very controversial. If you travel from Pakistan to Scotland, you will find different languages, different religions, different climates, different cultures, and different moral codes. That differing cultures have differing customs, standards, and moral codes is an empirical observation made by sociologists and anthropologists. That thesis might be called *sociological relativism,* and it is well supported by social scientific study. In contrast, *cultural relativism* is the claim that not only do differing ethical codes exist, but ethical judgments can only be made *relative to* a given culture: ethical principles have objective force only within a given culture. On this view, capital punishment is wrong in France, and right in Saudi Arabia; abortion is wrong in Italy, and right in the United States. According to the cultural relativist, it makes no sense to say that capital punishment is always or absolutely wrong, for right and wrong are strictly relative to culture.

Cultural relativism is *not* the view that ethical principles are relative to circumstances. That would fit the utilitarian perspective, not the cultural relativist. Utilitarians hold that we should do whatever—in those circumstances—would produce the best consequences (the greatest balance of pleasure over suffering) for everyone. So in specific instances we must consider the particular circumstances, but there is still a basic utilitarian principle that is cross-culturally true: you should always act in such a way that your act will produce the greatest balance of pleasure over pain for everyone. For utilitarians that principle is just as true in Australia as it is in Egypt. In contrast, cultural relativists do not believe that there are any universal ethical principles. Ethical principles are relative to cultures. In one culture, it might be right to be a utilitarian; in another culture, utilitarian ethics would be wrong.

Benefits of Cultural Relativism

Cultural relativism has some good points. Perhaps the most important is to shake us out of our ethical provincialism, and remind us that other cultures may have values that are not the same as our own, and that does not always mean theirs are wrong. Before we conclude that a different cultural ethic is mistaken, or even barbaric and evil, we should strive to understand how those values actually function in the culture. And as anthropologists constantly remind us, that is likely to be a much more complicated matter than we thought. For example, among some of the Aboriginal peoples of the Canadian Northwest, the basic ethical concept of "justice" is quite different from that in the rest of Canada as well as in the United States. Instead of focusing on who deserves punishment for a crime, and what degree of punishment should be meted out, they instead concentrate on how unity and harmony can be restored to the community, and on how both the harmed and those who did the harm can be restored to the community as a whole. If a young person breaks the law, this is seen as a symptom of something wrong in the community, and the goal is to restore the entire community to health. This leads to a very different concept of justice and a very different system of justice in that culture, but it is far from clear that it is an ethically inferior system. Even if we do not think it would work as a system of justice in our larger and more diverse culture, it may be a very good ethical system for a culture of closely united villages and deep family ties that interconnect almost all members. In any case, imposing the Western adversarial system of justice, with its punitive emphasis and atmosphere of confrontation and hostility, might well cause cultural disintegration and harmful repercussions we can hardly anticipate. And cultural destruction is a very serious danger. As Kate Brown and Andrew Jameton note:

> One reason for respecting cultural diversity rests on the observation that community membership, participation, and shared symbolism are important sources of human happiness and health, apart from any validity of the symbols with reference to science or to reality.[1]

Thus even if we conclude that the ethics of a particular culture don't entirely meet with our approval—or would not work in our system—we should exercise great caution in attempting reforms. It is easy to cause more harm than good, even with the best intentions.

Speaking of good intentions, it is worth noting that not infrequently the intentions of "cultural reformers" are not quite as good as they would have us believe. Some Europeans claimed they were coming to the 'New World' to carry out 'cultural reform' and convert the natives to the true religion. Judged by their actions, the "cultural reform" served only as a thin justification for plundering the wealth of the cultures they discovered, then killing or enslaving the people they found. A good example can be found in the "explanation" of why in 1832 the Seminoles were forcibly removed from their Florida homeland and moved to Oklahoma: it was the result of "the solicitude manifested by the President of the United States for the improvement of their condition, by recommending a removal to a country more suitable to their habits and wants."[2] Such "improvement in condition" and "cultural reform" often accompanies the theft of land. The blessings of "cultural reform" the United States brought to Central America often consisted in driving subsistence farmers and their families off their lands so U.S. corporations could have large plantations and cheap labor to grow pineapples or sugar cane for profitable export. Currently, some people suspect that the announced desire of some American politicians to bring cultural reform (and the "blessings of democracy") to countries in the Middle East is motivated more by love of oil than by love of reform. This does not imply that there is never room for 'cultural reform,' but the sordid history of such "reforms" reminds us to look closely at the actual motives of the reformers.

Criticisms of Cultural Relativism

Cultural relativism may broaden our understanding of other cultures and promote tolerance, and may prompt us to examine carefully both the motives and the consequences of promoting cultural reform. Notwithstanding those benefits, cultural relativism also faces some serious problems. The first is one that arises in the example previously cited. What culture does an Aboriginal Canadian youth belong to? She is a member of a tribal culture, such as the Dene. She is also part of the larger Aboriginal culture, comprised of many different tribes with distinct cultures and traditions. She is a Canadian citizen, and a member of that culture as well. The norms of those cultures may not always coincide. As noted before, the Canadian principles of justice may conflict with Aboriginal principles. This creates a problem for the ethical theory of cultural relativism: as a member of several different cultures, with conflicting norms, how can we decide what this Dene woman *should* do? That problem is very common. If you live in Pittsburgh you are a member of that culture (you probably have deep affection for the Steelers, you spend at least one summer day at Kennywood Park, and you drink Iron City beer); but you are also a member of a distinctive neighborhood culture, which may be distinguished by ethnicity, religious affiliation, and local tavern; and a member of the larger American culture as well. If what is right is set by the rules of your culture, you may find yourself pulled in several different directions by the conflicting rules of your several cultures. In the culture of small-town north Louisiana, dancing and drinking are regarded as sinful and immoral. When young people from those communities find oil field jobs along the South Louisiana coast, they find that an evening of drinking wine, playing music and dancing is considered a wholesome exercise of family and community values. Thus cultures are not as distinct and isolated as cultural relativism seems to require.

A second, and perhaps even more serious problem for cultural relativism, is the problem of ethical reform. Or perhaps we should say, the problem of the *impossibility* of ethical reform. If whatever my culture treats as right *is* right, then "reform" must always be wrong. In that case, when the U.S. culture approved of slavery, the abolitionists were mistaken; when women pushed for the right to vote and other basic rights (in a culture that denied such rights) then they were also wrong. Indeed, all our most revered reformers—Frederick Douglass, Susan B. Anthony, Mahatma Gandhi, Martin Luther King—would not only be wrong, but *morally* wrong: they fiercely opposed the moral and cultural norms of their societies, and by the principles of cultural relativism they were therefore opposing what was *right* in the societies in which they lived. Discrimination against homosexuals is a widespread cultural norm in the United States, but thankfully there seems to be gradual progress in overcoming that prejudice. Cultural relativism would stop such movements in their tracks.

Third, cultural relativism seems to weaken and trivialize our ethical concerns. The Southern rural farm culture in which I grew up ate a large meal (which we called dinner) at noon and a light 'supper' in the evening. In my present culture we eat a light lunch at noon, and the large dinner meal is served in the evening. No problem. That's analogous to I like apple pie and you prefer cherry. We can both have what we prefer, it's just a difference in tastes, we can live with the disagreement. Cultural relativism invites us to treat moral issues in the same manner. In our culture women are regarded as persons with full and equal rights; in your culture women are the property of fathers or husbands, and have no rights whatsoever. That's okay. You follow your cultural practices and we'll follow ours. But in this case, that solution is not so attractive. I may find your food too spicy and your dress too drab and the games in your culture a bit strange, but there is nothing morally offensive in them. But if you treat women as property, that's not just a difference in tastes, and I cannot comfortably 'tolerate' such practices as if they were merely taste preferences. That was the attitude taken by some "states' rights" advocates during the civil rights era: in our state Blacks have no right of equal protection under the law, no right to vote, no right to be safe from brutal racist attacks; if you want to have such rights in your state, that's fine, but leave us alone to follow our own cultural heritage. But tolerating racism and brutality and injustice is not like tolerating a preference for grits instead of potatoes with your scrambled eggs.

If you believe that racism is *morally wrong*, you cannot just dismiss it as a cultural quirk. Your family likes the beach, mine prefers to vacation in the mountains, and that's fine with you. But if your family believes that children should be treated with care and affection, and my family favors brutal child abuse, that is *not* a difference you can quietly tolerate. To do so would mean denying the importance and strength of your moral convictions.

Cultural relativists legitimately remind us that at least *some* of our notions of what is morally right or wrong have no basis other than cultural tradition. That reminder is useful in preventing us from condemning—or "reforming"—the practices and norms of other cultures simply because they differ from those with which we are more familiar. But frankly, that is a service that is probably performed better by teachers of cultural anthropology than by those who espouse the ethics of cultural relativism. Beyond that limited virtue, it is difficult to see many advantages to cultural relativist ethics. In fact, it is difficult to see any real basis for cultural relativist ethics. Certainly cultures are complex, and they develop in ways that allow them to perform useful functions. But there is no better reason to suppose that every culture is good than to suppose that every individual is good. The Nazi culture may have "kept order," but the order it kept was brutal, repressive, and murderous. The culture of the antebellum American South no doubt had some charming features: respect for elders, commitment to honesty and integrity, loyalty to friends and family. But its virtues were heavily weighted with a system that was built on slavery and brutality, promoted a rigid caste system, treated women as mere ornaments and not as full persons in their own right, and regarded labor with contempt. Any ethical theory that makes it impossible to intelligently critique a culture—including one's *own* culture—blocks consideration of some of the most important ethical issues we face.

Grounds for Cultural Relativism

The ethics of cultural relativism can be constructed on two very different foundations. First, one might adopt cultural relativism on the grounds that when it comes to cultures, "whatever is is right." That is, cultures always develop in such a manner that they are the best they could possibly be in that situation: every culture is the optimum fit for its circumstances. Thus colonial New England culture would not be a good fit for us, but it was the ideal culture for those who lived in New England during that period. The caste system of India would not work in twenty-first-century Montreal, but it was perfect for Bombay in 1900. The culture of ancient Rome would not be right for today's Minneapolis, but it was just right for ancient Rome. But that requires faith that cultures always 'evolve' or develop in such a way that they work as well as they possibly could. That faith has no foundation in empirical fact. There is no evidence of a guiding hand that shapes every culture to be the best it could possibly be. Indeed, there is abundant evidence that cultures can be and often are repressive and harmful and cruel, and far from the best possible culture that could possibly have developed in those settings. Consider, for example, certain European cultures of the sixteenth century, cultures that busied themselves by killing infidels, torturing heretics, burning witches, stifling dissent, blocking free inquiry, and maintaining a rigid hierarchy of caste and privilege. It is easy to imagine how such a culture could be improved, and of course reformers have brought many such improvements to pass. Indeed, it is considerably more difficult to imagine how you could make that culture worse than to imagine how you might have made it better. So if the ethics of cultural relativism is based on belief that whatever culture exists is always the best it could be, then it is based on a very weak foundation.

As noted earlier, we should be very cautious in concluding that a cultural practice is wrong: it may have a more complicated function and more complex relation to the larger conditions of that culture than we can readily appreciate. We can find an appropriate analogy in environmental studies. Often we discover that the destruction of an animal or insect "pest" that we thought useless or harmful has consequences for the entire ecosystem, and consequences we had neither anticipated nor desired. Still, it does not follow that when we look at cultural practices, then whatever is must be the best possible. It may well be that cultural practices that were once somewhat beneficial have been preserved by the force of custom or law or religious sanction to a time when they have long outlived their usefulness. And it is quite possible that some cultural practices that developed out of superstition or oppression survived though they were detrimental to most members of the culture. After all, cultures that were once successful often become inflexible, and perish because they cannot change and adapt. That being the case, it is hard to maintain that whatever cultural practices a culture is currently maintaining must be *right* for that culture.

But there is a second possible grounds for cultural relativism: the belief that there are no good grounds for ethical claims, and therefore no basis for criticizing any existing cultural practice. But this second path to cultural relativism seems no smoother than the first. If there are no grounds for any sort of ethical judgments, then there are no grounds for supposing that the norms of each culture *should* be accepted as good. On this approach to cultural relativism, attacking cultural practices would be as legitimate as supporting them. "There is no reason to think the norms of our culture are right. Therefore we should accept them without criticism." Somehow, that argument seems less than compelling.

In short, it is difficult to find reasonable grounds for cultural relativism as an ethical theory. It is surely desirable to have people understand and appreciate other cultures, and it is a good thing to get beyond the biased provincialism that leads one to suppose that any culture that deviates from our own cultural norms and traditions must therefore be inferior or even morally depraved. But there are much better ways to accomplish that laudable goal than by adopting the implausible ethics of cultural relativism.

Other Forms of Ethical Relativism

Cultural relativism is perhaps the best known relativist theory of ethics, but it is by no means the only one. The problem is when philosophers speak of ethical relativism, they often mean very different things. For example, there are 'methodological relativists,' and 'meta-ethical relativists,' and 'moral judgment relativists'; and to further complicate things, the advocates of these positions do not always define those categories in precisely the same way. We can't explore all those issues and distinctions here. However, one view that is sometimes classified—or misclassified—as ethical relativism will come in for more detailed examination. That is the view that ethical truths (like *all* truths) are not truths that "correspond to reality" or copy the world as it actually is. Instead, truths (including truths of ethics) are theories or beliefs that *work well*, that *lead us effectively*, that *function efficiently*. What is *true*—whether in ethics or physics or engineering—is what works best for us. Though people who take this view are sometimes described as (and less often describe themselves as) *relativists*, their views are very different from the 'cultural relativism' discussed in this chapter. For example, Richard Rorty, a leader of this "relativist" view (though he strongly rejects the relativist title), clearly opposes cultural relativism: "Truth is, to be sure, an absolute notion, in the following sense: 'true for me but not for you' and 'true in my culture but not in yours' are weird, pointless locutions."[3] To avoid confusing this with the many questions surrounding relativism, we'll call that view ethical *pragmatism*.

Pragmatism

Pragmatists believe that moral principles may indeed be *true*, just as true as scientific principles. But pragmatists insist that our traditional notion of *truth*—in philosophy and ethics as well as in science—is hopelessly muddled. According to the traditional account of truth, a claim is true when it corresponds to reality. Is the Copernican Theory true? The traditional correspondence theory of truth counts the theory as true just in case it corresponds to or matches or copies the way the world actually is. The Copernican Theory asserts that the Earth orbits the Sun; that theory is true (according to the correspondence account) just in case the Copernican Theory corresponds to or maps or copies the planetary reality. But according to pragmatists, that notion of matching or correspondence just doesn't work. In the first place, it doesn't work because there are many alternative theories that will all fit the data. For example, while the Copernican Theory fits all our observations of the solar system, so does the 'Yo-Yo Theory,' which claims that the Earth orbits the Sun until it completes its cycle (which will require another 10 million years), and then the Sun will begin to orbit a stationary Earth. The Yo-Yo Theory is perfectly silly, of course; but it fits all the data we currently have just as well as does the Copernican Theory. So why do we regard the Yo-Yo Theory as silly, and the Copernican Theory as sober truth? Not (according to the pragmatists) because the latter *corresponds* to reality and the former does not; but rather because the Copernican Theory is simpler and more useful and gives us better predictions and control. But that is what truth really consists in: not a correct matching to an external reality, but instead a coherent and workable system that *guides us well* and *works effectively*. (Incidentally, pragmatists are *not* claiming that there is no reality other than our ideas and minds. Pragmatists insist there certainly *is* a reality, and we must strive to understand it. The notion of understanding reality by copying it with our theories is what pragmatists/coherence theorists reject; not the idea of reality itself.)

What is true is not what copies or matches a "reality" independent of our theories and perceptions. That conception of reality is nonsense. It supposes that we can make sense of stepping outside our ideas and perceptions and beliefs and checking some pure "reality-as-it-is-in-itself." But such a "God's-eye view of the world"—or as Thomas Nagel called it, such a "view from nowhere"—is not possible. At the very least, it is not possible for beings like ourselves, animals firmly anchored within the natural world in which we evolved. As William James elegantly states the pragmatist position, "The trail of the human serpent is thus over everything," there is no separating the "real world" from our theories and beliefs and observations. And (pragmatists insist) it's not even clear that we can make sense of the notion of observing the world "as it is in itself," apart from our perceptions and theories. We *always* encounter reality as *part of* that reality, and we approach reality through our perceptions and ideas and theories. We are not 'outside observers.'

So rather than trying to *match* our theories to 'the world as it really and truly is, independently of us,' we must instead seek theories that *work best* in the world in which we live. Again, William James: "The true is the name of whatever proves itself to be good in the way of belief, and good, too, for definite, assignable reasons." If a theory works well, guides us effectively, functions well as a *tool* for making predictions and gaining control and living well, then that theory is *true*. It is true in the only sense of being true that makes sense. Of course it is not eternally true or absolutely true; such notions work only in the correspondence theory framework, in which we think of a theory as perfectly true when it is a perfect match for the world (the world "as it truly is," untouched by human hands or human perceptions or human theories). If a system of physics or astronomy works for us, leads us well into predictions and discoveries, then it is true; if a system of ethics works for us, guides us effectively in how to live well and successfully as the social animals we are, then it is true.

Pragmatic ethics, then, is an experimentalist approach to ethics, which seeks to find the ethical systems that work best for us, just as physicists and psychologists try to find the theories that work best for those purposes. It's not a social contract theory of ethics: pragmatists maintain that we must *discover* the best ethical theories, not simply choose one. We must discover which ethical systems work best for us, *not* which ethical systems match the "ethical truth" that exists independently of us. Our society might all agree to follow an ethical system that does *not* lead us well; in that case, we would be agreeing to a social contract that is wrong by pragmatic lights. Nor is pragmatism merely a new name for utilitarianism; pragmatists need not believe that an ethical system that maximizes pleasure and minimizes suffering will prove to be the ethical system that leads us best. Perhaps utilitarian ethics will prove itself best, but that is a matter to be decided by ethical experiment and practice, not utilitarian doctrine. And finally, pragmatic ethics is not relativism. Like relativists, pragmatists reject absolute eternal ethical truths that we *discover*; but unless one supposes that the *only* alternative to ethical absolutism is ethical relativism, then there seems little reason to classify pragmatists as relativists.

PHILOSOPHY AND SOCIAL HOPE

Richard Rorty

The following is excerpted from the introduction to Richard Rorty's *Philosophy and Social Hope*. Rorty is one of the best known and most controversial contemporary philosophers, who has been widely attacked by both right-wing and left-wing politicians and writers. In one of his essays[4] Rorty describes attacks aimed at him from both ends of the political spectrum. From the right, Neal Kozody denounces Rorty's "cynical and nihilistic view," and complains that for Rorty: "It is not enough . . . that American students should be merely mindless; he would have them positively mobilized for mindlessness." From the left, Rorty is sometimes condemned as a complacent elitist. The following passage gives a good introduction to Rorty's views on ethics, and you can draw your own conclusions.

Note that Rorty is *not* taking a cultural relativist view; instead Rorty considers himself a pragmatist. Whether he is a relativist at all—he denies it, though some critics assign him that label—is a conclusion you will have to draw for yourself.

The suggestion that everything we say and do and believe is a matter of fulfilling human needs and interests might seem simply a way of formulating the secularism of the Enlightenment—a way of saying that human beings are on their own, and have no supernatural light to guide them to the Truth. But of course the Enlightenment replaced the idea of such supernatural guidance with the idea of a quasi-divine faculty called 'reason'. It is this idea which American pragmatists and post-Nietzschean European philosophers are attacking. What seems most shocking about their criticisms of this idea is not their description of natural science as an attempt to manage reality rather than to represent it. Rather, it is their description of moral choice as always a matter of compromise between competing goods, rather than as a choice between the absolutely right and the absolutely wrong.

Controversies between foundationalists and antifoundationalists on the theory of knowledge look like the sort of merely scholastic quarrels which can safely be left to the philosophy professors. But quarrels about the character of moral choice look more important. We stake our sense of who we are on the outcome of such choices. So we do not like to be told that our choices are between alternative goods rather than between good and evil. When philosophy professors start saying that there is nothing either absolutely wrong or absolutely right, the topic of relativism begins to get interesting. The debates between the pragmatists and their opponents, or the Nietzscheans and theirs, begin to look too important to be left to philosophy professors. Everybody wants to get in on the act.

This is why philosophers like myself find ourselves denounced in magazines and newspapers which one might have thought oblivious of our existence. These denunciations claim that unless the youth is raised to believe in moral absolutes, and in objective truth, civilization is doomed. Unless the younger generation has the same attachment to firm moral principles as we have, these magazine and newspaper articles say, the struggle for human freedom and human decency will be over. When we philosophy teachers read this sort of article, we find ourselves being told that we have enormous power over the future of mankind. For all it will take to overturn centuries of moral progress, these articles suggest, is a generation which accepts the doctrines of moral relativism, accepts the views common to Nietzsche and Dewey.

Dewey and Nietzsche of course disagreed about a lot of things. Nietzsche thought of the happy, prosperous masses who would inhabit Dewey's social democratic utopia as 'the last men', worthless creatures incapable of greatness. Nietzsche was as instinctively antidemocratic in his politics as Dewey was instinctively democratic. But the two men agree not only on the nature of knowledge but on the nature of moral choice. Dewey said that every evil is a rejected good. William James said that every human need has a prima facie right to be gratified, and the only reason for refusing to gratify it is that it conflicts with another human need. Nietzsche would have entirely agreed. He would have phrased this point in terms of competition between bearers of the will to power, whereas James and Dewey would have found the term 'power', with its sadistic overtones, a bit misleading. But these three philosophers made identical criticisms of Enlightenment, and specifically Kantian, attempts to view moral principles as the product of a special faculty called 'reason'. They all thought that such attempts were disingenuous attempts to keep something like God alive in the midst of a secular culture.

Critics of moral relativism think that unless there is something absolute, something which shares God's implacable refusal to yield to human weakness, we have no reason to go on resisting evil. If evil is merely a lesser good, if all moral choice is a compromise between conflicting goods, then, they say, there is no point in moral struggle. The lives of those who have died resisting injustice become pointless. But to us pragmatists moral struggle is continuous with the struggle for existence, and no sharp break divides the unjust from the imprudent, the evil from the inexpedient. What matters for pragmatists is devising ways of diminishing human suffering and increasing human equality, increasing the ability of all human children to start life with an equal chance of happiness. This goal is not written in the stars, and is no more an expression of what Kant called 'pure practical reason' than it is of the Will of God. It is a goal worth dying for, but it does not require backup from supernatural forces.

The pragmatist view of what opponents of pragmatism call 'firm moral principles' is that such principles are abbreviations of past practices—way of summing up the habits of the ancestors we most admire. For example, Mill's greater-happiness principle and Kant's categorical imperative are ways of reminding ourselves of certain social customs—those of certain parts of the Christian West, the culture which has been, at least in words if not in deeds, more egalitarian than any other. The Christian doctrine that all members of the species are brothers and sisters is the religious way of saying what Mill and Kant said in non-religious terms: that considerations of family membership, sex, race, religious creed and the like should not prevent us from trying to do unto others as we would have them do to us—should not prevent us from thinking of them as people like ourselves, deserving the respect which we ourselves hope to enjoy.

But there are other firm moral principles than those which epitomize egalitarianism. One such principle is that dishonour brought to a woman of one's family must be paid for with blood. Another is that it would be better to have no son than to have one who is homosexual. Those of us who would like to put a stop to the blood feuds and the gaybashing produced by these firm moral principles call such principles 'prejudices' rather than 'insights'. It would be nice if philosophers could give us assurance that the principles which we approve of, like Mill's and Kant's, are 'rational' in a way that the principles of the blood-revengers and the gaybashers are not. But to say that they are more rational is just another way of saying that they are more universalistic—that they treat the differences between women of one's own family and other women, and the difference between gays and straights, as relatively insignificant. But it is not clear that failure to mention particular groups of people is a mark of rationality.

To see this last point, consider the principle 'Thou shalt not kill'. This is admirably universal, but is it more or less rational than the principle 'Do not kill unless one is a soldier defending his or her country, or is preventing a murder, or is a state executioner, or a merciful practitioner of euthanasia'? I have no idea whether it is more or less rational, and so do not find the term 'rational' useful in this area. If I am told that a controversial action which I have taken has to be defended by being subsumed under a universal, rational principle, I may be able to dream up such a principle to fit the occasion, but sometimes I may only be able to say, 'Well, it seemed like the best thing to do at the time, all things considered.' It is not clear that the latter defence is less rational than some universal-sounding principle which I have dreamed up *ad hoc* to justify my action. It is not clear that all the moral dilemmas to do with population control, the rationing of health care, and the like—should wait upon the formulation of principles for their solution.

As we pragmatists see it, the idea that there must be such a legitimating principle lurking behind every right action amounts to the idea that there is something like a universal, super-national court of law before which we stand. We know that the best societies are those which are governed by laws rather than by the whim of tyrants or mobs. Without the rule of law, we say, human life is turned over to emotion and to violence. This makes us think that there must be a sort of invisible tribunal of reason administering laws which we all, somewhere deep down inside, recognize as binding upon us. Something like this was Kant's understanding of moral obligation. But, once again, the Kantian picture of what human beings are like cannot be reconciled with history or with biology. Both teach us that the development of societies ruled by laws rather than men was a slow, late, fragile, contingent, evolutionary achievement.

Dewey thought that Hegel was right, against Kant, when he insisted that universal moral principles were useful only insofar as they were the outgrowth of the historical development of a particular society—a society whose institutions gave content to the otherwise empty shell of the principle. Recently Michael Walzer, a political philosopher best known for his earlier work *Spheres of Justice*, has come to Hegel's and Dewey's defence. In his more recent book *Thick and Thin*, Walzer argues that we should not think of the customs and institutions of particular societies as accidental accretions around a common core of universal moral rationality, the transcultural moral law. Rather, we should think of the thick set of customs and institutions as prior, and as what commands moral allegiance. The thin morality which can be abstracted out of the various thick moralities is not made up of the commandments of a universally shared human faculty called 'reason'. Such thin resemblances between these thick moralities as may exist are contingent, as contingent as the resemblances between the adaptive organs of diverse biological species.

Someone who adopts the anti-Kantian stance common to Hegel, Dewey and Walzer and is asked to defend the thick morality of the society with which she identifies herself will not be able to do so by talking about the rationality of her moral views. Rather, she will have to talk about the various concrete advantages of her society's practices over those of other societies. Discussion of the relative advantages of different thick moralities will, obviously, be as inconclusive as discussion of the relative superiority of a beloved book or person over another person's beloved book or person.

The idea of a universally shared source of truth called 'reason' or 'human nature' is, for us pragmatists, just the idea that such discussion *ought* to be capable of being made conclusive. We see this idea as a misleading way of expressing the hope, which we share, that the human race as a whole should gradually come together in a global community, a community which incorporates most of the thick morality of the European industrialized democracies. It is misleading because it suggests that the aspiration to such a community is somehow built into every member of the biological species. This seems to us pragmatists like the suggestion that the aspiration to be an anaconda is somehow built into all reptiles, or that the aspiration to be an anthropoid is somehow built into all mammals. This is why we pragmatists see the charge of relativism as simply the charge that we see luck where our critics insist on seeing destiny. We think that the utopian world community envisaged by the Charter of the United Nations and the Helsinki Declaration of Human Rights is no more

the *destiny* of humanity than is an atomic holocaust or the replacement of democratic governments by feuding warlords. If either of the latter is what the future holds, our species will have been unlucky, but it will not have been irrational. It will not have failed to live up to its moral obligations. It will simply have missed a chance to be happy.

I do not know how to argue the question of whether it is better to see human beings in this biologistic way or to see them in a way more like Plato's or Kant's. So I do not know how to give anything like a conclusive argument for the view which my critics call 'relativism' and which I prefer to call 'antifoundationalism' or 'antidualism'. It is certainly not enough for my side to appeal to Darwin and ask our opponents how they can avoid an appeal to the supernatural. That way of stating the issue begs many questions. It is certainly not enough for my opponents to say that a biologistic view strips human beings of their dignity and their self-respect. That too begs most of the questions at issue. I suspect that all that either side can do is to restate its case over and over again, in context after context. The controversy between those who see both our species and our society as a lucky accident, and those who find an immanent teleology in both, is too radical to permit of being judged from some neutral standpoint.

EXERCISES

1. Kant's ideal moral individual is one who feels no compassion for others, but helps them out of a pure sense of duty. Suppose that such a Kantian moralist lost her belief in rationally known objective moral truth. Would that person become an egoist? An amoralist? Or something else?

2. In Plato's *Republic*, Socrates considers a person who has been given a magical ring—the ring of Gyges—that makes him invisible. This person will be able to carry out all manner of crimes with no risk of being caught. Socrates attempts to show that a person who took advantage of such magic would end up miserable, rather than genuinely happy. Do you think Socrates could succeed in showing that?

3. In the criticism of psychological egoism, we said the psychological egoist claims her position is an empirical truth (everyone always seeks his or her own selfish interests). But that doesn't work as an empirical claim, the criticism goes; it is actually a self-sealing, definitional claim, because the psychological egoist cannot tell what would count *against* it. Is that a legitimate criticism? *Could* a psychological egoist give an example of what selfless behavior would be like?

4. The Western culture in which most of us live generally approves of eating meat. But many persons within that culture belong to groups that oppose eating at least some

forms of meat: Jainists oppose all meat-eating, Muslims and Jews abhor pork. If I am a relativist living in Texas, and am also a Jainist, and I refuse to eat barbecued ribs, have I done something wrong? Would I be doing something wrong—from a cultural relativist perspective—whether I refused ribs or not?

5. In the United States, abortion was once widely condemned, and was also illegal. Now abortion is widely accepted (though of course a minority fiercely opposes elective abortion). If you were a dedicated cultural relativist, at what point would you think abortion has changed from wrong to right? When a majority of U.S. citizens favored legalized abortion? When the Supreme Court ruled on *Roe. v. Wade*? Or when?

6. William James, one of the best known pragmatists, used his pragmatism to defend belief in God. According to James, belief in God helps some people (including James himself) to live better lives, by giving them greater confidence and more hope for the future; that is, belief in God enables them to *live better*. If that is the case, then belief in God "proves itself to be good in the way of belief, and good, too, for definite, assignable reasons"; and thus belief in God is a *true* belief. James's argument for belief in God has remained controversial to this day (and obviously not all pragmatists agree with it). What do you think of it?

    If you reject James's argument for belief in God, would that mean you must reject the pragmatic account of ethical truth? If you accept his argument, would that imply that you must also accept the pragmatic account of ethical truth?

7. Rorty's critics call him a relativist, though he himself rejects that title, preferring to call his position "pragmatic" or "antifoundationalist." *Is* Rorty a relativist, or not? (To answer this question in either the affirmative or the negative, you will have to make clear what *sense* of "relativism" you have in mind.)

ADDITIONAL READING

Psychological egoism was defended by Thomas Hobbes in *Leviathan*, and was promoted by Bernard de Mandeville in *The Fable of the Bees, or Private Vices, Public Benefits* (London, 1723). Mandeville's book is better written and more cogently argued than the more popular contemporary defense of ethical egoism by the novelist Ayn Rand in *The Virtue of Selfishness* (New York: New American Library, 1961). The classic critique of egoism is by Bishop Joseph Butler, *Fifteen Sermons upon Human Nature*, 1726 (Sermon 11 in particular). Another excellent critique (among many) of psychological egoism is by C. D. Broad, "Egoism as a Theory of Human Motives," in *Ethics and the History of Philosophy* (New York: Humanities Press, 1952). For arguments against ethical egoism, see (among many) Laurence Thomas, "Ethical Egoism and Psychological Dispositions," *American Philosophical Quarterly*, 17 (1980). Thomas Nagel's superb book, *The Possibility of Altruism* (Oxford: Clarendon Press, 1970) might also be useful in this context.

The anthropologist Ruth Benedict, in *Patterns of Culture* (New York: Penguin, 1934), was a major advocate of cultural relativism. Mary Midgley, *Heart and Mind* (New York: St. Martin's Press, 1981), offers a well-crafted critique of cultural relativism. For a more sophisticated version of relativism, and a defense of that view, see Gilbert Harman, *Explaining Value and Other Essays in Moral Philosophy* (Oxford: Clarendon Press, 2000). For a clear and fascinating debate on moral relativism versus moral objectivism, by two outstanding contemporary philosophers, see Gilbert Harman and Judith Jarvis Thomson, *Moral Relativism and Moral Objectivity* (Oxford: Blackwell, 1996).

The views of Richard Rorty—who is often classified as a relativist, though he himself prefers the title antidualist or antifoundationalist—can be found in his *Philosophy and the Mirror of Nature* (Princeton, N.J.: Princeton University Press, 1979), perhaps his most famous book, though it mentions ethics only briefly; *Contingency, Irony, and Solidarity* (Cambridge: Cambridge University Press, 1989), a very readable book that ranges through literature, social theory, and philosophy—Chapter 9, "Solidarity," contains very interesting elements of his views of ethics; *Truth and Progress: Philosophical Papers, Volume 3* (Cambridge: Cambridge University Press, 1998); and *Philosophy and Social Hope* (London: Penguin Books, 1999).

The pragmatist view was developed by Charles S. Peirce, William James, and John Dewey (among others) early in the twentieth century. It remains one of the leading schools of philosophical thought—though its boundaries are not altogether clear, and there is often dispute about who should be considered a pragmatist. For classic pragmatic views of ethics, see William James, *Pragmatism* (originally given as a series of lectures in 1907, it is available in a number of editions); John Dewey, *The Quest for Certainty* (originally given as the Gifford Lectures in 1929, it was published by G. P. Putnam's Sons, New York, in a paperback edition in 1960); John Dewey, *Human Nature and Conduct* (New York: Henry Holt and Company, 1922). For contemporary work on pragmatic ethics, see (in addition to the Rorty citations) Stanley Cavell, *In Quest of the Ordinary* (Chicago: University of Chicago Press, 1988); an excellent brief history and development of the view in Hugh Lafollette's "Pragmatic Ethics," in Hugh LaFollette, editor, *The Blackwell Guide to Ethical Theory* (Oxford: Blackwell Publishers, 2000); and the fascinating "prophetic pragmatism" of Cornel West, in *The American Evasion of Philosophy: A Genealogy of Pragmatism* (Madison, Wis.: University of Wisconsin Press, 1987).

NOTES

[1] K. Brown and A. Jameton, "Culture, Healing, and Professional Obligations: Commentary," *Hastings Center Report* (1993), 17.

[2] Jim Carnes, "Us and Them: A History of Intolerance in America," published by Teaching Tolerance, a project of the Southern Poverty Law Center (1995), p. 16. I discovered this passage in a quotation included in Judith A. Boss, *Ethics for Life* (Mountain View, Calif.: Mayfield Publishing, 1998).

[3] Richard Rorty, *Truth and Progress: Philosophical Papers, Volume 3* (Cambridge: Cambridge University Press, 1998), p. 2.

[4] Richard Rorty, "Trotsky and the Wild Orchids," included in *Philosophy and Social Hope* (London: Penguin Books, 1999).

CHAPTER  7

✦ VIRTUE ETHICS ✦

Our friend Sandra is a brilliant physicist. The physics faculty are in awe of her, the top graduate schools are competing for her, and she seems set to make major scientific discoveries in an outstanding career. Everyone agrees it's just a matter of time before she wins the Nobel Prize for her research. But in addition to physics, Sandra also loves video games; and Sandra surprises everyone by rejecting all graduate school offers, opting instead for a menial job that leaves her free to devote her evenings and weekends to the pursuit of simulated glory. What's our response? We're surprised, certainly, and probably disappointed: Sandra is throwing away a wonderful opportunity, she could have accomplished so much. We think she made a lousy decision. But is Sandra's choice *morally wrong*? Of course we are not going to put Sandra in jail for her choice, and we aren't going to *force* her to go to graduate school; still, is her choice *morally* wrong? Does Sandra's choice fall within the sphere of morality? If Sandra had obligations—say, to support her children—that her video-game playing was causing her to neglect, then she might be violating some special moral obligations. But Sandra is a free agent, unattached, with no dependents. Her choice is disappointing. She is wasting her talents (she is not even designing games, just playing them in blissful isolation). But is her life choice *morally* despicable?

No. Sandra's choice is purely personal. She is hurting no one except herself. This is a private matter, and morality has nothing to do with it. That's certainly one way of looking at it. In fact, that's how we'll see it from the social contract perspective. Ethics is designed to regulate our social behavior, our relations with others, and purely private behavior falls outside the scope of ethical judgment. That is the basis for an argument often made against utilitarians: they turn everything into a question of ethics, and leave no area of nonethical privacy. On the utilitarian view, your act is right if and only if it produces the greatest possible balance of good/pleasure over suffering. Does your Thursday night bowling league pass that test? No; you could accomplish more good by turning it into a Thursday night league for raising funds to eradicate hunger in impoverished countries. So not a single moment of your life escapes ethical scrutiny. But—so goes the criticism—we want a sphere of life that is private, where ethical evaluations don't intrude. Ethics is great, and moral obligations are important, but they aren't the *whole* of life. Whatever you think of this criticism of utilitarian ethics, it brings to the surface an underlying assumption of many contemporary ethical views: in the purely individual private sphere, ethics doesn't apply. (That means *purely* private, not just the privacy of my own family life. If I abuse my children within the privacy of my own home, that immoral act certainly does have an impact on others.) If the function of ethics is to regulate our social relations for the good and safety of us all, then it is hardly surprising that private nonsocial matters should fall outside its influence.

But of course from *other* ethical perspectives, Sandra's personal choice may be very much an ethical issue. Kant would have insisted that Sandra has an obligation to develop her talents: she could not will that everyone squander their talents rather than developing them for the common good. For the ancient Greeks and Romans, ethics starts at home: ethics is rooted in personal behavior, in the moral nature of the individual. For example, Plato regarded the state as the "soul writ large." Social ethics derive from individual ethics, not the other way around. Plato would consider Sandra's choice to be governed by her desire for pleasure, rather than controlled by reason, and thus evidence of a disordered and profoundly *immoral* and unjust soul. Aristotle's ethics was quite different from Plato's, but they shared at least one basic premise: both thought that ethics was first and foremost a personal and individual matter. Aristotle focused on how one becomes a good and virtuous person. A society comprised of virtuous persons would be a good society, but the starting point is the personal virtuous life of the individual. The Roman epicureans and stoics were fundamentally opposed in their concept of how to live a good moral life: the epicureans taught that you should seek pleasure (but do so intelligently and prudently, because many apparent pleasures have hidden costs); in contrast, the stoics counseled detachment and the minimization of needs and desires. But both believed that the basic question of ethics is how to live a good and virtuous life.

THE DISTINCTIVE FOCUS OF VIRTUE ETHICS

The ethical views we have examined in earlier chapters focused on what act is right or just or good, or on how—or whether—we can know what act is good. Is theft wrong? Could it ever be right? Is it wrong to lie? How do we know that telling lies is wrong? *Do* we know that telling lies is wrong? Should we share our wealth with those who are less fortunate? Does justice require such benevolence? Is it wrong to inflict suffering on animals to run medical experiments for human benefit?

All of these seem perfectly natural ethical questions; indeed, it may be difficult to imagine any other focus for ethics. But one ethical tradition, that traces its history to ancient Greece but also claims enthusiastic contemporary advocates, would consider such questions a very strange starting point for ethical inquiry. Rather than focusing on right or wrong actions, this tradition concentrates on the *character* of the actor. You can't tell whether an act is right or wrong just by observing the act itself; instead, you must look at the person performing the act.

Considering Character

In some ways, this approach makes perfect sense. After all, if you see me stretch out my hand and rescue a child about to fall from a tall building, you can't tell much about whether the act was good or bad. Of course the act was beneficial, and you're glad I saved the child (you are not some moral monster who delights in watching children plunge from tall buildings). But to know whether my act was actually morally good, you must probe much deeper. *Why* did I stretch out my hand and save the child? If I was having a brief seizure, and my hand shot out and involuntarily closed around the endangered child's arm, then that is certainly fortunate, but it is not morally worthy: an unusually strong gust of wind that blows the child back from the ledge is not a virtuous breeze. Neither the gusting wind nor my grasping seizure even counts as an *act*. And if I had intended to push the child over the ledge, but instead tripped and grasped for something to hold onto, and in so doing inadvertently grabbed the child's arm and pulled it to safety, then again the result is fortunate; but rather than being a good person, I am a moral scoundrel. Fortunately, I am also a clumsy oaf, and so I wound up saving the child instead of murdering it. But my act is nonetheless a vicious act of attempted murder rather than a heroic act of rescue (though I may never admit that). Or suppose I had been sublimely indifferent to the child's peril, caring not at all whether it tumbled or not. Just before the child slipped over the edge, I noticed the winning lottery ticket clutched in its grubby little fist, and so rescued the child strictly in hope of getting a significant share of the winnings. In that case, my act is again beneficial, and certainly better than allowing the child to perish, but it has lost most if not all of its moral luster.

The moral of this story is a simple one: judging an act as either good or bad requires us to examine the *character* and *motives* of the person who performed the act. The starting point for ethics is not the question of what acts are right or wrong, but what *characters* are virtuous or vicious. The virtuous person is not simply one who does the right act; rather, the virtuous person is one who consistently does right acts for the right motives. Aristotle, a virtue ethicist of ancient Athens, states the requirement thus: the virtuous agent first "must have knowledge, second he must choose the acts and choose them for their own sakes, and finally his action must proceed from a firm character."[1] One cannot be virtuous or perform genuinely good acts by accident. It requires deliberate practice and consistent effort at character building. We aren't naturally virtuous, but we have the capacity to become virtuous by practice, by consistently choosing good acts. And we become vicious in the same manner: by practicing vice, by not consistently making the effort to choose and act well. As you practice, so you become.

Practicing Virtue

Virtue theorists insist that we become good by doing good. If you cut corners in business, you are a shady operator, and you are developing the character of a shady operator. You are becoming practiced at it, it is becoming a habit. And if you tell yourself that you are really an honest and upright person who happens to practice deceit and chicanery in her daily behavior, then you are adding self-deception to the rest of your deceitful character. You are not what you wear, or what you drive, or what you eat; and you are not what you pretend to yourself to be, or wish you were; you are instead what you do. One who lies is a liar, and telling lies entrenches that character trait. If you do less than your best, you develop the habit, and you become—you make yourself—a slothful person. Becoming virtuous is not something we do at some later point when we gain true moral wisdom, or finally reach enlightenment, or have sufficient time for it; becoming virtuous is what we do in the everyday practice of our lives. When you consider whether to lie to your friend, or cut corners on your work, or cheat the newspaper seller, don't ask yourself whether it's right or wrong; rather, ask yourself whether you want to be the sort of person who engages in such behavior and has such a character. The acts you sow shape the character you reap.

> "We are what we repeatedly do. Excellence, then, is not an act, but a habit."
> Aristotle, *Nicomachean Ethics*

Virtue and Special Commitments

Virtue theory often appeals to those who set very high standards for themselves. *I* want to be the sort of person who does more than the minimum, who leaves the world a better place than she found it, who has the courage to combat injustice in high places. It's not that I think everyone is obligated to live by such a demanding code, but it's the standard I set for myself, it's who I want to become—and the only way to become that sort of person is by practicing what that sort of person would do, by going the extra mile, by acting bravely, by being willing to stand against the crowd or the fashion if that is what justice demands.

THE STRENGTHS OF VIRTUE ETHICS

Virtue theory has some distinct strengths. It emphasizes the strong connection between our acts and our character, and it encourages us to consider our characters as unified wholes rather than viewing each ethical decision in isolation. It reminds us that as moral actors we are more than merely placeholders who perform good or bad acts, but instead are persons with histories that shaped us, relations that matter to us, societies we value, and with goals and projects that give our lives meaning and significance.[2] In order to live healthy and satisfying lives we need commitments. Our commitments should not be *immoral* (if my goal in life is to run a stock scam that will net me $10 million, then virtue is likely to elude me). But neither must our commitments embrace a specifically *moral* goal: the goal of running an outstanding marathon, or composing a superb violin concerto, or discovering a new species of beetle is a legitimate goal. Such projects give my life *integrity*[3]: they are projects with which I identify, and which help to define who I am. Some *moral* ideals may also serve as personal life goals. For example, someone might have a deep commitment to honesty. Even in circumstances when it would be *useful* to fib, even when a lie might do more good than telling the truth, this person's commitment to honesty prevents her from telling a lie. Telling a lie would threaten the integrity and unity of *who she is,* just as for someone else giving up on the project of writing a great novel may undercut her sense of identity. Virtue theory allows space for such commitments. So your personal goals—whether moral (developing integrity) or nonmoral (running a marathon)—are morally relevant to your character development, even though there is more to your character than its moral commitments.

CRITICISMS OF VIRTUE THEORY

What Counts as Virtue?

Its positive features notwithstanding, virtue theory may seem to leave a few loose ends. We become virtuous by practicing virtuous acts. That is inspiring, and it does provide a useful reminder that what we sow is what we reap, and that it is easy to fall into undesirable habits—habits that are not easy to break, character traits that are not easy to change. But we still have the question: if we become virtuous by performing virtuous acts, how do we know which acts are virtuous in the first place? Juanita is a virtuous person because she consistently performs virtuous acts. And her acts count as virtuous because they are the product of a firm virtuous character with settled virtuous motives. But still: *which* acts are virtuous? Perhaps the answer is that virtuous acts are those done by virtuous persons. We then ask: but how do we recognize genuinely virtuous persons? At that point it will not be helpful to be told that virtuous persons are those who perform virtuous acts. Aristotle tried to escape the circle by suggesting that the genuinely virtuous person is the one who achieves true happiness and genuine satisfaction. But unless we have some independent criterion for "true happiness," we have made little progress.

Some virtue theorists would insist that the demand for "what counts as virtue" is shallow and premature. The goal of virtue theorists is to vividly describe the character traits that are genuinely admirable: ideal characteristics that are worthy of admiration. Virtue theory should not be criticized because it has not completed that project in advance. If we have not given a fully adequate account of genuinely virtuous character (so the virtue theorists would say), at least we have recognized the importance of developing such an account. That is a significant improvement over utilitarian and Kantian ethical theories, which focus too narrowly and superficially on what rules I should follow and acts I should perform, rather than on what I should strive to become and how I can shape a virtuous character.

Another answer that some virtue theorists—including Aristotle, and more recently Rosalind Hursthouse and Philippa Foot—might offer, is that virtue is what promotes *human flourishing* (or as Aristotle might call it, *true happiness*). Of course we cannot then say that what constitutes a genuinely happy and flourishing human life is a life in accordance with virtue, for that again spins in a circle. What virtue theorists generally have in mind is the idea of a life that is lived in such a way that it is a successful life for the sort of beings we are, for our natural kind. We are social beings, who live best in cooperative relations, exercising our distinctive rational capacities. Determining what is the best way of living for members of the human species is not an easy question, not by any means; but it is at least a real question, and seeking to answer it can provide substance and guidance to our account of virtuous character traits. It won't provide easy answers or simple ethical rules, but there is no reason to suppose ethics must be that easy.

Aristotle suggested another guide for what counts as virtuous: a guide that has come to be known as *The Golden Mean*. Aristotle describes it thus:

> Virtue, then, is a state of character concerned with choice, lying in a mean, i. e. the mean relative to us, this being determined by a rational principle, and by that principle by which the man of practical wisdom would determine it. Now it is a mean between two vices, that which depends on excess and that which depends on defect; and again it is a mean because the vices respectively fall short of or exceed what is right in both passions and actions, while virtue both finds and chooses that which is intermediate.[4]

Aristotle's golden mean is sometimes represented as merely "whatever is moderate is right." But that oversimplification turns the doctrine into something ridiculous, as Aristotle himself was well aware. To use Aristotle's own example, it would not be virtuous to commit a moderate number of murders or thefts. As Aristotle says, "they are themselves bad, and not the excesses or deficiencies of them." Furthermore, what counts as moderation may vary. Think of athletic training (another of Aristotle's examples). A moderate training session for a weekend jogger will be quite different from a moderate and well-balanced workout for an Olympic athlete; but both must try to avoid the extremes of overtraining (and wearing themselves down) or neglecting their training (and failing to improve). Trying to strike just the right balance is a difficult task, in both athletics and morality. Spendthrifts are too loose with their money, misers too tight. Bravery is a virtue, and it is the mean between rashness and cowardice. "Discretion is the better part of valor," as the saying goes; the challenge is in knowing exactly where the virtue of discretion ends and the vice of cowardice begins. But Aristotle does not pretend that virtue is easy: "It is no easy task to be good. For in everything it is no easy task to find the middle . . . ; wherefore goodness is both rare and laudable and noble."[5]

Virtue Theory and Individualism

Others have objected that virtue theory may be too individualistic: the focus should be on what acts contribute to the good of all, or at least the good of our society, rather than what acts will allow me to cultivate my own *individual* virtue. One might suggest that the cultivation of individual virtue will invariably contribute to the good of others and to the good of society; but that seems an article of faith, and in imperfect societies that faith may be misplaced. Imagine the following sort of case (which, unfortunately, at one time posed a very real quandary for some persons). It is 1948. You are the Black president of a small college deep in the southern United States. Your college is part of the segregated system of higher education in your state: White students attend one set of colleges, and Black students attend a different set. Separate but equal, in theory; in practice, the schools are certainly separate, but the White schools receive the lion's share of funds. You are struggling to provide a good education to the students who attend your college, but it's an uphill battle. The students at your college went to segregated elementary and secondary schools, where the same unequal distribution of educational resources meant that they studied in crowded classrooms in dilapidated buildings with inadequate school supplies; and now they have arrived on your campus, with strong goals but weak educational backgrounds, and you are trying to teach them without enough classrooms, in ancient laboratories, with a shortage of faculty, and a host of other problems. You are a shrewd and perceptive college president, and wise to the ways of the segregated state in which you live. You know that if you "play the game" for the exclusively White state legislature—bow and scrape, beg and plead, butter them up with flattery—they will give you the resources you desperately need to provide a good education for the students at your college. If you get those resources, you can educate thousands of young men and women, and give them an opportunity to escape the grinding poverty in which their families live, and an opportunity to eventually challenge and change the racist system in their state. Without such resources, these students have little or no chance of an education or a better life, and without those educated young people it will take much longer to break the ugly grip of racism in the region. But you have no illusions about the cost to you as a person. If you play the game for these racist legislators, you will become a person you detest: a toady to the White power structure, a living embodiment of racial stereotypes. In short, you will accomplish wonderful things and help many young people and contribute to the overthrow of a vicious apartheid system; but the cost is the sacrifice of your own integrity, your own honor, your own *virtue*. What *should* you do in such circumstances?

There are ways to avoid grappling with this question. You could say that in fact by playing the game for the White legislature, this Black college president will *not* make things better, but will in fact delay the needed changes by fostering the racist stereotypes that have hindered progress. Perhaps that's true. That's a question for sociologists. But it's a very difficult question, and it's at least *possible* that in such a vicious system there actually were people whose best way of helping others and bringing change was through obsequious flattery, rather than defiant resistance. That's an ugly thought; but the racist system was an ugly thing. So whether you think this would actually be the best way of helping others in this situation, suspend your doubts for a moment and suppose that you are in a situation where that is the case. (If you believe that there is no conceivable situation when sacrificing your own personal virtue would actually provide better overall results for others, then considering such a situation may be impossible for you. But that is a very strong claim. It strikes me as implausible, and in any case would require substantial argument to support.)

A second way to avoid this question is to claim that by practicing flattery, playing the game, bowing and scraping, one will *not* be sacrificing one's own virtue: it's just a show, a façade, and not what you really are. But if you take this position you have rejected virtue theory, for virtue theory asserts that you become what you practice: if you practice being a toady to the power system, then you become—you *are*—that sort of person. If we say of someone that "She acts bravely when she is around people weaker than she, but she acts like a coward when she is around powerful people," we are *not* saying that deep down she is really courageous. If I am a soldier who runs away whenever the bullets fly, but insist that deep down I am really very courageous, you will be legitimately skeptical of my bravery.

In this case, try to set aside your doubts, and consider what you think the college president—in this horrible but hardly impossible situation—*should* do. Should he sacrifice his virtue for the benefit of his students and their futures? Or should he insist on his own honor and dignity and integrity, even if the cost is not being able to provide educational resources to young people who desperately need them, and perhaps delaying the overthrow of the oppressive system in which he and his students live?

Don't move on too quickly. Take a few minutes out of your busy life and actually *think* about what this college president *should do*.

Virtue and Society

Some people will favor preserving one's own honor and dignity at all costs: "This above all, to thine own self be true." Others will find that too self-centered, and focus instead on the enormous benefits that might result from better educational resources: young people who otherwise would have been condemned to a life of grinding poverty—perhaps as sharecroppers growing cotton for a wealthy landowner—will instead live satisfying and dignified lives as physicians and lawyers and engineers. Most of us will agree that the best situation would be one in which we could live honorable and dignified and virtuous lives, and *also* contribute to advancing the welfare of others: both are good ends. But focus on the question of: Which is most basic, the cultivation of your individual virtue or the benefit to the whole? Which is most important? Then we find very different perspectives on what ethics is really about.

Virtue theorists would not all agree on the answer to that question. But many virtue theorists would say that this embattled college president *cannot* live a genuinely virtuous life. Not through any fault of his own, but rather because the full development of a virtuous life requires the support of the right kind of society, a society with a rich tradition of worthwhile values and long-term goals. This man is unlucky: he is living in a society in which living virtuously is not really possible.

But does development of individual virtue really depend on living in the right kind of society? Former U.S. Supreme Court Justice Thurgood Marshall lived in precisely the social setting in which our mythical college president is struggling. But he seems to me one of the greatest exemplars of a virtuous person the United States has to offer. Thurgood Marshall devoted his life and his profound intelligence and his outstanding legal skills to challenging the racist laws that shackled African Americans in the mid-twentieth century. He traveled into some of the most dangerous settings, where lynching was a constant threat, and challenged the institutionalized racism of the ruling powers. Marshall was a man of remarkable courage, deep commitment to a noble cause, and extraordinary ability that he used for high purposes. He lived in a vicious society—not a society that supported his development of virtue, but instead a society that he employed his own virtues to change. It is difficult for me to think of anyone who exhibited greater virtue.

Another great example of virtue for many people is Nelson Mandela, a leader in the struggle to overthrow the brutal apartheid system of South Africa: the apartheid society in which Mandela was born and lived. A man of great strength and fortitude, he spent years in the South African prison system—a dangerous place, where South African freedom fighters often "accidentally" died . He refused to give up his struggle for freedom even when offered a release from prison. And yet, when change finally came, and Mandela became the leader of a new South Africa, Mandela refused to seek vengeance and instead worked to heal the scars and suffering and distrust of the past. A remarkable person: very few people in history have combined the virtues of prerevolutionary courage and struggle with postrevolutionary compassion and restraint and wisdom. Mandela embodied the virtues of both. But the brutal society in which he developed those virtues was certainly not a virtuous society.

It seems doubtful that a good society is an essential condition to the development of virtuous character, since Thurgood Marshall and Nelson Mandela are powerful counter-examples to that claim. Virtue theory nonetheless performs a useful service by emphasizing the importance of community and society in fostering the development of virtue. After all, while the larger society did nothing to help Marshall and Mandela in their development of virtue, surely they were supported by a smaller subsociety (the courageous and committed community of civil rights workers and freedom fighters) that helped shape their characters. In any case, the question of *how* we become virtuous, and how good character is shaped, is an issue often neglected by traditional accounts of ethics. Virtue theory offers a useful focus on that important question.

Are There Multiple Sets of Virtues?

Nelson Mandela is a remarkable and almost unique person. He exhibited outstanding virtue as a revolutionary leader, and he also was wonderful—wise and patient and forgiving—as the leader of a new country. It is rare to find someone who can do either, and almost unheard of to find someone who excels at both. After all, the virtues required of a revolutionary are hardly the virtues needed as an elected leader. And that raises another important question concerning virtue theory: are there many *different* and perhaps incompatible sets of virtues? Are there different virtues for different societies, different sets of virtues for various roles in society, or even for different stages of life (are the virtues of youth the same as the virtues of age)? Or does every genuinely virtuous person share a common core of virtue? Though some virtue theorists have argued there is only one real set of universal virtues, many writers have doubted that there can be a single standard for virtue. Greg Pence offers the following example of radically different virtue sets for distinctly different societies:

> In frontier societies great heroes were often highly intelligent people who functioned beautifully outside the tight bounds of civilized cities with their churches, weddings, schools, lawyers, stores, police, and factories. Such frontier heroes lived by a simple hard code (horse thieves must be caught and killed, 'savages' are the enemy, each person pulls his own weight). When the frontiers became civilized, such heroes often found that their characters did not fit the society they had helped create. Society had required their types, and then moved on.[6]

Of course one might well decide that embodying the "hard code" of the "frontier heroes" is by no means an exercise of virtue: the genocidal murder of "savages" may have been admired in that society, but from a larger perspective it is abominably vicious rather than virtuous behavior. Still, Pence's example does bring out a key question for virtue theories: is virtue universal, or are virtues relative to societies? That is a large and difficult question, essentially the question of whether there are any universal truths of ethics. That's a question that will continue to concern us.

VIRTUE THEORY AND MEDICINE

Whatever the strengths or weaknesses of virtue theory as a general theory of ethics, there are some settings where virtue theory seems particularly helpful. When Aristotle wrote about the virtues almost 2,500 years ago, one of his favorite examples was the practice of medicine. And that still seems a productive setting for virtue theory: it seems especially useful to think about the *virtues* of a good nurse or therapist or physician. For example, one essential virtue for the practice of medicine is the ability to keep confidences, the ability to maintain confidentiality. People often gossip; it's a minor vice. But if a health professional "gossips" by revealing confidences about his or her patients, that is a betrayal of an essential virtue of medical caregivers. (It is not surprising that virtue theory should have its greatest successes in narrower and more tightly defined realms such as medicine: We have a relatively clear idea of what counts as "good medicine," while we have a much more difficult time agreeing on any *general* idea of human flourishing.)

Medical Beneficence

Another important medical virtue is the commitment to the good of the patient, rather than one's own self-interests. When I buy a used car, I know the salesperson is trying to sell the car for as much as possible. Her primary goal is to maximize her profit on the deal, whether it happens to be in my best interest or not. If I discover I overpaid for the car, I may be somewhat bitter; but (unless there was outright fraud such as rolling back the odometer) I won't blame the salesperson: she has no obligation to place my interests first. When the CEO of a major corporation cheats us we are bitter, but we really didn't expect much: whatever the slick advertising of noble motives, corporations and their officers have a primary commitment to increasing profit, not serving the public welfare (though betraying employees by gutting their pension plans may nonetheless be a special betrayal of trust, or at the very least a violation of a special obligation toward those who made the corporation a success). But if my physician performs unnecessary and dangerous surgery on me in order to put extra money in her own pocket, that's a different matter altogether. Healthcare workers are supposed to exhibit special virtues, and first among those virtues is a deep commitment to the good of the patient: a commitment to the patient's interests rather than the physician's own benefit. My physician might legitimately refuse to place me on the list for a heart transplant, judging that even though a transplant would benefit me, I can be treated effectively through medication, and other patients with greater need should get priority for the very scarce resource of transplantable hearts. But if my physician gives an available heart to someone else with less medical need but more money (who pays the physician a substantial bonus for the transplant), then I have been betrayed, and the physician has betrayed the virtues of her profession. If a dealer in classic restored cars is selling a beautiful '56 Chevy, and you offer more money than I, the dealer will sell the car to you. I may be disappointed, but the dealer has not failed any principle of virtue. But physicians are members of a profession with a profound tradition of virtue, not dealers of medicine.

When some physicians refused to treat AIDS patients—because it exposed the physician to a very small risk of infection—it was a betrayal of that medical virtue tradition, like a firefighter who only answers the call to "safe" fires or a police officer who pursues only nonviolent criminals. And that is also one of the reasons that profit-making Health Maintenance Organizations (HMOs) have been troubling to many physicians. Physicians have always been concerned with who receives medical benefits: if there is a shortage of a drug, which patients will benefit most from it? If there is a shortage of organs for transplant, which patients are most in need of a transplant, and which ones can be treated by other means? But in an HMO, the physician is expected to make treatment decisions on the basis of cost, rather than what is best for patients. The savings become profits for the HMO and monetary bonuses for the physician, rather than medical benefits for patients with more pressing needs. For many physicians, that threatens a basic value of medicine and undercuts a central virtue of the good physician.

A Virtuous Medical Hero

In 1994 and 1995 there was a terrible ethnic conflict in Rwanda between the Hutu and Tutsi; horrific, genocidal attacks were carried out by both sides. At one point in the conflict there was a hospital that cared for a number of disabled persons from one of the ethnic groups, and the area where the hospital was located was under attack by forces from the opposing group. It was clear the opposing forces would overrun the area within a few days, and would slaughter anyone who remained. A plane was sent in to evacuate the international aid workers who were caring for the disabled patients, but there were no resources for evacuating the patients. There was a young native doctor caring for the patients, and when the international medical workers were evacuated he was offered the opportunity to escape with them. He refused to go, though staying meant facing a brutal death within a few days. His reason for staying was simple: "I cannot abandon my patients."

Some people regard the behavior of this young doctor as foolish. His patients would soon die anyway, and he could have saved himself and provided medical care for others. His heroic act of caring probably went beyond what a Kantian ethic would require, and far beyond what a utilitarian would think wise. But it was in the virtue tradition of physicians who stayed in quarantined cities to nurse those afflicted with the death-dealing and highly contagious bubonic plague, and typically died with their patients. And it is in the tradition of the heroic firefighters who rushed into the collapsing World Trade Center in a doomed rescue effort. Those who were fleeing that terrible inferno reported their amazement at the firefighters rushing in the opposite direction, toward the collapsing buildings. If we could ask the firefighters who gave their lives in their attempts at rescue, many would no doubt say it was "just part of my job"; but if so, it was part of a "job"—part of a profession—with noble ideals of self-sacrifice, and a deep tradition of heroic virtues. Perhaps the behavior of the young Rwandan doctor does not make utilitarian sense. But it exemplifies an ideal of the medical profession, and physicians and nurses should celebrate him as a hero of a great tradition of virtue. Western doctors who refuse to treat AIDS patients could learn a very important lesson about medical virtues from that young African doctor.

NICOMACHEAN ETHICS

Aristotle

Aristotle was a student of Plato, and taught Alexander the Great. He wrote an enormous body of work, doing serious and influential work in almost every subject of knowledge known to the ancient world, ranging from logic to biology, metaphysics to ethics, poetry to rhetoric. His influence throughout the Medieval period was enormous. So great was his fame and authority that for many centuries Christian theologians simply referred to him as "The Philosopher." This translation is by W. D. Ross.

Now that we have spoken of the virtues, the forms of friendship, and the varieties of pleasure, what remains is to discuss in outline the nature of happiness, since this is what we state the end of human nature to be. Our discussion will be the more concise if we first sum up what we have said already. We said, then, that it is not a disposition; for if it were it might belong to some one who was asleep throughout his life, living the life of a plant, or, again, to some one who was suffering the greatest misfortunes. If these implications are unacceptable, and we must rather class happiness as an activity, as we have said before, and if some activities are necessary, and desirable for the sake of something else, while others are so in themselves, evidently happiness must be placed among those desirable in themselves, not among those desirable for the sake of something else; for happiness does not lack anything, but is self-sufficient. Now those activities are desirable in themselves from which nothing is sought beyond the activity. And of this nature virtuous actions are thought to be; for to do noble and good deeds is a thing desirable for its own sake.

Pleasant amusements also are thought to be of this nature; we choose them not for the sake of other things; for we are injured rather than benefited by them, since we are led to neglect our bodies and our property. But most of the people who are deemed happy take refuge in such pastimes, which is the reason why those who are ready-witted at them are highly esteemed at the courts of tyrants; they make themselves pleasant companions in the tyrants' favourite pursuits, and that is the sort of man they want. Now these things are thought to be of the nature of happiness because people in despotic posi-

tions spend their leisure in them, but perhaps such people prove nothing; for virtue and reason, from which good activities flow, do not depend on despotic position; nor, if these people, who have never tasted pure and generous pleasure, take refuge in the bodily pleasures, should these for that reason be thought more desirable; for boys, too, think the things that are valued among themselves are the best. It is to be expected, then, that, as different things seem valuable to boys and to men, so they should to bad men and to good. Now, as we have often maintained, those things are both valuable and pleasant which are such to the good man; and to each man the activity in accordance with his own disposition is most desirable, and, therefore, to the good man that which is in accordance with virtue. Happiness, therefore, does not lie in amusement; it would, indeed, be strange if the end were amusement, and one were to take trouble and suffer hardship all one's life in order to amuse oneself. For, in a word, everything that we choose we choose for the sake of something else—except happiness, which is an end. Now to exert oneself and work for the sake of amusement seems silly and utterly childish. But to amuse oneself in order that one may exert oneself, as Anacharsis puts it, seems right; for amusement is a sort of relaxation, and we need relaxation because we cannot work continuously. Relaxation, then, is not an end; for it is taken for the sake of activity.

If happiness is activity in accordance with virtue, it is reasonable that it should be in accordance with the highest virtue; and this will be that of the best thing in us. Whether it be reason or something else that is this element which is thought to be our natural ruler and guide and to take thought of things noble and divine, whether it be itself also divine or only the most divine element in us, the activity of this in accordance with its proper virtue will be perfect happiness. That this activity is contemplative we have already said.

Now this would seem to be in agreement both with what we said before and with the truth. For, firstly, this activity is the best (since not only is reason the best thing in us, but the objects of reason are the best of knowable objects); and, secondly, it is the most continuous, since we can contemplate truth more continuously than we can *do* anything. And we think happiness has pleasure mingled with it, but the activity of philosophic wisdom is admittedly the pleasantest of virtuous activities; at all events the pursuit of it is thought to offer pleasures marvellous for their purity and their enduringness, and it is to be expected that those who know will pass their time more pleasantly than those who inquire. And the self-sufficiency that is spoken of must belong most to the contemplative activity. For while a philosopher, as well as a just man or one possessing any other virtue, needs the necessaries of life, when they are sufficiently equipped with things of that sort the just man needs people towards whom and with whom he shall act justly, and the temperate man, the brave man, and each of the others is in the same case, but the philosopher, even when by himself, can contemplate truth, and the better the wiser he is; he can perhaps do so better if he has fellow-workers, but still he is the most self-sufficient. And this activity alone would seem to be loved for its own sake; for nothing arises from it apart from the contemplating, while from practical activities we gain more or less apart from the action. And happiness is thought to depend on leisure; for we are busy that we may have leisure, and make war that we may live in peace. Now the activity of the practical virtues is exhibited in political or military affairs, but the actions concerned with these seem to be unleisurely. Warlike actions are completely so (for no one chooses to be at war, or provokes war, for the sake of being at war; any one would seem absolutely murderous if he were to make enemies of his friends in order to bring about battle and slaughter); but the action of the statesman is also unleisurely, and—apart from the political action itself—aims at despotic power and

honours, or at all events happiness, for him and his fellow citizens—a happiness different from political action, and evidently sought as being different. So if among virtuous actions political and military actions are distinguished by nobility and greatness, and these are unleisurely and aim at an end and are not desirable for their own sake, but the activity of reason, which is contemplative, seems both to be superior in serious worth and to aim at no end beyond itself, and to have its pleasure proper to itself (and this augments the activity), and the self-sufficiency, leisureliness, unweariedness (so far as this is possible for man), and all the other attributes ascribed to the supremely happy man are evidently those connected with this activity, it follows that this will be the complete happiness of man, if it be allowed a complete term of life (for none of the attributes of happiness is *in*complete).

But such a life would be too high for man; for it is not in so far as he is man that he will live so, but in so far as something divine is present in him; and by so much as this is superior to our composite nature is its activity superior to that which is the exercise of the other kind of virtue. If reason is divine, then, in comparison with man, the life according to it is divine in comparison with human life. But we must not follow those who advise us, being men, to think of human things, and, being mortal, of mortal things, but must, so far as we can, make ourselves immortal, and strain every nerve to live in accordance with the best thing in us; for even if it be small in bulk, much more does it in power and worth surpass everything. This would seem, too, to be each man himself, since it is the authoritative and better part of him. It would be strange, then, if he were to choose not the life of his self but that of something else. And what we said before will apply now; that which is proper to each thing is by nature best and most pleasant for each thing; for man, therefore, the life according to reason is best and pleasantest, since reason more than anything else *is* man. This life therefore is also the happiest.

But in a secondary degree the life in accordance with the other kind of virtue is happy; for the activities in accordance with this befit our human estate. Just and brave acts, and other virtuous acts, we do in relation to each other, observing our respective duties with regard to contracts and services and all manner of actions and with regard to passions; and all of these seem to be typically human. Some of them seem even to arise from the body, and virtue of character to be in many ways bound up with the passions. Practical wisdom, too, is linked to virtue of character, and this to practical wisdom, since the principles of practical wisdom are in accordance with the moral virtues and rightness in morals is in accordance with practical wisdom. Being connected with the passions also, the moral virtues must belong to our composite nature; and the virtues of our composite nature are human; so, therefore, are the life and the happiness which correspond to these. The excellence of the reason is a thing apart; we must be content to say this much about it, for to describe it precisely is a task greater than our purpose requires. It would seem, however, also to need external equipment but little, or less than moral virtue does. Grant that both need the necessaries, and do so equally, even if the statesman's work is the more concerned with the body and things of that sort; for there will be little difference there; but in what they need for the exercise of their activities there will be much difference. The liberal man will need money for the doing of his liberal deeds, and the just man too will need it for the returning of services (for wishes are hard to discern, and even people who are not just pretend to wish to act justly); and the brave man will need power if he is to accomplish any of the acts that correspond to his virtue, and the temperate man will need opportunity; for how else is either he or any of the others to be recognized? It is debated, too, whether the will or the deed is more essential to virtue, which is assumed to involve both; it is surely clear that its perfection involves both; but for deeds many things are needed, and more, the greater and nobler the deeds are. But the man who is contemplating the truth needs no such thing, at least with a view to the exercise of his activity; indeed they are, one may say, even hindrances, at all events to his contemplation; but in so far as he is a man and lives with a number of people, he chooses to do virtuous acts; he will therefore need such aids to living a human life.

But that perfect happiness is a contemplative activity will appear from the following consideration as well. We assume the gods to be above all other beings blessed and happy; but what sort of actions must we assign to them? Acts of justice? Will not the gods seem absurd if they make contracts and return deposits, and so on? Acts of a brave man, then, confronting dangers and running risks because it is noble to do so? Or liberal acts? To whom will they give? It will be strange if they are really to have money or anything of the kind. And what would their temperate acts be? Is not such praise tasteless, since they have no bad appetites? If we were to run through them all, the circumstances of action would be found trivial and unworthy of gods. Still, every one supposes that they *live* and therefore that they are active; we cannot suppose them to sleep like Endymion. Now if you take away from a living being action, and still more production, what is left but contemplation? Therefore the activity of God, which surpasses all others in blessedness, must be contemplative; and of human activities, therefore, that which is most akin to this must be most of the nature of happiness.

This is indicated, too, by the fact that the other animals have no share in happiness, being completely deprived of such activity. For while the whole life of the gods is blessed, and that of men too in so far as some likeness of such activity belongs to them, none of the other animals is happy, since they in no way share in contemplation. Happiness extends, then, just so far as contemplation does, and those to whom contemplation more fully belongs are more truly happy, not as a mere concomitant but in virtue of the contemplation; for this is in itself precious. Happiness, therefore, must be some form of contemplation.

Now he who exercises his reason and cultivates it seems to be both in the best state of mind and most dear to the gods. For if the gods have any care for human affairs, as they are thought to have, it would be reasonable both that they should delight in that which was best and most akin to them (i.e. reason) and that they should reward those who love and honour this most, as caring for the things that are dear to them and acting both rightly and nobly. And that all these attributes belong most of all to the philosopher is manifest. He, therefore, is the dearest to the gods. And he who is that will presumably be also the happiest; so that in this way too the philosopher will more than any other be happy.

If these matters and the virtues, and also friendship and pleasure, have been dealt with sufficiently in outline, are we to suppose that our programme has reached its end? Surely, as the saying goes, where there are things to be done the end is not to survey and recognize the various things, but rather to do them; with regard to virtue, then, it is not enough to know, but we must try to have and use it, or try any other way there may be of becoming good. Now if arguments were in themselves enough to make men good, they would justly, as Theognis says, have won very great rewards, and such rewards should have been provided; but as things are, while they seem to have power to encourage and stimulate the generous-minded among our youth, and to make a character which is gently born, and a true lover of what is noble, ready to be possessed by virtue, they are not able to encourage the many to nobility and goodness. For these do not by nature obey the sense of shame, but only fear, and do not abstain from bad acts because of their baseness but through fear of punishment; living by passion they pursue their own pleasures and the means to them, and avoid the opposite pains, and have not even a conception of what is noble and truly pleasant, since they have never tasted it. What argument would remould such people? It is hard, if not impossible, to remove by argument the traits that have long since been incorporated in the character; and perhaps we must be content if, when all the influences by which we are thought to become good are present, we get some tincture of virtue.

Now some think that we are made good by nature, others by habituation, others by teaching. Nature's part evidently does not depend on us, but as a result of some divine causes is present in those who are truly fortunate; while argument and teaching, we may suspect, are not powerful with all men, but the soul of the student must first have been cultivated by means of habits for noble joy and noble hatred, like earth which is to nourish the seed. For he who lives as passion directs will not hear argument that dissuades him, nor understand it if he does; and how can we persuade one in such a state to change his ways? And in general passion seems to yield not to argument but to force. The character, then, must somehow be there already with a kinship to virtue, loving what is noble and hating what is base.

But it is difficult to get from youth up a right training for virtue if one has not been brought up under right laws; for to live temperately and hardily is not pleasant to most people, especially when they are young. For this reason their nurture and occupations should be fixed by law; for they will not be painful when they have become customary. But it is surely not enough that when they are young they should get the right nurture and attention; since they must, even when they are grown up, practise and be habituated to them, we shall need laws for this as well, and generally speaking to cover the whole of life; for most people obey necessity rather than argument, and punishments rather than the sense of what is noble.

This is why some think that legislators ought to stimulate men to virtue and urge them forward by the motive of the noble, on the assumption that those who have been well advanced by the formation of habits will attend to such influences; and that punishments and penalties should be imposed on those who disobey and are of inferior nature, while the incurably bad should be completely banished. A good man (they think), since he lives with his mind fixed on what is noble, will submit to argument, while a bad man, whose desire is for pleasure, is corrected by pain like a beast of burden. This is, too, why they say the pains inflicted should be those that are most opposed to the pleasures such men love.

However that may be, if (as we have said) the man who is to be good must be well trained and habituated, and go on to spend his time in worthy occupations and neither willingly nor unwillingly do bad actions, and if this can be brought about if men live in accordance with a sort of reason and right order, provided this has force—if this be so, the paternal command indeed has not the required force or compulsive power (nor in general has the command of one man, unless he be a king or something similar), but the law *has* compulsive power, while it is at the same time a rule proceeding from a sort of practical wisdom and reason. And while people hate *men* who oppose their impulses, even if they oppose them rightly, the law in its ordaining of what is good is not burdensome.

Exercises

1. Think of a profession you are considering as a career: engineering, or perhaps law or accounting or teaching. Could you develop a distinctive set of virtues for that profession? (That is, are there some virtues that would be particularly important for members of that profession?)

2. You are trying to decide what you should do in a particular case: say, should I purchase a term paper off the Internet and submit it as my own work? Would it be more helpful to think about that issue in terms of whether the *act* would be right or wrong, or in terms of whether this is contributing to development of the sort of *character* you approve?

3. Aristotle maintained that only persons of considerable wealth and resources would be able to develop the full range of virtues; Jesus seemed to think that to the contrary—it was almost impossible for wealthy persons to become genuinely virtuous. Obviously Aristotle and Jesus had very different concepts of what counts as a virtuous character, but they seemed to agree that one's social setting is very important for the development of virtue. For your own conception of virtue, whatever that may be, would you agree that only in an appropriate society or the right circumstances could one actually live a fully virtuous life?

4. Would it ever be right to sacrifice your own virtue for the good of others?

5. I have lived a dissolute life for many years: a life devoted to excessive eating, heavy drinking, laziness, deceitfulness, and pettiness. At age 45 I awaken one morning in the gutter, painfully sober after a three-day binge, and I resolve to change my ways and pursue virtue. Could I become a virtuous person within an hour? A week? A month? A year? Ever?

6. The dramatist George Bernard Shaw claimed that "Virtue consists, not in abstaining from vice, but in not desiring it." Would Aristotle agree? Would *you* agree?

7. You are a biology professor at the University of Wisconsin. You teach at the medical school, and are well-known for your research: your laboratory has carried out a number of important studies on various drugs. You are approached by ZQZ Pharmaceuticals. They would like you to run a test on the "off-label" effectiveness of one of their drugs, Zyloban. Zyloban has been approved for the treatment of stomach ulcers, but recently some doctors have used it for treatment of high blood pressure (after noticing that ulcer patients treated with Zyloban sometimes experienced a reduction in blood pressure readings). Such 'off-label' treatments are perfectly legal; the problem is, the drug has not really been tested for treatment of hypertension (high blood pressure), and we don't know if it actually works for that. True, a few doctors noticed their patients experienced lower blood pressure, but we have no idea whether that was caused by the Zyloban or by something else. Perhaps when their stomach ulcers cleared up that caused them to feel better, reduced their tense worrying about ulcers, and the reduction in tension caused lower blood pressure. Or maybe the patients started eating less because of their stomach problems, and they lost some weight and that caused the reduction in blood pressure. Or maybe they stopped smoking, and that was the cause. Without a controlled experiment, we have no idea whether Zyloban is effective in treating hypertension. Furthermore, since Zyloban was not tested initially for the treatment of hypertension, we don't know whether it causes problems for patients using it for long-term treatment of hypertension. The initial tests, which led the FDA to approve the drug, were for short-term

use with stomach ulcer patients. But treatment of hypertension would involve long-term use, and there might be side effects the earlier tests did not detect: Zyloban might cause special problems, even serious dangers, for patients who use it long-term. So ZQZ Pharmaceuticals wants you to run a long-term controlled study on the effectiveness of Zyloban for the treatment of hypertension. This will be a very large study, and they will pay you very generously to direct it. Also, with the money they pay for the study you can hire a number of medical students and graduate students at the university, to help you part-time and perhaps full-time in the summer; and they will also be paid well (and frankly, many of them could really use the money). The grant will also pay for much-needed laboratory equipment, the latest and best. And since this is a major, megabucks grant, the University of Wisconsin will be very happy about it: the dean will probably take you to lunch and lavish praise upon you.

No problems so far. This could be a worthwhile study, and it might provide information to aid in the treatment of hypertension, and thus improve the lives of many people; and it will make your students very happy, since they will make some much-needed extra income. But there's one catch: ZQZ Pharmaceuticals is paying for the study, and they want control over the publication of any results. They want the right to read any research report *before* it is published, and they want the right to veto publication of your research findings. That is, if your research shows that Zyloban is useless in the treatment of hypertension, or—even worse—reveals a harmful side effect that earlier studies had not detected, then ZQZ Pharmaceuticals can prevent the publication of your results; indeed, can require you not to discuss those results with anyone, nor publicize those results in any way. So if your research indicated that use of Zyloban might cause kidney failure—a potentially lethal side effect—you would be prohibited from publishing that result. Or if your study showed Zyloban was useless in treating hypertension, but the data from a separate study made by some other laboratory indicated Zyloban might be an effective hypertension drug, then ZQZ Pharmaceuticals could veto the publication of your results and allow the publication of the other study. Under that condition—ZQZ Pharmaceuticals has veto rights to the publication of your study—would you agree to run the study?

Suppose you want to refuse to run the study under those conditions: you would tell ZQZ Pharmaceuticals you are turning down their megabucks study grant. You are discussing it with one of your fellow researchers, and she wants to accept the grant and run the study. "Look," she says, "I understand your concerns about the publication veto. I feel the same way: I don't like it. But let's be realistic. If we turn down this research contract, they won't have any trouble at all finding another researcher who *will* run the study, and will accept the veto condition; and that researcher may not be quite as good as we are, so the study might not be quite as careful. And that researcher's students will get the money, rather than our students. So the study is going to be run anyway, with the veto condition. Refusing the research contract will just mean our students won't get the research funding, and the study may not be done as well as we could do it. So what will your principled refusal really accomplish? Nothing. At least nothing good. So I say: let's take the contract, and accept the veto power of ZQZ Pharmaceuticals."

What do you think of your colleague's argument? How would that argument look from the perspectives of virtue theory, utilitarian ethics, Humean ethics, and Kantian ethics?

Perhaps you have decided you should accept the research contract; perhaps you've decided you shouldn't. Suppose you *have* decided to accept the contract (maybe ZQZ Pharmaceuticals agreed to drop the veto requirement). The representative from ZQZ Pharmaceuticals drops by with a bottle of champagne to celebrate this wonderful new research partnership between ZQZ Pharmaceuticals and your laboratory, and hands you an envelope. "Look, we at ZQZ Pharmaceuticals consider you part of our family, and we want you to share in any success our company has. These are stock options on ZQZ Pharmaceuticals. Your study will be complete and ready for release next September 15; these options are on $1 million worth of ZQZ Pharmaceuticals stock. These options allow you to purchase ZQZ Pharmaceuticals stock at its September 1 price, and you can exercise the option anytime between September 15 and September 30. It's a pleasure having you as a member of the ZQZ Pharmaceuticals family!" Well, you know what this stock option means. If your research shows that Zyloban is not effective in treating hypertension, the value of ZQZ Pharmaceuticals stock will not rise, and your stock option will be worthless. But if your research shows Zyloban *is* safe and effective in treating hypertension, then Zyloban will be widely sold for hypertension, and ZQZ Pharmaceuticals will make a fortune in profits (there are *huge* numbers of hypertension patients), and the stock price will rise dramatically—and your stock option will be worth a *lot* of money. (Suppose ZQZ Pharmaceuticals stock was at $20 a share on September 1; on September 15, after release of your favorable research on Zyloban, the stock soars to $40 a share. You can buy a million dollars worth of Zyloft stock at the September 1 price, and immediately sell it for double what you paid: a neat little profit of $1 million, with absolutely no risk. (Actually, you would just take the stock option to your broker, and your broker would give you a check.) Sounds peachy. But you know what is really going on: ZQZ Pharmaceuticals is not doing this out of simple kindness; rather, they are giving you a huge incentive to do a study that shows Zyloban to be very effective and very safe (the better the drug, the more your stock option is worth). Of course, you are a highly principled researcher, and you would never let that influence you, right? But is it ethically legitimate for you to accept the stock option?

ADDITIONAL READING

The classic source for virtue ethics is Aristotle's *Nicomachean Ethics*. Perhaps the most influential contemporary book on virtue theory is by Alasdair MacIntyre, *After Virtue* (Notre Dame, Ind.: University of Notre Dame Press, 1981). An excellent exposition of contemporary virtue theory is found in Edmund Pincoffs, *Quandaries and Virtues* (Lawrence, Kan.: University of Kansas Press, 1986).

An intriguing brief case for virtue theory is presented by novelist and philosopher Iris Murdoch, in *The Sovereignty of Good* (New York: Schocken Books, 1971), though Murdoch's work encompasses a great deal more than just a defense of virtue theory. Other influential accounts of virtue theory include Philippa Foot, *Virtues and Vices* (Berkeley, Calif.: University of California, 1978); Michael Slote, *Goods and Virtues* (New York: Oxford University Press, 1984); and Michael Slote, *From Morality to Virtue* (New York: Oxford University Press, 1992). Major recent works in the virtue theory tradition are Philippa Foot, *Natural Goodness* (Oxford: Oxford University Press, 2001); Rosalind Hursthouse, *On Virtue Ethics* (Oxford: Oxford University Press, 1999); and Michael Slote, *Morals from Motives* (Oxford: Oxford University Press, 2000).

NOTES

[1] Aristotle, *Nichomachean Ethics*, trans. W. D. Ross, p. 1105a.

[2] A point noted by both Susan Wolf, "Moral Saints," *Journal of Philosophy*, 79 (1982), 419–439; and Bernard Williams, "A Critique of Utilitarianism," in J. J. C. Smart and Bernard Williams, *Utilitarianism For and Against* (Cambridge: Cambridge University Press, 1973).

[3] As Bernard Williams, 1973, describes it.

[4] Aristotle, *Nicomachean Ethics*, trans. W. D. Ross, p. 1107a.

[5] *Ibid*, p. 1109a.

[6] Greg Pence, "Virtue Theory," in Peter Singer, editor, *A Companion to Ethics* (Oxford: Blackwell, 1991), p. 255.

CHAPTER

✦ CARE ETHICS ✦

Men and women are different. Perhaps that's something you already knew. Still, it's worth mentioning, because at times we tend to forget it. For many decades in the United States almost all tests of new drugs were performed on men (often on male college students). And there is some reason for testing on young men, rather than on young women: some drugs may cause severe birth defects if a woman takes the drug early in pregnancy (the thalidomide tragedy is a terrible example); and since a woman might be pregnant without knowing it, testing experimental drugs on women poses special risks to the fetus. There's an easy solution to that problem: test all the new drugs on men.

It was an easy solution, but not a very good one. By testing exclusively on men, we discovered which drugs were safe and effective for men, and at what dosage; but when we prescribed those drugs for women, we had to guess at the correct dosage, and hope that what worked for men would also be safe and effective for women. Sometimes we were right, and sometimes we were wrong. In recent years we have adopted new policies requiring drugs to be tested on both men and women before gaining approval.

THE NEGLECT OF WOMEN'S ETHICAL VIEWS

Until recently, ethical theories—like drugs—were also tested exclusively on men. There were very few women writing about ethics, and many of those who were had been so thoroughly acculturated into a male-dominated philosophical outlook that they adopted the assumptions and perspectives of their male colleagues. Women's voices were largely silent. But this caused little alarm. As in drug testing, the operating assumption was simple: if it works for men, it will work for women. And like the analogous assumption in drug testing, the assumption that male-dominated ethics works universally has been scrutinized and found wanting.

When we recognize the importance of women's contributions to ethical thought, we must avoid the temptation to look for 'the women's perspective' on ethical questions. That would be as silly and as stereotypical as looking for 'the African-American perspective,' or 'the Arab-American viewpoint,' or 'the Hispanic perspective,' or 'the Irish-American ethical position.' African-American political views range from the leftist thought of Lani Guinier to the far right position of Clarence Thomas; likewise, there is no single "women's perspective" that can encompass both Janet Reno and Sandra Day O'Connor. Men have championed such diverse ethical views as utilitarianism, Kantianism, and social contract theory; and women have championed all those views, and more. To avoid supposing that there is a single "women's ethical theory," we'll talk about *care* ethics, rather than *feminist* ethics. Care ethics emphasizes the value of fostering relationships, paying as much attention to personal details as abstract principles, and recognizing the ethical importance of affection and care for others. Not all feminists favor care ethics—in fact, many feminists strongly object to care ethics. And some of the most dedicated advocates of care ethics are men.

Psychological Studies of Ethical Reasoning

The development of feminist/care ethics had important "extra-ethical" scientific influences: the recognition that much of past psychological research was based on a grossly unrepresentative sample that systematically excluded half the population. The result severely undervalued the importance of family and personal relationships in psychological health, misrepresented the process of psychological and moral development, and distorted our perspective of healthy psychological functioning. Contemporary psychological research has endeavored to correct that distortion, and contemporary care ethics has extended that correction to ethics.

In 1982 Harvard psychologist Carol Gilligan published *In a Different Voice*, a very influential study of how women reason about ethical issues. Gilligan had spent years working with Lawrence Kohlberg, a Harvard psychologist, researching the psychological processes involved in moral development. Kohlberg's research tracked a number of children over a period of many years, interviewing them periodically to examine the development of their moral perspectives. In the course of those interviews, Kohlberg posed moral quandaries to his subjects. For example, suppose there is a man, Heinz, whose wife is deathly ill. There is a very expensive drug that will save her life, but Heinz does not have enough money to buy the drug, and has no way of obtaining enough money. The pharmacist will neither give Heinz the drug nor lower the price. The only way Heinz can obtain the drug is by stealing it from the pharmacist. Should Heinz steal the drug?

When confronted with such a case, women often want more details: Why isn't it possible for Heinz to work out an agreement with the pharmacist? Has Heinz really explored every possibility? Is the pharmacist that indifferent to saving Heinz's wife? Also, if Heinz steals (or refuses to steal) the drug, what effect will that have on his relationship with his wife? In contrast, most men are happy to keep the problem at the abstract level: the details about Heinz and his wife and the pharmacist aren't important. It's the principle that counts, principles apply to everyone alike, and thus personal details are irrelevant.

This difference in desire for detail reflects another difference, which Kohlberg thought very significant. Kohlberg was primarily interested in 'stages of moral development,' and how we make moral progress through those successive stages. We start with self-centered interests, and most of us progress through further stages in which our concerns extend to the welfare of others (Stage 3), then some move forward to the recognition that rules take priority over particular interests (Stage 4), and ultimately a few reach Stages 5 and 6: recognition of abstract principles of universal justice. Women tend to get stuck at level three, focusing on the details of how to maintain relationships and promote the welfare of family and friends. Men are more likely to move on to the abstract principles, and therefore have less concern with the particulars of who is involved.

As Lawrence Kohlberg saw it, this indicated that most women failed to achieve the higher levels of moral development. He thought that might be due to their comparative isolation in the home and the community: maybe when women spend more time dealing with the larger issues of the outside world, they will also make greater moral progress. Carol Gilligan saw it differently. Rather than most women suffering arrested moral development, women tend to have a different perspective on ethics. Abstract principle is useful, but such principles should not be used to the detriment of actual people and their cares and concerns and relationships. As a Jewish carpenter once said, "The law is made for man; not man for the law." From the perspective of Carol Gilligan and many other women (and of course many men as well, including Jesus of Nazareth) abstract principles can lose their usefulness and become harmful if they become ends in themselves that are more important than their actual effects on specific people.

Watching 10-year-old boys play baseball, one might suppose that the best thing about the game is the excuse it gives for extended arguments about rules (and watching 30-year-old fathers arguing about rules at their children's little league games, one might suppose that the boys don't change much as they get older). Sometimes disputes are resolved, and the game continues to the next acrimonious argument; and sometimes the dispute shatters the game and the group, breaking the contestants into divided camps equally certain of their moral superiority and equally aggrieved at the perfidious folly of their former friends. On the same playground, the girls are also playing games, and they also face disagreements about the rules. But the disagreements are usually settled more quickly, and there is typically more concern with preserving friendships than with following rules. When a disagreement threatens group harmony, the girls are more likely to drop the game and play something else—still playing together—than allow the group to divide into warring factions. This general tendency shouldn't be exaggerated: little girls can be just as principled and unbending as little boys, and little league moms can be just as adamantly obnoxious as little league dads. Still, their general orientations are usually distinctly different: girls focus more on preserving the group, while boys emphasize following the rules.

Philosopher and educator Nel Noddings marks the relevant difference clearly:

> Women, perhaps the majority of women, prefer to discuss moral problems in terms of concrete situations. They approach moral problems not as intellectual problems to be solved by abstract reasoning but as concrete human problems to be lived and to be solved in living. . . .
>
> Faced with a hypothetical moral dilemma, women often ask for more information. It is not the case, certainly, that women cannot arrange principles hierarchically and derive conclusions logically. It is more likely that they see this process as peripheral to or even irrelevant to moral conduct. They want more information, I think, in order to form a picture. Ideally, they need to talk to the participants, to see their eyes and facial expressions, to size up the whole situation. Moral decisions are, after all, made in situations; they are qualitatively different from the solution to geometry problems. Women . . . give reasons for their acts, but the reasons point to feelings, needs, situational conditions, and their sense of personal ideal rather than universal principles and their application.[1]

THE CARE PERSPECTIVE ON ETHICS

The tendency observed on the playground can also be observed in philosophical perspectives on ethics. But the 'care' perspective on ethics has larger implications than simply the need to temper principle with concern for particular individuals and their relationships. Annette Baier notes that ethical debate often focuses on the choice between Kantian ethics (with its strong reliance on abstract principle) and utilitarian ethics (with its insistence on calculating consequences). But the emphasis on Kantian versus utilitarian ethics obscures the fact that *both* views share an important basic assumption: the assumption that *reason* is the key to ethical decision-making. Kantians reason from abstract principles (the question to be rationally resolved is what those principles are and how any particular act fits under those principles); utilitarians rationally calculate the balance of benefit over harm, and resolve ethical quandaries by adding up the accounts. But for both Kantians and utilitarians the essential element in ethics is the reasoning process.

Baier challenges that assumption. Rules and consequences have obvious importance, and sometimes our feelings must be governed by considerations of rules or consequences (my sympathetic impulse to rescue my toddler from the painful upcoming vaccination may be trumped by rational consideration of the dire consequences that might follow from not having the vaccination). But sympathy is the basic moral capacity, not law-discerning or consequence-calculating reason.

We neglect that to our peril. Teaching doctors and nurses and physical therapists the "rules" of morality, or how to do utilitarian calculations, may have some benefits. But if this merely coats them with a thin veneer of morality, while leaving them unsympathetic and uncaring and insensitive to the needs and fears and vulnerabilities of their patients, then learning the ethical rules may do more harm than good. Indeed, "ethical codes" more often serve to confer high status on the professionals and protect them from outside criticism ("only doctors are qualified to judge other doctors") rather than encouraging better moral behavior toward actual patients. In medical *care*—with patients who are often frightened and vulnerable—a caring perspective is very valuable.

When I go to my physician, I typically start from a position of grave concern over some health problem I do not understand, and I reveal myself in a way that makes me particularly vulnerable: not only the imperfections in my body, but also the flaws in my behavior. In seeking the right diagnosis and treatment, my doctor needs to know that I'm not getting enough exercise, that I occasionally drink too much, that I've been feeling depressed, and that I have very little will power when tempted by anything chocolate. The doctor may gently admonish me to give up smoking, or watch my diet, or take my daily medications; but she must avoid any suggestion that she is judging me. She is my confidante, perhaps my partner in seeking restoration of health, a coach who nudges me toward better health habits: but she is not my judge, and not someone who exploits my openness and vulnerability to pass judgment on me. (That is one reason that distributing medical resources on the basis of patient habits and lifestyles—chronic drinkers should be lower on the list for transplants, heavy smokers should have to wait longer for bypass surgery, overeaters should have to pay more for their surgery—is so destructive to medical *care:* it turns doctors into judges, rather than caregiving partners.)

The Relation of Caring to Rules

Important as a care-based perspective is in medicine, there is also a use for rules. My vulnerability may tempt my physician toward a benevolent but destructive paternalism: "This patient is sick, and doesn't really understand what is in his best interests; instead of giving him all this information and letting him make a choice that may be wrong, I'll just choose for him." The motive in this case may be kindness, and it may *feel* like the right thing to do; but most of us would deeply resent being treated in such a paternalistic manner, whatever the motives. It's my body, and I want to make my own decision about what treatments I will and will not have. The doctor's motives may be good, but it's not really a kindness to treat me like a child who is incapable of making his own decisions. Certainly we want our doctors to be caring and concerned, but we also want them to remember the *rule* that every competent person has the right to make his or her own informed decision about medical treatment. There are lots of people who could run my life better than I can, but I still want to run it myself, and I have the basic right to do so.

Trying to balance moral rules and moral feelings is a challenging task. One philosopher who has struggled with that issue is Jonathan Bennett, in an article—which we examined in Chapter 3—titled "The Conscience of Huckleberry Finn." You'll recall that at one point in Mark Twain's novel, Huck Finn is sharing a raft with his friend Jim, an escaped slave. As the raft moves closer and closer to the free states, Jim expresses his deep gratitude to Huck, calling Huck "the best friend I ever had." Soon Jim will be free, and—he tells Huck—he owes it all to his friend Huck. Without Huck, Jim could never had made the long dangerous trip up the river. As Huck thinks about this, he realizes that what Jim says is true, and Huck begins to feel terrible pangs of conscience. He is helping Jim escape from (what Huck considers) his rightful owner, poor old Miz Watson, who had always been kind to Huck. And Huck is repaying her kindness by practically stealing her property, and he knows what he is doing is wrong. So he resolves to put things right, and turn Jim in to some slave catchers. But when the opportunity comes, Huck can't do it: his deep feeling of friendship and affection for Jim outweighs his principled belief that slaves are property that should be returned to their owners.

In this case, Huck's "moral principles" are terribly wrong. Humans cannot be enslaved and treated as property, and we are glad Huck's feelings of affection and friendship triumphed over his flawed principles. But there also may be times when our principles should be a check on our feelings: the benevolent *feeling* of the kindly doctor who wishes to make my decisions for me should be trumped by the *principle* that competent patients have a right to make their own decisions. And if you find clear evidence that your friend has robbed a bank, and some innocent stranger is in the middle of a long prison term after being wrongly convicted of the crime committed by your friend, then probably your principled decision to turn in your friend should not be blocked by your feelings. There are plenty of other examples: A desire for vengeance is surely a natural feeling, but it is far from obvious that it is a reliable moral guide. Our 'Founding Fathers' often relied on their visceral "feeling" of revulsion for any skin hue other than pale pink in denying basic rights to those of African descent, and their "feeling" that it was unnatural for women to participate in political life led them to deny rights of self-government to half the population. Rules without feelings leave hollow and sometimes harmful ethics (if you provide for your children from a sense of duty rather than from affection, the result is likely to be resentful and deeply insecure children); but feelings without reflection and rules can produce policies based on the grossest prejudices. If we try to remove feelings and affections from ethics, we are likely to remove the engine that powers ethics, and we shall also destroy some of the most valuable elements of our ethical lives. But we also need to examine our feelings, to root out prejudices and narrow self-serving motives. It is often useful to subject our feelings to careful scrutiny and basic tests ("Would I think it fair if others treated *me* in that manner? Would I approve of everyone acting this way? Would I vote for such a rule from behind Rawls's 'veil of ignorance'? Will acting on this feeling cause more harm than good?") We can believe in the fundamental ethical importance of feelings without giving our feelings a blank check.

So which should be our moral guide? Our principles, or our feelings of warmth and friendship? That question poses a false dilemma. We need not think of ethics as being either pure principle or pure feeling; rather, the two can both serve useful functions, and they may work well to check and correct each other. My feelings of empathy and care are surely basic to ethics, whatever Kant may claim to the contrary. And rules are not an adequate substitute. When I am ill and frightened and lonely in the hospital, I am greatly cheered by your caring visit; but if I get the impression that you are visiting me purely from a sense of duty, and not out of simple care and affection, that will destroy much if not all of the comfort and pleasure gained from your visit. Even in this case, however, rules and reason may have some use: You are a busy person, with lots of demands on your schedule, and your hospitalized friend is not one of the obvious demands (and going to hospitals is not great fun). Thinking carefully about how your friend has helped and comforted you in the past, and about your duty to reciprocate such kindnesses, may be a useful reminder to buy some flowers and books and stop by the hospital. But a visit done strictly from duty, without genuine care, may be more depressing than uplifting to the patient. Thinking about our duties can certainly be helpful; but acting *purely* from duty—so far from being the ethical ideal that Kant thought it to be—often eviscerates the moral value and benefit of the dutiful act. Useful as such reasoned duty reminders are, they cannot substitute for affection and care.

Caring and Utilitarian Ethics

Care ethics does not ignore or disparage reason, but it does emphasize the importance of empathy and affection, friendships and relationships: elements of ethics (from the perspective of care ethics) Kantian systems woefully neglect. Care ethics also diverges significantly from the impersonal calculations of utilitarianism. By utilitarian standards, my duty is to maximize pleasure and minimize suffering for everyone involved, and the calculations demanded are quite impersonal: I must count my own pleasures and pains and those of my family and friends in the total, but I cannot give those concerns any greater weight than the pleasures and pains of strangers. Such utilitarian concerns have prompted many examples for utilitarian analysis, some of which seem to challenge that basic impersonal utilitarian perspective. One such example is this. My three children are suffering from a deadly disease, and I have just enough medicine to save them (and no possibility of securing more medicine). But across town live four unrelated smaller children who are suffering from the same disease, and the medicine I have would be just enough to save them. Should I save the four strangers or my three children? Simple utilitarian calculations seem to demand that I sacrifice my children to save the four strangers; but for most of us, such behavior would probably not be morally acceptable, much less morally obligatory. If someone sacrificed her three children to save the lives of four strangers, we would be more likely to regard such a person as a moral suspect (will she collect insurance on her children?) rather than a moral hero. She may qualify as a utilitarian saint, but that sort of sainthood strikes many as too cold and impersonal to be a worthy aspiration.

Utilitarians can devise ways of dealing with such examples. Some utilitarians bite the bullet, and insist that saving the four strangers *is* the right act, and our affection for our children should not blind us to the impersonal demands of our duty. Other utilitarians might take a gentler tone: you really *should* save the four strangers rather than your own three children, but that is such a strong ethical demand that you should not be blamed if you cannot meet it. Going still further, some utilitarians may attempt a utilitarian justification of the decision to save your three children in preference to the four strangers: bonds among family and friends are an important source of pleasure, and when we add in the benefits of preserving such relationships, then we see that this more comprehensive calculation of the balance of pleasure over suffering would justify saving the lives of the three family members. Perhaps such calculations do add up as the utilitarian suggests; but from the perspective of care ethics, that is still not a satisfactory solution: the bonds of affection and friendship and family must be recognized as an important and distinct ethical element, not just one pleasure calculation among others. Treating our special personal relationships as merely a subset of pleasurable sensations to be entered into the utilitarian calculation seems (to care theorists) an inadequate representation of the basic moral worth of these relations. After all, a very difficult and willful child, who brings more concern than pleasure to her parents, does not for that reason rank lower in ethical consideration or, one hopes, in parental affection.

"Many moral theories . . . employ the assumption that to increase the utility of individuals is a good thing to do. But if asked *why* it is a good thing to increase utility, or satisfy desire, or produce pleasure, or *why* doing so counts as a good reason for something, it is very difficult to answer. The claim is taken as a kind of starting assumption for which no *further* reason can be given. It seems to rest on a view that people seek pleasure, or that we can recognize pleasure as having more intrinsic value. But if women recognize quite different assumptions as more likely to be valid, that would certainly be of importance to ethics. We might then take it as one of our starting assumptions that creating good relations of care and concern and trust between ourselves and our children, and creating social arrangements in which children will be valued and well cared for, are more important than maximizing individual utilities. And the moral theories that might be compatible with such assumptions might be very different from those with which we are familiar." Virginia Held, "Feminism and Moral Theory," in Eva Feder Kittay and Diana T. Meyers, editors, *Women and Moral Theory* (Totowa, N.J.: Rowman and Littlefield, 1987), p. 126.

Care Ethics and Impersonal Duties

This last point leads to another distinctive feature of care ethics. On Kantian and utilitarian and social contract views, our duties tend to be *impersonal:* we have duties and obligations to others, of course, but they are duties due to anyone in the same position. On the care view, we may also have impersonal duties, but at least as important are duties of a very personal and individual nature: duties we owe specifically to family or friends, and not to just any generic moral placeholder. These are duties owed not because we are reciprocating benefits we have received but because of our special relations. Furthermore, such duties are typically not based on choices or voluntary contracts. We didn't 'ask to be born,' nor did we get any choice in our parents or siblings; and come to think of it, probably not a lot of choice in our oldest (and perhaps dearest) childhood friends. But few of us doubt that we have special obligations to them, obligations above and beyond the obligations we have to others generally. Perhaps we could give some sort of justification for those obligations in terms of reciprocating past care and affection; but such justifications are likely to strike us as artificial and unnecessary. If your sister or brother is in need, you feel a strong and special obligation to help. If someone has to stop and calculate that obligation on the basis of rules, and only then recognizes its moral force, we are more likely to think such a person morally impoverished than morally superior. Such basic felt obligations are probably more fundamental than any rule we could devise for their justification. Perhaps in the absence of deep feelings of affection and obligation, adherence to moral rules may serve as a substitute. But it is likely to be a very limited substitute: like a paint by number replacement for a work of art.

This is not to suggest that utilitarianism is useless. We may well make some rough utilitarian calculations when we are considering building a mansion for our family, and consider whether some of those resources might better be used to house homeless strangers. But care theorists would insist that we can and should consider such factors, but without reducing our special relations with friends and family to strict impersonal utilitarian calculations of pleasure and pain. Thus care theorists can find significant uses for moral rules. For example, at times when my affection for family and friends may be at low ebb, bringing a moral rule to mind may be useful. But for care theorists this is a backup system, not the core of morality. While recalling such rules may be useful in those circumstances, the same effect might be achieved though recalling special moments of shared affection and kindness. The care perspective does not deny that moral rules have their uses, but it insists that rules and reason are not the whole—or even the most vital element—of our moral lives.

WOMEN AND ETHICS
Perils of "Feminine" Ethics

Having examined care ethics, are we justified in describing that as "a feminine ethic," in contrast to more masculine Kantian or utilitarian theories? Or more generally, is there a distinctive "feminine" ethic at all? Or is ethics gender neutral? That is a much debated issue, and one on which feminists are deeply divided. That division is not surprising, since the notion of a 'distinctly feminine character' has a very mixed history. Women were often oppressed by the "chivalrous" thought systems that glorified their virtue. For example, in 1966 the Mississippi Supreme Court ruled women could legally be excluded from juries (so much for women defendants having a 'jury of their peers'); and they gave this reason:

> The legislature has a right to exclude women [from jury service] so they may contribute their services as mothers, wives, and homemakers, and also to protect them (in some areas they are still upon a pedestal) from the filth, obscenity, and noxious atmosphere that so often pervades a courtroom during a jury trial.[2]

Their cages (or "pedestals," as the Mississippi judges called them) may have been gilded, but the gilded bars were still there. In 1837 Sarah Grimke gave this analysis of the situation facing women:

> She has surrendered her dearest rights, and been satisfied with the privileges which man has assumed to grant her; she has been amused with the show of power, whilst man has absorbed all the reality into himself. He has adorned the creature whom God gave him as a companion with baubles and gewgaws, turned her attention to personal attractions, offered incense to her vanity, and made her the instrument of his selfish gratification, a plaything to please his eye and amuse his hours of leisure. 'Rule by obedience and by submission sway,' or in other words, study to be a hypocrite, pretend to submit, but gain your point, has been the code of household morality which woman has been taught.[3]

The notion of distinctly masculine/feminine moralities and roles is found in such sayings as "The man is the head, the woman the heart, " and "Behind every successful man is a good woman" (far behind, quietly at home, supportive and dependent). And lest one suppose this to be ancient history, there will probably be a wedding in your community this weekend in which the husband promises to love and cherish his wife and the wife promises to love, honor, and *obey* her husband, the head of the household.

Womanly Virtues

> "It would be an endless task to trace the variety of meannesses, cares, and sorrows into which women are plunged by the prevailing opinion that they were created rather to feel than reason, and that all the power they obtain must be obtained by their charms and weaknesses." Mary Wollstonecraft, A *Vindication of the Rights of Women*, 1792.

Think back to virtue theory. One common question is whether there are *multiple* sets of virtues—perhaps one set of virtues for the old, another for the young. But the one place where the notion of 'different sets of virtues' is most prominent is the contrast between *masculine* and *feminine* virtues. A virtuous woman is demure, quiet, modest, chaste. In fact, "Modesty" and "Chastity" were popular names for girls, not so many years ago. But no boys were named Modesty, because the virtuous male was not modest, but instead proud, ambitious, aggressive, brave, strong.

Given the history of a special "feminine morality"—designed to restrict the opportunities and influence of women—it is hardly surprising that most reformers have opposed the notion of 'feminine morality'. Mary Wollstonecraft (in her famous *Vindication of the Rights of Woman*) argued that there is only one moral system that applies to all: there is no distinctly feminine morality, and no life goals that are peculiarly appropriate for women rather than men.

The Value of Feminist Ethics

On the other side, women have sometimes claimed that the oppressive forms of "feminine morality" notwithstanding, there is a genuine and profoundly valuable feminine consciousness that is rooted in women's social development, a consciousness that must be valued and appreciated. For example, the sociologist Ariel Salleh maintains that through "women's lived experience" there is a special connection between woman and nature that offers the best prospect for "a sane, humane, ecological future."[4] But many remain deeply skeptical of such claims about special moral capacities. Jean Grimshaw, for example:

> If ethical concerns and priorities arise from different forms of social life, then those which have emerged from a social system in which women have so often been subordinate to men must be suspect. Supposedly 'female' values are not only the subject of little agreement among women: they are also deeply mired in conceptions of 'the feminine' which depend on the sort of polarization between 'masculine' and 'feminine' which has itself been so closely related to the subordination of women. There is no autonomous realm of female values, or of female activities which can generate 'alternative' values to those of the public sphere; and any conception of a 'female ethic' which depends on these ideas cannot, I think, be a viable one.[5]

This is only the edge of a difficult and ongoing debate. But whatever one's views on the question of whether 'care ethics' is distinctly feminine, it is difficult to deny that many of the central themes of care ethics have been ignored or undervalued in Western ethics.

THE NEED FOR MORE THAN JUSTICE

Annette Baier

Annette C. Baier was born in New Zealand, studied philosophy at Somerville College, Oxford, and has for some years been Distinguished Service Professor of Philosophy at the University of Pittsburgh. Though her work is wide-ranging, a central theme is the connection of principles of justice to caring relationships. She is the author of many important philosophical works, including *A Progress of Sentiments: Reflections on Hume's "Treatise," Postures of Mind,* and *Moral Prejudices* (from which this selection is taken).

In recent decades in North American social and moral philosophy, alongside the development and discussion of widely influential theories of justice, taken as John Rawls takes it as the "first virtue of social institutions," there has been a countermovement gathering strength, one coming from some interesting sources. Some of the most outspoken of the diverse group who have in a variety of ways been challenging the assumed supremacy of justice among the moral and social virtues are members of those sections of society whom one might have expected to be especially aware of the supreme importance of justice: blacks and women. Those who have only recently won recognition of their equal rights, who have only recently seen the correction or partial correction of long-standing racist and sexist injustices to their race and sex, are among the philosophers now suggesting that justice is only one virtue among many, and one that may need the presence of the others in order to deliver its own undenied value.

Let me say quite clearly at this early point that there is little disagreement that justice is *a* social value of very great importance, and injustice an evil. Nor would those who have worked on theories of justice want to deny that other things matter besides justice. Rawls, for example, incorporates the value of freedom into his account of justice, so that denial of basic freedoms counts as injustice. Rawls also leaves room for a wider theory of the right, of which the the-

ory of justice is just a part. Still, he does claim that justice is the "first" virtue of social institutions, and it is only that claim about priority that I think has been challenged. It is easy to exaggerate the differences of view that exist, and I want to avoid that. The differences are as much in emphasis as in substance, or we can say that they are differences in tone of voice. But these differences do tend to make a difference in approaches to a wide range of topics not just in moral theory but in areas such as medical ethics, where the discussion used to be conducted in terms of patients' rights, of informed consent, and so on, but now tends to get conducted in an enlarged moral vocabulary, which draws on what Gilligan calls the ethics of *care* as well as that of *justice.*

"Care" is the new buzzword. It is not, as Shakespeare's Portia demanded, mercy that is to season justice, but a less authoritarian humanitarian supplement, a felt concern for the good of others and for community with them. The "cold jealous virtue of justice" (Hume) is found to be too cold, and it is "warmer," more communitarian virtues and social ideals that are being called in to supplement it. One might say that liberty and equality are being found inadequate without fraternity, except that "fraternity" will be quite the wrong word if, as Gilligan initially suggested, it is *women* who perceive this value most easily. ("Sorority" will do no better, since it is too exclusive, and English has no gender-neutral word for the mutual concern of siblings.) She has since modified this claim, allowing that there are two perspectives on moral and social issues that we all tend to alternate between, and which are not always easy to combine, one of them what she calls the justice perspective, the other the care perspective. It is increasingly obvious that there are many male philosophical spokespersons for the care perspective (Laurence Thomas, Lawrence Blum, Michael Stocker), so it cannot be the prerogative of women. Nevertheless Gilligan still wants to claim that women are most unlikely to take *only* the justice perspective, as some men are claimed to, at least until some mid-life crisis jolts them into "bifocal" moral vision.

Is justice blind to important social values, or at least only one-eyed? What is it that comes into view from the "care perspective" that is not seen from the "justice perspective"?

Gilligan's position here is most easily described by contrasting it with that of Kohlberg, against which she developed it. Kohlberg, influenced by Jean Piaget and the Kantian philosophical tradition as developed by John Rawls, developed a theory about typical moral development which saw it to progress from a preconventional level, where what is seen to matter is pleasing or not offending parental authority figures, through a conventional level in which the child tries to fit in with a group, such as a school community, and to conform to its standards and rules, to a postconventional critical level, in which such conventional rules are subjected to tests and where those tests are of a Utilitarian or, eventually, a Kantian sort—clear ones that require respect for each person's individual rational will, or autonomy, and conformity to any implicit social contract such wills are deemed to have made or to any hypothetical ones they would make if thinking clearly. What was found when Kohlberg's questionnaires (mostly by verbal response to verbally sketched moral dilemmas) were applied to female as well as male subjects, Gilligan reports, is that the girls and women not only scored generally lower than the boys and men but tended to *revert* to the lower stage of the conventional level even after briefly (usually in adolescence) attaining the postconventional level. Piaget's finding that girls were deficient in "the legal sense" was confirmed.

These results led Gilligan to wonder if there might not be a quite different pattern of development to be discerned, at least in female subjects. She therefore conducted interviews designed to elicit not just how far advanced the subjects were toward an appreciation of the nature and importance of Kantian autonomy but also to find out what the subjects themselves saw as progress or lack of it, what conceptions of moral maturity they came to possess by the time they were adults. She found that although the Kohlberg version of moral maturity as respect for fellow persons and for their rights as equals (rights including that of free association) did seem shared by many young men, the women tended to speak in a different voice about morality itself and about moral maturity. To quote Gilligan, "Since the reality of connection is experienced by women as given rather than as freely contracted, they arrive at an understanding of life that reflects the limits of autonomy and control. As a result, women's development delineates the path not only to a less violent life but also to a maturity realized through interdependence and taking care." She writes that there is evidence that "women perceive and construe social reality differently from men and that these differences center around experiences of attachment and separation . . . because women's sense of integrity appears to be entwined with an ethic of care, so that to see themselves as women is to see themselves in a relationship of connection, the major transitions in women's lives would seem to involve changes in the understanding and activities of care." She contrasts this progressive understanding of care, from merely pleasing others to helping and nurturing, with the sort of progression that is involved in Kohlberg's stages, a progression in the understanding, not of mutual care, but of mutual *respect*, where this has its Kantian overtones of distance, even of some fear for the respected, and where personal autonomy and independence, rather than more satisfactory interdependence, are the paramount values.

This contrast, one cannot but feel, is one which Gilligan might have used the Marxist language of alienation to make. For the main complaint about the Kantian version of a society with its first virtue justice, construed as respect for equal rights to formal goods such as having contracts kept, due process,

equal opportunity including opportunity to participate in political activities leading to policy- and law-
making, to basic liberties of speech, free association
and assembly, and religious worship, is that none of
these goods does much to ensure that the people who
have and mutually respect such rights will have any
other relationships to one another than the minimal
relationship needed to keep such a "civil society"
going. They may well be lonely, driven to suicide,
apathetic about their work and about participation in
political processes, find their lives meaningless, and
have no wish to leave offspring to face the same
meaningless existence. Their rights, and respect for
rights, are quite compatible with very great misery,
and misery whose causes are not just individual misfortune and psychic sickness but social and moral
impoverishment.

Let me try to summarize the main differences, as I
see them, between on the one hand Gilligan's version
of moral maturity and the sort of social structures that
would encourage, express, and protect it and on the
other the orthodoxy she sees herself to be challenging. I shall from now on be giving my own interpretation of the significance of her challenges, not merely
reporting them. The most obvious point is the challenge to the individualism of the Western tradition,
to the fairly entrenched belief in the possibility and
desirability of each person pursuing his own good in
his own way, constrained only by a minimal formal
common good, namely, a working legal apparatus that
enforces contracts and protects individuals from
undue interference by others. Gilligan reminds us
that noninterference can, especially for the relatively
powerless, such as the very young, amount to neglect,
and even between equals can be isolating and alienat-
ing. On her less individualist version of individuality,
it becomes defined by responses to dependency and to
patterns of interconnection, both chosen and unchosen. It is not something a person *has*, and which she
then chooses relationships to suit, but something that
develops out of a series of dependencies and interde-
pendencies, and responses to them. This conception
of individuality is not flatly at odds with, say, Rawls's
Kantian one, but there is at least a difference of tone
of voice between speaking as Rawls does of each of us
having our own rational life plan, which a just society's moral traffic rules will allow us to follow, and

which may or may not include close association with
other persons, and speaking as Gilligan does of a satisfactory life as involving the "progress of affiliative
relationship" where "the concept of identity expands
to include the experience of interconnection." Rawls
can allow that progress to Gilligan-style moral maturity may be *a* rational life plan, but not a moral constraint on every life pattern. The trouble is that it will
not do just to say "let this version of morality be an
optional extra. Let us agree on the essential minimum, that is, on justice and rights, and let whoever
wants to go further and cultivate this more demanding ideal of responsibility and care." For, first, the
ideal of care cannot be satisfactorily cultivated without closer cooperation from others than respect for
rights and justice will ensure, and, second, the
encouragement of some to cultivate it while others do
not could easily lead to exploitation of those who do.
It obviously *has* suited some in most societies well
enough that others take on the responsibilities of care
(for the sick, the helpless, the young), leaving them
free to pursue their own less altruistic goods. Volunteer forces of those who accept an ethic of care, operating within a society where the power is exercised
and the institutions designed, redesigned, or maintained by those who accept a less communal ethic of
minimally constrained self-advancement, will not be
the solution. The liberal individualists may be able to
"tolerate" the more communally minded, if they keep
the liberals' rules, but it is not so clear that the more
communally minded can be content with just those
rules, nor be content to be tolerated and possibly
exploited.

For the moral tradition which developed the
concept of rights, autonomy, and justice is the same
tradition that provided "justifications" of the oppression of those whom the primary rights-holders
depended on to do the sort of work they themselves
preferred not to do. The domestic work was left to
women and slaves, and the liberal morality for rights-
holders was surreptitiously supplemented by a different set of demands made on domestic workers. As
long as women could be got to assume responsibility
for the care of home and children and to train their
children to continue the sexist system, the liberal
morality could continue to be the official morality, by
turning its eyes away from the contribution made by

those it excluded. The long unnoticed moral proletariat were the domestic workers, mostly female. Rights have usually been for the privileged. Talking about laws, and the rights those laws recognize and protect, does not in itself ensure that the group of legislators and rights-holders will not be restricted to some elite. Bills of rights have usually been proclamations of the rights of some in-group, barons, landowners, males, whites, nonforeigners. The "justice perspective" and the legal sense that goes with it are shadowed by their patriarchal past. What did Kant, the great prophet of autonomy, say in his moral theory about women? He said they were incapable of legislation, not fit to vote, that they needed the guidance of more "rational" males. Autonomy was not for them; it was only for first-class, really rational, persons. It is ironic that Gilligan's original findings in a way confirm Kant's views—it seems that autonomy really may not be for women. Many of them reject that ideal, and have been found not as good at making rules as are men. But where Kant concludes "so much the worse for women," we can conclude "so much the worse for the male fixation on the special skill of drafting legislation, for the bureaucratic mentality of rule worship, and for the male exaggeration of the importance of independence over mutual interdependence."

It is however also true that the moral theories that made the concept of a person's rights central were not just the instruments for excluding some persons but also the instruments used by those who demanded that more and more persons be included in the favored group. Abolitionists, reformers, women, used the language of rights to assert their claims to inclusion in the group of full members of a community. The tradition of liberal moral theory has in fact developed to include the women it had for so long excluded, to include the poor as well as rich, blacks as well as whites, and so on. Women such as Mary Wollstonecraft used the male moral theories to good purpose. So we should not be wholly ungrateful for those male moral theories, for all their objectionable earlier content. They were undoubtedly patriarchal, but they also contained the seeds of the challenge, or antidote, to this patriarchal poison.

Exploitation aside, why would women, once liberated, not be content to have their version of moral-ity merely tolerated? Why should they not see themselves as voluntarily, for their own reasons, taking on *more* than the liberal rules demand, while having no quarrel with the content of those rules themselves, nor with their remaining the only ones that are expected to be generally obeyed? To see why, we need to move on to three more differences between the Kantian liberals (usually contractarians) and their critics. These concern the relative weight put on relationships between equals, on freedom of choice, and on the authority of intellect over emotions. It is a typical feature of the dominant moral theories and traditions since Kant, or perhaps since Hobbes, that relationships between equals or those who are deemed equal in some important sense have been the relations that morality is primarily concerned to regulate. Relationships between those who are clearly unequal in power, such as parents and children, earlier and later generations in relation to one another, states and citizens, doctors and patients, the well and the ill, large states and small states, have had to be shunted to the bottom of the agenda and then dealt with by some sort of "promotion" of the weaker, so that an appearance of virtual equality is achieved. Citizens collectively become equal to states, children are treated as adults-to-be, the ill and dying are treated as continuers of their earlier more potent selves, so that their "rights" can be seen as the rights of equals. This pretense of an equality that is in fact absent may often lead to desirable protection of the weaker, or more dependent. But it somewhat masks the question of what our moral relationships *are* to those who are our superiors or our inferiors in power. A more realistic acceptance that we begin as helpless children, that at almost every point of our lives we deal with both the more and the less helpless, that equality of power and interdependency, between two persons or groups, is rare and hard to recognize when it does occur, might lead us to a more direct approach to questions concerning the design of institutions structuring these relationships between unequals (families, schools, hospitals, armies) and of the morality of our dealings with the more and the less powerful. One reason why those who agree with the Gilligan version of what morality is about will not want to agree that the liberals' rules are a good minimal set, the only ones we need pressure *everyone* to obey, is that these rules do little to protect the young or the dying or the starving or any of the relatively powerless against neglect, or to ensure an education that will form persons to be *capable* of conforming to an ethics of care and responsibility. Put baldly, and in a way Gilligan certainly has not put it, the liberal morality, if unsupplemented, may *unfit* people to be anything other than what its justifying theories suppose them to be, ones who have no interest in each other's interests. Yet some must take an interest in the next generation's interests. Women's traditional work, of caring for the less powerful, especially for the young, is obviously socially vital. One cannot regard any version of morality that does not ensure that caring for children gets well done as an adequate "minimal morality," anymore than we could so regard one that left any concern for more distant future generations an optional extra. A moral theory, it can plausibly be claimed, cannot regard concern for new and future persons as an optional charity left for those with a taste for it. If the morality the theory endorses is to sustain itself, it must provide for its own continuers, not just take out a loan on a carefully encouraged maternal instinct or on the enthusiasm of a self-selected group of environmentalists who make it their business or hobby to be concerned with what we are doing to mother earth.

The recognition of the importance for all parties of relations between those who are and cannot but be unequal, and of their effect on personality formation and so on other relationships, goes along with a recognition of the plain fact that not all morally important relationships can or should be freely chosen. So far I have discussed three reasons women have to be not content to pursue their own values within the framework of the liberal morality. The first was its dubious record. The second was its inattention to relations of inequality or its pretense of equality. The third reason is its exaggeration of the scope of choice, or its inattention to unchosen relations. Showing up the partial myth of equality among actual members of a community, and the undesirability of trying to pretend that we are treating all of them as equals, tends to go along with an exposure of the companion myth that moral obligations arise from freely *chosen* associations between such equals. Vulnerable future generations do not choose their dependence on earlier

generations. The unequal infant does not choose its place in a family or nation, nor is it treated as free to do as it likes until some association is freely entered into. Nor do parents always choose their parental role or freely assume their parental responsibilities, anymore than we choose our power to affect the conditions in which later generations will live. Gilligan's attention to the version of morality and moral maturity found in women, many of whom had faced a choice of whether or not to have an abortion, and who had at some point become mothers, is attention to the perceived inadequacy of the language of rights to help in such choices or to guide them in their parental role. It would not be much of an exaggeration to call the Gilligan "different voice" the voice of the potential parents. The emphasis on care goes with a recognition of the often unchosen nature of responsibilities of those who give care, both of children who care for their aged or infirm parents and of parents who care for the children they in fact have. Contract soon ceases to seem the paradigm source of moral obligation once we attend to parental responsibility, and justice as a virtue of social institutions will come to seem at best only first equal with the virtue, whatever its name, that ensures that the members of each new generation are made appropriately welcome and prepared for their adult lives.

This all constitutes a belated reminder to Western moral theorists of a fact they have always known, that, as Adam Ferguson and David Hume before him emphasized, we are born into families, and the first society we belong to, one that fits or misfits us for later ones, is the small society of parents (or some sort of child-attendants) and children, exhibiting as it may relationships both of near equality and of inequality in power. This simple reminder, with the fairly considerable implications it can have for the plausibility of contractarian moral theory, is at the same time a reminder of the role of human emotions as much as human reason and will in moral development as it actually comes about. The fourth feature of the Gilligan challenge to liberal orthodoxy is a challenge to its typical *rationalism*, or intellectualism, to its assumption that we need not worry what passions persons have, as long as their rational wills can control them. This Kantian picture of a controlling reason dictating to possibly unruly passions also tends to seem less useful when we are led to consider what sort of person we need to fill the role of parent or, indeed, want in any close relationship. It might be important for father figures to have rational control over their violent urges to beat to death the children whose screams enrage them, but more than control of such nasty passions seems needed in the mother or primary parent, or parent-substitute, according to most psychological theories. Primary parents need to love their children, not just to control their irritation. So the emphasis in Kantian theories on rational control of emotions, rather than on cultivating desirable forms of emotion, is challenged by Gilligan, along with her challenge to the assumption of the centrality of autonomy, or relations between equals, and of freely chosen relations.

It is clear, I think, that the best moral theory has to be a cooperative product of women and men, has to harmonize justice and care. The morality it theorizes about is after all for all persons, for men and for women, and will need their combined insights. As Gilligan said, what we need now is a "marriage" of the old male and the newly articulated female insights. If she is right about the special moral aptitudes of women, then it will most likely be the women who propose the marriage, since they are the ones with the more natural empathy, with the better diplomatic skills, the ones more likely to shoulder responsibility and take moral initiative, and the ones who find it easiest to empathize and care about how the other party feels. Then, once there is this union of male and female moral wisdom, we maybe can teach each other the moral skills each gender currently lacks, so that the gender difference in moral outlook that Gilligan found will slowly become less marked.

EXERCISES

1. On many ethical issues there is a significant difference between men and women. For example, women are more likely than men to oppose capital punishment (of course some women strongly favor capital punishment, and many men fervently oppose it; but on the whole, significantly higher percentages of women oppose capital punishment). Why do you suppose that difference exists?

2. The year was 1984. A middle-aged man named Leroy Reid was arrested in Milwaukee on a weapons violation charge. Reid was a convicted felon, who had spent several years in prison. After his release, he had lived for years as a quiet, law-abiding citizen. As was shown at his trial, Reid was a man of very limited intelligence—a psychologist who testified at the trial said he was not quite in the retarded range, but "substantially below average"—who read at a first-grade level. Reid wanted to find work, and he wanted to do something worthwhile. At some point he saw a magazine advertisement: "Study at home! You can become a private detective!" Reid sent a few dollars to the company, and they sent him a "private detective badge," of which he was very proud. He now believed he was a private detective, and would (as he put it) "be able to help people, like that man on television, the Equalizer." He thought he only needed one more thing to be a private detective: a gun. So he went to a sporting goods shop, and purchased a .22 caliber pistol. (The Brady Bill had not yet been passed, so Reid did not have to undergo a background check.)

   Unfortunately for Reid, Wisconsin had recently passed a new law: a law of which Reid had no knowledge. The law made it a crime for a convicted felon to knowingly possess a firearm. One day Reid was hanging around a Milwaukee courtroom, and a sheriff's deputy asked him for identification. Reid proudly showed him the bill of sale for the gun he had purchased, and his 'private detective' badge. The deputy asked Reid where the gun was, and Reid said he kept it at home. The deputy told Reid to go and get the gun and bring it to the sheriff's office. Reid did so. When he returned to the sheriff's office, Reid told them he had a gun he wanted to turn in. He was promptly arrested and held in jail until his trial several months later (he could not afford to post bail).

When the case came to trial, the Milwaukee district attorney's office prosecuted the case vigorously. There had recently been a murder of two Milwaukee police officers by a convicted felon who had been carrying a pistol, and the office was eager to prosecute anyone who broke the new law. Reid was defended by a lawyer from the public defender's office, who opened his case with a startling admission: Reid was guilty. Under the law, Reid *was guilty:* he was a convicted felon, he possessed a firearm, and he knew he possessed a firearm. That was all the law required, and there was no doubt on any of those three points. But Reid's lawyer implored the jury not to find Reid guilty: "You've heard all about people getting off on technicalities; this is a case of a man getting nailed on technicalities." True, Reid was guilty under the law. However, he had not intended to break the law (he only wanted a "career opportunity as a private detective" so he could "help people"); and he had no idea he was breaking the law. The prosecutor responded that "ignorance of the law is no excuse": Reid doesn't have to *know* he is breaking the law, or *intend* to break the law. The only requirements are that he be a convicted felon who possesses a firearm and knows he possesses a firearm. Reid meets those conditions; Reid is guilty.

You are the Milwaukee jury hearing Reid's case. You've heard the evidence and the arguments. What's your verdict? Guilty or not guilty?

3. In the previous case, you thought carefully about what your verdict should be. As you thought, which of the ethical theories—Kantian, Humean, utilitarian, social contract, care ethics—comes closest to fitting the process by which you reached your verdict? Did you employ more than one?

    Second, is the approach you applied the approach you would generally take to ethical issues, or is this a special case? (That is, perhaps you employed a utilitarian approach to this question, but you do not think utilitarian ethics is generally the best method, though it works best in this special case.)

4. It is surely no accident that as more women have gone to law school, and become lawyers and judges and law school professors, there have been some changes in the practice of law. One of the most obvious is the change in the way divorce and child custody cases are handled. Of course many such cases go forward in the traditional manner: each estranged spouse hires the toughest and most battle-hardened lawyer available, and the lawyers fight it out as adversaries, with each side striving to win as much as possible. If there are children, both sides fight to win exclusive custody and limit the opposing spouse to the bare minimum of visiting rights. This makes for exciting adversarial contests, but often the only real winner is the winning lawyer, and the biggest losers are the children who are largely deprived of one parent. In more and more cases, questions of divorce—and especially questions of child custody arrangements—are settled in special courts that place less emphasis on adversarial victory and more emphasis on reaching a settlement that meets the needs and interests of all the parties involved, especially the children. That is, many of these cases are now settled in settings that aim at cooperative conflict resolution (often including happy reconciliation of the couple that initially consider divorce, and whose tentative early moves in that direction would have been hardened by an adversarial contest) rather than a contest based on rights and principles.

Most people agree that expanding the opportunity for cooperative conflict resolution has been a good thing, and especially beneficial for the children who are often those who suffer most from divorce. If this is counted as a positive development, and if it has in fact been stimulated by having more women involved in the law (and consequently more people who favor a "care" perspective on ethics), *would* this count as some proof of the legitimacy of care ethics?

5. You are a physician, specializing in the treatment of kidney disease. One of your patients, Alan Durkin, is a relative—a cousin, the two of you share grandparents. Alan is two years younger than you, you have known him since childhood, and you are friends. Alan is not one of your closest friends, but—in addition to now seeing him as your patient for the last three years—you see one another at weddings and funerals and other large family gatherings, maybe two or three times a year. Alan is 45, and his kidney disease has become progressively worse, and now his kidneys have failed to the point that he requires dialysis twice weekly, and soon his need for dialysis will increase to every other day. He can continue with dialysis for some time, and his condition is not immediately life threatening—but a successful kidney transplant would greatly improve his quality of life. Alan is on the waiting list for a kidney transplant, but because his dialysis treatments are relatively successful in purifying his blood, Alan is not a high-priority transplant candidate. Given the acute shortage of organs available for transplant, you know Alan will not soon receive one of the precious kidneys. But as Alan's physician, you could fudge the data just a little bit—no one would know, and by making Alan's condition look somewhat worse, you could easily bump him higher on the list and greatly improve his chances of receiving a transplant within the next year or so. Of course if you do that, then someone who actually has a greater need for a kidney transplant will be passed over in favor of your cousin Alan. *Should* you fudge the data, or not?

    In attempting to answer that question, which ethical perspective—Kantian, feelings-based, utilitarian, virtue, social contract, care—is most useful to you?

6. You have finished college, found a good job, and you are now living in a city about a thousand miles from your childhood home, where your widowed mother still lives. One weekend your mother comes to visit you in your new home: she is very proud of you, delighted at your success. It is good to see her, and the two of you reminisce over dinner about events in your childhood. You remember the weekly violin lessons: she drove you there every week, and the two of you always stopped for ice cream on the way home, and how much you enjoyed your conversations on those occasions, and how proud and supportive she was of your violin playing. And your soccer team that almost disbanded because no coach was available, and she stepped in and coached the team—even though she had to study several books on soccer to prepare herself—and the team actually finished second in the league, and how much fun the season was. And how she was always there, cooking a hot breakfast for you every morning, caring for you when you were sick, teaching you to drive, not yelling at you when the fender got smashed, offering a soft shoulder when your first romance fizzled.

    Unfortunately, the next day your mom becomes rather ill; nothing life-threatening, but she needs medical attention. You call your regular doctor, but she's out of town at a medical convention. But she has two other doctors covering her patients in her absence: Dr. Jones and Dr. Smith. Dr. Jones is first on the list, so you take your sick mom to his office. You sign in with the receptionist, and you and your mom settle down in the waiting room to await your turn to see the doctor. As you are waiting, your mom notices a picture of Dr. Jones and his staff in the corner of the waiting room; she discovers that Dr. Jones is Black. You knew about your mother's racism already: for years it has been one of the few subjects of bitter arguments between you. Your mother immediately demands to leave: she refuses to be treated by a Black doctor, and she wants to go to Dr. Smith instead. You find your mother's racist attitudes profoundly repugnant, morally repulsive. But your mother—whom you love, her faults notwithstanding, and who dearly loves you—is sick, and she is deeply disturbed about the prospect of being treated by a Black doctor. You aren't likely to get her past her deep racism in the next few minutes; after all, you've been trying for many years. And she will be much more comfortable seeing a White doctor. You have the car and the keys, and you can force her to see Dr. Jones; or you can agree to take her to Dr. Smith.

The standard question for such cases is: What should you do? But that is *not* the question being asked here. Instead, think about *how* care theorists would approach this problem: what steps would they take, what process might a care theorist follow? And second, how does the approach of the care theorist *differ* from the approach of some other ethical theorist (of your own choice: say, from a Kantian).

7. You are a physician at a tissue match laboratory. Ben Thomas makes an appointment to be tested. Ben's daughter, Rebecca, is 25. Rebecca has lost most of the functioning in her kidneys as a result of a severe blow suffered in a bicycle accident. She requires dialysis twice a week, and her health is poor. A kidney transplant would very likely restore her to full health, and she is on a waiting list for a kidney; but the list is long, and Rebecca's chances of getting a kidney are small. Because relatives have the best chance of having a close tissue match (and thus greatly reducing the likelihood of the patient's body *rejecting* the transplanted kidney), Ben hopes his kidney will be a close match. Ben is in good health, with two healthy kidneys, and if there is a good match, he plans to donate one of his kidneys to Rebecca (an increasingly common procedure). Since Rebecca is on the waiting list for a kidney transplant, you already have complete data on her; you just need to run tests on Ben.

You run the tests, as Ben requests, and unfortunately the tests show that Ben is not a good tissue match, and cannot contribute a kidney to Rebecca. But the tests also show something else, that neither you nor Ben had anticipated: Ben is not the biological father of Rebecca. Should you tell Ben this additional information? What factors or principles should you weigh in making your decision? Does Ben have a right to this information? Would care theorists and Kantians be likely to reach very different conclusions on this issue? *Must* they reach different conclusions?

8. Suppose someone suggested that "care ethics" is important in the home and among family and friends, but that an ethics of justice must govern our larger and more impersonal ethical lives. What do you think would be Annette Baier's response?

ADDITIONAL READING

Carol Gilligan, *In a Different Voice: Psychological Theory and Women's Development* (Cambridge, Mass: Harvard University Press, 1982), had a powerful impact on the contemporary development of care ethics. Nel Noddings's work has been influential in both philosophy and education; see her *Caring: A Feminine Approach to Ethics and Moral Education* (Berkeley, Calif.: University of California Press, 1984); and *Educating Moral People: A Caring Alternative to Character Education* (New York: Teachers College Press, 2002). Annette

C. Baier is a clear and cogent writer on this topic, who is particularly insightful in placing care ethics in a larger philosophical perspective. See her *Moral Prejudices* (Cambridge, Mass.: Harvard University Press, 1994). Among the best advocates of care ethics is Lawrence A. Blum, *Friendship, Altruism and Morality* (London: Routledge & Kegan Paul, 1980). Virginia Held's edited collection, *Justice and Care* (Boulder, Colo.: Westview Press, 1995), is an excellent collection of essays on the subject. A very good and wide-ranging anthology is Eva Feder Kittay and Diana Meyers, editors, *Women and Moral Theory* (Totowa, N.J.: Rowman & Littlefield, 1987).

Notes

[1]Nel Noddings, *Caring: A Feminine Approach to Ethics & Moral Education* (Berkeley, Calif.: University of California Press, 1984), p. 96.

[2]Quoted in Valerie P. Hans and Neil Vidmar, *Judging the Jury* (New York: Plenum Press, 1986), p. 53.

[3]Sarah Grimke, "The Pastoral Letter of the General Association of Congregational Ministers of Massachusetts, 1837," printed in David A. Hollinger and Charles Capper, editors, *The American Intellectual Tradition*, vol. 1, 4th ed. (New York: Oxford University Press, 2001), p. 274.

[4]Ariel Kay Salleh, "Working with Nature: Reciprocity or Control?" in *Environmental Philosophy: From Animal Rights to Radical Ecology*, 2nd ed., Michael E. Zimmerman, J. Baird Callicott, George Sessions, Karen J. Warren, and John Clark, editors (Upper Saddle River, N.J.: Prentice-Hall, 1998), p. 323.

[5]Jean Grimshaw, "The Idea of a Female Ethic," in *A Companion to Ethics*, Peter Singer, editor (Oxford: Blackwell, 1991), p. 498.

CHAPTER

Who counts morally? If a moral code orders "Thou shalt not kill," who is included in the scope of the commandment? That actually involves two questions. First, who is expected to *follow* the order? Second, who is *protected* by the order? Or another way of phrasing those questions: First, what is the scope of moral *agency*? Who are numbered among the moral *actors*? And second, who are the legitimate *subjects* of moral consideration, those to whom moral consideration is owed? To continue with the example, consider the range of that commandment as it is given by the Hebrew God. Obviously the commandment is to be interpreted quite narrowly, since this same God has just led the children of Israel on a campaign that destroys city after city, and all their inhabitants. So apparently the commandment applies to the children of Israel: *they* are not to kill one another.

Who Is Due Moral Consideration?

Social Contract Ethics

For social contract theorists, the answer to who counts morally seems obvious: those who count are those who enter into the contract. If you haven't agreed to the contract, then you are in a state of nature, and you are not covered by any moral rules. Those who *have* agreed to the moral rules—who have agreed to the contract—have obligations toward those who have also accepted the contract, and *no* moral obligations to those who have not. But perhaps the answer is not quite that easy. After all, social contract theorists do not believe that anyone has literally signed the contract. The contract is a myth, a story that offers a model of how morality works: we agree to act decently toward others (not rob from them or kill them) in exchange for such treatment for ourselves. So on this more sophisticated interpretation of social contract theory, who is—and who is not—covered by the contract? Under the contract model, to qualify as part of the ethical community (and as a moral agent) one must be capable of understanding and following rules. Those who lack that capacity have no moral standing. We might decide to be nice to children, to those who have become childlike due to the infirmities of age or accident, to kittens and puppies; but we have no moral *obligations* to them. (Of course if a full member of our social contract has special interest in and affection for a child, then the other full members should refrain from harming that child. But not because the child is a holder of rights. In a similar manner, other social contractors should not damage your car; but that is because of your interest in the car, not because the car has a right not to be damaged.)

Perhaps social contract theorists can find other ways of dealing with questions regarding what falls outside the scope of the social contract; but the social contract theory itself seems to be of little help for such questions. Contract theorist John Rawls explicitly recognizes this limitation: "We should recall . . . the limits of a theory of justice. Not only are many aspects of morality left aside, but no account can be given of right conduct in regard to animals and the rest of nature."[1]

Kantian Ethics

Under the Kantian model, the requirements for admission to the moral community are even more stringent. To qualify for moral consideration you must be able to use the power of reason to derive and understand the moral law, and you must follow the law *because* you recognize it as a moral imperative (and for no other motive). If you are admitted to the world of moral lawmakers, then you merit very special treatment: you are a member of the kingdom of ends, and you must always be treated as an end, never as merely a means to someone else's ends. But the gatekeeper for this moral community allows very few to pass. And notoriously, Kant has little use for you if you aren't part of the moral community. For example, he thinks there is nothing inherently wrong with torturing dogs: they have no moral standing, and we can do with them as we wish. The only reason for refraining from such acts is that it might cause the torturer to become callous, and that might lead him or her to harm some who *are* members of the moral kingdom of ends. (Consistency would seem to require that Kant also find nothing inherently wrong with torturing small children who have not yet learned to reason, or older people whom age has robbed of the capacity for abstract reason, or the unfortunates who are incapable of such reasoning.)

Tom Regan's Kantian Account of Animal Rights

Kantian ethics appears barren ground in which to sow the idea of animal rights. However, one of the leading proponents of animal rights—Tom Regan—has developed a Kantian argument that fiercely defends the rights of a broad range of nonhuman animals. Not surprisingly, turning Kantian ethics into an animal rights doctrine requires a few modifications, and the most important modification is in who counts as "ends in themselves." For Kant, the only ends in themselves are rational beings who are capable of using reason to ascertain universal ethical principles. It is wrong to treat such rational lawgivers as merely means to someone else's ends, and it is wrong to treat anyone *else* as having inherent value. But Regan claims this sets the bar too high. Why should reason be the distinguishing mark that qualifies you as worthy of moral consideration? According to Kant reason enables you to recognize and understand the truth of the moral law; but why should it follow that only those capable of such reasoning should be counted as ends in themselves?

The ability to reason about rules and principles is surely a useful capacity, and we are happy to have that ability. But why should anyone suppose that such abstract reasoning ability is the only thing that makes a life worthwhile or valuable in itself? Philosophers might favor abstract reason as the vital element for moral worth; but other equally legitimate candidates are the ability to feel affection, the ability to appreciate beauty, the ability to wire a house. No doubt some degree of abstract reasoning ability is essential for formulating a system of moral law, but why should it follow that abstract reasoning ability must be the sole criterion for moral worth? Of course if those who formalize the rules get to choose the rules, then it is not surprising that abstract reasoning ability is chosen as the standard for moral worth. But in the Kantian system, those abstract reasoners who formalize the moral law are supposed to be discovering the moral law, not drawing it up to suit themselves.

Regan proposes that in order to possess inherent worth (and be a member of the 'kingdom of ends') you need only be "the subject of a life," not a rational lawmaker. That is, you must be conscious of having a life that can go better or worse. You need not be able to place it on a graph, or reflect deeply about it, or set ultimate goals, or develop rule-governed justifications of your evaluations, or even give a verbal description of the progress of your life. You must *have* a life, and have sufficient self-awareness that you can recognize things are going well or ill.

If we adopt Regan's revision of Kantian morality, then the moral community becomes considerably more inclusive. Who has a sense of having a life that can go better or worse? Well, you do, of course. If the cafeteria hired Emeril as their head chef, your life would go considerably better. If your lover became madly attracted to your best friend, your life would go much worse. You might or might not spend a lot of time contemplating it, but you would certainly be aware of it. Who else? Obviously there are humans of all shapes, sizes, genders, and ethnic backgrounds who also meet the standard. But not only humans. Chimpanzees are certainly the subjects of lives that can go better or worse (and in the hands of some researchers, can go considerably worse). Your dog clearly finds life much better when you return home for the summer. Pigs discover that life has taken a turn for the worse when they are squeezed into huge trucks and driven to slaughter. Your gerbils have enjoyed life more since you installed the tunnels and toys for them. And even Perky, your parakeet, is quite delighted to be sitting on your shoulder, and may show clear signs of distress when you leave for the fall semester. Obviously almost all humans—including most of those who cannot formulate abstract rules—are the subjects of lives, in Regan's sense. So are chimpanzees, gorillas, dogs, mice, and pigs. Crabgrass, bacteria, and viruses are not.

Chimpanzees, humans, dogs, cats, pigs, cows, and laboratory mice have moral standing, according to Regan. They are subjects of lives that can go better or worse. But what animals fall within that range? Are walleye pikes included? Oysters? Spiders? Beetles? Where is the dividing line? That is a very difficult question, and philosophers, psychologists, and biologists might puzzle over it for many years (I think there is likely to be a large area of gray rather than a clear dividing line). But we need no clear line to recognize that the animals we subject to the greatest abuse—the pigs we eat and the chimps and mice we experiment on—fall on this side of the divide. (I can't set a precise moment when day turns into night. That's why we have the notion of twilight. But I know the difference between night and day.) Thus we have a Kantian (or neo-Kantian) moral obligation to treat many animals we now treat merely as means to our experimental or culinary ends as instead ends in themselves, with their own inherent worth. And we mustn't say that while chimpanzees may have inherent worth, they don't have as *much* inherent worth as we humans do (and thus their rights are not as strong as ours). For if we take the Kantian view, this is not a matter of degree. There are no *degrees* of moral standing. You are smarter, better at abstract reasoning, better looking, warmer and kinder, more imaginative, more industrious than I; if we are competing for a slot in medical school, you should get it. But there are no second-class members of the kingdom of ends: we are both *equally* entitled to be treated as ends, rather than merely as means to someone else's ends. You don't have greater inherent worth or stronger rights than I just because you are considerably smarter and wiser than I am. My IQ is 85, and yours is twice that; but from a Kantian perspective, you do not have twice the inherent worth I have. We both are entitled to be treated as ends, not merely as means, and we both are entitled to be treated with dignity and respect, rather than *used* as instruments.

Utilitarians and the Moral Community

Though Regan modifies Kantian ethics to encompass concern for nonhuman animals, utilitarian ethics has generally been regarded as a more congenial environment for broadened ethical consideration of other species. Utilitarians have no trouble casting a wide moral net. On the utilitarian view, the morally right act is that act that maximizes pleasure and minimizes pain for *all* who are affected. On this view, minimizing suffering is morally good, whether the suffering afflicts a human or a chimpanzee or a dog. Even Mill—who rated human pleasures as much higher *quality*, and thus more important, than the pleasures enjoyed by other animals—had no doubt that the pleasures and pains of nonhuman animals were morally significant.

Thus utilitarians count all suffering and all pleasure as morally significant, regardless of the species of the sufferer. Jeremy Bentham, the modern founder of utilitarian ethics, insisted that it doesn't matter how many legs an animal has. What matters is simply: can it suffer? If it can, it is due *moral* consideration. Suffering is suffering, and the goal of utilitarian ethics is to minimize suffering wherever it is found.

The contemporary utilitarian philosopher Peter Singer takes the same view, and argues that any attempt to count the pleasure and suffering of other species as of less moral significance is gross prejudice. You are considerably smarter, but when it comes to making the moral utilitarian calculation of what policy will minimize suffering and maximize pleasure, your pleasures and pains do not weigh more heavily than mine just because you're smarter, or better looking, or a better athlete. All of those things are (from the utilitarian perspective) irrelevant, since what counts is simply that we suffer or feel pleasure, not how smart or cute we are. If I agree that the policy I am proposing will cause you suffering, but claim your suffering should count for less because you are a woman, that would obviously be rank prejudice: your gender is irrelevant, the only question is whether you are capable of suffering. Likewise, Singer says, if you agree that your proposed policy will cause me suffering, but claim my suffering should count for less because I am not a member of your species, that is just as prejudiced and irrational a conclusion as discounting my suffering because I am of a different gender. So utilitarianism casts a wide moral net: all who are capable of feeling pleasure or pain must be *counted* in our moral decision-making.

Eastern Views

If we are looking for the most *inclusive* moral systems, we must turn to the East. Buddhist morality emphasizes the personal moral development of the individual; but this moral development process requires concern for all in the community, and for Buddhists that community embraces all living things. Perhaps the strongest insistence on moral concern for all living things comes from Jainism, a philosophical system developed around 500 BCE in India by Mahavira. Jainists insist on an uncompromising reverence for all living things, including dogs and cats and pigs, but also insects. In fact, Jainists refuse to eat root crops, such as carrots, because the plant must be killed. (Though this attitude is based on moral reverence for all living things, the concern is not *exclusively* for the living things in their own right. For Jainism, the emphasis is on self-purification, and harming any living being brings harm and corruption on oneself.)

MORAL AGENTS

Kant regards the treatment of animals as morally irrelevant, since nonhuman animals have no moral standing whatsoever. Torturing a stray dog is neither moral nor immoral; rather, for Kant it is amoral. Some social contract theorists agree, but most other ethical views—whether neo-Kantian, utilitarian, intuitionist, or emotion-based—would consider the welfare of nonhuman animals at least morally *relevant*. Thus many ethical views regard nonhuman animals as *subjects* of moral behavior. Could nonhuman animals also count as moral agents? That is, could nonhuman animals act morally or immorally?

If one is a pure Kantian, the answer is easy. Genuine ethical behavior must be driven entirely and exclusively by ethical principles derived from pure reason. No nonhuman animals (and probably very few human animals, for that matter) are capable of such rational devotion to duty, and thus they cannot act morally. But Kant sets very severe standards for what counts as *acting morally*. Kant's standards exclude from the realm of moral action many acts (for example, acts of kindness motivated by sympathy or affection) most of us would count as genuine moral acts. So for those who are not doctrinaire Kantians: What would you count as a moral act? Under what conditions does one qualify as a moral *agent*?

Moral Agency and Intent

"Acting morally" seems to require moral *intent*; but that leads to ambiguity and confusion. I can fully intend to do a generous act without intending to follow a moral rule of generosity. A Boy Scout may specifically intend to do a good deed daily; but you can perform a good deed, and do so *intentionally*, without planning to perform a morally good act. If you misplace your lunch pail, and it is found by a hungry person, then you have fed a hungry person; but it's not at all clear that you performed a moral act, since you didn't *intend* to feed the hungry. But if you see someone who is hungry, and give that person your lunch with the purpose of relieving that person's distress, then you have *intentionally* performed a morally worthy act. If we ask you about it later, you may report that you were not intending to perform a morally good act; rather, you were just intending to relieve a hungry person's suffering. But we would still say you intentionally performed what was a morally good act, and for morally worthy reasons (you wanted to relieve suffering). In fact, some might think that one who has to think about some moral rule to 'feed the hungry' is not quite as morally upright as is someone who simply strives to relieve suffering (without having to think about what *rule* that falls under). Pure Kantians would not count feeding the hungry as a moral act unless it was done purely from a sense of moral duty and moral principle, but few of us have that narrow an interpretation of moral behavior.

Almost everyone agrees that genuine moral behavior requires more than merely good results. That is a point on which Kantians and utilitarians and care theorists and virtue ethicists concur. If you save a child from toppling over the ledge, we require further inquiry before judging the act virtuous. If you are a clumsy would-be murderer who was attempting to shove the child off the ledge, the act was vicious. If your hand stretched out due to a sudden seizure the motion is fortunate but not morally significant. If you were motivated solely by hope of rich reward, then the act loses its positive moral worth. So we must look deeper than your extended hand to determine moral worth. But motives—rather than reasons—must be examined, and those motives need not stem from deliberation. If I am a vicious and mercurial but clumsy killer, my spontaneous *non*deliberative attempt to shove you from a ledge is morally vicious though it accidentally saves your life. A mother's spontaneous loving *un*reflective rescue of her child is morally virtuous: if the act is motivated by affection[2] for the child[3] the absence of deliberation does not imply absence of moral worth. (That is, *most* would count the mother's loving rescue as a moral act. Kant would not.)

Moral acts such as the rescue of children or friends require the right intent, the proper motive. To act morally I must genuinely *intend* to rescue the child. Giving a verbal account of that intent is a complicated process. *Having* the intent is comparatively simple.

Many animals, human and nonhuman, can form and act upon intentions they cannot conceptually order and explain. A hyena intends to feed upon an animal carcass, is threatened by a lion (a lion that intends to chase it away), and quickly revises its intentions in favor of safety. A male chimp carefully searches for heavy stones, weighs each in his hand, and selects the heaviest before carrying it some distance to his rival, where—holding the stone as a potential weapon—the chimp begins the long *intended* intimidation display.[4] A subordinate male chimp *intends* to mate with a female, sees the dominant male in the vicinity, and abruptly changes his intentions. Indeed, there are reports of chimps finding their amorous intentions thwarted by the presence of a dominant male and then *intentionally* feigning the intent to forage in another area in order to draw the desired mate out of the dominant's view.[5] Such intentional deception is not rare: a subordinate chimp amidst dominants may continue to "search" for food after he has found it, then later return alone to claim the treat.[6] (The hard-wired reaction of the robin to a dangerous intruder near its nest—the robin limps away from the nest, and since it appears to be easy prey the predator follows—may be classified as deceptive, but it is certainly not intentional deception; in contrast, the much more variable and flexible deceptive behavior of the chimp is intentional.) It is one thing to question the chimp's conceptual apparatus for distinguishing truth from deception; it is quite another—and much simpler—to conclude that the chimp intends to deceive; simpler still to note that the chimp intends to find food, seek cover, threaten a rival, or rescue a friend.

Rather than verbal conceptualization being a necessary condition of specific intentions, it is probably more common for the manifestation of intentions to serve as the prompt for teaching verbal categorizations of intent. Hearing the sound of breaking glass, I rush to the dining room where my child is playing. He is sitting on the floor, next to a crumpled tablecloth that covers some strange bulges.

"What happened?"

"I don't know, Daddy; there was a crash in the kitchen."

"What's under the tablecloth?"

"Oh, nothing."

When I pick up the cloth I discover a broken lamp, and reprimand my son. "Darling, accidents happen, and I know you didn't mean to pull the tablecloth down and break the lamp. But you shouldn't have tried to deceive me."

"But I wasn't trying to deceive you, Daddy. I was just trying to keep you from finding out I had broken the lamp."

"But that's what deception *is*. When you told me the crash came from the other room and you hid the broken lamp under the tablecloth, you *were* trying to deceive me. You didn't know it was *deception*; but you were intending to mislead me, and that's what it is to intentionally deceive."

In that manner my child may learn to verbally conceptualize and describe intending to deceive. But he needs no instruction in *intending* to deceive: he is quite accomplished at such intentions long before his verbal categorizations match his devious motives.

Limits to the complex conceptualization of intentions are not confined to children and nonhumans, of course. The defendant in a breaking and entering trial may rightly insist he did not intend to commit a felony (a necessary condition for being guilty of breaking and entering); all he intended was to break the window and steal the television set.[7] The defendant may lack the conceptual sophistication to intend the commission of a felony, yet be fully capable of intending and committing one: by intentionally and knowingly stealing another's property. Likewise, a chimp who is incapable of "intending to act morally" may be quite capable of intending a rescue and thereby *intentionally* performing a morally good act.

Michael Bradie claims that "Animals can act on the basis of altruistic motives but they do not and cannot form intentions to so act."[8] But in fact animals—humans and nonhumans—can act on, and intend to act on, altruistic[9] motives as well as hunger and thirst and concupiscence motives. Other animals may not conceptualize their motives quite as elegantly: they may not know they are intending to act altruistically, just as the hapless defendant may not know he intends to commit a felony. That does not bar them from forming and acting on altruistic intentions. Of course a chimpanzee cannot intend to perform an altruistic act purely because it is in the category "altruistic." That is, a chimp cannot resolve to 'do a good (altruistic) deed daily'. A chimpanzee can, however, be motivated by affection to *intend* the rescue of a friend. When a human performs such an act for identical motives, we count it a moral act. Does simple consistency require the same categorization for chimp altruism?

Humans can, as Bradie insists, form intentions to act altruistically in the strong sense of intending to do an altruistic deed *because* it falls under the altruistic classification. Other animals cannot. But that does not preclude other animals performing genuinely altruistic moral acts. In fact, the wonders of (uniquely human) decisions to do altruistic moral acts because they are altruistic are greatly exaggerated. Humans do occasionally form such intentions—"I will do a good altruistic deed this day"—though such elaborate moral machinations are rare and exotic exceptions among common everyday moral behavior. And except to Kantians, they are not a source of moral delight and wonderment. "Why did you rescue me?" "What a question; you're my friend; when I saw you in danger, my affection for you immediately prompted me to rush to your rescue." Compare that to: "Why did you rescue me?" "It was an act of altruism; and I always strive to do an altruistic deed daily." The latter may be a moral act, but it is not quintessentially moral, and it is certainly not moral to the exclusion of the former. Proper intent is essential for moral behavior; reasoned deliberation is not (unless you are a strict Kantian). If reasoned deliberation were essential for moral behavior, that would indeed exclude nonhumans from moral behavior, along with a substantial part of what we normally consider moral behavior by humans. The Kantian will applaud such narrowing of the moral sphere, but it is not a narrowing required by other views of ethics.

An Experiment in Moral Agency

Imagine you are imprisoned in a glass cubicle, that you have been deprived of food for a couple of days, and you are desperately hungry. You can see another person who is also imprisoned in another glass cubicle; but apparently you are looking through a one-way mirror, for although you can see and hear this person, he cannot see or hear you, and so you have no means of communicating with him. Finally your jailer brings you food. Indeed, a very attractive and delicious buffet is spread before you. You immediately rush to the table and begin to eat, but you are stopped by a scream coming from the other cubicle. As you started to eat, the person imprisoned in the other cubicle apparently was given a severely painful electrical shock. You take another bite, and the other person again screams in pain. You soon realize that your jailers have arranged things so that if you satisfy your hunger, the stranger in the other cubicle will suffer severe pain during the process. You don't think deeply about it, or formulate a rule, or run a utilitarian calculation; but you put down your plate, and tempting as the food is you refuse to eat more. The food remains before your hungry eyes for many hours, but you never eat. Are you acting morally?

Most of us would say you have indeed acted morally, perhaps even heroically. You did not refuse the food by accident (it wasn't as if you simply never noticed it in your cell). Rather, you purposefully refrained from eating because you did not want someone else to suffer. You didn't base your acts on Kantian reason, or utilitarian calculations, but you purposefully deprived yourself of considerable pleasure (and the relief of your own hunger pains) in order to prevent the suffering of another. And you had no ulterior motive: you weren't expecting to win a gold star for good morality, or a large monetary award from the person you saved from suffering (you don't know the other person, and have no idea whether you will ever encounter that person again). Though a pure Kantian would want to know more before deciding that you acted morally—did you refuse food strictly from duty, or did you instead merely feel sympathy for the other person?—most of us would have no trouble in swiftly concluding that your act was a positive and virtuous *moral act*.

It turns out that this experiment has been done.[10] But the persons involved were rhesus monkeys, rather than humans. And though some hungry monkeys ate the food, a significant number did not. Was the behavior of the rhesus monkeys moral? A *nonreflective human* who refused food under such circumstances—with the intention of preventing the suffering of her fellows—would be considered to have acted morally (by all except the most doctrinaire Kantians). If the cases are analogous, should we draw the same conclusion about the rhesus monkey?

Arguments Against Nonhuman Moral Agency

A quick and easy answer to this argument is available: the rhesus monkeys are not humans, so their behavior cannot be moral. That is a quick and easy answer that has (as Bertrand Russell once phrased it) all the advantages of theft over honest labor. The question we are examining is whether nonhuman animals *could* behave morally. Starting with the assumption they cannot does not take us very far in that inquiry. If we say the rhesus monkeys could *not* act morally, because they are not humans *and* only humans have souls and souls are required for moral behavior, then at least that argument does not beg the question. Still, it does not shed much light on the issue. It is notoriously difficult to get a clear notion of what a soul might be, and in any case, it is not at all clear that if humans have souls then monkeys do not. Neither is it clear why having a soul is a necessity for moral behavior. Perhaps a soul is necessary for immortality, but can only the immortals act morally?

There is another closely related argument against counting nonhuman behavior as moral. If a mother—human, chimp, or feline—caresses a distressed and crying infant, she (most commonly) *intends* to comfort it. Povinelli and Godfrey disparage such comforting as merely the mother seeking relief from the discomfort caused by the infant's crying. For example:

> Chimpanzees show patterns of behavior that appear, from a psychological perspective, only weakly altruistic. Much of what might qualify as chimpanzee altruism may be based on the arousal of feelings of emotional distress in the helper, perhaps through emotional contagion, and the role of social attribution is unclear when helping is prompted by emotional contagion.[11]

But while 'feelings of distress' may certainly be aroused in the mother, it is still generally the case that the mother genuinely *intends* to relieve the infant's distress. Were her motive only the relief of her own 'emotional contagion' discomfort, the purpose might be achieved more readily by moving out of earshot or tossing the infant from a high branch.

Given the ease of escape from 'the emotional contagion' of distress, it is hardly plausible that 'apparent altruism' is caused by the "altruistic" helper's self-interest in reducing his or her own suffering. But just as it is invoked by Povinelli and Godfrey to explain away "chimpanzee altruism," so also it has been a favorite psychological explanation for apparent acts of human altruism. Social psychologists call this the "aversive-arousal reduction" account of altruism: a sufferer arouses aversive feelings among those nearby, and in order to reduce their own aroused discomfort they attempt to aid the sufferer. Such aid is (as Batson[12] characterizes it) more "pseudoaltruistic" than genuinely altruistic, since the motive of the aid giver is relief of his or her own distress (when such reduction of aversive stimuli is most conveniently achieved by giving aid).

In a series of cleverly designed experiments, Daniel Batson has demonstrated the implausibility of the popular aversive-arousal reduction account of "altruism." Batson and other researchers have shown that the behavior *predicted* by the aversive-arousal reduction hypothesis simply does not occur. For example, if the hypothesis were correct, then when escape behavior becomes increasingly easy (escape is one way of reducing the supposed aversive arousal from another's suffering) subjects should help less and escape more. But in fact ease of escape has no influence on willingness to help another in distress.[13]

So the aversive-arousal reduction hypothesis fails to account for the altruistic behavior of animals, including human animals. But the fact that it is so readily embraced as an explanation is significant in its own right, for it reveals a good deal about some insidiously influential assumptions. Suppose I am suffering, and that my suffering makes you feel bad (through "emotional contagion"); it need not follow that your efforts to relieve my suffering are directed exclusively at the reduction of your *own* suffering. That may be one of your motives, but another motive—alongside the first, and not in conflict with the first, nor lessened nor cheapened nor "pseudofied" due to the presence of the first—may be the genuinely altruistic motive of relieving *my* suffering. Indeed, it should be rather surprising if in most instances altruistic behavior were motivated purely by either such motive, rather than a combination of the two. Why should there be such a strong temptation—among philosophers, and even among some social psychologists—to draw such a radical distinction between them? The motive of the social psychologist may be innocent enough: setting up artificial distinctions is necessary in order to test competing hypotheses. But why should philosophers assume that being motivated by 'emotional contagion' *excludes* the influence of genuine altruism? Lurking in the philosophical shadows is the ghost of Kant. Only from a Kantian assumption that a genuinely moral act must be done *purely* from duty (and not at all from inclination) could it seem that a genuine act of altruistic virtue is fatally contaminated by any taint of pleasure or pain reduction or inclination for oneself.

The Kantian view is designed to set moral behavior—particularly rule-governed, duty-driven, human rational moral behavior—dramatically apart from the natural world. It secures for humanity a special god-like sphere *apart* from other animals. But it achieves that radical separation at a high cost. If your motive in rescuing me is purely to perform a dutiful deed, then I may be glad of being rescued, but I shall hardly regard your motives as purer or nobler or more virtuous than the motives of one who rushes to my rescue from immediate affection and heartfelt concern for my welfare, with no dutiful deliberations entering into it.

There is a competitor to the Kantian moral tradition that is more easily accommodated into the natural world and the actual behavior of humans and other animals: to be virtuous is to be moved by the right sorts of concerns and affections and revulsions. One who takes genuine delight in the pleasures of others and feels deep sympathy with the sufferings of others is a Kantian moral cipher, but perhaps a moral hero for Aristotle or Hume. If you rescue me or feed me or house me because it would cause you great sorrow to know I am suffering, that need not be a 'pseudoaltruistic' motive: you are genuinely aiming to relieve *my* suffering. Likewise, if making others happy is a source of genuine joy for you, then you are still striving to make others happy. That your activities also bring you joy does not mean you are primarily seeking your own selfish pleasure, nor does it lessen your genuine striving for the happiness of others. Playing tennis makes me happy, but I don't play tennis in order to be happy. I play tennis because I want to play tennis. If you offered me the happiness, but without the bother of playing tennis, I should think that no bargain. Likewise, a virtuous person who is made happy by bringing joy to others is acting altruistically (not pseudoaltruistically). If she were offered the experience of joy but without the bother of helping others, she would find it a poor and detestable offer. She takes great joy in helping others, but she does not help others in order to make herself joyful. (Of course should she become depressed, and her kind acts no longer bring her any pleasure, her kind behavior might eventually extinguish; but the fact that her pleasure holds her altruistic behavior steadily in force does *not* imply that her altruism is actually *aimed* at her own pleasure.)

DARWIN AND THE MORAL STATUS OF NONHUMAN ANIMALS

Those who believe animals are moral beings, or at the very least have moral standing (are moral *subjects*), generally oppose the use of animals for research. But that is not because they are "antiresearch," or because they doubt the value of such research. Rather, it is because they believe that the treatment of animals as mere means to our ends is wrong. It would also be valuable to use *humans* any way we wish in conducting scientific research, with no concern for their safety or their interests. That would no doubt be a great benefit for scientific research, but the fact that we would regard such policies as morally loathsome does not imply an antiresearch bias.

Scientists often want to draw a strict line between human research and nonhuman research. Human research must be tightly regulated and restricted: you can't just experiment on a human because you have a special research project you want to pursue, without regard to the interests of the human research subjects, and that rule applies even if the research project is very valuable and beneficial. But such a strict line between humans (who have moral capacities and are ends in themselves) and nonhumans (who are regarded as not themselves moral beings but instead merely as things that may be treated as means to our ends) is inconsistent with contemporary evolutionary science. As Michael Ruse points out:

> Darwinism insists that features evolve gradually, and something as important as morality should have been present in our (very recent) shared ancestors. Furthermore, if morality is as important biologically to humans as is being claimed, it would be odd indeed had all traces now been eliminated from the social interactions of other high-level primates.[14]

Thus from the perspective of contemporary science, there is no clear moral gap between humans and other species.

If ethics is essentially Kantian, then it is silly to include animals. If ethics is utilitarian, we can include animals as ethical objects, but perhaps not as ethical actors (who make careful calculations). If ethics is a natural, nontranscendent phenomenon, rooted in affections, then its roots are shared with other animals.

THE DESCENT OF MAN

Charles Darwin

Charles Darwin lived in England from 1809 to 1892. Though he is often described as having developed 'the theory of evolution,' in fact there were evolutionary theories (such as LaMarck's) well before Darwin's. His distinctive contribution was his 'theory of natural selection,' which provided a mechanistic account of how evolution proceeds. He described his theory in two great books, *The Origin of Species* and *The Descent of Man*.

CHAPTER IV.

COMPARISON OF THE MENTAL POWERS OF MAN AND THE LOWER ANIMALS—*continued*.

I subscribe to the judgment of those writers who maintain that of all the differences between man and the lower animals, the moral sense or conscience is by far the most important. This sense, as Mackintosh remarks, "has a rightful supremacy over every other principle of human action;" it is summed up in that short but imperious word *ought*, so full of high significance. It is the most noble of all the attributes of man, leading him without a moment's hesitation to risk his life for that of a fellow-creature; or after due deliberation, impelled simply by the deep feeling of right or duty, to sacrifice it in some great cause. Immanuel Kant exclaims, "Duty! Wondrous thought, that workest neither by fond insinuation, flattery, nor by any threat, but merely by holding up thy naked law in the soul, and so extorting for thyself always

reverence, if not always obedience; before whom all appetites are dumb, however secretly they rebel; whence thy original?"

This great question has been discussed by many writers of consummate ability; and my sole excuse for touching on it, is the impossibility of here passing it over; and because, as far as I know, no one has approached it exclusively from the side of natural history. The investigation possesses, also, some independent interest, as an attempt to see how far the study of the lower animals throws light on one of the highest psychical faculties of man.

The following proposition seems to me in a high degree probable—namely, that any animal whatever, endowed with well-marked social instincts, the parental and filial affections being here included, would inevitably acquire a moral sense or conscience, as soon as its intellectual powers had become as well, or nearly as well developed, as in man. For, *firstly*, the social instincts lead an animal to take pleasure in the society of its fellows, to feel a certain amount of sympathy with them, and to perform various services for them. The services may be of a definite and evidently instinctive nature; or there may be only a wish and readiness, as with most of the higher social animals, to aid their fellows in certain general ways. But these feelings and services are by no means extended to all the individuals of the same species, only to those of the same association. *Secondly,* as soon as the mental faculties had become highly developed, images of all past actions and motives would be incessantly passing through the brain of each individual: and that feeling of dissatisfaction, or even misery, which invariably results, as we shall hereafter see, from any unsatisfied instinct, would arise, as often as it was perceived that the enduring and always present social instinct had yielded to some other instinct, at the time stronger, but neither enduring in its nature, nor leaving behind it a very vivid impression. It is clear that many instinctive desires, such as that of hunger, are in their nature of short duration; and after being satisfied, are not readily or vividly recalled. *Thirdly,* after the power of language had been acquired, and the wishes of the community could be expressed, the common opinion how each member ought to act for the public good, would naturally become in a paramount degree the guide to action. But it should be borne in mind that however great weight we may attribute to public opinion, our regard for the approbation and disapprobation of our fellows depends on sympathy, which, as we shall see, forms an essential part of the social instinct, and is indeed its foundation-stone. *Lastly,* habit in the individual would ultimately play a very important part in guiding the conduct of each member; for the social instinct, together with sympathy, is, like any other instinct, greatly strengthened by habit, and so consequently would be obedience to the wishes and judgment of the community. These several subordinate propositions must now be discussed, and some of them at considerable length.

It may be well first to premise that I do not wish to maintain that any strictly social animal, if its intellectual faculties were to become as active and as highly developed as in man, would acquire exactly the same moral sense as ours. In the same manner as various animals have some sense of beauty, though they admire widely different objects, so they might have a sense of right and wrong, though led by it to follow widely different lines of conduct. If, for instance, to take an extreme case, men were reared under precisely the same conditions as hive-bees, there can hardly be a doubt that our unmarried females would, like the worker-bees, think it a sacred duty to kill their brothers, and mothers would strive to kill their fertile daughters; and no one would think of interfering. Nevertheless, the bee, or any other social animal, would gain in our supposed case, as it appears to me, some feeling of right or wrong, or a conscience. For each individual would have an inward sense of possessing certain stronger or more enduring instincts, and others less strong or enduring; so that there would often be a struggle as to which impulse should be followed; and satisfaction, dissatisfaction, or even misery would be felt, as past impressions were compared during their incessant passage through the mind. In this case an inward monitor would tell the animal that it would have been better to have followed the one impulse rather than the other. The one course ought to have been followed, and the other ought not; the one would have been right and the other wrong; but to these terms I shall recur.

The more enduring Social Instincts conquer the less persistent Instincts.—We have not, however, as yet considered the main point, on which, from our present point of view, the whole question of the moral sense turns. Why should a man feel that he ought to obey one instinctive desire rather than another? Why is he bitterly regretful, if he has yielded to a strong sense of self-preservation, and has not risked his life to save that of a fellow-creature? or why does he regret having stolen food from hunger?

It is evident in the first place, that with mankind the instinctive impulses have different degrees of strength; a savage will risk his own life to save that of a member of the same community, but will be wholly indifferent about a stranger: a young and timid mother urged by the maternal instinct will, without a moment's hesitation, run the greatest danger for her own infant, but not for a mere fellow-creature. Nevertheless many a civilized man, or even boy, who never before risked his life for another, but full of courage and sympathy, has disregarded the instinct of self-preservation, and plunged at once into a torrent to save a drowning man, though a stranger. In this case man is impelled by the same instinctive motive, which made the heroic little American monkey, formerly described, save his keeper, by attacking the great and dreaded baboon. Such actions as the above appear to the simple result of the greater strength of the social or maternal instincts than that of any other instinct or motive; for they are performed too instantaneously for reflection, or for pleasure or pain to be felt at the time; though, if prevented by any cause, distress or even misery might be felt. In a timid man, on the other hand, the instinct of self-preservation might be so strong, that he would be unable to force himself to run any such risk, perhaps not even for his own child.

I am aware that some persons maintain that actions performed impulsively, as in the above cases, do not come under the dominion of the moral sense, and cannot be called moral. They confine this term to actions done deliberately, after a victory over opposing desires, or when prompted by some exalted motive. But it appears scarcely possible to draw any clear line of distinction of this kind. As far as exalted motives are concerned, many instances have been recorded of savages, destitute of any feeling of general benevolence towards mankind, and not guided by any religious motive, who have deliberately sacrificed their lives as prisoners, rather than betray their comrades; and surely their conduct ought to be considered as moral. As far as deliberation, and the victory over opposing motives are concerned, animals may be seen doubting between opposed instincts, in rescuing their offspring or comrades from danger; yet their actions, though done for the good of others, are not called moral. Moreover, anything performed very often by us, will at last be done without deliberation or hesitation, and can then hardly be distinguished from an instinct; yet surely no one will pretend that such an action ceases to be moral. On the contrary, we all feel that an act cannot be considered as perfect, or as performed in the most noble manner, unless it be done impulsively, without deliberation or effort, in the same manner as by a man in whom the requisite qualities are innate. He who is forced to overcome his fear or want of sympathy before he acts, deserves, however, in one way higher credit than the man whose innate disposition leads him to a good act without effort. As we cannot distinguish between motives, we rank all actions of a certain class as moral, if per-

formed by a moral being. A moral being is one who is capable of comparing his past and future actions or motives, and of approving or disapproving of them. We have no reason to suppose that any of the lower animals have this capacity; therefore, when a Newfoundland dog drags a child out of the water, or a monkey faces danger to rescue its comrade, or takes charge of an orphan monkey, we do not call its conduct moral. But in the case of man, who alone can with certainty be ranked as a moral being, actions of a certain class are called moral, whether performed deliberately, after a struggle with opposing motives, or impulsively through instinct, or from the effects of slowly-gained habit.

But to return to our more immediate subject. Although some instincts are more powerful than others, and thus lead to corresponding actions, yet it is untenable, that in man the social instincts (including the love of praise and fear of blame) possess greater strength, or have, through long habit, acquired greater strength than the instincts of self-preservation, hunger, lust, vengeance, &c. Why then does man regret, even though trying to banish such regret, that he has followed the one natural impulse rather than the other; and why does he further feel that he ought to regret his conduct? Man in this respect differs profoundly from the lower animals. Nevertheless we can, I think, see with some degree of clearness the reason of this difference.

Man, from the activity of his mental faculties, cannot avoid reflection: past impressions and images are incessantly and clearly passing through his mind. Now with those animals which live permanently in a body, the social instincts are ever present and persistent. Such animals are always ready to utter the danger-signal, to defend the community, and to give aid to their fellows in accordance with their habits; they feel at all times, without the stimulus of any special passion or desire, some degree of love and sympathy for them; they are unhappy if long separated from them, and always happy to be again in their company. So it is with ourselves. Even when we are quite alone, how often do we think with pleasure or pain of what others think of us,—of their imagined approbation or disapprobation; and this all follows from sympathy, a fundamental element of the social instincts. A man who possessed no trace of such instincts would be an unnatural monster. On the other hand, the desire to satisfy hunger, or any passion such as vengeance, is in its nature temporary, and can for a time be fully satisfied. Nor is it easy, perhaps hardly possible, to call up with complete vividness the feeling, for instance, of hunger; nor indeed, as has often been remarked, of any suffering. The instinct of self-preservation is not felt except in the presence of danger; and many a coward has thought himself brave until he has met his enemy face to face. The wish for another man's property is perhaps as persistent a desire as any that can be named; but even in this case the satisfaction of actual possession is generally a weaker feeling than the desire: many a thief, if not a habitual one, after success has wondered why he stole some article.

A man cannot prevent past impressions often repassing through his mind; he will thus be driven to make a comparison between the impressions of past hunger, vengeance satisfied, or danger shunned at other men's cost, with the almost ever-present instinct of sympathy, and with his early knowledge of what others consider as praiseworthy or blameable. This knowledge cannot be banished from his mind, and from instinctive sympathy is esteemed of great moment. He will then feel as if he had been baulked in following a present instinct or habit, and this with all animals causes dissatisfaction, or even misery.

At the moment of action, man will no doubt be apt to follow the stronger impulse; and though this may occasionally prompt him to the noblest deeds, it will more commonly lead him to gratify his own desires at the expense of other men. But after their gratification when past and weaker impressions are judged by the ever-enduring social instinct, and by his deep regard for the good opinion of his fellows, retribution will surely come. He will then feel remorse, repentance, regret, or shame; this latter feeling, however, relates almost exclusively to the judgment of others. He will consequently resolve more or less firmly to act differently for the future; and this is conscience; for conscience looks backwards, and serves as a guide for the future.

The nature and strength of the feelings which we call regret, shame, repentance or remorse, depend apparently not only on the strength of the violated instinct, but partly on the strength of the temptation, and often still more on the judgment of our fellows. How far each man values the appreciation of others, depends on the strength of his innate or acquired feel-

ing of sympathy; and on his own capacity for reasoning out the remote consequences of his acts. Another element is most important, although not necessary, the reverence or fear of the Gods, or Spirits believed in by each man: and this applies especially in cases of remorse. Several critics have objected that though some slight regret or repentance may be explained by the view advocated in this chapter, it is impossible thus to account for the soul-shaking feeling of remorse. But I can see little force in this objection. My critics do not define what they mean by remorse, and I can find no definition implying more than an overwhelming sense of repentance. Remorse seems to bear the same relation to repentance, as rage does to anger, or agony to pain. It is far from strange that an instinct so strong and so generally admired, as maternal love, should, if disobeyed, lead to the deepest misery, as soon as the impression of the past cause of disobedience is weakened. Even when an action is opposed to no special instinct, merely to know that our friends and equals despise us for it is enough to cause great misery.

Man prompted by his conscience, will through long habit acquire such perfect self-command, that his desires and passions will at last yield instantly and without a struggle to his social sympathies and instincts, including his feeling for the judgment of his fellows. The still hungry, or the still revengeful man will not think of stealing food, or of wreaking his vengeance. It is possible, or as we shall hereafter see, even probable, that the habit of self-command may, like other habits, be inherited. Thus at last man comes to feel, through acquired and perhaps inherited habit, that it is best for him to obey his more persistent impulses. The imperious word *ought* seems merely to imply the consciousness of the existence of a rule of conduct, however it may have originated. Formerly it must have been often vehemently urged that an insulted gentleman *ought* to fight a duel. We even say that a pointer *ought* to point, and a retriever to retrieve game. If they fail to do so, they fail in their duty and act wrongly.

If any desire or instinct leading to an action opposed to the good of others still appears, when recalled to mind, as strong as, or stronger than, the social instinct, a man will feel no keen regret at having followed it; but he will be conscious that if his conduct were known to his fellows, it would meet with their disapprobation; and few are so destitute of sympathy as not to feel discomfort when this is realised.

Finally the social instincts, which no doubt were acquired by man as by the lower animals for the good of the community, will from the first have given to him some wish to aid his fellows, some feeling of sympathy, and have compelled him to regard their approbation and disapprobation. Such impulses will have served him at a very early period as a rude rule of right and wrong. But as man gradually advanced in intellectual power, and was enabled to trace the more remote consequences of his actions; as he acquired sufficient knowledge to reject baneful customs and superstitions; as he regarded more and more, not only the welfare, but the happiness of his fellow-men; as from habit, following on beneficial experience, instruction and example, his sympathies became more tender and widely diffused, extending to men of all races, to the imbecile, maimed, and other useless members of society, and finally to the lower animals,—so would the standard of his morality rise higher and higher. And it is admitted by moralists of the derivative school and by some intuitionists, that the standard of morality has risen since an early period in the history of man.

As a struggle may sometimes be seen going on between the various instincts of the lower animals, it is not surprising that there should be a struggle in man between his social instincts, with their derived virtues, and his lower, though momentarily stronger impulses or desires. This, as Mr. Galton has remarked, is all the less surprising, as man has emerged from a state of barbarism within a comparatively recent period. After having yielded to some temptation we feel a sense of dissatisfaction, shame, repentance, or remorse, analogous to the feelings caused by other powerful instincts or desires, when left unsatisfied or baulked. We compare the weakened impression of a past temptation with the ever present social instincts, or with habits, gained in early youth and strengthened during our whole lives, until they have become almost as strong as instincts. If with the temptation still before us we do not yield, it is because either the social instinct or some custom is at the moment predominant, or because we have learnt that it will appear to us hereafter the stronger, when compared with the weakened impression of the temptation, and

we realise that its violation would cause us suffering. Looking to future generations, there is no cause to fear that the social instincts will grow weaker, and we may expect that virtuous habits will grow stronger, becoming perhaps fixed by inheritance. In this case the struggle between our higher and lower impulses will be less severe, and virtue will be triumphant.

There can be no doubt that the difference between the mind of the lowest man and that of the highest animal is immense. An anthropomorphous ape, if he could take a dispassionate view of his own case, would admit that though he could form an artful plan to plunder a garden—though he could use stones for fighting or for breaking open nuts, yet that the thought of fashioning a stone into a tool was quite beyond his scope. Still less, as he would admit, could he follow out a train of metaphysical reasoning, or solve a mathematical problem, or reflect on God, or admire a grand natural scene. Some apes, however, would probably declare that they could and did admire the beauty of the coloured skin and fur of their partners in marriage. They would admit, that though they could make other apes understand by cries some of their perceptions and simpler wants, the notion of expressing definite ideas by definite sounds had never crossed their minds. They might insist that they were ready to aid their fellow-apes of the same troop in many ways, to risk their lives for them, and to take charge of their orphans; but they would be forced to acknowledge that disinterested love for all living creatures, the most noble attribute of man, was quite beyond their comprehension.

Nevertheless the difference in mind between man and the higher animals, great as it is, certainly is one of degree and not of kind. We have seen that the senses and intuitions, the various emotions and faculties, such as love, memory, attention, curiosity, imitation, reason, &c., of which man boasts, may be found in an incipient, or even sometimes in a well-developed condition, in the lower animals. They are also capable of some inherited improvement, as we see in the domestic dog compared with the wolf or jackal. If it could be proved that certain high mental powers, such as the formation of general concepts, self-consciousness, &c., were absolutely peculiar to man, which seems extremely doubtful, it is not improbable that these qualities are merely the incidental results of other highly-advanced intellectual faculties; and these again mainly the result of the continued use of a perfect language. At what age does the newborn infant possess the power of abstraction, or become self-conscious, and reflect on its own existence? We cannot answer; nor can we answer in regard to the ascending organic scale. The half-art, half-instinct of language still bears the stamp of its gradual evolution. The ennobling belief in God is not universal with man; and the belief in spiritual agencies naturally follows from other mental powers.

The moral sense perhaps affords the best and highest distinction between man and the lower animals; but I need say nothing on this head, as I have so lately endeavoured to shew that the social instincts,—the prime principle of man's moral constitution—with the aid of active intellectual powers and the effects of habit, naturally lead to the golden rule, "As ye would that men should do to you, do ye to them likewise;" and this lies at the foundation of morality.

EXERCISES

1. As an intelligent and scientifically literate person, you recognize the human species is very closely connected to other species. Yet you may be very skeptical of the idea that other species could be ethical actors, and perhaps even skeptical that nonhuman animals have any moral standing whatsoever. If so, what distinct step in the human evolutionary process sets humans apart in their special and unique moral status?

2. Think back to social contract ethics. Is there any plausible way for an animal rights advocate to favor some variety of social contract theory?

3. If studies showed that vegetarians are *healthier*—they live longer and suffer fewer diseases—would that provide any support for the claim that killing animals for food is morally wrong? Would it count against the claim that eating meat is *natural?*

4. The dominant Christian view is that nonhuman animals have no moral standing, and certainly do not qualify as moral agents. But there is one remarkable exception to that rule: St. Francis of Assisi. (St. Francis was such a striking exception that many in the Church campaigned—unsuccessfully—to have him declared a heretic. His views are recognized as part of orthodox Roman Catholic belief, and the Franciscan Order—which he founded—promotes his teachings.) St. Francis was well-known for preaching to the birds and animals, and his views are honored in the annual blessing of the animals. One famous event in his life involves a large and ferocious wolf: a wolf that was terrorizing a small village, and had killed a number of its residents. St. Francis spoke to the wolf, the wolf repented of his sinful acts, and was buried in consecrated ground. One may have doubts about some of the details, but the point is that according to this traditional account, the wolf was certainly a moral *agent:* a moral agent who did wrong, and then reformed and lived a good moral life. So: must orthodox Catholics hold that nonhuman animals are not only moral *subjects,* but can—at least in some instances—be moral *agents?*

5. Darwin speaks highly of Kant's writings on ethics; what do you think Kant would say about Darwin's ethical views?

ADDITIONAL READING

There are a number of excellent books that address the implications of Darwinian evolution for ethics, and for our relation to other species. Among the best are: Jeffrie G. Murphy, *Evolution, Morality, and the Meaning of Life* (Totowa, N.J.: Rowman and Littlefield,

1982); James Rachels, *Created from Animals: The Moral Implications of Darwinism* (Oxford: Oxford University Press, 1990); Michael Ruse, *Taking Darwin Seriously* (Oxford: Basil Blackwell, 1986); and Peter Singer, *The Expanding Circle* (New York: Farrar, Straus & Giroux, 1981). Good anthologies on the subject include *Evolutionary Ethics*, Matthew H. Nitecki and Doris V. Nitecki, editors (Albany, N.Y.: SUNY Press, 1993); *Issues in Evolutionary Ethics*, Paul Thompson, editor (Albany, N.Y.: SUNY Press, 1995); and *Evolutionary Origins of Morality*, Leonard D. Katz, editor (Thorverton, UK: Exeter Imprint Academic, 2000).

Frans de Waal has written a number of fascinating books that explore in detail the behavior of other primate species, including the possibility of moral acts by nonhuman primates; see especially his *Chimpanzee Politics* (London: Jonathan Cape, 1982); *Peacemaking Among Primates* (Cambridge, Mass.: Harvard University Press, 1989); and *Good Natured: The Origins of Right and Wrong in Humans and Other Animals* (Cambridge, Mass.: Harvard University Press, 1996).

Notes

[1] John Rawls, *A Theory of Justice* (Oxford University Press: Oxford, 1972), p. 512.

[2] Of course there is a "deeper" cause for such solicitude: the preservation of one's genetic legacy. But though that may be the ultimate cause, it does not alter or diminish the genuine selfless concern for the child. Genetic preservation may cause my love, but the rush to rescue is no less motivated by genuine love for the child. (Genetic preservation also fuels my sex drive, but my passion is not directed at the preservation of my genes.) Even if solicitude has its origins in "selfish genes," that does not diminish its genuine moral value. Frans de Waal offers an apt analogy:

> Even if a diamond owes its beauty to millions of years of crushing pressure, we rarely think of this fact when admiring the gem. So why should we let the ruthlessness of natural selection distract from the wonders it has produced? Humans and other animals have been endowed with a capacity for genuine love, sympathy, and care—a fact that can and will one day be fully reconciled with the idea that genetic self-promotion drives the evolutionary process. *Good Natured: The Origins of Right and Wrong in Humans and Other Animals* (Cambridge, Mass.: Harvard University Press, 1996), pp. 16–17.

[3] A similar point is made by Lawrence Blum in his account of "direct altruism":

> The direct altruism view means to express a kind of virtue which does not depend on moral reflectiveness or self-consciousness. It depends only on being responsive to the weal and woe of others. . . . The compassionate or kind person does not necessarily or typically act in order to be virtuous. . . . He need not *aim* at being kind or compassionate. . . . What is necessary is only that he aim to meet the other's need, relieve her suffering, etc. *Friendship, Altruism and Morality* (London: Routledge & Kegan Paul,1980), p. 100

[4] Frans de Waal, *Peacemaking Among Primates* (Cambridge, Mass.: Harvard University Press, 1989), p. 39.

[5] Frans de Waal, *Chimpanzee Politics* (London: Jonathan Cape, 1982), pp. 48ff.

[6] Frans de Waal, 1982, pp. 73–74.

[7] This is an example of the confusions and complications that can grow in contexts of referential opacity; see Willard van Orman Quine, *Word & Object* (Cambridge, Mass.: MIT Press,1960).

[8]Michael Bradie, *The Secret Chain: Evolution and Ethics* (Albany, N.Y.: SUNY Press, 1994), p. 136.

[9]Lawrence Blum (1980, pp. 9–10) uses "altruism" in the sense of "a regard for the good of another person for his own sake, or conduct motivated by such a regard." As he notes, this usage does not require that altruism involve self-sacrifice.

[10]The research is described in Jules H. Masserman, Stanley Wechkin, and William Tetris, "'Altruistic' Behavior in Rhesus Monkeys," *American Journal of Psychiatry*, 121: 584–585.

[11]Daniel J. Povinelli and Laurie R. Godfrey, "The Chimpanzee's Mind: How Noble in Reason? How Absent of Ethics?" In *Evolutionary Ethics*, Matthew H. Nitecki and Doris V. Nitecki, editors (Albany, N.Y.: SUNY Press, 1993), p. 310.

[12]C. Daniel Batson, *The Altruism Question: Toward a Social-Psychological Answer* (Hillsdale, N.J.: Lawrence Erlbaum, 1991), pp. 43ff.

[13]Batson, 1991, pp. 109–127.

[14]Ruse, 1986, p. 227. Frans de Waal (1996, p. 210) makes a similar point:

A chimpanzee stroking and patting a victim of attack or sharing her food with a hungry companion shows attitudes that are hard to distinguish from those of a person picking up a crying child, or doing volunteer work in a soup kitchen. To classify the chimpanzee's behavior as based on instinct and the person's behavior as proof of moral decency is misleading, and probably incorrect. First of all, it is uneconomic in that it assumes different processes for similar behavior in two closely related species.

CHAPTER 10

◆ ETHICAL ◆ NONOBJECTIVISM

We have looked at a variety of ways people have tried to find—or create—ethical standards. Perhaps one of those methods, or some combination of them, or some system we haven't examined will establish ethical truths. But there is another possibility: there are no ethical truths. Science may establish facts, but in ethics there are no facts to discover. There are neither transcendent nor natural moral facts. (Nonobjectivists may allow the possibility of *synthetic* moral facts: that is, the "moral facts" created synthetically by social contracts. We adopt a rule in our contract that it is wrong to steal, so in our society it is wrong to steal. But nonobjectivists would not regard that as an *objective* moral fact. Moral nonobjectivists would say: "True, in your society you have a rule that stealing is wrong; but that doesn't show that stealing is in fact wrong. And if tomorrow you adopted a rule that stealing is right, that would not make the legitimacy of theft a moral fact. You may establish *rules* by force or referendum, but you can't legislate moral *facts* any more than you can legislate biological or astronomical or chemical facts.")

The Nature of Ethical Nonobjectivism

Nonobjectivism Is Not Neutral

Note that nonobjectivism is not a neutral position. Nonobjectivists claim that there are *not* objective moral truths. The skeptic maintains that neither side has proved its case, and she can sit quietly, waiting for someone to offer her proof. The nonobjectivist has a case to make, and the case is not an easy one. After all, most people are firmly convinced there *are* objective moral facts: Slavery is morally wrong, it is and always was and always will be morally wrong. If tomorrow we passed a law making slavery legal, that would not eliminate the moral wrongness of slavery; instead, the moral fact that slavery is wrong would make the new law morally wrong. Bringing books and flowers and encouragement to a hospitalized friend is objectively right. Perhaps in another culture one would bring some other present, or write a poem or sing a song; but caring for a friend—however that care may be manifested in different settings—is morally good, and that's a fact. The nonobjectivist must explain away such supposed moral facts.

Noncognitivism

In recent years many nonobjectivists marched under the banner of *noncognitivism* or *emotivism*. Noncognitivists claimed such assertions as "stealing is wrong" or "generosity is a virtue" were not real statements at all; that is, they did not make real claims and were not true or false. Instead, such sentences *express* approval or disapproval. They are really saying: "Go generosity!" or "Down with stealing!" Or alternatively, they are imperatives, rather than statements: "Don't steal!" If I say to you "Please close the door," or "Go Steelers," it wouldn't make sense for you to ask: "Is that true?" (You could ask whether I am sincere. Perhaps I really don't like the Steelers, and am simply afraid to cheer for the Browns in the midst of belligerent Steelers fans. But it makes no sense to ask whether "Go Steelers" is *true*.) Likewise (according to the noncognitivists) it makes no sense to ask whether "Honesty is good" is true or false. It expresses feelings of approval, rather than making a claim.

Nonobjectivists are fairly common, but noncognitivists are an endangered philosophical species. However convenient it might be for philosophical theory, it is hard to convince Sarah that when she says "slavery is wrong" she is merely *expressing* her distaste for slavery. "The hell I am," she will reply. "It's not a matter of taste. Slavery is morally wrong. If you think slavery is okay, that's not like saying you like sushi. I like sushi, you don't, *that's* a matter of taste. When I say I like sushi and you say you don't like sushi, we aren't really in conflict. But when I say slavery is wrong, and you say it's not, we are in deep conflict." If I delight in strawberry ice cream, but hate strawberry shortcake, you may think my tastes a bit unusual, but you will not charge me with inconsistency. However, if I claim all people should be treated as ends in themselves and never merely as means, but then insist there is nothing wrong with slavery, you can correctly point out that my views about slavery are inconsistent with my other moral principles. My moral principle that all persons should be treated as ends in themselves logically implies slavery is wrong. But expressions of feeling don't have logical implications. So whatever status we ascribe to moral principles and moral assertions, it seems implausible to suppose they are merely expressions of feeling.

If we grant that moral claims are genuine statements, that still leaves a lot of questions. In particular, are they statements of *fact*? Are moral statements (such as "stealing is wrong") and moral principles ("you should always treat others as ends in themselves, never merely as means") objectively true, the way "Jupiter is the largest planet in our solar system" is objectively true? Moral objectivists insist moral statements are true (or at least we may yet *discover* they are true). Moral nonobjectivists deny that moral statements are true. We may feel strongly about them, and we may be passionately committed to them, and some may be inconsistent with others; but in all that huge class of true statements—"the Earth is the third planet from the Sun," "George Washington was the first president of the United States," "the Cubs play in Chicago"—moral statements are nowhere to be found.

ARGUMENTS FOR ETHICAL NONOBJECTIVISM

The Argument from Moral Diversity

The ethical nonobjectivist has a number of arguments for her position. Perhaps the most obvious, and the one most frequently heard, is the argument from the *diversity* of moral views. One needn't go to distant climes and exotic cultures to observe such diversity. We are quite familiar with the bitter differences between those who consider abortion a heinous crime and those who view banning abortion as an egregious violation of women's rights to control their own bodies. And other conflicts are abundant. One group believes capital punishment to be the only morally appropriate punishment for those who commit the most terrible crimes, while the opposing view regards capital punishment as barbaric. Some view sex before marriage as a violation of moral principles, and others regard such lengthy sexual abstinence as a wrongful deprivation of an enjoyable and enriching experience.

Objectivists have two possible answers. One, that the great divergence of moral opinion is more apparent than real. At a deeper level, there is convergence. For example, there is surely deep division concerning the question of abortion, but there are also some important points of growing consensus. Both sides to the dispute tend to agree that women have the right to control over their own bodies (those who oppose abortion believe the rights of the fetus trump the woman's right to control over her own body, but do not eliminate that right). There are those who believe women should be subject to the wills of their husbands, and have no control over anything. But take away the distorting prism of religious zealotry, and few would favor such a view. And of course no moral objectivist would claim that everyone agrees on any moral principle. There is surely consensus among competent astronomers that Jupiter is the planet in our solar system with the greatest mass. But if some astronomers persist in looking through the wrong end of the telescope, or their viewing suffers some other distorting influence, then the fact that they do not agree with this scientific consensus is no reason to think the scientific consensus is wrong. Likewise, moral consensus leaves room for a few dissenters.

That brings us to the second reply objectivists offer to the nonobjectivist argument from moral diversity. That reply is simple: If there is divergence of opinion, it just means that some opinions are wrong. Some people reject Darwin, but that doesn't mean there is no truth in evolutionary theory. And some people approve of child abuse, but that doesn't change the fact that child abuse is wrong. This second answer may be especially attractive to those who claim special access to moral truth (for example, if one believes one has received a special religious revelation, and others have not had that privilege). Even without belief in one's own special knowledge of moral truth, it is quite possible to hope that moral consensus will emerge. It just takes time, and examination of morality has been hamstrung by political and religious oppression. However, we have been making serious inquiries into morality for well over 2,500 years, and there still seem to be precious few points of solid agreement; in any case, significantly fewer than in the sciences. So the nonobjectivist might be justified in asking just how long we are supposed to wait for this emerging moral consensus.

The Argument from the Impossibility of Argument About Ethics

A second argument for moral nonobjectivism was developed by a famous twentieth century British philosopher. A. J. Ayer claims we cannot really argue about ethics, and that the impossibility of ethical argument shows ethics to be nonobjective.

On the surface, Ayer's claim seems bizarre. Go to any clash between prolifers and prochoicers and you will get plenty of arguments about ethics. But Ayer is not impressed by such cases. Look carefully at those "arguments," Ayer would say. For the most part they are just name calling, rather than argument. And when there really is argument, it's not actually about *ethics*. Instead, there are disputes over whether a fetus has consciousness, or whether a fetus has a soul, or whether abortion is "natural," or about the psychological effects on a woman who is forced to carry an unwanted pregnancy to term. But those are questions of biology and theology and psychology, not really questions about ethics. When we encounter a genuine ethical issue—Does the fetus have rights? Does a woman's right to control her own body trump any rights the fetus may have to be born?—then we *cannot argue* about that issue. We might try to discover inconsistencies in the views of the other side, and point out that the position they are holding is inconsistent with some of their other views. For example, the prochoice group might argue that *if* people maintain that pregnant women should be compelled to give birth because the fetus has "a right to be born," then they ought to also believe that any woman who is not now pregnant should be compelled to implant the excess embryos from fertility clinics, embryos that will die unless they are implanted. But no one believes a woman should be compelled to have an embryo implanted, and so consistency requires that no one be compelled to carry a fetus against her will. The prolife side might respond that in the case of abortion, one is actively killing the fetus, while in the case of not implanting an embryo, one is simply allowing the embryo to die, but not purposefully killing it. Now the argument turns to the question of whether there is a moral difference between killing and letting die, and again we may turn to examples, but (Ayer would maintain) if we really have a conflict over that *basic ethical* question, we can't argue about that. One group feels strongly one way, and the other group feels strongly for the other side, but argument becomes impossible.

Consider an example. Lowell Kleiman is a moral realist, who believes in objective moral facts. In support of his moral objectivism he notes "cultures that are opposed to genocide, and to killing in general, are more likely to be at peace with their neighbors." From this observation, Kleiman poses the following rhetorical question: "Peace among nations is a moral goal. Why is it difficult to see any moral facts behind the achievement of a moral goal?"[1] And surely for most of us peace *is* a moral goal. But not everyone shares this deeply held value. One of Ezra Pound's poems celebrates "the battle's rejoicing, when our elbows and swords drip the crimson" and pronounces this curse: "May God damn for ever all who cry 'Peace!'" And Pound's warlike values are but an echo of King David's, who sings verses of praise (Psalm 18) to the "God that girdeth me with strength" and "teacheth my hands to war." Most of us will fervently oppose such brutal values, and we will try to convince those who hold them of the error of their ways. "Look, war isn't like the knights of the Round Table. People really get killed, and they suffer terrible injuries, and innocents are caught up in the deadly struggle and are killed or displaced and left homeless, and children die from bombs and land mines and starvation, and the countries engaged in war become more repressive: they lock up citizens suspected of favoring the other side, and rights of free speech are overwhelmed by the demands of propaganda. There's nothing beautiful or glorious about it. In war, life is nasty, brutish, and short." Such points may convince those who held a false picture of what war really involves. During the American Civil War, spectators packed picnic lunches and rode their carriages out to the fields of northern Virginia, near Manassas, to watch the glorious battle unfold, with its stirring music and bright flags and heroic charges. What they saw instead was a terrible slaughter. Men and horses were blown to bits by rows of cannon and ranks of muskets, confusion and terror reigned on all sides. Many people had their myths about war exploded that day. The reality was very different from what they had fantasized.

But what if someone experiences such brutality and instead finds it thrilling and desirable? "Consider how many innocent people are slaughtered," we say. "That is a small price to pay for the glories of war," is the response. "But if you engage in war, you yourself are likely to meet a swift and brutal end." "Better an hour of war than 70 years of peace," our opponent answers. If someone really holds such a fundamentally different moral out-look from our own, we can certainly *oppose* her, and we may revile her as a moral monster; but can we really *argue* with her? Of course there are facts we *can* argue about: Is this war necessary to secure a more lasting peace? Is this war essential to preventing other terrible harms? Are there actually lots of civilian casualties in war? Does war in fact make a country more repressive? But suppose our disagreement is not about those issues, but instead about the basic value question: Alice says war, in all its brutal savagery, is good. We say it is morally bad (even if we believe war is sometimes justified, we still believe it to be in itself a bad thing, and something to be avoided when possible). Can we argue with Alice about that *basic* moral issue? Ayer says we cannot; and the impossibility of argument, Ayer main-tains, shows that the basic moral issue is not a matter of objective fact.

To answer Ayer's argument, you could go either of two directions. First, you could try to demonstrate that there *is* room for genuine argument on even the most basic ethical issues. Or second, you could accept Ayer's assertion that argument on ethical issues is not possible, but insist that ethics is objective nonetheless: some basic ethical truths are simply known immediately, they are *intuitively* obvious to anyone who thinks clearly and looks objectively at the issue. True, if Alice fails to recognize these basic ethical truths, we can-not argue with her. But that doesn't show that there are no ethical truths. Instead, it reveals that Alice is morally blind.

The Argument from Simplicity: Ockham's Razor

This response to Ayer brings us to a third argument for moral nonobjectivism. It was devel-oped by another twentieth-century British philosopher, J. L. Mackie, and it is known as the "argument from queerness." Mackie argues that belief in moral objectivity would commit us to a very weird sort of thing: moral facts. Moral facts are weird because they have two dis-tinct properties. First, they must be facts that exist independently of us. They are *objective* facts, which are true whether we recognize them or not. It's an objective fact that Jupiter is the largest planet in our solar system whether I—or anyone else—knows it. (That's why nonobjectivists do not count the rules devised by social contracts as *objective* moral facts.) And second, they must be facts that have the very special and queer property of command-ing our approval.

We finally arrive at the basic question that divides objectivists and nonobjectivists. Can we account for ethics and ethical behavior *without* the assumption of objective moral facts? If we can, then a system without moral facts will have the advantage of *simplicity*, and that is a very substantial advantage indeed. " 'Tis a blessing to be simple," says the opening line of the famous folk song, and contemporary scientists and philosophers tend to agree. If we favored more complicated explanations over simpler ones, then we could explain any-thing. But the "explanations" would be quite strange, and they wouldn't offer much help. My watch has stopped. "Must need a new battery," you say. "No," I reply, "it's not the bat-tery; the problem is that my little watch elf is taking a nap, and so he's stopped moving the gears." "There's no watch elf! It's just an old battery." "No, I'll show you." I bang the watch briskly on a table, and the hands start to move again. "You see, I awakened the elf, and he started moving the gears." When the watch soon stops again, it's because the elf returned to slumber. You open the watch, and find no elf. "You see, there's no elf there." "He's there alright," I reply. "But he's very shy, and he hides. Besides, he can make himself invisible." You place a new battery in the watch, and now it runs fine, without stopping. "You see, it's the battery that drives the watch; there's no elf." "There is too an elf," I insist; "but he's a battery-powered elf, and he was getting really run down. That's why he was sleeping so much. Now that he has a new battery, he's back on the job driving the gears and running the watch."

This is a silly dialogue, of course. But it's silly only because of a deeply held principle by which we reason, a principle so common that we hardly know it's there. The principle was formally stated by William of Ockham, back in the early fourteenth century, and we now call it the principle of "Ockham's razor." The principle is this: when giving explanations, don't make assumptions that are not required. Or another way of stating it: when there are competing explanations, both of which give adequate accounts of what is to be explained, then the *simpler* explanation is better; that is, the more *parsimonious* explanation, the *thriftier* explanation, is better. I can "explain" the workings of my watch quite effectively by means of my elf hypothesis. When the watch stops, the elf is asleep. When the watch slows down, the elf is tired. When the watch keeps accurate time, the elf is on top of his game. When the watch is inaccurate, the elf has been drinking. The problem is that this explanation is not as *parsimonious* as the competing explanation. It adds to the explanatory story a very special additional entity: an elf (and not just any elf, but an elf that can make itself invisible). If you let me add elves and ghosts and miracles to my explanatory scheme, then I can "explain" anything; but the explanations violate the principle of Ockham's razor, and are not as efficient and effective as the simpler explanations in terms of rundown batteries and rust.

That's a long detour, but it leads us back to Mackie's argument from queerness. Mackie makes use of Ockham's razor to argue that while moral objectivism might "explain" ethics and ethical behavior, we can give simpler, thriftier, more parsimonious explanations of the same phenomena *without* appealing to objective moral facts. If we can explain ethical experiences without assuming the existence of objective moral facts, then we have a *better* (because simpler) explanation. And like the invisible watch elf, objective moral facts aren't just one more entity in the universe: they are very strange things indeed, and we shouldn't assume they exist unless no simpler explanation is available. Why would objective moral facts be such a strange and exotic addition to the world? As we noted earlier, Mackie claims they must have two distinct properties. First, they must exist in our world (that is a property they share with deck chairs and wombats and rowboats—nothing special about that). Second (and this is the special property) they must automatically and powerfully motivate us. If we recognize that something is *objectively good,* then recognition of that fact motivates us to pursue it. (Of course something else may block or prevent our pursuit, but recognition of the inherent goodness of the object will nonetheless provide a strong motive for pursuing it.) If I acknowledge that something is in *fact* morally good, but I have no interest in pursuing or preserving that good, then you are justified in concluding that I did not really understand or appreciate its goodness. I'm mouthing the words, but I don't really see the good. Thus objective moral facts must be very special. They are facts about the world, *and* they automatically arouse in us—in anyone who recognizes them—both approval and motive to pursue. And these special objective moral facts, which are unlike anything else in the world, will also require a special perceptual power if we are to comprehend them. So the moral objectivist is not only burdened with special strange moral facts, but also with special perceptual faculties as well. Moral objectivism might still be true, but we should not accept such a cumbersome theory if some simpler hypothesis provides a workable alternative account.

How could the moral objectivist attempt to answer Mackie's argument that moral facts are too complicated? One way is to deny that moral facts are as complicated as Mackie suggests. They *are* facts about the world, but they do not necessarily motivate us to *favor* the moral facts. This leads to a spirited debate between "internalists" (who insist that any real moral fact *must* motivate those who recognize the fact, and "externalists" (who hold that the motive to act morally is separate from—external to—the recognition of objective moral facts). It's an interesting debate, but far beyond the scope of this discussion.

In a second possible answer to Mackie's queerness argument, the objectivist might reply that moral facts *are* rather complicated, but not everything is nice and simple. Besides, there are other facts about the world that we recognize as *scientifically* objective that are also quite complicated: consider the many perplexities generated by space and time, not to mention quarks and antimatter. So objective morality is complicated, but that's what morality requires.

But *does* an explanation of morality require something that complicated? That is a very tough and controversial question. If there is a moral *fact*, perhaps the best candidate is something like this: treating others as you would wish to be treated is good. Many different religious traditions, as well as a number of secular philosophical views, have favored this principle—or something quite similar—as the most basic principle of ethics. And even among those who do not think ethics is *objectively true*, most would regard this as good moral guidance. What is the best explanation for the popularity of this moral principle? The explanation favored by the moral objectivists is: there is widespread allegiance to this moral principle because all these various perspectives and cultures and traditions have discovered the same basic moral fact, that it is right and good to treat others as you yourself wish to be treated. That is certainly one possible explanation, and perhaps it is the most satisfactory explanation (though it may involve some rather complicated elements, as we noted before). What *alternative* explanations would be proposed by the nonobjectivists?

Nonobjectivists might hypothesize that any uniformity in moral principles is the result of our common biological heritage. For example, Michael Ruse maintains that our most basic ethical impulses are shaped by our evolutionary history:

> We are what we are because we are recently evolved from savannah-dwelling primates. Suppose that we had evolved from cave-dwellers, or some such thing. We might have as our highest principle of moral obligation the imperative 'to eat each others' faeces. Not simply the desire, but the obligation.[2]

However plausible or implausible you may find this evolutionary account of our basic values, it does have at least one distinct virtue: it makes no appeal to special ethical powers or complicated moral facts. Instead, this account of ethics is fashioned from materials that are already at hand (our knowledge of evolution). It does not require any special additional resources, and so—by the principle of Ockham's razor—it scores points for simplicity. We do have deep ethical 'intuitions,' but we don't require special moral facts to account for them.

If the evolutionary explanation does not take your fancy, then you might consider explanations formulated by sociologists and psychologists. We are shaped from an early age to live in at least a minimal degree of harmony with those around us, and we gradually internalize that training. I am happily playing with a bright red shiny fire engine, complete with bell and siren and a nifty ladder. Quite naturally Susie is also attracted to the new toy, and grabs it away. My screams of frustration quickly bring the attention of powerful adults: "No, Susie, he was playing with it first; you can't just take it away from him, that wouldn't be nice." This seems like a peachy result to me, until a few minutes later when the same powerful adult again arrives on the scene: "You've been playing with the fire engine for quite a while. Wouldn't you like to let Susie play with it now?" Well, actually, I wouldn't.

I would prefer that Susie go soak her head. But young as I am, I've already learned that this is not really a question about how I feel, but an order—politely phrased, but no less an order—to yield the fire engine to Susie. I can try to hang on to the fire engine at all costs—"Mine! I had it first!"—but I soon discover that is not a very effective strategy: I wind up without the fire engine, sitting in timeout, feeling bitter and powerless. On the other hand, if I cheerfully share the fire engine with that damned Susie, I may get to continue playing with it, and I might even cop an extra cookie or two at snack time. And perhaps best of all, I feel that I am sharing the fire engine with Susie from my own choice: and so I feel powerful rather than powerless, and I also feel like a paragon of virtue. So it's not long before I discover that "treat others as you would like to be treated" has serious benefits. Of course at 4 years old I don't follow it as a moral principle, but I have been effectively shaped into that pattern of behavior. When someone does suggest that principle to me, I am now predisposed to see it as an obvious and basic truth. In different cultures the acculturation process will take somewhat different forms. But we are highly social beings, who live together in close groups. Without some such learning of basic cooperation skills, cooperative projects and harmonious communities would be impossible. So all viable cultures promote the learning of cooperative behavior. And it works a lot better—both socially and psychologically—if that cooperative behavior is *internalized*. I am generous and cooperative with others because I *want* to be, not because I am forced to be. Again, however plausible you find that account, it gets high marks by the standard of Ockham's razor. It is a simple account, that requires no special additional special resources such as "objective moral facts." (However, some moral realists will insist that "cooperative cultures work better" is *itself* a statement of moral fact; but that is a question we'll consider in the next chapter.)

Some might criticize the nonobjectivist explanations provided as somewhat speculative, and in any case not so neat and complete as the explanations in terms of special moral faculties that recognize special moral facts. That's a legitimate criticism. The nonobjectivists will answer that their explanations are based on empirical scientific materials from biology and sociology and psychology, and that such explanations are not complete but instead depend on ongoing scientific research. We may not be able to give explanations that are as neat and easy as the moral objectivists offer; but at least we are not appealing to special faculties or special forces or special facts, but instead trying to give real explanations based on empirical research. It's easy to give neat explanations if you can appeal to moral facts or watch elves, but the *quality*—and particularly the *simplicity*—of the explanations may leave something to be desired.

The Continuing Struggle Between Objectivists and Nonobjectivists

So the controversy between moral objectivists and moral nonobjectivists rages on. This is an issue on which you will have to decide for yourself which view is more plausible and more promising. Even though this dispute runs deep, both sides can find some common ground. Whether I think there are objective moral truths or only useful moral guidelines shaped by our cultural or evolutionary history, in either case I think it is important that people cooperate and live in peace. As noted earlier, there *are* people who would disagree, and favor brutal war over peaceful harmony; but fortunately, there are very few—whether objectivists or nonobjectivists—who take that view. For the most part, we prefer to live in communities where people are cooperative and pleasant, kind and considerate. We want to raise our children in such communities, and have them become productive, virtuous members of such communities. Objectivists and nonobjectivists alike tend to share such ideals, so perhaps it doesn't matter so much which side of the divide one falls on.

Still, this is a difference that makes a difference. For example, objectivists and nonobjectivists may have significant differences in the details of how best to shape their children to be cooperative moral citizens. The moral objectivist will aim at placing children in a position to *recognize* the basic moral truths. The nonobjectivist aims at *instilling* or *shaping* a positive moral outlook and desirable moral behavioral patterns. (This is perhaps the source of the controversy between those who believe it is important to reward and reinforce good behavior, and those who believe that such external rewards make it difficult for the child to recognize the intrinsic objective worth of the good behavior.)

Alternatives to Nonobjectivism

If you have always thought of ethics as *transcendent*—perhaps given by God—and you no longer (or perhaps never did) believe in those transcendent sources, then you may suppose nonobjectivism is the inevitable result. It certainly is one possibility. It is favored by a number of philosophers, and may well be the view you find most plausible. But there are other alternatives to consider. We have already looked at some nontranscendent objectivist views (such as utilitarianism and social contract theory and pragmatism). The next chapter presents another form of natural moral objectivism—a form of moral realism that was crafted in direct response to some of the nonobjectivist arguments of this chapter.

LANGUAGE, TRUTH, AND LOGIC

A. J. Ayer

A. J. Ayer was a very influential twentieth-century British philosopher, who early in his career helped to bring the ideas of the European logical positivists into British, American, and Australian philosophy. Logical positivism was a complex philosophical movement, but among its major goals was making philosophy more scientific and logical, and eliminating from philosophy many of the traditional metaphysical questions that logical positivists regarded as illegitimate *pseudo*questions: questions that had endured for so long because they were either literally nonsensical or because they turned on basic errors in either logic or language. In the following excerpt, Ayer is turning his logical positivist methodology to questions of ethics.

For more details on Ayer's life and work—and on the development of twentieth-century Anglo-American philosophy—see Ayer's fascinating autobiography, *Part of My Life* (London: Collins, 1977; a paperback version was published by Oxford University Press in 1978). It is one of the most honest, revealing, and entertaining autobiographies ever written by a philosopher, as Ayer chronicles the highlights of his love life and his military service with as much enthusiasm as he describes his many philosophical controversies. Another good source for the study of Ayer's work is *The Philosophy of A. J. Ayer*, edited by Lewis Edwin Hahn (LaSalle, Ill.: Open Court, 1992). For Ayer's later work on moral philosophy—in which he revises some of his earlier views, though he vigorously defends the essentials of his position—see Ayer's *Philosophical Essays* (London: Macmillan, 1969), especially "On the Analysis of Moral Judgments."

It is advisable here to make it plain that it is only normative ethical symbols, and not descriptive ethical symbols, that are held by us to be indefinable in factual terms. There is a danger of confusing these two types of symbols, because they are commonly constituted by signs of the same sensible form. Thus a complex sign of the form "x is wrong" may constitute a sentence which expresses a moral judgement concerning a certain type of conduct, or it may constitute a sentence which states that a certain type of conduct is repugnant to the moral sense of a particular society. In the latter case, the symbol "wrong" is a descriptive ethical symbol, and the sentence in which it occurs expresses an ordinary sociological proposition; in the former case, the symbol "wrong" is a normative ethical symbol, and the sentence in which it occurs does not, we maintain, express an empirical proposition at all. It is only with normative ethics that we are at present concerned; so that whenever ethical symbols are used in the course of this argument without qualification, they are always to be interpreted as symbols of the normative type.

In admitting that normative ethical concepts are irreducible to empirical concepts, we seem to be leaving the way clear for the "absolutist" view of ethics—that is, the view that statements of value are not controlled by observation, as ordinary empirical propositions are, but only by a mysterious "intellectual intuition." A feature of this theory, which is seldom recognized by its advocates, is that it makes statements of value unverifiable. For it is notorious that what seems intuitively certain to one person may seem doubtful, or even false, to another. So that unless it is possible to provide some criterion by which one may decide between conflicting intuitions, a mere appeal to intuition is worthless as a test of a proposition's validity. But in the case of moral judgements, no such criterion can be given. Some moralists claim to settle the matter by saying that they "know" that their own moral judgements are correct. But such an assertion is of purely psychological interest, and has not the slightest tendency to prove the validity of any moral judgement. For dissentient moralists may equally well "know" that their ethical views are correct. And, as far as subjective certainty goes, there will be nothing to choose between them. When such differences of opinion arise in connection with an ordinary empirical proposition, one may

attempt to resolve them by referring to, or actually carrying out, some relevant empirical test. But with regard to ethical statements, there is, on the "absolutist" or "intuitionist" theory, no relevant empirical test. We are therefore justified in saying that on this theory ethical statements are held to be unverifiable. They are, of course, also held to be genuine synthetic propositions.

Considering the use which we have made of the principle that a synthetic proposition is significant only if it is empirically verifiable, it is clear that the acceptance of an "absolutist" theory of ethics would undermine the whole of our main argument. And as we have already rejected the "naturalistic" theories which are commonly supposed to provide the only alternative to "absolutism" in ethics, we seem to have reached a difficult position. We shall meet the difficulty by showing that the correct treatment of ethical statements is afforded by a third theory, which is wholly compatible with our radical empiricism.

We begin by admitting that the fundamental ethical concepts are unanalysable, inasmuch as there is no criterion by which one can test the validity of the judgements in which they occur. So far we are in agreement with the absolutists. But, unlike the absolutists, we are able to give an explanation of this fact about ethical concepts. We say that the reason why they are unanalysable is that they are mere pseudo-concepts. The presence of an ethical symbol in a proposition adds nothing to its factual content. Thus if I say to someone, "You acted wrongly in stealing that money," I am not stating anything more than if I had simply said, "You stole that money." In adding that this action is wrong I am not making any further statement about it. I am simply evincing my moral disapproval of it. It is as if I had said, "You stole that money," in a peculiar tone of horror, or written it with the addition of some special exclamation marks. The tone, or the exclamation marks, adds nothing to the literal meaning of the sentence. It merely serves to show that the expression of it is attended by certain feelings in the speaker.

If now I generalise my previous statement and say, "Stealing money is wrong," I produce a sentence which has no factual meaning—that is, expresses no proposition which can be either true or false. It is as if I had written "Stealing money!!"—where the shape and thickness of the exclamation marks show, by a suitable convention, that a special sort of moral disapproval is the feeling which is being expressed. It is clear that there is nothing said here which can be true or false. Another man may disagree with me about the wrongness of stealing, in the sense that he may not have the same feelings about stealing as I have, and he may quarrel with me on account of my moral sentiments. But he cannot, strictly speaking, contradict me. For in saying that a certain type of action is right or wrong, I am not making any factual statement, not even a statement about my own state of mind. I am merely expressing certain moral sentiments. And the man who is ostensibly contradicting me is merely expressing his moral sentiments. So that there is plainly no sense in asking which of us is in the right. For neither of us is asserting a genuine proposition.

What we have just been saying about the symbol "wrong" applies to all normative ethical symbols. Sometimes they occur in sentences which record ordinary empirical facts besides expressing ethical feeling about those facts: sometimes they occur in sentences which simply express ethical feeling about a certain type of action, or situation, without making any statement of fact. But in every case in which one would commonly be said to be making an ethical judgement, the function of the relevant ethical word is purely "emotive." It is used to express feeling about certain objects, but not to make any assertion about them.

It is worth mentioning that ethical terms do not serve only to express feeling. They are calculated also to arouse feeling, and so to stimulate action. Indeed some of them are used in such a way as to give the sentences in which they occur the effect of commands. Thus the sentence "It is your duty to tell the truth" may be regarded both as the expression of a certain sort of ethical feeling about truthfulness and as the expression of the command "Tell the truth." The sentence "You ought to tell the truth" also involves the command "Tell the truth," but here the tone of the command is less emphatic. In the sentence "It is good to tell the truth" the command has become little more than a suggestion. And thus the "meaning" of the word "good," in its ethical usage, is differentiated from that of the word "duty" or the word "ought." In fact we may define the meaning of the various ethical words in terms both of the differ-

ent feelings they are ordinarily taken to express, and also the different responses which they are calculated to provoke.

We can now see why it is impossible to find a criterion for determining the validity of ethical judgements. It is not because they have an "absolute" validity which is mysteriously independent of ordinary sense-experience, but because they have no objective validity whatsoever. If a sentence makes no statement at all, there is obviously no sense in asking whether what it says is true or false. And we have seen that sentences which simply express moral judgements do not say anything. They are pure expressions of feeling and as such do not come under the category of truth and falsehood. They are unverifiable for the same reason as a cry of pain or a word of command is unverifiable—because they do not express genuine propositions.

Thus, although our theory of ethics might fairly be said to be radically subjectivist, it differs in a very important respect from the orthodox subjectivist theory. For the orthodox subjectivist does not deny, as we do, that the sentences of a moralizer express genuine propositions. All he denies is that they express propositions of a unique non-empirical character. His own view is that they express propositions about the speaker's feelings. If this were so, ethical judgements clearly would be capable of being true or false. They would be true if the speaker had the relevant feelings, and false if he had not. And this is a matter which is, in principle, empirically verifiable. Furthermore they could be significantly contradicted. For if I say, "Tolerance is a virtue," and someone answers, "You don't approve of it," he would, on the ordinary subjectivist theory, be contradicting me. On our theory, he would not be contradicting me, because, in saying that tolerance was a virtue, I should not be making any statement about my own feelings or about anything else. I should simply be evincing my feelings, which is not at all the same thing as saying that I have them.

The distinction between the expression of feeling and the assertion of feeling is complicated by the fact that the assertion that one has a certain feeling often accompanies the expression of that feeling, and is then, indeed, a factor in the expression of that feeling. Thus I may simultaneously express boredom and say that I am bored, and in that case my utterance of the words, "I am bored," is one of the circumstances which make it true to say that I am expressing or evincing boredom. But I can express boredom without actually saying that I am bored. I can express it by my tone and gestures, while making a statement about something wholly unconnected with it, or by an ejaculation, or without uttering any words at all. So that even if the assertion that one has a certain feeling always involves the expression of that feeling, the expression of a feeling assuredly does not always involve the assertion that one has it. And this is the important point to grasp in considering the distinction between our theory and the ordinary subjectivist theory. For whereas the subjectivist holds that ethical statements actually assert the existence of certain feelings, we hold that ethical statements are expressions and excitants of feeling which do not necessarily involve any assertions.

We have already remarked that the main objection to the ordinary subjectivist theory is that the validity of ethical judgements is not determined by the nature of their author's feelings. And this is an objection which our theory escapes. For it does not imply that the existence of any feelings is a necessary and sufficient condition of the validity of an ethical judgement. It implies, on the contrary, that ethical judgements have no validity.

There is, however, a celebrated argument against subjectivist theories which our theory does not escape. It has been pointed out by Moore that if ethical statements were simply statements about the speaker's feelings, it would be impossible to argue about questions of value. To take a typical example: if a man said that thrift was a virtue, and another replied that it was a vice, they would not, on this theory, be disputing with one another. One would be saying that he approved of thrift, and the other that *he* didn't; and there is no reason why both these statements should not be true. Now Moore held it to be obvious that we do dispute about questions of value, and accordingly concluded that the particular form of subjectivism which he was discussing was false.

It is plain that the conclusion that it is impossible to dispute about questions of value follows from our theory also. For as we hold that such sentences as "Thrift is a virtue" and "Thrift is a vice" do not express propositions at all, we clearly cannot hold that they express incompatible propositions. We must therefore admit that if Moore's argument really refutes the ordinary subjectivist theory, it also refutes ours. But, in fact, we deny that it does refute even the ordinary subjectivist theory. For we hold that one really never does dispute about questions of value.

This may seem, at first sight, to be a very paradoxical assertion. For we certainly do engage in disputes which are ordinarily regarded as disputes about questions of value. But, in all such cases, we find, if we consider the matter closely, that the dispute is not really about a question of value, but about a question of fact. When someone disagrees with us about the moral value of a certain action or type of action, we do admittedly resort to argument in order to win him over to our way of thinking. But we do not attempt to show by our arguments that he has the "wrong" ethical feeling towards a situation whose nature he has correctly apprehended. What we attempt to show is that he is mistaken about the facts of the case. We argue that he has misconceived the agent's motive: or that he has misjudged the effects of the action, or its probable effects in view of the agent's knowledge; or that he has failed to take into account the special circumstances in which the agent was placed. Or else we employ more general arguments about the effects which actions of a certain type tend to produce, or the qualities which are usually manifested in their performance. We do this in the hope that we have only to get our opponent to agree with us about the nature of the empirical facts for him to adopt the same moral attitude towards them as we do. And as the people with whom we argue have generally received the same moral education as ourselves, and live in the same social order, our expectation is usually justified. But if our opponent happens to have undergone a different process of moral "conditioning" from ourselves, so that, even when he acknowledges all the facts, he still disagrees with us about the moral value of the actions under discussion, then we abandon the attempt to convince him by argument. We say that it is impossible to argue with him because he has a distorted or undeveloped moral sense; which signifies merely that he employs a different set of values from our own. We feel that our own system of values is superior, and therefore speak in such derogatory terms of his. But we cannot bring forward any arguments to show that our system is superior. For our judgement that it is so is itself a judgement of value, and accordingly outside the scope of argument. It is because argument fails us when we come to deal with pure questions of value, as distinct from questions of fact, that we finally resort to mere abuse.

In short, we find that argument is possible on moral questions only if some system of values is presupposed. If our opponent concurs with us in expressing moral disapproval of all actions of a given type *t*, then we may get him to condemn a particular action A, by bringing forward arguments to show that A is of type *t*. For the question whether A does or does not belong to that type is a plain question of fact. Given that a man has certain moral principles, we argue that he must, in order to be consistent, react morally to certain things in a certain way. What we do not and cannot argue about is the validity of these moral principles. We merely praise or condemn them in the light of our own feelings.

If anyone doubts the accuracy of this account of moral disputes, let him try to construct even an imaginary argument on a question of value which does not reduce itself to an argument about a question of logic or about an empirical matter of fact. I am confident that he will not succeed in producing a single example. And if that is the case, he must allow that its involving the impossibility of purely ethical arguments is not, as

Moore thought, a ground of objection to our theory, but rather a point in favour of it.

Having upheld our theory against the only criticism which appeared to threaten it, we may now use it to define the nature of all ethical enquiries. We find that ethical philosophy consists simply in saying that ethical concepts are pseudo-concepts and therefore unanalysable. The further task of describing the different feelings that the different ethical terms are used to express, and the different reactions that they customarily provoke, is a task for the psychologist. There cannot be such a thing as ethical science, if by ethical science one means the elaboration of a "true" system of morals. For we have seen that, as ethical judgements are mere expressions of feeling, there can be no way of determining the validity of any ethical system, and, indeed, no sense in asking whether any such system is true. All that one may legitimately enquire in this connection is, What are the moral habits of a given person or group of people, and what causes them to have precisely those habits and feelings? And this enquiry falls wholly within the scope of the existing social sciences.

It appears, then, that ethics, as a branch of knowledge, is nothing more than a department of psychology and sociology.

EXERCISES

1. It was suggested that objectivists and nonobjectivists might use different methods in attempting to "morally educate" their children. Are there *other* important differences between the views of objectivists and nonobjectivists? That is, are there other ways in which this difference makes a difference in the way they live?

2. Are your friends moral objectivists or moral nonobjectivists? Perhaps you have discussed this question with some of your friends, and so you have a clear idea of their views. But think of a friend or two with whom you have not had such a discussion. Do you think you could *tell*—from their behavior, or their views on some other issue, or their appearance, or by the clothes they wear, or however—whether they are objectivists?

3. Find someone who disagrees with your views on capital punishment; spend a few minutes trying to convince the other to change his/her mind on this question.

   Certainly you *argued* about the issue. But were any of the arguments genuine *ethical* arguments? For example, if one of you maintained that capital punishment deters crime, and the other insisted that it does not, then you may well have been arguing; but it's an argument about sociology, and not about ethics. If you both simply insisted on the intuitively obvious correctness of your respective positions, then you certainly disagreed, but you didn't really argue about an ethical issue. Was there any point at which you actually argued about values (which Ayer insists is not possible)?

4. In the dispute between objectivists and nonobjectivists, who should have the burden of proof? The nonobjectivist, since she is denying what seems to many quite obvious? Or the objectivist, who is trying to establish the existence of moral truths, something positive? Placing the burden of proof is very important. For example, if I am charged with a crime, the *prosecution*—who is making the claim that I committed the crime—bears the burden of proving it. I don't have to prove my innocence, and that's obviously a good thing. If the burden of proof were reversed, then you could be convicted of all sorts of crimes you did not commit. Where were you on August 25, at 4 a.m., when the State Street Convenience Store was robbed? You say you were home asleep; but can you *prove* that's where you were? Can you prove you did not commit the robbery? Of course not. Fortunately, you don't have to prove you are innocent. The prosecution has the burden of proving you are guilty. So in the case of objectivism versus nonobjectivism: Who has the burden of proof?

5. Ockham's razor—the principle that the simpler explanation is better—is central to the nonobjectivists' arguments against moral objectivism. Suppose an objectivist responded that Ockham's razor is useful in science, but not in ethics. What would you think of that moral objectivist counterargument?

ADDITIONAL READING

A number of contemporary philosophers have argued against moral objectivity. Among the most influential are A. J. Ayer, *Language, Truth and Logic* (London: Gollancz, 1970), from which the previous reading was taken; Gilbert Harman, *The Nature of Morality* (Oxford: Oxford University Press, 1977); John Mackie, *Ethics: Inventing Right and Wrong* (Hammondsworth, UK: Penguin, 1977); C. L. Stevenson, *Ethics and Language* (New Haven Conn.: Yale University Press, 1944); and C. L. Stevenson, *Facts and Values* (New Haven Conn.: Yale University Press, 1963).

There is a very interesting debate between Richard Rorty (defending a nonobjectivist view) and Hilary Putnam (who favors a moral realist perspective); Rorty's part of the debate can be found in "Putnam and the Relativist Menace," *Journal of Philosophy*, 90 (1993), 443–461. For more on Rorty's views, see the suggested readings at the end of Chapter 6. Putnam's position is elaborated in *Realism with a Human Face* (Cambridge, Mass.: Harvard University Press, 1990); and *The Many Faces of Realism* (LaSalle, Ill.: Open Court, 1987).

One of the strongest nonobjectivist writers is Herbert Feigl. See his "Validation and Vindication," in *Readings in Ethical Theory*, C. Sellars and J. Hospers, editors (New York: Appleton-Century-Crofts, 1952); "'De Principiis non Disputandum . . . ?' On the Meaning and the Limits of Justification," in *Philosophical Analysis*, Max Black, editor (Ithaca, N.Y.: Cornell University Press, 1950).

An interesting recent version of nonobjectivism has been proposed by Simon Blackburn; see his *Essays on Quasi-Realism* (Oxford: Oxford University Press, 1993).

NOTES

[1]Lowell Kleiman, "Morality as the Best Explanation," *American Philosophical Quarterly* 26 (1989), 166.

[2]Michael Ruse, *Taking Darwin Seriously* (Oxford: Basil Blackwell, 1986), p. 263.

CHAPTER 11

✧ MORAL REALISM ✧

Moral realism is the position that there are real moral facts, objective moral truths. But exactly what such moral facts are, and how they are known, is a matter of great dispute. Traditionally, moral facts have been very special stuff, known by special faculties. For Plato, moral facts are moral ideals that exist above and beyond our natural world, and are known only through rigorous use of reason. Some have held that moral facts are established by divine will, or through special divine creation, and they are known to us by intuitive powers implanted by God or by special revelation. Kant believed that discovering objective moral truths is analogous to discovering truths of geometry.

CONTEMPORARY MORAL REALISM

The Modesty of Moral Realism

Many people claim to know objective moral facts with absolute certainty: perhaps through reason, or special intuitive powers, or by revelation from a deity. You have heard people (perhaps heard yourself) say: "Everybody knows the difference between right and wrong, I don't care who you are." Such claims usually imply that everyone knows objective moral truths, plain moral facts (though there may be disagreement about whether they are known through reason or intuition or revelation or social training). But in contemporary moral philosophy, the philosophers who march under the banner of "moral realism" mean something much more modest. In fact, many contemporary moral realists would deny that they *know* moral facts at all. However, they do insist that objective moral facts are possible, and that it may be possible to discover them. But moral realists maintain that discovering moral facts is not an easy task—they aren't known through special intuition, or by pure reflective reason. Instead, finding real moral facts (if any exist) will require diligent research, including careful inquiry into the moral lives and moral beliefs of a variety of people and cultures. Maybe such research will yield evidence of real moral facts. Maybe it will not. But we should not decide the question before we do the research. In any case, the existence of objective moral facts is a genuine possibility, which further research might indicate is a reality.

This is not your grandmother's moral realism. And it is certainly not the moral realism of Kant or Plato. First of all, it is a lot less certain of itself. Kant knows moral truths through the exercise of pure reason, and he has absolutely no doubts about either the existence or the absolute truth of objective moral facts. The contemporary moral realists, in contrast, champion a more modest thesis: while we are not sure that there are objective moral facts, their existence has not been disproved; and it is possible that careful research will provide reasonable and legitimate grounds for accepting the hypothesis that moral facts exist. So (the moral realists say) let's continue to study the issue with open minds, and see if ultimately the hypothesis of objective moral facts proves more useful and productive and plausible than the hypothesis that there are no such facts.

Moral Realism and Empirical Research

That is about as mild and moderate a claim of moral realism as one can imagine. But it is also a very interesting claim, and it reveals a great deal not only about contemporary ethics, but also about contemporary views of science. First of all, contemporary moral realists do not suppose they can drag an objective moral fact out of the bushes, shine a bright light on it for everyone to see, and thus conclusively establish the truth of moral realism. Kant thought he could do that through the use of reason; some believe that intuitions reveal indubitable objective moral truths to those who look carefully; and others announce moral truths carved by God's own finger on tablets of stone (or even gold). But moral realists do not believe the issue will be settled that easily. Instead, contemporary moral realists hold that the existence of moral facts is a complex and challenging issue, requiring both empirical research and a clearer picture of the way facts—whether moral or scientific—are actually established.

Contemporary moral realism is a response to some of the nonobjectivist arguments considered in the previous chapter. Thus moral realists directly challenge the key nonobjectivist arguments. And contemporary moral realists make no appeal to mysteries or miracles or intuitions, nor to any exalted powers of reason. They argue that moral realism is an empirically and scientifically plausible hypothesis that *may* well be true.

Moral Realism and the Argument from Simplicity

Central to contemporary moral realism is its answer to the *simplicity* argument for nonobjectivism (the argument that nonobjectivism is simpler and thus more scientifically satisfactory than moral objectivism; that is, the argument that the principle of Ockham's razor favors nonobjectivism). Moral realists respond that a more subtle and sophisticated view of science shows that moral realism is not refuted by such accusations of scientific inadequacy. Instead, moral realism remains a scientifically plausible contender for the most satisfactory ethical theory. The following section examines that claim: the claim that contemporary moral realism is compatible with good scientific practice, and that moral realism might prove the most scientifically adequate account of ethics and ethical behavior (or at least might be an important element of such an empirical account).

Establishing Facts

Think for a moment of Nessie, the notoriously shy 'Loch Ness Monster' that Scots have been sighting and scientists seeking for many decades. Is there a small herd of fantastic sea creatures that were trapped in Loch Ness many millennia ago, and have survived there while the rest of their species and their close relatives died out many centuries ago? Well, not so many years ago a fisherman hauled up a very strange-looking fish from a species scientists had believed long extinct. So it's possible that some remnant of a nearly extinct species survives in Loch Ness, however implausible it might be that a sufficiently large breeding population could have survived there this long. Several scientific expeditions have thought it worth examining, and if tomorrow one of those expeditions should entrap Nessie or one of her cousins and bring her to the surface while the television cameras crowd around, then those who believe in Nessie will be proved right. Once the Loch Ness Monster is placed in front of us, and we see it and touch it and smell it, then that settles the matter. Of course we'll have to check for forgeries. Barnum and Bailey once exhibited a unicorn in their circus, but that didn't establish the existence of unicorns. But barring fraud, this is a straightforward scientific question: Does Nessie exist? If she does, then a species scientists had once thought extinct will be moved to the endangered list, but it will not require a major shakeup of our scientific beliefs.

Not all scientific questions are that simple. Suppose that instead of Nessie, scientists discover a small community of Medusa: people with fierce snakes growing out of their scalps instead of hair. Hitherto we had thought the Medusa a character of Greek mythology, but now we find that they're real. If that happened, scientists wouldn't just add another species, grouped somewhere among the primates. Scientists already have a niche ready for Nessie, however unlikely it is that Nessie's niche will be filled. But if a Medusa shows up, that would involve a lot more than adding a new branch to the evolutionary tree. It would mean a radical rethinking of our fundamental biological theories. In fact, biologists would spend years looking for the hoax before even considering the possibility that the Medusa is real.

Consider another example. What happens when something burns? Place yourself back in the eighteenth century, sitting comfortably in a Philadelphia tavern and sharing a glass of ale with Benjamin Franklin. Ben pokes a long thin oak splinter in the fireplace, and then lights his clay pipe with the flame. Since you are both fascinated with scientific questions, the discussion soon turns to the nature of fire. What happens when a thick oak log burns in the fireplace? No fair looking through your twenty-first century science textbook. Look deep into the fire, observe carefully: what do you see? As the fire burns, it consumes the wood, ultimately leaving only the ash and embers. A nice spit of oak burns readily, but the heavy iron grate on which the oak rests does not flame and is not consumed by the flames, though it may glow red-hot. So, what is the scientific explanation? Well, it's fairly obvious, even after an evening sipping ale. The oak logs contain something that is burned, something that the fire consumes: phlogiston. Paper is high in phlogiston, so it burns easily and swiftly and leaves only a small residue of ash. Oak also contains a significant amount of phlogiston, so it burns well. Iron bars, by contrast, contain little or no phlogiston, so they do not burn.

That's a very nice account of burning, and it's certainly the account a good amateur scientist like Ben Franklin would have given in the mid-eighteenth century. Phlogiston theory explains a lot, and it proved valuable for chemists studying the nature of air. Phlogiston can't just disappear when it burns, of course, so it must be absorbed into the air (you can almost see it happen as the smoke rises from the fire). If you light a candle and then place it inside a closed container, the candle soon sputters out: the air has become saturated with phlogiston, and cannot absorb any more, so burning must stop. And if we isolate a type of air in which burning occurs very rapidly and vigorously, then obviously we have found air that contains little or no phlogiston, and thus absorbs phlogiston readily and promotes rapid burning. Joseph Priestley, the great British scientist of the late eighteenth century, called it "dephlogisticated air."

But Antoine Lavoisier, a French contemporary of Priestley's, had different ideas. He called the gas oxygen, and proposed a very different account of burning: an account that turns burning into rapid oxidation, rather than loss of phlogiston. That is, something burns when it reacts rapidly with oxygen.

What will decide the issue between phlogiston and oxidation? It won't be simple; in fact, Priestley died a firm believer in phlogiston, decades after Lavoisier developed his account. The scientific debate over phlogiston and oxygen was not like the scientific discovery of a new species of beetle. Rather, it involved a radical and systematic shift in scientific theory (what Thomas Kuhn called a "paradigm shift"). The traditional phlogiston theory viewed air as a single substance, while the new theory of oxygen divided air into many distinct elements, such as oxygen, nitrogen, and hydrogen. How do we decide which theory is right? The issue won't be settled by one observation, or even one key experiment. Instead, the question is: which theory works best, which theoretical model accounts for more, which theory is less cumbersome, and which theory proves more productive?

Establishing Moral Facts

With our look at Nessie and oxygen in the background, consider now the controversy over moral facts. Opponents of moral realism maintain that we don't need special objective moral facts to account for our ethical data. Of course people feel strongly about lots of 'moral issues,' and have strong convictions about right and wrong; but those phenomena can be explained more simply and productively through examining the cultures that shaped us, and the evolutionary process that formed us. Moral realists propose a radically different explanation, positing a different sort of fact—objective moral facts—that cannot simply be added into the opposing view. That is, objective moral facts are more like the Medusa than Nessie. Should the moral realist view be accepted, or the opposing nonrealist, nonobjectivist position?

Contemporary moral realists believe that this issue is similar to the issue that divided believers in phlogiston from proponents of the new gas theories. Resolving that conflict will require looking not just at the specific event, but at the larger question of what explanatory account ultimately works best for a wide range of questions.

Consider a prime candidate for the status of "objective moral fact." On her way to class, Rita sees a small and overly curious child fall into a flood-swollen river. Rita does not know the child, nor the child's mother who is screaming for help. At grave risk to her own safety, Rita plunges into the raging maelstrom and rescues the child. Rita's act is heroic, virtuous, morally good. And moral realists will say that the sentence "Rita performed a morally good act" states a *moral fact*. In contrast, those who deny the existence of moral facts will agree that Rita is heroic, and will agree that Rita's heroism warms their hearts and inspires their admiration; but their warm approval of Rita's act notwithstanding, they will deny that it constitutes an objective moral fact. It is simpler (they will say) to explain Rita's act, and our deep approval of her act, in terms of social conditioning and other facts of psychology and biology and sociology. We don't really require a special category of "moral facts" to make sense of her heroic act, and adding the special category of moral facts makes for a more cumbersome and less economical explanatory scheme. Both the moral realist and her opponent observe the same phenomenon (the heroic rescue), but one observes oxygen while the other sees dephlogisticated air.

MORAL FACTS AND SCIENTIFIC REVOLUTIONS

So what is the *truth* about moral objectivity? Are there real moral facts, or not? According to contemporary moral realists, that is not a simple question, and the verdict isn't in. The verdict will be delivered analogously to the way we get the verdict on the truth of new scientific theories. What happens when a radically new theory is proposed: a theory like the gas theory, that ultimately triumphed over phlogiston? Or Newton's theory, which revolutionized physics? Or Copernicus's theory (the Earth travels around the Sun), that overturned the Ptolemaic theory (the Earth is stationary, and the Sun and all the other planets orbit the Earth)?

Kuhn on the History of Science

Thomas Kuhn, in *The Structure of Scientific Revolutions*, argued that we have a false image of the progress of science. We tend to think that when a new scientific theory is proposed, a crucial experiment is devised to determine whether the old or the new theory is correct, the experiment is carried out, and the old theory survives the challenge or the new theory is proved true. But Kuhn notes that actual scientific practice is not always so neat and clean. Sometimes a new theory does something so impressive that it quickly wins many followers: Halley's prediction of the return of the comet, using Newtonian theory, is a good example of a very impressive scientific prediction. But in that case, most scientists had already adopted Newton's theory years before the comet was sighted, and the failure of the comet to appear would not have caused them to reject Newtonian physics.

Think of the long battle between the Copernicans and followers of Ptolemy. Who is right? Place yourself in the middle of the sixteenth century: you know nothing about gravity, there are no telescopes, there are certainly no space stations. Copernicus proposes a new theory that challenges the longstanding Ptolemaic system. Who is right? How would you decide? Is there some experiment you could do (using only sixteenth-century materials and sixteenth-century science) to decide which theory is true?

Not easy, is it? Well, think about what the two theories claim. Ptolemy claims the Earth is the fixed center of the universe, and everything revolves around it. Copernicus, on the other hand, says the Earth is traveling at a high rate of speed, fast enough to make a complete orbit of the Sun every 365 days: quite a trip. How do we—living in the sixteenth century—decide? Someone devised a brilliant experiment. Suppose that today is the first day of November. According to the Ptolemaic theory, next May the Earth will be exactly where it is right now. But the Copernican theory says that six months from now we'll be a long way from here, all the way over on the other side of the Sun. Suppose Copernicus is right. We make a star sighting tonight, and measure the precise angle between two stars. When we make the same measurement six months from now, the angle should be somewhat different; after all, we are taking measurements from very different locations (on opposite sides of the Sun). The difference between the two angles is called the stellar parallax. The Copernican theory says there should be one; the Ptolemaic theory predicts there will not (because the Earth has not moved).

Back in the late 1500s the astronomers got out their instruments, made meticulous observations, and then repeated the process six months later. And they found: no stellar parallax. The crucial experiment was finished. Copernicus lost, the Ptolemaic theory is true. So scientists rejected the Copernican theory, and the Ptolemaic theory triumphed. But of course that wasn't what happened. Many scientists continued to believe in the

Copernican theory, even after the crucial stellar parallax experiment seemed to prove the Ptolemaic theory true. Instead of rejecting the Copernican theory, they looked for reasons to explain why the stellar parallax didn't show up. Maybe the measurements weren't accurate. Or maybe the distance to the stars is so enormous (when compared to the distance that the Earth travels around the Sun) that the angle of the stellar parallax is too small to detect it with our measuring instruments. (That was the problem. We eventually did develop instruments that could detect the stellar parallax, but centuries later).

So—as Thomas Kuhn notes—the Copernican theory triumphed, despite the fact that a "crucial experiment" went against it. What actually happens, then, when a scientific theory is accepted? It's not a matter of this or that 'crucial experiment' (although experiments obviously have great influence). Rather, the scientific community studies the evidence, conducts experiments, debates the competing theories, revises and amends the competing theories ("The Earth travels around the Sun, *and* the distance between the Sun and the other stars is much greater than we had previously thought"). Eventually out of this debate there emerges a scientific consensus. Usually the dissenters aren't really converted (the dedicated Ptolemaic theorists don't become Copernicans); instead, the defenders of the losing theory gradually die out, and the winning theory gains the allegiance of future generations of scientists.

Moral Realism and Theoretical Revolution

A similar situation exists in ethics, according to the moral realists. Moral realism is one of the competing theories. There's no 'crucial experiment' that will establish either the truth or falsity of moral realism. The question is whether moral realism works better, proves itself more valuable, and whether a consensus forms around our moral judgments in such a way that moral realism emerges as the most plausible explanation. After all, that would be the best evidence we could have for moral realism: we reach some consensus in our moral judgments, we reach general agreement on at least some basic set of moral judgments. If there is such agreement, then the most plausible and productive theory to account for that agreement is that there are *real moral facts* to agree upon.

TWO WAYS THAT MORAL REALISM MIGHT FAIL

One: A Better Theory

There are two ways moral realism can fail. First, we might reach some general agreement concerning ethical principles, but some other theory might prove more useful in explaining that agreement: the agreement is not the result of common perception of moral facts, but instead results from a widespread delusion or large-scale social conditioning or a common biological heritage. But we can't know that in advance, so moral realism—at least for the present—remains a viable and plausible ethical theory. It can't be ruled out in advance by skeptical philosophers. Moral realism must have a fair chance to compete.

Two: No Moral Consensus

The second way that moral realism could fail is if there is no general agreement on moral principles. After all, it is precisely that general agreement that the theory of moral realism is designed to explain. (Some moral realists would argue that moral realism is the best explanation for *other* moral phenomena as well, so even without moral consensus moral realism might serve a legitimate explanatory function.) Moral realism is proposed as the most plausible and productive account of moral consensus. But if there is no moral consensus, then there is nothing for moral realism to explain. That being the case, it might appear that moral realism is a nonstarter. After all, isn't it obvious that there is no general moral agreement? (The raging controversies over abortion, capital punishment, and affirmative action should swiftly dispel any belief in general moral agreement.)

But the moral realist believes that beneath this troubled and controversial surface, we may find a deep calm of moral consensus. That moral consensus won't be found in the shouted confrontations between prolife and prochoice demonstrators, nor will it be found in heated dorm room arguments fueled by too much beer and too little sleep; nor should we expect to find moral consensus among politicians jockeying for votes, or among religious zealots who claim the exclusive right to speak for God. But if we put ourselves in a position to think calmly, observe carefully and without prejudice, and consider thoughtfully, then we may find more convergence than we would have thought at first glance.

When we tone down the rhetoric, and sit down and talk calmly together (a rare event in the highly charged abortion controversy), everyone agrees that killing babies is wrong. There is disagreement, obviously, over whether a fetus is a baby; but that disagreement is important precisely because everyone agrees that it's wrong to kill babies. Of course there are, tragically, times and places where babies have been killed. A parent sometimes murders a child. But when that happens, we usually find that the murderer was suffering severe depression, or perhaps was unhinged by drugs, or inflamed by wild passions. It was not a case when the parent was guided by cool reason. (Of course there are also cultures in which a baby—especially a baby girl—is sometimes killed shortly after birth. Again, we think that in such circumstances the murderers are not guided by cool collected thought, but instead by religious bigotry or deep biases or cultural pressures.) And while the abortion rhetoric may suggest that prolifers have no respect for women's rights to control their own bodies, that again is not really the case. No one on either side believes women should be subject to rape or physical abuse. In fact, both sides agree that women have a basic moral right to control over their own bodies (though one side believes that the right to life of the "unborn baby" trumps the rights of the pregnant woman). Unfortunately there are cultures that deny women any rights whatsoever. Moral realists believe such cultures have not looked at the question calmly and thoughtfully, but instead are swayed by religious indoctrination. So when we turn down the heat in the struggle over abortion, we find a deep cool reservoir of moral agreement beneath the hot and contentious surface.

Perhaps when we put aside religious fervor and cultural biases and heated rhetoric, and instead consider calmly and reflectively, then we shall find that there is a substantial area of moral consensus. Or perhaps not. But—so the moral realist insists—the jury is still out. And so the possibility that objective *moral facts* are the best and most plausible explanation remains a legitimate hypothesis, worthy of continued investigation. Contemporary moral realists do not claim certain knowledge of absolute moral truths. Like nonobjectivists, they agree that absolute moral principles are not discoverable through pure reason or God's will or deep emotions. But they insist that the question of objective moral facts remains to be resolved. Maybe such moral facts don't exist. But just because they aren't absolutes dictated by God or pure reason, we shouldn't conclude that the issue is settled.

REALISM

Michael Smith

Michael Smith, who wrote the essay from which the following passage is excerpted, is a leading contemporary advocate of moral realism. He currently teaches philosophy at Monash University, in Melbourne.

Imagine that you are giving the baby a bath. As you do, it begins to scream uncontrollably. Nothing you do seems to help. As you watch it scream, you are overcome with a desire to drown the baby in the bathwater. Certainly you may now be *motivated* to drown the baby. (You may even actually drown it.) But does the mere fact that you have this desire, and are thus motivated, mean that you have a *reason* to drown the baby?

One commonsensical answer is that, since the desire is not *worth* satisfying, it does not provide you with such a reason; that, in this case, you are motivated to do something you have *no* reason to do. However, the standard picture seems utterly unable to accept this answer. After all, your desire to drown the baby need be based on no false belief. As such, it is entirely beyond rational criticism—or so that standard picture tells us.

The problem, here, is that the standard picture gives no special privilege to what we would want if we were 'cool, calm and collected' (to use a flippant phrase). Yet we seem ordinarily to think that not being cool, calm and collected may lead to all sorts of irrational emotional outbursts. Having those desires that we would have if we were cool, calm and collected thus seems to be an independent rational ideal. When cool, calm and collected, you would wish for the baby not to be drowned, no matter how much it screams, and no matter how overcome you may be, in your uncool, uncalm and uncollected state, with a desire to drown it. This is why you have no reason to drown the baby.

Perhaps we have already said enough to reconcile the objectivity of moral judgement with its practicality. Judgements of right and wrong are judgements about what we have reason to do and reason not to do. But what sort of fact is a fact about what we have reason to do? The preceding discussion suggests an

answer. It suggests that facts about what we have reason to do are not facts about what we *do* desire, as the standard picture would have it, but are rather facts about what we *would* desire if we were in certain idealized conditions of reflection; if, say, we were well-informed, cool, calm and collected. According to this account then, I have a reason to give to famine relief in my particular circumstances just in case, if I were in such idealized conditions of reflection. I would desire that, even when in my particular circumstances, I give to famine relief. And this sort of fact may certainly be the object of a belief.

Moreover, this account of what it is to have a reason makes it plain why the standard picture of human psychology is wrong to insist that beliefs and desires are altogether distinct; why, on the contrary, having certain beliefs, beliefs about that we have reason to do, does make it rational for us to have certain desires, desires to do what we believe we have reason to do.

In order to see this, suppose I believe that I would desire to give to famine belief if I were cool, calm and collected—i.e. more colloquially, I believe I have a reason to give to famine relief—but, being uncool, uncalm and uncollected, I don't desire to give to famine relief. Am I rationally criticizable for not having the desire? I surely am. After all, from my own point of view my beliefs and desires form a more coherent, and thus a rationally preferable, package if I do in fact desire to do what I believe I would desire to do if I were cool, calm and collected. This is because, since it is an independent rational ideal to have the desires I would have if I were cool, calm and collected, so, from my own point of view, if I believe that I would have a certain desire under such conditions and yet fail to have it, then my beliefs and desires fail to meet this ideal. To believe that I would desire to give to famine relief if I were cool, calm and collected, and yet to fail to desire to give to famine relief, is thus to manifest a commonly recognizable species of rational failure.

If this is right, then it follows that, contrary to the standard picture of human psychology, there is in fact no problem at all in supposing that I may have genuine *beliefs* about what I have reason to do, where having those beliefs makes it rational for me to have the corresponding *desires*. And if there is no problem at all in supposing that this may be so, then there is no problem in reconciling the practicality of moral judgement with the claim that moral judgements express our beliefs about the reasons we have.

However, this doesn't yet suffice to solve the problem facing the moral realist. For moral judgements aren't *just* judgements about the reasons we have. They are judgements about the reasons we have *where those reasons are supposed to be determined entirely by our circumstances*. As I put it earlier, people in the same circumstances face the same moral choice: if they did the same action then either they both acted rightly (they both did what they had reason to do) or they both acted wrongly (they both did what they had reason not to do). Does the account of what it is to have a reason just given entail that this is so?

Suppose our circumstances are identical, and let's ask whether it is right for each of us to give to famine relief: that is, whether we each have a reason to do so. According to the account on offer it is right that I give to famine relief just in case I have a reason to give to famine relief, and I have such a reason just in case, if I were in idealized conditions of reflection— well-informed, cool, calm and collected—I would desire to give to famine relief. And the same is true of you. If our circumstances are the same then, suppos- edly, we should both have such a reason or both lack such a reason. But do we?

The question is whether, if we were well-informed, cool, calm and collected we would tend to *converge* in the desires we have. Would we converge or would there always be the possibility of some non-rationally- explicable difference in our desires *even under such conditions?* The standard picture of human psychology now returns to centre-stage. For it tells us that there is *always* the possibility of some non-rationally-explicable difference in our desires even under such idealized

conditions of reflection. This is the residue of the stan- dard picture's conception of desire as a psychological state that is beyond rational criticism.

If this is right then the moral realist's attempt to combine the objectivity and the practicality of moral judgement must be deemed a failure. We are forced to accept that there is a *fundamental relativity* in the rea- sons we have. What we have reason to do is relative to what we would desire under certain idealized con- ditions of reflection, and this may differ from person to person. It is not wholly determined by our circum- stances, as moral facts are supposed to be.

Many philosophers accept the standard picture's pronouncement on this point. But accepting there is such a fundamental relativity in our reasons seems altogether premature to me. It puts the cart before the horse. For surely moral practice is itself the forum in which we will *discover* whether there is a fundamental relativity in our reasons.

After all, in moral practice we attempt to change people's moral beliefs by engaging them in rational argument: i.e. by getting their beliefs to approximate those they would have under more idealized condi- tions of reflection. And sometimes we succeed. When we succeed, other things being equal, we succeed in changing their desires. But if we accept that there is a fundamental relativity in our reasons then we can say, in advance, that this procedure will never result in a massive *convergence* in moral beliefs; for we know in advance that there will never be a convergence in the desires we have under such idealized conditions of reflection. Or rather, and more accurately, if there is a fundamental relativity in our reasons then it follows that any convergence we find in our moral beliefs, and thus in our desires, must be entirely contingent. It could in no way be explained by, or suggestive of, the fact that the desires that emerge have some *privileged* rational status.

My question is: 'Why accept this?' Why not think, instead, that if such a convergence emerged in moral practice then that would itself suggest that these particular moral beliefs, and the corresponding desires, *do* enjoy a privileged rational status? After all, something like such a convergence in mathematically practice lies behind our conviction that mathemati- cal claims enjoy a privileged rational status. So why not think that a like convergence in moral practice would show that moral judgements enjoy the same privileged rational status? At this point, the standard picture's insistence that there is a fundamental relativity in our reasons begins to sound all too much like a hollow dogma.

The kind of moral realism described here endorses a conception of moral facts that is a far cry from the picture presented at the outset: moral facts as queer facts about the universe whose recognition necessarily impacts upon our desires. Instead, the realist has eschewed queer facts about the universe in favour of a more 'subjectivist' conception of moral facts. This emerged in the realist's analysis of what it is to have a reason. The realist's point, however, is that such a conception of moral facts may make them subjective only in the innocuous sense that they are facts about what we would *want* under certain idealized conditions of reflection, where wants are, admittedly, a kind of psychological state enjoyed by subjects. But moral facts remain objective insofar as they are facts about what *we*, not just *you* or *I*, would

want under such conditions. The existence of a moral fact—say, the rightness of giving to famine relief in certain circumstances—requires that, under idealized conditions of reflection, rational creatures would *converge* upon a desire to give to famine relief in such circumstances.

Of course, it must be agreed on all sides that moral argument has not yet produced the sort of convergence in our desires that would make the idea of a moral fact—a fact about the reasons we have entirely determined by our circumstances—look plausible. But neither has moral argument had much of a history in times in which we have been able to engage in free reflection unhampered by a false biology (the Aristotelian tradition) or a false belief in God (the Judeo-Christian tradition). It remains to be seen whether sustained moral argument can elicit the requisite convergence in our moral beliefs, and corresponding desires, to make the idea of a moral fact look plausible. The kind of moral realism described here holds out the hope that it will. Only time will tell.

EXERCISES

1. There is a major press conference at the University of Michigan. A group of distinguished researchers from psychology, sociology, philosophy, and biology have all gathered to announce an important discovery: the clear and confirmed discovery of a moral fact. Would you find that more or less plausible than the announcement by a similarly distinguished group of researchers from the physics department that they have discovered a new subatomic particle?

2. Suppose you look at the evidence presented by this distinguished group from the University of Michigan and decide their announced discovery of a moral fact is well-supported, reasonable, very plausible. You are now convinced these researchers have made the confirmed *scientific discovery* of a moral fact. Would that please you or disappoint you?

3. Many moral realists insist that the question of objective moral facts remains an open question, not yet resolved. If that is the case, how long should we wait before deciding that failure to discover an objective moral fact is strong evidence that such facts do not exist?

4. If we never reach moral consensus, might the moral realists still be able to make a case for moral realism?

5. Moral realists claim we are most likely to discover objective moral facts when we think calmly and reflectively and carefully—and the main reason we haven't reached moral consensus is that we have not thought calmly and carefully. Could the moral realist offer any proof that calm reflection is the best approach to achieving moral consensus?

6. Contemporary moral realism is a type of moral *objectivism*—along with Kantian and intuitionist theories. But although all three are *objectivist* views, the intuitionist and the

Kantian hold very different views from the contemporary moral realist. What would you consider the most *basic* difference between the Kantian and the moral realist? Between the intuitionist and the contemporary moral realist?

ADDITIONAL READING

Geoff Sayre-McCord, *Essays on Moral Realism* (Ithaca, N.Y.: Cornell University Press, 1988) is a superb anthology, bringing together many of the best papers on moral realism. Another excellent anthology—which discusses moral realism and a great deal more—is *Morality, Reason and Truth: New Essays on the Foundations of Ethics* David Copp and David Zimmerman, editors (Totowa, N. J.: Rowman & Allanheld, 1984).

One of the best and clearest accounts of moral realism is a paper by Peter Railton: *The Philosophical Review,* 95 (1986), 163–207. An excellent book-length study of moral realism is David O. Brink's *Moral Realism and the Foundations of Ethics* (Cambridge: Cambridge University Press, 1989).

CHAPTER 12

♦ HOW HARD IS ETHICS? ♦

We have looked at several contrasting views concerning ethics. First, the contrast between those who think ethical principles must be transcendent absolutes, and those who believe ethics is a matter of grubby, worldly, contingent truths. And second, the contrast between those who believe ethics is fundamentally based in reason, and the contrasting position of those who regard feelings as the basis of ethics. Third, the difference between ethical *objectivists* and *non*objectivists. There is a fourth perspective for looking at ethics: How *hard* is ethics?

How hard is ethics? This is not a question about how hard this ethics *course* is. Is it a gut course, in which you're guaranteed at least a B if you occasionally show up? Or is it a monster that leaves brilliant students in tears and their GPAs in tatters? Rather, this is a question of how hard it is to *live ethically*.

THE DEMANDS OF ETHICAL LIVING

Obviously there are circumstances when morality makes very difficult demands. Imagine yourself living in Poland under the Nazi regime. The Nazis have already murdered many Jews, and are now sending others to the death camps. One of your friends at the university is Jewish, and fleeing from the Nazis she shows up late one night at your door, desperately seeking a hiding place. You know the Nazi regime is committing terrible crimes against Jews, and that your friend will certainly be murdered without your help. But you also know that the Nazis execute those who are caught hiding Jews, and that protecting your friend could cost you your life. You have no doubt that you *ought* to hide your friend, but this is a case in which the demands of morality are very high indeed.

Important though such cases may be, they are also special circumstances. Set them aside for a moment, and consider your current life. You are at college, in reasonably decent circumstances. College students don't live in luxury, the cafeteria food is not exactly haute cuisine, and your roommate may be something of a toxic hazard. But at least you have food to eat and a roof over your head and no immediate threats to your life. So consider life in your current situation. Is living a good moral life easy? Or is it a difficult and demanding task? Is the moral path straight and narrow, or broad and easy?

Are We Naturally Moral?

The way you answer that question reveals a lot about how you view morality, and also about how you view humanity. Are we naturally moral? This cuts across the previous distinctions, and often divides those who otherwise hold very similar views. Among social contract theorists, Rousseau believed our natural state (without the constraints of rules and laws) was one of simple harmony. In contrast, Hobbes believed the "state of nature"— with no laws, and no powerful authorities to enforce the laws—was a war of all against all, in which our natural greed and aggressiveness resulted in constant conflict. And among the nonobjectivists, Sartre believes making moral choices is a heavy and frightening burden: we must make important choices, and we bear the total responsibility for our choices, but we have absolutely no guidance or knowledge to aid us with our choices. Other nonobjectivists—perhaps Hume—believe there are no objectively true moral principles, but we don't much miss them. Our moral lives are guided by deep natural inclinations, and we need not spend a lot of time reasoning or worrying about it. Still other nonobjectivists may regard the whole question as hopeless. It's like asking how difficult it is to work out a reliable astrological chart: since the notion of a reliable astrological chart is nonsense, it makes no sense to ask whether it is hard or easy to cast reliable charts.

Your view of the *difficulty* of living a moral life is likely to be one of those deep hidden assumptions that subtly shapes your judgment of which moral theory seems most plausible. For some people, it seems clear and obvious that living a moral life is a difficult and demanding endeavor. It's like staying on a diet. All the things you really *want* to eat— chocolate chip cookies, fettuccini alfredo with heavy cream sauce, eggs benedict, chocolates with gooey centers—are bad for you. Evil comes in very attractive packages, and resistance requires constant vigilance. The path of virtue is straight and narrow, and it's terribly easy to take a wrong turn down the back roads with their neon lights, flashy appeal, and sweet temptations. In the late sixteenth century, Michel Montaigne summed up this view eloquently: "The easy, gentle, and sloping path . . . is not the path of true virtue. It demands a rough and thorny road."

In contrast, others see moral behavior as an easy and natural process. You don't need to think hard about it, or devote all your energies to resisting temptation. We are social beings, with natural feelings of pity and sympathy, and living morally comes naturally to us. Obviously there are people who are profoundly bad, and all of us do bad things occasionally, but these are special cases. Except in particularly problematic or stressful circumstances, moral behavior is a natural part of our social lives.

Starting Assumptions About Ethics

Probably one of those views—living morally is easy, living morally is hard—seems approximately right to you, and the other may strike you as rather ridiculous, the sort of view that no one could seriously hold. Stop and think for a moment about *why* one perspective seems more plausible than the other. Do you have any clear *evidence* that one perspective is the right one? Could you give a cogent argument for one view and against the other? More importantly, did you adopt your own perspective on the basis of argument or evidence?

Probably not. In fact, your perspective on this issue is likely to color what you regard as plausible argument concerning morality. It acts as a filter on what you consider evidence on moral issues. And it may strongly and subtly influence what you consider a *live option* in morality.

Comparing Ethical Systems on the Basis of Difficulty

Let's look at specific moral views in terms of whether they portray morality as hard or easy. We might start by examining some religious traditions. In orthodox Judaism, living a good moral life is a rigorous and demanding process. There are myriad rules that must be followed precisely, and the rules govern almost every detail of life: how to eat, how to dress, how to worship, when to work; and the rules themselves require rigorous examination, extensive commentary, and long study. (Though those are *difficult* demands, Orthodox Jews need not regard them as onerous and burdensome. Strict dietary laws may be demanding, but for some people such laws also afford the opportunity to invest the most ordinary elements of their lives with deep moral or spiritual significance. What they eat and wear, how they travel, when they work—all these mundane activities are given religious and moral importance.) Some of the later Jewish prophets seemed to take a very different view. For example, the prophet Micah asked: "What doth the Lord require of thee, but to do justly, and to love mercy, and to walk humbly with thy God?" And Micah was clearly implying that these requirements were simple and easy to keep (though obviously not everyone met them). Jesus, as he wandered and preached, seemed to teach that living a good moral life is simple and easy; child's play, so to speak: "Suffer the little children to come unto me, for such is the kingdom of Heaven." Simply love God and love your neighbor, feed the hungry, care for the sick, help those in need—and all of that is natural and easy, a "light burden." Don't think about the morrow, don't worry about the rules; just love and help your neighbor, and that is what we are naturally inclined to do anyway (like children showing spontaneous affection). Of course some are corrupted, and refuse to feed the hungry, but those are people who have been corrupted by wealth, and have become greedy and cold. Absent such corruption, we have a natural inclination (as children of God) toward kindness to one another. In dramatic contrast, traditional Christianity—especially as formulated by Martin Luther and John Calvin, but also embedded in the Catholic doctrine of original sin—insists that we are profoundly and hopelessly and *naturally* evil and selfish, wicked and loathsome, and only by a rare and special miraculous dispensation from God do a few overcome their natural evil tendencies and become morally good.

Eastern Views

The Taoist tradition treats the development of moral tendencies as a natural process, and Taoism *discourages* hard striving. To the contrary, we live better when we devote less attention to ethical rules and principles and instead follow natural ethical feelings (though we do an improved job of this as we come to realize the connectedness, the oneness, of everything and everyone). In the words of Lao-tse (who was advising Confucius to do less moralizing):

> All this talk of goodness and duty, these perpetual pin-pricks unnerve and irritate the hearer. You had best study how it is that Heaven and Earth maintain their eternal course, that the sun and moon maintain their light, the stars their seried ranks, the birds and beasts their flocks, the trees and shrubs their station. Thus you too should learn to guide your steps by Inward Power, to follow the course that the Way of Nature sets; and soon you will no longer need to go round laboriously advertising goodness and duty.[1]

Mencius, a Chinese Confucian philosopher of the fourth century BCE, also believed our natural tendency is toward virtue:

If you let people follow their feelings (original nature), they will be able to do good. This is what is meant by saying that human nature is good. If man does evil, it is not the fault of his natural endowment. The feeling of commiseration is found in all men, the feeling of shame and dislike is found in all men; the feeling of respect and reverence is found is all men; and the feeling of right and wrong is found in all men. . . . Humanity, righteousness, propriety, and wisdom are not drilled into us from outside. We originally have them with us.[2]

This natural tendency toward goodness can be destroyed, but only by placing the person in a horrific environment in which good character cannot grow naturally.

Taoism, along with Mencius, counsels a natural and easy path toward moral goodness. In contrast, perhaps the most severe and demanding ethical tradition—an Eastern parallel to Kant's rationalist moral austerity—can be found in Jainism, a version of Hindu thought. For the Jainists, all pleasure is evil, a distraction from the path of enlightenment. The moral path requires the renouncing of all pleasures, and adherence to an austere and ascetic life. Pleasure should be avoided, and suffering quietly endured. The path of true morality has nothing to do with feelings, whether of pleasure or kindness; rather, genuine morality requires the ascetic control or suppression of all feelings, in order to reach higher consciousness.

Kant's Austere Ethics

Turning to the ethical theories we examined in earlier chapters, it seems clear that Kantian rationalism is far removed from the view that there is anything natural or easy or agreeable in ethics. As you recall, Kant insisted that if your kind or generous act is motivated by a *feeling* of warm affection, then your agreeable act has no moral worth. To act morally, one must be motivated *exclusively* by rational commitment to the universal moral law. There is nothing easy or natural about acting morally; to the contrary, it requires the rational power to recognize absolute moral laws that transcend our natural world, as well as the special—almost miraculous—power of will to rise above all natural feelings and inclinations. Some might suggest this is a moral code more suited to gods than humans, but for Kant, our special capacity to act morally is what raises us above the natural world and makes us godlike.

Plato takes a similar position. Plato believed our natural desires are greedy and depraved, and that they must be held in tight check by the powers of reason. He compared the human soul to a city-state made up of wise philosophers, strong soldiers, and the unruly and undisciplined mob of ordinary people. So long as the wise philosophers rule, through the power of reason, and are supported by the strong and courageous soldiers, then the masses of workers can be kept under control and the nation will function well. But if the mass of workers seize control, then the nation will become disordered and chaotic, since the masses are not well-suited for governing (Plato was no friend of democracy). Likewise, so long as the individual is governed by the power of reason, and reason is assisted by courage and willpower (the soldiers), then the mass of unruly desires can be suppressed, and the person will live a good moral life. But if reason for a moment lets down its guard, then the desires will exert their power and seize control and lead the person to corruption and immorality.

Care Ethics

At the polar opposite of Kantian-Platonic ethics we find ethical systems that—rather than *rejecting* natural feelings as a temptation or distraction—make such feelings the ethical cornerstone. In care ethics, our feelings of affection originate with our family and friends, and extend outward from that basic natural foundation, and these natural feelings are the heart and soul of ethics. Rather than starting from rationally derived universal principles, ethics starts at home: in caring relationships with specific individuals. If your kindness toward your family, your friends, and your neighbors is motivated by impersonal rules rather than personal affection, then you are morally impaired rather than morally heroic.

While ethical systems based on feelings are certainly less strenuous than Kantian rationalism, they need not maintain that ethics is always *easy*. Their slogan is *not* "If it feels good, do it." Feelings are important. They are the foundation and the motivation for ethical behavior. But feelings are not to be followed blindly. As Jonathan Bennett pointed out, sometimes our feelings must be subjected to rational scrutiny. There is no doubt that many people have strong *feelings* of racial or ethnic or gender prejudice, but such feelings cannot withstand critical examination. Aware of the problems with some of our feelings, some ethical theorists who believe feelings are the foundation of ethics insist that not just any feelings will do. Feelings must be schooled, developed, and examined before we use them as the basis of moral behavior. In fact, one might maintain that ethics is based on feelings and inclinations, but there is nothing easy about it: shaping the right sorts of feelings is a difficult and demanding process. Aristotle seemed to favor that position.

Aristotle and Virtue

According to Aristotle, we are naturally suited to moral goodness, but we don't *automatically* develop such inclinations. Rather, they must be carefully cultivated and developed by rigorous practice. For Aristotle, the ideal of virtuous behavior is doing the right thing because you *want* to do the right thing, because you desire to act virtuously. But in order to reach that point, you must carefully and consistently practice doing right until it becomes habitual and natural. If instead you act selfishly and deceitfully, then you will become a selfish and deceitful person. The idea that you might cheat on exams, lie to your friends, and act selfishly throughout your high school and college life, but then turn around and become a profoundly virtuous physician or lawyer or accountant after you graduate: that is nonsense. If you practice deceitful, dissolute, selfish behavior, then what feels right to you may be very wrong. Your habits and inclinations and desires develop with practice, and what you sow is what you reap. With practice and effort, you can develop the habits and inclinations of an honest, generous, virtuous person; but you can no more become virtuous without diligent practice than you can become a great runner or a superb violinist just by choosing to be so.

Intuitionists

When we turn to the intuitionists, we find a range of views concerning the difficulty of ethics. For some, our intuitions of right and wrong are obvious and clear (whether we are intuiting the truth of moral principles or the justice of a specific act). If you fail to have the correct intuitions, then you are a moral monster who has been hopelessly corrupted by either terrible influences or by your own recklessly dissolute life. Other intuitionists hold that intuitive insights must be preceded by careful preparation. You must purify your thoughts in order to see the moral intuition clearly, or perhaps you must scrutinize all the details of the situation you are considering in order to intuit what is right in these specific circumstances. (When dealing with intuitionism, this is largely a question of how difficult it is to intuit *what* we ought to do; the difficulty of actually *doing* what we know is right is not an issue intuitionists worry about as much. Intuitionists tend to believe that *if* we really get in touch with this deep moral reservoir of intuition, we will be more than halfway toward doing the right thing.)

Utilitarians

You might think that ethics is easy for utilitarians. Decide what will produce the greatest balance of pleasure over pain for everyone, and do it. But it's not as easy as it sounds. In the first place, as we noted earlier, the calculations can be difficult to make: our acts may have consequences that are tough to predict. But it is not only difficult to make utilitarian calculations; it is also difficult to follow utilitarian principles. Under the utilitarian model, almost every aspect of our lives is permeated by ethical considerations. If I decide to go bowling tonight with my friends, that seems an innocent way to pass an evening, and does not appear to raise serious moral issues. But from a utilitarian perspective, I must calculate whether going bowling is likely to produce the greatest possible balance of pleasure over pain. My friends and I will gain moderate pleasure from an evening of bowling, but wouldn't working in a homeless shelter and contributing the cost of bowling to famine relief do considerably more to reduce suffering? Some moderate pleasures (from bowling) will be lost, but the gains in reduction of suffering more than offset those losses. Since I *ought* to do whatever will produce the greatest balance of pleasure over suffering, my apparently innocent night of bowling becomes morally problematic. And we can extend such questions much further. My home is not a luxurious estate, but it does contain several rooms and a couple of baths, and there are many around the world who are homeless. By living in a smaller home, and devoting the extra money to providing homes for the homeless, a small amount of convenience would be sacrificed for a substantial reduction in suffering. Thus utilitarian calculations seem to demand that I move to a smaller house and use the extra resources for housing others in severe need. And indeed, every aspect of my life will have to be evaluated by that utilitarian measure. Utilitarian calculations don't quite demand that we sell *all* we have and give it to the poor, but they make strong demands on our resources. In particular, they leave no moral room for enjoying luxuries while others suffer the lack of necessities. Utilitarian ethics is sometimes disparaged as low and mean-spirited, concerned only with pleasure. Examined more closely, it is a very demanding ethical system for those who attempt to live by its calculations.

DUTY AND FEELINGS

The question of whether ethics is difficult or easy goes back to the debate between Christina and Dekisha. Dekisha believes in the stern demands of *duty:* if you're merely doing what feels good, you may be doing something good in caring for the homeless, but you haven't really acted ethically. In Dekisha's Kantian view, if it doesn't require real effort of will, morally it's not worth doing. This sort of view is common in many areas, ethical and otherwise. If the medicine doesn't taste bad, it's probably not very effective. Gaining wisdom is hard and laborious work. William Butler Yeats, the great Irish poet, expressed the opposing view: "Wisdom is a butterfly, and not a gloomy bird of prey." Or in the immortal words of Homer Simpson, "If something is hard to do, then it's not worth doing." On this opposing view, if you are striving and struggling to be ethical, then you haven't reached the right level of ethical development. Christina's joyous caring is more morally wholesome than Dekisha's dutiful struggle. Or maybe neither side is quite right, and Aristotle is closer to the truth: ethical behavior is something you learn by doing. Acting ethically is like learning to type: it's hard when you start, but it gets easier as you practice.

The question of whether ethics is hard or easy has a parallel in questions concerning free will. Does genuine free will require a special effort of will, or is free will simply the free following of your own desires? Is free will a special human power that requires great effort, or is it a natural and easy process? But that's a question we'll save for the next chapter.

THE BOOK OF MENCIUS

Mencius

Mencius was a fourth century BCE Confucian philosopher. The *Book of Mencius* was probably put together after his death by his students. Mencius actively campaigned against other philosophers he thought mistaken; thus his own teachings are typically presented in contrast to the views of someone he is critiquing. Though Mencius defends the Confucian tradition, he emphasizes our natural intuitive inclination to goodness, whereas Confucius had focused more on preservation of the social code of conduct.

BOOK SIX, PART I

6A:1. Kao Tzu said, "Human nature is like the willow tree, and righteousness is like a cup or a bowl. To turn human nature into humanity and righteousness is like turning the willow into cups and bowls." Mencius said, "Sir, can you follow the nature of the willow tree and make the cups and bowls, or must you violate the nature of the willow tree before you can make the cups and bowls? If you are going to violate the nature of the willow tree in order to make cups and bowls, then must you also violate human nature in order to make it into humanity and righteousness? Your words, alas! would lead all people in the world to consider humanity and righteousness as calamity [because they required the violation of human nature]!"

6A:2. Kao Tzu said, "Man's nature is like whirling water. If a breach in the pool is made to the east it will flow to the east. If a breach is made to the west it will flow to the west. Man's nature is indifferent to good and evil, just as water is indifferent to east and west." Mencius said, "Water, indeed, is indifferent to the east and west, but is it indifferent to high and low? Man's nature is naturally good just as water naturally flows downward. There is no man without this good nature; neither is there water that does not flow downward. Now you can strike water and cause it to splash upward over your forehead, and by damming and leading it, you can force it uphill. Is this the nature of water? It is the forced circumstance that makes it do so. Man can be made to do evil, for his nature can be treated in the same way."

6A:6. Kung-tu Tzu said, "Kao Tzu said that man's nature is neither good nor evil. Some say that man's

nature may be made good or evil, therefore when King Wen and King Wu were in power the people loved virtue, and when Kings Yu and Li were in power people loved violence. Some say that some men's nature is good and some men's nature is evil. Therefore even under (sage-emperor) Yao there was Hsiang [who daily plotted to kill his brother], and even with a bad father Ku-sou, there was [a most filial] Shun (Hsiang's brother who succeeded Yao), and even with (wicked king) Chou as uncle and ruler, there were Viscount Ch'i of Wei and Prince Pi-kan. Now you say that human nature is good. Then are those people wrong?"

Mencius said, "If you let people follow their feelings (original nature), they will be able to do good. This is what is meant by saying that human nature is good. If man does evil, it is not the fault of his natural endowment. The feeling of commiseration is found in all men; the feeling of shame and dislike is found in all men; the feeling of respect and reverence is found in all men; and the feeling of right and wrong is found in all men. The feeling of commiseration is what we call humanity; the feeling of shame and dislike is what we called righteousness; the feeling of respect and reverence is what we called propriety (*li*); and the feeling of right and wrong is what we called wisdom. Humanity, righteousness, propriety, and wisdom are not drilled into us from outside. We originally have them with us. Only we do not think [to find them]. Therefore it is said, 'Seek and you will find it, neglect and you will lose it.' [Men differ in the development of their endowments], some twice as much as others, some five times, and some to an incalculable degree, because no one can develop his original endowment to the fullest extent. *The Book of Odes* says, 'Heaven produces the teeming multitude. As there are things there are their specific principles. When the people keep their normal nature they will love excellent virtue.' Confucius said, 'The writer of this poem indeed knew the Way (Tao). Therefore as there are things, there must be their specific principles, and since people keep to their normal nature, therefore they love excellent virtue.'"

6A:7. Mencius said, "In good years most of the young people behave well. In bad years most of them abandon themselves to evil. This is not due to any difference in the natural capacity endowed by Heaven. The abandonment is due to the fact that the mind is allowed to fall into evil. Take for instance the growing of wheat. You sow the seeds and cover them with soil. The land is the same and the time of sowing is also the same. In time they all grow up luxuriantly. When the time of harvest comes, they are all ripe. Although there may be a difference between the different stalks of wheat, it is due to differences in the soil, as rich or poor, to the unequal nourishment obtained from the rain and the dew, and to differences in human effort. Therefore all things of the same kind are similar to one another. Why should there be any doubt about men? The sage and I are the same in kind.

6A:8. Mencius said, "The trees of the Niu Mountain were once beautiful. But can the mountain be regarded any longer as beautiful since, being in the borders of a big state, the trees have been hewed down with axes and hatchets? Still with the rest given them by the days and nights and the nourishment provided them by the rains and the dew, they were not without buds and sprouts springing forth. But then the cattle and the sheep pastured upon them once and again. That is why the mountain looks so bald. When people see that it is so bald, they think that there was never any timber on the mountain. Is this the true nature of the mountain? Is there not [also] a heart of humanity and righteousness originally existing in man? The way in which he loses his originally good mind is like the way in which the trees are hewed down with axes and hatchets. As trees are cut down day after day, can a mountain retain its beauty? To be sure, the days and nights do the healing, and there is the nourishing air of the calm morning which keeps him normal in his likes and dislikes. But the effect is slight, and is disturbed and destroyed by what he does during the day. When there is repeated disturbance, the restorative influence of the night will not be sufficient to preserve (the proper goodness of the mind). When the influence of the night is not sufficient to preserve it, man becomes not much different from the beast. People see that he acts like an animal, and think that he never had the original endowment (for goodness). But is that his true character? Therefore with proper nourishment and care, everything grows, whereas without proper nourishment and care, everything decays.

EXERCISES

1. "Feeding the hungry because you hope to gain reward—either an award as 'outstanding all-round student at North State University,' or treasure in heaven—is morally empty. Feeding the hungry because you believe it is your duty (and you do your duty, but you take no joy in it) is morally minimal. Feeding the hungry because you share their sorrow and rejoice in their comfort is to become a genuinely moral person." Would you agree or disagree?

2. Consider the statement in Question 1. Would a utilitarian say that those are differences that make no difference, that the act is morally equivalent in all three cases? *Must* a utilitarian take that view?

3. "Acting morally is like swinging a golf club. When it seems easy and natural and comfortable, then you know you have it right." Is that true?

4. "Anyone who genuinely and profoundly *understands* what is right and what is wrong would never be tempted to do wrong." Is that true?

5. Think of three friends: friends with whom you have not discussed ethical theory (if indeed you can think of three friends with whom you haven't discussed these issues).

Would you be able to predict their answers to Question 3, on the basis of what you know about their personalities? Would they be able to predict *your* answer?

6. If you discovered your fiancee had views that were the polar opposite of yours on the question of whether ethics is hard or easy, would that cause you to think twice about your wedding plans?

ADDITIONAL READING

Some of the most important sources for this topic—such as Hume and Kant—are listed in other suggested readings. Plato's *Republic* is an excellent example of the view that genuinely ethical behavior requires great struggle. The contrasting view, that ethical behavior is natural and relatively easy, is found in Mencius (excerpted previously). A good English translation can be found in Wing-Tsit Chan, *A Sourcebook in Chinese Philosophy* (Princeton, N.J.: Princeton University Press, 1963). Jean-Jacques Rousseau takes a position somewhat similar to that of Mencius; see *A Discourse on the Origin of Inequality*, trans. Franklin Philip (Oxford: Oxford University Press, 1994; originally published in 1755).

NOTES

[1] Quotation taken from Raymond M. Smullyan's delightful "Is God a Taoist?" in *The Tao Is Silent* (New York: Harper & Row, 1977).

[2] *The Book of Mencius*, from *A Source Book in Chinese Philosophy*, trans. and comp. by Wing-Tsit Chan (Princeton University Press, N.J., 1963), p. 55. Written c.350 BCE.

CHAPTER 13

✧ FREE WILL ✧

Questions about free will are closely linked to questions about ethics. But the nature of that link is more controversial. Is free will essential to ethics? What's the relation between free will and moral responsibility? Between moral responsibility and ethics? Before we can examine these issues we must know what free will *is*. That turns out to be a difficult and contentious question.

DETERMINISM

Questions about free will are often prompted by concerns about *determinism*. Determinism is the thesis that for absolutely every event that happens—every leaf that falls, star that explodes, word that is spoken, idea considered—there is a set of past events that caused it to happen; and given the state of the cosmos at any point in time together with the fixed laws that govern all events, everything that will follow is inevitable. The eighteenth-century French philosopher, LaPlace, expressed the idea through the picture of "LaPlace's demon": if there were some all-knowing being, who knew the exact state of the entire cosmos at any given time, and all the laws governing the cosmos, then it could predict every detail of the world at any future time. There are two special sources for belief in determinism. One is based in religion, and the other in natural science.

God and Determinism

Consider some of the major characteristics attributed to God by Jews, Christians, and Muslims. God has no limits, and is thus omnipresent. God is not merely very strong, but *all*-powerful: omnipotent. And not just bright, but *all*-knowing: omniscient. This awe-inspiring concept of God also inspires some serious questions. If God knows everything, then God knows everything I have ever done. Furthermore, God knows everything I *will* do, and has known it *forever* (an *omniscient* God—Who knows *everything*—obviously can't add knowledge as He goes along, because there's no additional knowledge to add). But if a thousand years ago God already knew all my thoughts, choices, and behavior, then am I really acting freely? Am I making genuine choices, or is my life just a script I am destined to follow? And if God has all power, how can I have independent power to choose and act?

Science and Determinism

So the concept of God as an all-knowing, all-powerful being was one source of determinist belief. A second source was the development of Newtonian physics. Building on the work of Copernicus, Galileo, and Kepler, Isaac Newton developed a system of mathematically precise and elegantly simple laws that explained the motion of the planets, the falling of a rock, the orbit of the moon, and even the path of a comet. Before Newton, comets were considered strange and inexplicable, bright moving lights with long tails that disrupted the clockwork precision of the starry skies, glowing alien invaders that threatened established order. They were messages from an angry God, or perhaps harbingers of doom. But using Newtonian principles and ancient observations, Edmund Halley predicted the return of the comet that now bears his name: not only its return, but when it would appear, at what point in the sky, and what path it would follow. The British poet Alexander Pope captured the triumphant spirit:

> Nature and Nature's laws lay hid in night:
> God said, Let Newton be! and all was light.

In the heady excitement of Newtonian physics many wondered if similar laws might be found for other elements of our world. Newtonian physics predicted the paths of comets. Might science also discover precise laws governing the apparent spontaneity and unpredictability of human behavior? Thus people began to consider the possibility that human behavior (and everything else in the universe) was governed by fixed laws. Those laws might be difficult to discover—after all, human behavior seems at least as complex as the orbit of a comet, and it took many years to understand that—but such explanations may at least be possible. If so, such laws govern a *determined* universe.

Hume's Argument for Determinism

David Hume was a strong champion of determinism. Indeed, Hume maintained that determinism is the only reasonable possibility, and that we *all* believe in determinism. Suppose that just now, as you are sitting quietly in your chair contemplating the joys of philosophy, the door to your room very slowly (and rather mysteriously) creaks open. "Why did my door open?" you ask yourself. Probably you don't give it much thought, fascinated as you are by your philosophical inquiries. But concentrate on the opening door for just a moment: why did it open? "Probably a breeze in the hall," you suggest, but the air is absolutely still. "Maybe the door is not quite level." So you get out your level and check the door—and it turns out to be dead level. "Maybe there was a very small tremor." But seismic reports show that not even the tiniest tremor was recorded. "I'll bet one of my friends is playing a trick on me; there must be some nylon filament attached to the door, and someone is pulling on it." But a careful check reveals no such trickery. The outside door is locked, and there is no one else in the house. You start to get a bit concerned. "Maybe some vile terrorist group is testing a new gamma ray machine, and they are aiming a stream of microparticles at my door." But no such particle stream can be detected. "Well, maybe my room is haunted; perhaps the ghost of some distressed student who perished trying to read philosophy has been troubled by the presence of philosophy books in my room, and opened the door to escape." Okay, I don't know why your door opened, and maybe you won't be able to discover why. But notice the process you went through in trying to discover the cause. You looked at air currents, earthquakes, uneven floors; you considered trickery and terrorist plots; and finally you were driven to a hypothesis about ghosts and goblins. But one explanation never occurred to you at all: There was *no* cause for your door opening; it just happened, with no cause whatsoever. To suppose that doors open without any cause is so alien to your thinking that you will turn instead to terrorist conspiracies and supernatural forces. The cause may be natural or supernatural, mundane or extraordinary, but there *has* to be a cause. Things don't happen without a cause.

The same thinking applies to human behavior. Your friend Nawal has a kind word and a friendly smile for everyone: the most cheerful, warm-hearted person you have ever known. You meet Nawal crossing campus, and bid her good morning. "Go to hell," she replies with a sneer. You are so surprised you drop your books and almost spill your mocha latte. A few seconds later you spot a mutual friend, and you inquire about Nawal's strange behavior: "What's bugging Nawal? She just told me to go to hell." The two of you may consider a variety of explanations for Nawal's unusual cantankerousness. Perhaps she just flunked a calculus exam, or maybe she had a fight with her boyfriend; perhaps her hard drive crashed, or she just left a long and boring philosophy lecture. If no such explanation is available we may consider other possibilities: her brain has been invaded by space aliens, or the C.I.A. drugged her coffee, or she suffers from demon possession. But again, no matter how far-fetched the causal hypothesis—from space aliens to demon possession—it is still more plausible than concluding that there was no cause, and she just changed from cheerful to cranky with no cause whatsoever. The moral of the story is simple. Whether we are thinking of doors opening or comets orbiting or people cursing, we believe *everything* that happens has a cause. That is, we all believe in *determinism*. Far from being a strange and exotic doctrine, determinism is—according to Hume—the plainest common sense.

> Men are deceived if they think themselves free, an opinion which consists only in this, that they are conscious of their actions and ignorant of the causes by which they are determined. Benedict Spinoza, *Ethics*

Reactions to Determinism

Some see determinism as a doctrine of promise: everything that happens has a cause, and thus it is always worthwhile to examine why events occur. Wars and crime, disease and famine are not random inexplicable mysteries, but instead have definite causes that we might come to understand. By understanding them we may learn to prevent them. And acts of kindness, creations of genius, and periods of social harmony are not just matters of good luck. They are caused, and by understanding their causes we might promote them. In stark contrast, others see determinism as a doctrine of hopelessness and helplessness: determinism means that we are ridiculous puppets whose strings are pulled by forces beyond our understanding, and the *illusion* that we act freely only makes us more absurd.

The negative perspective on determinism was voiced by the American philosopher William Barrett. According to Barrett determinism conflicts with our "desire for freshness, novelty, genuine creation—in short, an open rather than a closed universe."[1] In Barrett's view, a determined world "would stifle us with boredom."[2]

But why should determinism dictate such boredom? If my life is entirely determined, that does not imply I know the outcome. It's all new and fresh and exciting to me. In theological determinism God is omniscient and knows everything that will happen. God knows the details of our future lives, but even then we ourselves do not. In natural determinism every event is determined by natural laws; but obviously we do not know all those laws, and so we cannot even roughly predict the details of our future lives. Either way, the events of our lives remain new and fresh to us. Indeed, they may be new and fresh in the sense that they are original, and have never before occurred (though the conditions that brought them about were already in place).

FATALISM

So if I don't know what will happen, why should determinism frighten me? Why should it threaten me with terrible boredom? Perhaps it is not determinism that is so scary, but a doctrine often confused with determinism: fatalism. Fatalists believe that your "fate" is fixed, your destiny sealed, and struggle as you will there is nothing you can do to change it. Think of a late-night war movie, starring the tough old sergeant with a gruff voice and kind heart. The squad has wandered into an ambush, and is trapped by an enemy machine gun that blocks their advance and prevents their retreat. The sergeant grabs a grenade and prepares to charge the machine gun nest. "You can't go out there, Sarge," pleads the frightened private. "That machine gunner will cut you to ribbons." Sarge tightens his helmet, clutches the grenade, and utters the immortal late-night movie line: "Don't worry, kid. Somewhere out there, there's a bullet with my name on it. When it's my time, that bullet'll catch up with me. And it'll find me whether I'm hiding in a foxhole or charging up a hill. But when that bullet finds me, I'm gonna' be charging straight into it, not hiding in a hole." That's classic fatalism: my ultimate destiny is set, no matter what I do. The trivial details may be up to me—I can charge or cower—but I cannot escape my fate.

> "Our hour is marked, and no one can claim a moment of life beyond what fate has predestined." Napoleon Bonaparte, to Dr. Arnott, April 1821

But for most of us fatalism prompts a feeling of resentment and helplessness. Some powerful force we cannot understand—a power that seems to delight in toying with us and thwarting our best plans—manipulates our destiny. In ancient Greek drama, Oedipus is fated to murder his father and marry his mother. Oedipus resolves to escape his fate, and so leaves his home and travels to a distant country. There is a battle in which Oedipus kills that country's king, and following local tradition is crowned king and marries the queen. But Oedipus had been adopted as an infant, an event of which he has no memory. The country to which he fled (to escape his fate) is the country of his birth. And as you probably already guessed, the king he killed was his father and the queen was his mother.

Not everyone fears fatalism. To the contrary, some find fatalism comforting. The Roman stoics told the story of a dog tied to a horse-drawn cart that is on its way to market. The dog may fight and bite and struggle and be dragged through the dust behind the cart, or the dog may trot quietly beside the cart and take what pleasures the day offers. In either case the dog will arrive at its destiny. The moral is, don't struggle and worry: whatever will be, will be.

Fatalism has its charms, but it seems a very implausible doctrine. It disconnects all our efforts and acts from the system of real causes, and replaces them with a notion of God as a cosmic con man. We feel as if we are having an effect on the world, but the real strings are invisible to us, and are being pulled by a devious deity who thwarts our plans and makes our best efforts work against us. But I see no reason whatsoever to suppose that such a malevolent power exists. Of course our best laid plans do sometimes go awry, but that sad fact does not imply some diabolical controlling force. As Shakespeare writes in *Julius Caesar*: "Men some time are masters of their fates; the fault, dear Brutus, is not in our stars but in ourselves."

One of the great philosophical poems, *The Rubaiyat of Omar Khayyam*, was written by an eleventh-century Persian poet and astronomer. It was translated into English by Edward Fitzgerald. One major theme of the poem is fatalism, as indicated by the following two verses:

> Oh, Thou, who didst with pitfall and with gin
> Beset the Road I was to wander in,
>   thou wilt not with Predestined Evil round
> Enmesh, and then impute my Fall to sin!
>
> Oh, Thou, who Man of baser Earth didst make,
> And ev'n with Paradise devise the Snake:
>   For all the Sin the Face of wretched Man
> Is black with—Man's forgiveness give—and take!

Determinism and Fatalism

If determinism is true, then who we are, what we do, what we think, and what we become are all shaped by—determined by—past causal events in conjunction with complex causal laws. Will you ace your philosophy exam, or bomb it? Will you run a great race on Saturday, or finish far back in the pack? Will your current fling blossom into a great romance, or wither away? Will you join the Green Party? get into medical school? move to the coast? Every detail of your life, great and small, is completely determined by past causes. But what distinguishes determinism from fatalism is that those past causes are *not* alien forces that control you against your own will and wishes, forces that thwart your choices and frustrate your efforts. If you are *fated* to slay your father then so it shall be, no matter how hard you struggle: your struggles have nothing to do with it. But determinism is a very different matter. If it is determined that you will run a great race, then given the causes in operation you will certainly run a great race. But it is not as if you would run a great race even if you were trying to throw the race, or if you did not train hard. For among the key causes that determine your racing success are your own hard training, your fortitude, and your racing skill. Without those key causal factors you would not run well. If determinism is true, then all those factors are determined: you are shaped by your causal history to be a skillful racer, a tireless trainer, and a tough competitor. But those are not *alien* forces that conspire to *make* you run a great race whether you wish it or not. Instead, among the key causal elements are your own efforts, desires, and skills.

DETERMINISM AND FREE WILL

Having distinguished fatalism from determinism, let's look more closely at the latter. For while there seems little reason to believe in fatalism, determinism is a much more serious question. As Hume noted, when something happens we *do* think there must have been some cause. And if we apply that idea universally, determinism is the result. If determinism is true, could we still have free will? Many have answered no. However, there are also many who deny that determinism undercuts free will. They are called *compatibilists*, because they believe free will and determinism are *compatible*; they can peacefully coexist.

Simple Compatibilism

David Hume claimed that all the puzzles and disputes about free will result from sloppy and confused use of language. If we think about it carefully, and avoid verbal entanglements, then free will is a simple and obvious matter, and "all mankind, both learned and ignorant, have always been of the same opinion"[3] about the nature and existence of free will. What does free will mean? Hume answers:

> By liberty [free will] we can only mean a power of acting or not acting according to the determinations of the will; that is, if we choose to remain at rest, we may; if we choose to move, we also may. Now this hypothetical liberty is universally allowed to belong to everyone who is not a prisoner and in chains.[4]

Free will consists in having the power to act in accordance with your own will. If you want to play the oboe, you can play the oboe; if you choose not to attend the anniversary party for Uncle Fred and Aunt Ethyl, then no one will place you in chains and drag you there against your will; if you choose to eat six chocolate chip cookies, then you eat six chocolate chip cookies.

What does it mean for a person to be free? Forget about abstract philosophical principles, and don't be misled by the confusing language philosophers use. We all know what it means to be free: when you can follow your own wishes, make your own plans, pursue your own goals, then you are free. Of course your wishes and desires were shaped by the determining factors in your past, but that doesn't make them any less your own. If you are not being coerced or restrained against your will and against your wishes, then you are free. As we noted, this view of free will is called *compatibilism*: Determinism is *compatible* with free will. We'll call Hume's version *simple* compatibilism: doing what *you want* (you are not coerced) is acting freely, and that simple freedom is compatible with your desires and choices and acts being *determined*.

Consider a case of simple compatibilism. The Human Genome Project has finished mapping human genetic structure, and they have discovered a new and interesting gene: the football fan gene. It turns out that all persons who have this gene are dedicated football fans, and persons who lack the football fan gene (geneticists have labeled it the FFG) find football boring. Joline lives and dies with the Green Bay Packers, and sure enough, she tests positive for the FFG. On Sunday morning she is putting on her green and yellow earmuffs, her Packers stocking cap, her Packers mittens, and her heavy Packers coat, and loading her car with beer and a sturdy grill on the way to a tailgate party with her friends at Lambeau Field, to be followed by a football game at which she will yell herself hoarse in support of her beloved Packers. As she rushes around the house she hums the Packer fight song, interspersed with occasional shouts of "Go to Hell Bears." She has been looking forward to this game all week, and can hardly wait to get to the stadium. We manage to stop her just long enough to ask a question: "Are you going to the Packers game of your own free will?"

Joline thinks it's the dumbest question she's ever heard. "Of course I'm going of my own free will. Does it look like anyone is forcing me to go to the game? I go because I love football, and I love the Packers. Stop bothering me, I've got to get this bratwurst in the van."

"No, you're mistaken," we reply. "We just got the tests back, and you tested positive for the FFG. You are genetically programmed to love football. Your mom also loved football, didn't she? You probably inherited it from her. So you are going because you have the football fan gene, not because of your own free choice. You may think you are going freely, but in fact you are not."

Joline is not convinced. "Geneshmeen. So maybe I have the FFG. Or maybe I love football because I was conditioned to love football by my mother: my first toys were a soft green and yellow football and a cuddly teddy bear wearing a Green Bay Packers jersey. Of course there must be causes for why I love football, but whatever *caused* me to love football, that doesn't change the fact that I go to football games because I *like football*. That's how I *choose* to spend my Sunday afternoons. No one forces me to go to football games, I go from my *own free choice*."

Does Joline choose and act freely when she goes to a football game? Let's up the ante. Suppose that given her exact circumstances she *could not* do otherwise than what she does. Of course if Joline wanted to spend her afternoon at the movies, she could do so; but given her genetic heritage, she will *not* want to miss the football game. And if there were some special circumstances—one of her friends is deathly ill, and Joline must rush her to the hospital—then Joline would respond to that emergency and skip the football game. But in the circumstances that she is actually in, and being the person she actually is, Joline will inevitably go to the football game. We could predict it with just as much certainty as we can predict the return of Halley's comet: both Joline's path to the football game and the orbit of Halley's comet are completely fixed by natural causes (the natural causes determining Joline's behavior are of course quite different from the natural causes setting the orbit of Halley's comet, but there is no difference in the determined regularity of their movements). If a medical emergency occurs, Joline's path will deviate from the football field; and if a large meteorite collides with Halley's comet, then the comet will deviate from its orbit. But given the *actual circumstances*—no meteorite, and no medical emergency—both will follow their determined natural courses. (And of course, the meteorite and medical emergency would *also* be part of the determined system.) You might wish to dispute that description of Joline's behavior. But suppose you *agree* with that completely naturalistic-deterministic account of Joline's movements. She is still moving due to her *own intentions* (and Halley's comet is not). Is she acting freely? Does she have free will? She certainly thinks she is free. Is her sense of freedom an illusion? Or is the key factor just that she acts from her own intentions (however determined those intentions may be), and so she is still free?

Joline insists that she *is* free. "It's not your genes, nor your early conditioning, nor determinism that destroys freedom. What destroys your freedom is not being allowed to do what you really want to do. I know something about that. When I was a junior in high school, my family moved for a year to a country where women were not allowed to do any athletic activity in public. I love to run, and I love competing in road races. For that whole year, I couldn't go out and run. I was miserable, and had no freedom. Fortunately, now my circumstances allow me to run, and I have good friends who encourage my running, and good safe places to run, and I am able to do what I love to do and freely choose to do. That's freedom, and the fact that you can dig out the determining causes that made me a runner in no way compromises my free will."

Many people will say that Joline has all the freedom anyone could want. She is doing what she wants to do, nobody forces her to act against her own wishes, she is following her own goals and preferences and intentions. Of course Joline does not *choose* her own genes, nor her own early conditioning; but *those* choices are nonsense. If (before her birth, even before her conception) Joline could choose her own genetic makeup and the environment that would shape her, then *who* would be doing the choosing?

So Joline's behavior is *determined,* in every detail: her genetics and her environmental history shape the person she is. But Joline still acts *freely*, because she follows her own wishes and desires, and can successfully act as she wants to act. Her wants and desires and goals are determined by past causes, but they are still her own goals and intentions, and thus she acts freely. Joline's free choices are determined, but not *fated*. Joline goes to the Packers game because that is what she wants: she can successfully pursue her own goals, without some fatalistic trickster intervening to frustrate her plans. If Joline follows her own goals and acts successfully on her own preferences, the fact that her goals and her acts are shaped and *determined* by past causes does not threaten her freedom. That is the view of David Hume and other simple compatibilists.

Deep Compatibilism

Joline goes to Packers games because she *wants* to go. But one October Monday morning, the day after a particularly painful Packer loss, we find Joline in a reflective mood. "I dearly love the Packers, and love going to games. But you know, I wish I didn't. It takes up an enormous amount of time and energy, and for every year of Super Bowl glory there's several years of bitter frustration. I really wish that I didn't care at all about football, and instead loved music. If I liked music as much as I like the Packers, I would have learned a great deal about music, and I would have become a decent musician. Perhaps I would have composed some good songs. That would be very satisfying. It would be better than spending my days waving a green and yellow banner, and I think it would have brought me greater joy. Don't get me wrong, I love cheering for the Packers. But I wish I loved the Packers a lot less and music a lot more."

If Joline loves going to Packers games, but at a deeper reflective level would prefer *not* to have that Packer passion, then is Joline's behavior *free*? A contemporary American philosopher who has worried a great deal about this question is Harry G. Frankfurt. Consider the case of a drug addict (one of Frankfurt's favorite examples). The addict takes drugs because he desires drugs. No one forces him to take drugs; rather, he takes drugs because of his own addictive desire for drugs. (Let's not get bogged down just now in questions about why he started taking drugs. To make the case easier, suppose our addict became addicted to drugs quite innocently, when someone slipped drugs into his morning oatmeal.) The addict certainly has the desire for drugs, and he acts on his own desire, and no one forces him to act on his desire. Yet few of us would call this unfortunate addict free. To the contrary, he seems to be enslaved by his addiction. His enslavement seems worse because it operates internally. It is a terrible thing to be enslaved by some tyrant who holds us in chains; but surely it is just as bad, perhaps even worse, to be enslaved by our own desires.

The drug addict pushes us to think harder about the conditions of genuine freedom. The addict acts on his desires when he consumes drugs, but it is hard to count such acts as genuinely free. Frankfurt proposes that to decide whether the addict is free, we must look deeper into his motivational structure. We might call this *deep* compatibilism, to distinguish it from Hume's *simple* compatibilism. If the addict desires drugs, but experiences that desire as alien and oppressive, then he is not really free: he does not have the will he wants to have. He certainly desires drugs, but at a deeper (or higher-order) level he does not approve of his own desire. Now imagine a very different addict: he desires drugs, and strongly approves of his addictive desire for drugs. He is, in Frankfurt's felicitous phrase, a "willing addict." He has the will he prefers to have, and he can act in accordance with desires he recognizes as his own.

This seems immediately appealing. If I am acting from a will I *approve* and acknowledge as my own, I act freely and have free will. Yet there is something disturbing about counting the willing addict as an exemplar of free will. It's easy to imagine an *unwilling* addict; but who would *willingly* be enslaved to drug addiction?

Consider Sandra, a woman who grows up in an oppressive society in which women are expected to be submissive and subservient. The men make all the decisions, and the women smile sweetly, follow their orders, and praise their wisdom. Sandra doesn't buy it. Sandra believes she has just as much right and certainly as much ability to make decisions, take leadership roles, and choose her own path as does any man. And so Sandra struggles valiantly against the oppressive society that attempts to control and subdue her. But the struggle is long and difficult, Sandra has no support, and she endures constant harsh disapproval. Gradually her spirit and fortitude are worn down, and she begins to submit to the subservient role assigned her. The more she submits, the more approval and affection she receives from those around her. Finally Sandra is broken, and she embraces the rules and roles of her oppressive society. She now sees her earlier struggles as youthful sinful pride, and she is glad that her "willfulness" is gone, and she is grateful to have become a properly subservient woman. She is now submissive, and willingly so. By embracing the culture and rules that subordinate her, she has gained free will. Or so deep compatibilists would say.

But surely not. Sandra didn't have much freedom when she struggled against her oppressive society; but when she *internalizes* the oppressive forces, she does not thereby gain free will. The *unwilling* slave is not free, but the *willing* slave is not freer. To the contrary, the "willingly subservient" Sandra is more deeply oppressed than ever. Or so some might think, in opposition to Frankfurt's account of free will.

So it seems that genuine free will requires more. Sandra has deeply embraced her culture's oppressive rules, and when she thinks about it, she is profoundly grateful to her community for leading her back to the straight and narrow path of submissive righteousness. Otherwise, she might have remained a willful, rebellious, independent woman—and Sandra now sees that as a violation of God's glorious plan, and she is glad to play her own submissive role in God's design. Indeed, she does everything possible to insure that her own daughters avoid their mother's errors, and she endeavors to raise them as good submissive women. Sandra is deeply, reflectively, and willingly subservient and submissive. Sandra may now be a willing slave, but she hardly seems a free one.

Sandra deeply approves of her subservience. She chooses to be submissive, likes being submissive, and profoundly approves of her desire to be submissive. She acts as she wants to act, and reflectively approves of her wants and desires, and thus has the will she prefers and approves. But in Sandra's case this does not seem to add up to free will. To the contrary, the more profoundly and completely she favors her subservience, the less free she seems. This leads some philosophers to propose stronger conditions for genuine free will. It is not enough that one do what one *wishes* (as Hume's simple compatibilism suggested), nor is it enough that one deeply approve of the wishes and will that one has (as Frankfurt's deep compatibilism demands). Genuine free will requires something more.

Rationalist Compatibilism

So what is this something more that genuine free will requires? Many different proposals have been offered: perhaps all that is required is some capacity to reflect on one's values. But submissive Sandra has that capacity, and it is by no means clear that she enjoys free will. A contemporary American philosopher, Susan Wolf, proposes a very strong additional condition for genuine free will. To have free will you must will the right path, the *truly good*. If you will what is wrong and harmful—an empty life of drug addiction, or a life of subservience—then you are not thinking clearly and accurately. To be truly free requires more than just following your own desires (Hume's simple compatibilism), more than following your own *deep* values and preferences (Frankfurt's deep compatibilism). Real freedom requires doing the *right thing* for the *right reason*. Thus we might call Wolf's version of free will *rationalist* compatibilism.

According to rationalist compatibilism, the genuinely free person is "an agent who can form (and act on) right values because they are right—that is, an agent who is able to 'track' the True and Good in her value judgments . . . ." If a driver is profoundly and unswervingly committed to following a road that will end at a washed out bridge, the driver's dedication to that path does not change the fact that he has chosen the wrong route. His deep dedication to that route looks more like the constraint of obsession than genuine freedom.

In Susan Wolf's view, real freedom does not require open alternatives or the ability to choose otherwise. From Wolf's perspective, that is a false freedom, a capacity to make stupid and arbitrary mistakes. As Wolf sees it, wanting the ability to choose among open alternatives is:

> . . . not only to want the ability to make choices even where there is no basis for choice but to want the ability to make choices on no basis even when a basis exists. But the latter ability would seem to be an ability no one could ever have reason to want to exercise. Why would one want the ability to pass up the apple when to do so would merely be unpleasant or arbitrary? Why would want the ability to stay planted on the sand when to do so would be cowardly or callous?[5]

The ability to pursue open alternatives does not enhance your freedom. To suppose otherwise would be like preferring a train that has the capacity to jump the tracks. True freedom is the capacity to recognize the true track, and then follow it unswervingly. (You do not follow it *mindlessly*, like a puppet or robot; rather, you follow the true path because reason reveals to you what is True and Good, and it is your own rational preference to follow the true path, and you track that path accurately through your own reason and will power.) This requires strong powers of both reason (to discover what is genuinely good and right) and willpower (to control the passions and inclinations that would lead one astray, and instead follow the stern narrow path of duty). Those who favor this view (such as Kant) often celebrate the dual powers of reason and will, which enable them to follow the straight and narrow path of the moral law:

> Two things fill the mind with ever new and increasing admiration and awe, the oftener and more steadily they are reflected on: the starry heavens above me and the moral law within me.[6]

Whether you accept or reject Wolf's view, she has (building on the tradition of Plato and Kant) established a philosophical landmark that will help us stay oriented as we explore other views. Whether it is a landmark to guide you on the right path, or a monument to philosophical error, is a question you will have to decide for yourself.

LIBERTARIAN FREE WILL AND THE REJECTION OF DETERMINISM

Libertarian Free Will

As appealing as some find Wolf's rational compatibilist view of freedom—real freedom consists in following a steadfast path, and requires no turnoffs or alternatives—it is vehemently rejected by others. From the opposing perspective, what Wolf leaves out (and what *all* compatibilist accounts of free will lack) is the single most important ingredient in free will: the ability to actually choose, the ability to do otherwise, the opportunity to select among *genuine alternatives*. Even if the one true path is dictated by reason, that will not satisfy the desire for open alternatives and free choices. As the Russian novelist, Fyodor Dostoyevsky, insists in *The Underground Man*:

> What he [humanity] wants to preserve is precisely his noxious fancies and vulgar trivialities, if only to assure himself that men are still men . . . and not piano keys responding to the laws of nature.[7]

And being a highly rational piano key will not satisfy that craving. Instead, real free will is the power to make choices that are not determined by *anything*—not by our genetics, our conditioning, nor even by our reason.

This view of free will has long been popular among philosophers and theologians, as well as among butchers, bakers, and candlestick makers. Roderick Chisholm, a contemporary American philosopher, describes it thus:

> If we are responsible [and Chisholm thinks our power of free will does make us responsible] then we have a prerogative which some would attribute only to God; each of us, when we really act, is a prime mover unmoved. In doing what we do, we cause events to happen, and nothing and no one, except ourselves, causes us to cause those events to happen.[8]

This account of free will is called the *libertarian* position. According to libertarians, free will requires a very special power: the power to choose among genuinely open alternatives, and thus make yourself according to your own plans and preferences.

In the libertarian version of free will, we make ourselves from scratch. That's what Chisholm means by saying that when we act freely we are "unmoved movers": we make free choices that cause things to happen (including causing ourselves to develop our characters and attributes), but those choices are not themselves caused by *anything* other than ourselves (and *we* are not caused by anything outside ourselves to be the way we are). God does not assign us our characters, nature does not shape us, our genes do not limit us. When we make genuinely free choices, exercising our "special godlike prerogative" of free will, then the causal sequence starts and ends with us. We initiate our free choices, and nothing—neither God nor environment nor genetic heritage—causes us to choose as we do.

Existentialist Versions of Libertarian Free Will

Chisholm celebrates this great self-making and self-choosing power, but no one has endorsed the libertarian view more enthusiastically than Jean-Paul Sartre and the existentialists. Existentialists take their name from their fundamental premise: existence precedes essence. It seems a strange rallying cry, hardly up there with "Remember the Alamo." But for existentialists, "existence precedes essence" is the glorious solution to the problem of free will. We do not have assigned characters, fixed essences, given natures: we make ourselves by our own choices. We make ourselves by our own self-defining *choices* (we first exist, and then by our *choices* we make our own characters, our own essences, what we are).

Chisholm explicitly recognizes that this notion of free will grants to humans "a prerogative which some would attribute only to God; each of us, when we really act, is a prime mover unmoved." In the existentialist version humans stake their own claim to this special power of free will. Sartre notes the joys and perils of this extraordinary unconditional freedom:

> Everything is indeed permitted if God does not exist, and man is in consequence forlorn, for he cannot find anything to depend upon either within or outside himself. He discovers forthwith, that he is without excuse. For if indeed existence precedes essence, one will never be able to explain one's action by reference to a given and specific human nature, in other words, there is no determinism—man is free, man *is* freedom. Nor, on the other hand, if God does not exist, are we provided with any values or commands that could legitimize our behavior. Thus we have neither behind us, nor before us in a luminous realm of values, any means of justification or excuse. We are left alone, without excuse. That is what I mean when I say that man is condemned to be free. Condemned, because he did not create himself, yet is nevertheless at liberty, and from the moment that he is thrown into this world he is responsible for everything he does. The existentialist . . . thinks that every man, without any support or help whatever, is condemned at every instant to invent man.[9]

So the free will of the existentialists is a miracle working power of self-creation. There is no essence to define you, no fixed values to guide you, no causal factors to determine you: you have the godlike power to make yourself, and what you do with this power is completely and inescapably your responsibility. Free will is a miraculous power of self-making and self-transformation.

It's not surprising that many people find this view of free will attractive. In the first place, it ascribes to all who possess free will a remarkable status. Rather than grubby mortal beings shaped out of clay, we are godlike in our power of self-creation. Furthermore, this miracle-working view of free will is appealing because it makes us totally responsible for everything we do. Whatever we accomplish, whatever we become, we did it ourselves with no help from anyone; so we get full credit for what we do, and we don't owe anything to anyone. Since most people who read philosophy have significant accomplishments (you graduated from high school, made it into college, and are enjoying a reasonably successful college career with excellent prospects of success when you graduate) they are happy to believe that they deserve full and absolute credit for whatever they have done with their lives.

The existentialist model of miraculous self-creative free will has some significant advantages. It is a dashing, daring, swashbuckling, swaggering view of free will. It plays well in action movies, but does it hold up under closer scrutiny? Is this radical self-creation view of free will really plausible?

However flattering it may be to think that we have godlike powers of self-creation, in the harsh light of our actual lives it seems a difficult proposition to believe. All of us are well aware—sometimes painfully, sometimes thankfully—of the many forces and influences that shaped us. We may debate the relative impact of "nature" and "nurture": that is, does our genetic legacy have a larger influence on our lives, or does our social and cultural environment carry greater weight? But there is no debate over whether these factors have a profound influence. You have arms instead of wings, and that was set by your genes, not your godlike choice; and you find cannibalism disgusting, a result of cultural shaping rather than an existential choice of your own values. If we "create ourselves" uniquely and entirely, then all the empirical studies of human society, psychology, and biology would seem to be impossible. But given the fact that we know a great deal about how our genetic, social, cultural, and family influences shape us, it is difficult to take seriously the notion that we "make ourselves."

But there is a second problem for the existential notion of self-creation, and it is even more severe. The problem lies in making *sense* of what such self-creation could possibly be. Obviously the choices you make have a profound influence on your life and your character. Your choice to go to college instead of looking for work; your choice to attend a large state university or a small private college; your choice to major in sociology, or secondary education, or civil engineering, or to drop out of college and become a surfer; your choice to live with John, or marry John, or maybe dump John; your choice to work for the small start-up company in Albuquerque or the huge corporation based in Boston. All these choices have a resounding influence on your character, your future, your life, the person you become. So obviously we do, to some extent, make ourselves by our choices. And sometimes those choices seem like pivotal, life-changing choices: the choice to become a musician, rather than joining the wholesale foods company that was founded by your grandfather and where your father has worked his entire career; the choice to renounce your family's religion and become a Taoist; the choice to leave your unhappy marriage. Such choices are important, and they shape our lives and our characters. But *who* is making those choices?

In Sartre's scheme, the self-defining choices are made *before* we have values, preferences, ideals, characters. We are pure existential points, and the choices we make set the course of how the lines of our character will be drawn. But how is it possible to choose without values, convictions, preferences? It doesn't seem to be *my* choice at all, but instead just a random, capricious event. I can understand making a choice that reflects my own values and preferences, and I can understand making a choice to reject some of the values I have previously held (because I now hold a different value system). But I can make no sense of what it would be like to choose *before* I have *any* values, direction, preferences. If I completely "make myself" through my choices, then there seems to be no one originally there to set the choices in motion. The question is not whether Sartre's account is correct;

rather, it's a question of whether the account makes enough sense to be *evaluated* for accuracy. Saying that I "make myself through my choices" and that no real self exists prior to those choices (existence precedes essence) leaves a very perplexing question: Who is this "I" who makes the choices?

C. A. Campbell's Libertarian Free Will

Many philosophers like the idea of free choices that are somehow our own choices but are not shaped and determined by who we are. But trying to make *sense* of this notion of free will has long been a challenge. A common way of trying to make this notion of free choice work is to isolate the choice into as small and unobtrusive a space as possible. One of the most interesting and inventive of those minimizing libertarian approaches to free will is offered by C. A. Campbell.

Campbell acknowledges that our preferences, our values, and the largest part of our characters are formed—even determined—by our cultures, our genes, and our environmental histories. Knowledge of these powerful influences enables us to predict, with considerable accuracy, the future choices and behavior of those we know well. Arthur grew up in a permissive, indulgent environment, and he has developed a strong desire for alcohol. He realizes that he is fast sinking into severe alcohol dependence, and is now trying to avoid drinking. But Arthur is not very strong, and his desire for alcohol is. Thus we can predict, with some confidence, that Arthur will attend Joe's party, where alcohol will be plentiful; that Arthur will attempt to avoid drinking, and will fail; and that Arthur will end the evening passed out on the floor. Carolyn also enjoys parties, and enjoys having a few drinks. Drinking heavily has some appeal for Carolyn, but the appeal is not very powerful, and Carolyn is a strong and self-disciplined person who sets a careful limit on her alcohol intake and refuses to go beyond that limit. We can confidently predict that Carolyn will end the evening sober, while Arthur will conclude his evening unconscious.

And yet (Campbell claims) our predictions may go wrong. Carolyn's temptation to drink heavily is not very strong, and she has powerful resources for combating that temptation; but tonight she may fail to exercise her willpower, and instead yield to temptation. Arthur confronts the powerful temptation to drink excessively, and his powers of resistance are flabby; but tonight Arthur might rise to the occasion, take courage, and triumph over temptation. We cannot be certain about what Carolyn and Arthur will do, because—according to Campbell—they have a special small domain of 'contracausal free will' that enables them to overcome their conditioning and their genes and their social shaping. They have a special power of choice and will that allows them to defy their history and rise to duty and act in a new way (or instead choose to *withhold* the effort of will and follow their desires). C. A. Campbell describes it thus:

> Here, and here alone, so far as I can see, in the act of deciding whether to put forth or withhold the moral effort required to resist temptation and rise to duty, is to be found an act which is free in the sense required for moral responsibility; an act of which the self is sole author, and of which it is true to say that 'it could be' (or, after the event, 'could have been') 'otherwise'.[10]

And Campbell insists that when we observe from "the inner standpoint of the practical consciousness in its actual functioning" we recognize in our moral decisions a "*creative activity*, in which . . . nothing determines the act save the agent's doing of it".[11]

In Campbell's scenario we are not entirely self-made and self-chosen—our desires, affections, inclinations are the product of our genetic and conditioning histories—but in some of our critical choices (especially choices in which our desire conflicts with out sense of what we should do) we make special free creative choices. This view has several advantages. First and foremost, Campbell's view avoids the existential quandary about who is doing the choosing: *I* make the choice of whether to resist temptation and rise to duty, and the temptation and the duty and the willpower are my own. Second, Campbell's account leaves room for the obvious shaping and conditioning of our characters by our genetic makeup and environmental surroundings and cultural milieu: these forces shape our desires, our tastes, and perhaps also our sense of duty. And third, the area of free will is a special small niche of willpower, rather than (as in existentialism) the wholesale creation of ourselves. (Of course existentialists may not see that as an advantage: the idea of totally creating ourselves has a romantic and dashing appeal; as long as we're going to be deities exercising special miraculous creative powers of free will, why be minor deities? Instead of miraculously touching up the details, why not create ourselves from scratch?)

But even Campbell's more modest account of "contracausal free will" raises some serious questions. Suppose that Arthur, our friend who typically drinks himself into oblivion, tonight remains stone sober, resisting all offers of alcoholic refreshment. What shall we say about such a case? And Carolyn, our paragon of self-control, tonight goes on a bender and brings in the dawn dancing on a table, singing Broadway show tunes, and calling for more bourbon. What would you regard as the most plausible account of her unusual behavior?

According to Campbell, Arthur exerted his willpower and rose to duty while Carolyn withheld the effort of will and succumbed to desire. There is nothing more to say, no further explanation is possible. In both cases, it was an act of free choice in which "nothing determines the act save the agent's doing of it." In Arthur's case, the desire was strong and the resources to combat that desire weak. But it was still *possible* for Arthur to overcome his desire by his choice to exert free will, and that's what happened. For Carolyn the desire was weak and the powers of self-control strong, but still Carolyn could and did choose *not* to exert the (comparatively small) amount of willpower necessary to resist temptation.

In neither case is there any question *who* is doing the choosing, who is exercising contracausal free will; but there is a question of *how* such processes occur. Let's look at this more closely. Carolyn *desires* to drink heavily, but she believes she *should not*. Last weekend Carolyn went to a party and drank moderately. This weekend she gets blotto. What happened? On Campbell's libertarian view, there need be no difference in circumstances whatsoever. She might have had exactly the same moral principles, reflectiveness, willpower; she wasn't feeling sadder, she wasn't feeling more adventurous, her values hadn't changed. In fact, *everything* might have been exactly the same, molecule for molecule. In precisely the same circumstances, one time she exerted the effort of will to control her drinking and the other time she withheld the effort of will. No further explanation is possible: she just did it. She made her own choices, and in identical circumstances she could have chosen otherwise, and that's all there is to say. (If you think there must have been *some* difference in circumstances to account for the difference in behavior—she was tired, or a bit depressed, or had just broken up with her boyfriend—then you are rejecting Campbell's libertarian view. Of course no two situations will actually be exactly identical. But the point is that on Campbell's view there is nothing in the circumstances or environment that accounts for the different acts; the difference must come *solely* from the contracausal free will.)

Campbell's acts of contracausal free will avoid the existentialist question of who is doing the choosing; but they encounter another version of the same problem, though on a smaller scale. We know *who* is making the choice; but it is difficult to understand *how* the choice is being made. Campbell insists that the moral effort one exerts (or withholds) is the essence of free will: ". . . in moral effort we have something for which a man is responsible *without qualification*, something that is *not* affected by heredity and environment but depends *solely* upon the self itself."[12] No further explanation is possible, but (Campbell claims) no further explanation is needed. To see and understand such acts of free will, you must consult your own personal experience: you must look to the inside, introspect, and observe the internal creative process at work. I can't observe it in you, and you can't observe it in me, and there is no distinctive brain wave pattern that can identify it. But when you look carefully, internally, at your own *creative* process of deciding whether to follow your strongest desire or your sense of duty, then you have the best evidence of this creative free will that anyone could possibly have: your own introspective experience.

So on Campbell's narrow libertarian view, *why* does Carolyn choose differently this weekend? Not because of differences in her character, or desires, or abilities; not because she desires more, or cares less, or thinks less clearly; rather, because of a special *creative choice*. But if the choice does not come from her own character or desires or moral principles, in what sense is this her choice at all? Obviously the desires, the moral concerns, and the thinking are Carolyn's own; but this special creative choice that comes from none of those personal characteristics, in what sense does that choice really *belong* to her, rather than being an event that merely *happened* to her? The answer from the libertarians is simple: when you look carefully, when you introspect, you have no doubt that the choice is profoundly your own. You are confident, from your own experience, that such choices exist. No further explanation is possible, and from the perspective of external observation such choices must remain unknowable mysteries. But these ultimate, internal, self-defining choices are the essence of genuine free will.

Whether Campbell's libertarian solution is adequate or inadequate, you will have to decide for yourself. Likewise, you must decide for yourself whether such radical libertarian free will is required for genuine free will, or whether some more modest account offers all you want in the way of free will.

Suppose that we make our own choices, but the choices are not miraculous acts of contracausal self-creation (as the libertarians demand) and neither are they inexorably guided by the True and Good (Wolf's condition for genuine freedom). Instead, we make fallible choices, choices that are sometimes wise and other times stupid, choices that we recognize as being our own. We acknowledge that our choices and our characters were shaped by our rich histories—social, environmental, and genetic. Whatever shaped them, and however good or bad our free choices may be, we recognize them as our own choices, and we find making choices a healthy and desirable element of our lives. In some circumstances our choice-making is so badly restricted and compromised by a harsh background that it hardly qualifies as free choice at all: the woman who is worn down to favor submissiveness, and the child raised in a brutal environment, would be examples of such severe cases that we have doubts about their genuine freedom. But in most cases our histories and opportunities are not so brutally narrow, and the fact that there are causes that shaped our characters and choices is not really troubling. Some will regard such a naturalistic (even deterministic) account of free choice as perfectly adequate for human free will. Others will see it as a sham: real choice and real freedom must transcend such grubby natural boundaries, and be based on special human capacities that have no natural explanation.

There is an interesting parallel between views of free will and views of ethics. Just as some anchor ethics in natural powers (utilitarians and care theorists, for example), others (such as Kantians) insist that real ethical principles must transcend any natural phenomena.

Likewise, some place free will squarely within the natural world, growing out of the environments that shaped our characters and choices; while others (libertarians) view free will as our special power to rise above any natural influences. Which view you find most plausible has deep connections to your views on the nature of humans and the nature of the world.

In any case, those are the major competing accounts of free will, and in the next chapter we'll be looking further at some of their ethical implications. If you are not at all sure which of those views is correct, or even which of those views you favor, you're in good company. Debates about the nature of free will, and the plausibility of the competing accounts, has been a major part of the history of philosophy, and the debate goes on.

ASYMMETRICAL FREEDOM

Susan Wolf

Susan Wolf, professor of philosophy at University of North Carolina at Chapel Hill, presents a fascinating version of rationalist free will, and she draws out some implications of that view you may find surprising. In addition to her many insightful essays on the subject, her *Freedom Within Reason* (New York: Oxford University Press, 1990) is a rich and very readable study of questions related to both free will and moral responsibility.

In order for a person to be morally responsible, two conditions must be satisfied. First, he must be a free agent—an agent, that is, whose actions are under his own control. For if the actions he performs are not up to him to decide, he deserves no credit or discredit for doing what he does. Second, he must be a moral agent—an agent, that is, to whom moral claims apply. For if the actions he performs can be neither right nor wrong, then there is nothing to credit or discredit him with. I shall call the first condition, *the condition of freedom*, and the second, *the condition of value*. Those who fear that the first condition can never be met worry about the problem of free will. Those who fear that the second condition can never be met worry about the problem of moral skepticism. Many people believe that the condition of value is dependent on the condition of freedom—that moral prescriptions make sense only if the concept of free will is coherent. In what follows, I shall argue that the converse is true—that the condition of freedom depends on the condition of value. Our doubts about the existence of true moral values, however, will have to be left aside.

I shall say that an agent's action is *psychologically determined* if his action is determined by his interests—that is, his values or desires—and his interests are determined by his heredity or environment. If all our actions are so determined, then the thesis of psychological determinism is true. This description is admittedly crude and simplistic. A more plausible description of psychological determination will include among possible determining factors a wider range of psychological states. There are, for example, some beliefs and emotions which cannot be analyzed as values or desires and which clearly play a role in the psychological explanations of why we act as we do. For my purposes, however, it will be easier to leave the description of psychological determinism uncluttered. The context should be sufficient to make the intended application understood.

Many people believe that if psychological determinism is true, the condition of freedom can never be satisfied. For if an agent's interests are determined by heredity and environment, they claim, it is not up to the agent to have the interests he has. And if his actions are determined by his interests as well, then he cannot but perform the actions he performs. In order for an agent to satisfy the condition of freedom, then, his actions must not be psychologically determined. Either his actions must not be determined by his interests, or his interests must not be determined by anything external to himself. They therefore conclude that the condition of freedom requires the absence of psychological determinism. And they think this is what we mean to express when we state the condition of freedom in terms of the requirement that the agent "could have done otherwise".

Let us imagine, however, what an agent who satisfied this condition would have to be like. Consider first what it would mean for the agent's actions not to be determined by his interests—for the agent, in other words, to have the ability to act despite his interests. This would mean, I think, that the agent has the ability to act against everything he believes in and everything he cares about. It would mean, for example, that if the agent's son were inside a burning building, the agent could just stand there and watch the house go up in flames. Or that the agent, though he thinks his neighbor a fine and agreeable fellow, could just get up one day, ring the doorbell, and punch him in the nose. One might think such pieces of behavior should not be classified as actions at all—that they are rather more like spasms that the agent cannot control. If they are actions, at least, they are very bizarre, and an agent who performed them would have to be insane. Indeed, one might think he would have to be insane if he had even the ability to perform them. For the rationality of an agent who could perform such irrational actions as these must hang by a dangerously thin thread.

So let us assume instead that his actions are determined by his interests, but that his interests are not determined by anything external to himself. Then of any of the interests he happens to have, it must be the case that he does not have to have them. Though perhaps he loves his wife, it must be possible for him not to love her. Though perhaps he cares about people in general, it must be possible for him not to care. This agent, moreover, could not have reasons for his interests—at least no reasons of the sort we normally have. He cannot love his wife, for example, because of the way his wife is—for the way his wife is is not up to him to decide. Such an agent, presumably, could not be much committed to anything; his interests must be something like a matter of whim. Such an agent must be able not to care about the lives of others, and, I suppose, he must be able not to care about his own life as well. An agent who didn't care about these things, one might think, would have to be crazy. And again, one might think he would have to be crazy if he had even the ability not to care.

In any case, it seems, if we require an agent to be psychologically undetermined, we cannot expect him to be a moral agent. For if we require that his actions not be determined by his interests, then *a fortiori* they cannot be determined by his moral interests. And if we require that his interests not be determined by anything else, then *a fortiori* they cannot be determined by his moral reasons.

When we imagine an agent who performs right actions, it seems, we imagine an agent who is rightly determined: whose actions, that is, are determined by the right sorts of interests, and whose interests are determined by the right sorts of reasons. But an agent who is not psychologically determined cannot perform actions that are right in this way. And if his actions can never be appropriately right, then in not performing right actions, he can never be wrong. The problem seems to be that the undetermined agent is so free as to be free *from moral reasons*. So the satisfaction of the condition of freedom seems to rule out the satisfaction of the condition of value.

This suggests that the condition of freedom was previously stated too strongly. When we require that a responsible agent "could have done otherwise" we cannot mean that it was not determined that he did what he did. It has been proposed that 'he could have done otherwise' should be analyzed as a conditional instead. For example, we might say that 'he could have done otherwise' means that he would have done otherwise, if he had tried. Thus the bank robber is responsible for robbing the bank, since he would have restrained himself if he had tried. But the man he locked up is not responsible for letting him escape, since he couldn't have stopped him even if he had tried.

Incompatibilists, however, will quickly point out that such an analysis is insufficient. For an agent who would have done otherwise if he had tried cannot be blamed for his action if he could not have tried. The compatibilist might try to answer this objection with a new conditional analysis of 'he could have tried'. He might say, for example, that 'he could have tried to do otherwise' be interpreted to mean he would have tried to do otherwise, if he had chosen. But the incompatibilist now has a new objection to make: namely, what if the agent could not have chosen?

It should be obvious that this debate might be carried on indefinitely with a proliferation of conditionals and a proliferation of objections. But if an agent is determined, no conditions one suggests will be conditions that an agent could have satisfied.

Thus, any conditional analysis of 'he could have done otherwise' seems too weak to satisfy the condition of freedom. Yet if 'he could have done otherwise' is not a conditional, it seems too strong to allow the satisfaction of the condition of value. We seem to think of ourselves one way when we are thinking about freedom, and to think of ourselves another way when we are thinking about morality. When we are thinking about the condition of freedom, our intuitions suggest that the incompatibilists are right. For they claim that an agent can be free only insofar as his actions are not psychologically determined. But when we are thinking about the condition of value, our intuitions suggest that the compatibilists are right. For they claim that an agent can be moral only insofar as his actions are psychologically determined. If our intuitions require that both these claims are right, then the concept of moral responsibility must be incoherent. For then a free agent can never be moral, and a moral agent can never be free.

In fact, however, I believe that philosophers have generally got our intuitions wrong. There is an asymmetry in our intuitions about freedom which has generally been overlooked. As a result, it has seemed that the answer to the problem of free will can lie in only one of two alternatives: Either the fact that an agent's action was determined is always compatible with his being responsible for it, or the fact that the agent's action was determined will always rule his responsibility out. I shall suggest that the solution lies elsewhere—that both compatibilists and incompatibilists are wrong. What we need in order to be responsible beings, I shall argue, is a suitable combination of determination and indetermination.

When we try to call up our intuitions about freedom, a few stock cases come readily to mind. We think of the heroin addict and the kleptomaniac, of the victim of hypnosis, and the victim of a deprived childhood. These cases, I think, provide forceful support for our incompatibilist intuitions. For of the kleptomaniac it may well be true that he would have done otherwise if he had tried. The kleptomaniac is not responsible because he could not have tried. Of the victim of hypnosis it may well be true that he would have done otherwise if he had chosen. The

victim of hypnosis is not responsible because he could not have chosen.

The victim of the deprived childhood who, say, embezzles some money, provides the most poignant example of all. For this agent is not coerced nor overcome by an irresistible impulse. He is in complete possession of normal adult faculties of reason and observation. He seems, indeed, to have as much control over his behavior as we have of ours. He acts on the basis of his choice, and he chooses on the basis of his reasons. If there is any explanation of why this agent is not responsible, it would seem that it must consist simply in the fact that his reasons are determined.

These examples are all peculiar, however, in that they are examples of people doing bad things. If the agents in these cases were responsible for their actions, this would justify the claim that they deserve to be blamed. We seldom look, on the other hand, at examples of agents whose actions are morally good. We rarely ask whether an agent is truly responsible if his being responsible would make him worthy of praise.

There are a few reasons why this might be so which go some way in accounting for the philosophers' neglect. First, acts of moral blame are more connected with punishment than acts of moral praise are connected with reward. So acts of moral blame are likely to be more public, and examples will be readier to hand. Second, and more important, I think, we have stronger reasons for wanting acts of blame to be justified. If we blame someone or punish him, we are likely to be causing him some pain. But if we praise someone or reward him, we will probably only add to his pleasures. To blame someone undeservedly is, in any case, to do him an injustice. Whereas to praise someone undeservedly is apt to be just a harmless mistake. For this reason, I think, our intuitions about praise are weaker and less developed than our intuitions about blame. Still, we do have some intuitions about cases of praise, and it would be a mistake to ignore them entirely.

When we ask whether an agent's action is deserving of praise, it seems we do not require that he could have done otherwise. If an agent does the right thing for just the right reasons, it seems absurd to ask whether he could have done the wrong. "I cannot tell a lie," "He couldn't hurt a fly" are not exemptions from praiseworthiness but testimonies to it. If a friend presents you with a gift and says "I couldn't resist," this suggests the strength of his friendship and not the weakness of his will. If one feels one "has no choice" but to speak out against injustice, one ought not to be upset about the depth of one's commitment. And it seems I should be grateful for the fact that if I were in trouble, my family "could not help" but come to my aid.

Of course, these phrases must be given an appropriate interpretation if they are to indicate that the agent is deserving of praise. "He couldn't hurt a fly" must allude to someone's gentleness—it would be perverse to say this of someone who was in an iron lung. It is not admirable in George Washington that he cannot tell a lie, if it is because he has a tendency to stutter that inhibits his attempts. 'He could not have done otherwise' as it is used in the context of praise, then, must be taken to imply something like 'because he was too good'. An action is praiseworthy only if it is done for the right reasons. So it must be only in light of and because of these reasons that the praiseworthy agent "could not help" but do the right thing.

But when an agent does the right thing for the right reasons, the fact that, having the right reasons, he *must* do the right should surely not lessen the credit he deserves. For presumably the reason he cannot do otherwise is that his virtue is so sure or his moral commitment so strong.

One might fear that if the agent really couldn't have acted differently, his virtue must be *too* sure or his commitment *too* strong. One might think, for example, that if someone literally couldn't resist buying a gift for a friend, his generosity would not be a virtue—it would be an obsession. For one can imagine situations in which it would be better if the agent did resist—if, for example, the money that was spent on the gift was desperately needed for some other purpose. Presumably, in the original case, though, the money was not desperately needed—we praise the agent for buying a gift for his friend rather than, say, a gift for himself. But from the fact that the man could not resist in this situation it doesn't follow that he couldn't resist in another. For part of the explanation of why he couldn't resist in this situation is that in this situation he has no reason to try to resist. This man, we assume, has a generous nature—a disposition, that

is, to perform generous acts. But, then, if he is in a situation that presents a golden opportunity, and has no conflicting motive, how could he act otherwise?

One might still be concerned that if his motives are determined, the man cannot be truly deserving of praise. If he cannot help but have a generous character, then the fact that he is generous is not up to him. If a man's motives are determined, one might think, then *he* cannot control them, so it cannot be to his credit if his motives turn out to be good. But whether a man is in control of his motives cannot be decided so simply. We must know not only whether his motives are determined, but how they are determined as well.

We can imagine, for example, a man with a generous mother who becomes generous as a means of securing her love. He would not have been generous had his mother been different. Had she not admired generosity, he would not have developed this trait. We can imagine further that once this man's character had been developed, he would never subject it to question or change. His character would remain unthinkingly rigid, carried over from a childhood over which he had no control. As he developed a tendency to be generous, let us say, he developed other tendencies—a tendency to brush his teeth twice a day, a tendency to avoid the company of Jews. The explanation for why he developed any one of these traits is more or less the same as the explanation for why he has developed any other. And the explanation for why he has retained any one of these tendencies is more or less the same as the explanation for why he has retained any other. These tendencies are all, for him, merely habits which he has never thought about breaking. Indeed, they are habits which, by hypothesis, it was determined he would never think about breaking. Such a man, perhaps, would not deserve credit for his generosity, for his generosity might be thought to be senseless and blind. But we can imagine a different picture in which no such claim is true, in which a generous character might be determined and yet under the agent's control.

We might start again with a man with a generous mother who starts to develop his generosity out of a desire for her love. But his reasons for developing a generous nature need not be his reasons for retaining it when he grows more mature. He may notice, for example, that his generous acts provide an independent pleasure, connected to the pleasure he gives the person on whom his generosity is bestowed. He may find that being generous promotes a positive fellow feeling and makes it easier for him to make friends than it would otherwise be. Moreover, he appreciates being the object of the generous acts of others, and he is hurt when others go to ungenerous extremes. All in all, his generosity seems to cohere with his other values. It fits in well with his ideals of how one ought to live.

Such a picture, I think, might be as determined as the former one. But it is compatible with the exercise of good sense and an open frame of mind. It is determined, because the agent does not create his new reasons for generosity any more than he created his old ones. He does not *decide* to feel an independent pleasure in performing acts of generosity, or decide that such acts will make it easier for him to make friends. He discovers that these are consequences of a generous nature—and if he is observant and perceptive, he cannot help but discover this. He does not choose to be the object of the generous acts of others, or to be the victim of less generous acts of less virtuous persons. Nor does he choose to be grateful to the one and hurt by the other. He cannot help but have these experiences—they are beyond his control. So it seems that what reasons he *has* for being generous depends on what reasons there *are*.

If the man's character is determined in this way, however, it seems absurd to say that it is not under his control. His character is determined on the basis of his reasons, and his reasons are determined by what reasons there are. What is not under his control, then, is that generosity be a virtue, and it is only because he realizes this that he remains a generous man. But one cannot say for *this* reason that his generosity is not praiseworthy. This is the best reason for being generous that a person could have.

So it seems that an agent can be morally praiseworthy even though he is determined to perform the action he performs. But we have already seen that an agent cannot be morally blameworthy if he is determined to perform the action he performs. Determination, then, is compatible with an agent's responsibility for a good action, but incompatible with an agent's responsibility for a bad action. The metaphysical conditions required for an agent's responsibility will vary according to the value of the action he performs.

The condition of freedom, as it is expressed by the requirement that an agent could have done otherwise, thus appears to demand a conditional analysis after all. But the condition must be one that separates the good actions from the bad—the condition, that is, must be essentially value-laden. An analysis of the condition of freedom that might do the trick is:

He could have done otherwise if there had been good and sufficient reason.

where the 'could have done otherwise' in the analysans is not a conditional at all. For presumably an action is morally praiseworthy only if there are no good and sufficient reasons to do something else. And an action is morally blameworthy only if there are good and sufficient reasons to do something else. Thus, when an agent performs a good action, the condition of freedom is a counterfactual: though it is required that the agent would have been able to do otherwise *had there been* good and sufficient reason to do so, the situation in which the good-acting agent actually found himself is a situation in which there was no such reason. Thus, it is compatible with the satisfaction of the condition of freedom that the agent in this case could not actually have done other than what he actually did. When an agent performs a bad action, however, the condition of freedom is not a counterfactual. The bad-acting agent does what he does in the face of good and sufficient reasons to do otherwise. Thus the condition of freedom requires that the agent in this case could have done otherwise in just the situation in which he was actually placed. An agent, then, can be determined to perform a good action and still be morally praiseworthy. But if an agent is to be blameworthy, he must unconditionally have been able to do something else.

It may be easier to see how this analysis works, and how it differs from conditional analyses that were suggested before, if we turn back to the case in which these previous analyses failed—namely, the case of the victim of a deprived childhood.

We imagined a case, in particular, of a man who embezzled some money, fully aware of what he was doing. He was neither coerced nor overcome by an irresistible impulse, and he was in complete possession of normal adult faculties of reason and observation. Yet it seems he ought not to be blamed for committing his crime, for, from his point of view, one cannot reasonably expect him to see anything wrong with his action. We may suppose that in his childhood he was given no love—he was beaten by his father, neglected by his mother. And that the people to whom he was exposed when he was growing up gave him examples only of evil and selfishness. From his point of view, it is natural to conclude that respecting other people's property would be foolish. For presumably no one had ever respected his. And it is natural for him to feel that he should treat other people as adversaries.

In light of this, it seems that this man shouldn't be blamed for an action we know to be wrong. For if we had had his childhood, we wouldn't have known it either. Yet this agent seems to have as much control over his life as we are apt to have over ours: he would have done otherwise, if he had tried. He would have tried to do otherwise, if he had chosen. And he would have chosen to do otherwise, if he had had reason. It is because he couldn't have had reason that this agent should not be blamed.

Though this agent's childhood was different from ours, it would seem to be neither more nor less binding. The good fortune of our childhood is no more to our credit than the misfortune of his is to his blame. So if he is not free because of the childhood he had, then it would appear that we are not free either. Thus it seems no conditional analysis of freedom will do—for there is nothing internal to the agent which distinguishes him from us.

My analysis, however, proposes a condition that is not internal to the agent. And it allows us to state the relevant difference: namely that, whereas our childhoods fell within a range of normal decency, his was severely deprived. The consequence this has is that he, unlike us, could not have had reasons even though there were reasons around. The problem is not that his reason was functioning improperly, but that his data were unfortuitously selective. Since the world for him was not suitably cooperating, his reason cannot attain its appropriate goal.

The goal, to put it bluntly, is the True and the Good. The freedom we want is the freedom to find it. But such a freedom requires not only that we, as agents, have the right sorts of abilities—the abilities, that is, to direct and govern our actions by our most fundamental selves. It requires as well that the world cooperate in such a way that our most fundamental selves have the opportunity to develop into the selves they ought to be.

If the freedom necessary for moral responsibility is the freedom to be determined by the True and the Good, then obviously we cannot know whether we have such a freedom unless we know, on the one hand, that there *is* a True and a Good and, on the other, that there *are* capacities for finding them. As a consequence of this, the condition of freedom cannot be stated in purely metaphysical terms. For we cannot know which capacities and circumstances are necessary for freedom unless we know which capacities and circumstances will enable us to form the *right* values and perform the *right* actions. Strictly speaking, I take it, the capacity to reason is not enough—we need a kind of sensibility and perception as well. But these are capacities, I assume, that most of us have. So when the world co-operates, we are morally responsible.

I have already said that the condition of freedom cannot be stated in purely metaphysical terms. More specifically, the condition of freedom cannot be stated in terms that are value-free. Thus, the problem of free will has been misrepresented insofar as it has been thought to be a purely metaphysical problem. And, perhaps, this is why the problem of free will has seemed for so long to be hopeless.

That the problem should have seemed to be a purely metaphysical problem is not, however, unnatural or surprising. For being determined by the True and the Good is very different from being determined by one's garden variety of causes, and I think it not unnatural to feel as if one rules out the other. For to be determined by the Good is not to be determined by the Past. And to do something because it is the right thing to do is not to do it because one has been taught to do it. One might think, then, that one can be determined only by one thing or the other. For if one is going to do whatever it is right to do, then it seems one will do it whether or not one has been taught. And if one is going to do whatever one has been taught to do, then it seems one will do it whether or not it is right.

In fact, however, such reasoning rests on a category mistake. These two explanations do not necessarily compete, for they are explanations of different kinds. Consider, for example, the following situation: you ask me to name the capital of Nevada, and I reply

"Carson City." We can explain why I give the answer I do give in either of the following ways: First, we can point out that when I was in the fifth grade I had to memorize the capitals of the fifty states. I was taught to believe that Carson City was the capital of Nevada, and was subsequently positively reinforced for doing so. Second, we can point out that Carson City *is* the capital of Nevada, and that this was, after all, what you wanted to know. So on the one hand, I gave my answer because I was taught. And on the other, I gave my answer because it was right.

Presumably, these explanations are not unrelated. For if Carson City were not the capital of Nevada, I would not have been taught that it was. And if I hadn't been taught that Carson City was the capital of Nevada, I wouldn't have known that it was. Indeed, one might think that if the answer I gave weren't right, I *couldn't* have given it because I was taught. For no school board would have hired a teacher who got such facts wrong. And if I hadn't been taught that Carson City was the capital of Nevada, perhaps I couldn't have given this answer because it was right. For that Carson City is the capital of Nevada is not something that can be known a priori.

Similarly, we can explain why a person acts justly in either of the following ways: First, we can point out that he was taught to act justly, and was subsequently positively reinforced for doing so. Second, we can point out that it is right to act justly, and go on to say why he knows this is so. Again, these explanations are likely to be related. For if it weren't right to act justly, the person may well not have been taught that it was. And if the person hadn't been taught that he ought to act justly, the person may not have discovered this on his own. Of course, the explanations of both kinds in this case will be more complex than the explanations in the previous case. But what is relevant here is that these explanations are compatible: that one can be determined by the Good and determined by the Past.

In order for an agent to be morally free, then, he must be capable of being determined by the Good. Determination by the Good is, as it were, the goal we need freedom to pursue. We need the freedom *to* have our actions determined by the Good, and the freedom to be or to become the sorts of persons whose actions will continue to be so determined. In light of this, it should be clear that no standard incompatibilist views about the conditions of moral responsibility can be right, for, according to these views, an agent is free only if he is the sort of agent whose actions are not causally determined at all. Thus, an agent's freedom would be incompatible with the realization of the goal for which freedom is required. The agent would be, in the words, though not in the spirit, of Sartre, "condemned to be free"—he could not both be free and realize a moral ideal.

Thus, views that offer conditional analyses of the ability to do otherwise, views that, like mine, take freedom to consist in the ability *to be determined* in a particular way, are generally compatibilist views. For insofar as an agent *is* determined in the right way, the agent can be said to be acting freely. Like the compatibilists, then, I am claiming that whether an agent is morally responsible depends not on whether but on how that agent is determined. My view differs from theirs only in what I take the satisfactory kind of determination to be.

However, since on my view the satisfactory kind of determination is determination by reasons that an agent ought to have, it will follow that an agent can be both determined and responsible only insofar as he performs actions that he ought to perform. If an agent performs a morally bad action, on the other hand, then his actions can't be determined in the appropriate way. So if an agent is ever to be responsible for a bad action, it must be the case that his action is not psychologically determined at all. According to my view, then, in order for both moral praise and moral blame to be justified, the thesis of psychological determinism must be false.

Is it plausible that this thesis is false? I think so. For though it appears that some of our actions are psychologically determined, it appears that others are not. It appears that some of our actions are not determined by our interests, and some of our interests are not determined at all. That is, it seems that some of our actions are such that no set of psychological facts are sufficient to explain them. There are occasions on which a person takes one action, but there seems to be no reason why he didn't take another.

For example, we sometimes make arbitrary choices—to wear the green shirt rather than the blue, to have coffee rather than tea. We make such choices on the basis of no reason—and it seems that we might, in these cases, have made a different choice instead.

Some less trivial and more considered choices may also be arbitrary. For one may have reasons on both sides which are equally strong. Thus, one may have good reasons to go to graduate school and good reasons not to; good reasons to get married, and good reasons to stay single. Though we might want, in these cases, to choose on the basis of reasons, our reasons simply do not settle the matter for us. Other psychological events may be similarly undetermined, such as the chance occurrence of thoughts and ideas. One is just struck by an idea, but for no particular reason—one might as easily have had another idea or no idea at all. Or one simply forgets an appointment one has made, even though one was not particularly distracted by other things at the time.

On retrospect, some of the appearance of indetermination may turn out to be deceptive. We decide that unconscious motives dictated a choice that seemed at the time to be arbitrary. Or a number of ideas that seemed to occur to us at random reveal a pattern too unusual to be the coincidence we thought. But if some of the appearances of indetermination are deceptive, I see no reason to believe that all of them should be.

Let us turn, then, to instances of immoral behavior, and see what the right kind of indetermination would be. For indetermination, in this context, is indetermination among some number of fairly particular alternatives—and if one's alternatives are not of the appropriate kind, indetermination will not be sufficient to justify moral blame. It is not enough, for example, to know that a criminal who happened to rob a bank might as easily have chosen to hold up a liquor store instead. What we need to know, in particular, is that when an agent performs a wrong action, he could have performed the right action for the right reasons instead. That is, first, the agent could have had the interests that the agent ought to have had, and second, the agent could have acted on the interests on which he ought to have acted.

Corresponding to these two possibilities, we can imagine two sorts of moral failure: the first corresponds to a form of negligence, the second to a form of weakness. Moral negligence consists in a failure to recognize the existence of moral reasons that one

ought to have recognized. For example, a person hears that his friend is in the hospital, but fails to attend to this when planning his evening. He doesn't stop to think about how lonely and bored his friend is likely to be—he simply reaches for the *TV Guide* or for his novel instead. If the person could have recognized his friend's sorry predicament, he is guilty of moral negligence. Moral weakness, on the other hand, consists in the failure to act on the reasons that one knows one ought, for moral reasons, to be acting on. For example, a person might go so far as to conclude that he really ought to pay his sick friend a visit, but the thought of the drive across town is enough to convince him to stay at home with his book after all. If the person could have made the visit, he is guilty of moral weakness.

There is, admittedly, some difficulty in establishing that an agent who performs a morally bad action satisfies the condition of freedom. It is hard to know whether an agent who did one thing could have done another instead. But presumably we decide such questions now on the basis of statistical evidence—and, if, in fact, these actions are not determined, this is the best method there can be. We decide, in other words, that an agent could have done otherwise if others in his situation have done otherwise, and these others are like him in all apparently relevant ways. Or we decide that an agent could have done otherwise if he himself has done otherwise in situations that are like this one in all apparently relevant ways.

It should be emphasized that the indetermination with which we are here concerned is indetermination only at the level of psychological explanation. Such indetermination is compatible with determination at other levels of explanation. In particular, a sub-psychological, or physiological, explanation of our behavior may yet be deterministic. Some feel that if this is the case, the nature of psychological explanations of our behavior cannot be relevant to the problem of free will. Though I am inclined to disagree with this view, I have neither the space nor the competence to argue this here.

Restricting the type of explanation in question appropriately, however, it is a consequence of the condition of freedom I have suggested that the explanation for why a responsible agent performs a morally bad action must be, at some level, incomplete. There must be nothing that made the agent perform the action he did, nothing that prevented him from performing a morally better one. It should be noted that there may be praiseworthy actions for which the explanations are similarly incomplete. For the idea that an agent who could have performed a morally bad action actually performs a morally good one is no less plausible than the idea that an agent who could have performed a morally good action actually performs a morally bad one. Presumably, an agent who does the right thing for the right reasons deserves praise for his action whether it was determined or not. But whereas indetermination is compatible with the claim that an agent is deserving of praise, it is essential to the justification of the claim that an agent is deserving of blame.

Seen from a certain perspective, this dealing out of praise and blame may seem unfair. In particular, we might think that if it is truly undetermined whether a given agent in a given situation will perform a good action or a bad one, then it must be a matter of chance that the agent ends up doing what he does. If the action is truly undetermined, then it is not determined by the agent himself. One might think that in this case the agent has no more control over the moral quality of his action than does anything else.

However, the fact that it is not determined whether the agent will perform a good action or a bad one does not imply that which action he performs can properly be regarded as a matter of chance. Of course, in some situations an agent might choose to make it a matter of chance. For example, an agent struggling with the decision between fulfilling a moral obligation and doing something immoral that he very much wants to do might ultimately decide to let the toss of a coin settle the matter for him. But, in normal

cases, the way in which the agent makes a decision involves no statistical process or randomizing event. It appears that the claim that there is no complete explanation of why the agent who could have performed a better action performed a worse one or of why the agent who could have performed a worse action performed a better one rules out even the explanation that it was a matter of chance.

In order to have control over the moral quality of his actions, an agent must have certain requisite abilities—in particular, the abilities necessary to see and understand the reasons and interests he ought to see and understand and the abilities necessary to direct his actions in accordance with these reasons and interests. And if, furthermore, there is nothing that interferes with the agent's use of these abilities—that is, no determining cause that prevents him from using them and no statistical process that, as it were, takes out of his hands the control over whether or not he uses them—then it seems that these are all the abilities that the agent needs to have. But it is compatible with the agent's having these abilities and with there being no interferences to their use that it is not determined whether the agent will perform a good action or a bad one. The responsible agent who performs a bad action fails to exercise these abilities sufficiently, though there is no complete explanation of why he fails. The responsible agent who performs a good action does exercise these abilities—it may or may not be the case that it is determined that he exercise them.

The freedom required for moral responsibility, then, is the freedom to be good. Only this kind of freedom will be neither too much nor too little. For then the agent is not so free as to be free from moral reasons, nor so unfree as to make these reasons ineffective.

EXERCISES

1. In the biblical account, the children of Israel are held in slavery in Egypt for many years. At one point Pharaoh apparently considers freeing them, but God "hardened Pharaoh's heart" and thus Pharaoh refused to free the Israeli slaves. Most of us, surely, would say that what Pharaoh did was *morally wrong*: it is wrong to hold slaves in bondage. But if Almighty God *hardened* Pharaoh's heart, then it is difficult to suppose that Pharaoh acted with *free will*. So *is* free will necessary for performing morally wrong

(and morally right) acts? If you still believe that free will is essential for acting wrongly or rightly, how would you explain away this apparent counterexample?

2. If I do something I don't really want to do—such as attending the golden wedding anniversary celebration of Aunt Ethyl and Uncle Fred, or writing a required term paper on "The Accomplishments of Herbert Hoover"—can I still be acting freely?

3. If I give in to temptation, and—against my better judgment and in violation of the diet I'm striving to follow—munch down six large gooey chocolate chip cookies, am I acting freely? Is that an exercise of free will?

4. You are a music major, specializing in oboe performance. Ever since you first heard the oboe, as a small child, you loved the instrument; and as soon as you were old enough for middle school orchestra, you chose the oboe as your instrument. Other kids played soccer; you played oboe. Other kids had favorite rock bands; you had favorite woodwind ensembles.

    Recent research on the human genome reveals an exciting discovery: a profound love of the oboe is caused by a specific gene; and all—and only—those who have that gene really love the oboe. Apparently one can like the oboe without the gene, but all who really love the oboe have the gene; and all who have the gene are deeply and permanently drawn to the oboe immediately upon hearing that instrument. (Of course if one lives one's entire life isolated deep in a rain forest, and never hears the sweet sound of the oboe, then one will have no passion for the oboe; but all who have the very rare oboe gene, and have an opportunity to hear the oboe, are immediately and passionately dedicated to the oboe.) So your passion for the oboe is genetically programmed. Do you act freely when you practice the oboe? Is your oboe-playing an exercise of free will? Was your choice to study music rather than medicine a free choice?

5. It's quite obvious that most of us prefer to have choices, and to exercise control over our choices. Psychologists have made extensive studies of this preference. (Not everyone prefers to make their own choices; some prefer to have others choose for them, or believe that they cannot really exercise effective control. However, that preference for not making choices is strongly associated with a number of psychological problems: those who do not wish to make their own choices are more likely to become depressed, they suffer pain more acutely, and they generally have less fortitude when working on a difficult project). Could people have a healthy belief in choice-making and their own choice-making effectiveness, and still believe in determinism?

6. Rafia is the youngest vice president at a major financial corporation. She is a brilliant stock analyst, and her future looks bright: gossip around the firm has her on the inside track to become CEO within a decade. But Rafia discovers some deceptive accounting practices that the company has been exploiting to inflate its profits and artificially boost its stock price. When Rafia reports her concerns to the current CEO and to the company's chief financial officer, they tell her not to worry about it, and not to tell anyone: "Nobody outside the company knows about this, and it won't be revealed for many years. By that time we will have sold off our stock and we'll all be very, very rich. The company may go bankrupt, and some stockholders will lose their investments: but that's their tough luck. Lots of companies do this. One of the things you have to learn, as you climb up the corporate ladder, is how to keep secrets. By keeping this secret, you will become a very successful and wealthy woman." Rafia is appalled. Rafia would love to be rich, and she would love to become a top corporate officer for a major corporation: that's what she went to college for, that's why she has put in incredibly long hours for many years. But the idea of making millions of dollars through fraudulent stock

deals while small investors lose their life savings and many employees lose their pension benefits: Rafia believes that is dead wrong, and she refuses to go along. She takes company documents to the Securities and Exchange Commission; the commission investigates, and levies large penalties against Rafia's corporation, and forces them to stop their fraudulent practices. Rafia, however, is fired. Other financial companies see her as a whistle-blowing risk, and refuse to hire her. Rafia winds up in a low-level position working for a small local bank as a loan officer, at a fraction of her former income.

One of Rafia's friends asks her about why she revealed the company fraud: "Rafia, you're smart and savvy. You knew that employees who 'blow the whistle' on their employers usually wind up suffering reprisals, and lose their jobs, and never find jobs that good. You were on the fast track to the very top of the corporate world; it was what you always wanted, it was what you had worked so hard for. Why did you do it?"

"I had to," Rafia replies. "I simply could not go along with that kind of fraud, in which so many people would get hurt. I could never have lived with myself if I had been a party to that. Once I discovered the fraud, I did what I had to do; I simply couldn't have done anything else."

A. Suppose that Rafia, being who she is, and given the deep moral principles she holds, really *could not* do otherwise. Did Rafia act freely?

B. Most of us will find Rafia a morally admirable person. Would she be *more* or *less* admirable if she had wrestled with her conscience, been severely tempted to go along with the fraud and pocket her fortune, agonized over her decision, and after days of indecisiveness decided to reveal the fraud?

C. In what sense, if any, is it true that Rafia "could not do otherwise"? Is *decisive* Rafia more, less, or equally as free as *indecisive* Rafia (of the previous question)?

D. Rafia is planning to take her information to the Securities and Exchange Commission early tomorrow morning: it is the right thing to do, she believes; and she also believes it is what she *must* do; but still, if we ask Rafia, she will tell us she is acting freely. The phone rings. Rafia answers, and finds she is talking to an F.B.I. agent: "We have been investigating the company you work for," the agent tells Rafia, "and we have uncovered evidence of fraud. We know that you made copies of some of the documents that show evidence of the fraudulent practices. Turn those documents in to the Securities and Exchange Commission first thing tomorrow morning, or we will charge you with fraud." "That's exactly what I was planning to do with them," Rafia replies. "Fine," the F.B.I. agent replies; "just be sure that you do, otherwise you'll be arrested." Rafia's resolve to give the documents to the SEC is unchanged; but now she feels that her act is somewhat less free. Is it reasonable for Rafia to feel that the F.B.I. call has somehow diminished her freedom, when the agent is demanding that she do what she had already decided to do anyway?

7. Your friend Saul is the world's greatest procrastinator. If a term paper is due Wednesday at 8 a.m., he *never* starts it before Tuesday night. More likely he will plead for an extension, and start the paper Wednesday afternoon. His ethics term paper is due November 15. On the first day of October, you find Saul at his desk with stacks of ethics books around him, while he works furiously at his keyboard. Looking at the monitor, you discover Saul is on page 12 of the ethics paper that is not due for another six weeks.

You are amazed. "What got into you? That paper isn't due for weeks yet. You *never* work on anything until the very last minute. What's the deal?"

"Nothing happened," Saul replies; "I just exercised my free will and chose to write my term paper punctually, and not procrastinate."

"Yeah, sure," you reply. "I bet your parents threatened to cut off your funds if you flunked another course. Or maybe the dean called you in for a stern lecture. Or I know, your coach read you the riot act about your low grades. No, I've got it: Allison said she was dumping you if you don't shape up and get your act together. That's got to be it, right?"

"No, nothing like that. I know I have a tendency to procrastinate. And I was sorely tempted to put this paper off until the last minute. But this time I simply chose to do otherwise. It was an act of free will; nothing else has changed; that's the only explanation I can give."

Would you find that a plausible explanation? Or would you suppose that there must be something your friend Saul is not telling you? And what does your answer say about your own view of free will?

8. If psychologists accepted Campbell's libertarian view of free will, would that mean psychology could *never* be a complete science? That there would always be human behavior that would remain completely beyond scientific psychological explanation?

ADDITIONAL READING

A number of recent books consider the question of free will in light of recent research in biology and psychology. John M. Doris, in *Lack of Character: Personality and Moral Behavior* (Cambridge: Cambridge University Press, 2002), organizes and reviews several decades of psychological research (particularly social psychology research), and he draws out in detail and depth its philosophical implications in the areas of free will and moral responsibility. One of the most interesting and important books written on free will is by a neuropsychologist, Daniel M. Wegner. *The Illusion of Conscious Will* (Cambridge, Mass.: Bradford Books, 2002) is a very readable book that draws out the implications of decades of neuropsychological research, and its often surprising results. A superb collection of essays—and commentary—on the implications of contemporary neuroscience for questions of free will can be found in *The Volitional Brain: Towards a Neuroscience of Free Will*, Benjamin Libet, Anthony Freeman, and Keith Sutherland, editors (Thorverton, Exeter UK: Imprint Academic, 1999). Bruce N. Waller, *The Natural Selection of Autonomy* (Albany, N.Y.: SUNY Press, 1998) uses recent research in biology and psychology in an attempt to uncover some of the motives common to both libertarian and compatibilist views of free will, and to attack traditional justifications for moral responsibility.

For the best, clearest, and most even-handed guide to the issues surrounding the free will debate (and also for a very creative addition to that debate), see two books by Richard Double: *The Non-Reality of Free Will* (New York: Oxford University Press, 1991), and *Metaphilosophy and Free Will* (New York: Oxford University Press, 1996).

For a fascinating libertarian account of free will from the Italian Renaissance, see Giovanni Pico della Mirandola, "The Dignity of Man" (sometimes titled "Oration on the Dignity of Man"); it is available in several renaissance anthologies. C. A. Campbell's *On Selfhood and Godhood* (London: George Allen & Unwin, 1957) is the classic modern source. Robert Kane has developed what is undoubtedly the most sophisticated and interesting contemporary defense of libertarian free will, in *Free Will and Values* (Albany, N.Y.:

SUNY Press,1985) and *The Significance of Free Will* (Oxford: Oxford University Press, 1996). Kane's edited work, *The Oxford Handbook of Free Will* (Oxford: Oxford University Press, 2002), is a wonderful guide to contemporary thought concerning free will. Two other influential sources for incompatibilist views of free will are William James, "The Dilemma of Determinism," (1884, available in a number of anthologies); and Jean-Paul Sartre, *Being and Nothingness* (New York: Philosophical Library, 1956).

The classic presentation of both determinism and compatibilism is David Hume, *An Inquiry Concerning Human Understanding*, Section 8, and in his *Treatise of Human Nature*, Book II, Part III. Thomas Hobbes developed an earlier similar account (1651) in *Leviathan*, Chapter 2. A more recent argument for compatibilism can be found in A. J. Ayer, "Freedom and Necessity," in his *Philosophical Essays* (London: Macmillan, 1954). For a delightful critique of compatibilism, presented in a spirited dialogue by an Italian humanist philosopher of the fifteenth century, see Lorenzo Valla, "Dialogue on Free Will." It can be found in *The Renaissance Philosophy of Man*, Ernst Cassirer, Paul Oskar Kristeller, and John Herman Randall, editors (Chicago: The University of Chicago Press, 1948). The book also contains an excellent translation of Giovanni Pico della Mirandola's "The Dignity of Man."

The position we called deep compatibilism is championed by Harry G. Frankfurt. Frankfurt developed his views in a number of essays, all of them collected in *The Importance of What We Care About* (Cambridge: Cambridge University Press, 1988). Another excellent deep compatibilist source is Gerald Dworkin's *The Theory and Practice of Autonomy* (Cambridge: Cambridge University Press, 1988).

Rationalist compatibilism is presented most effectively by Susan Wolf, in *Freedom Within Reason* (New York: Oxford University Press, 1990).

Daniel Dennett has written two very entertaining and readable books that take a compatibilist view on free will: *Elbow Room* (Cambridge, Mass.: Bradford Books, 1985); and *Freedom Evolves* (New York: Viking, 2003). P. F. Strawson's "Freedom and Resentment" was originally published in 1962; it is now widely anthologized, including in the Gary Watson anthology, *Free Will*, listed here. Strawson's essay has been a very influential compatibilist view, arguing that we simply can't get along without our basic concepts of freedom and responsibility, whatever scientists might discover about determinism.

Philosophers who deny the existence of free will altogether (generally because they favor determinism and believe determinism and free will are incompatible) include Baron D'Holbach (1770); Arthur Schopenhauer, *Essay on the Freedom of the Will* (first published in 1841, reissued by New York: Liberal Arts Press, 1960). More recently, John Hospers has denied free will (making extensive use of Freudian psychology in his arguments); see "What Means This Freedom," in *Determinism and Freedom in the Age of Modern Science*, Sidney Hook, editor (New York: New York University Press, 1958). B. F. Skinner, in *Beyond Freedom and Dignity* (New York: Alfred A. Knopf, 1971), as well as in his utopian novel, *Walden Two* (first published in 1948; available in paperback, New York: Macmillan, 1976), is often thought to be rejecting free will altogether. In fact, his writings reject *libertarian* free will (and moral responsibility), but he strongly champions compatibilist free will.

There are many excellent free will anthologies; perhaps the best small collection is edited by Gary Watson: *Free Will* (Oxford: Oxford University Press, 1982). An excellent recent anthology is edited by Laura Waddell Ekstrom, *Agency and Responsibility* (Boulder, Colo.: Westview Press, 2001).

NOTES

[1]William Barrett, "Determinism and Novelty," in *Determinism and Freedom in the Age of Modern Science*, Sidney Hook, editors (New York: Collier Books, 1961), p. 46.

[2]Barrett, 1961, pp. 46–47.

[3]David Hume, "Of Liberty and Necessity," *Enquiry Concerning the Human Understanding* (Oxford: Clarendon Press, 1902), p. 80.

[4]Hume, "Of Liberty and Necessity," p. 100.

[5]Susan Wolf, *Freedom Within Reason* (Oxford: Oxford University Press, 990), p. 55.

[6]Kant, 1788, p. 259.

[7]F. Dostoyevsky, *Notes from Underground*, trans. Andrew R. MacAndrew (New York: New American Library,1961), p. 114. Originally published in 1864.

[8]Roderick Chisholm, "Human Freedom and the Self," The Lindley Lecture, University of Kansas, 1964; reprinted in *Free Will*, Gary Watson, editor (Oxford: Oxford University Press, 1982), 24–35.

[9]Jean-Paul Sartre, "Existentialism Is a Humanism," in *Existentialism from Dostoevsky to Sartre*, W. Kaufmann, editor (New York: New Arena Library, 1975), pp. 352–353. First published in 1946.

[10]C. A. Campbell, *On Selfhood and Godhood* (London: George Allen & Unwin, 1957), p. 163.

[11]Campbell, p. 177.

[12]C. A. Campbell; italics in original.

CHAPTER 14

✦ FREEDOM, MORAL ✦ RESPONSIBILITY, AND ETHICS

The question of free will is closely related to a major ethical issue: Are we *morally responsible* for what we do? Do we justly deserve blame and punishment for our transgressions, and reward for our triumphs? Many philosophers have treated the questions of free will and moral responsibility (or "just deserts") as two sides of a single coin. C. A. Campbell, for example, insists that:

> It is not seriously disputable that the kind of freedom in question is the freedom which is commonly recognised to be in some sense a precondition of moral responsibility. Clearly, it is on account of this integral connection with moral responsibility that such exceptional importance has always been felt to attach to the Free Will problem. But in what precise sense is free will a precondition of moral responsibility, and thus a postulate of the moral life in general?[1]

Psychiatrist Willard Gaylin, former director of the Hastings Center for Applied Ethics, sums up his view of the question thus:

> Freedom demands responsibility; autonomy demands culpability.[2]

That's the entire paragraph, and that's all Gaylin has to say on the subject: the connection between freedom (autonomy) and moral responsibility (culpability) is so obvious that it need only be stated.

But the connection has not seemed so obvious to everyone. Some have thought we could be morally responsible (justly deserving of punishment) even though we are not free. For example, Jonathan Edwards (a famous preacher and theologian of colonial New England) denied that humans have free will. God is *omnipotent*, *all* powerful, and therefore humans have no power to make choices. Instead a few are saved by the gift of God's grace, and not from their own free choices. But though we are not *free*, we are nonetheless sinful and wicked, and thus God *justly* punishes us. On the other side, some believe we have *free will* (in Hume's compatibilist sense of being free to choose as we wish, though our wishes are determined), but such free will cannot justify moral responsibility. (For moral responsibility we would need *libertarian* free will, and we do not have that.) Thus—on this view—we might have compatibilist free will, but not be morally responsible.

But just as there are differing accounts of free will, there are also many different views of moral responsibility. Before trying to navigate our way through that labyrinth, it is important to be clear on exactly what moral responsibility is.

TYPES OF RESPONSIBILITY

Role Responsibility

Not all responsibility is *moral* responsibility. Moral responsibility is the foundation for judgments that a person justly deserves blame or punishment, praise or reward. There is a very different type of responsibility we might call *role* responsibility,[3] that unfortunately is often confused with moral responsibility. You're planning a picnic with some friends, and it's your job—your responsibility, your *role* responsibility—to bring a keg of beer. Suppose you succeed splendidly, the keg is there on time, nicely chilled, pumping perfectly. Then you have fulfilled your role responsibility. But your *moral* responsibility is another question altogether. It is something very different to suppose that you justly deserve praise or blame, reward or punishment, for how you carry out your role responsibility. Suppose someone says "Susan did a great job providing the keg; she carried out her role splendidly, and deserves our praise." Someone else might deny that Susan deserves any praise for her role responsibility success: "Yeah, Susan provided the keg; but her mom owns the brewery! Susan just told one of the delivery guys when and where to set the keg up, and that's all she had to do. She doesn't deserve any special credit." Maybe Susan does deserve credit, or maybe she doesn't. That is, maybe she is morally responsible for what she did, maybe she is not. But that's a different question from the question of whether she met her role responsibility. If it is clear that she carried out her role responsibility, but her moral responsibility remains in doubt, then obviously these are two different sorts of responsibility.

Suppose the opposite occurs: everyone arrives at the picnic, but there's no beer. Susan had the role responsibility for making sure the keg was at the picnic, but she neglected to do it. She failed at her role responsibility. But the question of whether she is morally responsible is quite a different matter. "Susan had role responsibility for the keg, and she blew it. But you can't really blame her: she's been under so much stress from finishing her senior project and waiting to hear from medical schools; it was just more than she could handle." So Susan has *role* responsibility, but it's not at all clear that she also has *moral* responsibility. Again, that marks two distinctly different sorts of responsibility (even if you believe that Susan *is* morally responsible, that is clearly a distinct issue from whether she is role responsible).

Taking Role Responsibility

Another way of marking the distinction between role and moral responsibility is that often one can *take* role responsibility. When we are planning the picnic, Susan can *take* responsibility for bringing a keg, simply by agreeing to do so. But you can't take moral responsibility: If we are debating whether Susan *deserves credit* (is morally responsible) for securing a keg—since her Mom did all the work—Susan can't settle the issue by claiming or taking moral responsibility. Her claim of moral responsibility will not establish that she justly deserves reward. Likewise, if someone claims moral responsibility for a bad act, that will not settle the issue of his actual moral responsibility. John Spenkelink was the first person to be executed by Florida after it reinstated capital punishment. A few days before his execution Spenkelink *claimed* full moral responsibility for the murder he had committed. What had led him on this path to murder? John had been a well-behaved kid until at age 11 he returned home from school to discover the body of his beloved father, who had committed suicide. After that John lost interest in school, began to get into trouble while skipping school, dropped out, began drinking heavily, and was drifting around the Southeast until he killed a fellow drifter in a violent argument. So was John Spenkelink morally responsible for the path he followed after discovering his father's suicide? Suicide often has a devastating psychological impact on family and friends, and it is hard to imagine the traumatic effect on an adolescent boy who is the first to discover his father's body. Traumatized or not, perhaps John did have full moral responsibility for his further behavior, and for the murder he committed. Perhaps not. But his *claim* of moral responsibility carries no weight in trying to resolve that question. Claiming or taking *role* responsibility is one thing; *moral* responsibility is a different matter.

Role responsibility for a keg at a summer picnic is hardly insignificant. But role responsibility for yourself, and for who you are, and for what you do: that's considerably more important. If I cannot make my own moral decisions, follow my own drummer, and exercise control over my plans and purposes—in short, *take* role responsibility for my own moral life—then I cannot be a full moral being. If you make all my moral decisions for me, usurp my authority, and prevent me from taking responsibility, then I am a puppet rather than a moral agent. I must be able to take responsibility for my own moral life if I am to have a moral life at all. But though I take role responsibility for my own moral life, it is a very different matter to judge that I am *morally responsible*.

Donna makes her own moral decisions, she takes responsibility for them, and she rightly resents interference. But one might acknowledge that Donna takes full role responsibility for her moral life while still questioning whether she justly deserves credit or blame (whether she is *morally* responsible). After all, it is quite legitimate to say: Donna has taken full (role) responsibility for her moral life; but when we understand how vilely she was treated as a child, and how few psychological resources she has for living a virtuous life, we should not blame her for exercising her taken responsibility so miserably.[4] And the same issues arise if Donna lives a life of great moral worth: Donna takes role responsibility for her own moral life and moral decisions; but is she *morally* responsible for her virtuous life, or is she instead lucky to have the early environment and moral fortitude and generous sympathies that enabled her to choose and follow a virtuous life course? (Of course some will maintain that Donna really is *morally* responsible. But that will be a different issue from judging that she has *taken* responsibility, that she has *role responsibility* for her life.)

Of course if you are severely incompetent—a small child, or badly brain damaged, or suffering severe dementia—then you are incapable of exercising role responsibility for your life, and someone else has to make decisions for you. But if (perhaps because of an abusive or overindulgent childhood) I am *lousy* at exercising role responsibility for myself (I repeatedly make bad marriage choices and poor career decisions, and I choose impulsively), I may still have *full* role responsibility for my own life. If you try to interfere, or offer unsolicited advice, I shall feel resentful. After all, it's *my* life, and I want to make my *own* choices. You may be able to make better choices for me than I could for myself, but I still insist on making my own choices and exercising full role responsibility for my own life. But moral responsibility is quite different. While I may have full role responsibility for running my own life, it does not follow that I am *morally responsible*—that I *justly deserve* reward or punishment—for managing my life well or ill. It makes perfectly good sense to say: "Doug has full role responsibility for his life, he makes his own choices; but (for whatever reason— his early environment or his genetic makeup or his natural impetuosity) Doug is so lousy at exercising responsibility that he deserves no blame for making such a mess of his life." That is, Doug takes role responsibility for his life but may still lack moral responsibility. (You may believe that anyone who exercises role responsibility for her life *is* morally responsible for the choices she makes. Perhaps that's true. The point here is that it is a *separate* issue: the question of whether one is role responsible is not the same as the question of whether one is morally responsible).

In sum, *role* responsibility for yourself and your acts is essential for morality. To live morally, I must make my own choices, rather than being pulled by someone else's strings. But that role responsibility requirement for morality is not *moral* responsibility. So if someone confidently asserts that morality requires responsibility, it is possible they are thinking of role responsibility, and then confusing it with moral responsibility.

Moral Responsibility and the Utility of Punishment

When we are considering moral responsibility, the first task is to distinguish it from role responsibility. But with the focus squarely on moral responsibility, there are still serious questions about what justifies claims and ascriptions of moral responsibility. Does Ikram *deserve blame or punishment* (or praise and reward)? That is, is Ikram *morally responsible* for what he did? It is sometimes suggested that this is simply a question of whether it is useful to punish Ikram, but that hardly seems adequate to justify claims of moral responsibility. It's easy to think of cases in which punishment might be *useful*, but would not be justified because the victim of the punishment is not morally responsible: does not justly deserve punishment. For example, suppose that we experience a wave of brutal murders, apparently committed almost randomly by a number of unrelated people, but we have not been able to catch any of the murderers. We become convinced that if one murderer were caught and executed, the others would become frightened and stop their crimes, but unfortunately we cannot apprehend a murderer. However, there is an innocent, harmless, friendless, home- less man roaming the streets, and it would be easy to frame him. So someone might be tempted to frame this poor innocent, and punish him: execute him. And it might even be *useful* to do so (though of course there would be great risks of this plot being discovered, with terrible consequences). But however useful it might or might not be, it certainly would not be *just*: the man does not justly deserve punishment. Or consider another case: a person in our community becomes a carrier for a terrible deadly disease, and spreads it to all those with whom she comes in contact. She herself is not affected by the disease, and lives in perfect health while she spreads the disease—unknowingly—to others. When we dis- cover that she is carrying this deadly disease, we will take measures to stop her from spread- ing this infection. If we cannot destroy the disease in her, we shall have to quarantine her, perhaps even place her in isolation on an island. This will be useful, perhaps even essential; but she certainly does not *deserve* to be placed in solitary confinement.

One more example. A nefarious chemist invents a drug that transforms those who ingest it into violent and dangerous thugs. Our gentle friend Joe is given the drug (the chemist slips it into a glass of orange juice in the cafeteria line, and Joe happens to get that glass). It turns out that the only way to rehabilitate someone who has taken this drug is to punish him severely after he commits a violent act. Most of us will have doubts about Joe *deserving* punishment (Joe merely drew the unlucky juice glass), but the punishment will be quite *useful* if it results in Joe's rehabilitation. In similar manner, when a child touches a hot stove and is burned, it may be a useful learning experience. That does not imply that she justly deserved to be burned. So genuine moral responsibility cannot be established on the basis of the usefulness of punishment and reward. If a person justly deserves punishment, then that person must be morally responsible for the punished act, and the utility or disutility of the punishment is irrelevant; likewise, if a person justly deserves the reward for winning a race, the fact that more people would be made happy by giving the reward to someone else has no bearing on the winner's just deserts. (Of course if everyone hates the winner, we might decide to give the award to someone else. But then we will be deciding that there is something more important than just deserts, *not* that the winner does not justly deserve the reward.)

CONDITIONS FOR MORAL RESPONSIBILITY

So moral responsibility carries very strong conditions. But whatever else moral responsibility may require, *most* have believed that at the very least it requires freedom. I am not morally responsible for shooting someone if I am placed in steel restraints that force my hand to grip a pistol and my finger to close on the trigger. I am not morally responsible for robbing a bank if you have drugged me and turned me into a compulsive bank robber who cannot help robbing banks.

Could You Do Otherwise?

But exactly what sort of freedom—and what sort of free will—does moral responsibility require? C. A. Campbell answers that the only account of free will that can support moral responsibility is the libertarian view, in which you are acting freely (and thus you are morally responsible for your acts) *if and only if* you could have actually done otherwise. So obviously one reason for embracing the rather mysterious, miracle-working model of libertarian free will is because of the libertarian conviction that only such a radical account of free will can make sense of moral responsibility: How could we *blame* someone for doing wrong (or credit someone for doing right) if they could not have done otherwise?

This question plunges us into a dispute that has raged for many centuries. Consider our profoundly virtuous friend Alexandra. She is a paragon of virtue, who does good joyfully and brushes aside "temptations" easily. Alexandra is offered an opportunity to pick up a huge windfall by profiting on inside information from a corporation CEO: the stock price on Shady Deal Industries is currently very high, but their books have been manipulated to hide enormous losses, and when those losses are revealed Shady Deal Industries stock will be almost worthless. Alexandra can sell the stock short, and cash in on a small fortune. There is no way her devious insider trading will be discovered. She will simply look like a shrewd investor who profited by her careful analysis of the market. Alexandra cannot even imagine doing such a thing: "I couldn't possibly do that; it would be unfair to other people who will lose the money I gain through this inside information." Is Alexandra *morally responsible*—does she deserve credit—for her virtuous choice?

Alexandra *cannot* do a devious and dishonest act. Of course she could *if* she wanted to; but given who she is, there is no way she could *want* to do such a thing. (Saying that she could nonetheless do so is just silly; it's like saying that if you had wings, then you could fly—so even though you don't have wings, you could still fly.) So Alexandra cannot consider insider trading. But does it follow that Alexandra deserves no credit, that she is not morally responsible for her virtuous behavior?

It may seem from such examples that one might deserve credit or blame even if one could not do otherwise. But there are cases that seem to lead to the opposite conclusion. Patty Hearst is the daughter of the fabulously wealthy Hearst family. She was kidnapped (and supposedly brainwashed) by a group of revolutionaries calling themselves the Symbionese Liberation Army. She was present and heavily armed during robberies carried out by the Symbionese Liberation Army. At her trial, the prosecution claimed that Patty had been converted to the Symbionese Liberation Army cause, and that she was a willing participant in the robberies. The Hearst case is difficult and controversial, and raises many questions: Was Patty Hearst actually "brainwashed"? Did she genuinely convert to the Symbionese Liberation Army, or was she forced to participate? To avoid those complications, consider a fictional case: Nancy Wurst is a law-abiding college student, the daughter of a wealthy family. She is kidnapped by a band of revolutionaries and bank robbers (the Anarchist Brigade) and *effectively* brainwashed into becoming a dedicated convert to their values (suspend your doubts about whether brainwashing is really possible). She now deeply believes in the values of the Anarchist Brigade, and she robs banks because she *wants* to. She is so profoundly dedicated to the cause that she *cannot* choose otherwise. But she is not some mindless zombie: she discusses the values she now holds, she effectively plans bank robberies, she reads books and watches movies and talks intelligently with her friends. In the course of one of the robberies, Nancy is captured. She remains steadfast in her commitment to the Anarchist Brigade, so we shall certainly have to take steps to protect society from her attacks. But the question is: Does Nancy *deserve punishment?* Is she *morally responsible* for her criminal behavior?

Suppose the Anarchist Brigade has developed *very* effective brainwashing techniques, and they have the ability to convert—brainwash—anyone they capture. Nancy was unlucky: she happened to be the one they caught. Before they kidnapped her, she was just as peaceful and law abiding as you are (probably more). If you had been the one kidnapped, then you would now be an enthusiastic bank-robbing member of the Anarchist Brigade. Would you deserve punishment for your crimes? That is, would *you* be morally responsible under those circumstances?

The "brainwashing" carried out by the Symbionese Liberation Army on Patty Hearst required several weeks to convert her. The Anarchist Brigade is much better, and they do the job in a couple of weeks. Suppose they become even more sophisticated, and can do the trick by simply slipping a pill into your coffee, a pill that takes effect in about 30 seconds and radically alters your entire worldview, transforming you into a dedicated disciple of the Anarchist Brigade. The pill was placed in Nancy's coffee while she was having breakfast at the local diner. Several of you were having breakfast together, and she just happened to get the cup with the pill. Does that change anything?

Suppose the process takes a much longer time: not 30 seconds, or 30 days, but about 20 years. That is, suppose that Nancy was born into a family that belonged to the Anarchist Brigade, and the course of her development—her environment together with her genetic heritage—shaped her into a dedicated member of the Brigade. Of course she now robs banks because she *wants* to; she *chooses* to rob banks. But her desires and choices are the determined result of how she was shaped. Like getting the unlucky cup of coffee, Nancy drew the unlucky long-term environment. You, a person who is not tempted to rob banks, drew a more fortunate environmental history. You were lucky, and Nancy unlucky; but can we establish *just deserts* and *moral responsibility* on a foundation of good or bad luck?

If Nancy rejects the Anarchist Brigade (she was a rebellious teenager and rejected her parents' values) then that choice was also the product of her conditioning history. There was some environmental cause that, fortunately, led her to reject a life of bank robbery. Or at least there was such a cause, unless you believe in the special godlike libertarian power to make choices with no causal antecedents. This is not to deny that Nancy makes choices and decisions, follows her own goals and values and preferences. That may be sufficient to count Nancy and ourselves as *free* (according to compatibilist views of free will). But when we look very closely at the causes that shaped her, and that shape the choices we make and the values we cherish, the notion of *moral responsibility* becomes more problematic. Of course we can insist that Nancy really *is* a bank robber. That's true, certainly. But the question is whether she *justly deserves punishment* for being a bank robber. Furthermore, Nancy *chooses* to be a bank robber, and she *values* her career of bank robbery. But if those choices and values are the product of her good or bad fortune, there remains the question of whether she is morally responsible for them.

So the question of moral responsibility leaves us with three alternatives. One, we can embrace the libertarian position—a position that strikes some as being hard to swallow, perhaps even incoherent, but which may be the only account that will provide a foundation for moral responsibility. Second, we can try to find a way to justify moral responsibility on compatibilist grounds: Nancy's choices and values and character are the determined product of good or bad fortune, but she still deserves credit or blame for them. Or third, we can reject moral responsibility. Philosophers are deeply divided over what alternative is best. You'll have to decide for yourself. But before deciding, you might want to consider how this question is related to your larger views concerning ethics.

MORAL RESPONSIBILITY AND ETHICS

What is the relation between moral responsibility and ethics? Many philosophers believe that without moral responsibility, there could be no real ethics. The libertarian C. A. Campbell insists that denial of justly deserved praise and blame would destroy "the reality of the moral life." You may recall that Susan Wolf is a Kantian, for whom genuine freedom consists in rationally following the True and the Good; but she concurs with Campbell that if we deny moral responsibility then we must:

> . . . stop thinking in terms of what ought and ought not to be. We would have to stop thinking in terms that would allow the possibility that some lives and projects are better than others.[5]

A similar view is voiced by the Catholic philosopher F. C. Copleston, who asserts that without moral responsibility "there would be no objective moral distinction between the emperor Nero and St. Francis of Assisi."[6]

Ethics Without Moral Responsibility

But would the denial of moral responsibility really mean the end of all morality? Consider morality in its most majestic form: true morality is whatever God pronounces good, and it derives its authority and truth solely from God's holy will. Martin Luther and John Calvin had no difficulty proclaiming such a transcendent moral law while simultaneously rejecting all moral responsibility. God hardens whom He will harden, and shows mercy to whom He will show mercy; and thus, as Paul asserted, "it is not of him that willeth, nor of him that runneth, but of God that showeth mercy." So it is wrong that "any man should boast" of his just deserts; rather, God by His grace makes some righteous while leaving others in depraved wickedness. The virtuous have no grounds for boasting, for they have no moral responsibility for their righteousness. That does not alter the fact that they truly are virtuous (by God's grace) and the wicked are morally loathsome. One may find such moral views repugnant, but it seems clear that Luther and Calvin could consistently champion an *ethical* doctrine and make moral judgments while *rejecting* moral responsibility.

It appears that other ethical systems can also survive without moral responsibility. Suppose Wanda adopts the Kantian view that moral principles are derived from rational deduction, and she deduces that her basic moral obligation is to live by a rule that she could will as a universal law. Wanda further believes that whether one is able to conform one's will to that high rational moral standard is a matter of one's good or bad fortune, and thus we are not morally responsible for either success or failure in our moral lives. It is Wanda's good fortune to have the clear reason and strong willpower required for Kantian moral goodness, but she deserves no credit for her severe moral virtue. Kant himself would agree with Wanda's rationalist ethics, but reject her views on moral responsibility. But it seems that Kantian rationalist ethics does not *require* moral responsibility.

Clearly if all our acts were purely luck, then morality and moral judgments would be impossible. It's not by *luck* that the Kantian performs a virtuous act: she performs the act purposefully and reflectively, and as a result of her own careful deliberations. But that is consistent with holding that she deserves no *credit* for her purposeful virtuous behavior, since she is ultimately lucky to have developed the capacities for such virtuous rational reflection. Thus it is not inconsistent to judge her life *virtuous*—by the most severe rationalistic ethical laws—while *denying* that she is morally responsible.[7] They are separate issues, and establishing the existence of moral acts does not automatically entail the existence of moral responsibility.

Moral Judgments and Moral Responsibility

Without moral responsibility, some moral judgments do become impossible. We can no longer say things like: Jones justly deserves praise for her virtuous character, and Smith deserves blame for his vicious acts. But that is obviously not the whole of morality. In the absence of moral responsibility we can continue to judge Jones's character virtuous, and Smith's acts vicious. And we can strive to shape our children like the virtuous Jones, and struggle to eliminate vicious acts in ourselves and others, and consciously shape an environment that maximizes virtue and minimizes vice. Without moral responsibility there is still a wide range for ethical judgments and behavior and planning.

Consider Ebeneezer Scrooge, the famous Dickens character. Scrooge (pre-ghosts) is the paradigm for a thoroughly greedy and sordid person. Scrooge has sharp intelligence, and he weighs alternatives and makes his own choices, and through his iron self-control he resolutely follows his miserly pattern of life. Scrooge is utterly vile, and his miserly character is thoroughly his own. But is he morally responsible, does he deserve blame for his selfish character and his selfish acts? Dickens shows us how Scrooge's early poverty marked him with a terrible fear of the cruel treatment the world metes out to the impoverished— "there is nothing on which it [the world] is so hard as poverty," Scrooge asserts—and his early love, Belle, describes his resulting character accurately:

You fear the world too much. . . . All your other hopes have merged into the hope of being beyond the chance of its sordid reproach. I have seen your nobler aspirations fall off one by one, until the master passion, Gain, engrosses you.

But miserliness is a characteristic which Scrooge considers and approves: "What then?" he retorted. "Even if I have grown so much wiser, what then?"

Scrooge is a thoroughly sordid and greedy character. But when Dickens lets us glimpse the grinding poverty that shaped him we feel less confident that he deserves blame. Certainly Scrooge has moral faults (such as miserliness) and they are his *own* moral flaws. But does it follow that he is morally responsible for his moral faults? Scrooge intentionally pursues—profoundly and reflectively pursues—a life of greed that enriches himself and impoverishes others. Scrooge is not incompetent, and he follows his own deeply held goal: the goal of accumulating as much wealth as he possibly can, with no regard for who gets hurt or exploited in the process (given the "accounting irregularities" of the past few years, he seems a depressingly familiar figure). Ebeneezer Scrooge is certainly someone most of us would regard as morally loathsome. But is Scrooge morally responsible for his intentional avaricious acts? When we look more deeply into Scrooge's all-consuming and purposeful selfishness we find a history of desperate deprivation that shaped his greedy character. Scrooge is now a purposefully greedy, cold-hearted, single-minded pursuer of riches, whose acts are morally vicious because his own deepest intentions are vile. But like all of us, he was shaped by forces that made him what he is; and if he has—or lacks—the reflective and self-evaluative[8] capacities to change, then those capacities are themselves the product of forces that were ultimately beyond his control. So is Scrooge morally responsible for the greedy acts he intentionally performs?

Some answer yes, some no. Clearly libertarians would reject this accout of how Scrooge became what he is. But if you can regard this as even a legitimate *question,* then obviously you believe that judgments of moral responsibility are distinct from moral judgments. If you can judge someone morally bad, and still have some question of whether that morally bad person is *morally responsible*, then you do not believe that morality requires moral responsibility.

Retribution

There is no doubt that retribution is a powerful motive: "revenge is sweet," as the saying goes. When wronged, we desire revenge, and we feel that taking revenge is *just*. Those whose loved ones have been harmed or killed commonly feel that justice requires retribution, and we generally feel that those who work hard and make a contribution justly deserve reward. So obviously we have deep feelings about "retributive justice" and "getting even" and "just rewards." But how reliable are those feelings as moral guides?

That returns us to one of the most basic questions we have examined. Most (Kant is the great exception) believe that our *feelings*, especially our "moral feelings" (such as affection and pity and sympathy), are important. Granted the strength and importance of such feelings, it also seems clear that our feelings can sometimes benefit from guidance. You are walking through the autumn woods with a friend; as you pass along a narrow tree-lined path, your friend holds back a large limb to let you pass—and then just as you draw even, she releases the limb, and it swings back and smacks you in the mouth. You are livid, and every impulse in your being cries out for retribution. But then you discover that your friend suffered a mild stroke, which caused her to lose strength in her arms, and she was unable to hold the branch back. Your improved knowledge of the situation swiftly changes your retributive emotions into feelings of solicitude. Would wider knowledge of the causes of character and behavior have a similar effect on our retributive feelings in other cases? Some say that "To know all is to forgive all." That is, if we really understood what shaped people to be the way they are (if we "walked a mile in their shoes") we would feel less inclined to demand retribution. Scrooge is a vile and greedy man, but when we look more closely at the harsh forces that shaped him we perhaps feel less inclined to demand retributive punishment for the wrongs he has committed. We want him to change, of course. We believe that he really is morally bad, and we're glad the ghosts paid him a transforming visit—and in the absence of ghosts, we may seek other means of modifying his character. But we may feel less desire to gain revenge for his miserly treatment of his employees. Or perhaps we still feel a desire for revenge but judge that this is a desire we ought to hold in check (like the desire you sometimes feel to choke the person sitting in the airport lounge talking loudly on his cell phone, or your desire to have a wild fling with your best friend's sweetheart).

Conclusion

So we return to the question of the respective roles of feelings and rationality in ethics. As T. S. Eliot says, "in our end is our beginning." Or perhaps we've just been going in circles. Maybe, in the course of examining ethical theories, you have found one that fits perfectly the way you look at ethics. Or possibly you have emerged less certain, and just a bit dizzy, without any clear ethical recipes. If you have also emerged with a better understanding of some of the key issues in ethics, and the connections among those issues, and an interest in those issues, then perhaps that's not a bad thing. One of the most important things in ethics is being sensitive to ethical questions and ethical issues. When people go wrong— they cheat their investors, or abuse their patients, or betray their friends—the problem *may* be that they don't have a clear ethical code to follow. More likely, they didn't really think about what they were doing as having an ethical component at all ("I'm just maximizing profits, there's nothing else to consider"). If we wonder how so many otherwise decent people could have been slaveholders—or more recently, could have supported apartheid in South Africa or the Jim Crow racist oppression of the American South—one likely reason is that they failed to recognize what they were doing as a *moral issue*. Slavery and apartheid were "just the ways things have always worked," or "simply an economic decision." Of course being bothered by or concerned about ethical issues is not itself sufficient for ethical behavior. (Many slaveholders worried about the moral wrong of enslaving fellow humans, but years and lifetimes passed while they did nothing to correct that wrong.) Still, reflective awareness of ethical issues is an important element of ethical development. So if you are encouraged to think more about ethical issues, and to be more alert to ethical quandaries, then perhaps you've made some ethical gains, even if you are more ethically confused than when you started. And gaining some practice at thinking hard about ethical issues is valuable, even if you are currently confident of your own ethical principles. For new and unsettling ethical issues constantly emerge: Is cloning morally legitimate? Should we allow genetic therapy for human enhancement (to make people taller or faster or smarter, rather than to treat genetic diseases)? Whatever combination of reason, emotion, or intuition comprises your moral capacities, it is important to keep those powers in good working order and give them regular exercise. You're going to need them.

MORAL LUCK

Thomas Nagel

Thomas Nagel is a professor of philosophy and law at New York University. Generally recognized as a leading Kantian, he is certainly not doctrinaire in his views. In particular, he is known for raising serious philosophical perplexities to which he offers at most only tentative solutions; and the philosophically famous essay on moral luck, printed here, is a good example. Among Nagel's major works are *The Possibility of Altruism* (Princeton: Princeton University Press, 1970), *Mortal Questions,* which contains the essay "Moral Luck," (Cambridge: Cambridge University Press, 1979); and *The View from Nowhere* (Oxford: Oxford University Press, 1986). All of Nagel's works are delightful to read; the questions they raise, however, are not easy to answer.

Kant believed that good or bad luck should influence neither our moral judgment of a person and his actions, nor his moral assessment of himself.

> The good will is not good because of what it effects or accomplishes or because of its adequacy to achieve some proposed end; it is good only because of its willing, i.e., it is good of itself. And, regarded for itself, it is to be esteemed incomparably higher than anything which could be brought about by it in favor of any inclination or even of the sum total of all inclinations. Even if it should happen that, by a particularly unfortunate fate or by the niggardly provision of a stepmotherly nature, this will should be wholly lacking in power to accomplish its purpose, and if even the greatest effort should not avail it to achieve anything of its end, and if there remained only the good will (not as a mere wish but as the summoning of all the means in our power), it would sparkle like a jewel in its own right, as something that had its full worth in itself. Usefulness or fruitlessness can neither diminish nor augment this worth.

He would presumably have said the same about a bad will: whether it accomplishes its evil purposes is morally irrelevant. And a course of action that would be condemned if it had a bad outcome cannot be vindicated if by luck it turns out well. There cannot be moral risk. This view seems to be wrong, but it arises in response to a fundamental problem about moral responsibility to which we possess no satisfactory solution.

The problem develops out of the ordinary conditions of moral judgment. Prior to reflection it is intuitively plausible that people cannot be morally assessed for what is not their fault, or for what is due to factors beyond their control. Such judgment is different from the evaluation of something as a good or bad thing, or state of affairs. The latter may be present in addition to moral judgment, but when we blame someone for his actions we are not merely saying it is bad that they happened, or bad that he exists: we are judging *him,* saying he is bad, which is different from his being a bad thing. This kind of judgment takes only a certain kind of object. Without being able to explain exactly why, we feel that the appropriateness of moral assessment is easily undermined by the discovery that the act or attribute, no matter how good or bad, is not under the person's control. While other evaluations remain, this one seems to lose its footing. So a clear absence of control, produced by involuntary movement, physical force, or ignorance of the circumstances, excuses what is done from moral judgment. But what we do depends in many more ways than these on what is not under our control—what is not produced by a good or a bad will, in Kant's phrase. And external influences in this broader range are not usually thought to excuse what is done from moral judgment, positive or negative.

Let me give a few examples, beginning with the type of case Kant has in mind. Whether we succeed or fail in what we try to do nearly always depends to some extent on factors beyond our control. This is true of murder, altruism, revolution, the sacrifice of certain interests for the sake of others—almost any morally important act. What has been done, and what is morally judged, is partly determined by external factors. However jewel-like the good will may be in its own right, there is a morally significant difference between rescuing someone from a burning building and dropping him from a twelfth-storey window while trying to rescue him. Similarly, there is a morally significant difference between reckless driving and manslaughter. But whether a reckless driver hits a pedestrian depends on the presence of the pedestrian at the point where he recklessly passes a red light. What we do is also limited by the opportunities and choices with which we are faced, and these are largely determined by factors beyond our control. Someone who was an officer in a concentration camp might have led a quiet and harmless life if the Nazis had never come to power in Germany. And someone who led a quiet and harmless life in Argentina might have become an officer in a concentration camp if he had not left Germany for business reasons in 1930.

I shall say more later about these and other examples. I introduce them here to illustrate a general point. Where a significant aspect of what someone does depends on factors beyond his control, yet we continue to treat him in that respect as an object of moral judgment, it can be called moral luck. Such luck can be good or bad. And the problem posed by this phenomenon, which led Kant to deny its possibility, is that the broad range of external influences here identified seems on close examination to undermine moral assessment as surely as does the narrower range of familiar excusing conditions. If the condition of control is consistently applied, it threatens to erode most of the moral assessments we find it natural to make. The things for which people are morally judged are determined in more ways than we at first realize by what is beyond their control. And when the seemingly natural requirement of fault or responsibility is applied in light of these facts, it leaves few pre-reflective moral judgments intact. Ultimately, nothing or almost nothing about what a person does seems to be under his control.

Why not conclude, then, that the condition of control is false—that it is an initially plausible hypothesis refuted by clear counter-examples? One could in that case look instead for a more refined condition which picked out the *kinds* of lack of control that really undermine certain moral judgments, with-

out yielding the unacceptable conclusion derived from the broader condition, that most or all ordinary moral judgments are illegitimate.

What rules out this escape is that we are dealing not with a theoretical conjecture but with a philosophical problem. The condition of control does not suggest itself merely as a generalization from certain clear cases. It seems *correct* in the further cases to which it is extended beyond the original set. When we undermine moral assessment by considering new ways in which control is absent, we are not just discovering what *would* follow given the general hypothesis, but are actually being persuaded that in itself the absence of control is relevant in these cases too. The erosion of moral judgment emerges not as the absurd consequence of an over-simple theory, but as a natural consequence of the ordinary idea of moral assessment, when it is applied in view of a more complete and precise account of the facts. It would therefore be a mistake to argue from the unacceptability of the conclusions to the need for a different account of the conditions of moral responsibility. The view that moral luck is paradoxical is not a *mistake*, ethical or logical, but a perception of one of the ways in which the intuitively acceptable conditions of moral judgment threaten to undermine it all.

Moral luck is like this because while there are various respects in which the natural objects of moral assessment are out of our control or influenced by what is out of our control, we cannot reflect on these facts without losing our grip on the judgments.

There are roughly four ways in which the natural objects of moral assessment are disturbingly subject to luck. One is the phenomenon of constitutive luck—the kind of person you are, where this is not just a question of what you deliberately do, but of your inclinations, capacities, and temperament. Another category is luck in one's circumstances—the kind of problems and situations one faces. The other two have to do with the causes and effects of action: luck in how one is determined by antecedent circumstances, and luck in the way one's actions and projects turn out. All of them present a common problem. They are all opposed by the idea that one cannot be more culpable or estimable for anything than one is for that fraction of it which is under one's control. It seems irrational to take or dispense credit or blame for matters over which a person has no control, or for their influence on results over which he has partial control. Such things may create the conditions for action, but action can be judged only to the extent that it goes beyond these conditions and does not just result from them.

Let us first consider luck, good and bad, in the way things turn out. Kant, in the above-quoted passage, has one example of this in mind, but the category covers a wide range. It includes the truck driver who accidentally runs over a child, the artist who abandons his wife and five children to devote himself to painting, and other cases in which the possibilities of success and failure are even greater. The driver, if he is entirely without fault, will feel terrible about his role in the event, but will not have to reproach himself. Therefore this example of agent-regret is not yet a case of *moral* bad luck. However, if the driver was guilty of even a minor degree of negligence—failing to have his brakes checked recently, for example— then if that negligence contributes to the death of the child, he will not merely feel terrible. He will blame himself for the death. And what makes this an example of moral luck is that he would have to blame himself only slightly for the negligence itself if no situation arose which required him to brake suddenly and violently to avoid hitting a child. Yet the *negligence* is the same in both cases, and the driver has no control over whether a child will run into his path.

The same is true at higher levels of negligence. If someone has had too much to drink and his car swerves on to the sidewalk, he can count himself morally lucky if there are no pedestrians in its path. If there were, he would be to blame for their deaths, and would probably be prosecuted for manslaughter. But if he hurts no one, although his recklessness is exactly the same, he is guilty of a far less serious legal offence and will certainly reproach himself and be reproached by others much less severely. To take another legal example, the penalty for attempted murder is less than that for successful murder—however similar the intentions and motives of the assailant may be in the two cases. His degree of culpability can depend, it would seem, on whether the victim happened to be wearing a bullet-proof vest, or whether a bird flew into the path of the bullet—matters beyond his control.

Finally, there are cases of decision under uncertainty—common in public and in private life. Anna Karenina goes off with Vronsky, Gauguin leaves his family, Chamberlain signs the Munich agreement, the Decembrists persuade the troops under their command to revolt against the czar, the American colonies declare their independence from Britain, you introduce two people in an attempt at match-making. It is tempting in all such cases to feel that some decision must be possible, in the light of what is known at the time, which will make reproach unsuitable no matter how things turn out. But this is not true; when someone acts in such ways he takes his life, or his moral position, into his hands, because how things turn out determines what he has done. It is possible *also* to assess the decision from the point of view of what could be known at the time, but this is not the end of the story. If the Decembrists had succeeded in overthrowing Nicholas I in 1825 and establishing a constitutional regime, they would be heroes. As it is, not only did they fail and pay for it, but they bore some responsibility for the terrible punishments meted out to the troops who had been persuaded to follow them. If the American Revolution had been a bloody failure resulting in greater repression, then Jefferson, Franklin and Washington would still have made a noble attempt, and might not even have regretted it on their way to the scaffold, but they would also have had to blame themselves for what they had helped to bring on their compatriots. (Perhaps peaceful efforts at reform would eventually have succeeded.) If Hitler had not overrun Europe and exterminated millions, but instead had died of a heart attack after occupying the Sudetenland, Chamberlain's action at Munich would still have utterly betrayed the Czechs, but it would not be the great moral disaster that has made his name a household word.

In many cases of difficult choice the outcome cannot be foreseen with certainty. One kind of assessment of the choice is possible in advance, but another kind must await the outcome, because the outcome determines what has been done. The same degree of culpability or estimability in intention, motive, or concern is compatible with a wide range of judgments, positive or negative, depending on what happened beyond the point of decision. The *mens rea* which could have existed in the absence of any consequences does not exhaust the grounds of moral judgment. Actual results influence culpability or esteem in a large class of unquestionably ethical cases ranging from negligence through political choice.

That these are genuine moral judgments rather than expressions of temporary attitude is evident from the fact that one can say *in advance* how the moral verdict will depend on the results. If one negligently leaves the bath running with the baby in it, one will realize, as one bounds up the stairs toward the bathroom, that if the baby has drowned one has done something awful, whereas if it has not one has merely been careless. Someone who launches a violent revolution against an authoritarian regime knows that if he fails he will be responsible for much suffering that is in vain, but if he succeeds he will be justified by the outcome. I do not mean that *any* action can be retroactively justified by history. Certain things are so bad in themselves, or so risky, that no results can make them all right. Nevertheless, when moral judgment does depend on the outcome, it is objective and timeless and not dependent on a change of standpoint produced by success or failure. The judgment after the fact follows from an hypothetical judgment that can be made beforehand, and it can be made as easily by someone else as by the agent.

From the point of view which makes responsibility dependent on control, all this seems absurd. How is it possible to be more or less culpable depending on whether a child gets into the path of one's car, or a bird into the path of one's bullet? Perhaps it is true that what is done depends on more than the agent's state of mind or intention. The problem then is, why is it not irrational to base moral assessment on what people do, in this broad sense? It amounts to holding them responsible for the contributions of fate as well as for their own—provided they have made some contribution to begin with. If we look at cases of negligence or attempt, the pattern seems to be that overall culpability corresponds to the product of mental or intentional fault and the seriousness of the outcome. Cases of decision under uncertainty are less easily explained in this way, for it seems that the overall judgment can even shift from positive to negative depending on the outcome. But here too it seems rational to subtract the effects of occurrences subse-

quent to the choice, that were merely possible at the time, and concentrate moral assessment on the actual decision in light of the probabilities. If the object of moral judgment is the *person,* then to hold him accountable for what he has done in the broader sense is akin to strict liability, which may have its legal uses but seems irrational as a moral position.

The result of such a line of thought is to pare down each act to its morally essential core, an inner act of pure will assessed by motive and intention. Adam Smith advocates such a position in *The Theory of Moral Sentiments*, but notes that it runs contrary to our actual judgments.

> But how well soever we may seem to be persuaded of the truth of this equitable maxim, when we consider it after this manner, in abstract, yet when we come to particular cases, the actual consequences which happen to proceed from any action, have a very great effect upon our sentiments concerning its merit or demerit, and almost always either enhance or diminish our sense of both. Scarce, in any one instance, perhaps, will our sentiments be found, after examination, to be entirely regulated by this rule, which we all acknowledge ought entirely to regulate them.

Joel Feinberg points out further that restricting the domain of moral responsibility to the inner world will not immunize it to luck. Factors beyond the agent's control, like a coughing fit, can interfere with his decisions as surely as they can with the path of a bullet from his gun. Nevertheless the tendency to cut down the scope of moral assessment is pervasive, and does not limit itself to the influence of effects. It attempts to isolate the will from the other direction, so to speak, by separating out constitutive luck. Let us consider that next.

Kant was particularly insistent on the moral irrelevance of qualities of temperament and personality that are not under the control of the will. Such qualities as sympathy or coldness might provide the background against which obedience to moral requirements is more or less difficult, but they could not be objects of moral assessment themselves, and might well interfere with confident assessment of its proper object—the determination of the will by the motive of duty. This rules out moral judgment of many of the virtues and vices, which are states of character that influence choice but are certainly not exhausted by dispositions to act deliberately in certain ways. A person may be greedy, envious, cowardly, cold, ungenerous, unkind, vain, or conceited, but *behave* perfectly by a monumental effort of will. To possess these vices is to be unable to help having certain feelings under certain circumstances, and to have strong spontaneous impulses to act badly. Even if one controls the impulses, one still has the vice. An envious person hates the greater success of others. He can be morally condemned as envious even if he congratulates them cordially and does nothing to denigrate or spoil their success. Conceit, likewise, need not be displayed. It is fully present in someone who cannot help dwelling with secret satisfaction on the superiority of his own achievements, talents, beauty, intelligence, or virtue. To some extent such a quality may be the product of earlier choices; to some extent it may be amenable to change by current actions. But it is largely a matter of constitutive bad fortune. Yet people are morally condemned for such qualities, and esteemed for others equally beyond control of the will: they are assessed for what they are *like*.

To Kant this seems incoherent because virtue is enjoined on everyone and therefore must in principle be possible for everyone. It may be easier for some than for others, but it must be possible to achieve it by making the right choices, against whatever temperamental background. One may want to have a generous spirit, or regret not having one, but it makes no sense to condemn oneself or anyone else for a quality which is not within the control of the will. Condemnation implies that you should not be like that, not that it is unfortunate that you are.

Nevertheless, Kant's conclusion remains intuitively unacceptable. We may be persuaded that these moral judgments are irrational, but they reappear involuntarily as soon as the argument is over. This is the pattern throughout the subject.

The third category to consider is luck in one's circumstances, and I shall mention it briefly. The things we are called upon to do, the moral tests we face, are importantly determined by factors beyond our control. It may be true of someone that in a dangerous situation he would behave in a cowardly or heroic fashion, but if the situation never arises, he will never have the chance to distinguish or disgrace himself in this way, and his moral record will be different.

A conspicuous example of this is political. Ordinary citizens of Nazi Germany had an opportunity to behave heroically by opposing the regime. They also had an opportunity to behave badly, and most of them are culpable for having failed this test. But it is a test to which the citizens of other countries were not subjected, with the result that even if they, or some of them, would have behaved as badly as the Germans in like circumstances, they simply did not and therefore are not similarly culpable. Here again one is morally at the mercy of fate, and it may seem irrational upon reflection, but our ordinary moral attitudes would be unrecognizable without it. We judge people for what they actually do or fail to do, not just for what they would have done if circumstances had been different.

This form of moral determination by the actual is also paradoxical, but we can begin to see how deep in the concept of responsibility the paradox is embedded. A person can be morally responsible only for what he does; but what he does results from a great deal that he does not do; therefore he is not morally responsible for what he is and is not responsible for. (This is not a contradiction, but it is a paradox.)

It should be obvious that there is a connection between these problems about responsibility and control and an even more familiar problem, that of freedom of the will. That is the last type of moral luck I want to take up, though I can do no more within the scope of this essay than indicate its connection with the other types.

If one cannot be responsible for consequences of one's acts due to factors beyond one's control, or for antecedents of one's acts that are properties of temperament not subject to one's will, or for the circumstances that pose one's moral choices, then how can one be responsible even for the stripped-down acts of the will itself, if *they* are the product of antecedent circumstances outside of the will's control?

The area of genuine agency, and therefore of legitimate moral judgment, seems to shrink under this scrutiny to an extensionless point. Everything seems to result from the combined influence of factors, antecedent and posterior to action, that are not within the agent's control. Since he cannot be responsible for them, he cannot be responsible for their results—though it may remain possible to take up the aesthetic or other evaluative analogues of the moral attitudes that are thus displaced.

It is also possible, of course, to brazen it out and refuse to accept the results, which indeed seem unacceptable as soon as we stop thinking about the arguments. Admittedly, if certain surrounding circumstances had been different, then no unfortunate consequences would have followed from a wicked intention, and no seriously culpable act would have been performed; but since the circumstances were *not* different, and the agent *in fact* succeeded in perpetrating a particularly cruel murder, *that* is what he did, and that is what he is responsible for. Similarly, we may admit that if certain antecedent circumstances had been different, the agent would never have developed into the sort of person who would do such a thing; but since he *did* develop (as the inevitable result of those antecedent circumstances) into the sort of swine he is, and into the person who committed such a murder, *that* is what he is blameable for. In both cases one is responsible for what one actually does—even if what one actually does depends in important ways on what is not within one's control. This compatibilist account of our moral judgments would leave room for the ordinary conditions of responsibility—the absence of coercion, ignorance, or involuntary movement—as part of the determination of what someone has done—but it is understood not to exclude the influence of a great deal that he has not done.

The only thing wrong with this solution is its failure to explain how skeptical problems arise. For they arise not from the imposition of an arbitrary external requirement, but from the nature of moral judgment itself. Something in the ordinary idea of what someone does must explain how it can seem necessary to subtract from it anything that merely happens—even though the ultimate consequence of such subtraction is that nothing remains. And something in the ordinary idea of knowledge must explain why it seems to be undermined by any influences on belief not within the control of the subject—so that knowledge seems impossible without an impossible foundation in autonomous reason. But let us leave epistemology aside and concentrate on action, character, and moral assessment.

The problem arises, I believe, because the self which acts and is the object of moral judgment is threatened with dissolution by the absorption of its acts and impulses into the class of events. Moral judgment of a person is judgment not of what happens to him, but of him. It does not say merely that a certain event or state of affairs is fortunate or unfortunate or even terrible. It is not an evaluation of a state of the world, or of an individual as part of the world. We are not thinking just that it would be better if he were different, or did not exist, or had not done some of the things he has done. We are judging *him*, rather than his existence or characteristics. The effect of concentrating on the influence of what is not under his control is to make this responsible self seem to disappear, swallowed up by the order of mere events.

What, however, do we have in mind that a person must *he* to be the object of these moral attitudes? While the concept of agency is easily undermined, it is very difficult to give it a positive characterization. That is familiar from the literature on Free Will.

I believe that in a sense the problem has no solution, because something in the idea of agency is incompatible with actions being events, or people being things. But as the external determinants of what someone has done are gradually exposed, in their effect on consequences, character, and choice itself, it becomes gradually clear that actions are events and people things. Eventually nothing remains which can be ascribed to the responsible self, and we are left with nothing but a portion of the larger sequence of events, which can be deplored or celebrated, but not blamed or praised.

Though I cannot define the idea of the active self that is thus undermined, it is possible to say something about its sources. There is a close connexion between our feelings about ourselves and our feelings about others. Guilt and indignation, shame and contempt, pride and admiration are internal and external sides of the same moral attitudes. We are unable to view ourselves simply as portions of the world, and from inside we have a rough idea of the boundary between what is us and what is not, what we do and what happens to us, what is our personality and what is an accidental handicap. We apply the same essentially internal conception of the self to others. About ourselves we feel pride, shame, guilt, remorse—and agent-regret. We do not regard our actions and our characters merely as fortunate or unfortunate episodes—though they may also be that. We cannot *simply* take an external evaluative view of ourselves—of what we most essentially are and what we do. And this remains true even when we have seen that we are not responsible for our own existence, or our nature, or the choices we have to make, or the circumstances that give our acts the consequences they have. Those acts remain ours and we remain ourselves, despite the persuasiveness of the reasons that seem to argue us out of existence.

It is this internal view that we extend to others in moral judgment—when we judge *them* rather than their desirability or utility. We extend to others the refusal to limit ourselves to external evaluation, and we accord to them selves like our own. But in both cases this comes up against the brutal inclusion of humans and everything about them in a world from which they cannot be separated and of which they are nothing but contents. The external view forces itself on us at the same time that we resist it. One way this occurs is through the gradual erosion of what we do by the subtraction of what happens.

The inclusion of consequences in the conception of what we have done is an acknowledgment that we are part of the world, but the paradoxical character of moral luck which emerges from this acknowledgment shows that we are unable to operate with such a view, for it leaves us with no one to be. The same thing is revealed in the appearance that determinism obliterates responsibility. Once we see an aspect of what we or someone else does as something that happens, we lose our grip on the idea that it has been done and that we can judge the doer and not just the happening. This explains why the absence of determinism is no more hospitable to the concept of agency than is its presence—a point that has been noticed often. Either way the act is viewed externally, as part of the course of events.

The problem of moral luck cannot be understood without an account of the internal conception of agency and its special connection with the moral attitudes as opposed to other types of value. I do not have such an account. The degree to which the problem has a solution can be determined only by seeing whether in some degree the incompatibility between this conception and the various ways in which we do not control what we do is only apparent. I have nothing to offer on that topic either. But it is not enough to say merely that our basic moral attitudes toward ourselves and others are determined by what is actual; for they are also threatenedbythesourcesofthatactuality, and by the external view of action which forces itself on us when we see how everything we do belongs to a world that we have not created.

EXERCISES

1. If there *are* objective moral facts—suppose, say, that "stealing is wrong" is an objective fact on the same order as "Jupiter is the largest planet in our solar system"—would that *strengthen* human freedom, restrict freedom, or have no bearing on freedom?

2. Suppose that we have two possible prison systems, and you as judge may sentence this convicted bank robber to either: One is Attica, where he will suffer terribly during his eight-year incarceration, and come out unreformed, or maybe worse; the other is Shangrila, where the robber will enjoy interesting work and learn important skills and live a decent and not unpleasant eight years, and will be very unlikely to return to crime. You may think that actually the opposite would result; put that aside for a moment. In this situation, which would you choose for the sentence you impose?

3. All week you have been trying to decide whether to go to the mountains for a Saturday skiing holiday, stay at the university and study for your biology exam, go home to spend the weekend with your family, or volunteer to spend the weekend helping at a homeless shelter. You carefully weigh the benefits and detriments of each course of action, and finally on Friday night—after a week of deliberation—choose to go skiing. On Monday of that week, a close friend, who knows you are trying to decide whether or

not to go skiing, confidently writes down what your choice will be, places it in a sealed envelope, and locks it in a safe. As you pack your skiing gear, she hands you the envelope: "I knew all along you would decide to go skiing," she says. Assuming that she really was certain (this is not some "mind-reading" trickery), does this mean that you did not really choose? Does it imply that your choice was not free? Would it lessen or destroy your moral responsibility for that choice?

4. In the previous example, will it make any difference if the reasons that convinced you to go skiing are really good reasons? Will it make any difference if they were *not* good reasons, but were instead the product of elaborate self-deception? (You tell yourself—and convince yourself—that you are going for the exercise, when all your friends know that your real motivation is a glimpse of a ski instructor with whom you once had a passionate relation, but who is now indifferent to you, but for whom you still carry a torch—though you will not admit it to your friends nor even yourself. You say things like "I wouldn't spend two minutes with that ski instructor, even if she begged me"; meanwhile, your friends exchange knowing smiles.)

5. One fiercely debated philosophical issue is whether *determinism* destroys *reason*. That is, if determinism is true, and everything you do—including your cognitive activities—is determined by past causal events, could you still *reason* about what to do?

    We are spending the afternoon at Saratoga, and I'm trying to pick a horse for the seventh race. God already knows what horse I'll pick (though of course I do not), and the deliberative process I will follow is *determined* by my complex history (what I learned about racehorses from my Aunt Louise, the critical thinking skills I picked up in my logic classes, the statistical analysis I learned from Professor Sykes in my undergraduate stats class, and so on and so forth). I study the racing form carefully, watch the horses and the jockeys in the post parade, check the odds board—and finally settle on Dilapidated Darling, and run up to the window to wager five bucks on her nose. Did I *really* reason about my choice? If the whole process was *determined*, was my "reasoning process" only a sham?

6. Do people really *deserve* punishment for their wrong acts? That is, is it right and fair and just to hold people morally responsible for what they do? Suppose we have been discussing this question for quite some time, and we still disagree: I insist that Arthur *justly deserves* punishment for his bad acts, and you believe that punishment is *not* morally justified. Though we disagree on this fundamental issue, suppose we agree on a number of points: We agree that moral responsibility is different from role responsibility; we agree that punishment is not the best way to reform Arthur and change his bad behavior; and we agree that Arthur's genetics and environment shaped him to be what he is and to act as he does, and given who he is and how he developed, he could not have done otherwise than he did. But even with all these points of *agreement*, our basic *disagreement* over moral responsibility remains: I still believe Arthur *ought* to be punished, and you believe that punishing Arthur is *wrong*. Is there anything further that either of us could do to resolve our conflict, or must we just disagree? Does your answer to that question turn on whether you hold a moral objectivist or nonobjectivist view?

NOTES

[1] Campbell, 1957, p. 159.

[2] Willard Gaylin, *The Killing of Bonnie Garland* (Hammondsworth, UK: Penguin Books, 1983), p. 338.

[3]The distinguished British legal theorist, H. L. A. Hart, makes a similar distinction, and first uses the phrase *role* responsibility; see *Punishment and Responsibility* (Oxford: Clarendon Press, 1968).

[4]Just because she does a lousy job at taking responsibility, that does not imply that we should deny her the opportunity. After all, practice at taking responsibility may help her become better at it. And even those of us who are incurably lousy at taking responsibility for ourselves may well prefer our own inept decision-making to having someone else make all our decisions for us.

[5]Susan Wolf, "The Importance of Free Will," *Mind*, 90 (1981), 386–405.

[6]F. C. Copleston, "The Existence of God: A Debate," in Paul Edwards and Arthur Pap, editors, *A Modern Introduction to Philosophy*, rev. ed. (New York: The Free Press, 1965), p. 488.

[7]Some claim there can be no real rationality and deliberation if our reasoning is entirely shaped by past causes (if determinism is true). Richard Taylor, for example, makes that the cornerstone of his argument for libertarian free will in *Metaphysics* (Englewood Cliffs, N.J.: Prentice-Hall, 1963), pp. 50–55; and many others have made similar claims: Daniel D. Colson, "The Transcendental Argument Against Determinism: A Challenge Yet Unmet," *Southern Journal of Philosophy*, 20 (1982), 15–24; John C. Eccles, "Brain and Free Will," in Gordon Globus, Grover Maxwell, and Irwin Savodnik, editors, *Consciousness and the Brain: A Scientific and Philosophical Inquiry* (New York: Plenum Press, 1976), pp. 101–121; Antony Flew, "Rationality and Unnecessitated Choice," in Newton Garver and Peter H. Hare, editors *Naturalism and Rationality* (Buffalo, N.Y.: Prometheus Books, 1986), pp. 41–51; J. E. Llewelyn, "The Inconceivability of Pessimistic Determinism," *Analysis*, 27 (1966), 39–44; Alasdair MacIntyre, "Determinism," *Mind*, 66 (1957), 28–41; and Susan Wolf, "The Importance of Free Will," *Mind*, 90 (1981), 386–405. But that cannot account for the consensus philosophical belief that denying moral responsibility entails denying genuine morality; for (although a number of philosophers have claimed that genuine rationality cannot coexist with determinism) rather than being a consensus view (as would be required to support the consensus view that morality requires moral responsibility) it is probably a minority view in contemporary philosophy (opponents include Patricia Churchland, "Is Determinism Self-refuting?" *Mind*, 40 (1981), 99–101; Daniel Dennett, 1984, Chapter 2; Stephen Toulmin, "Reasons and Causes," in Robert Borger and Frank Cioffi, editors, *Explanation in the Behavioural Sciences* (Cambridge: Cambridge University Press, 1970), pp. 1–26; and Bruce N. Waller, "Deliberating About the Inevitable," *Analysis*, 45 (1985), 48–52.

[8]As emphasized by Charles Taylor, in "Responsibility for Self," in Amelie Rorty, editor, *Identities of Persons* (Berkeley: University of California Press, 1976), pp. 281–299.

CHAPTER 15

✦ CURRENT ETHICAL ✦ DEBATES

THE ETHICS OF WAR

The first pair of essays examines the ethics of war, through consideration of a specific event that occurred in the 1991 Gulf War. The event in question was the U.S. air attack on a column of Iraqi soldiers and civilians who were fleeing along the road to Basra. A key question raised by both essays is whether the sustained attack on that column was justified, given the number of civilians present, the disorganized state of the Iraqi military forces at that point, and the scattered surrender attempts of those in the column.

THE ROAD TO BASRA

A Case Study in Military Ethics

Martin L. Cook & Phillip A. Hamann

I. MORAL CHALLENGES OF THE GULF WAR

The recent Persian Gulf War provides opportunity for reflection from a number of perspectives. Military planners are just beginning to digest the many lessons for desert war tactics, the psychological effects of high-tech cyber wars on individual soldiers, the performance of a new generation of precision weapons, and the logistical, political, and economic challenges of addressing regional conflicts.

For ethics, too, the Gulf War has raised a number of challenges for the inherited framework of the just

war tradition. In this essay, we . . . will assess one much-discussed episode of that war—the so-called "turkey shoot" of fleeing vehicles and personnel from Kuwait City near the end of the ground war.

Ironically, most of the important and profound challenges regarding just conduct in this war emerge from the very success of the execution of the Gulf War—success both in the military and in the ethical dimensions of combat. Most historians agree that never in the history of air warfare has the power of military aviation been applied so definitively, yet so discriminately and precisely. The capabilities of computer and laser-guided munitions made it possible for aerial bombardment of populated areas to be limited, with very few exceptions, to targets of clear military status and to inflict an unprecedentedly low degree of collateral damage. The remote desert environment in which the pivotal hostilities were conducted likewise allowed the Coalition forces to use massive bombardments with weapons (so called "dumb bombs," cluster munitions, and even fuel-air explosives) that could not be precisely targeted in a theater of operations where it could reasonably be surmised that only soldiers and their military hardware would be their targets. Even the end of the war, by stopping well short of the occupation and political reconstruction of Iraqi society, spared the Coalition forces the agonizing choices of an army of occupation or of urban house-to-house warfare.

No modern war can achieve the unequivocal goals of political justice in the absence of a regrettable loss of life. But considering the scale of the resources on both sides of the conflict, the Gulf War was in many respects a close approximation of the ideal of the just war *in bello*. Yet despite the Coalition's obvious successes by comparative standards, these very successes raise questions in a number of areas about the adequacy of traditional measures for the moral assessment of future conflicts. To mention only a few examples:

Although they were used only against combatants away from populated areas, fuel-air explosive munitions and "bouncing Betty" cluster bombs seem to many to be excessive in their cruelty and lethality. Precision munitions were orders of magnitude more likely to hit their intended targets than those of any previous air campaign, yet questions continued to be raised about legitimate targeting. Such skepticism was founded on both foreseeable consequences and intentionality. The American decision to target the Iraqi electrical power system is an excellent case in point. By inherited standards, bombing electrical generation and distribution facilities is a legitimate means of disabling an enemy's command, communication, and control efforts. This targeting priority was especially effective given the centralized political structure of Saddam Hussein's dictatorship, and was made more necessary by deliberate Iraqi intermingling of civilian use and military facilities. Yet the effect of such

bombing also involves the severe damage to civilian sanitation, health care, and many other essential life functions for a society at large. The degradation of Iraqi military function was certainly real, but hardly total. In that light, do we need to rethink the legitimacy of such "dual-use" targets?

Perhaps the single event which most troubled observers during the war was the "Basra Road" engagement, commonly reported in the headlines as "The Highway of Death." In stark contrast to the official briefing photographs of the clinical and bloodless precision of the weapons of the air war, the images of mile after mile of burned out vehicles and twisted, charred bodies suddenly appeared on the front pages of newspapers and news updates on television in the homes of most Americans.

Besides the obvious reaction of horror to the scene of such carnage, principled questions were also raised. Many of the vehicles on the road appeared to be civilian cars and trucks. If the rumor is true that special Saudi mortuary units (the first Coalition units on the scene) buried some 5,000 casualties, then this particular attack may well have been the most devastating single engagement of the war.

As we will see later, this episode points to a difficulty in the laws and customs of war regarding surrender, the return of individual soldiers to the status of noncombatant, and the circumstances in which the tokens of surrender may be offered and accepted. In the laws and customs of war, the need to clearly identify oneself and others as belonging wholly either to the class of combatants or noncombatants is, perhaps, the most crucial issue. Each class has distinct rights and liabilities—and a great deal of the law of war concerns itself with attempting to eliminate any ambiguities about the status of individuals in this respect. Specifically and most importantly, noncombatants are to be held immune from direct and deliberate targeting, whereas with a few exceptions, combatants may be attacked at any time.

Was this an indiscriminate attack on civilians and soldiers alike? Scattered among the ruins were toys and household goods. What and who was in this convoy? American pilots described this engagement as a classic "turkey shoot"—a kill box of a target-rich environment reminiscent of the free-fire zones in Vietnam. Is there something wrong morally when this type of killing gets too easy? This single aerial attack has borne a great deal of the brunt of the criticism of the *in bello* dimensions of the war. This attack was unique also because it was a staggering display of the power of modern aerial weapons against ground troops. For good or ill, it probably has a lot to say about future regional conflicts in which ground troops are pitted against an enemy with overwhelming air superiority.

Certainly first appearances were disturbing. Of the approximately 1400 vehicles at the Mutlah Ridge site along two to four miles of road, only 28 were counted as military vehicles. White flags were reportedly being flown by the people on the road *during the attack*, and yet no opportunity for surrender was allowed. Various news agencies reported that anywhere from 4,000 to 40,000 Kuwaiti citizens had been kidnapped and were being transported with the convoy to Iraq. What was their status in the midst of such a withering attack? There were reports of the strafing of fleeing soldiers on foot up to a quarter of a mile away from the highway itself. There were reports of "overkill"—of zealous pilots, overcome with a delight in destruction to the point that they disregarded directives, including the ATO and the directives of the airborne command posts, all in order to get to the "kill box" quickly and not to "miss out" on the engagement.

The destruction of the column on the road to Basra raises many important questions for the military historian and the military ethicist. What were the facts regarding this engagement? This paper will, for the first time, draw on a wealth of materials from within the Defense Department to clarify numerous questions of fact about this particular engagement, which now seems to be a rather formidable critical challenge. Who ordered the attack? What did the commanders and pilots believe they were attacking? What, in the event, were the facts about the targets in question? What were the casualties, and what military alternatives, short of allowing a full-scale armed retreat of elite Iraqi troops, were there to this destruction? Alternatively, should the retreat have been allowed? After all, the convoy, precisely by withdrawing from Kuwaiti territory, was contributing to the achievement of one of the stated major Coalition war aims! We believe the following to be the definitive explanation of this crucial event in the Gulf War.

II. THE FACTS

On Monday, 25 February (the second day of the ground war), American intelligence agencies passed reports from the Kuwaiti Resistance inside Kuwait City to the military command center in Riyadh that the Iraqi occupation forces were preparing to leave the city. Kuwaiti Resistance reported that members of the Iraqi secret police, the Mukhabarat, were attempting to destroy evidence of war crimes (killing all tortured Kuwaitis for example) and pillaging as much property as possible. The Resistance also boasted of mounting a small offensive against the panic-stricken Iraqis. This offensive did not really amount to much—the resistance movement was known to exaggerate at times. But the resistance movement never suggested that the convoy that was preparing to leave Kuwait City contained kidnapped Kuwaiti citizens. (Most of the kidnapped Kuwaiti citizens had already been sent to Basra and other locations weeks prior to this incident.) Air Force intelligence therefore surmised with high confidence that the convoy consisted exclusively of panicked stragglers from the decimated front line divisions (the Iraqi III Corps) and the Iraqi secret police.

In addition, at the start of the ground campaign, American intelligence agencies intercepted an uncoded telephone message from a general officer of the Iraqi Republican Guard. The officer appeared to issue a general order of retreat to Republican Guard units in Kuwait and to order the setting up of a screening or blocking maneuver to allow the Republican Guard to get out of the Kuwait Theater of Operation and into Basra. Hence, American intelligence was aware of preparation for a sudden and massive exodus of Iraqis from Kuwait.

The Mukhabarat secret police is a paramilitary organization with little access to heavy military armor. Its members frequently do not wear uniforms. Therefore, the fact that some individuals on the road were not uniformed was consistent with their identity as Iraqi secret police.

The evening of the same day, a JSTARS aircraft (a recently modified Boeing 707, with discriminating air-to-ground radar tasked to report where and how enemy traffic was moving) detected the large number of vehicles massing in Kuwait City. There are conflicting reports, even within the military sources, here. One Defense Department document claims that there were up to 200 tanks in this convoy. This is inconsistent with post-battle inventories, which show few military vehicles in the convoy. Although we are not certain, the best explanations of this Defense Department report are either that it confused the Mutlah Ridge convoy with another farther north or that the Arab forces, which were allowed on the highway first to perform Islamic burials of the dead, took advantage of the opportunity to "recover" as much military hardware as possible for their own use. The latter is a quite real possibility in the case of the Soviet built tanks, in particular, since they would have provided spare parts for the same kinds of tanks in the inventories of most Arab armies.

In a ground survey conducted several days after the attack, the Department of Defense confirmed that only 28 of the vehicles destroyed or left abandoned in the convoy were military. The character of the vehicles is ultimately of less moral importance than the question of the *identity of the convoy drivers and passengers* and the *nature of the convoy's activities*.

The tactical thinking of American military commanders was heavily influenced by close study of the eight-year war with Iran that Iraq fought before its invasion of Kuwait. Iraqi tactics during the Iran-Iraq war were a source of considerable concern regarding this convoy from Kuwait city, and focused the minds of the planners on two major issues. First, the Iraqis demonstrated their will to use their superiority in armor wherever the terrain allowed for it. The Iraqi army favored a "defense-in-depth" strategy. Such a strategy required two to three layers of front line troops. These troops were used both to slow the oncoming Iranian offensive, and as "intelligence fodder" to announce what avenues of attack the Iranians were attempting to exploit. If the Iranian offensive was slowed or stalled by these forces, the rear Iraqi echelons (consisting of the highly mobile Republican Guard armor divisions) quickly crushed the offensive. The success of this type of tactic depends on both the initiative and the ability to maneuver—precisely what a retreating convoy would be attempting to gain.

The second major lesson, and the one that concerned the American commanders most, was the Iraqis' use of chemical munitions. If the situation did not allow the use of rear echelon armored divisions,

then the Iraqis on several occasions retreated as quickly as possible in order to leave an open no-man's land between their forces and those of the Iranians. This area was then saturated with artillery shells containing chemical and nerve agents. The results were devastating and militarily effective. In fact, this type of attack accounted for the overwhelming success of the Iraqis in securing Iranian territory in 1988 and forcing a cease-fire.

In light of this history, planners in Riyadh considered it very possible that the Iraqi convoy at Mutlah Ridge was not running *from* the Coalition forces but instead *from an artillery attack by Iraqi chemical and biological weapons* they had every reason to expect would soon be launched.

That night, after the JSTARS confirmation of the resistance reports, General Schwarzkopf decided not to attack the convoy right away because it was still in the city. This decision reduced the collateral damage to Kuwaiti citizens. In fact, Kuwait City was off-limits to any aerial bombardment. For obvious reasons, Coalition planners were politically sensitive to postwar criticisms of having "destroyed the city in order to save it."

The convoy managed to leave the city that night, move through the small town of Al-Jahra, and in the early morning hours of the 26th (still dark) was headed north to Basra near a ridge line known as Mutlah Ridge.

Now that the convoy was out in the open, the problem was no longer *whether* to attack the convoy, but *how to attack it*. The tactical difficulty was that it was dark and the weather was bad. The visibility was low and the ceiling had dropped below eight-thousand feet. Most attack aircraft had been ordered to stay above that altitude to avoid Iraqi antiaircraft fire. There was also the so-called "petroleum overcast" resulting from Iraqis setting alight Kuwaiti oilwells. These conditions required the use of the F-15E Strike Eagles. These night and all-weather air-to-ground fighters were ordered to hit the front and back of the convoy at certain choke points along the highway, immobilizing it along the road. They accomplished this mission quite successfully, and the convoy was brought to a halt by bottlenecking it at Mutlah Ridge.

The next morning, in daylight and with better weather, the "kill box" method of air interdiction was employed to funnel attacking aircraft into the Mutlah

Ridge area. In this method, latitude and longitude demarcations were given that designated a thirty-mile by thirty-mile area. In this region were large numbers of mobile targets and aircraft were authorized to acquire targets and fire at will. Safe separation of aircraft was maintained by airborne command posts, which gave individual aircraft time on target commands and monitored the numbers and types of aircraft in the box at any given moment. Throughout the rest of the day, a large number of Air Force, Marine, and Navy aircraft of different types attacked and strafed this now "target-rich environment" of two to four miles length. Many pilots described the result as a "feeding frenzy" or a "turkey shoot."

Another significant aspect of this attack involved the actions of those being attacked. Several reports indicated that the Iraqis were waving white flags along the highway. But this fact must be coupled with an event that occurred two days earlier. An Iraqi unit in southern Kuwait had used the white flag as an illegitimate ruse to expose a Saudi regiment during the initial stages of the Coalition attack. Iraqi forces had engaged in other such illegal tactics such as parking combat aircraft by mosques and archeological sites. Such acts of illegal perfidy by the Iraqis posed tough challenges on the commanders in the field.

As a result of these previous episodes, as well as the immediate circumstances of this attack, white flags on the highway were generally ignored (although some pilots did express reservations about this to their commanders). Even though some white flags were present, civilian vehicles in the same convoy were directing antiaircraft fire at the attacking aircraft. Several pilots reported that the antiaircraft fire was apparently coordinated with respect to the variable cloud ceilings throughout the day. This suggests that elements of the convoy retained at least some capability to communicate with each other and that elements, at least, were still under effective command and control—i.e., that they were still organized military units. In other words, despite the initial appearance of an enemy force withdrawing in chaos, the convoy, according to pilots, continued to show signs of organized retreat and command and control.

The attacks were aimed specifically at the vehicles on the highway. The goal of the air campaign throughout the theater of operations at this time was the attrition of Iraqi military hardware. This fit well with the stated U.S. national security objective of restoring security and stability to the Gulf region, which translated operationally into the destruction of the Republican Guard units of the Iraqi army.

The convoy in the area around Mutlah Ridge was the only one of several convoys throughout the Kuwaiti theater area that included a large number of civilian vehicles. It was also the only convoy that received media attention because the others were too far north inside of Iraq for press pool coverage. These convoy attacks continued into the next day (the 27th) at several other locations throughout northern Kuwait and southeastern Iraq, primarily against military vehicles, and were terminated only with the cease-fire at midnight.

III. MORAL QUESTIONS RAISED BY BASRA ROAD

In this section we will focus on three moral themes: 1) noncombatant immunity and the question of surrender, 2) military necessity and proportionality, and 3) observations regarding the psychology of combat and the possibilities of right intent in combatants.

First, regarding noncombatant immunity and surrender. As we saw above, popular concern that large numbers of civilian hostages were in the Basra convoy was unwarranted. Convoy participants were almost exclusively Iraqi soldiers and un-uniformed paramilitary Iraqis—and were reasonably believed to be so at the time. Although not morally decisive, they were, in fact, many of the perpetrators of the worst horrors of the occupation of Kuwait City. Many military officers interviewed did appeal to the language of reprisals as justification for this attack. We are not suggesting that their destruction on the road to Basra was a kind of morally justified "rough justice" for war crimes. But these facts show, at least, that the objects of the attack were not innocents, either in the technical legal sense or in the more general moral sense.

There is, therefore, no question that the Iraqis on the road to Basra were not *hors de combat*. Although many in the press failed to make this distinction, it is crucial to note that they were and remained combatants. Mere armed retreat does not, and should not, be construed as tantamount to surrender. Participation in such a retreat does not entitle one to any of the rights of immunity from attack granted to civilians or to surrendered military personnel. Whether we view this convoy as retreating or withdrawing, given the stated military objectives of this campaign and the imminence of the chemical threat, retreat and withdrawal were synonymous and in all likelihood will continue to be viewed as such in future conflicts. Prior to any surrender or cease-fire agreement, both are military maneuvers, and therefore subject to legitimate attack.

There is, however, a legitimate and important question about surrender. As we indicated above, some Iraqi troops apparently did display tokens of surrender and, in the normal case, such tokens should be accepted. But in the case at hand, the failure of the American air forces to accept these tokens seems warranted. The previous perfidious use of white flags and other indicia of surrender, the fact that flags were interspersed with elements of the convoy still engaged in coordinated hostile fire against American aircraft, and the lack of ground or even helicopter-borne troops in the area to accept the surrender and provide benevolent quarantine all justify dismissing these displays.

Perfidious use of the white flag is governed explicitly by the Annex to the Hague Conventions, summarized in the United States Army's *The Law of Land Warfare*, as follows: "Flags of truce must not be used surreptitiously to obtain military information or to obtain time to effect a retreat or secure reinforcements or to feign a surrender in order to surprise an enemy." Perfidious acts are prohibited for a variety of reasons. Such acts reduce the mutual respect for the laws of war and the humanitarian principles they attempt to express. Such acts also promote the unnecessary escalation of the conflict and impede the restoration of peace. Although there does not appear to have been any centrally directed Iraqi policy to carry out acts of perfidy, actions during the Iran-Iraq conflict and several isolated incidents during Desert Storm did, in fact, color the Coalition's perceptions of Iraqi attempts to offer surrender. Good faith efforts are required, insofar as they do not involve unreasonable risks to one's own troops, to determine the legitimacy of each and every white flag. In this case, it was readily apparent that surrender was not being offered on the part of entire units and that the white flags in question were the result of uncoordinated actions of individuals. In light of these facts, we do not judge

there to have been any moral requirement that the attack be ended because of these flags.

There is a larger in-principle question here, and one that deserves further thought and elaboration in the laws of war. There are actually no well understood conditions with respect to the concept of surrender. In fact, in the field the opposite is the case and presents yet another challenge to individual commanders and the just war tradition alike. An enemy who wishes to surrender must manifest an unconditional and unambiguous intent to surrender by way of customary indicia. Traditionally, these include laying down of arms and no longer demonstrating a willingness to resist.

Unfortunately, there is no recognized universal procedure for conveying this message. One might expect and hope for a clearer description of the means of conveying this message. Yet even the current U.S. Army field manual on the law of land warfare does not delineate acceptable methods of indicating an intention to surrender. The onus at present falls on the would-be prisoner to communicate the will to surrender unambiguously.

Also, even if we leave aside the perfidy question, there is a difficulty with determining whether the white flag represents the desire of the *individual soldier* to surrender, or that of *the entire unit*. The U.S. Army Field Manual, *The Law of Land Warfare*, includes the following instruction: "[The] white flag, when used by troops, indicates a desire to communicate with the enemy. The hoisting of a white flag has no other signification in international law. . . . If hoisted in action by an individual soldier or a small party, it may signify merely the surrender of that soldier or party. It is essential, therefore, to determine with reasonable certainty that the flag is shown by actual authority of the enemy commander before basing important action on that assumption. The enemy is not required to cease firing when a white flag is raised." This regulation incorporates an important moral point. There is a trade-off between allowing for the return of combatants to non-combatant status, on the one hand, and the practical constraint that although *individuals* may, in the face of attack, be quite prepared to quit their combatant status, surrender is normally the action of military units. Certainly, when it is practical to allow individual surrender, individuals should be granted such rights. And if, indeed, pilots deliberately targeted individual soldiers who manifested an apparent intent to surrender *as individuals* (something which we do not, in fact, know occurred) then a moral and, at least arguably, legal violation occurred. But individuals flying a white flag in the midst of an organized and armed military unit engaged in hostilities with aircraft are rarely going to find themselves in a position for surrender, nor is it practically realistic or morally requisite that the laws of war attempt to incorporate such a possibility.

On the other hand, had the facts been slightly different and entire units or even the whole column wished to surrender, there is no provision in current law or regulation that clearly indicates applicable and unambiguous indicia for such an air-to-ground engagement. Nor is it clear in such engagements what the practical implications of surrender would be, since obviously air forces can neither gain practical control over ground forces nor provide them with the benevolent quarantine required by the laws governing surrender. Hence, law and moral thought are at a conceptual limit here, and further thought needs to be given about the moral meaning of conflict and surrender during such engagements.

The second set of considerations concerns military necessity and proportionality. Was it *necessary*, in military terms, to attack this convoy, or could it have been allowed safely to withdraw from Kuwait (thereby fulfilling the announced goal of the war)?

In light of the historical patterns of Iraqi tactics, and the fact that these units included some of the most elite of the Iraqi army, the attack seems well justified. As we noted above, the Coalition air commanders had every reason to fear that this withdrawal was the precursor to renewed attack or even to artillery attack using gas or biological warheads (warheads which we now know were in fact deployed and available for use with Iraqi troops). General Schwarzkopf's intention was to keep such pressure on troops engaged in armed retreat that they would not be given the opportunity to regroup for attack or to set up artillery emplacements necessary to execute this tactic. Therefore, attacking the column seems well warranted indeed, and militarily desirable and necessary.

But even if necessary, was it proportionate? Probably not, at least not in the full scope of the attack. Certainly bottling up the column was warranted. The intention to destroy the armor and artillery in the column, and perhaps even the other vehicles, seems likewise warranted. But there seems little question that gratuitous destruction was wreaked upon individual soldiers and groups far off the road and well away from the vehicles and weapons. If reports of the use of cluster bombs against soldiers on foot are true, there seems to be little justification indeed.

On the other hand, determinations of proportionality require specification of both sides of the balance. In this case, much depends on what one thinks is the military and political goal of this attack. The real goal and hope in the minds of the planners went considerably farther than the destruction of this unit. Indeed, the hope was the long term crippling of the Iraqi Republican Guard, that is, rendering it incapable of inflicting further damage on the Shiites of the south and the Kurds of the north. But even this intention was in careful balance with the recognition that Iraq should not be left defenseless in the face of Iran at the end of the war.

The third and last topic we wish to explore here is, we think, too rarely seriously entertained by academic discussions of military ethics. This is the psychological effect of modern combat on the soldiers and airmen who fight the battles. From St. Augustine's letter to Boniface to the present day, the Christian just war tradition has always had an emphasis on the proper mental and intentional state of the warrior. Boniface, Augustine counseled, was to go to war "mournfully"—without hate or rancor, letting "necessity" and not his will do the killing.

Similarly, much of the "moral armor" of the military professional consists in the belief that the destruction they bring on others is not personally or emotionally motivated, but is instead simply an instance of professionalism in conduct.

Yet much in the human dimension of the Basra Road engagement raises questions about the limits of human ability to retain such attitudes in the heat of battle. Major Hamann's interviews with many veterans of Basra Road reveal a fairly wide range of intense emotional reactions to this situation.

On the one hand, there was clearly a kind of overwhelming excitement in the minds of many pilots. Some disregarded even considerations of personal safety, neglecting to check in with and receive clearance from forward air controllers, which suggests eagerness to join in the "turkey shoot" some pilots themselves called a "feeding frenzy." Perhaps precisely because these were units directly from Kuwait City widely reported to have committed outrages against the civilians of Kuwait, the motive of revenge seems to have joined with the technical thrill of videogame-like opportunities to fire on multiple targets at will. On the other hand, some pilots felt revulsion at what they were doing and requested permission *not* to return to the scene of battle following refueling and rearming.

Besides the previously mentioned reservations about the Iraqi attempts to surrender and admissions that some pilots disregarded command and control in this engagement (aberrations in the context of the entire air campaign), the attacks on the roads to Basra revealed some startling yet persistent behaviors that can be classified into three general areas.

First some pilots delighted in the amount of destruction they could wreak on the convoy. They expressed an odd sense of pleasure in shooting a large number of live targets after weeks of destroying only hardened stationary targets. This sometimes resulted in the expenditure of a large number of antitank rounds into civilian vehicles and regret only at having wasted extra rounds of ammunition. But the general delight in destruction is also a well documented psychological phenomenon of war. To quote a classic passage from Glenn Gray's *The Warriors*:

> Men who have lived in the zone of combat long enough to be veterans are sometimes possessed by a fury that makes them capable of anything. Blinded by the rage to destroy and supremely careless of the consequences. . . . it is as if they are seized by a demon, or are no longer in control of themselves. From the Homeric account of the sacking of Troy to the conquest of Dienbienphu, Western literature is filled with descriptions of soldiers as berserkers and mad destroyers.

This phenomenon of battle is a constant, a constant which the technological evolution of modern weapons probably will never eliminate.

Second, several pilots expressed a certain satisfaction in demonstrating the full capabilities of their aircraft on the convoys retreating into Basra. Pilots have always developed an attachment for their flying machines, even to the point where the machine seems to take on a personality of its own. This devo-

tion varies from one type of aircraft to another, and frequently evolves into a competition amongst pilots of different weapons systems. The attacks on the roads to Basra are an illustration of this competition.

While the fighters were either striking downtown Baghdad or searching for the glorious and elusive air-to-air dogfight, the results of which were guaranteed to be replayed on CNN, the A-10 was tasked for missions (search and rescue, SCUD hunts, and even battle damage reconnaissance) that it was not designed to do and its pilots were never trained to fly. Although the aircraft and crews performed those missions with distinction, the retreating convoys on the road to Basra provided them a real opportunity to demonstrate to the Air Force chain of command (primarily consisting of fast fighter pilots) the capabilities of A-10 aircraft. Several pilots boasted to Major Hamann that it was gratifying after so many years of frustration to show those idiots in command post "how much killing an A-10 could really do!" A certain amount of enthusiasm is sometimes warranted and even desirable in terms of the motivation needed to face combat. But the indulgent exhibition of machines—machines with unprecedented lethality—comes precariously close to excessive violence and threatens to ignore the just war tradition's plea for restraint and virtuous conduct on the part of soldiers, even in war.

The mystique regarding soldiers' attachment to their weapons has received very little attention in the study of war. "The fear engendered by these weapons—a backdrop of unimaginable horror lying just beneath the surface—has led to a sort of paralysis of inquiry. . . . By virtue of an odd sort of consensus of opposites, weapons are generally perceived as matter-of-fact objects, mechanisms with little more symbolic and cultural significance than a pair of pliers." But to understand weapons in this way is to *misunderstand* them.

Of Arms and Men by Robert O'Connell, a military intelligence officer and historian, explores this complex relationship between soldiers and their weapons. In his review of military history from the perspective of the evolution of weapons, O'Connell distinguishes between *predatory* and *intraspecific* aggression.

Intraspecific conflicts are characterized by ritual and ceremonial restraint, he claims. Weapons are symmetrical in size and lethality and are employed with much posturing. The virtues of the military hero in this type of conflict are coupled with an aesthetic valuing of the weapons, almost to the point where actual killing becomes a secondary objective.

In predatory conflict killing is no longer an art form. Instead, it is a mechanical process governed by an objective scientific pattern of thinking. The enemy is hunted down with casual ruthlessness, is shown no sympathy, and is not the object of feelings of shared humanity. It is here that we find language that dehumanizes the enemy.

A third observation regarding the psychology of combat was this: in Major Hamann's interviews, all of the pilots who expressed both their love of their machines and a delight in destruction also referred to the Iraqis in animal or subhuman terms. John Keegan, a noted military historian, has commented that the impersonalization of battle is one of the indices of divergence between the facts of everyday morality and battle-field morality. Reflexive comments by participants on the roads into Basra are a manifestation of this index. Several pilots even went as far as to describe the enemy as a creature of indeterminate qualities—an eerie coping strategy reminiscent of the testimonials of veterans of World War II and Vietnam.

There are several possible explanations for this particular psychological mechanism for coping with combat stress. All of these can be generalized as attempts to perceive as simple what is in reality very complex and, therefore, frustrating to the individual decision maker. A compartmentalized, prejudiced environment is much easier to deal with. "It must be counted as one of the particular cruelties of modern warfare that, by inducing even in the fit and willing soldier a sense of his unimportance it encouraged his treating the lives of disarmed and demoralized opponents as equally unimportant." This observation brings us back to one of the most obscure of all battle-field transactions—how soldiers get their offer of surrender communicated and accepted. Insofar as these psychological dynamics are at play, clearly this too complicates that transaction.

Religious and cultural differences also contributed to the common language for this dehumanization. What they were destroying were not individual persons whose plight one could sympathize with, but "camel jockeys," "rag heads," and other labels of segregation. Clearly O'Connell is right when he notes that aversion to weapons and to tactics that are deemed less than honorable is sharply reduced when the enemy is seen as fundamentally alien.

IV. CONCLUSIONS

The attack on the convoy to Basra was not what it seemed in the immediate flush of press reporting. It was, in fact, a justified attack on combatants who had no moral claim to immunity from attack, and whose destruction served important and legitimate ends of the war.

On the other hand, we have seen that the image of air war as clinical and precise is only a half-truth. True, laser guided munitions and careful planning of targeting (such as that of the ATO procedures of the Gulf War) can go a long way to make air war discriminate and to reduce collateral damage. Still, the Gulf War brings us close to the limitations of human psychology under stress. Pilots seem unable to restrain, under some circumstances, perhaps understandable human emotions of revenge, and the dehumanizing rhetoric of both pilots and commanders almost certainly weakens those restraints there are.

Furthermore, although we have argued that there was no obligation to accept isolated white flags as evidence of a desire to surrender in this engagement, there is a deeper question about surrender and air war—perhaps most clearly revealed in close air support missions. When one side enjoys total air supremacy in the theater of operations and engages ground forces, do the laws of war need to be extended to think about providing such overwhelmed troops with some means of surrender? Further thought needs to be given to clarifying both the means signaling the intent to lay down arms and the tactical means of accepting surrender on the part of the attacker.

WHITE FLAGS ON THE ROAD TO BASRA
Surrendering Soldiers in the Persian Gulf War

Gabriel Palmer-Fernández

It is true that in war soldiers are killed who could be taken prisoner. Perhaps this happens more often than we would like to admit. Sometimes surrendering soldiers are killed in the heat of battle, in a kind of frenzy. At that moment, consumed by the sight of wounded and dead comrades, by fear, shock, and other emotions in extreme, the soldier hardly knows what goes on. "If you start a man killing, you can't turn him off like an engine." Sometimes, too, the killing takes a more insidious form. Captured soldiers are killed for the success of a mission or the safety of the unit, or soldiers fleeing the battlefield and others bearing white flags are killed simply because they can be killed. Combat then turns into crime. That is one of the grave temptations in war. But surrendering soldiers are immune from direct attack and have the right to quarter. Their captors will impose upon them the burdens of submission and grant them those rights and privileges that belong to the prisoner of war. Once surrendered, soldiers regain their innocence. That is the tradition of civilized war.

But between combat and surrender, between the right to kill enemy soldiers and the duty to protect them, lies a zone of ambiguity wherein it is not clear whether that right or that duty is paramount. The ambiguity partly arises from the psychological nature of combat itself. When exactly does combat stop? With the last soldier? With the last round? When the enemy is overpowered? With the display of the tokens of surrender? Or with their acceptance? The epistemology is somewhat disorderly. Nor does just-war theory, as Michael Walzer observes, "readily cover cases of this sort." That theory does tell us when we may (perhaps must) fight and how we ought to. It does not clearly tell us when we ought to stop the fight. The ambiguity arises also from technological developments and strategic doctrines, especially in air and space power, that can quickly erode some of the established boundaries defining war as a rule-governed activity and challenge fundamental moral assumptions about war itself.

If war is a moral condition between states, then we need to know a fair amount about the nature of the rules that govern it, the relation of those rules to purely strategic considerations of what will and will not contribute to victory, and the circumstances under which enemy soldiers have a moral claim to immunity from direct attack. It is the aim of this paper to examine some of the conditions relevant to the cessation of armed hostilities at the tactical or unit level. I will suggest, in the third section, that once enemy soldiers have neither the will nor the means to fight, they are no longer legitimate targets of attack. I begin with an incident in the Persian Gulf War in which Iraqi soldiers displaying white flags were killed.

1. SURRENDERING SOLDIERS

On February 25, 1991, Kuwaiti resistance tipped off U.S. military intelligence that Iraqi forces occupying Kuwait City were preparing to retreat, and by evening of that day, air-to-ground radar confirmed that a large convoy of Iraqi vehicles and troops was heading out of the city. The next day, once the convoy was in the open along Mutlah Ridge, F-15E Strike Eagles hit its front and rear, creating a target-rich environment that would stretch for nearly sixty miles. Beginning on the early hours of February 27 and throughout the rest of the day, Air Force, Marine, and Navy pilots were authorized to acquire targets on the convoy and to fire at will. A few vehicles in the convoy, some of them reportedly civilian, fired at attacking aircraft but without inflicting any damage. Many pilots described the scene as a "turkey shoot" and a "feeding frenzy," expressing a certain delight in the havoc and destruction they wreaked. "It was like a dream come true. When you're flying in the States you look around and imagine that everything is a target, fuel tankers, trucks, tanks, whatever. Well now it was all laid out right in front of us. Kids in a candy store." A-10 pilots seem to have enjoyed a special enthusiasm in demonstrating the kind of destruction their plane, with its

Gatling-type 30-millimeter gun, could produce on enemy tanks, armored personnel carriers, and infantry when more than a few of them boasted of "how much killing an A-10 could really do."

Damage to the Iraqi convoy was extensive. The Department of Defense report to Congress (hereafter DoD report) states that more than 200 Iraqi tanks and hundreds of other military and civilian vehicles were destroyed in the attack. Michael Kelly reports that "large quantities of tanks, trucks, howitzers, and armoured personnel carriers" were destroyed. General H. Norman Schwarzkopf, Commander, U.S. Central Command, recalls that "more than a thousand military vehicles and stolen civilian trucks, buses and cars" were destroyed. And a U.S. Air Force report puts the number of vehicles "at more than 1,400, which included only 14 tanks and 14 other armored vehicles." Although none of these reports cites the number of enemy casualties, Saudi mortuary units, the first coalition units on the scene, claim to have buried some 5,000 Iraqi soldiers.

In an effort to avoid the fight, the DoD report states, "most Iraqi soldiers . . . immediately abandoned their vehicles and fled into the desert." Many of these soldiers were conscripts and some of them "weren't but 13, 14 years old." Whether on foot or vehicles, they were hunted as far as a half mile from the road and some of them killed by cluster bombs. There are also reports that the retreat was disorderly, rather than a coordinated withdrawal that could reform into an offensive line, and that some Iraqi soldiers in the convoy were waving white flags. Killing soldiers in war is acceptable under most conditions. But is it still acceptable when they are, as Stanley Hoffmann puts it, "neither volunteers nor mercenaries but the forcibly drafted cannon fodder of a tyrant and plainly in full flight from an overwhelming enemy"? When a belligerent so clearly overpowers the enemy, some of whom flee while others display the token of surrender, is there a duty to cease fire and give quarter? Might the convoy have been captured "rather than," as Hoffman says, "slaughtered during rout"?

2. THE RULE OF MILITARY NECESSITY

Military writers and journalists refer to the incident on the road to Basra as the "Highway of Death." Almost unanimously they describe the destruction

wreaked on the convoy by air power as "more complete, more total" than any seen before, a "scene of utter devastation," as Schwarzkopf recounts. The justification for the attack was hardly novel, however.

The DoD report recounts the incident on the road to Basra after a brief discussion on the rule of military necessity that quotes U.S. Army General Orders 100, Lieber's Code: military necessity "consists in the necessity of those measures which are indispensable for securing the ends of war, and which are lawful according to the modern law and usages of war." It then declares that "[a]ttacks on retreating enemy forces have been common throughout history"—that they are, in other words, customary and hence compatible with the laws of war—and cites a few historical examples. Whereas the report does not explicitly appeal to the rule of military necessity to justify the attack upon the convoy, a recent article by Martin Cook and Phillip Hamann does. "The attack seems well justified," they assert, "and militarily desirable and necessary." Yet they provide hardly any discussion to support that assertion. They do state, and rightly so, that there is no "question that gratuitous destruction was wreaked upon individual soldiers" and that "the use of cluster bombs against soldiers on foot . . . [has] little justification." By their account, the attack failed to meet the *in bello* rule of proportionality in violating the prohibition on unnecessary suffering, suggesting that the level of violence used was excessive with regard to its military end.

Cook and Hamann's account raises an important set of questions. What is military necessity? Does it refer to the success of a tactical goal, the safety of a unit that is critically threatened, or, as Lieber put it, "the ends of war"? Under what conditions may it justifiably be invoked? Were those conditions met on the road to Basra? In each case the thinking is utilitarian, looking to produce a favorable state of affairs. But not all that might contribute to victory or to tactical success is permissible in war. Thus the Nuremberg Military Tribunal suggested when it declared that were military necessity to confer the right to do anything that would contribute to winning a war "it would eliminate all humanity and decency and all law from the conduct of war, and it is a contention which the Tribunal repudiates as contrary to the accepted usages of civilized nations."

There is a sense in which the attack was militarily necessary. The retreating Iraqi convoy did consist of armed enemies, and the law and customs of war permit attacking such a force. Most of the soldiers belonged to the Iraqi front-line divisions, the III Corps. But among them were also members of the Iraqi secret police, the Mukhabarat, and the elite Republican Guard, a major worry of the coalition forces, particularly in the first days of the ground war. Moreover, there was a concern over the use of chemical and biological munitions. Iraq had used chemical and nerve agents quite effectively against its own citizens and Iran, and Iraqi Prime Minister Saddam Hussein had threatened their use against coalition forces. Given this concern, there was reason to think that the convoy was not retreating from the rapid advance of coalition forces. It may instead have been protecting itself from a planned Scud or artillery attack using chemical and biological weapons, after which it would re-form into an offensive force. It was, therefore, "imperative," as Richard Hallion puts it, "that these forces not be allowed to retire so that they could regroup and threaten coalition ground forces."

But by February 26, the ground war was practically over, and Hussein had ordered his troops to withdraw from Kuwait. Moreover, the condition of Iraqi troops, especially the units in and around Kuwait City, was chaotic—hardly worth calling such a multitude an army capable of mounting a counterattack. Cook and Hamann admit that the convoy "consisted exclusively of panicked stragglers from the decimated front line divisions (the Iraqi III Corps)." And Schwarzkopf himself says:

> There was no longer any communication between Baghdad and Basra and the remaining divisions in the field—each had to fend for itself. . . . I sat back to watch victory unfold.

The claim that the attack was militarily necessary then is not well established by the facts, and the appeal to that rule needs closer examination. Legal and military texts variously define military necessity as a legal prerequisite for any use of force, as a qualification of specific rules of war, as a right of self-preservation of a state to disregard the rules of war, and as a legally valid reason for the abrogation of the rules of war. But Cook and Hamann's remark on military necessity does not rely on any of these established interpretations. The first version refers to political and not tactical considerations. War is an instrument, this version asserts, and its employment is permissible only if there is no alternative means of achieving the political objective sought. Moreover, war is a limited instrument, proscribing acts of violence that make the return to peace difficult and those that inflict unnecessary suffering or are motivated by the desire for revenge or the lust to kill. The second refers to specific rules of war that are qualified by reference to military necessity and can, under particular circumstances, justify violence, as might be the case, for example, with scorched-earth policies and the bombing of unfortified towns. Although these are forbidden strategies, their prohibition is sometimes qualified by military necessity. If military necessity is taken as the right of self-preservation of a state (the so-called *Kriegsräison* doctrine, that whatever victory demands is permissible), then any act of violence that contributes to victory is militarily necessary. On this view, necessity would override all moral and legal claims, and for that reason this view has been almost universally condemned. Nor, finally, does there appear to be a breach of the rules of war by the Iraqi army that allows coalition forces to reciprocate in kind, as is the case with reprisals. None of these versions, then, fits well with Cook and Hamann's aim of justifying the attack on the convoy.

There is another sense of military necessity that does fit, however, as follows. Military necessity consists in those acts of violence relevant to achieving a tactical or military objective and compatible with the laws and customs of war. Assuming the retreat was a coordinated maneuver affording the convoy an opportunity to reorganize itself into an offensive force, then the attack would clearly be relevant to the important objective of defeating such an opportunity and compatible with established practices of war. One would want, however, to determine whether military necessity so defined justifies violence when it is essential or only reasonably required to achieving such an objective. The former would be a more stringent test for application of the rule than the latter. So conceived, I suspect that either test would justify the attack. But at least we can say, on this account, that when an act of violence is neither essential nor reasonably required to achieving a tactical or military end, then it is an unnecessary and prohibited act. Killing, enemy soldiers under such conditions would be a criminal, and not a belligerent, act.

Military necessity requires, in addition to the relevancy of an act of violence, that violence be proportionate to its tactical end, thereby forbidding violence that produces gratuitous or excessive harm. For example, W. G. Downey argues that a 30-caliber explosive having the same military purpose as an ordinary 30-caliber "increases the suffering of the recipient without furthering the military purpose of the projectile." Such suffering is gratuitous, and instruments of war producing gratuitous or excessive suffering are prohibited. Cook and Hamann's judgment that the attack on the convoy was "gratuitous" can only mean that it increased the "suffering of the recipients without furthering the military purpose of the attack." It ought, therefore, to be condemned.

Suppose, however, the attack was desirable or necessary for a different reason. Cook and Hamann suggest that our judgment "depends on what one thinks is the . . . political goal of this attack." Here necessity refers not to tactical or military objectives, but to the larger strategic or political goals of the war. We ought "to inflict maximum destruction, *maximum destruction* on the entire Iraqi military machine . . . destroy all war-fighting equipment . . . eliminate Iraq's ability to threaten the Arab world," Schwarzkopf says. The attack on the convoy would then be necessary to achieving that goal, provided military necessity refers to what is strategically or politically desirable. But the complete destruction of the Iraqi war machine neither was a stated goal of that war nor is a legitimate goal of any war. Hence, on this account the killing on the road to Basra cannot be justified.

3. ACTS OF PERFIDY OR SURRENDER?

On the afternoon of February 27, General Colin Powell, then Chairman of the Joint Chiefs of Staff, informed Schwarzkopf that White House staff had become quite uncomfortable over the attack on the convoy. "The reports made it sound like wanton killing. . . . The President is thinking about going on the air tonight at nine o'clock and announcing we're cutting it off," Schwarzkopf recounts Powell saying. Schwarzkopf had just told the American people in a televised briefing that "there wasn't enough left of Iraq's army for it to be a regional military threat. . . . Our objective was the destruction of the enemy forces,

and for all intents and purposes we've accomplished that objective." When war's objective is accomplished and enemy soldiers are overrun and unwilling to fight, why kill rather than subdue and capture them? What is conscientious conduct toward a belligerent who has neither the will nor the means to fight?

Cook and Hamann admit that the attack on the convoy raises important issues about the conditions of surrender. The laws of war do not provide "well understood conditions with respect to the concept of surrender. . . . There is no recognized universal procedure for conveying this message." Nonetheless, they say,

> the failure of the American air forces to accept tokens of surrender seems warranted. The previous perfidious use of white flags and other indicia of surrender, the fact that flags were interspersed with elements of the convoy still engaged in coordinated hostile fire against American aircraft, and the lack of ground or even helicopter-borne troops in the area to accept the surrender and provide benevolent quarantine all justify dismissing these displays.

It was, they conclude, "a justified attack on combatants who had no moral immunity from attack." I want now to examine the reasons leading to that conclusion, which seem to be flawed in important ways.

The first of these is the alleged perfidy in the use of white flags by Iraqi troops. In the normal case, the hoisting of the white flag is taken as indicative of an intent to communicate with the enemy, to initiate negotiations towards capitulation, or to surrender and is accompanied by the cessation of fire from the side displaying the flag. Although there are questions regarding the exact legal significance of the white flag—for example, who has the authority to display it, and whether it indicates the intent of the individual soldier or the entire unit to surrender—in practice it has long been held that when a soldier submits to the opponent's control by displaying the token of surrender, the latter is obligated to cease fire and to grant immunity from direct attack.

But Cook and Hamann contend that Iraqi troops did not express a genuine intent to surrender in displaying the white flag. Its use was perfidious, and so there was no obligation to extend protection to them under quarter. The statement is a factual one, the truth of which is difficult to confirm or to deny. Grant, for the sake of argument, that during the Iran-Iraq war, Iraqi troops made frequent use of the white flag in order to deceive the enemy. Is there any evidence suggesting that this, too, was the case in the Persian Gulf War? Cook and Hamann's own report on this matter is vague. They say at one point that there were "several *isolated* incidents during Desert Storm" of acts of perfidy, yet cite only two such instances. One occurred several days prior to the attack on the convoy when "an Iraqi unit in Southern Kuwait had used the white flag as an illegitimate ruse to expose a Saudi regiment." The other refers to the illegal tactic of parking combat aircraft near mosques and archeological sites. But those are the only acts of perfidy they report. Suppose there were a few more. How many are sufficient to motivate the view that the white flags on the road to Basra did not express a genuine intent to surrender and were instead acts of perfidy? And how many flags must an enemy display to communicate a genuine intent to surrender?

The conduct of Iraqi troops in this war provides no evidence suggesting the view held by Cook and Hamann, that displays of the white flag by Iraqi troops were perfidious. On the contrary, after weeks of daylight and nighttime bombing, an aggressive leaflet campaign encouraging Iraqi soldiers to defect or to surrender, and the very large number of soldiers who did surrender during the ground war without putting up a fight, one can only presume that any use of the white flag in this war was indeed genuine.

Suppose, however, that the use of white flags was perfidious. Cook and Hamann then missed the opportunity to provide a robust justification for the attack on the convoy. Perfidious use of the white flag can, with further requirements, justify reprisals against enemy soldiers, acts of violence that otherwise are prohibited but are allowed in order to neutralize the benefits of, or to punish, illegality. Even a mere appeal, without full justification, to the language of reprisal might have bolstered their contention that Iraqi troops on the road to Basra committed perfidy. The crucial reason why perfidious acts are prohibited and justify reprisal is that they undermine the rules of war and particularly many of the humanitarian concerns they express. But is that not also the case when a belligerent goes headlong into a devastating attack

against an enemy already overwhelmed and who does not really wish to fight? Iraqi soldiers waving white flags on the road to Basra and those on the platforms in the Ad-Dawrah offshore oil fields had reason to suspect that American forces would not honor their tokens of surrender. In that regard American forces may have undermined respect for the rules of war and the humanitarian concerns they express, even if we cannot attach criminality to their actions.

The second reason Cook and Hamann give is that white flags "were interspersed with elements of the convoy still engaged in coordinated hostile fire." I noted above that an important condition of surrender is that the side seeking quarter cease hostile fire; otherwise the token of surrender may be dismissed.

Suppose American pilots attacking the convoy on the road to Basra were under heavy antiaircraft fire, of the kind that would reasonably have led them to wonder whether they would pull out of their mission alive. Certainly they would have seen some of their fellow pilots eject into enemy territory or crash to death. Air-to-surface warfare has its own distinct dangers. Suppose further that in the heat of this battle some Iraqi soldiers waved white flags. What should we make of these flags? Do we say the Iraqis wished to surrender? It is all or only some of them? Obviously not all. Should we then have effected a partial surrender? If so, how? Absent the cessation of hostile fire in this instance, honoring the white flag would have placed American pilots at even greater risk. Let us grant then that, as conceived, American pilots were in the heat of battle and therefore justified in continuing the attack.

The facts about the incident on the road to Basra, however, are different. Cook and Hamann contend that Iraqi fire was "coordinated," but only so with regards to some, not most or all, of the elements in the convoy. That only some elements were engaged in hostile fire gives us reason to think that the fire was less than coordinated, otherwise there would have been a determined resistance. "There was some 'triple-A' [antiaircraft artillery] fire from the retreating Iraqis," one pilot from the USS *Ranger* said, "but they were basically 'sitting ducks.'" And pilots returning to the *Ranger* described not a military unit under clear command of a superior, but "a massive, disorderly retreat." Even if hostile fire was coordinated, it was certainly feeble. It produced no American casualties, no damage to attacking aircraft, not even those emotions that typically accompany real battle—not only because American forces were far superior to the Iraqi army in every meaningful way, but also because the Iraqis did not have the will or the means to put up a fight.

The third reason Cook and Hamann give can also be dismissed. Suppose there was, as they contend, a "lack of ground or even helicopter-borne troops to accept the surrender." Should we conclude that the lack of troops to accept surrender is sufficient to deny quarter? Were any options available other than continued violence? One option was to stop the killing upon appearance of white flags and to let the soldiers retreat into Iraq. As Schwarzkopf recounts, by February 26 the Iraqi army had been defeated and he was ready to "[sit] back and watch victory unfold." A second, related option was to let the convoy proceed north to Basra and to attack with ground forces near the Iraqi border town of Safwan. If white flags were again displayed, then any of several coalition forces that had pushed the Iraqis on their left flank on February 25 and the following day was in good position to receive prisoners. Among these units were U.S. 1st and 2nd Marine Divisions and British 1st Armored Division, south of Kuwait City on the evening before the attack. By the following day, these units had advanced west and north of Kuwait City, past Mutlah Ridge where the attack on the convoy took place. U.S. Army 1st Squadron, 4th Cavalry, 1st Division was particularly well positioned to take prisoners in this area of operations. On February 26 this unit was ordered to conduct a flank screen on the road from Kuwait City north to Safwan and moved into position with tanks, Bradleys, and nearly a dozen attack helicopters. It easily engaged the enemy destroying most of its equipment, including T-55 and T-62 Soviet-made tanks (the same as those destroyed by air power on the road to Basra), taking many prisoners, and suffering no casualties. A similar maneuver by this unit might have been possible against the retreating convoy. Either option would surely have spared many human lives. But even if Cook and Hamann are correct, the lack of American troops on the road to Basra available to accept surrendering Iraqi soldiers cannot, itself, justify killing them.

There is an important form of argument directly condemning the killing on the road to Basra that I only sketch here. Suppose one admits the reasonableness of the Kantian principle that humanity in each person must always be treated as an end in itself, never merely as a means. Killing soldiers in war would still be acceptable, for this principle does not lead to pacifism. But one would have to give very good reasons why a particular act of killing is morally permissible, reasons that would be acceptable to any rational agent when the matter is looked at from the viewpoint of the humanity principle. As Thomas Hill puts it, "to be justified in a deliberate killing, a person would need to be able to face the victim and say, sincerely and truthfully, 'I choose to kill you (when I have an option not to); but still I regard you as more than a *mere* means, in fact as a person with a worth that is incalculable.'"

Consider now a battlefield condition that is like the one on the road to Basra except that American and Iraqi soldiers are face to face. Upon the initial attack some Iraqi soldiers shoot back. But the fire is sporadic and ineffective. Others wave white flags, and still more run away from the fight leaving their weapons and the war behind. Can one look at one of those soldiers (at any one of them) with rifle trained on him and say, sincerely and truthfully, "I choose deliberately to kill you, although you have neither the will nor the means to fight"? I suspect it would not be hard to kill soldiers engaged in armed resistance. Any plausible doctrine of self-defense or of war as a moral enterprise can support those killings. But we cannot say the same regarding the others. The crucial reason why these soldiers cannot morally be killed is that, absent the will and means to fight, they are no longer engaged in an activity that is internally connected with war such that their suffering or death is the consequence of their own chosen actions. Those soldiers bearing white flags and others fleeing the battlefield are hors de combat, and thus killing them is much like killing the innocent.

Some might object to the above analogy. They will assert that modern technological warfare, particularly the kind that employs air and space weapons, cannot be made to fit the morality of face-to-face encounters. War is not a contest of individual wills, and so individual morality does not apply to it. They might add that recent developments in weaponry have radically changed the nature of the battlefield in the same way the machine gun did on the Western Front between 1914 and 1918. Today we don't fight wars in which the enemy is within visual range but those in which the enemy is beyond it and mediated by electronic systems. We must, therefore, develop our moral ideas to fit this new environment. But those who endorse this objection will have to explain just how a person's immunity from attack is suspended in modern warfare and how one's innocence in war is not a shield from deliberate death. If innocence is no longer a shield, then modern war cannot draw the important distinction between legitimate and illegitimate targets of deliberate attack. It can thereby come dangerously close to murder on a mass scale.

4. CONCLUSION: TO KILL OR TO CAPTURE?

My aim in this paper was to examine some conditions relevant to the concept of surrender at the tactical or unit level. To that end, my discussion focused on an incident in which soldiers displaying the traditional token of surrender were intentionally killed. In conclusion, I briefly speculate on what my discussion of that incident tells us about the conditions of surrender.

First, the purpose of attack is to secure a military objective, and this objective is attained by disabling, wounding, killing enemy soldiers, or by capturing them. But once that objective is achieved and enemy soldiers come under the power of a belligerent, further violence against them is unjustified. Initially, the attack upon the retreating convoy on the road to Basra may have served the military objective of preventing a counterattack. So, when the convoy was disabled, the purpose of attack was achieved, and further use of violence turned this belligerent act into a criminal one. Second, although further discussion is needed, intentionally killing another human being may be justified when the death of the victim is in some reasonable way connected with self-chosen activity. Such may be the case with self-defense killing of an unjust aggressor. It may be the case, too, with others who choose to share in the activities of the aggressor. But it is always wrong intentionally to kill those who do not have the will (choose not) and have not the means to fight. And third, in war when killing enemy soldiers is unjustified because they have come under one's power, even if no tokens of surrender are offered, one ought to extend to them the benefit of quarter. But when their surrender cannot be effected, as may have been the case on the road to Basra, one ought to let them go.

ADDITIONAL READING

Paul Christopher, *The Ethics of War and Peace: An Introduction to Legal and Moral Issues* (Englewood Cliffs, N.J.: Prentice-Hall, 1994) is a basic and readable overview and analysis of just war theory. Jenny Teichman's *Pacifism and the Just War* (Oxford: Basil Blackwell, 1986) is a brief but very insightful sudy of just war theory, pacificism, guerrilla war, and terrorism.

Michael Walzer, *Just and Unjust Wars: A Moral Argument with Historical Illustrations* (New York: Basic Books, 1977), is a modern classic on questions concerning the morality of war. Colm McKeogh, *Innocent Civilians: The Morality of Killing in War* (New York: Palgrave, 2002), is both a historical study and a philosophical analysis of the status of civilians in war. Richard B. Miller, *Interpretations of Conflict: Ethics, Pacifism, and the Just War Tradition* (Chicago: University of Chicago Press, 1991), offers a rational reconstruction of rival moral traditions concerning just war. Richard Norman, *Ethics, Killing, and War* (Cambridge: Cambridge University Press, 1995), examines just war theory form the viewpoint of contemporary moral philosophy, and includes discussion of such recent conflicts as the 1991 Gulf War and the Falklands/Malvinas War.

James T. Johnson has written two excellent analyses of the history of just war theory: *Just War Tradition and the Restraint of War: A Moral and Historical Inquiry* (Princeton, N.J.: Princeton University Press, 1981), and *The Quest for Peace: Three Moral Traditions in Western Cultural History* (Princeton, N.J.: Princeton University Press, 1987). Frederick Russell,

The Just War in the Middle Ages (Cambridge: Cambridge University Press, 1977) examines the history and development of medieval doctrines of just war, from Cicero and Augustine to Aquinas.

For an interesting comparison of Western and Islamic traditions on war and peace, see John Kelsay, *Islam and War: A Study in Comparative Ethics* (Louisville, Ky.: Westminster/John Knox Press, 1993).

Encyclopedia of Religion and War, Gabriel Palmer-Fernández, editor (New York: Routledge, 2003) is a comprehensive historical and cross-cultural analysis of the relation between religion and war, covering the major religious traditions of the world, religious wars, and contemporary movements.

DEATH PENALTY

Though capital punishment has been abolished in most countries, it remains a profoundly controversial issue in the United States. Robert S. Gerstein offers a straightforward retributivist justification for the death penalty, while Justice Thurgood Marshall (who was discussed in the chapter on virtue) argues against capital punishment (Marshall's argument was a *dissenting* opinion in the case of *Gregg* v. *Georgia*; that is, the majority of the court approved capital punishment).

CAPITAL PUNISHMENT—"CRUEL AND UNUSUAL"?

A Retributivist Response

Robert S. Gerstein

Thomas Long, in his article "Capital Punishment—'Cruel and Unusual'?"[1] canvasses the various arguments made for the view that capital punishment is cruel and unusual punishment and comes to the conclusion that the only argument with substantial merit is that which holds that capital punishment is unconstitutional because the pain and suffering it involves cannot be shown to be justified by its effectiveness as a deterrent. It must therefore be regarded as an irrational imposition of pain and suffering until such time as it can be shown that it is a more effective deterrent than less severe punishments would be. He then goes on to admit that this argument has its "sinister" aspects: it is probably true that no punishment could meet the burden of proof required by this standard of rationality. The force of the argument then is to undermine the justification for punishment generally.

I would suggest that Long arrives at this surprising result largely because he has chosen to restrict his consideration of the legitimacy of capital punishment to utilitarian considerations. The key to understanding this restriction is to be found, I believe, in his decision to disregard the retributivist view because "nonretributive views are today predominant among theoreticians of crime and punishment."[2] Having rejected retributivism, and any consideration of whether people "deserve" certain sorts of punishments or not, he is left with a classic utilitarian calculus in which the pain caused to the criminal is to be balanced against the benefits society would gain from the example his punishment sets to others. The dilemma in which he finds himself at the end of his indecisive calculations serves to underline Kant's warning to the penologist who stops being concerned with giving people what they deserve and instead "rummages around in the winding paths of a theory of happiness"[3] for guidance.

It is true that many judges and scholars simply reject retributivism out of hand.[4] It is also true, however, that there has in recent years been a revival of interest in retributive theory.[5] I would like to suggest that the rejection of retributivism is largely a product of misunderstanding and that, properly understood, the retributive view offers a more plausible basis for the solution of the problems surrounding cruel and unusual punishment generally, and capital punishment in particular, than do utilitarian views such as Long's.

The most common way of misunderstanding retributivism is to take it to be a fancy word for revenge. Those who assume that it is simply a rationalization for the venting of our passion for vengeance[6] quite rightly conclude that retributivism can offer us little help in deciding what is cruel and unusual punishment. Obviously this passion is not subject to any inherent limits on cruelty: it has been known to lead people to kill not only wrongdoers, but their whole families as well; it has led to boilings in oil and burnings at the stake. Others who connect retributivism with revenge construe it as a kind of utilitarian argument. In this view the retributivist is not one who justifies the urge to vengeance, but one who thinks that punishment is useful because it allows people to vent this emotion in a (relatively) harmless and orderly way.[7] People who see retributivism in this way also quite rightly come to the conclusion that it offers us no help in deciding what kinds of punishments should be ruled out as cruel and unusual.

These misunderstandings have at their heart the equation of vengeance with retribution. The equation is made understandable by the fact that there are connections, historical and conceptual, between these two ideas. It is mistaken because it misses the enormous and crucial differences between them.

Vengefulness is an emotional response to injuries done to us by others: we feel a desire to injure those who have injured us. Retributivism is not the idea that it is good to have and satisfy this emotion. It is rather the view that there are good arguments for including that kernel of rationality to be found in the passion for vengeance as a part of any just system of laws. Assuming the existence of a generally just legal system, the argument for making retributive punishment a part of it has been succinctly stated in this way:

In order to enjoy the benefits that a legal system makes possible, each man must be prepared to make an important sacrifice—namely, the sacrifice of obeying the law even when he does not desire to do so. Each man calls on others to do

this, and it is only just or fair that he bear a comparable burden when his turn comes. Now if the system is to remain just, it is important to guarantee that those who disobey will not thereby gain an unfair advantage over those who obey voluntarily. Criminal punishment thus attempts to maintain the proper balance between benefit .and obedience by insuring that there is no profit in criminal wrongdoing.[8]

It has been seen that some critics of retributivism regard it as a theory that would lead us to use criminals as objects upon which to vent our emotions, as scapegoats to be dealt with without regard to their value as people. In fact, nothing could be further from the truth. It is a major tenet of the standard form of retributivism that "a human being can never be manipulated merely as a means to the purposes of someone else."[9] Punishment is not, in this view, a matter of injuring people because it is useful to us but of dealing with them in the way they deserve to be dealt with. The question for the retributivist is not: what will be the most advantageous way of disposing of this criminal? Rather it is: what is the just way to treat one of our fellow citizens who has willfully taken unjust advantage of the rest of us?

It is especially surprising that critics suggest that retributivism leads to the destruction of all limits on the severity of punishment. Retributivism in its classic form has within it a standard which measures out the severity of the punishment with great care: lex talionis.[10] Indeed, if the purpose of punishment is to restore the balance of advantages necessary to a just community, then punishment must be proportioned to the offense: any unduly severe punishment would unbalance things in the other direction.

In fact, one of the great advantages of retributivism over other views is that it serves not only as a justification for punishment but also as a guide to the appropriate kind of punishment and a limit on the severity of punishment. Most other views require us to balance various utilitarian considerations against each other to come to our conclusions. So, for example, a very harsh punishment might be warranted for a particular crime from the point of view of the needs of deterrence, but we might decide to mitigate it because it would simply be too painful to those that would undergo it. Understood from this perspective, the problem of deciding whether some particular punishment was cruel and unusual would, of course, be a matter of weighing the social advantages to be derived from it against the pain it would cause the criminal. A variety of policies, including deterrence, security, and rehabilitation, must all be taken into account.

In retributivism, on the other hand, we have a single coherent perspective from which to make a principled judgment as to the punishment appropriate for this offense and this person. Because punishment is justified as the deserved response of the community to a member who has acted unjustly, it is essential that the punishment meted out to him be consistent with his position as a member of the community. He is not to be treated as an object or even as an enemy. Our duty to treat him justly is no less stringent than that which we have toward any other member of the community. The purpose of punishment is to restore the balance of justice within the community, not further to derange it.

What then would retributivism regard as cruel and unusual punishment? Clearly, any punishment the severity of which was out of proportion with the offense. But further, any punishment which would be inconsistent with the criminal's status as a member of the community whose capacity for a sense of justice (a capacity of which he did not make use when he committed his crime)[11] is worthy of our respect. This is not to say that we may not cause him pain, and even very great pain. To say that punishment is justified is to say that a man with the capacity for a sense of justice ought to feel guilty and recognize that he should suffer for what he has done. The line is not to be drawn in terms of the degree, but in terms of the kind of suffering that is inflicted. As Plato pointed out, it can never be the business of a just man to make another man less just than he was.[12] An affliction which undermines a man's self-respect rather than awakening his conscience, which impairs his capacity for justice rather than stimulating it, could not serve as just punishment.

In fact, one of the most widely accepted views of the meaning of "cruel and unusual punishment," that developed by Justice Brennan,[13] fits very well into the retributivist perspective. Brennan argues that cruel and unusual punishments are those which "treat members of the human race as nonhumans, as objects to be toyed with and discarded."[14] He sums up his view in terms of the "primary principle . . . that a punishment must not in its severity be degrading to human dignity."[15] Brennan's position gains both force and clarity when it is seen in the context of retributivism. In this context the distinction between punishments which destroy human dignity and those which do not becomes more plausible because the theory shows us how we can justify the imposition of some afflictive punishments on a person while giving full respect to his human dignity. The idea of human dignity is also given content when it is explicated in terms of the capacity for a sense of justice. Just as we justify punishment as a response to those who abuse this capacity, so we shape and limit punishment out of the desire to preserve and stimulate it.

How does capital punishment fit into this scheme? The retributivist view, to the extent it is dealt with at all, is dealt with only as providing arguments in favor of capital punishment.[16] This is, first, because it does offer a justification for punishment in general, and, second, because the *lex talionis* can be seen as a justification for capital punishment in particular: "life for life, eye for eye, tooth for tooth." Of course, this should make it clear that retributivism would almost certainly rule out as cruel and unusual the use of capital punishment for rape, or for any other crime but murder. But is the retributivist committed to the support of capital punishment for murder? Kant argued that because there is "no sameness of kind between death and remaining alive even under the most miserable conditions" only capital punishment can restore the balance of justice where murder has been committed.[17]

The retributive theory contains the foundation of a very different sort of argument, however.[18] It can lead us to ask how it is possible for us to continue to respect the moral capacity of another while we prepare for and carry out his execution. The answer to this question might depend on attitudes that do change over time. Perhaps the people involved in the ceremony surrounding the public beheading of a nobleman in the eighteenth century could continue to have profound respect for him as a moral being.[19] But ceremonial public executions would not be tolerated among us today. Given our surreptitious and mechanical approach to execution, it is hard to see that the condemned are treated as anything more than "objects to be . . . discarded." The condemned man's physical suffering may be minimized, but that is no more than we would do for a domestic animal to be disposed of. It is not the degree of suffering which might lead the retributivist to regard capital punishment as cruel and unusual, but its dehumanizing character, its total negation of the moral worth of the person to be executed.

I have not attempted here to give a justification of retributivism but only to establish that it would be a serious mistake not to include it among the alternative positions to be considered in gaining a full understanding of the issues involved in declaring the death penalty unconstitutional. Retributivism does offer a coherent and intuitively sound approach to understanding what the phrase "cruel and unusual punishment" can be taken to mean. It is not subject to the difficulties that beset positions like that developed by Long. And if it does not give us an easy answer to the question whether the death penalty is cruel and unusual, it does present the question to us in a form which presses us to make a principled judgment of the most serious sort: when, if ever, can we say that a person whom we continue to respect as a fellow member of a community founded on the principles of justice is deserving of death at our hands?

NOTES

[1] *Ethics* 83 (April 1973): 214–23.

[2] *Ibid.*, p. 220, n. 21.

[3] Kant, *The Metaphysical Elements of Justice*, trans. John Ladd (Indianapolis: Bobbs-Merrill Co., 1965), p. 100.

[4] See *Furman v. Georgia*, 92 S.Ct. 2726, 2779–80 (Marshall, J., concurring 1972), and the authorities cited at 2780, no. 86.

[5] See Moberly, *The Ethics of Punishment* (London: Faber & Faber, 1968); Herbert Morris, "Persons and Punishment," *Monist* 52 (October 1968); 475; Jeffrie Murphy, "Three Mistakes about Retributivism," *Analysis* 31 (April 1971): 166.

[6] See *Furman v. Georgia*, 92 S.Ct., 2726, 2779 (Marshall, J., concurring 1972).

[7] *Ibid.*, at 2761 (Stewart, J., concurring), 2836 (Powell, J., dissenting); Goldberg and Dershowitz, "Declaring the Death Penalty Unconstitutional," *Harvard Law Review* 83 (June 1970): 1773, 1796.

[8] Murphy, p. 166.

[9] Kant, p. 100.

[10] *Ibid.*, p. 101.

[11] The concept of the capacity for a sense of justice is developed in Rawls, "The Sense of Justice," *The Philosophical Review* 72 (1963); 281.

[12] *Republic*, trans. Cornford (Oxford: Oxford University Press, 1941), p. 13.

[13] Concurring in Trop v. Dulles, 356 U.S. 86, 102 (1958), and *Furman v. Georgia*, 92 S.Ct. 2726, 2742–48 (1972).

[14] *Furman v. Georgia*, at 2743.

[15] *Ibid.*, at 2748.

[16] See *Ibid.*, 92 S.Ct. 2726, 2779 (Marshall, J., concurring), 2761 (Stewart, J., concurring), 2836 (Powell, J., dissenting).

[17] Kant, p. 102.

[18] Moberly, on whose view I have drawn extensively here, is one leading retributivist who opposes capital punishment (see *The Ethics of Punishment*, pp. 296–99).

[19] See Kant, p. 103, where such an execution is used as an example.

DISSENTING OPINION IN GREGG v. GEORGIA

Justice Thurgood Marshall

The inquiry here is simply whether the death penalty is necessary to accomplish the legitimate legislative purposes in punishment, or whether a less severe penalty—life imprisonment—would do as well.

The two purposes that sustain the death penalty as nonexcessive in the Court's view are general deterrence and retribution. In Furman, I canvassed the relevant data on the deterrent effect of capital punishment. The state of knowledge at that point, after literally centuries of debate, was summarized as follows by a United Nations Committee:

"It is generally agreed between the retentionists and abolitionists, whatever their opinions about the validity of comparative studies of deterrence, that the data which now exist show no correlation between the existence of capital punishment and lower rates of capital crime."

The available evidence, I concluded in Furman, was convincing that "capital punishment is not necessary as a deterrent to crime in our society."

The Solicitor General in his amicus brief in these cases relies heavily on a study by Isaac Ehrlich, reported a year after Furman, to support the contention that the death penalty does deter murder. Since the Ehrlich study was not available at the time of Furman and since it is the first scientific study to suggest that the death penalty may have a deterrent effect, I will briefly consider its import.

The Ehrlich study focused on the relationship in the Nation as a whole between the homicide rate and "execution risk"—the fraction of persons convicted of murder who were actually executed. Comparing the differences in homicide rate and execution risk for the years 1933 to 1969, Ehrlich found that increases in execution risk were associated with increases in the homicide rate. But when he employed the statistical technique of multiple regression analysis to control for the influence of other variables posited to have an impact on the homicide rate, Ehrlich found a negative correlation between changes in the homicide rate and changes in execution risk. His tentative conclusion was that for the period from 1933 to 1967

each additional execution in the United States might have saved eight lives.

The methods and conclusions of the Ehrlich study have been severely criticized on a number of grounds. It has been suggested, for example, that the study is defective because it compares execution and homicide rates on a nationwide, rather than a state-by-state, basis. The aggregation of data from all States—including those that have abolished the death penalty—obscures the relationship between murder and execution rates. Under Ehrlich's methodology, a decrease in the execution risk in one State combined with an increase in the murder rate in another State would, all other things being equal, suggest a deterrent effect that quite obviously would not exist. Indeed, a deterrent effect would be suggested if, once again all other things being equal, one State abolished the death penalty and experienced no change in the murder rate, while another State experienced an increase in the murder rate.

The most compelling criticism of the Ehrlich study is that its conclusions are extremely sensitive to the choice of the time period included in the regression analysis. Analysis of Ehrlich's data reveals that all empirical support for the deterrent effect of capital punishment disappears when the five most recent years are removed from his time series—that is to say, whether a decrease in the execution risk corresponds to an increase or a decrease in the murder rate depends on the ending point of the sample period. This finding has cast severe doubts on the reliability of Ehrlich's tentative conclusions. Indeed, a recent regression study, based on Ehrlich's theoretical model but using cross-section state data for the years 1950 and 1960, found no support for the conclusion that executions act as a deterrent.

The Ehrlich study, in short, is of little, if any, assistance in assessing the deterrent impact of the death penalty. The evidence I reviewed in Furman remains convincing, in my view, that "capital punishment is not necessary as a deterrent to crime in our society." The justification for the death penalty must be found elsewhere.

The other principal purpose said to be served by the death penalty is retribution. The notion that retribution can serve as a moral justification for the sanction of death finds credence in the opinion of my Brothers STEWART, POWELL, and STEVENS, and that of my Brother WHITE in Roberts v. Louisiana. It is this notion that I find to be the most disturbing aspect of today's unfortunate decisions.

The concept of retribution is a multifaceted one, and any discussion of its role in the criminal law must be undertaken with caution. On one level, it can be said that the notion of retribution or reprobation is the basis of our insistence that only those who have broken the law be punished, and in this sense the notion is quite obviously central to a just system of criminal sanctions. But our recognition that retribution plays a crucial role in determining who may be punished by no means requires approval of retribution as a general justification for punishment. It is the question whether retribution can provide a moral justification for punishment—in particular, capital punishment—that we must consider.

My brothers STEWART, POWELL, and STEVENS offer the following explanation of the retributive justification for capital punishment:

> "'The instinct for retribution is part of the nature of man, and channeling that instinct in the administration of criminal justice serves an important purpose in promoting the stability of a society governed by law. When people begin to believe that organized society is unwilling or unable to impose upon criminal offenders the punishment they 'deserve,' then there are sown the seeds of anarchy—of self-help, vigilante justice, and lynch law.'"

This statement is wholly inadequate to justify the death penalty. As my Brother BRENNAN stated in Furman, "[t]here is no evidence whatever that utilization of imprisonment rather than death encourages private blood feuds and other disorders." It simply defies belief to suggest that the death penalty is necessary to prevent the American people from taking the law into their own hands.

In a related vein, it may be suggested that the expression of moral outrage through the imposition of the death penalty serves to reinforce basic moral values—that it marks some crimes as particularly offensive and therefore to be avoided. The argument is akin to a deterrence argument, but differs in that it contemplates the individual's shrinking from antisocial conduct, not because he fears punishment, but because he has been told in the strongest possible way that the conduct is wrong. This contention, like the previous one, provides no support for the death penalty. It is inconceivable that any individual concerned about conforming his conduct to what society says is "right" would fail to realize that murder is "wrong" if the penalty were simply life imprisonment.

The foregoing contentions—that society's expression of moral outrage through the imposition of the death penalty pre-empts the citizenry from taking the law into its own hands and reinforces moral values—are not retributive in the purest sense. They are essentially utilitarian in that they portray the death penalty as valuable because of its beneficial results. These justifications for the death penalty are inadequate because the penalty is, quite clearly I think, not necessary to the accomplishment of those results.

There remains for consideration, however, what might be termed the purely retributive justification for the death penalty—that the death penalty is appropriate, not because of its beneficial effect on society, but because the taking of the murderer's life is itself morally good. Some of the language of the opinion of my Brothers STEWART, POWELL, and STEVENS appears positively to embrace this notion of retribution for its own sake as a justification for capital punishment. They state:

> "[T]he decision that capital punishment may be the appropriate sanction in extreme cases is an expression of the community's belief that certain crimes are themselves so grievous an affront to humanity that the only adequate response may be the penalty of death."

They then quote with approval from Lord Justice Denning's remarks before the British Royal Commission on Capital Punishment:

> "'The truth is that some crimes are so outrageous that society insists on adequate punishment, because the wrong-doer deserves it, irrespective of whether it is a deterrent or not.'"

Of course, it may be that these statements are intended as no more than observations as to the popular demands that it is thought must be responded to in order to prevent anarchy. But the implication of the statements appears to me to be quite different— namely, that society's judgment that the murderer "deserves" death must be respected not simply because the preservation of order requires it, but because it is appropriate that society make the judgment and carry it out. It is this latter notion, in particular, that I consider to be fundamentally at odds with the Eighth Amendment. The mere fact that the community demands the murderer's life in return for the evil he has done cannot sustain the death penalty, for as JUSTICES STEWART, POWELL, and STEVENS remind us, "the Eighth Amendment demands more than that a challenged punishment be acceptable to contemporary society." To be sustained under the Eighth Amendment, the death penalty must "compor[t] with the basic concept of human dignity at the core of the Amendment,"; the objective in imposing it must be "[consistent] with our respect for the dignity of [other] men." Under these standards, the taking of life "because the wrongdoer deserves it" surely must fall, for such a punishment has as its very basis the total denial of the wrongdoer's dignity and worth.

The death penalty, unnecessary to promote the goal of deterrence or to further any legitimate notion of retribution, is an excessive penalty forbidden by the Eighth and Fourteenth Amendments. I respectfully dissent from the Court's judgment upholding the sentences of death imposed upon the petitioners in these cases.

ADDITIONAL READING

Franklin E. Zimring and Gordon Hawkins, *Capital Punishment and the American Agenda* (Cambridge, Mass.: Cambridge University Press, 1986). This excellent book places capital punishment within a world setting and draws the historical and sociological background for use of capital punishment in the United States.

Bruce N. Waller places the issue of capital punishment in the larger context of philosophical theories for the justification of punishment, in "From Hemlock to Lethal Injection: The Case for Self-Execution," *The International Journal of Applied Philosophy*, vol. 4, no. 4 (Fall 1989) 53–58.

Michael A. Mello has been a defense lawyer involved in death row cases for many years; his very readable book on the subject is *Dead Wrong: A Death Row Lawyer Speaks out Against Capital Punishment* (Madison: The University of Wisconsin Press, 1997).

A particularly interesting book, which examines the death penalty in light of the many mistaken convictions that have recently been overturned (many involving prisoners on death row), is Barry Scheck, Peter Neufeld, and Jim Dwyer, *Actual Innocence* (New York: Doubleday, 2000).

Two books offer interesting debates on the subject. E. Van den Haag and J. P. Conrad, *The Death Penalty: A Debate* (New York: Plenum, 1983) focuses more narrowly on the death penalty; for a fascinating debate that places the issue in a much larger context, see Jean Hampton and Jeffrie Murphy, *Forgiveness and Mercy* (Cambridge, Mass.: Cambridge University Press, 1988).

Among the many anthologies are Hugo Adam Bedau, *The Death Penalty in America*, 3rd ed. (New York: Oxford University Press, 1982); J. Feinberg and H. Gross, editors, *Punishment: Selected Readings* (Belmont, Calif.: Dickinson, 1975); and Austin Sarat, editor, *The Killing State: Capital Punishment in Law, Politics, and Culture* (New York: Oxford University Press, 1999).

Excellent anthologies on the more general issue of punishment are Robert M. Baird and Stuart E. Rosenbaum, *Philosophy of Punishment* (Buffalo, N.Y.: Prometheus, 1988); and Jeffrie G. Murphy, *Punishment and Rehabilitation*, 2nd ed. (Belmont, Calif.: Wadsworth, 1985).

EUTHANASIA

There are a few terms that will be useful in following this discussion. "Passive euthanasia" involves allowing death to occur when further treatment might have prolonged life; that is, passive euthanasia "allows nature to take its course." If a patient is dying of a painful cancer, and has only a few days to live, and the patient develops pneumonia that is treatable but will cause her death more swiftly if it is not treated, then *not* treating the pneumonia in order to allow a swifter and less painful death would count as *passive* euthanasia. If I cannot breathe without the help of a respirator, but I choose to stop the use of the respirator and thus soon die, that is again passive euthanasia. But if I am suffering from cancer, and wish to die more swiftly, and my physician injects me with a drug that will swiftly *cause* my death, that is a case of *active* euthanasia. In the Netherlands (where active euthanasia has been openly practiced for many years, and where it has recently been legalized by statute), no distinction is made between whether my doctor gives me a drug I take myself, or whether my doctor actually injects me with the drug: they simply count both as active euthanasia. In the United States, however, those two cases are carefully distinguished, and many writers consider 'physician-assisted suicide' (in which my physician prepares a lethal dose for me, but I take it myself) very different from 'active euthanasia' (in which my physician actually administers the lethal drug). Whether that difference is morally significant is a judgment you will have to make.

Euthanasia has been a controversial issue for many years, and the controversy shows no signs of going away. The literature on this controversy is immense, but two of the most interesting and insightful essays are by John D. Arras and Margaret P. Battin. They debate the ethics of 'physician-assisted suicide,' in which physicians provide terminally ill patients with a means of ending their lives swiftly and painlessly, thereby avoiding further suffering and deterioration; but the patients themselves must actually take the deadly potion (thus the physician *assists* in suicide, but does not actually carry out the killing). While Arras opposes and Battin favors physician-assisted suicide, they agree on what issues are important: particularly, the question of the effects of physician-assisted suicide on society and on medical practice and on the protection of vulnerable patients. Thus the essays not only debate a vital ethical question, but also demonstrate the difficulties in gauging the consequences of our acts and our policies.

PHYSICIAN-ASSISTED SUICIDE

A Tragic View

John D. Arras

INTRODUCTION

For many decades now, the call for physician-assisted suicide (PAS) and euthanasia have been perennial lost causes in American society. Each generation has thrown up an assortment of earnest reformers and cranks who, after attracting their fifteen minutes of fame, inevitably have been defeated by the combined weight of traditional law and morality. Incredibly, two recent federal appellate court decisions suddenly changed the legal landscape in this area, making the various states within their respective jurisdictions the first governments in world history, excepting perhaps the Nazi regime in Germany, to officially sanction PAS. Within the space of a month, both an eight to three majority of the United States Court of Appeals for the Ninth Circuit[1] on the West Coast, and a three-judge panel in the United States Court of Appeals for the Second Circuit,[2] in the Northeast, struck down long-standing state laws forbidding physicians to aid or abet their patients in acts of suicide. Within a virtual blink of an eye, the unthinkable had come to pass: PAS and euthanasia had emerged from their exile beyond the pale of law to occupy center stage in a dramatic public debate that eventually culminated in the United States Supreme Court's unanimous reversal of both lower court decisions in June 1997. . . .[3]

As a firm believer in patient autonomy, I find myself to be deeply sympathetic to the central values motivating the case for PAS and euthanasia; I have concluded, however, that these practices pose too great a threat to the rights and welfare of too many people to be legalized in this country at the present time. Central to my argument in this paper will be the claim that the recently overturned decisions of the circuit courts employ a form of case-based reasoning that is ill-suited to the development of sound social policy in this area. I shall argue that in order to do justice to the very real threats posed by the widespread social practices of PAS and euthanasia, we need to adopt precisely the kind of policy perspective that the circuit courts rejected on principle. Thus, this essay thus presents the case for a forward-looking, legislative approach to PAS and euthanasia, as opposed to an essentially backward-looking, judicial or constitutional approach.[4] Although I suggest below that the soundest legislative policy at the present time would be to extend the legal prohibition of PAS into the near future, I remain open to the possibility that a given legislature, presented with sufficient evidence of the reliability of various safeguards, might come to a different conclusion.

ARGUMENTS AND MOTIVATIONS IN FAVOR OF PAS/EUTHANASIA

Let us begin, then, with the philosophical case for PAS and euthanasia, which consists of two distinct prongs, both of which speak simply, directly, and powerfully to our commonsensical intuitions. First, there is the claim of autonomy, that all of us possess a right to self-determination in matters profoundly touching on such religious themes as life, death, and the meaning of suffering. . . . Second, PAS and/or euthanasia are merciful acts that deliver terminally ill patients from painful and protracted death. . . . For patients suffering from the final ravages of end-stage AIDS or cancer, a doctor's lethal prescription or injection can be, and often is, welcomed as a blessed relief. Accordingly, we should treat human beings at least as well as we treat grievously ill or injured animals by putting them, at their own request, out of their misery.

These philosophical reflections can be supplemented with a more clinical perspective addressed to the motivational factors lying behind many requests to die. Many people advocate legalization because they fear a loss of control at the end of life. They fear falling victim to the technological imperative; they fear dying in chronic and uncontrolled pain; they fear the psychological suffering attendant upon the relentless disintegration of the self; they fear, in short, a bad death. All of these fears, it so happens, are eminently justified. Physicians routinely ignore the documented wishes of patients and all-too-often allow patients to die with uncontrolled pain.[5] Studies of cancer patients have shown that over fifty percent suffer from unrelieved pain,[6] and many researchers have found that uncontrolled pain, particularly when accompanied by feelings of hopelessness and untreated depression, is a significant contributing factor for suicide and suicidal ideation.

Clinical depression is another major factor influencing patients' choice of suicide. Depression, accompanied by feelings of hopelessness, is the strongest predictor of suicide for both individuals who are terminally ill and those who are not. Yet most doctors are not trained to notice depression, especially in complex cases such as the elderly suffering from terminal illnesses. Even when doctors succeed in diagnosing depression, they often do not successfully treat it with readily available medications in sufficient amounts.

Significantly, the New York Task Force found that the vast majority of patients who request PAS or euthanasia can be treated successfully both for their depression and their pain, and that when they receive adequate psychiatric and palliative care, their requests to die usually are withdrawn.[7] In other words, patients given the requisite control over their lives and relief from depression and pain usually lose interest in PAS and euthanasia.

With all due respect for the power of modern methods of pain control, it must be acknowledged that a small percentage of patients suffer from conditions, both physical and psychological, that currently lie beyond the reach of the best medical and humane care. Some pain cannot be alleviated short of inducing a permanent state of unconsciousness in the patient, and some depression is unconquerable. For such unfortunate patients, the present law on PAS/euthanasia can represent an insuperable barrier to a dignified and decent death.[8]

OBJECTIONS TO PAS/EUTHANASIA

Opponents of PAS and euthanasia can be grouped into three main factions. One strongly condemns both practices as inherently immoral, as violations of the moral rule against killing the innocent. Most members of this group tend to harbor distinctly religious objections to suicide and euthanasia, viewing them as violations of God's dominion over human life. They argue that killing is simply wrong in itself, whether or not it is done out of respect for the patient's autonomy or out of concern for her suffering. Whether or not this position ultimately is justifiable from a theological point of view, its imposition on believers and non-believers alike is incompatible with the basic premises of a secular, pluralistic political order.

A second faction primarily objects to the fact that physicians are being called upon to do the killing. While conceding that killing the terminally ill or assisting in their suicides might not always be morally wrong for others to do, this group maintains that the participation of physicians in such practices undermines their role as healers and fatally compromises the physician-patient relationship.

Finally, a third faction readily grants that neither PAS nor active euthanasia, practiced by ordinary citizens or by physicians, are always morally wrong. On the contrary, this faction believes that in certain rare instances early release from a painful or intolerably degrading existence might constitute both a positive good and an important exercise of personal autonomy for the individual. Indeed, many members of this faction concede that should such a terrible fate befall them, they would hope to find a thoughtful, compassionate, and courageous physician to release them from their misery. But in spite of these important concessions, the members of this faction shrink from endorsing or regulating PAS and active euthanasia due to fears bearing on the social consequences of liberalization. This view is based on two distinct kinds of so-called "slippery slope" arguments: one bears on the inability to cabin PAS/euthanasia within the confines envisioned by its proponents; the other focuses on the likelihood of abuse, neglect, and mistake.

An Option Without Limits

The first version of the slippery slope argument contends that a socially sanctioned practice of PAS would in all likelihood prove difficult, if not impossible, to cabin within its originally anticipated boundaries. Proponents of legalization usually begin with a wholesomely modest policy agenda, limiting their suggested reforms to a narrow and highly specified range of potential candidates and practices. "Give us PAS," they ask, "not the more controversial practice of active euthanasia, for presently competent patients who are terminally ill and suffering unbearable pain." But the logic of the case for PAS, based as it is upon the twin pillars of patient autonomy and mercy, makes it highly unlikely that society could stop with this modest proposal once it had ventured out on the slope. As numerous other critics have pointed out, if autonomy is the prime consideration, then additional constraints based upon terminal illness or unbearable pain, or both, would appear hard to justify. Indeed, if autonomy is crucial, the requirement of unbearable suffering would appear to be entirely subjective. Who is to say, other than the patient herself, how much suffering is too much? Likewise, the requirement of terminal illness seems an arbitrary standard against which to judge patients' own subjective evaluation of their quality of life. If my life is no longer worth living, why should a terminally ill cancer patient be granted PAS but not me, merely because my suffering is due to my "non-terminal" amyotrophic lateral sclerosis (ALS) or intractable psychiatric disorder?

Alternatively, if pain and suffering are deemed crucial to the justification of legalization, it is hard to see how the proposed barrier of contemporaneous consent of competent patients could withstand serious erosion. If the logic of PAS is at all similar to that of forgoing life-sustaining treatments, and we have every reason to think it so, then it would seem almost inevitable that a

case soon would be made to permit PAS for incompetent patients who had left advance directives. That
would then be followed by a "substituted judgment"
test for patients who "would have wanted" PAS, and
finally an "objective" test would be developed for
patients (including newborns) whose best interests
would be served by PAS or active euthanasia even in
the absence of any subjective intent.

In the same way, the joint justifications of autonomy and mercy combine to undermine the plausibility
of a line drawn between PAS and active euthanasia.
As the authors of one highly publicized proposal have
come to see, the logic of justification for active
euthanasia is identical to that of PAS.[9] Legalizing
PAS, while continuing to ban active euthanasia,
would serve only to discriminate unfairly against
patients who are suffering and wish to end their lives,
but cannot do so because of some physical impair-
ment. Surely these patients, it will be said, are "the
worst-off group," and therefore they are the most in
need of the assistance of others who will do for them
what they can no longer accomplish on their own.

None of these initial slippery slope considerations amount to knock-down objections to further
liberalization of our laws and practices. After all, it is
not obvious that each of the highly predictable shifts
(e.g., from terminal to "merely" incurable, from contemporaneous consent to best interests, and from
PAS to active euthanasia), are patently immoral and
unjustifiable. Still, in pointing out this likely slippage,
the consequentialist opponents of PAS/euthanasia
are calling on society to think about the likely consequences of taking the first tentative step onto the
slope. If all of the extended practices predicted above
pose substantially greater risks for vulnerable patients
than the more highly circumscribed initial liberalization proposals, then we need to factor in these additional risks even as we ponder the more modest
proposals.[10]

The Likelihood of Abuse

The second prong of the slippery slope argument
argues that whatever criteria for justifiable PAS and
active euthanasia ultimately are chosen, abuse of the
system is highly likely to follow. In other words,
patients who fall outside the ambit of our justifiable

criteria will soon be candidates for death. This prong
resembles what I have elsewhere called an "empirical
slope" argument, as it is based not on the close logical
resemblance of concepts or justifications, but rather
on an empirical prediction of what is likely to happen
when we insert a particular social practice into our
existing social system.

In order to reassure skeptics, the proponents of
PAS/euthanasia concur that any potentially justifiable social policy in this area must meet at least the
following three requirements. The policy would have
to insist first, that all requests for death be truly voluntary; second, that all reasonable alternatives to
PAS and active euthanasia must be explored before
acceding to a patient's wishes; and, third, that a reliable system of reporting all cases must be established
in order to effectively monitor these practices and
respond to abuses. As a social pessimist on these matters, I believe, given social reality as we know it, that
all three assumptions are problematic.

With regard to the voluntariness requirement,
we pessimists contend that many requests would not
be sufficiently voluntary. In addition to the subtly
coercive influences of physicians and family members,
perhaps the most slippery aspect of this slope is the
highly predictable failure of most physicians to diagnose reliably and treat reversible clinical depression,
particularly in the elderly population. As one geriatric psychiatrist testified before the New York Task
Force, we now live in the "golden age" of treating
depression, but the "lead age" of diagnosing it. We
have the tools, but physicians are not adequately
trained and motivated to use them. Unless dramatic
changes are effected in the practice of medicine, we
can predict with confidence that many instances of
PAS and active euthanasia will fail the test of
voluntariness.

Second, there is the lingering fear that any legislative proposal or judicial mandate would have to be
implemented within the present social system marked
by deep and pervasive discrimination against the poor
and members of minority groups. We have every reason to expect that a policy that worked tolerably well
in an affluent community like Scarsdale or Beverly
Hills, might not work so well in a community like
Bedford-Stuyvesant or Watts, where your average citizen has little or no access to basic primary care, let

alone sophisticated care for chronic pain at home or in the hospital. There is also reason to worry about any policy of PAS initiated within our growing system of managed care, capitation, and physician incentives for delivering less care. Expert palliative care no doubt is an expensive and time-consuming proposition, requiring more, rather than less, time spent just talking with patients and providing them with humane comfort. It is highly doubtful that the context of physician-patient conversation within this new dispensation of "turnstile medicine" will be at all conducive to humane decisions untainted by subtle economic coercion.

In addition, given the abysmal and shameful track record of physicians in responding adequately to pain and suffering,[11] we also can confidently predict that in many cases all reasonable alternatives will not have been exhausted. Instead of vigorously addressing the pharmacological and psycho-social needs of such patients, physicians no doubt will continue to ignore, undertreat or treat many of their patients in an impersonal manner. The result is likely to be more depression, desperation, and requests for physician-assisted death from patients who could have been successfully treated. The root causes of this predictable failure are manifold, but high on the list is the inaccessibility of decent primary care to over thirty-seven million Americans. Other notable causes include an appalling lack of training in palliative care among primary care physicians and cancer specialists alike; discrimination in the delivery of pain control and other medical treatments on the basis of race and economic status; various myths shared by both physicians and patients about the supposed ill effects of pain medications; and restrictive state laws on access to opioids.

Finally, with regard to the third requirement, pessimists doubt that any reporting system would adequately monitor these practices. A great deal depends here on the extent to which patients and practitioners will regard these practices as essentially private matters to be discussed and acted upon within the privacy of the doctor-patient relationship. As the Dutch experience has conclusively demonstrated, physicians will be extremely loath to report instances of PAS and active euthanasia to public authorities, largely for fear of bringing the harsh glare of publicity upon the patients' families at a time when privacy is

most needed. The likely result of this predictable lack of oversight will be society's inability to respond appropriately to disturbing incidents and long-term trends. In other words, the practice most likely will not be as amenable to regulation as the proponents contend.

The moral of this story is that deeply seated inadequacies in physicians' training, combined with structural flaws in our health care system, can be reliably predicted to secure the premature deaths of many people who would in theory be excluded by the criteria of most leading proposals to legalize PAS. If this characterization of the status quo is at all accurate, then the problem will not be solved by well meaning assurances that abuses will not be tolerated, or that patients will, of course, be offered the full range of palliative care options before any decision for PAS is ratified.[12] While such regulatory solutions are possible in theory, and may well justly prevail in the future, we should be wary of legally sanctioning any negative right to be let alone by the state when the just and humane exercise of that right will depend upon the provision of currently nonexistent services. The operative analogy here, I fear, is our failed and shameful policy of "deinstutionalization," which left thousands of vulnerable and defenseless former residents of state psychiatric hospitals to fend for themselves on the streets, literally "rotting with their rights on." It is now generally agreed that the crucial flaw in this well-intended but catastrophic policy was our society's willingness to honor such patients' negative right to be free of institutional fetters without having first made available reliable local alternatives to institutionalization. The operative lesson for us here is that judges and courts are much better at enunciating negative rights than they are at providing the services required for their successful implementation. . . .

TOWARDS A POLICY OF PRUDENT (LEGAL) RESTRAINT AND AGGRESSIVE (MEDICAL) INTERVENTION

In contrast to the judicial approach, which totally vindicates the value of patient autonomy at the expense of protecting the vulnerable, my own preferred approach to a social policy of PAS and euthanasia conceives of this debate as posing an essentially "tragic choice."[13] It frankly acknowledges that whatever choice we make, whether we opt for a reaffirmation of the current legal restraints or for a policy of legitimization and regulation, there are bound to be "victims." The victims of the current policy are easy to identify: They are on the news, the talk shows, the documentaries, and often on Dr. Kevorkian's roster of so-called "patients." The victims of legalization, by contrast, will be largely hidden from view; they will include the clinically depressed eighty-year-old man who could have lived for another year of good quality if only he had been adequately treated, and the fifty-year-old woman who asks for death because doctors in her financially stretched HMO cannot, or will not, effectively treat her unrelenting, but mysterious, pelvic pain. Perhaps eventually, if we slide far enough down the slope, the uncommunicative stroke victim, whose distant children deem an earlier death to be a better death, will fall victim. There will be others besides these, many coming from the ranks of the uninsured and the poor. To the extent that minorities and the poor already suffer from the effects of discrimination in our health care system, it is reasonable to expect that any system of PAS and euthanasia will exhibit similar effects, such as failure to access adequate primary care, pain management, and psychiatric diagnosis and treatment. Unlike Dr. Kevorkian's "patients," these victims will not get their pictures in the papers, but they all will have faces and they will all be cheated of good months or perhaps even years.

This "tragic choice" approach to social policy on PAS/euthanasia takes the form of the following argument formulated at the legislative level. First, the number of "genuine cases" justifying PAS, active euthanasia, or both, will be relatively small. Patients who receive good personal care, good pain relief, treatment for depression, and adequate psycho-social supports tend not to persist in their desire to die.

Second, the social risks of legalization are serious and highly predictable. They include the expansion of these practices to nonvoluntary cases, the advent of active euthanasia, and the widespread failure to pursue readily available alternatives to suicide motivated by pain, depression, hopelessness, and lack of access to good primary medical care.

Third, rather than propose a momentous and dangerous policy shift for a relatively small number of "genuine cases"—a shift that would surely involve a great deal of persistent social division and strife analogous to that involved in the abortion controversy—we should instead attempt to redirect the public debate toward a goal on which we can and should all agree, namely the manifest and urgent need to reform the way we die in America. Instead of pursuing a highly divisive and dangerous campaign for PAS, we should attack the problem at its root with an ambitious program of reform in the areas of access to primary care and the education of physicians in palliative care. At least as far as the "slippery slope" opponents of PAS are concerned, we should thus first see to it that the vast majority of people in this country have access to adequate, affordable, and nondiscriminatory primary and palliative care. At the end of this long and arduous process, when we finally have an equitable, effective, and compassionate health care system in place, one that might be compared favorably with that in the Netherlands, then we might well want to reopen the discussion of PAS and active euthanasia.

Finally, there are those few unfortunate patients who truly are beyond the pale of good palliative, hospice, and psychiatric care. The opponents of legalization must face up to this suffering remnant and attempt to offer creative and humane solutions. One possibility is for such patients to be rendered permanently unconscious by drugs until such time, presumably not a long time, as death finally claims them. Although some will find such an option to be aesthetically unappealing, many would find it a welcome relief. Other patients beyond the reach of the best palliative and hospice care could take their own lives, either by well-known traditional means, or with the help of a physician who could sedate them while they refused further food and (life extending) fluids. Finally, those who find this latter option to be unacceptable might still be able to find a compassionate physician who, like Dr. Timothy Quill, will ultimately be willing, albeit in fear and trembling, to "take small risks for people they really know and care about." Such actions will continue to take place within the privacy of the patient-physician relationship, however, and thus will not threaten vulnerable patients and the social fabric to the same extent as would result from full legalization and regulation.

As the partisans of legalized PAS correctly point out, the covert practice of PAS will not be subject to regulatory oversight, and is thus capable of generating its own abuses and slippery slope. Still, I believe that the ever-present threat of possible criminal sanctions and revocation of licensure will continue to serve, for the vast majority of physicians, as powerful disincentives to abuse the system. Moreover, as suggested earlier, it is highly unlikely that the proposals for legalization would result in truly effective oversight.

CONCLUSION

Instead of conceiving this momentous debate as a choice between, on the one hand, legalization and regulation with all of their attendant risks, and on the other hand, the callous abandonment of patients to their pain and suffering, enlightened opponents must recommend a positive program of clinical and social reforms. On the clinical level, physicians must learn how to really listen to their patients, to unflinchingly engage them in sensitive discussions of their needs and the meaning of their requests for assisted death, to deliver appropriate palliative care, to distinguish fact from fiction in the ethics and law of pain relief, to diagnose and treat clinical depression, and finally, to ascertain and respect their patients' wishes for con-

trol regarding the forgoing of life-sustaining treatments. On the social level, opponents of PAS must aggressively promote major initiatives in medical and public education regarding pain control, in the sensitization of insurance companies and licensing agencies to issues of the quality of dying, and in the reform of state laws that currently hinder access to pain-relieving medications.

In the absence of an ambitious effort in the direction of aggressive medical and social reform, I fear that the medical and nursing professions will have lost whatever moral warrant and credibility they might still have in continuing to oppose physician-assisted suicide and active euthanasia. As soon as these reforms are in place, however, we might then wish to proceed slowly and cautiously with experiments in various states to test the overall benefits of a policy of legalization. Until that time, however, we are not well served as a society by court decisions allowing for legalization of PAS. The Supreme Court has thus reached a sound decision in ruling out a constitutional right to PAS. As the Justices acknowledged, however, this momentous decision will not end the moral debate over PAS and euthanasia. Indeed, it should and hopefully will intensify it.

NOTES

[1] *Compassion in Dying* v. *Washington,* 79 F.3d 790, 838 (9th Cir. 1996).

[2] *Quill* v. *Vacco,* 80 F.3d 716, 731 (2nd Cir. 1996).

[3] *Vacco, Attorney General of New York. et al.* v. *Quill et al.,* certiorari to the United States Court of Appeals for the Second Circuit, No. 95–1858. Argued January 8, 1997—Decided June 26, 1997. *Washington et al.* v. *Glucksberg et al.,* certiorari to the United States Court of Appeals for the Ninth Circuit, No. 96–110. Argued January 8, 1997—Decided June 26, 1997.

[4] My stance on these issues has been profoundly influenced by my recent work with the New York State Task Force on Life and the Law (hereinafter "Task Force") to come to grips with this issue.

[5] "A Controlled Trial to Improve Care for Seriously Ill Hospitalized Patients: The Study to Understand Prognoses and Preferences for Outcomes and Risks of Treatments" (SUPPORT), *Journal of the American Medical Association* 274 (Nov. 22, 1995): 1591–92.

[6] Task Force, *When Death Is Sought,* x–xi.

[7] Task Force, *When Death Is Sought,* xiv.

[8] The preceding section thus signals two important points of agreement with the so-called "Philosophers' Brief" submitted to the Supreme Court in *Compassion in Dying* and *Vacco* by Ronald Dworkin, Thomas Nagel, Robert Nozick, John Rawls, Thomas Scanlon, and Judith Jarvis Thomson. I agree that individuals in the throes of a painful or degrading

terminal illness may well have a very strong moral and even legal interest in securing PAS. I also agree that the pain and suffering of a small percentage of dying patients cannot be adequately controlled by currently available medical interventions. As we shall see, however, I disagree with the philosophers' conclusion that this interest is sufficiently strong in the face of current medical and social inadequacies as to justify a legal right that would void the reasonably cautious prohibitions of PAS and euthanasia in effect in every state.

[9]Cassel et al., "Care of the Hopelessly Ill," 1380–84. See also Franklin G. Miller et al., "Regulating Physician-Assisted Death," *New England Journal of Medicine* 331(1994): 199–23 (conceding by the untenability of the previous distinction).

[10]Professors Dworkin, et al. consistently fail to mention the possibility, let alone the high likelihood, of this first sort of slippage; I take this to be a serious omission both in their joint brief and in Dworkin's individually authored articles on this subject. These authors simply assume (with the plaintiffs and circuit court majority opinions) that this right will be restricted by means of procedural safeguards to presently competent, incurably ill individuals manifesting great pain and suffering due to physical illness. (For evidence of Dworkin's continuing failure to acknowledge this problem, see his assessment of the Supreme Court opinions in "Assisted Suicide: What the Court Really Said," *New York Review of Books* 44, no. 14 (Sept. 25, 1997); 40–44. Failure to notice this sort of dynamic might be due either to the philosophers' lack of familiarity with the recent history of bioethics or to their belief that the social risks of PAS are equivalent to the risks inherent in the widely accepted practice of forgoing life-sustaining treatments, and thus that such slippage would not present any additional risk. The latter assumption is, of course, vigorously contested by the opponents of PAS and euthanasia.

[11]Task Force, *When Death Is Sought*, 43–47. "Despite dramatic advances in pain management, the delivery of pain relief is grossly inadequate in clinical practice. . . . Studies have shown that only 2 to 60 percent of cancer pain is treated adequately." *Ibid.*, 43.

[12]See, e.g., Ronald Dworkin, "Introduction to the Philosophers' Brief," *New York Review of Books*, 41–42; and Dworkin, "Assisted Suicide: What the Court Really Said," 44.

[13]For an explication of the notion of a "tragic choice" in the sense that I employ here, see Guido Calabresi and Philip Bobbit, *Tragic Choices* (New York: W.W. Norton, 1978).

EUTHANASIA

The Way We Do It, the Way They Do It

Margaret P. Battin

Because we tend to be rather myopic in our discussions of death and dying, especially about the issues of active euthanasia and assisted suicide, it is valuable to place the question of how we go about dying in an international context. We do not always see that our own cultural norms may be quite different from those of other nations and that our background assumptions and actual practices differ dramatically—even when the countries in question are all developed industrial nations with similar cultural ancestries, religious traditions, and economic circumstances. I want to explore the three rather different approaches to end-of-life dilemmas prevalent in the United States, the Netherlands, and Germany—developments mirrored in Australia, Belgium, Switzerland, and elsewhere in the developed world—and consider how a society might think about which model of approach to dying is most appropriate for it.

THREE BASIC MODELS OF DYING

The Netherlands, Germany, and the United States are all advanced industrial democracies. They all have sophisticated medical establishments and life expectancies over 75 years of age; their populations are all characterized by an increasing proportion of older persons. They are all in what has been called the fourth stage of the epidemiologic transition[1]—that stage of societal development in which it is no longer the case that the majority of the population dies of acute parasitic or infectious diseases, often with rapid, unpredictable onsets and sharp fatality curves (as was true in earlier and less developed societies); rather, in modern industrial societies, the majority of a population—perhaps as much as two-thirds, or more—dies of degenerative diseases, especially delayed-degenerative diseases that are characterized by late, slow onset and extended decline. This is the case throughout the developed world. Accidents and suicide claim some, as do infectious diseases like AIDS, pneumonia, and influenza, but most people in highly industrialized countries die from heart disease (by no means always suddenly fatal); cancer; atherosclerosis; chronic obstructive pulmonary disease; diabetes, liver, kidney, or other organ disease; or degenerative neurological disorders. In the developed world, we die not so much from attack by outside diseases but from gradual disintegration. Thus, all three of these modern industrial countries—the United States, the Netherlands, and Germany—are alike in facing a common problem: how to deal with the characteristic new ways in which we die.

Dealing with Dying in the United States

In the United States, we have come to recognize that the maximal extension of life-prolonging treatment in these late-life degenerative conditions is often inappropriate. Although we could keep the machines and tubes—the respirators, intravenous lines, feeding tubes—hooked up for extended periods, we recognize that this is inhumane, pointless, and financially impossible. Instead, as a society we have developed a number of mechanisms for dealing with these hopeless situations, all of which involve withholding or withdrawing various forms of treatment.

Some mechanisms for withholding or withdrawing treatments are exercised by the patient who is confronted by such a situation or who anticipates it. These include refusal of treatment, the patient-executed Do Not Resuscitate (DNR) order, the Living Will, and the Durable Power of Attorney. Others are mechanisms for decision by second parties about a patient who is no longer competent or never was competent, reflected in a long series of court cases from *Quinlan, Saikewicz, Spring, Eichner, Barber, Bartling, Conroy, Brophy*, the trio *Farrell, Peter*, and *Jobes*, to *Cruzan*. These cases delineate the precise circumstances under which it is appropriate to withhold or withdraw various forms of therapy, including respiratory support, chemotherapy, dialysis, antibiotics in intercurrent infections, and artificial nutrition and hydration. Thus, during the past quarter-century, roughly since *Quinlan* (1976), the U.S. has developed an impressive body of case law and state statutes that protects, permits, and facilitates the characteristic American strategy of dealing with end-of-life situations. These cases provide a framework for withholding or withdrawing treatment when physicians and family members believe there is no medical or moral point in going on. This has sometimes been termed *passive euthanasia;* more often, it is simply called *allowing to die*.

Indeed, "allowing to die" has become ubiquitous in the United States. For example, a 1988 study found that of the 85% of deaths in the United States that occurred in health care institutions, including hospitals, nursing homes, and other facilities, about 70% involved electively withholding some form of life-sustaining treatment.[2] A 1989 study found that 85–90% of critical care professionals said they were withholding or withdrawing life-sustaining treatments from patients who were "deemed to have irreversible disease and are terminally ill."[3] A 1997 study of limits to life-sustaining care found that between 1987–88 and 1992–93, recommendations to withhold or withdraw life support prior to death increased from 51% to 90% in the intensive-care units studied.[4] Rates of withholding therapy such as ventilator support, surgery, and dialysis were found in yet another study to be substantial, and to increase with age.[5] A 1994/95 study of 167 intensive-care units—all the ICUs associated with U.S. training programs in critical care medicine or pulmonary and critical care medicine—found that in 75% of deaths, some form of care was withheld or withdrawn.[6] It has been estimated that 1.3 million American deaths a year follow decisions to withhold life support;[7] this is a majority of the just over 2 million American deaths per year.

In recent years, the legitimate use of withholding and withdrawing treatment has increasingly been understood to include practices likely or certain to result in death. The administration of escalating doses of morphine in a dying patient, which, it has been claimed, will depress respiration and so hasten death, is accepted under the (Catholic) principle of double effect provided the medication is intended to relieve pain and merely foreseen but not intended to result in death; this practice is not considered killing or active hastening of death. The use of "terminal sedation," in which a patient dying in pain is sedated into unconsciousness while artificial nutrition and hydration are withheld, is also recognized as medically and legally acceptable; it too is understood as a form of "allowing to die," not active killing. With the single exception of Oregon, where physician-assisted suicide became legal in 1997[8], withholding and withdrawing treatment and related forms of allowing to die are the only legally recognized ways we in the United States go about dealing with dying. A number of recent studies have shown that many physicians—in all states studied—do receive requests for assistance in suicide or active euthanasia and that a substantial number of these physicians have complied with one or more such requests; however, this more direct assistance in dying takes place entirely out of sight of the law. Except in Oregon, *allowing to die,* but not *causing to die,* has been the only legally protected alternative to maximal treatment legally recognized in the United States; it remains America's—and American medicine's—official posture in the face of death.

Dealing with Dying in the Netherlands

In the Netherlands, although the practice of withholding and withdrawing treatment is similar to that in the United States, voluntary active euthanasia and physician assistance in suicide are also available responses to end-of-life situations.[9] Active euthanasia, understood as the termination of the life of the patient at the patient's explicit and persistent request, is the more frequent form of directly assisted dying and most discussion in the Netherlands has concerned it rather than assistance in suicide, though the

conceptual difference is not regarded as great: many cases of what the Dutch term *voluntary active euthanasia* involve initial self-administration of the lethal dose by the patient but procurement of death by the physician, and many cases of what is termed *physician-assisted suicide* involve completion of the lethal process by the physician if a self-administered drug does not prove fully effective. Although until 2001 they were still technically illegal under statutory law, and even with legalization remain an "exception" to those provisions of the Dutch Penal Code which prohibit killing on request and intentional assistance in suicide, active euthanasia and assistance in suicide have long been widely regarded as legal, or rather *gedoogd*, legally "tolerated," and have in fact been deemed justified (not only non-punishable) by the courts when performed by a physician if certain conditions were met. Voluntary active euthanasia (in the law, called "life-ending on request") and physician-assisted suicide are now fully legal by statue under these guidelines. Dutch law protects the physician who performs euthanasia or provides assistance in suicide from prosecution for homicide if these guidelines, known as the conditions of "due care," are met.

Over the years, the guidelines have been stated in various ways. They contain six central provisions:

1. that the patient's request be voluntary and well-considered;
2. that the patient be undergoing or about to undergo intolerable suffering, that is, suffering which is lasting and unbearable;
3. that all alternatives acceptable to the patient for relieving the suffering have been tried, and that in the patient's view there is no other reasonable solution;
4. that the patient have full information about his situation and prospects;
5. that the physician consult with a second physician who has examined the patient and whose judgment can be expected to be independent;
6. that in performing euthanasia or assisting in suicide, the physician act with due care.

Of these criteria, it is the first that is held to be central: euthanasia may be performed only at the *voluntary* request of the patient. This criterion is also understood to require that the patient's request be a stable, enduring, reflective one—not the product of a transitory impulse. Every attempt is to be made to rule out depression, psychopathology, pressures from family members, unrealistic fears, and other factors compromising voluntariness, though depression is not in itself understood to preclude such choice. Euthanasia may be performed *only* by a physician, not by a nurse, family member, or other party.

In 1990, a comprehensive, nationwide study requested by the Dutch government, popularly known as the Remmelink Commission report, provided the first objective data about the incidence of euthanasia and physician-assisted suicide.[10] This study also provided information about other medical decisions at the end of life, particularly withholding or withdrawal of treatment and the use of life-shortening doses of opioids for the control of pain, as well as direct termination. The Remmelink report was supplemented by a study focusing particularly carefully on the characteristics of patients and the nature of their euthanasia requests.[11] Five years later, the researchers from these two studies jointly conducted a major new nationwide study replicating much of the previous Remmelink inquiry, providing empirical data both about current practice in the Netherlands and change over a five-year period.[12] A third nationwide study was published in 2003,[13] thus providing sixteen years of comprehensive data.

About 140,000 people die in the Netherlands every year, and of these deaths, about 30% are sudden and unexpected, while the majority are predictable and foreseen, usually the result of degenerative illness comparatively late in life. Of the total deaths in the Netherlands, about 20.2% involve decisions to withhold or withdraw treatment in situations where continuing treatment would probably have prolonged life; another 20.1% involve the "double effect" use of opioids to relieve pain but in dosages probably sufficient to shorten life. Only a small fraction of people who die receive euthanasia—in 2001, about 2.4%—and an even smaller fraction, 0.2%, receive physician-assisted suicide. Of patients who do receive euthanasia or physician-assisted suicide, about 80% are dying of cancer, while 3% have cardiovascular disease and 4% neurological disease, primarily ALS.

However, the 1990 Remmelink report also revealed that another 0.8% of patients who died did so as the result of life-terminating procedures not techni-cally called euthanasia, without explicit, current request. These cases, known as "the 1000 cases," unleashed highly exaggerated claims that patients were being killed against their wills. In fact, in about half of these cases, euthanasia had been previously discussed with the patient or the patient had expressed in a previous phase of the disease a wish for euthanasia if his or her suffering became unbearable ("Doctor, please don't let me suffer too long"); and in the other half, the patient was no longer competent and was near death, clearly suffering grievously although verbal contact had become impossible.[14] In 91% of these cases without explicit, current request, life was shortened by less than a week, and in 33% by less than a day.

Over the next decade, as revealed in the 1995 and 2003 nationwide studies, the proportion of cases of euthanasia rose slightly (associated, the authors conjectured, with the aging of the population and an increase in the proportion of deaths due to cancer, that condition in which euthanasia is most frequent); the proportion of cases of assisted suicide had remained about the same. The proportion of cases of life termination without current explicit request declined slightly to 0.7%, down from the notorious 1000 to about 900. In 1990, a total of 2.9% of all deaths had involved euthanasia and related practices; by 2001 this total was about 3.7%.[15] In the early days of openly tolerated euthanasia, comparatively few cases were reported as required to the Public Prosecutor; there has been a dramatic gain since reporting procedures have been revised to require reporting to a review committee rather than to the police, and about 54% are now reported. However, there are no major differences between reported and unreported cases in terms of the patient's characteristics, clinical conditions, or reasons for the action.[16] Euthanasia is performed in about 1:25 of deaths that occur at home, about 1:75 of hospital deaths, and about 1:800 of nursing home deaths. The Netherlands has now established regional review committees for such cases, and has initiated hospice-style pain management programs complete with a 24-hour phone-in consultation services for physicians confronted by euthanasia requests.

Although euthanasia is thus not frequent, a small fraction of the total annual mortality, it is nevertheless a conspicuous option in terminal illness, well-known to both physicians and the general public. There has been very widespread public discussion of the issues that arise with respect to euthanasia during the last quarter-century, and surveys of public opinion show that public support for a liberal euthanasia policy has been growing: from 40% in 1966 to 81% in 1988, then to about 90% by 2000. Doctors, too, support the practice, and although there has been a vocal opposition group, it has remained in the clear minority. Some 57% of Dutch physicians say that they have performed euthanasia or provided assistance in suicide, and an additional 30% say that although they have not actually done so, they can conceive of situations in which they would be prepared to do so. Ten percent say they would never perform it but would refer the patient to another physician. The proportion of physicians who say they not only would not do so themselves but would not refer a patient who requested it to a physician who would dropped from 4% in 1990 to 3% in 1995 to 1% in 2001. Thus, although many physicians who have performed euthanasia say that they would be most reluctant to do so again and that "only in the face of unbearable suffering and with no alternatives would they be prepared to take such action,"[17] all three nationwide studies have shown that the majority of Dutch physicians accept the practice. Surveying the changes over the 5-year period between 1990–1995, the authors of the nationwide study also commented that the data do not support claims of a slippery slope,[18] and the more recent studies show no such pattern either.

In general, pain alone is not the basis for deciding upon euthanasia, since pain can, in most cases, be effectively treated; only a third of Dutch physicians think that adequate pain control and terminal care make euthanasia redundant, and that number has been dropping. Rather, the "intolerable suffering" mentioned in the second criterion is understood to mean suffering that is intolerable in the patient's (rather than the physician's) view, and can include a fear of or unwillingness to endure *entluistering*, that gradual effacement and loss of personal identity that characterizes the end stages of many terminal illnesses. In very exceptional circumstances, the Supreme Court ruled in the *Chabot* case of 1994, physician-assisted suicide may be justified for a patient with non-somatic, psychiatric illness like intractable depression, but such cases are extremely rare and require heightened scrutiny.

In a year, about 35,000 patients seek reassurance from their physicians that they will be granted euthanasia if their suffering becomes severe; there are about 9,700 explicit requests, and about two-thirds of these are turned down, usually on the grounds that there is some other way of treating the patient's suffering. In 14% of cases in 1990, the denial was based on the presence of depression or psychiatric illness.

In the Netherlands, many hospitals now have protocols for the performance of euthanasia; these serve to ensure that the legal guidelines have been met. However, euthanasia is often practiced in the patient's home, typically by the general practitioner who is the patient's long-term family physician. Euthanasia is usually performed after aggressive hospital treatment has failed to arrest the patient's terminal illness; the patient has come home to die, and the family physician is prepared to ease this passing. Whether practiced at home or in the hospital, it is believed that euthanasia usually takes place in the presence of the family members, perhaps the visiting nurse, and often the patient's pastor or priest. Many doctors say that performing euthanasia is never easy but that it is something they believe a doctor ought to do for his or her patient when the patient genuinely wants it and nothing else can help.

Thus, in the Netherlands a patient who is facing the end of life has an option not openly practiced in the United States, except Oregon: to ask the physician to bring his or her life to an end. Although not everyone in the Netherlands does so—indeed, over 96% of people who die in a given year do not do so in this way—it is a choice legally recognized and widely understood.

Facing Death in Germany

In part because of its very painful history of Nazism, Germany medical culture has insisted that doctors should have no role in directly causing death. As in the other countries with advanced medical systems, withholding and withdrawing of care is widely used to avoid the unwanted or inappropriate prolongation of life when the patient is already dying, but there has been vigorous and nearly universal opposition in German public discourse to the notion of active euthanasia, at least in the horrific, politically-motivated sense associated with Nazism. In the last few years, some

Germans have begun to approve of euthanasia in the Dutch sense, based on the Greek root *eu-thanatos*, or "good death," a voluntary choice by the patient for an easier death, but many Germans still associate euthanasia with the politically-motivated exterminations by the Nazis, and view the Dutch as stepping out on a dangerously slippery slope.

However, although under German law killing on request (including voluntary euthanasia) is illegal, German law has not prohibited assistance in suicide since the time of Frederick the Great (1742), provided the person is *tatherrschaftsfähig*, capable of exercising control over his or her actions, and also acting out of *freiverantwortliche Wille*, freely responsible choice. Doctors are prohibited from assistance in suicide not by law but by the policies and code of ethics of the *Bundesärztekammer*, the German medical association.[19] Furthermore, any person, physician or otherwise, has a duty to rescue a person who is unconscious. Thus, medical assistance in suicide is limited, but it is possible for a family member or friend to assist in a person's suicide, for instance by providing a lethal drug, as long as the person is competent and acting freely and the assister does not remain with the person after unconsciousness sets in.

Taking advantage of this situation, there has developed a private organization, the *Deutsche Gesellschaft für Humanes Sterben* (DGHS), or German Society for Dying in Dignity, which provides support to its very extensive membership in many end-of-life matters, including choosing suicide as an alternative to terminal illness. Of course, not all Germans are members of this organization and many are not sympathetic with its aims, yet the notion of self-directed ending of one's own life in terminal illness is widely understood as an option. Although since 1993 the DGHS has not itself supplied such information for legal reasons, it tells its members how to obtain the booklet "Departing Drugs," published in Scotland, and other information about ending life, if they request it, provided they have been a member for one year and have not received medical or psychotherapeutic treatment for depression or other psychiatric illness during the last three years. The information includes a list of prescription drugs, together with the specific dosages necessary for producing a certain, painless death. The DGHS does not itself sell or supply lethal drugs[20]; rather, it recommends that the member approach a physician for a prescription for the drug desired, asking, for example, for a barbiturate to help with sleep. If necessary, the DGHS has been willing to arrange for someone to obtain drugs from neighboring countries, including France, Italy, Spain, Portugal, and Greece, where they may be available without prescription. It also makes available the so-called Exit Bag, a plastic bag used with specific techniques for death by asphyxiation. The DGHS provides and trains family members in what it calls *Sterbebegleitung* (accompaniment in dying), which may take the form of simple presence with a person who is dying, but may also involve direct assistance to a person who is committing suicide, up until unconsciousness sets in. The *Sterbebegleiter* is typically a layperson, not someone medically trained, and physicians play no role in assisting in these cases of suicide. Direct active *Sterbehilfe*—active euthanasia—is illegal under German law. But active indirect *Sterbehilfe*, understood as assistance in suicide, is not illegal, and the DGHS provides counseling in how a "death with dignity" may be achieved in this way.

To preclude suspicion by providing evidence of the person's intentions, the DGHS also provides a form—printed on a single sheet of distinctive purple paper—to be signed once when joining the organization, documenting that the person has reflected thoroughly on the possibility of "free death" (*Freitod*) or suicide in terminal illness as a way of releasing oneself from severe suffering, and expressing the intention to determine the time and character of one's own death. The person then signs this "free death directive" or "suicide decision declaration" (*Freitodverfügung*) again at the time of the suicide, leaving it beside the body as evidence that the act is not impetuous or coerced. The form also requests that, if the person is discovered before the suicide is complete, no rescue measures be undertaken. Because assisting suicide is not illegal in Germany (provided the person is competent and in control of his or her own will, and thus not already unconscious), there has been no legal risk for family members, the *Sterbebegleiter*, or others in reporting information about the methods and effectiveness of suicide attempts, and at least in the past the DGHS has encouraged its network of regional bureaus, located in major cities throughout the country, to facilitate feedback. On this basis, it has regularly updated and revised the drug information provided. There has been no legal risk in remaining with the patient to assist him or her at the bedside, that is, at least until recent legal threats.

Open, legal assistance in suicide has been supported by a feature of the German language that makes it possible to conceptualize it in a comparatively benign way. While English, French, Spanish, and many other languages have just a single primary word for suicide, German has four: *Selbstmord, Selbsttötung, Suizid,* and *Freitod,* of which the latter has comparatively positive, even somewhat heroic connotations.[21] Thus German-speakers can think about the deliberate termination of their lives in a linguistic way not easily available to speakers of other languages. The negatively-rooted term *Selbstmord* ("self-murder") can be avoided; the comparatively neutral terms *Selbsttötung* ("self-killing") and *Suizid* ("suicide") can be used, and the positively-rooted term *Freitod* ("free death") can be reinforced. The DGHS has frequently used *Freitod* rather than German's other, more negative terms to describe the practice with which it provides assistance.

No reliable figures are available about the number of suicides with which the DGHS has assisted, and, as in the Netherlands, the actual frequency of directly assisted death is probably small: most Germans who die as a result of medical decision-making, like most Dutch and most Americans, die as treatment is withheld or withdrawn or as opiates are administered in doses that foreseeably but not intentionally shorten life—that is, by being "allowed to die." Yet it is fair to say, both because of the legal differences and the different conceptual horizons of German-speakers, that the option of self-produced death outside the medical system is more clearly open in Germany than it has been in the Netherlands or the United States.

In recent years, the DGHS has decreased its emphasis on suicide, now thinking of it as a "last resort" when pain control is inadequate—and turned much of its attention to the development of other measures for protecting the rights of the terminally ill, measures already available in many other countries. It distributes newly legalized advance directives, including living wills and durable powers of attorney, as well as organ-donation documents. It provides information about pain control, palliative care, and Hospice. It offers information about suicide prevention. Yet, despite various legal threats, it remains steadfast in

defense of the terminally ill patient's right to self-determination, including the right to suicide, and continues to be supportive of patients who make this choice.

To be sure, assisted suicide is not the only option open to terminally ill patients in Germany, and the choice may be infrequent. Reported suicide rates in Germany are only moderately higher than in the Netherlands or the United States, though there is reason to think that terminal-illness suicides in all countries are often reported as deaths from the underlying disease. Although there is political pressure from right-to-die organizations to change the law to permit voluntary active euthanasia in the way understood in the Netherlands, Germany is also seeing increasing emphasis on help in dying, like that offered by Hospice, that does not involve direct termination. Whatever the pressures, the DGHS is a conspicuous, widely known organization, and many Germans appear to be aware that assisted suicide is available and not illegal even if they do not use its services.

OBJECTIONS TO THE THREE MODELS OF DYING

In response to the dilemmas raised by the new circumstances of death, in which the majority of people in the advanced industrial nations die after an extended period of terminal deterioration, different countries develop different practices. The United States, with the sole exception of Oregon, legally permits only withholding and withdrawal of treatment, "double effect" uses of high doses of opiates, and terminal sedation, all conceived of as "allowing to die." The Netherlands permits these, but also permits voluntary active euthanasia and physician-assisted suicide. Germany rejects physician-performed euthanasia, but, at least until recent legal threats, permits assisted suicide not assisted by a physician. These three serve as the principal types or models of response to end-of-life dilemmas in the developed world. To be sure, all of these practices are currently undergoing evolution, and in some ways they are becoming more alike: Germany is paying new attention to the rights of patients to execute advance directives and thus to have treatment withheld or withdrawn, and public surveys reveal considerable support for euthanasia in the

Dutch sense, voluntary active aid-in-dying under careful controls. In the Netherlands, a 1995 policy statement of the Royal Dutch Medical Association expressed a careful preference for physician-assisted suicide in preference to euthanasia, urging that physicians encourage patients who request euthanasia to administer the lethal dose themselves as a further protective of voluntary choice. And, in the United States, the Supreme Court's 1997 ruling there is no constitutional right to physician-assisted suicide has been understood to countenance the emergence of a "laboratory of the states" in which individual states, following the example of Oregon, may in the future move to legalize physician-assisted suicide, though following an attempt in 2001 by the U.S. Attorney General to undercut Oregon's law by prohibiting the use of scheduled drugs for the purpose of causing death, it appears that the issue will return to the U.S. Supreme Court. Nevertheless, among these three countries that serve as the principal models of approaches to dying, there remain substantial difference, and while there are ethical and practical advantages to each approach, each approach also raises serious moral objections.

Objections to the German Practice

German law does not prohibit assisting suicide, but postwar German culture and the Germany physicians' code of ethics discourages physicians from taking an active role in causing death. This gives rise to distinctive moral problems. For one thing, if the physician is not permitted to assist in his or her patient's suicide, there may be little professional help or review provided for the patient's choice about suicide. If patients make such choices essentially outside the medical establishment, medical professionals may not be a position to detect or treat impaired judgment on the part of the patient, especially judgment impaired by depression. Similarly, if the patient must commit suicide assisted only by persons outside the medical profession, there are risks that the patient's diagnosis and prognosis will be inadequately confirmed, that the means chosen for suicide will be unreliable or inappropriately used, that the means used for suicide will fall into the hands of other persons, and that the patient will fail to recognize or be able to resist intrafamilial pres-

sures and manipulation. While it now makes efforts to counter most of these objections, even the DGHS itself has been accused in the past of promoting rather than simply supporting choices of suicide. Finally, as the DGHS now emphasizes, assistance in suicide can be a freely chosen option only in a legal context that also protects the many other choices a patient may make—declining treatment, executing advance directives, seeking Hospice care—about how his or her life shall end.

Objections to the Dutch Practice

The Dutch practice of physician-performed active voluntary euthanasia and physician-assisted suicide also raises a number of ethical issues, many of which have been discussed vigorously both in the Dutch press and in commentary on the Dutch practices from abroad. For one thing, it is sometimes said that the availability of physician-assisted dying creates a disincentive for providing good terminal care. There is no evidence that this is the case; on the contrary, Peter Admiraal, the anesthesiologist who has been perhaps the Netherlands' most vocal defender of voluntary active euthanasia, insists that pain should rarely or never be the occasion for euthanasia, as pain (in contrast to suffering) is comparatively easily treated.[22] In fact, pain is the primary reason for the request in only about 5% of cases. Instead, it is a refusal to endure the final stages of deterioration, both mental and physical, that primarily motivates the majority of requests.

It is also sometimes said that active euthanasia violates the Hippocratic Oath. The original Greek version of the Oath does prohibit the physician from giving a deadly drug, even when asked for it; but the original version also prohibits the physician from performing surgery and from taking fees for teaching medicine, neither of which prohibitions has survived into contemporary medical practice. At issue is whether deliberately causing the death of one's patient—killing one's patient, some claim—can ever be part of the physician's role. "Doctors must not kill," insist opponents,[23] but Dutch physicians often say that they see performing euthanasia—where it is genuinely requested by the patient and nothing else can be done to relieve the patient's condition—as part of their duty to the patient, not as a violation of it. As the 1995 nationwide report commented, "a large majority of Dutch physicians consider euthanasia an exceptional but accepted part of medical practice."[24] Some Dutch do worry, however, that too many requests for euthanasia or assistance in suicide are refused—only about 1/3 of explicit requests are actually honored. One well-known Dutch commentator points to another, seemingly contrary concern: that some requests are made too early in a terminal course, even shortly after diagnosis, when with good palliative care the patient could live a substantial amount of time longer.[25] However, these are concerns about how euthanasia and physician-assisted suicide are practiced, not about whether they should be legal at all.

The Dutch are also often said to be a risk of starting down the slippery slope, that is, that the practice of voluntary active euthanasia for patients who meet the criteria will erode into practicing less-than-voluntary euthanasia on patients whose problems are not irremediable and perhaps by gradual degrees will develop into terminating the lives of people who are elderly, chronically ill, handicapped, mentally retarded, or otherwise regarded as undesirable. This risk is often expressed in vivid claims of widespread fear and wholesale slaughter—claims based on misinterpretation of the 1,000 cases of life-ending treatment without explicit, current request, claims that are often repeated in the right-to-life press in both the Netherlands and the U.S. although they are simply not true. However, it is true that in recent years the Dutch have begun to agonize over the problems of the incompetent patient, the mentally ill patient, the newborn with serious deficits, and other patients who cannot make voluntary choices, though these are largely understood as issues about withholding or withdrawing treatment, not about direct termination.[26]

What is not often understood is that this new and acutely painful area of reflection for the Dutch—withholding and withdrawing treatment from incompetent patients—has already led in the United States to the emergence of a vast, highly developed body of law: namely, that long series of cases beginning with *Quinlan* and culminating in *Cruzan*. Americans have been discussing these issues for a long time and have developed a broad set of practices that are regarded as routine in withholding and withdrawing treatment

from persons who are no longer or never were competent. The Dutch see Americans as much further out on the slippery slope than they are because Americans have already become accustomed to second-party choices that result in death for other people. Issues involving second-party choices are painful to the Dutch in a way they are not to Americans precisely because *voluntariness* is so central in the Dutch understanding of choices about dying. Concomitantly, the Dutch see the Americans' squeamishness about first-party choices—voluntary euthanasia, assisted suicide—as evidence that we are not genuinely committed to recognizing voluntary choice after all. For this reason, many Dutch commentators believe that the Americans are at a much greater risk of sliding down the slippery slope into involuntary killing than they are.

Objections to the American Practice

The German, Dutch, and American practices all occur within similar conditions—in industrialized nations with highly developed medical systems where a majority of the population die of illnesses exhibiting characteristically extended downhill courses—but the issues raised by the American response to this situation—relying on withholding and withdrawal of treatment—may be even more disturbing than those of the Dutch or the Germans. We Americans often assume that our approach is "safer" because, except in Oregon, it involves only letting someone die, not killing them; but it, too, raises very troubling questions.

The first of these issues is a function of the fact that withdrawing and especially withholding treatment are typically less conspicuous, less pronounced, less evident kinds of actions than direct killing, even though they can equally well lead to death. Decisions about nontreatment have an invisibility that decisions about directly causing death do not have, even though they may have the same result, and hence there is a much wider range of occasions in which such decisions can be made. One can decline to treat a patient in many different ways, at many different times—by not providing oxygen, by not instituting dialysis, by not correcting electrolyte imbalances, and so on—all of which will cause the patient's death. Open medical killing also brings about death, but is much more overt and conspicuous. Consequently, letting die offers many fewer protections. In contrast to the standard slippery-slope argument, which sees killing as riskier than letting die, the more realistic slippery-slope argument warns that because our culture relies primarily on decisions about nontreatment and practices like terminal sedation construed as "allowing to die," grave decisions about living or dying are not as open to scrutiny as they are under more direct life-terminating practices, and hence are more open to abuse. Indeed, in the view of one influential commentator, the Supreme Court's 1997 decision in effect legalized active euthanasia, voluntary and nonvoluntary, in the form of terminal sedation, even as it rejected physician-assisted suicide.[27]

Second, reliance on withholding and withdrawal of treatment invites rationing in an extremely strong way, in part because of the comparative invisibility of these decisions. When a health care provider does not offer a specific sort of care, it is not always possible to discern the motivation; the line between believing that it would not provide benefit to the patient and that it would not provide benefit worth the investment of resources in the patient can be very thin. This is a particular problem where health care financing is decentralized, profit-oriented, and non-universal, as in the United States, and where rationing decisions without benefit of principle are not always available for easy review.

Third, relying on withholding and withdrawal of treatment can often be cruel. Even with Hospice or with skilled palliative care, it requires that the patient who is dying from one of the diseases that exhibits a characteristic extended, downhill course (as the majority of patients in the developed world all do) must, in effect, wait to die until the absence of a certain treatment will cause death. For instance, the cancer patient who forgoes chemotherapy or surgery does not simply die from this choice; he or she continues to endure the downhill course of the cancer until the tumor finally destroys some crucial bodily function or organ. The patient with amyotrophic lateral sclerosis who decides in advance to decline respiratory support does not die at the time this choice is made but continues to endure increasing paralysis until breathing is impaired and suffocation occurs. Of course, attempts are made to try to ameliorate these situations by administering pain medication or symptom control at the time treatment is withheld—for instance, by using opiates and paralytics as a respirator is withdrawn—but these are all ways of disguising the fact that we are letting the disease kill the patient rather than directly bringing about death. But the ways diseases kill people can be far more cruel than the ways physicians kill patients when performing euthanasia or assisting in suicide.

END-OF-LIFE PRACTICES IN OTHER COUNTRIES

In most of the developed world dying looks much the same. As in the United States, the Netherlands, and Germany, the other industrialized nations also have sophisticated medical establishments, enjoy extended life expectancies, and find themselves in the fourth stage of the epidemiological transition, in which the majority of their populations die of diseases with extended downhill courses. Dying takes place in much the same way in all these countries, though the exact frequency of withholding and withdrawing treatment, of double-effect use of opiates, and euthanasia and physician-assisted suicide varies among them. Indeed, new data is rapidly coming to light.

In Australia, a replication of the Remmelink Commission study originally performed in the Netherlands found that of deaths in Australia that involved a medical end-of-life decision, 28.6% involved withholding or withdrawing treatment; 30.9% involved the use of opiates under the principle of double effect, and 1.8% involved voluntary active euthanasia (including 0.1% physician-assisted suicide), though neither are legal.[28] But the study also found—this is the figure that produced considerable surprise—that some 3.5% of deaths involved termination of the patient's life without the patient's concurrent explicit request. This figure is five times as high as that in the Netherlands. In slightly more than a third of these cases (38%), there was some discussion with the patient, though not an explicit request for death to be hastened, and in virtually all of the rest, the doctor did not consider the patient competent or capable of making such a decision. In 0.5% of all deaths involving medical end-of-life decisions, doctors did not discuss the choice of hastening of death with the patient because they thought it was "clearly the best one for the patient" or that "discussion would have done more harm than good."[29]

A 2003 study of six European countries—Belgium, Denmark, Italy, the Netherlands, Sweden, and Switzerland—found that in all countries studied, about a third of deaths are sudden and unexpected; among the other two-thirds, the frequency of death following end-of-life decisions ranged from 23% in Italy to 51% in Switzerland. "Double effect" deaths and direct termination without explicit current request were found everywhere. However, patients and relatives were more likely to be involved in decision-making where the frequency of legal voluntary euthanasia is comparatively high—Switzerland and the Netherlands—and while rates of voluntary euthanasia were highest in the Netherlands, rates of euthanasia without current, explicit consent were higher in all five other countries. Rates of physician-assisted suicide were highest in Switzerland (0.36% of all deaths), of which 92% involved the participation of a right-to-die organization.[30]

End-of-life practices in these and other developed countries tend to follow one of the three models explored here. For example, Canada's practices are much like those of the United States, in that it relies on withholding and withdrawing treatment and other forms of allowing to die, but, in the 1993 case *Rodriquez v. British Columbia*, the Canadian Supreme Court narrowly rejected physician-assisted suicide. Australia's Northern Territory briefly legalized assisted dying in 1997, but the law was overturned after just four cases. The United Kingdom, the birthplace of the Hospice movement, stresses palliative care but also rejects physician-assisted suicide and active euthanasia. Late in 2001, Belgium has legalized active euthanasia but not physician-assisted suicide; despite the latter, Belgium's law is patterned fairly closely after the Dutch law. Switzerland's law, like that of Germany, does not criminalize assisted suicide, but does not impose a duty to rescue that makes medical assistance in suicide difficult. Switzerland now has at least four right-to-die organizations, including *Exit* and *Dignitas*, in part analogues of Oregon's Compassion in Dying and Germany's DGHS, that provide information, counseling, and other support to terminally ill patients who choose suicide, *Freitod*, but the Swiss

groups are also able to provide such patients an accompaniment team which consults with the patient to make sure that the choice of suicide is voluntary, to secure a prescription for the lethal medication, and to deliver it to the person at a preappointed time. They also maintain "safe houses" where a person can go to die. These organizations encourage family members to be present when the patient takes the drug, if he or she still wants to use it, and *Dignitas* operates a safe house for patients traveling from abroad for this purpose. In general, the Swiss organizations provide extensive help to the patient who chooses this way of dying, though in keeping with Swiss law, they all insist that the patient take the drug him- or herself: as in Germany, assisted suicide is legal, but euthanasia is not. In 2002, about 500 people, approximately 0.4% of the 60,000 people in German-speaking Switzerland who died, died in this way.[31]

In contrast, practices in less developed countries look very, very different. In these countries, especially the least developed, background circumstances are different: life spans are significantly shorter, health care systems are only primitively equipped and grossly underfunded, and many societies have not passed through to the fourth stage of the epidemiologic transition: in these countries, people die earlier, they are more likely to die of infectious and parasitic disease, including AIDS, and degenerative disease is more likely to be interrupted early by death from pneumonia, sepsis, malnutrition, and other factors in what would otherwise have been a long downhill course. Dying in the poorer countries remains different from dying in the richer countries, and the underlying ethical problem in the richer countries—what practices concerning the end of life to adopt when the majority of a population dies of late-life degenerative diseases with long downhill courses—is far less applicable in the less developed parts of the world.

THE PROBLEM: A CHOICE OF CULTURES

In the developed world, we see three sorts of models in the three countries we've examined in detail. While much of medical practice in them is similar, they do offer three quite different basic options in approaching death. All three of these options generate moral problems; none of them, nor any others we might devise, is free of moral difficulty. The question, then, is this: for a given society, which practices about dying are, morally and practically speaking, best?

It is not possible to answer this question in a less-than-ideal world without attention to the specific characteristics and deficiencies of the society in question. In asking which of these practices is best, we must ask which is best *for us*. That we currently employ one set of these options rather than others does not prove that it is best for us; the question is, would practices developed in other cultures or those not yet widespread in any culture be better for our own culture than that which has so far developed here? Thus, it is necessary to consider the differences between our own society and these other societies in the developed world that have real bearing on which model of approach to dying we ought to adopt. This question can be asked by residents of any country or culture: which model of dying is best *for us*? I have been addressing this question from the point of view of an American, but the question could be asked by any member of any culture, anywhere.

First, notice that different cultures exhibit different degrees of closeness between physicians and patients—different patterns of contact and involvement. The German physician is sometimes said to be more distant and more authoritarian than the American physician; on the other hand, the Dutch physician is often said to be closer to his or her patients than either the American or the German is. In the Netherlands, basic primary care is provided by the *huisarts*, the general practitioner or family physician, who typically lives in the neighborhood, makes house calls frequently, and maintains an office in his or her own home. This physician usually also provides care for the other members of the patient's family and will remain the family's physician throughout his or her practice. Thus, the patient for whom euthanasia becomes an issue—say, the terminal cancer patient who has been hospitalized in the past but who has returned home to die—will be cared for by the trusted family physician on a regular basis. Indeed, for a patient in severe distress, the physician, supported by the visiting nurse, may make house calls as often as once a day, twice a day, or even more frequently (after all, the physician's office is right in the neighborhood) and is in continuous contact with the family.

In contrast, the traditional American institution of the family doctor who makes house calls has largely become a thing of the past, and although some patients who die at home have access to hospice services and receive house calls from their long-term physician, many have no such long-term care and receive most of it from staff at a clinic or from house staff rotating through the services of a hospital. Most Americans die in institutions, including hospitals and nursing homes; in the Netherlands, in contrast, the majority of people die at home. The degree of continuing contact that the patient can have with a familiar, trusted physician and the degree of institutionalization clearly influence the nature of his or her dying and also play a role in whether physician-performed active euthanasia, assisted suicide, and/or withholding and withdrawing treatment is appropriate.

Second, the United States has a much more volatile legal climate than either the Netherlands or Germany; its medical system is highly litigious, much more so than that of any other country in the world. Fears of malpractice actions or criminal prosecution color much of what physicians do in managing the dying of their patients. Americans also tend to develop public policy through court decisions and to assume that the existence of a policy puts an end to any moral issue. A delicate legal and moral balance over the issue of euthanasia, as has been the case in the Netherlands throughout the time it was understood as *gedoogd*, tolerated but not fully legal, would hardly be possible here.

Third, we in the United States have a very different financial climate in which to do our dying. Both the Netherlands and Germany, as well as virtually every other industrialized nation, have systems of national health insurance or national health care. Thus the patient is not directly responsible for the costs of treatment, and consequently the patient's choices about terminal care and/or euthanasia need not take personal financial considerations into account. Even for the patient who does have health insurance in the United States, many kinds of services are not covered, whereas the national health care or health insurance programs of many other countries provide multiple relevant services, including at-home physician care, home-nursing care, home respite care, care in a nursing home or other long-term facility, dietitian care, rehabilitation care, physical therapy, psychological counseling, and so on. The patient in the United States needs to attend to the financial aspects of dying in a way that patients in many other countries do not, and in this country both the patient's choices and the recommendations of the physician are very often shaped by financial considerations.

There are many other differences between the United States, on the one hand, and the Netherlands and Germany, with their different options for dying, on the other hand, including differences in degrees of paternalism in the medical establishment, in racism, sexism, and ageism in the general culture, and in awareness of a problematic historical past, especially Nazism. All of these cultural, institutional, social, and legal differences influence the appropriateness or inappropriateness of practices such as active euthanasia and assisted suicide. For instance, the Netherlands' tradition of close physician-patient contact, its comparative absence of malpractice-motivated medicine, and its provision of comprehensive health insurance, together with its comparative lack of racism and ageism and its experience in resistance to Nazism, suggest that this culture is able to permit the practice of voluntary active euthanasia, performed by physicians, as well as physician-assisted suicide, without risking abuse. On the other hand, it is sometimes said that Germany still does not trust its physicians, remembering the example of Nazi experimentation, and given a comparatively authoritarian medical climate in which the contact between physician and patient is quite distanced, the population could not be comfortable with the practice of physician-performed active euthanasia or physician-assisted suicide. There, only a wholly patient-controlled response to terminal situations, as in non-physician-assisted suicide, is a reasonable and prudent practice.

But what about the United States? This is a country where (1) sustained contact with a personal physician has been decreasing, (2) the risk of malpractice action is perceived as substantial, (3) much medical care is not insured, (4) many medical decisions are financial decisions as well, (5) racism remains high, and (6) the public has not experienced direct contact with Nazism or similar totalitarian movements. Thus, the United States is in many respects an untrustworthy candidate for practicing active euthanasia. Given the pressures on individuals in an often atomized society, encouraging solo suicide, assisted if at all only by nonprofessionals, might well be open to considerable abuse too.

However, there are several additional differences between the United States and both the Netherlands and Germany that may seem peculiarly relevant here. First, American culture is more confrontational than many others, including Dutch culture. While the Netherlands prides itself rightly on a long tradition of rational discussion of public issues and on toleration of others' views and practices, the United States (and to some degree also Germany) tends to develop highly partisan, moralizing oppositional groups, especially over social issues like abortion. In general, this is a disadvantage, but in the case of euthanasia it may serve to alert the public to issues and possibilities it might not otherwise consider, especially the risks of abuse. Here the role of religious groups may be particularly strong, since in discouraging or prohibiting suicide and euthanasia (as many, though by no means all, religious groups do), they may invite their members to reinspect the reasons for such choices and encourage families, physicians, and health care institutions to provide adequate, humane alternatives.

Second, though this may at first seem to be not only a peculiar but a trivial difference, it is Americans who are particularly given to self-analysis. This tendency not only is evident in the United States' high rate of utilization of counseling services, including religious counseling, psychological counseling, and psychiatry, but also is more clearly evident in its popular culture: its diet of soap operas, situation comedies, and pop psychology books. It is here that the ordinary American absorbs models for analyzing his or her personal relationships and individual psychological characteristics. While, of course, things are changing rapidly and America's cultural tastes are widely exported, the fact remains that the ordinary American's cultural diet contains more in the way of professional and do-it-your-self amateur psychology and self-analysis than anyone else's. This long tradition of self-analysis may put Americans in a better position for certain kinds of end-of-life practices than many other cultures. Despite whatever other deficiencies U.S. society has, we live in a culture that encourages us to inspect our own motives, anticipate the impact of our actions on others, and scrutinize our own relationships with others, including our physicians. This disposition is of importance in euthanasia and assisted-suicide contexts because these are the kinds of fundamental choices about which one may have somewhat mixed motives, be subject to various interpersonal and situational pressures, and so on. If the voluntary character of choices about one's own dying is to be protected, it may be a good thing to inhabit a culture in which self-inspection of one's own mental habits and motives, not to mention those of one's family, physician, and others who might affect one's choices, is culturally encouraged. Counseling specifically addressed to end-of-life choices is not yet easily or openly available, especially if physician-assisted suicide is at issue—though some groups like Seattle-based Compassion in Dying now provide it—but I believe it will become more frequent in the future as people facing terminal illnesses characterized by long downhill, deteriorative courses consider how they want to die.

Finally, the United States population, varied as it is, is characterized by a kind of do-it-yourself ethic, an ethic that devalues reliance on others and encourages individual initiative and responsibility. (To be sure, this ethic is little in evidence in the series of court cases from *Quinlan* to *Cruzan*, but these were all cases about patients who had become or always were incapable of decision-making.) This ethic seems to be coupled with a sort of resistance to authority that perhaps also is basic to the American temperament, even in all its diversity. If this is really the case, Americans might be especially well served by end-of-life practices that emphasize self-reliance and resistance to authority.

These, of course, are mere conjectures about features of American culture relevant to the practice of euthanasia or assisted suicide. These are the features that one would want to reinforce should these practices become general, in part to minimize the effects of the negative influences. But, of course, these positive features will differ from one country and culture to another, just as the negative features do. In each country, a different architecture of antecedent assumptions and cultural features develops around end-of-life issues, and in each country the practices of euthanasia and assisted or physician-assisted suicide,

if they are to be free from abuse, must be adapted to the culture in which they take place.

What, then, is appropriate for the United States' own cultural situation? Physician-performed euthanasia, even if not in itself morally wrong, is morally jeopardized where legal, time-related, and especially financial pressures on both patients and physicians are severe; thus, it is morally problematic in our culture in a way that it is not in the Netherlands. Solo suicide outside the institution of medicine (as in Germany) may be problematic in a country (like the United States) that has an increasingly alienated population, offers deteriorating and uneven social services, is increasingly racist and classist, and in other ways imposes unusual pressures on individuals, despite opportunities for self-analysis. Reliance only on withholding and withdrawing treatment and allowing to die (as in the United States) can be cruel, and its comparative invisibility invites erosion under cost-containment and other pressures. These are the three principal alternatives we have considered, but none of them seems wholly suited to our actual situation for dealing with the new fact that most of us die of extended-decline, deteriorative diseases.

Perhaps, however, there is one that would best suit the United States, certainly better than its current reliance on allowing to die, and better than the Netherlands' more direct physician involvement or Germany's practices entirely outside medicine. The "arm's-length" model of physician-assisted suicide—permitting physicians to supply their terminally ill patients who request it with the means for ending their own lives (as has become legal in Oregon) still grants physicians some control over the circumstances in which this can happen—only, for example, when the prognosis is genuinely grim and the alternatives for symptom control are poor—but leaves the fundamental decision about whether to use these means to the patient alone. It is up to the patient then—the independent, confrontational, self-analyzing, do-it-yourself, authority-resisting patient—and his or her advisors, including family members, clergy, the physician, and other health care providers, to be clear about whether he or she really wants to use these means or not. Thus, the physician is involved but not directly, and it is the patient's decision, although the patient is not making it alone.

Thus also it is the patient who performs the action of bringing his or her own life to a close, though where the patient is physically incapable of doing so or where the process goes awry the physician must be allowed to intercede. We live in an imperfect world, but of the alternatives for facing death—which we all eventually must—I think that the practice of permitting this somewhat distanced though still medically supported form of physician-assisted suicide is the one most nearly suited to the current state of our own flawed society. This is a model not yet central in any of the three countries examined here—the Netherlands, Germany, or (except in Oregon) the United States, or any of the other industrialized nations with related practices—but it is the one, I think, that suits us best.

NOTES

[1] S. J. Olshansky and A. B. Ault, "The Fourth Stage of the Epidemiological Transition: The Age of Delayed Degenerative Diseases," *Milbank Memorial Fund Quarterly Health and Society* 64 (1986): 355–91.

[2] S. Miles and C. Gomez, *Protocols for Elective Use of Life-Sustaining Treatment* (New York: Springer-Verlag, 1988).

[3] C. L. Sprung, "Changing Attitudes and Practices in Forgoing Life-Sustaining Treatments," *JAMA* 262 (1990):2213.

[4] T. J. Prendergast and J. M. Luce, "Increasing Incidence of Withholding and Withdrawal of Life Support from the Critically Ill," *American Journal of Respiratory and Critical Care Medicine* 155 (1): 1–2 (January 1997).

[5] M. B. Hamel et al. (SUPPORT Investigators), "Patient age and decisions to withhold life-sustaining treatments from seriously ill, hospitalized adults," *Annals of Internal Medicine* 130(2): 116–125 (Jan. 19, 1999).

[6] John M. Luce, "Withholding and Withdrawal of Life Support: Ethical, Legal, and Clinical Aspects," *New Horizons* 5(1):30–37 (Feb. 1997).

[7] *New York Times,* 23 July 1990. A13.

[8] Accounts of the use of Oregon's Death With Dignity Act (Measure 16) begin with A. E. Chin, K. Hedberg, G. K. Higginson, D. W. Fleming, "Legalized Physician-Assisted Suicide in Oregon—the first year's experience," *New England Journal of Medicine* 340:577–83 (1999) and are updated annually in this journal and at the website of the Oregon Department of Human Services. The 129 cases of legal physician-assisted suicide that have taken place in the first five years since it became legal in Oregon—a five-year period during which a total of about 6 million deaths occurred in the U.S.—represent at most about 0.00116% of the total annual mortality for the U.S.; it is less than 0.1% of the annual mortality in Oregon. As of this writing new legal challenges have been directed against this law; the outcome remains in question.

[9] For a fuller account, see my remarks "A Dozen Caveats Concerning the Discussion of Euthanasia in the Netherlands," in Margaret P. Battin, *The Least Worst Death: Essays in Bioethics on the End of Life* (New York and London: Oxford University Press, 1994): 130–44.

[10] P. J. van der Maas, J. J. M. van Delden, L. Pijnenborg, "Euthanasia and Other Medical Decisions Concerning the End of Life," published in full in English as a special issue of *Health Policy,* 22, nos. 1-2 (1992) and, with C. W. N. Looman, in summary in *The Lancet* 338 (1991):669–674.

[11] G. van der Wal et al., "Euthanasie en hulp bij zelfdoding door artsen in de thuissituatie," parts 1 and 2, *Nederlands Tijdschrift voor Geneeskunde* 135 (1991): 1593–98, 1600–03.

[12]P. J. van der Maas, G. van der Wal, et al., "Euthanasia, Physician-Assisted Suicide, and Other Medical Practices Involving the End of Life in the Netherlands, 1990–1995," *New England Journal of Medicine* 335:22 (1996): 1699–1705.

[13]Bregje D. Onwuteaka-Philipsen, Agnes van der Heide, Dirk Koper, Ingeborg Keij-Deerenberg, Judith A. C. Rietjens, Mette Rurup, Astrid M. Vrakking, Jean Jacques Georges, Martien T. Muller, Gerrit van der Wal, Paul J. van der Maas, "Euthanasia and other end-of-life decisions in the Netherlands in 1990, 1995, and 2001," *The Lancet* 2003: 362, 395–399. A full account is available in Gerrit van der Wal, Agnes van der Heide, Bregje D. Onwuteaka-Philipsen, Paul. J. van der Maas, *Medische besluitvorming aan het einde van het leven: De praktijk en de toetsingsprocedure euthanasie*. Utrecht: De Tijdstroom, 2003.

[14]L. Pijnenborg, P. J. van der Maas, J. J. M. van Delden, C. W. N Looman, "Life Terminating Acts without Explicit Request of Patient," *The Lancet* 341 (1993): 1196–99.

[15]Onwuteaka-Philipsen, 2003. These figures are an average of the results of the two principal parts of the 1990, 1995, and 2001 nationwide studies, the interview study and the death-certificate study.

[16]G. van der Wal et al., "Evaluation of the Notification Procedure for Physician-Assisted Death in the Netherlands," *New England Journal of Medicine* 335:22 (1996):1706–1711.

[17]van der Maas et al., "Euthanasia and other Medical Decisions Concerning the End of Life," 673.

[18]van der Maas et al., "Euthanasia, Physician-Assisted Suicide, and Other Medical Practices Involving the End of Life in the Netherlands, 1990–1995," p. 1705.

[19]Kurt Schobert, "Physician-assisted Suicide in Germany and Switzerland, with focus on some developments in recent years," MSS in preparation, citing "Grundsätze der Bundesärztekammer zur ärztlichen Sterbebegleitung," in Urban Wiesing, ed., *Ethik in der Medizin*, Stuttgart 2002, pp. 203–208.

[20]That is, it no longer sells or supplies such drugs. A scandal in 1992–93 engulfed the original founder and president of the DGHS, Hans Hennig Atrott, who had been secretly providing some members cyanide in exchange for substantial contributions; he was convicted of violating the drug laws and tax evasion, though not charged with or convicted or assisting suicides.

[21]See my "Assisted Suicide: Can We Learn from Germany?" in Margaret P. Battin, *The Least Worst Death: Essays in Bioethics on the End of Life* (New York and London: Oxford University Press, 1994): 254–70.

[22]P. Admiraal, "Euthanasia in a General Hospital," paper read at the Eighth World Congress of the International Federation of Right-to-Die Societies, Maastricht, the Netherlands, June 8, 1990.

[23]See the editorial "Doctors Must Not Kill," *Journal of the American Medical Association* 259:2139–40 (1988), signed by Willard Gaylin, M.D., Leon R. Kass, M.D., Edmund D. Pellegrino, M.D., and Mark Siegler, M.D.

[24]van der Maas et al., "Euthanasia, Physician-Assisted Suicide, and Other Medical Practices," 1705.

[25]Govert den Hartogh, personal communication.

[26]H. ten Have, "Coma: Controversy and Consensus," *Newsletter of the European Society for Philosophy of Medicine and Health Care* (May 1990): 19–20.

[27]David Orentlicher, "The Supreme Court and Terminal Sedation: Rejecting Assisted Suicide, Embracing Euthanasia," *Hastings Constitutional Law Quarterly* 24(4):947–968 (1997); see also *The New England Journal of Medicine* 337(17):1236–39 (1997).

[28]Physician-assisted suicide was briefly legal in the Northern Territory of Australia in 1997 and four cases were performed before the law was overturned, but these cases did not occur during the study period.

[29]Helga Kuhse, Peter Singer, Peter Baume, Malcolm Clark, and Maurice Rickard, "End-of-life Decisions in Australian Medical Practice," *The Medical Journal of Australia* 166:191–196 (1997).

[30]van der Heide, Agnes, Luc Deliens, Karin Faisst, Tore Nilstun, Michael Norup, Eugenio Paci, Gerrit van der Wal, Paul. J. van der Maas, on behalf of the EURELD consortium, End-of-life decision-making in six European countries: descriptive study. *The Lancet* 361: (August 2, 2003), 345–350.

[31]Swissinfo June 19, 2003, citing a University of Zurich study.

Additional Reading

There is an enormous literature on euthanasia. The following is just a small sample.

James Rachels's brief paper, "Active and Passive Euthanasia," *New England Journal of Medicine,* 292 (1975), which is widely anthologized, is perhaps the best source for a clear and cogent argument for allowing *active* euthanasia if we approve of *passive* euthanasia; that is, Rachels argues that if we believe it is alright to stop the treatment of a suffering patient and allow that patient to die (when further treatment would prolong the patient's life and therefore her suffering), then we should also approve of purposefully *causing* death (perhaps by administering a drug) in order to hasten death and relieve suffering. Rachels's ideas are expanded in his book, *The End of Life: Euthanasia and Morality* (New York: Oxford University Press, 1986).

Dan W. Brock's "Voluntary Active Euthanasia," *Hastings Center Report,* (March–April 1992) is a careful examination of both pro and con points in favor of active euthanasia. Brock favors active euthanasia, but not without serious misgivings, and he is quick to acknowledge the strong points made against such a policy.

Edmund D. Pellegrino's "Distortion of the Healing Relationship," in *Ethical Issues in Death and Dying,* 2nd ed., Tom L. Beauchamp and Robert M. Veatch, editors (Upper Saddle River, N.J.: Prentice-Hall, 1996) is a good brief argument against active euthanasia. For a longer examination of the arguments against euthanasia, see David C. Thomasma and Glenn C. Graber, *Euthanasia: Toward an Ethical Social Policy* (New York: Continuum, 1990).

Margaret P. Battin has an excellent book on the subject: *The Least-Worth Death: Essays in Bioethics on the End of Life* (New York: Oxford University Press, 1994).

Ronald Dworkin's *Life's Dominion: An Argument About Abortion, Euthanasia, and Individual Freedom* (New York: Alfred A. Knopf, 1993) is careful and reflective, and treats all sides on these difficult issues with respect and fairness. His chapter "Dying and Living" is particularly good in examining the psychological aspects of why some patients would prefer to have the option of active euthanasia.

Susan Wolf's "Gender, Feminism, and Death: Physician-Assisted Suicide and Euthanasia," in Susan M. Wolf, editor, *Feminism & Bioethics: Beyond Reproduction* (New York: Oxford University Press, 1996) raises doubts about active euthanasia, and offers original insights in a debate where many of the arguments are becoming rather standardized.

Active euthanasia has been openly practiced in the Netherlands for many years, originally as a result of court rulings that authorized it. The Dutch experience with euthanasia has been closely watched, and one of the best sources for examining the issue from the

Dutch perspective is a book edited by David C. Thomasma, Thomasine Kimbrough-Kushner, Gerrit K. Kimsma, and Chris Ciesielski-Carlucci, *Asking To Die: Inside the Dutch Debate About Euthanasia* (Dordrecht, Netherlands: Kluwer Academic Publishers, 1998).

An interesting debate on physician-assisted suicide can be found in *The New England Journal of Medicine* (January 2, 1977): Marcia Angell, "The Supreme Court and Physician-Assisted Suicide—The Ultimate Right" argues in favor of legalizing physician-assisted suicide, while the opposing view is given by Kathleen M. Foley, "Competent Care for the Dying Instead of Physician-Assisted Suicide." An excellent recent debate is found in Gerald Dworkin, R. G. Frey, and Sissela Bok, *Euthanasia and Physician-Assisted Suicide* (Cambridge, Mass.: Cambridge University Press, 1998); Dworkin and Frey argue for allowing physician-assisted suicide in some circumstances, while Sissela Bok opposes it.

There are many good anthologies on euthanasia, including: Bonnie Steinbock and Alastair Norcross, editors, *Killing and Letting Die*, 2nd ed. (New York: Fordham University Press, 1994); Margaret Battin, Rosamond Rhodes, and Anita Silvers, editors, *Physician-Assisted Suicide: Expanding the Debate* (London: Routledge, 1998); Loretta M. Kopelman and Kenneth A. De Ville, editors, *Physician-Assisted Suicide: What Are the Issues?* (Dordrecht Netherlands: Kluwer, 2001); Robert F. Weir, editor, *Physician-Assisted Suicide* (Bloomington: Indiana University Press, 1997); and the Beauchamp and Veatch anthology, *Ethical Issues in Death and Dying*, cited previously.

THE JUST DISTRIBUTION OF SCARCE MEDICAL RESOURCES: SHOULD ALCOHOLICS RECEIVE EQUAL CONSIDERATION FOR LIVER TRANSPLANTS?

Transplant surgery has been literally a lifesaver for many people in need of hearts, lungs, kidneys, and livers. Unfortunately, the demand for transplanted organs far exceeds the available supply, and while many patients are saved by transplants, many more die on the waiting list. This situation has raised difficult ethical issues concerning how scarce organs should be distributed. One particularly controversial question has been whether those whose liver damage is a result of their own behavior—their own excessive use of alcohol—should be considered equally for receiving scarce organs. Alvin H. Moss and Mark Siegler favor penalizing alcoholics, while Carl Cohen and Martin Benjamin are opposed. The issue is important not only in relation to issues of distributive justice, but also in connection with arguments about free will and moral responsibility.

SHOULD ALCOHOLICS COMPETE EQUALLY FOR LIVER TRANSPLANTATION?

Alvin H. Moss, MD & Mark Siegler, MD

The circumstances of liver transplantation are unique among organ transplantation because of the dire, absolute scarcity of donor livers and the predominance of one disease—alcohol-related end-stage liver disease—as the principal cause of liver failure. We propose that patients who develop end-stage liver disease through no fault of their own should have higher priority for receiving a liver transplant than those whose end-stage liver disease results from failure to obtain treatment for alcoholism. We base our proposal on considerations of fairness and on whether public support for liver transplantation can be maintained if, as a result of a first-come, first-served approach, patients with alcohol-related end-stage liver disease receive more than half the available donor livers. We conclude that since not all can live, priorities must be established for the use of scarce health care resources.

(JAMA. 1991;265: 1295–1298)

Until recently, liver transplantation for patients with alcohol-related end-stage liver disease (ARESLD) was not considered a treatment option. Most physicians in the transplant community did not recommend it because of initial poor results in this population and because of a predicted high recidivism rate that would preclude long-term survival. In 1988, however, Starzl and colleagues reported 1-year survival rates for patients with ARESLD comparable to results in patients with other causes of end-stage liver disease (ESLD). Although the patients in the Pittsburgh series may represent a carefully selected population, the question is no longer Can we perform transplants in patients with alcoholic liver disease and obtain acceptable results? but Should we? This question is particularly timely since the Health Care Financing Administration (HCFA) has recommended that Medicare coverage for liver transplantation be offered to patients with alcoholic cirrhosis who are abstinent. The HCFA proposes that the same eligibility criteria be used for patients with ARESLD as are used for patients with other causes of ESLD, such as primary biliary cirrhosis and sclerosing cholangitis.

SHOULD PATIENTS WITH ARESLD RECEIVE TRANSPLANTS?

At first glance, this question seems simple to answer. Generally, in medicine, a therapy is used if it works and saves lives. But the circumstances of liver transplantation differ from those of most other lifesaving therapies, including long-term mechanical ventilation and dialysis, in three important respects:

Nonrenewable Resource

First, although most lifesaving therapies are expensive, liver transplantation uses a nonrenewable, absolutely scarce resource—a donor liver. In contrast

to patients with end-stage renal disease, who may receive either a transplant or dialysis therapy, every patient with ESLD who does not receive a liver transplant will die. This dire, absolute scarcity of donor livers would be greatly exacerbated by including patients with ARESLD as potential candidates for liver transplantation. In 1985, 63 737 deaths due to hepatic disease occurred in the United States, at least 36 000 of which were related to alcoholism, but fewer than 1000 liver transplants were performed. Although patients with ARESLD represent more than 50% of the patients with ESLD, patients with ARESLD account for less than 10% of those receiving transplants (*New York Times.* April 3, 1990:B6[col 1]). If patients with ARESLD were accepted for liver transplantation on an equal basis, as suggested by the HCFA, there would potentially be more than 30 000 additional candidates each year. (No data exist to indicate how many patients in the late stages of ARESLD would meet transplantation eligibility criteria.) In 1987, only 1182 liver transplants were performed; in 1989, fewer than 2000 were done. Even if all donor livers available were given to patients with ARESLD, it would not be feasible to provide transplants for even a small fraction of them. Thus, the dire, absolute nature of donor liver scarcity mandates that distribution be based on unusually rigorous standards—standards not required for the allocation of most other resources such as dialysis machines and ventilators, both of which are only *relatively* scarce.

Comparison with Cardiac Transplantation

Second, although a similar dire, absolute scarcity of donor hearts exists for cardiac transplantation, the allocational decisions for cardiac transplantation differ from those for liver transplantation. In liver transplantation, ARESLD causes more than 50% of the cases of ESLD; in cardiac transplantation, however, no one predominant disease or contributory factor is responsible. Even for patients with end-stage ischemic heart disease who smoked or who failed to adhere to dietary regimens, it is rarely clear that one particular behavior caused the disease. Also, unlike our proposed consideration for liver transplantation, a history of alcohol abuse is considered a contraindication and is a common reason for a patient with heart disease to be denied cardiac transplantation. Thus, the allocational decisions for heart transplantation differ from those for liver transplantation in two ways: determining a cause for end-stage heart disease is less certain, and patients with a history of alcoholism are usually rejected from heart transplant programs.

Expensive Technology

Third, a unique aspect of liver transplantation is that it is an expensive technology that has become a target of cost containment in health care. It is, therefore, essential to maintain the approbation and support of the public so that organs continue to be donated under appropriate clinical circumstances—even in spite of the high cost of transplantation.

General Guideline Proposed

In view of the distinctive circumstances surrounding liver transplantation, we propose as a general guideline that patients with ARESLD should not compete equally with other candidates for liver transplantation. We are *not* suggesting that patients with ARESLD should *never* receive liver transplants. Rather, we propose that a priority ranking be established for the use of this dire, absolutely scarce societal resource and that patients with ARESLD be lower on the list than others with ESLD.

OBJECTIONS TO PROPOSAL

We realize that our proposal may meet with two immediate objections: (1) Some may argue that since alcoholism is a disease, patients with ARESLD should be considered equally for liver transplantation. (2) Some will question why patients with ARESLD should be

singled out for discrimination, when the medical profession treats many patients who engage in behavior that causes their diseases. We will discuss these objections in turn.

Alcoholism: How Is It Similar to and Different from Other Diseases?

We do not dispute the reclassification of alcoholism as a disease. Both hereditary and environmental factors contribute to alcoholism, and physiological, biochemical, and genetic markers have been associated with increased susceptibility. Identifying alcoholism as a disease enables physicians to approach it as they do other medical problems and to differentiate it from bad habits, crimes, or moral weaknesses. More important, identifying alcoholism as a disease also legitimizes medical interventions to treat it.

Alcoholism is a chronic disease, for which treatment is available and effective. More than 1.43 million patients were treated in 5586 alcohol treatment units in the 12-month period ending October 30, 1987. One comprehensive review concluded that more than two thirds of patients who accept therapy improve. Another cited four studies in which at least 54% of patients were abstinent a minimum of 1 year after treatment. A recent study of alcohol-impaired physicians reported a 100% abstinence rate an average of 33.4 months after therapy was initiated. In this study, physician-patients rated Alcoholics Anonymous, the largest organization of recovering alcoholics in the world, as the most important component of their therapy.

Like other chronic diseases—such as type I diabetes mellitus, which requires the patient to administer insulin over a lifetime—alcoholism requires the patient to assume responsibility for participating in continuous treatment. Two key elements are required to successfully treat alcoholism: the patient must accept his or her diagnosis and must assume responsibility for treatment. The high success rates of some alcoholism treatment programs indicate that many patients can accept responsibility for their treatment. ARESLD, one of the sequelae of alcoholism, results from 10 to 20 years of heavy alcohol consumption. The risk of ARESLD increases with the amount of alcohol consumed and with the duration of heavy consumption. In view of the quantity of alcohol consumed, the years, even decades, required to develop ARESLD, and the availability of effective alcohol treatment, attributing personal responsibility for ARESLD to the patient seems all the more justified. We believe, therefore, that even though alcoholism is a chronic disease, alcoholics should be held responsible for seeking and obtaining treatment that could prevent the development of late-stage complications such as ARESLD. Our view is consistent with that of Alcoholics Anonymous: alcoholics are responsible for undertaking a program for recovery that will keep their disease of alcoholism in remission.

Are We Discriminating Against Alcoholics?

Why should patients with ARESLD be singled out when a large number of patients have health problems that can be attributed to so-called voluntary health-risk behavior? Such patients include smokers with chronic lung disease; obese people who develop type II diabetes; some individuals who test positive for the human immunodeficiency virus; individuals with multiple behavioral risk factors (inattention to blood pressure, cholesterol, diet, and exercise) who develop coronary artery disease; and people such as skiers, motorcyclists, and football players who sustain activity-related injuries. We believe that the health care system should respond based on the actual medical needs of patients rather than on the factors (eg, genetic, infectious, or behavioral) that cause the problem. We also believe that individuals should bear some responsibility—such as increased insurance premiums—for medical problems associated with voluntary choices. The critical distinguishing factor for treatment of ARESLD is the scarcity of the resource needed to treat it. The resources needed to treat most of these other conditions are only moderately or relatively scarce, and patients with these diseases or injuries can receive a share of the resources (ie, money, personnel, and medication) roughly equivalent to their need. In contrast, there are insufficient donor livers to sustain the lives of all with ESLD who are in need. This difference permits us to make some discriminating choices—or to establish priorities—in selecting candidates for liver transplantation based on notions of fairness. In addition, this reasoning enables us to offer patients with alcohol-related medical and surgical problems their fair share of relatively scarce resources, such as blood products, surgical care, and intensive care beds, while still maintaining that their claim on donor livers is less compelling than the claims of others.

REASONS PATIENTS WITH ARESLD SHOULD HAVE A LOWER PRIORITY ON TRANSPLANT WAITING LISTS

Two arguments support our proposal. The first argument is a moral one based on considerations of fairness. The second one is based on policy considerations and examines whether public support of liver transplantation can be maintained if, as a result of a first-come, first-served approach, patients with ARESLD receive more than half the available donor livers. Finally, we will consider further research necessary to determine which patients with ARESLD should be candidates for transplantation, albeit with a lower priority.

Fairness

Given a tragic shortage of donor livers, what is the fair or just way to allocate them? We suggest that patients who develop ESLD through no fault of their own (eg, those with congenital biliary atresia or primary biliary cirrhosis) should have a higher priority in receiving a liver transplant than those whose liver disease results from failure to obtain treatment for alcoholism. In view of the dire, absolute scarcity of donor livers, we believe it is fair to hold people responsible for their choices, including decisions to refuse alcoholism treatment, and to allocate organs on this basis.

It is unfortunate but not unfair to make this distinction. When not enough donor livers are available for all who need one, choices have to be made, and they should be founded on one or more proposed principles of fairness for distributing scarce resources. We shall consider four that are particularly relevant:

- To each, an equal share of treatment.
- To each, similar treatment for similar cases.
- To each, treatment according to personal effort.
- To each, treatment according to ability to pay.

It is not possible to give each patient with ESLD an equal share, or, in this case, a functioning liver. The problem created by the absolute scarcity of donor livers is that of inequality; some receive livers while others do not. But what is fair, need not be equal. Although a first-come, first-served approach has been suggested to provide each patient with an equal chance, we believe it is fairer to give a child dying of biliary atresia an opportunity for a *first* normal liver than it is to give a patient with ARESLD who was born with a normal liver a *second* one.

Because the goal of providing each person with an equal share of health care sometimes collides with the realities of finite medical resources, the principle of *similar treatment for similar cases* has been found to be helpful. Outka stated it this way: "If we accept the case for equal access, but if we simply cannot, physically cannot, treat all who are in need, it seems more just to discriminate by virtue of categories of illness, rather than between rich ill and poor ill." This principle is derived from the principle of formal justice, which, roughly stated, says that people who are equal in relevant respects should be treated equally and that people who are unequal in relevant respects should be treated differently. We believe that patients with ARESLD are unequal in a relevant respect to others with ESLD, since their liver failure was preventable; therefore, it is acceptable to treat them differently.

Our view also relies on the principle of *To each, treatment according to personal effort*. Although alcoholics cannot be held responsible for their disease, once their condition has been diagnosed they can be held responsible for seeking treatment and for preventing the complication of ARESLD. The standard of personal effort and responsibility we propose for alcoholics is the same as that held by Alcoholics Anonymous. We are not suggesting that some lives and behaviors have greater value than others—an approach used and appropriately repudiated when dialysis machines were in short supply. But we are holding people responsible for their personal effort.

Health policymakers have predicted that this principle will assume greater importance in the future. In the context of scarce health care resources, Blank foresees a reevaluation of our health care priorities, with a shift toward individual responsibility and a renewed emphasis on the individual's obligation to society to maximize one's health. Similarly, more than a decade ago, Knowles observed that prevention of disease requires effort. He envisioned that the next

major advances in the health of the American people would be determined by what individuals are willing to do for themselves.

To each, treatment according to ability to pay has also been used as a principle of distributive justice. Since alcoholism is prevalent in all socioeconomic strata, it is not discrimination against the poor to deny liver transplantation to patients with alcoholic liver disease. In fact, we believe that poor patients with ARESLD have a stronger claim for a donor liver than rich patients, precisely because many alcohol treatment programs are not available to patients lacking in substantial private resources or health insurance. Ironically, it is precisely this group of poor and uninsured patients who are most likely not to be eligible to receive a liver transplant because of their inability to pay. We agree with Outka's view of fairness that would discriminate according to categories of illness rather than according to wealth.

Policy Considerations Regarding Public Support for Liver Transplantation

Today, the main health policy concerns involve issues of financing, distributive justice, and rationing medical care. Because of the many deficiencies in the US health care system—in maternal and child health, in the unmet needs of the elderly, and in the millions of Americans without health insurance—an increasing number of commentators are drawing attention to the trade-offs between basic health care for the many and expensive, albeit lifesaving care for the few.

Because of its high unit cost, liver transplantation is often at the center of these discussions, as it has been in Oregon, where the legislature voted to eliminate Medicaid reimbursement for all transplants except kidneys and corneas. In this era of health care cost containment, a sense of limits is emerging and allocational choices are being made. Oregon has already shown that elected officials and the public are prepared to face these issues.

In our democracy, it is appropriate that community mores and values be regarded seriously when deciding the most appropriate use of a scarce and nonrenewable organ symbolized as a "Gift of Life." As if to underscore this point, the report of the Task Force on Organ Transplantation recommended that each donated organ be considered a national resource for the public good and that the public must participate in decisions on how to use this resource to best serve the public's interests.

Much of the initial success in securing public and political approval for liver transplantation was achieved by focusing media and political attention not on adults but on children dying of ESLD. The public may not support transplantation for patients with ARESLD in the same way that they have endorsed this procedure for babies born with biliary atresia. This assertion is bolstered not only by the events in Oregon but also by the results of a Louis Harris and Associates national survey, which showed that lifesaving therapy for premature infants or for patients with cancer was given the highest health care priority by the public and that lifesaving therapy for patients with alcoholic liver disease was given the lowest. In this poll, the public's view of health care priorities was shared by leadership groups also polled: physicians, nurses, employers, and politicians.

Just because a majority of the public holds these views does not mean that they are right, but the moral intuition of the public, which is also shared by its leaders, reflects community values that must be seriously considered. Also indicative of community values are organizations such as Mothers Against Drunk Driving, Students Against Drunk Driving, corporate employee assistance programs, and school student assistance programs. Their existence signals that many believe that a person's behavior can be modified so that the consequences of behavior such as alcoholism can be prevented. Thus, giving donor livers to patients with ARESLD on an equal basis with other patients who have ESLD might lead to a decline in public support for liver transplantation.

SHOULD ANY ALCOHOLICS BE CONSIDERED FOR TRANSPLANTATION? NEED FOR FURTHER RESEARCH

Our proposal for giving lower priority for liver transplantation to patients with ARESLD does not completely rule out transplantation for this group. Patients with ARESLD who had not previously been offered therapy and who are now abstinent could be acceptable candidates. In addition, patients lower on the waiting list, such as patients with ARESLD who have been treated and are now abstinent, might be eligible for a donor liver in some regions because of the increased availability of donor organs there. Even if only because of these possible conditions for transplantation, further research is needed to determine which patients with ARESLD would have the best outcomes after liver transplantation.

Transplant programs have been reluctant to provide transplants to alcoholics because of concern about one unfavorable outcome: a high recidivism rate. Although the overall recidivism rate for the Pittsburgh patients was only 11.5%, in the patients who had been abstinent less than 6 months it was 43%. Also, compared with the entire group in which 1-year survival was 74%, the survival rate in this subgroup was lower, at 64%.

In the recently proposed Medicare criteria for coverage of liver transplantation, the HCFA acknowledged that the decision to insure patients with alcoholic cirrhosis "may be considered controversial by some." As if to counter possible objections, the HCFA listed requirements for patients with alcoholic cirrhosis: patients must meet the transplant center's requirement for abstinence prior to liver transplantation and have documented evidence of sufficient social support to ensure both recovery from alcoholism and compliance with the regimen of immunosuppressive medication.

Further research should answer lingering questions about liver transplantation for ARESLD patients: Which characteristics of a patient with ARESLD can predict a successful outcome? How long is abstinence necessary to qualify for transplantation? What type of a social support system must a patient have to ensure good results? These questions are being addressed. Until the answers are known, we propose that further transplantation for patients with ARESLD be limited to abstinent patients who had not previously been offered alcoholism treatment and to abstinent treated patients in regions of increased donor liver availability and that it be carried out as part of prospective research protocols at a few centers skilled in transplantation and alcohol research.

COMMENT

Should patients with ARESLD compete equally for liver transplants? In a setting in which there is a dire, absolute scarcity of donor livers, we believe the answer is no. Considerations of fairness suggest that a first-come, first-served approach for liver transplantation is not the most just approach. Although this decision is difficult, it is only fair that patients who have not assumed equal responsibility for maintaining their health or for accepting treatment for a chronic disease should be treated differently. Considerations of public values and mores suggest that the

public may not support liver transplantation if patients with ARESLD routinely receive more than half of the available donor livers. We conclude that since not all can live, priorities must be established and that patients with ARESLD should be given a lower priority for liver transplantation than others with ESLD.

ALCOHOLICS AND LIVER TRANSPLANTATION

Carl Cohen, PhD, Martin Benjamin, PhD,
and the Ethics and Social Impact Committee of the
Transplant and Health Policy Center,
Ann Arbor, Michigan

Two arguments underlie a widespread unwillingness to consider patients with alcoholic cirrhosis of the liver as candidates for transplantation. First, alcoholics are morally blameworthy, their condition the result of their own misconduct; such blameworthiness disqualifies alcoholics in unavoidable competition for organs with others who are equally sick but blameless. Second, because of their habits, alcoholics will not exhibit satisfactory rates of survival after transplantation; good stewardship of a scarce lifesaving resource therefore requires that alcoholics not be considered for liver transplantation. These arguments are carefully analyzed and shown to be defective. There is not good moral or medical reason for categorically precluding alcoholics as candidates for liver transplantation. It would, in addition, be unjust to implement such a preclusion simply because others might respond negatively if we do not.

(*JAMA.* 1991;265:1299–1301)

Alcoholic cirrhosis of the liver—severe scarring due to the heavy use of alcohol—is by far the major cause of end-stage liver disease. For persons so afflicted, life may depend on receiving a new, transplanted liver. The number of alcoholics in the United States needing new livers is great, but the supply of available livers for transplantation is small. *Should those whose end-stage liver disease was caused by alcohol abuse be categorically excluded from candidacy for liver transplantation?* This question, partly medical and partly moral, must now be confronted forth-rightly. Many lives are at stake.

Reasons of two kinds underlie a widespread unwillingness to transplant livers into alcoholics: First, there is a common conviction—explicit or tacit—that alcoholics are morally blameworthy, their condition the result of their own misconduct, and

that such blameworthiness disqualifies alcoholics in unavoidable competition for organs with others equally sick but blameless. Second, there is a common belief that because of their habits, alcoholics will not exhibit satisfactory survival rates after transplantation, and that, therefore, good stewardship of a scarce lifesaving resource requires that alcoholics not be considered for liver transplantation. We examine both of these arguments.

THE MORAL ARGUMENT

A widespread condemnation of drunkenness and a revulsion for drunks lie at the heart of this public policy issue. Alcoholic cirrhosis—unlike other causes of end-stage liver disease—is brought on by a person's conduct, by heavy drinking. Yet if the dispute here were only about whether to treat someone who is seriously ill because of personal conduct, we would not say—as we do not in cases of other serious diseases resulting from personal conduct—that such conduct disqualifies a person from receiving desperately needed medical attention. Accident victims injured because they were not wearing seat belts are treated without hesitation; reformed smokers who become coronary bypass candidates partly because they disregarded their physicians' advice about tobacco, diet, and exercise are not turned away because of their bad habits. But new livers are a scarce resource, and transplanting a liver into an alcoholic may, therefore, result in death for a competing candidate whose liver disease was wholly beyond his or her control. Thus we seem driven, in this case unlike in others, to reflect on the weight given to the patient's personal conduct. And heavy drinking—unlike smoking, or overeating, or failing to wear a seat belt—is widely regarded as morally wrong.

Many contend that alcoholism is not a moral failing but a disease. Some authorities have recently reaffirmed this position, asserting that alcoholism is "best regarded as a chronic disease." But this claim cannot be firmly established and is far from universally believed. Whether alcoholism is indeed a disease, or a moral failing, or both, remains a disputed matter surrounded by intense controversy.

Even if it is true that alcoholics suffer from a somatic disorder, many people will argue that this disorder results in deadly liver disease only when coupled with a weakness of will—a weakness for which part of the blame must fall on the alcoholic. This consideration underlies the conviction that the alcoholic needing a transplanted liver, unlike a nonalcoholic competing for the same liver, is at least partly responsible for his or her need. Therefore, some conclude, the alcoholic's personal failing is rightly considered in deciding upon his or her entitlement to this very scarce resource.

Is this argument sound? We think it is not. Whether alcoholism is a moral failing, in whole or in part, remains uncertain. But even if we suppose that it is, it does not follow that we are justified in categorically denying liver transplants to those alcoholics suffering from end-stage cirrhosis. We could rightly preclude alcoholics from transplantation only if we assume that qualification for a new organ requires

some level of moral virtue or is canceled by some level of moral vice. But there is absolutely no agreement—and there is likely to be none—about what constitutes moral virtue and vice and what rewards and penalties they deserve. The assumption that undergirds the moral argument for precluding alcoholics is thus unacceptable. Moreover, even if we could agree (which, in fact, we cannot) upon the kind of misconduct we would be looking for, the fair weighting of such a consideration would entail highly intrusive investigations into patients' moral habits—investigations universally thought repugnant. Moral evaluation is wisely and rightly excluded from all deliberations of who should be treated and how.

Indeed, we do exclude it. We do not seek to determine whether a particular transplant candidate is an abusive parent or a dutiful daughter, whether candidates cheat on their income taxes or their spouses, or whether potential recipients pay their parking tickets or routinely lie when they think it is in their best interests. We refrain from considering such judgments for several good reasons: (1) We have genuine and well-grounded doubts about comparative degrees of voluntariness and, therefore, *cannot pass judgment fairly*. (2) Even if we could assess degrees of voluntariness reliably, we *cannot know what penalties different degrees of misconduct deserve*. (3) *Judgments of this kind could not be made consistently in our medical system*—and a fundamental requirement of a fair system in allocating scarce resources is that it treat all in need of certain goods on the same standard, without unfair discrimination by group.

If alcoholics should be penalized because of their moral fault, then all others who are equally at fault in causing their own medical needs should be similarly penalized. To accomplish this, we would have to make vigorous and sustained efforts to find out whose conduct has been morally weak or sinful and to what degree. That inquiry, as a condition for medical care or for the receipt of goods in short supply, we certainly will not and should not undertake.

The unfairness of such moral judgments is compounded by other accidental factors that render moral assessment especially difficult in connection with alcoholism and liver disease. Some drinkers have a greater predisposition for alcohol abuse than others. And for some who drink to excess, the predisposition to cirrhosis is also greater; many grossly intemperate drinkers do not suffer grievously from liver disease. On the other hand, alcohol consumption that might be considered moderate for some may cause serious liver disease in others. It turns out, in fact, that the disastrous consequences of even low levels of alcohol consumption may be much more common in women than in men. Therefore, penalizing cirrhotics by denying them transplant candidacy would have the effect of holding some groups arbitrarily to a higher standard than others and would probably hold women to a higher standard of conduct than men.

Moral judgments that eliminate alcoholics from candidacy thus prove unfair and unacceptable. The alleged (but disputed) moral misconduct of alcoholics with end-stage liver disease does not justify categorically excluding them as candidates for liver transplantation.

MEDICAL ARGUMENT

Reluctance to use available livers in treating alcoholics is due in some part to the conviction that, because alcoholics would do poorly after transplant as a result of their bad habits, good stewardship of organs in short supply requires that alcoholics be excluded from consideration.

This argument also fails, for two reasons: First, it fails because the premise—that the outcome for alcoholics will invariably be poor relative to other groups—is at least doubtful and probably false. Second, it fails because, even if the premise were true, it could serve as a good reason to exclude alcoholics only if it were an equally good reason to exclude other groups having a prognosis equally bad or worse. But equally low survival rates have not excluded other groups; fairness therefore requires that this group not be categorically excluded either.

In fact, the data regarding the post-transplant histories of alcoholics are not yet reliable. Evidence gathered in 1984 indicated that the 1-year survival rate for patients with alcoholic cirrhosis was well below the survival rate for other recipients of liver transplants, excluding those with cancer. But a 1988 report, with a larger (but still small) sample number, shows remarkably good results in alcoholics receiving transplants: 1-year survival is 73.2%—and of 35 carefully selected (and possibly nonrepresentative) alcoholics who received transplants and lived 6 months

or longer, only two relapsed into alcohol abuse. Liver transplantation, it would appear, can be a very sobering experience. Whether this group continues to do as well as a comparable group of non-alcoholic liver recipients remains uncertain. But the data, although not supporting the broad inclusion of alcoholics, do suggest that medical considerations do not now justify categorically excluding alcoholics from liver transplantation.

A history of alcoholism is of great concern when considering liver transplantation, not only because of the impact of alcohol abuse upon the entire system of the recipient, but also because the life of an alcoholic tends to be beset by general disorder. Returning to heavy drinking could ruin a new liver, although probably not for years. But relapse into heavy drinking would quite likely entail the inability to maintain the routine of multiple medication, daily or twice-daily, essential for immunosuppression and survival. As a class, alcoholic cirrhotics may therefore prove to have substantially lower survival rates after receiving transplants. All such matters should be weighed, of course. But none of them gives any solid reason to exclude alcoholics from consideration categorically.

Moreover, even if survival rates for alcoholics selected were much lower than normal—a supposition now in substantial doubt—what could fairly be concluded from such data? Do we exclude from transplant candidacy members of other groups known to have low survival rates? In fact we do not. Other things being equal, we may prefer not to transplant organs in short supply into patients afflicted, say, with liver cell cancer, knowing that such cancer recurs not long after a new liver is implanted. Yet in some individual cases we do it. Similarly, some transplant recipients have other malignant neoplasms or other conditions that suggest low survival probability. Such matters are weighed in selecting recipients, but they are insufficient grounds to categorically exclude an entire group. This shows that the argument for excluding alcoholics based on survival probability rates alone is simply not just.

THE ARGUMENTS DISTINGUISHED

In fact, the exclusion of alcoholics from transplant candidacy probably results from an intermingling, perhaps at times a confusion, of the moral and medical arguments. But if the moral argument indeed does not apply, no combination of it with probable survival rates can make it applicable. Survival data, carefully collected and analyzed, deserve to be weighed in selecting candidates. These data do not come close to precluding alcoholics from consideration. Judgments of blameworthiness, which ought to be excluded generally, certainly should be excluded when weighing the impact of those survival rates. Some people with a strong antipathy to alcohol abuse and abusers may, without realizing it, be relying on assumed unfavorable data to support a fixed moral judgment. The arguments must be untangled. Actual results with transplanted alcoholics must be considered without regard to moral antipathies.

The upshot is inescapable: there are no good grounds at present—moral or medical—to disqualify a patient with end-stage liver disease from consideration for liver transplantation simply because of a history of heavy drinking.

SCREENING AND SELECTION OF LIVER TRANSPLANT CANDIDATES

In the initial evaluation of candidates for any form of transplantation, the central questions are whether patients (1) are sick enough to need a new organ and (2) enjoy a high enough probability of benefiting from this limited resource. At this stage the criteria should be noncomparative. Even the initial screening of patients must, however, be done individually and with great care.

The screening process for those suffering from alcoholic cirrhosis must be especially rigorous—not for moral reasons, but because of factors affecting survival, which are themselves influenced by a history of heavy drinking—and even more by its resumption. Responsible stewardship of scarce organs requires that the screening for candidacy take into consideration the manifold impact of heavy drinking on long-term transplant success. Cardiovascular problems brought on by alcoholism and other systematic contraindications must be looked for. Psychiatric and social evaluation is also in order, to determine whether patients understand and have come to terms with their condition and whether they have the social support essential for continuing immunosuppression and follow-up care.

Precisely which factors should be weighed in this screening process have not been firmly established. Some physicians have proposed a specified period of alcohol abstinence as an "objective" criterion for selection—but the data supporting such a criterion are far from conclusive, and the use of this criterion to exclude a prospective recipient is at present medically and morally arbitrary.

Indeed, one important consequence of overcoming the strong presumption against considering alcoholics for liver transplantation is the research opportunity it presents and the encouragement it gives to the quest for more reliable predictors of medical success. As that search continues, some defensible guidelines for case-by-case determination have been devised, based on factors associated with sustained recovery from alcoholism and other considerations related to liver transplantation success in general. Such guidelines appropriately include (1) refined diagnosis by those trained in the treatment of alcoholism, (2) acknowledgment by the patient of a serious drinking problem, (3) social and familial stability, and (4) other factors experimentally associated with long-term sobriety.

The experimental use of guidelines like these, and their gradual refinement over time, may lead to more reliable and more generally applicable predictors. But those more refined predictors will never be developed until prejudices against considering alcoholics for liver transplantation are overcome.

Patients who are sick because of alleged self-abuse ought not be grouped for discriminatory treatment—unless we are prepared to develop a detailed calculus of just deserts for health care based on good conduct. Lack of sympathy for those who bring serious disease upon themselves is understandable, but the temptation to institutionalize that emotional response must be tempered by our inability to apply such considerations justly and by our duty *not* to apply them unjustly. In the end, some patients with alcoholic cirrhosis may be judged, after careful evaluation, as good risks for a liver transplant.

OBJECTION AND REPLY

Providing alcoholics with transplants may present a special "political" problem for transplant centers. The public perception of alcoholics is generally negative.

The already low rate of organ donation, it may be argued, will fall even lower when it becomes known that donated organs are going to alcoholics. Financial support from legislatures may also suffer. One can imagine the effect on transplantation if the public were to learn that the liver of a teenager killed by a drunken driver had been transplanted into an alcoholic patient. If selecting even a few alcoholics as transplant candidates reduces the number of lives saved overall, might that not be good reason to preclude alcoholics categorically?

No. The fear is understandable, but excluding alcoholics cannot be rationally defended on that basis. Irresponsible conduct attributable to alcohol abuse should not be defended. No excuses should be made for the deplorable consequences of drunken behavior, from highway slaughter to familial neglect and abuse. But alcoholism must be distinguished from those consequences; not all alcoholics are morally irresponsible, vicious, or neglectful drunks. If there is a general failure to make this distinction, we must strive to overcome that failure, not pander to it.

Public confidence in medical practice in general, and in organ transplantation in particular, depends on the scientific validity and moral integrity of the policies adopted. Sound policies will prove publicly defensible. Shaping present health care policy on the basis of distorted public perceptions or prejudices will, in the long run, do more harm than good to the process and to the reputation of all concerned.

Approximately one in every 10 Americans is a heavy drinker, and approximately one family in every three has at least one member at risk for alcoholic cirrhosis. The care of alcoholics and the just treatment of them when their lives are at stake are matters a democratic polity may therefore be expected to act on with concern and reasonable judgment over the long run. The allocation of organs in short supply does present vexing moral problems; if thoughtless or shallow moralizing would cause some to respond very negatively to transplanting livers into alcoholic cirrhotics, that cannot serve as good reason to make such moralizing the measure of public policy.

We have argued that there is now no good reason, either moral or medical, to preclude alcoholics categorically from consideration for liver transplantation. We further conclude that it would therefore be unjust to implement that categorical preclusion simply because others might respond negatively if we do not.

ADDITIONAL READING

Leon Kass is a severe advocate of holding patients responsible for their own health problems, and limiting treatment accordingly; see his "Regarding the End of Medicine and the Pursuit of Health," *The Public Interest*, 40 (1975), 11–42. Walter Glannon, in "Responsibililty, Alcoholism, and Liver Transplantation," *Journal of Medicine and Philosophy*, 23 (1998), argues for a position very similar to that of Moss and Siegler (reprinted here). E. Haavi Morreim, "Lifestyles of the Risky and Infamous: From Managed Care to Managed Lives," *Hastings Center Report* vol. 25, no. 6 (1995), 5–12, holds similar views, though his position is much more moderate than that of Kass and Glannon. Robert Veatch, in "Voluntary Risks to Health: The Ethical Issues," in *JAMA* 243 (January 4, 1980) shares this perspective.

For arguments *against* allowing judgments concerning patients' moral flaws and bad choices to influence treatment decisions, see: Robert Crawford, "Individual Responsibility and Health Politics," in P. Conrad and R. Kern, editors, *The Sociology of Health and Illness: Critical Perspectives,* 2nd ed. (New York: St. Martin's Press, 1986); Marcia Millman, "The Ideology of Self-Care: Blaming the Victims of Illness," in A. W. Johnson, O. Grusky, and B. H. Raven, editors, *Contemporary Health Services: Social Science Perspectives* (Boston: Auburn House, 1982); L. Harris, "Autonomy Under Duress," in H. E. Flack and E. D. Pellegrino, editors. *African-American Perspectives on Biomedical Ethics* (Washington, D.C.: Georgetown University Press, 1992); V. M. Gonzalez, J. Goeppinger, and K. Lorig, "Four

Psychosocial Theories and Their Application to Patient Education and Clinical Practice," *Arthritis Care and Research*, 3 (1990), 132–143.

James Childress, "Who Shall Live When Not All Can Live?" *Soundings*, 53 (Winter 1970), and widely anthologized) is the classic examination of the problem of scarce life-saving resources (such as transplant organs). Though it was written over 30 years ago—a very long time in the rapidly changing world of medicine—its insights and the clarity of the writing make it a landmark article.

ABORTION

Of all the social controversies, the issue of abortion is perhaps the most heated. There are many opposing essays to choose from, but the ones by John T. Noonan, Jr. (opposed to elective abortion) and Jane English (who argues in favor of legalized elective abortion) are particularly clear, and draw strong accounts of the opposing positions.

THE IMMORALITY OF ABORTION

John T. Noonan, Jr.

The most fundamental question involved in the long history of thought on abortion is: How do you determine the humanity of a being? To phrase the question that way is to put in comprehensive humanistic terms what the theologians either dealt with as an explicitly theological question under the heading of "ensoulment" or dealt with implicitly in their treatment of abortion. The Christian position as it originated did not depend on a narrow theological or philosophical concept. It had no relation to theories of infant baptism. It appealed to no special theory of instantaneous ensoulment. It took the world's view on ensoulment as that view changed from Aristotle to Zacchia. There was, indeed, theological influence affecting the theory of ensoulment finally adopted, and, of course, ensoulment itself was a theological concept, so that the position was always explained in theological terms. But the theological notion of ensoulment could easily be translated into humanistic language by substituting "human" for "rational soul"; the problem of knowing when a man is a man is common to theology and humanism.

If one steps outside the specific categories used by the theologians, the answer they gave can be analyzed as a refusal to discriminate among human beings on the basis of their varying potentialities. Once conceived, the being was recognized as man because he had man's potential. The criterion for humanity, thus, was simple and all-embracing: if you are conceived by human parents, you are human.

The strength of this position may be tested by a review of some of the other distinctions offered in the contemporary controversy over legalizing abortion. Perhaps the most popular distinction is in terms of viability. Before an age of so many months, the fetus is not viable, that is, it cannot be removed from the mother's womb and live apart from her. To that extent, the life of the fetus is absolutely dependent on the life of the mother. This dependence is made the basis of denying recognition to its humanity.

There are difficulties with this distinction. One is that the perfection of artificial incubation may make the fetus viable at any time: it may be removed and artifically sustained. Experiments with animals already show that such a procedure is possible. This hypothetical extreme case relates to an actual difficulty: there is considerable elasticity to the idea of viability. Mere length of life is not an exact measure. The viability of the fetus depends on the extent of its anatomical and functional development. The weight and length of the fetus are better guides to the state of its development than age, but weight and length vary.

Moreover, different racial groups have different ages at which their fetuses are viable. Some evidence, for example, suggests that Negro fetuses mature more quickly than white fetuses. If viability is the norm, the standard would vary with race and with many individual circumstances.

The most important objection to this approach is that dependence is not ended by viability. The fetus is still absolutely dependent on someone's care in order to continue existence; indeed a child of one or three or even five years of age is absolutely dependent on another's care for existence; uncared for, the older fetus or the younger child will die as surely as the early fetus detached from the mother. The unsubstantial lessening in dependence at viability does not seem to signify any special acquisition of humanity.

A second distinction has been attempted in terms of experience. A being who has had experience, has lived and suffered, who possesses memories, is more human than one who has not. Humanity depends on formation by experience. The fetus is thus "unformed" in the most basic human sense.

This distinction is not serviceable for the embryo which is already experiencing and reacting. The embryo is responsive to touch after eight weeks and at least at that point is experiencing. At an earlier stage the zygote is certainly alive and responding to its environment. The distinction may also be challenged by the rare case where aphasia has erased adult memory: has it erased humanity? More fundamentally, this distinction leaves even the older fetus or the younger child to be treated as an unformed inhuman thing. Finally, it is not clear why experience as such confers humanity. It could be argued that certain central experiences such as loving or learning are necessary to make a man human. But then human beings who have failed to love or to learn might be excluded from the class called man.

A third distinction is made by appeal to the sentiments of adults. If a fetus dies, the grief of the parents is not the grief they would have for a living child. The fetus is an unnamed "it" till birth, and is not perceived as personality until at least the fourth month of existence when movement in the womb manifests a vigorous presence demanding joyful recognition by the parents.

Yet feeling is notoriously an unsure guide to the humanity of others. Many groups of humans have had difficulty in feeling that persons of another tongue, color, religion, sex, are as human as they. Apart from reactions to alien groups, we mourn the loss of a ten-year-old boy more than the loss of his one-day-old brother or his 90-year-old grandfather. The difference felt and the grief expressed vary with the potentialities extinguished, or the experience wiped out; they do not seem to point to any substantial difference in the humanity of baby, boy, or grandfather.

Distinctions are also made in terms of sensation by the parents. The embryo is seen only at birth. What can be neither seen nor felt is different from what is tangible. If the fetus cannot be seen or touched at all, it cannot be perceived as man.

Yet experience shows that sight is even more untrustworthy than feeling in determining humanity. By sight, color became an appropriate index for saying who was a man, and the evil of racial discrimination was given foundation. Nor can touch provide the test; a being confined by sickness, "out of touch" with others, does not thereby seem to lose his humanity. To the extent that touch still has appeal as a criterion, it appears to be a survival of the old English idea of "quickening"—a possible mistranslation of the Latin *animatus* used in the canon law. To that extent touch as a criterion seems to be dependent on the Aristotelian notion of ensoulment, and to fall when this notion is discarded.

Finally, a distinction is sought in social visibility. The fetus is not socially perceived as human. It cannot communicate with others. Thus, both subjectively and objectively, it is not a member of society. As moral rules are rules for the behavior of members of society to each other, they cannot be made for behavior toward what is not yet a member. Excluded from the society of men, the fetus is excluded from the humanity of men.

By force of the argument from the consequences, this distinction is to be rejected. It is more subtle than that founded on an appeal to physical sensation, but it is equally dangerous in its implications. If humanity depends on social recognition, individuals or whole groups may be dehumanized by being denied any status in their society. Such a fate is fictionally portrayed in *1984* and has actually been the lot of many men in many societies. In the Roman empire, for example, condemnation to slavery meant the practical denial of most human rights; in the Chinese Communist world, landlords have been classified as enemies of the people and so treated as nonpersons by the state. Humanity does not depend on social recognition, though often the failure of society to recognize the prisoner, the alien, the heterodox as human has led to the destruction of human beings. Anyone conceived by a man and a woman is human. Recognition of this condition by society follows a real event in the objective order, however imperfect and halting the recognition. Any attempt to limit humanity to exclude some group runs the risk of furnishing authority and precedent for excluding other groups in the name of the consciousness or perception of the controlline group in the society.

A philosopher may reject the appeal to the humanity of the fetus because he views "humanity" as a secular view of the soul and because he doubts the existence of anything real and objective which can be identified as humanity. One answer to such a philosopher is to ask how he reasons about moral questions without supposing that there is a sense in which he and the others of whom he speaks are human. Whatever group is taken as the society which determines who may be killed is thereby taken as human. A second answer is to ask if he does not believe that there is a right and wrong way of deciding moral questions. If there is such a difference, experience may be appealed to: to decide who is human on the basis of the sentiment of a given society has led to consequences which rational men would characterize as monstrous.

The rejection of the attempted distinctions based on viability and visibility, experience and feeling, may be buttressed by the following considerations: Moral judgments often rest on distinctions, but if the distinctions are not to appear arbitrary fiat, they should relate to some real difference in probabilities. There is a kind of continuity in all life, but the earlier stages of the elements of human life possess tiny probabilities of development. Consider for example, the spermatozoa in any normal ejaculate: There are about 200,000,000 in any single ejaculate, of which one has a chance of developing into a zygote. Consider the oocytes which may become ova: there are 100,000 to 1,000,000 oocytes in a female infant, of which a maximum of 390 are ovulated. But once spermatozoon and ovum meet and the conceptus is formed, such studies as have been made show that roughly in only 20 percent of the cases will spontaneous abortion occur. In other words, the chances are about 4 out of

5 that this new being will develop. At this stage in the life of the being there is a sharp shift in probabilities, an immense jump in potentialities. To make a distinction between the rights of spermatozoa and the right of the fertilized ovum is to respond to an enormous shift in possibilities. For about twenty days after conception the egg may split to form twins or combine with another egg to form a chimera, but the probability of either event happening is very small.

It may be asked, What does a change in biological probabilities have to do with establishing humanity? The argument from probabilities is not aimed at establishing humanity but at establishing an objective discontinuity which may be taken into account in moral discourse. As life itself is a matter of probabilities, as most moral reasoning is an estimate of probabilities, so it seems in accord with the structure of reality and the nature of moral thought to found a moral judgment on the change in probabilities at conception. The appeal to probabilities is the most commensensical of arguments, to a greater or smaller degree all of us base our actions on probabilities, and in morals, as in law, prudence and negligence are often measured by the account one has taken of the probabilities. If the chance is 200,000,000 to 1 that the movement in the bushes into which you shoot is a man's, I doubt if many persons would hold you careless in shooting; but if the chances are 4 out of 5 that the movement is a human being's few would acquit you of blame. Would the argument be different if only one out of ten children conceived came to term? Of course this argument would be different. This argument is an appeal to probabilities that actually exist, not to any and all states of affairs which may be imagined.

The probabilities as they do exist do not show the humanity of the embryo in the sense of a demonstration in logic any more than the probabilities of the movement in the bush being a man demonstrate beyond all doubt that the being is a man. The appeal is a "buttressing" consideration, showing the plausibility of the standard adopted. The argument focuses on the decisional factor in any moral judgment and assumes that part of the business of a morality is drawing lines. One evidence of the nonarbitrary character of the line drawn is the difference of probabilities on either side of it. If a spermatozoon is destroyed, one destroys a being which had a chance of far less than 1 in 200 billion of developing into a reasoning being, possessed of the genetic code, a heart and other organs, and capable of pain. If a fetus is destroyed, one destroys a being already possessed of the genetic code, organs, and sensitivity to pain, and one which had an 80 percent chance of developing further into a baby outside the womb who, in time, would reason.

The positive argument for conception as the decisive moment of humanization is that at conception the new being receives the genetic code. It is this genetic information which determines his characteristics, which is the biological carrier of the possibility of human wisdom, which makes him a self-evolving being. A being with a human genetic code is man.

This review of current controversy over the humanity of the fetus emphasizes what a fundamental question the theologians resolved in asserting the inviolability of the fetus. To regard the fetus as possessed of equal rights with other humans was not, however, to decide every case where abortion might be employed. It did decide the case where the argument was that the fetus should be aborted for its own good. To say a being was human was to say it had a destiny to decide for itself which could not be taken from it by another man's decision. But human beings with equal rights often come in conflict with each other, and some decision must be made as whose claims are to prevail. Cases of conflict involving the fetus are different only in two respects: the total inability of the fetus to speak for itself and the fact that the right of the fetus regularly at stake is the right to life itself.

The approach taken by the theologians to these conflicts was articulated in terms of "direct" and "indirect." Again, to look at what they were doing from outside their categories, they may be said to have been drawing lines or "balancing values." "Direct" and "indirect" are spatial metaphors; "line-drawing" is another. "To weigh" or "to balance" values is a metaphor of a more complicated mathematical sort hinting at the process which goes on in moral judgments. All the metaphors suggest that, in the moral judgments made, comparisons were necessary, that no value completely controlled. The principle of double effect was no doctrine fallen from heaven, but a method of analysis appropriate where two relative values were being compared. In Catholic moral theology, as it developed, life even of the innocent was not taken as an absolute. Judgments on acts affecting life

issued from a process of weighing. In the weighing, the fetus was always given a value greater than zero, always a value separate and independent from its parents. This valuation was crucial and fundamental in all Christian thought on the subject and marked it off from any approach which considered that only the parents' interests needed to be considered.

Even with the fetus weighed as human, one interest could be weighed as equal or superior: that of the mother in her own life. The casuists between 1450 and 1895 were willing to weigh this interest as superior. Since 1895, that interest was given decisive weight only in the two special cases of the cancerous uterus and the ectopic pregnancy. In both of these cases the fetus itself had little chance of survival even if the abortion were not performed. As the balance was once struck in favor of the mother whenever her life was endangered, it could be so struck again. The balance reached between 1895 and 1930 attempted prudentially and pastorally to forestall a multitude of exceptions for interests less than life.

The perception of the humanity of the fetus and the weighing of fetal rights against other human rights constituted the work of the moral analysts. But what spirit animated their abstract judgments? For the Christian community it was the injunction of Scripture to love your neighbor as yourself. The fetus as human was a neighbor; his life had parity with one's own. The commandment gave life to what otherwise would have been only rational calculation.

The commandment could be put in humanistic as well as theological terms: Do not injure your fellow man without reason. In these terms, once the humanity of the fetus is perceived, abortion is never right except in self-defense. When life must be taken to save life, reason alone cannot say that a mother must prefer a child's life to her own. With this exception, now of great rarity, abortion violates the rational humanist tenet of the equality of human lives.

For Christians the commandment to love had received a special imprint in that the exemplar proposed of love was the love of the Lord for his disciples. In the light given by this example, self-sacrifice carried to the point of death seemed in the extreme situations not without meaning. In the less extreme cases, preference for one's own interests to the life of another seemed to express cruelty or selfishness irreconcilable with the demands of love.

ABORTION AND THE CONCEPT OF A PERSON

Jane English

The abortion debate rages on. Yet the two most popular positions seem to be clearly mistaken. Conservatives maintain that a human life begins at conception and that therefore abortion must be wrong because it is murder. But not all killings of humans are murders. Most notably, self defense may justify even the killing of an innocent person.

Liberals, on the other hand, are just as mistaken in their argument that since a fetus does not become a person until birth, a woman may do whatever she pleases in and to her own body. First, you cannot do as you please with your own body if it affects other people adversely. Second, if a fetus is not a person, that does not imply that you can do to it anything you wish. Animals, for example, are not persons, yet to kill or torture them for no reason at all is wrong.

At the center of the storm has been the issue of just when it is between ovulation and adulthood that a person appears on the scene. Conservatives draw the line at conception, liberals at birth. In this paper I first examine our concept of a person and conclude that no single criterion can capture the concept of a person and no sharp line can be drawn. Next I argue that if a fetus is a person, abortion is still justifiable in many cases; and if a fetus is not a person, killing it is still wrong in many cases. To a large extent, these two solutions are in agreement. I conclude that our concept of a person cannot and need not bear the weight that the abortion controversy has thrust upon it.

I

The several factions in the abortion argument have drawn battle lines around various proposed criteria for determining what is and what is not a person. For example, Mary Anne Warren lists five features (capacities for reasoning, self-awareness, complex communication, etc.) as her criteria for personhood and argues for the permissibility of abortion because a fetus falls outside this concept. Baruch Brody uses brain waves. Michael Tooley picks having-a-concept-of-self as his criterion and concludes that infanticide and abortion

are justifiable, while the killing of adult animals is not. On the other side, Paul Ramsey claims a certain gene structure is the defining characteristic. John Noonan prefers conceived-of-humans and presents counterexamples to various other candidate criteria. For instance, he argues against viability as the criterion because the newborn and infirm would then be non-persons, since they cannot live without the aid of others. He rejects any criterion that calls upon the sorts of sentiments a being can evoke in adults on the grounds that this would allow us to exclude other races as non-persons if we could just view them sufficiently unsentimentally.

These approaches are typical: foes of abortion propose sufficient conditions for personhood which fetuses satisfy, while friends of abortion counter with necessary conditions for personhood which fetuses lack. But these both presuppose that the concept of a person can be captured in a strait jacket of necessary and/or sufficient conditions. Rather, 'person' is a cluster of features, of which rationality, having a self concept and being conceived of humans are only part.

What is typical of persons? Within our concept of a person we include, first, certain biological factors: descended from humans, having a certain genetic makeup, having a head, hands, arms, eyes, capable of locomotion, breathing, eating, sleeping. There are psychological factors: sentience, perception, having a concept of self and of one's own interests and desires, the ability to use tools, the ability to use language or symbol systems, the ability to joke, to be angry, to doubt. There are rationality factors: the ability to reason and draw conclusions, the ability to generalize and to learn from past experience, the ability to sacrifice present interests for greater gains in the future. There are social factors: the ability to work in groups and respond to peer pressures, the ability to recognize and consider as valuable the interests of others, seeing oneself as one among "other minds," the ability to sympathize, encourage, love, the ability to evoke from others the responses of sympathy, encouragement, love, the ability to work with others for mutual advantage. Then there are legal factors: being subject to the law and protected by it, having the ability to sue and enter contracts, being counted in the census, having a name and citizenship, the ability to own property, inherit, and so forth.

Now the point is not that this list is incomplete, or that you can find counter-instances to each of its points. People typically exhibit rationality, for instance, but someone who was irrational would not thereby fail to qualify as a person. On the other hand, something could exhibit the majority of these features and still fail to be a person, as an advanced robot might. There is no single core of necessary and sufficient features which we can draw upon with the assurance that they constitute what really makes a person; there are only features that are more or less typical.

This is not to say that no necessary or sufficient conditions can be given. Being alive is a necessary condition for being a person, and being a U.S. Senator is sufficient. But rather than falling inside a sufficient condition or outside a necessary one, a fetus lies in the penumbra region where our concept of a person is not so simple. For this reason I think a conclusive answer to the question whether a fetus is a person is unattainable.

Here we might note a family of simple fallacies that proceed by stating a necessary condition for personhood and showing that a fetus has that characteristic. This is a form of the fallacy of affirming the consequent. For example, some have mistakenly reasoned from the premise that a fetus is human (after all, it is a human fetus rather than, say, a canine fetus), to the conclusion that it is *a* human. Adding an equivocation on 'being', we get the fallacious argument that since a fetus is something both living and human, it is a human being.

Nonetheless, it does seem clear that a fetus has very few of the above family of characteristics, whereas a newborn baby exhibits a much larger proportion of them—and a two-year-old has even more. Note that one traditional anti-abortion argument has centered on pointing out the many ways in which a fetus resembles a baby. They emphasize its development ("It already has ten fingers . . .") without mentioning its dissimilarities to adults (it still has gills and a tail). They also try to evoke the sort of sympathy on our part that we only feel toward other persons

("Never to laugh . . . or feel the sunshine?"). This all seems to be a relevant way to argue, since its purpose is to persuade us that a fetus satisfies so many of the important features on the list that it ought to be treated as a person. Also note that a fetus near the time of birth satisfies many more of these factors than a fetus in the early months of development. This could provide reason for making distinctions among the different stages of pregnancy, as the U.S. Supreme Court has done.

Historically, the time at which a person has been said to come into existence has varied widely. Muslims date personhood from fourteen days after conception. Some medievals followed Aristotle in placing ensoulment at forty days after conception for a male fetus and eighty days for a female fetus. In European common law since the Seventeenth Century, abortion was considered the killing of a person only after quickening, the time when a pregnant woman first feels the fetus move on its own. Nor is this variety of opinions surprising. Biologically, a human being develops gradually. We shouldn't expect there to be any specific time or sharp dividing point when a person appears on the scene.

For these reasons I believe our concept of a person is not sharp or decisive enough to bear the weight of a solution to the abortion controversy. To use it to solve that problem is to clarify *obscurum per obscurius*.

II

Next let us consider what follows if a fetus is a person after all. Judith Jarvis Thomson's landmark article, "A Defense of Abortion," correctly points out that some additional argumentation is needed at this point in the conservative argument to bridge the gap between the premise that a fetus is an innocent person and the conclusion that killing it is always wrong. To arrive at this conclusion, we would need the additional premise that killing an innocent person is always wrong. But killing an innocent person is sometimes permissible, most notably in self defense. Some examples may help draw out our intuitions or ordinary judgments about self defense.

Suppose a mad scientist, for instance, hypnotized innocent people to jump out of the bushes and attack innocent passers-by with knives. If you are so attacked, we agree you have a right to kill the attacker in self defense, if killing him is the only way to protect your life or to save yourself from serious injury. It does not seem to matter here that the attacker is not malicious but himself an innocent pawn, for your killing of him is not done in a spirit of retribution but only in self defense.

How severe an injury may you inflict in self defense In part this depends upon the severity of the injury to be avoided: you may not shoot someone merely to avoid having your clothes torn. This might lead one to the mistaken conclusion that the defense may only equal the threatened injury in severity; that to avoid death you may kill, but to avoid a black eye you may only inflict a black eye or the equivalent. Rather, our laws and customs seem to say that you may create an injury somewhat, but not enormously, greater than the injury to be avoided. To fend off an attack whose outcome would be as serious as rape, a severe beating or the loss of a finger, you may shoot; to avoid having your clothes torn, you may blacken an eye.

Aside from this, the injury you may inflict should only be the minimum necessary to deter or incapacitate the attacker. Even if you know he intends to kill you, you are not justified in shooting him if you could equally well save yourself by the simple expedient of running away. Self defense is for the purpose of avoiding harms rather than equalizing harms.

Some cases of pregnancy present a parallel situation. Though the fetus is itself innocent, it may pose a threat to the pregnant woman's well-being, life prospects or health, mental or physical. If the pregnancy presents a slight threat to her interests, it seems self defense cannot justify abortion. But if the threat is on a par with a serious beating or the loss of a finger, she may kill the fetus that poses such a threat, even if it is an innocent person. If a lesser harm to the fetus could have the same defensive effect, killing it would not be justified. It is unfortunate that the only way to free the woman from the pregnancy entails the death of the fetus (except in very late stages of pregnancy). Thus a self defense model supports Thomson's point that the woman has a right only to be freed from the fetus, not a right to demand its death.

The self defense model is most helpful when we take the pregnant woman's point of view. In the pre-Thomson literature, abortion is often framed as a question for a third party: do you, a doctor, have a right to choose between the life of the woman and that of the fetus? Some have claimed that if you were a passer-by who witnessed a struggle between the innocent hypnotized attacker and his equally innocent victim, you would have no reason to kill either in defense of the other. They have concluded that the self defense model implies that a woman may attempt to abort herself, but that a doctor should not assist her. I think the position of the third party is somewhat more complex. We do feel some inclination to intervene on behalf of the victim rather than the attacker, other things equal. But if both parties are innocent, other factors come into consideration. You would rush to the aid of your husband whether he was attacker or attackee. If a hypnotized famous violinist were attacking a skid row bum, we would try to save the individual who is of more value to society. These considerations would tend to support abortion in some cases.

But suppose you are a frail senior citizen who wishes to avoid being knifed by one of these innocent hypnotics, so you have hired a bodyguard to accompany you. If you are attacked, it is clear we believe that the bodyguard, acting as your agent, has a right to kill the attacker to save you from a serious beating. Your rights of self defense are transferred to your agent. I suggest that we should similarly view the doctor as the pregnant woman's agent in carrying out a defense she is physically incapable of accomplishing herself.

Thanks to modern technology, the cases are rare in which a pregnancy poses as clear a threat to a woman's bodily health as an attacker brandishing a switchblade. How does self defense fare when more subtle, complex and long-range harms are involved?

To consider a somewhat fanciful example, suppose you are a highly trained surgeon when you are kidnapped by the hypnotic attacker. He says he does not intend to harm you but to take you back to the mad scientist who, it turns out, plans to hypnotize you to have a permanent mental block against all your knowledge of medicine. This would automatically destroy your career which would in turn have a serious adverse impact on your family, your personal relationships and your happiness. It seems to me that if the only way you can avoid this outcome is to shoot the innocent attacker, you are justified in so doing. You are defending yourself from a drastic injury to your life prospects. I think it is no exaggeration to claim that unwanted pregnancies (most obviously among teenagers) often have such adverse life-long consequences as the surgeon's loss of livelihood.

Several parallels arise between various views on abortion and the self defense model. Let's suppose further that these hypnotized attackers only operate at night, so that it is well known that they can be avoided completely by the considerable inconvenience of never leaving your house after dark. One view is that since you could stay home at night, therefore if you go out and are selected by one of these hypnotized people, you have no right to defend yourself. This parallels the view that abstinence is the only acceptable way to avoid pregnancy. Others might hold that you ought to take along some defense such as Mace which will deter the hypnotized person without killing him, but that if this defense fails, you are obliged to submit to the resulting injury, no matter how severe it is. This parallels the view that contraception is all right but abortion is always wrong, even in cases of contraceptive failure.

A third view is that you may kill the hypnotized person only if he will actually kill you, but not if he will only injure you. This is like the position that abortion is permissible only if it is required to save a woman's life. Finally we have the view that it is all right to kill the attacker, even if only to avoid a very slight inconvenience to yourself and even if you knowingly walked down the very street where all these incidents have been taking place without taking along any Mace or protective escort. If we assume that a fetus is a person, this is the analogue of the view that abortion is always justifiable, "on demand."

The self defense model allows us to see an important difference that exists between abortion and infanticide, even if a fetus is a person from conception. Many have argued that the only way to justify abortion without justifying infanticide would be to find some characteristic of personhood that is acquired at birth. Michael Tooley, for one, claims infanticide is justifiable because the really significant characteristics of person are acquired some time after birth. But all such approaches look to characteristics of the developing human and ignore the relation between the fetus and the woman. What if, after birth, the presence of an infant or the need to support it posed a grave threat to the woman's sanity or life prospects? She could escape this threat by the simple expedient of running away. So a solution that does not entail the death of the infant is available. Before birth, such solutions are not available because of the biological dependence of the fetus on the woman. Birth is the crucial point not because of any characteristics the fetus gains, but because after birth the woman can defend herself by a means less drastic than killing the infant. Hence self defense can be used to justify abortion without necessarily thereby justifying infanticide.

III

On the other hand, supposing a fetus is not after all a person, would abortion always be morally permissible? Some opponents of abortion seem worried that if a fetus is not a full-fledged person, then we are justified in treating it in any way at all. However, this does not follow. Non-persons do get some consideration in our moral code, though of course they do not have the same rights as persons have (and in general they do not have moral responsibilities), and though their interests may be overridden by the interests of persons. Still, we cannot just treat them in any way at all.

Treatment of animals is a case in point. It is wrong to torture dogs for fun or to kill wild birds for no reason at all. It is wrong Period, even though dogs and birds do not have the same rights persons do. However, few people think it is wrong to use dogs as experimental animals, causing them considerable suffering in some cases, provided that the resulting research will probably bring discoveries of great benefit to people. And most of us think it all right to kill birds for food or to protect our crops. People's rights are different from the consideration we give to animals, then, for it is wrong to experiment on people, even if others might later benefit a great deal as a result of their suffering. You might volunteer to be a subject, but this would be supererogatory; you certainly have a right to refuse to be a medical guinea pig.

But how do we decide what you may or may not do to non-persons? This is a difficult problem, one for which I believe no adequate account exists. You do not want to say, for instance, that torturing dogs is all right whenever the sum of its effects on people is good—when it doesn't warp the sensibilities of the torturer so much that he mistreats people. If that were the case, it would be all right to torture dogs if you did it in private, or if the torturer lived on a desert island or died soon afterward, so that his actions had no effect on people. This is an inadequate account, because whatever moral consideration animals get, it has to be indefeasible, too. It will have to be a general proscription of certain actions, not merely a weighing of the impact on people on a case-by-case basis.

Rather, we need to distinguish two levels on which consequences of actions can be taken into account in moral reasoning. The traditional objections to Utilitarianism focus on the fact that it operates solely on the first level, taking all the consequences into account in particular cases only. Thus Utilitarianism is open to "desert island" and "lifeboat" counterexamples because these cases are rigged to make the consequences of actions severely limited.

Rawls' theory could be described as a teleological sort of theory, but with teleology operating on a higher level. In choosing the principles to regulate society from the original position, his hypothetical choosers make their decision on the basis of the total consequences of various systems. Furthermore, they are constrained to choose a general set of rules which people can readily learn and apply. An ethical theory must operate by generating a set of sympathies and attitudes toward others which reinforces the functioning of that set of moral principles. Our prohibition against killing people operates by means of certain moral sentiments including sympathy, compassion and guilt. But if these attitudes are to form a coherent set, they carry us further: we tend to perform supererogatory actions, and we tend to feel similar compassion toward person-like non-persons.

It is crucial that psychological facts play a role here. Our psychological constitution makes it the case that for our ethical theory to work, it must prohibit certain treatment of non-persons which are sig-

nificantly person-like. If our moral rules allowed people to treat some person-like non-persons in ways we do not want people to be treated, this would undermine the system of sympathies and attitudes that makes the ethical system work. For this reason, we would choose in the original position to make mistreatment of some sorts of animals wrong in general (not just wrong in the cases with public impact), even though animals are not themselves parties in the original position. Thus it makes sense that it is those animals whose appearance and behavior are most like those of people that get the most consideration in our moral scheme.

It is because of "coherence of attitudes," I think, that the similarity of a fetus to a baby is very significant. A fetus one week before birth is so much like a newborn baby in our psychological space that we cannot allow any cavalier treatment of the former while expecting full sympathy and nurturative support for the latter. Thus, I think that anti-abortion forces are indeed giving their strongest arguments when they point to the similarities between a fetus and a baby, and when they try to evoke our emotional attachment to and sympathy for the fetus. An early horror story from New York about nurses who were expected to alternate between caring for six-week premature infants and disposing of viable 24-week aborted fetuses is just that—a horror story. These beings are so much alike that no one can be asked to draw a distinction and treat them so very differently.

Remember, however, that in the early weeks after conception, a fetus is very much unlike a person. It is hard to develop these feelings for a set of genes which doesn't yet have a head, hands, beating heart, response to touch or the ability to move by itself. Thus it seems to me that the alleged "slippery slope" between conception and birth is not so very slippery. In the early stages of pregnancy, abortion can hardly be compared to murder for psychological reasons, but in the latest stages it is psychologically akin to murder.

Another source of similarity is the bodily continuity between fetus and adult. Bodies play a surprisingly central role in our attitudes toward persons. One has only to think of the philosophical literature on how far physical identity suffices for personal identity or Wittgenstein's remark that the best picture of the human soul is the human body. Even after death, when all agree the body is no longer a person, we still observe elaborate customs of respect for the human body; like people who torture dogs, necrophiliacs are not to be trusted with people. So it is appropriate that we show respect to a fetus as the body continuous with the body of a person. This is a degree of resemblance to persons that animals cannot rival.

Michael Tooley also utilizes a parallel with animals. He claims that it is always permissible to drown newborn kittens and draws conclusions about infanticide. But it is only permissible to drown kittens when their survival would cause some hardship. Perhaps it would be a burden to feed and house six more cats or to find other homes for them. The alternative of letting them starve produces even more suffering than the drowning. Since the kittens get their rights second-hand, so to speak, *via* the need for coherence in our attitudes, their interests are often overridden by the interests of full-fledged persons. But if their survival would be no inconvenience to people at all, then it is wrong to drown them, *contra* Tooley.

Tooley's conclusions about abortion are wrong for the same reason. Even if a fetus is not a person, abortion is not always permissible, because of the resemblance of a fetus to a person. I agree with Thomson that it would be wrong for a woman who is seven months pregnant to have an abortion just to avoid having to postpone a trip to Europe. In the early months of pregnancy when the fetus hardly resembles a baby at all, then, abortion is permissible whenever it is in the interests of the pregnant woman or her family. The reasons would only need to outweigh the pain and inconvenience of the abortion itself. In the middle months, when the fetus comes to resemble a person, abortion would be justifiable only when the continuation of the pregnancy or the birth of the child would cause harms—physical, psychological, economic or social—to the woman. In the late months of pregnancy, even on our current assumption that a fetus is not a person, abortion seems to be wrong except to save a woman from significant injury or death.

The Supreme Court has recognized similar gradations in the alleged slippery slope stretching between conception and birth. To this point, the present paper has been a discussion of the moral status of abortion only, not its legal status. In view of the great physical, financial and sometimes psychological costs of abortion, perhaps the legal arrangement most compatible with the proposed moral solution would be the absence of restrictions, that is, so-called abortion "on demand."

So I conclude, first, that application of our concept of a person will not suffice to settle the abortion issue. After all, the biological development of a human being is gradual. Second, whether a fetus is a person or not, abortion is justifiable early in pregnancy to avoid modest harms and seldom justifiable late in pregnancy except to avoid significant injury or death.

ADDITIONAL READING

Judith Jarvis Thomson's "In Defense of Abortion" remains the classic prochoice argument, though very limited in scope. It originally appeared in *Philosophy & Public Affairs*, vol. 1, no. 1 (1971), and is now widely anthologized. Another well-known prochoice essay is by Mary Anne Warren: "On the Moral and Legal Status of Abortion," *The Monist*, vol. 57, no. 1 (1973).

A widely anthologized argument opposing abortion is by Don Marquis, "Why Abortion Is Immoral," *Journal of Philosophy*, 86 (April 1989).

Among the anthologies on abortion are Susan Dwyer and Joel Feinberg's *The Problem of Abortion*, 3rd ed. (Belmont, Calif.: Wadsworth, 1997).

Ronald Dworkin's *Life's Dominion: An Argument About Abortion, Euthanasia, and Individual Freedom* (New York: Alfred A. Knopf, 1993) treats the issue very carefully, showing respect for both sides of this deeply contentious issue. Frances Myrna Kamm, *Creation and*

Abortion: A Study in Moral and Legal Philosophy (New York: Oxford University Press, 1992) is another excellent and thoughtful book on the subject. Laurence Tribe, *Abortion: The Clash of Absolutes* (New York: W. W. Norton, 1990) is the work of a distinguished legal scholar. Daniel Callahan criticizes many of the arguments on *both* sides of the issue. His own conclusion may not satisfy either side of the conflict, but it is well worth noting:

> Although the contending sides in the abortion debate commonly ignore, or systematically deride, the essentially positive impulses lying behind their opponents' positions, the conflict is nonetheless best seen as the pitting of essentially valuable impulses against one another. The possibility of a society which did allow women the right and the freedom to control their own lives is a lofty goal. No less lofty is that of a society which, with no exceptions, treated all forms of human life as equally valuable. In the best of all possible worlds, it might be possible to reconcile these goals. In the real world, however, the first goal requires the right of abortion, and the second goal excludes that right. This, I believe, is a genuine and deep dilemma. That so few are willing to recognize the dilemma, or even to admit that any choice must be less than perfect, is the most disturbing element of the whole debate.
>
> —Daniel Callahan, "Abortion: Some Ethical Issues"

AFFIRMATIVE ACTION

The views of Lisa Newton and Ronald Dworkin offer a stark contrast on the issue of affirmative action, an issue that remains controversial, and that is likely to be involved in a number of future Supreme Court rulings.

AGAINST AFFIRMATIVE ACTION

Lisa H. Newton

I have heard it argued that "simple justice" requires that we favor women and blacks in employment and educational opportunities, since women and blacks were "unjustly" excluded from such opportunities for so many years in the not so distant past. It is a strange argument, an example of a possible implication of a true proposition advanced to dispute the proposition itself, like an octopus absent-mindedly slicing off his head with a stray tentacle. A fatal confusion underlies this argument, a confusion fundamentally relevant to our understanding of the notion of the rule of law.

Two senses of justice and equality are involved in this confusion. The root notion of justice, progenitor of the other, is the one that Aristotle (*Nichomachean Ethics* 5. 6; *Politics* 1.2; 3. 1) assumes to be the founda-

tion and proper virtue of the political association. It is the condition which free men establish among themselves when they "share a common life in order that their association bring them self-sufficiency"—the regulation of their relationship by law, and the establishment, by law, of equality before the law. Rule of law is the name and pattern of this justice; its equality stands against the inequalities—of wealth, talent, etc.—otherwise obtaining among its participants, who by virtue of that equality are called "citizens." It is an achievement—complete, or, more frequently, partial—of certain people in certain concrete situations. It is fragile and easily disrupted by powerful individuals who discover that the blind equality of rule of law is inconvenient for their interests. Despite its obvious instability, Aristotle assumed that the establishment of justice in this sense, the creation of citizenship, was a permanent possibility for men and that the resultant association of citizens was the natural home of the species. At levels below the political association, this rule-governed equality is easily found; it is exemplified by any group of children agreeing together to play a game. At the level of the political association, the attainment of this justice is more difficult, simply because the stakes are so much higher for each participant. The equality of citizenship is not something that happens of its own accord, and without the expenditure of a fair amount of effort it will collapse into the rule of a powerful few over an apathetic many. But at least it has been achieved, at some times in some places; it is always worth trying to achieve, and eminently worth trying to maintain, wherever and to whatever degree it has been brought into being.

Aristotle's parochialism is notorious; he really did not imagine that persons other than Greeks could associate freely in justice, and the only form of association he had in mind was the Greek *polis*. With the decline of the *polis* and the shift in the center of political thought, his notion of justice underwent a sea change. To be exact, it ceased to represent a political type and became a moral ideal: the ideal of equality as we know it. This ideal demands that all men be included in citizenship—that one Law govern all equally, that all men regard all other men as fellow citizens, with the same guarantees, rights, and protections. Briefly, it demands that the circle of citizenship achieved by any group be extended to include the entire human race. Properly understood, its effect on our associations can be excellent: it congratulates us on our achievement of rule of law as a process of government but refuses to let us remain complacent until we have expanded the associations to include others within the ambit of the rules, as often and as far as possible. While one man is a slave, none of us may feel truly free. We are constantly prodded by this ideal to look for possible unjustifiable discrimination, for inequalities not absolutely required for the functioning of the society, and advantageous to all. And after twenty centuries of pressure, not at all constant, from this ideal, it might be said that some progress has been made. To take the cases in point for this problem, we are now prepared to assert, as Aristotle would never have been, the equality of sexes and of persons

of different colors. The ambit of American citizenship, once restricted to white males of property, has been extended to include all adult free men, then all adult males including ex-slaves, then all women. The process of acquisition of full citizenship was for these groups a sporadic trail of half-measures, even now not complete; the steps on the road to full equality are marked by legislation and judicial decisions which are only recently concluded and still often not enforced. But the fact that we can now discuss the possibility of favoring such groups in hiring shows that over the area that concerns us, at least, full equality is presupposed as a basis for discussion. To that extent, they are full citizens, fully protected by the law of the land.

It is important for my argument that the moral ideal of equality be recognized as logically distinct from the condition (or virtue) of justice in the political sense. Justice in this sense exists *among* a citizenry, irrespective of the number of the populace included in that citizenry. Further, the moral ideal is parasitic upon the political virtue, for "equality" is unspecified—it means nothing until we are told in what respect that equality is to be realized. In a political context, "equality" is specified as "equal rights"—equal access to the public realm, public goods and offices, equal treatment under the law—in brief, the equality of citizenship. If citizenship is not a possibility, political equality is unintelligible. The ideal emerges as a generalization of the real condition and refers back to that condition for its content.

Now, if justice (Aristotle's justice in the political sense) is equal treatment under law for all citizens, what is injustice? Clearly, injustice is the violation of that equality, discriminating for or against a group of citizens, favoring them with special immunities and privileges or depriving them of those guaranteed to the others. When the southern employer refuses to hire blacks in white-collar jobs, when Wall Street will only hire women as secretaries with new titles, when Mississippi high schools routinely flunk all black boys above ninth grade, we have examples of injustice, and we work to restore the equality of the public realm by ensuring that equal opportunity will be provided in such cases in the future. But of course, when the employers and the schools *favor* women and blacks, the same injustice is done. Just as the previous discrimination did, this reverse discrimination violates the public equality which defines citizenship and destroys the rule of law for the areas in which these favors are granted. To the extent that we adopt a program of discrimination, reverse or otherwise, justice in the political sense is destroyed, and none of us, specifically affected or not, is a citizen, a bearer of rights—we are all petitioners for favors. And to the same extent, the ideal of equality is undermined, for it has content only where justice obtains, and by destroying justice we render the ideal meaningless. It is, then, an ironic paradox, if not a contradiction in terms, to assert that the ideal of equality justifies the violation of justice; it is as if one should argue, with William Buckley, that an ideal of humanity can justify the destruction of the human race.

Logically, the conclusion is simple enough: all discrimination is wrong *prima facie* because it violates justice, and that goes for reverse discrimination too. No violation of justice among the citizens may be justified (may overcome the *prima facie* objection) by appeal to the ideal of equality, for that ideal is logically dependent upon the notion of justice. Reverse discrimination, then, which attempts no other justification than an appeal to equality, is wrong. But let us try to make the conclusion more plausible by suggesting some of the implications of the suggested practice of reverse discrimination in employment and education. My argument will be that the problems raised there are insoluble, not only in practice but in principle.

We may argue, if we like, about what "discrimination" consists of. Do I discriminate against blacks if I admit none to my school when none of the black applicants are qualified by the tests I always give? How far must I go to root out cultural bias from my application forms and tests before I can say that I have not discriminated against those of different cultures? Can I assume that women are not strong enough to be roughnecks on my oil rigs, or must I test them individually? But this controversy, the most popular and well-argued aspect of the issue, is not as fatal as two others which cannot be avoided: if we are regarding the blacks as a "minority" victimized by discrimination, what is a "minority"? And for any group—blacks, women, whatever—that has been discriminated against, what amount of reverse discrimination wipes out the initial discrimination? Let us grant as true that women and blacks were discriminated against, even when laws forbade such discrimination, and grant for the sake of argument that a

history of discrimination must be wiped out by reverse discrimination. What follows?

First, are there other groups which have been discriminated against? For they should have the same right of restitution. What about American Indians, Chicanos, Appalachian Mountain whites, Puerto Ricans, Jews, Cajuns, and Orientals? And if these are to be included, the principle according to which we specify a "minority" is simply the criterion of "ethnic (sub) group," and we're stuck with every hyphenated American in the lower-middle class clamoring for special privileges for *his* group—and with equal justification. For be it noted, when we run down the Harvard roster, we find not only a scarcity of blacks (in comparison with the proportion in the population) but an even more striking scarcity of those second-, third-, and fourth-generation ethnics who make up the loudest voice of Middle America. Shouldn't they demand *their* share? And eventually, the WASPs will have to form their own lobby, for they too are a minority. The point is simply this: there is no "majority" in America who will not mind giving up just a bit of their rights to make room for a favored minority. There are only other minorities, each of which is discriminated against by the favoring. The initial injustice is then repeated dozens of times, and if each minority is granted the same right of restitution as the others, an entire area of rule governance is dissolved into a pushing and shoving match between self-interested groups. Each works to catch the public eye and political popularity by whatever means of advertising and power politics lend themselves to the effort, to capitalize as much as possible on temporary popularity until the restless mob picks another group to feel sorry for. Hardly an edifying spectacle, and in the long run no one can benefit: the pie is no larger—it's just that instead of setting up and enforcing rules for getting a piece, we've turned the contest into a free-for-all, requiring much more effort for no larger a reward. It would be in the interest of all the participants to reestablish an objective rule to govern the process, carefully enforced and the same for all.

Second, supposing that we do manage to agree in general that women and blacks (and all the others) have some right of restitution, some right to a privileged place in the structure of opportunities for a while, how will we know when that while is up? How much privilege is enough? When will the guilt be gone, the price paid, the balance restored? What recompense is right for centuries of exclusion? What criterion tells us when we are done? Our experience with the Civil Rights movement shows us that agreement on these terms cannot be presupposed: a process that appears to some to be going at a mad gallop into a black takeover appears to the rest of us to be at a standstill. Should a practice of reverse discrimination be adopted, we may safely predict that just as some of us begin to see "a satisfactory start toward righting the balance," others of us will see that we "have already gone too far in the other direction" and will suggest that the discrimination ought to be reversed again. And such disagreement is inevitable, for the point is that we could not *possibly* have any criteria for evaluating the kind of recompense we have in mind. The context presumed by any discussion of restitution is the context of rule of law: law sets the rights of men and simultaneously sets the method for remedying the violation of those rights. You may exact suffering from others and/or damage payments for yourself if and only if the others have violated your rights; the suffering you have endured is not sufficient reason for them to suffer. And remedial rights exist only where there is law: primary human rights are useful guides to legislation but cannot stand as reasons for awarding remedies

for injuries sustained. But then, the context presupposed by any discussion of restitution is the context of preexistent full citizenship. No remedial rights could exist for the excluded; neither in law nor in logic does there exist a right to *sue* for a standing to sue.

From these two considerations, then, the difficulties with reverse discrimination become evident. Restitution for a disadvantaged group whose rights under the law have been violated is possible by legal means, but restitution for a disadvantaged group whose grievance is that there was no law to protect them simply is not. First, outside of the area of justice defined by the law, no sense can be made of "the group's rights," for no law recognizes that group or the individuals in it, qua members, as bearers of rights (hence *any* group can constitute itself as a disadvantaged minority in some sense and demand similar restitution). Second, outside of the area of protection of law, no sense can be made of the violation of rights (hence the amount of the recompense cannot be decided by any objective criterion). For both reasons, the practice of reverse discrimination undermines the foundation of the very ideal in whose name it is advocated; it destroys justice, law, equality, and citizenship itself, and replaces them with power struggles and popularity contests.

THE JUSTICE OF AFFIRMATIVE ACTION

Ronald Dworkin

I

In 1945 a black man named Sweatt applied to the University of Texas Law School, but was refused admission because state law provided that only whites could attend. The Supreme Court declared that this law violated Sweatt's rights under the Fourteenth Amendment to the United States Constitution, which provides that no state shall deny any man the equal protection of its laws. In 1971 a Jew named DeFunis applied to the University of Washington Law School; he was rejected although his test scores and college grades were such that he would have been admitted if he had been a black or a Filipino or a Chicano or an American Indian. DeFunis asked the Supreme Court to declare that the Washington practice, which

required less exacting standards of minority groups, violated his rights under the Fourteenth Amendment.

The Washington Law School's admission procedures were complex. Applications were divided into two groups. The majority—those not from the designated minority groups—were first screened so as to eliminate all applicants whose predicted average, which is a function of college grades and aptitude test scores, fell below a certain level. Majority applicants who survived this initial cut were then placed in categories that received progressively more careful consideration. Minority-group applications, on the other hand, were not screened; each received the most careful consideration by a special committee consisting of a black professor of law and a white professor who had taught in programs to aid black law students. Most of the minority applicants who were accepted in the year in which DeFunis was rejected had predicted averages below the cutoff level, and the law school conceded that any minority applicant with his average would certainly have been accepted.

The *DeFunis* case split those political action groups that have traditionally supported liberal causes. The B'nai B'rith Anti-Defamation League and the AFL-CIO, for example, filed briefs as amici curiae in support of DeFunis's claim, while the American Hebrew Women's Council, the UAW, and the UMWA filed briefs against it.

These splits among old allies demonstrate both the practical and the philosophical importance of the case. In the past liberals held, within one set of attitudes, three propositions: that racial classification is an evil in itself; that every person has a right to an educational opportunity commensurate with his abilities; and that affirmative state action is proper to remedy the serious inequalities of American society. In the last decade, however, the opinion has grown that these three liberal propositions are in fact not compatible, because the most effective programs of state action are those that give a competitive advantage to minority racial groups.

That opinion has, of course, been challenged. Some educators argue that benign quotas are ineffective, even self-defeating, because preferential treatment will reinforce the sense of inferiority that many blacks already have. Others make a more general objection. They argue that any racial discrimination, even for the purpose of benefiting minorities, will in fact harm those minorities, because prejudice is fostered whenever racial distinctions are tolerated for any purpose whatever. But these are complex and controversial empirical judgments, and it is far too early, as wise critics concede, to decide whether preferential treatment does more harm or good. Nor is it the business of judges, particularly in constitutional cases, to overthrow decisions of other officials because the judges disagree about the efficiency of social policies. This empirical criticism is therefore reinforced by the moral argument that even if reverse discrimination does benefit minorities and does reduce prejudice in the long run, it is nevertheless wrong because distinctions of race are inherently unjust. They are unjust because they violate the

rights of individual members of groups not so favored, who may thereby lose a place, as DeFunis did.

DeFunis presented this moral argument, in the form of a constitutional claim, to the courts. The Supreme Court did not, in the end, decide whether the argument was good or bad. DeFunis had been admitted to the law school after one lower court had decided in his favor, and the law school said that he would be allowed to graduate however the case was finally decided. The Court therefore held that the case was moot and dismissed the appeal on that ground. But Justice Douglas disagreed with this neutral disposition of the case; he wrote a dissenting opinion in which he argued that the Court should have upheld DeFunis's claim on the merits. Many universities and colleges have taken Justice Douglas's opinion as handwriting on the wall, and have changed their practices in anticipation of a later Court decision in which his opinion prevails. In fact, his opinion pointed out that law schools might achieve much the same result by a more sophisticated policy than Washington used. A school might stipulate, for example, that applicants from all races and groups would be considered together, but that the aptitude tests of certain minority applicants would be graded differently, or given less weight in overall predicted average, because experience had shown that standard examinations were for different reasons a poorer test of the actual ability of these applicants. But if this technique is used deliberately to achieve the same result, it is devious, and it remains to ask why the candid program used by the University of Washington was either unjust or unconstitutional.

II

DeFunis plainly has no constitutional right that the state provide him a legal education of a certain quality. His rights would not be violated if his state did not have a law school at all, or if it had a law school with so few places that he could not win one on intellectual merit. Nor does he have a right to insist that intelligence be the exclusive test of admission. Law schools do rely heavily on intellectual tests for admission. That seems proper, however, not because applicants have a right to be judged in that way, but because it is reasonable to think that the community as a whole is better off if its lawyers are intelligent. That is, intellectual standards are justified, not because they reward the clever, but because they seem to serve a useful social policy.

Law schools sometimes serve that policy better, moreover, by supplementing intelligence tests with other sorts of standards: they sometimes prefer industrious applicants, for example, to those who are brighter but lazier. They also serve special policies for which intelligence is not relevant. The Washington Law School, for example, gave special preference not only to minority applicants but also to veterans who had been at the school before entering the military, and neither DeFunis nor any of the briefs submitted in his behalf complained of that preference.

DeFunis does not have an absolute right to a law school place, nor does he have a right that only intelligence be used as a standard for admission. He says he nevertheless has a right that race *not* be used as a standard, no matter how well a racial classification might work to promote the general welfare or to reduce social and economic inequality. He does not claim, however, that he has this right as a distinct and independent political right that is specifically protected by the Constitution, as is his right to freedom of speech and religion. The Constitution does not condemn racial classification directly, as it does condemn censorship or the establishment of a state religion. DeFunis claims that his right that race not be used as a criterion of admission follows from the more abstract right of equality that is protected by the Fourteenth Amendment, which provides that no state shall deny to any person the equal protection of the law.

But the legal arguments made on both sides show that neither the text of the Constitution nor the prior decisions of the Supreme Court decisively settle the question whether, as a matter of law, the Equal Protection Clause makes all racial classifications unconstitutional. The Clause makes the concept of equality a test of legislation, but it does not stipulate any particular conception of that concept. Those who wrote the clause intended to attack certain consequences of slavery and racial prejudice, but it is unlikely that they intended to outlaw all racial classifications, or that they expected such a prohibition to be the result of what they wrote. They outlawed whatever policies would violate equality, but left it to others to decide, from time to time, what that means.

There cannot be a good legal argument in favor of DeFunis, therefore, unless there is a good moral argument that all racial classifications, even those that make society as a whole more equal, are inherently offensive to an individual's right to equal protection for himself.

There is nothing paradoxical, of course, in the ideal that an individual's right to equal protection may sometimes conflict with an otherwise desirable social policy, including the policy of making the community more equal overall. Suppose a law school were to charge a few middle-class students selected by lot, double tuition in order to increase the scholarship fund for poor students. It would be serving a desirable policy—equality of opportunity—by means that violated the right of the students selected by lot to be treated equally with other students who could also afford the increased fees. It is, in fact, part of the importance of DeFunis's case that it forces us to acknowledge the distinction between equality as a policy and equality as a right, a distinction that political theory has virtually ignored. He argues that the Washington Law School violated his individual right to equality for the sake of a policy of greater equality overall, in the same way that double tuition for arbitrarily chosen students would violate their rights for the same purpose.

We must therefore concentrate our attention on that claim. We must try to define the central concept on which it turns, which is the concept of an individual right to equality made a constitutional right by the Equal Protection Clause. What rights to equality do citizens have as individuals which might defeat programs aimed at important economic and social policies, including the social policy of improving equality overall?

There are two different sorts of rights they may be said to have. The first is the right to *equal treatment,* which is the right to an equal distribution of some opportunity or resource or burden. Every citizen, for example, has a right to an equal vote in a democracy; that is the nerve of the Supreme Court's decision that one person must have one vote even if a different and more complex arrangement would better secure the collective welfare. The second is the right to *treatment as an equal,* which is the right, not to receive the same distribution of some burden or benefit, but to be treated with the same respect and concern as anyone else. If I have two children, and one is dying from a disease that is making the other uncomfortable, I do not show equal concern if I flip a coin to decide which should have the remaining dose of a drug. This example shows that the right to treatment as an equal is fundamental, and the right to equal treatment, derivative. In some circumstances the right to treatment as an equal will entail a right to equal treatment, but not, by any means, in all circumstances.

DeFunis does not have a right to equal treatment in the assignment of law school places; he does not have a right to a place just because others are given places. Individuals may have a right to equal treatment in elementary education, because someone who is denied elementary education is unlikely to lead a useful life. But legal education is not so vital that everyone has an equal right to it.

DeFunis does have the second sort of right—a right to treatment as an equal in the decision as to which admissions standards should be used. That is, he has a right that his interests be treated as fully and sympathetically as the interests of any others when the law school decides whether to count race as a pertinent criterion for admission. But we must be careful not to overstate what that means.

Suppose an applicant complains that his right to be treated as an equal is violated by tests that place the less intelligent candidates at a disadvantage against the more intelligent. A law school might properly reply in the following way. Any standard will place certain candidates at a disadvantage as against others, but an admission policy may nevertheless be justified if it seems reasonable to expect that the overall gain to the community exceeds the overall loss, and if no other policy that does not provide a comparable disadvantage would produce even roughly the same gain. An individual's right to be treated as an equal means that his potential loss must be treated as a matter of concern, but that loss may nevertheless be outweighed by the gain to the community as a whole. If it is, then the less intelligent applicant cannot claim that he is cheated of his right to be treated as an equal just because he suffers a disadvantage others do not.

Washington may make the same reply to DeFunis. Any admissions policy must put some applicants at a disadvantage, and a policy of preference for minority applicants can reasonably be supposed to benefit the community as a whole, even when the loss to candidates such as DeFunis is taken into account. If there are more black lawyers, they will help to provide better legal services to the black community, and so reduce social tensions. It might well improve the quality of legal education for all students, moreover, to have a greater number of blacks as classroom discussants of social problems. Further, if blacks are seen as successful law students, then other blacks who do meet the usual intellectual standards might be encouraged to apply and that, in turn, would raise the intellectual quality of the bar. In any case, preferential admissions of blacks should decrease the difference in wealth and power that now exists between different racial groups, and so make the community more equal overall. It is, as I said, controversial whether a preferential admissions program will in fact promote these various policies, but it cannot be said to be implausible that it will. The disadvantage to applicants such as DeFunis is, on that hypothesis, a cost that must be paid for a greater gain; it is in that way like the disadvantage to less intelligent students that is the cost of ordinary admissions policies.

We now see the difference between DeFunis's case and the case we imagined, in which a law school charged students selected at random higher fees. The special disadvantage to these students was not necessary to achieve the gain in scholarship funds, because the same gain would have been achieved by a more equal distribution of the cost amongst all the students who could afford it. That is not true of DeFunis. He did suffer from the Washington policy more than those majority applicants who were accepted. But that discrimination was not arbitrary; it was a consequence of the meritocratic standards he approves. DeFunis's argument therefore fails. The Equal Protection Clause gives constitutional standing to the right to be treated as an equal, but he cannot find, in that right, any support for his claim that the clause makes all racial classification illegal.

III

If we dismiss DeFunis's claim in this straightforward way, however, we are left with this puzzle. How can so many able lawyers, who supported his claim both in morality and law, have made that mistake? These lawyers all agree that intelligence is a proper criterion for admission to law schools. They do not suppose that anyone's constitutional right to be treated as an equal is compromised by that criterion. Why do they deny that race, in the circumstances of this decade, may also be a proper criterion?

They fear, perhaps, that racial criteria will be misused; that such criteria will serve as an excuse for prejudice against the minorities that are not favored, such as Jews. But that cannot explain their opposition. Any criteria may be misused, and in any case they think that racial criteria are wrong in principle and not simply open to abuse.

Why? The answer lies in their belief that, in theory as well as in practice, *DeFunis* and *Sweatt* must stand or fall together. They believe that it is illogical for liberals to condemn Texas for raising a color barrier against Sweatt, and then applaud Washington for raising a color barrier against DeFunis. The difference between these two cases, they suppose, must be only the subjective preference of liberals for certain minorities now in fashion. If there is something wrong with racial classifications, then it must be something that is wrong with racial classifications as such, not just classifications that work against those groups currently in favor. That is the inarticulate premise behind the slogan, relied on by defendants of DeFunis, that the Constitution is colorblind. That slogan means, of course, just the opposite of what it says: it means that the Constitution is so sensitive to color that it makes any institutional racial classification invalid as a matter of law.

It is of the greatest importance, therefore, to test the assumption that Sweatt and DeFunis must stand or fall together. If that assumption is sound, then the straightforward argument against DeFunis must be fallacious after all, for no argument could convince us that segregation of the sort practiced against Sweatt is justifiable or constitutional. Superficially, moreover, the arguments against DeFunis do indeed seem available against Sweatt, because we can construct an argument that Texas might have used to show that segregation benefits the collective welfare, so that the special disadvantage to blacks is a cost that must be paid to achieve an overall gain.

Suppose the Texas admissions committee, though composed of men and women who themselves held no prejudice, decided that the Texas economy demanded more white lawyers than they could educate, but could find no use for black lawyers at all. That might

have been, after all, a realistic assessment of the commercial market for lawyers in Texas just after World War II. Corporate law firms needed lawyers to serve booming business but could not afford to hire black lawyers, however skillful, because the firms' practices would be destroyed if they did. It was no doubt true that the black community in Texas had great need of skillful lawyers, and would have preferred to use black lawyers if they were available. But the committee might well have thought that the commercial needs of the state as a whole outweighed that special need.

Or suppose the committee judged, no doubt accurately, that alumni gifts to the law school would fall off drastically if it admitted a black student. The committee might deplore that fact, but nevertheless believe that the consequent collective damage would be greater than the damage to black candidates excluded by the racial restriction.

It may be said that these hypothetical arguments are disingenuous, because any policy of excluding blacks would in fact be supported by a prejudice against blacks as such, and arguments of the sort just described would be accepted by men who do not have the prejudices the objection assumes. It therefore does not follow from the fact that the admissions officers were prejudiced, if they were, then they would have rejected these arguments if they had not been.

In any case, arguments such as those I describe were in fact used by officials who might have been free from prejudice against those they excluded. Many decades ago, as the late Professor Bickel reminds us in his brief for the B'nai B'rith, President Lowell of Harvard University argued in favor of a quota limiting the number of Jews who might be accepted by his university. He said that if Jews were accepted in numbers larger than their proportion of the population, as they certainly would have been if intelligence were the only test, then Harvard would no longer be able to provide to the world men of the qualities and temperament it aimed to produce, men, that is, who were more well-rounded and less exclusively intellectual that Jews tended to be, and who, therefore, were better and more likely leaders of other men, both in and out of government. It was no doubt true, when Lowell spoke, that Jews were less likely to occupy important places in government or at the heads of large public companies. If Harvard wished to serve the general welfare by improving the intellectual qualities of the nation's leaders, it was rational not to allow its classes to be filled up with Jews. The men who reached that conclusion might well prefer the company of Jews to that of the Wasps who were more likely to become senators. Lowell suggested he did, though perhaps the responsibilities of his office prevented him from frequently indulging his preference.

It might now be said, however, that discrimination against blacks, even when it does serve some plausible policy, is nevertheless unjustified because it is invidious and insulting. The briefs opposing DeFunis make just that argument to distinguish his claim from Sweatt's. Because blacks were the victims of slavery and legal segregation, they say, any discrimination that excludes blacks will be taken as insulting by them, whatever arguments of general welfare might be made in its support. But it is not true, as a general matter, that any social policy is unjust if those whom it puts at a disadvantage feel insulted. Admission to law school by intelligence is not unjust because those who are less intelligent feel insulted by their exclusion. Everything depends upon whether the feeling of insult is produced by some more objective feature that would disqualify the policy even if the insult were not felt. If segregation does improve the general welfare, even when the disadvantage to blacks is fully taken into account, and if no other reason can be found why segregation is nevertheless unjustified, then the insult blacks feel, while understandable, must be based on misperception.

It would be wrong, in any case, to assume that men in the position of DeFunis will not take *their* exclusion to be insulting. They are very likely to think of themselves, not as members of some large majority group that is privileged overall, but as members of some other minority, such as Jews or Poles or Italians, whom comfortable and successful liberals are willing to sacrifice in order to delay more violent social change. If we wish to distinguish *DeFunis* from *Sweatt* on some argument that uses the concept of an insult, we must show that the treatment of the one, but not the other, is in fact unjust.

IV

So these familiar arguments that might distinguish the two cases are unconvincing. That seems to confirm that Sweatt and DeFunis must be treated alike,

and therefore that racial classification must be outlawed altogether. But fortunately a more successful ground of distinction can be found to support our initial sense that the cases are in fact very different. This distinction does not rely, as these unconvincing arguments do, on features peculiar to issues of race or segregation, or even on features peculiar to issues of educational opportunity. It relies instead on further analysis of the idea, which was central to my argument against DeFunis, that in certain circumstances a policy which puts many individuals at a disadvantage is nevertheless justified because it makes the community as a whole better off.

Any institution which uses that idea to justify a discriminatory policy faces a series of theoretical and practical difficulties. There are, in the first place, two distinct senses in which a community may be said to be better off as a whole, in spite of the fact that certain of its members are worse off, and any justification must specify which sense is meant. It may be better off in a *utilitarian* sense, that is, because the average or collective level of welfare in the community is improved even though the welfare of some individuals falls. Or it may be better off in an *ideal* sense, that is, because it is more just, or in some other way closer to an ideal society, whether or not average welfare is improved. The University of Washington might use either utilitarian or ideal arguments to justify its racial classification. It might argue, for example, that increasing the number of black lawyers reduces racial tensions, which improves the welfare of almost everyone in the community. That is a utilitarian argument. Or it might argue that, whatever effect minority preference will have on average welfare, it will make the community more equal and therefore more just. That is an ideal, not a utilitarian, argument.

The University of Texas, on the other hand, cannot make an ideal argument for segregation. It cannot claim that segregation makes the community more just whether it improves the average welfare or not. The arguments it makes to defend segregation must therefore all be utilitarian arguments. The arguments I invented, like the argument that white lawyers could do more than black lawyers to improve commercial efficiency in Texas, are utilitarian, since commercial efficiency makes the community better off only if it improves average welfare.

Utilitarian arguments encounter a special difficulty that ideal arguments do not. What is meant by
average or collective welfare? How can the welfare of
an individual be measured, even in principle, and
how can gains in the welfare of different individuals
be added and then compared with losses, so as to justify the claim that gains outweigh losses overall? The
utilitarian argument that segregation improves average welfare presupposes that such calculations can be
made. But how?

Jeremy Bentham, who believed that only utilitarian arguments could justify political decisions, gave
the following answer. He said that the effect of a policy on an individual's welfare could be determined by
discovering the amount of pleasure or pain the policy
brought him, and that effect of the policy on the collective welfare could be calculated by adding together
all the pleasure and subtracting all of the pain it
brought to everyone. But, as Bentham's critics
insisted, it is doubtful whether there exists a simple
psychological state of pleasure common to all those
who benefit from a policy or of pain common to all
those who lose by it; in any case it would be impossible to identify, measure, and add the different pleasures and pains felt by vast numbers of people.

Philosophers and economists who find utilitarian
arguments attractive, but who reject Bentham's psychological utilitarianism, propose a different concept
of individual and overall welfare. They suppose that
whenever an institution or an official must decide
upon a policy, the members of the community will
each prefer the consequences of one decision to the
consequences of others. DeFunis, for example, prefers
the consequences of the standard admissions policy to
the policy of minority preference Washington used,
while the blacks in some urban ghetto might each
prefer the consequences of the latter policy to the former. If it can be discovered what each individual
prefers, and how intensely, then it might be shown
that a particular policy would satisfy on balance more
preferences, taking into account their intensity, than
alternative policies. On this concept of welfare, a policy makes the community better off in a utilitarian
sense if it satisfies the collection of preferences better
than alternative policies would, even though it dissat-
isfies the preferences of some.

Of course, a law school does not have available
any means of making accurate judgments about the
preferences of all those whom its admissions policies
will affect. It may nevertheless make judgments
which, though speculative, cannot be dismissed as
implausible. It is, for example, plausible to think that
in postwar Texas, the preferences of the people were
overall in favor of the consequences of segregation in
law schools, even if the intensity of the competing
preference for integration, and not simply the number
of those holding that preference, is taken into
account. The officials of the Texas law school might
have relied upon voting behavior, newspaper editori-
als, and simply their own sense of their community in
reaching that decision. Though they might have been
wrong, we cannot now say, even with the benefit of
hindsight, that they were.

So even if Bentham's psychological utilitarianism
is rejected, law schools may appeal to preference utilitarianism to provide at least a rough and speculative
justification for admissions policies that put some
classes of applicants at a disadvantage. But once it is
made clear that these utilitarian arguments are based
on judgments about the actual preferences of members of the community, a fresh and much more serious
difficulty emerges.

The utilitarian argument, that a policy is justified
if it satisfies more preferences overall, seems at first
sight to be an egalitarian argument. It seems to
observe strict impartiality. If the community has only
enough medicine to treat some of those who are sick,
the argument seems to recommend that those who
are sickest be treated first. If the community can
afford a swimming pool or a new theater, but not
both, and more people want the pool, then it recommends that the community build the pool, unless
those who want the theater can show that their preferences are so much more intense that they have
more weight in spite of the numbers. One sick man is
not to be preferred to another because he is worthier
of official concern: the tastes of the theater audience
are not to be preferred because they are more
admirable. In Bentham's phrase, each man is to count
as one and no man is to count as more than one.

These simple examples suggest that the utilitarian argument not only respects, but embodies, the
right of each citizen to be treated as the equal of any
other. The chance that each individual's preferences
have to succeed, in the competition for social policy,
will depend upon how important his preference is to

him, and how many others share it, compared to the intensity and number of competing preferences. His chance will not be affected by the esteem or contempt of either officials or fellow citizens, and he will therefore not be subservient or beholden to them.

But if we examine the range of preferences that individuals in fact have, we shall see that the apparent egalitarian character of a utilitarian argument is often deceptive. Preference utilitarianism asks officials to attempt to satisfy people's preferences so far as this is possible. But the preferences of an individual for the consequences of a particular policy may be seen to reflect, on further analysis, either a *personal* preference for his own enjoyment of some goods or opportunities, or an *external* preference for the assignment of goods and opportunities to others, or both. A white law school candidate might have a personal preference for the consequences of segregation, for example, because the policy improves his own chances of success, or an external preference for those consequences because he has contempt for blacks and disapproves social situations in which the races mix.

The distinction between personal and external preferences is of great importance for this reason. If a utilitarian argument counts external preferences along with personal preferences, then the egalitarian character of that argument is corrupted, because the chance that anyone's preferences have to succeed will then depend, not only on the demands that the personal preferences of others make on scarce resources, but on the respect or affection they have for him or for his way of life. If external preferences tip the balance, then the fact that a policy makes the community better off in a utilitarian sense would *not* provide a justification compatible with the right of those it disadvantages to be treated as equals.

This corruption of utilitarianism is plain when some people have external preferences because they hold political theories that are themselves contrary to utilitarianism. Suppose many citizens, who are not themselves sick, are racists in political theory, and therefore prefer that scarce medicine be given to a white man who needs it rather than a black man who needs it more. If utilitarianism counts these political preferences at face value, then it will be, from the standpoint of personal preferences, self-defeating, because the distribution of medicine will

then not be, from that standpoint, utilitarian at all. In any case, self-defeating or not, the distribution will not be egalitarian in the sense defined. Blacks will suffer, to a degree that depends upon the strength of the racist preference, from the fact that others think them less worthy of respect and concern.

There is a similar corruption when the external preferences that are counted are altruistic or moralistic. Suppose many citizens, who themselves do not swim, prefer the pool to the theater because they approve of sports and admire athletes, or because they think that the theater is immoral and ought to be repressed. If the altruistic preferences are counted, so as to reinforce the personal preferences of swimmers, the result will be a form of double counting: each swimmer will have the benefit not only of his own preference, but also of the preference of someone else who takes pleasure in his success. If the moralistic preferences are counted, the effect will be the same: actors and audiences will suffer because their preferences are held in lower respect by citizens whose personal preferences are not themselves engaged.

In these examples, external preferences are independent of personal preferences. But of course political, altruistic, and moralistic preferences are often not independent, but grafted on to the personal preferences they reinforce. If I am white and sick, I may also hold a racist political theory. If I want a swimming pool for my own enjoyment I may also be altruistic in favor of my fellow athlete, or I may also think that the theater is immoral. The consequences of counting these external preferences will be as grave for equality as if they were independent of personal preference, because those against whom the external preferences run might be unable or unwilling to develop reciprocal external preferences that would right the balance.

External preferences therefore present a great difficulty for utilitarianism. That theory owes much of its popularity to the assumption that it embodies the right of citizens to be treated as equals. But if external preferences are counted in overall preferences, then this assumption is jeopardized. That is, in itself, an important and neglected point in political theory; it bears, for example, on the liberal thesis, first made prominent by Mill, that the government has no right to enforce popular morality by law. It is often said that this liberal thesis is inconsistent with utilitarianism, because if the preferences of the majority that homosexuality should be repressed, for example, are sufficiently strong, utilitarianism must give way to their wishes. But the preference against homosexuality is an external preference, and the present argument provides a general reason why utilitarians should not count external preferences of any form. If utilitarianism is suitably reconstituted so as to count only personal preferences, then the liberal thesis is a consequence, not an enemy, of that theory.

It is not always possible, however, to reconstitute a utilitarian argument so as to count only personal preferences. Sometimes personal and external preferences are so inextricably tied together, and so mutually dependent, that no practical test for measuring preferences will be able to discriminate the personal and external elements in any individual's overall preference. That is especially true when preferences are affected by prejudice. Consider, for example, the associational preference of a white law student for white classmates. This may be said to be a personal preference for an association with one kind of colleague rather than another. But it is a personal preference that is parasitic upon external preferences: except in very rare cases a white student prefers the company of other whites because he has racist social and political convictions, or because he has contempt for blacks as a group. If these associational preferences are counted in a utilitarian argument used to justify segregation, then the egalitarian character of the argument is destroyed just as if the underlying external preferences were counted directly. Blacks would be denied their right to be treated as equals because the chance that their preferences would prevail in the design of admissions policy would be crippled by the low esteem in which others hold them. In any community in which prejudice against a particular minority is strong, then the personal preferences upon which a utilitarian argument must fix will be saturated with that prejudice; it follows that in such a community no utilitarian argument purporting to justify a disadvantage to the minority can be fair.

This final difficulty is therefore fatal to Texas' utilitarian arguments in favor of segregation. The preferences that might support any such argument are either distinctly external, like the preferences of the community at large for racial separation, or are inextricably combined with and dependent upon external preferences, like the associational preferences of white students for white classmates and white lawyers for white colleagues. These external preferences are so widespread that they must corrupt any such argument. Texas' claim, that segregation makes the community better off in a utilitarian sense, is therefore incompatible with Sweatt's right to treatment as an equal guaranteed by the Equal Protection Clause.

It does not matter, to this conclusion, whether external preferences figure in the justification of a fundamental policy, or in the justification of derivative policies designed to advance a more fundamental policy. Suppose Texas justifies segregation by pointing to the apparently neutral economic policy of increasing community wealth, which satisfies the personal preferences of everyone for better homes, food, and recreation. If the argument that segregation will improve community wealth depends upon the fact of external preference; if the argument notices, for example, that because of prejudice industry will run more efficiently if factories are segregated; then the argument has the consequence that the black man's personal preferences are defeated by what others think of him. Utilitarian arguments that justify a disadvantage to members of a race against whom prejudice runs will always be unfair arguments, unless it can be shown that the same disadvantage would have been justified in the absence of the prejudice. If the prejudice is widespread and pervasive, as in fact it is in the case of blacks, that can never be shown. The preferences on which any economic argument justifying segregation must be based will be so intertwined with prejudice that they cannot be disentangled to the degree necessary to make any such contrary-to-fact hypothesis plausible.

We now have an explanation that shows why any form of segregation that disadvantages blacks is, in the United States, an automatic insult to them, and why such segregation offends their right to be treated as equals. The argument confirms our sense that utilitarian arguments purporting to justify segregation are not simply wrong in detail but displaced in principle. This objection to utilitarian arguments is not, however, limited to race or even prejudice. There are other cases in which counting external preferences would offend the rights of citizens to be treated as equals, and it is worth briefly noticing these, if only to protect the argument against the charge that it is constructed ad hoc for the racial case. I might have a moralistic preference against professional women, or an altruistic preference for virtuous men. It would be unfair for any law school to count preferences like these in deciding whom to admit to law schools; unfair because these preferences, like racial prejudices, make the success of the personal preferences of an applicant depend on the esteem and approval, rather than on the competing personal preferences, of others.

The same objection does not hold, however, against a utilitarian argument used to justify admission based on intelligence. That policy need not rely, directly or indirectly, on any community sense that intelligent lawyers are intrinsically more worthy of respect. It relies instead upon the law school's own judgment, right or wrong, that intelligent lawyers are more effective in satisfying personal preferences of others, such as the preference for wealth or winning law suits. It is true that law firms and clients prefer the services of intelligent lawyers; that fact might make us suspicious of any utilitarian argument that is said not to depend upon that preference, just as we are suspicious of any argument justifying segregation that is said not to depend on prejudice. But the widespread preference for intelligent lawyers is, by and large, not parasitic on external preferences: law firms and clients prefer intelligent lawyers because they also hold the opinion that such lawyers will be more effective in serving their personal preferences. Instrumental preferences, of that character, do not themselves figure in utilitarian arguments, though a law school may accept, on its own responsibility, the instrumental hypothesis upon which such preferences depend.

V

We therefore have the distinctions in hand necessary to distinguish *DeFunis* from *Sweatt*. The arguments for an admissions program that discriminates against blacks are all utilitarian arguments, and they are all utilitarian arguments that rely upon external preferences in such a way as to offend the constitutional right of blacks to be treated as equals. The arguments for an admissions program that discriminates in favor of blacks are both utilitarian and ideal. Some of the utilitarian arguments do rely, at least indirectly, on external preferences, such as the preference of certain blacks for lawyers of their own race; but the utilitarian arguments that do not rely on such preferences are strong and may be sufficient. The ideal arguments do not rely upon preferences at all, but on the independent argument that a more equal society is a better society even if its citizens prefer inequality. That argument does not deny anyone's right to be treated as an equal himself.

We are therefore left, in *DeFunis*, with the simple and straightforward argument with which we began. Racial criteria are not necessarily the right standards for deciding which applicants should be accepted by law schools. But neither are intellectual criteria, nor indeed, any other set of criteria. The fairness—and constitutionality—of any admissions program must be tested in the same way. It is justified if it serves a proper policy that respects the right of all members of the community to be treated as equals, but not otherwise. The criteria used by schools that refused to consider blacks failed that test, but the criteria used by the University of Washington Law School do not.

We are all rightly suspicious of racial classifications. They have been used to deny, rather than to respect, the right of equality, and we are all conscious of the consequent injustice. But if we misunderstand the nature of that injustice because we do not make the simple distinctions that are necessary to understand it, then we are in danger of more injustice still. It may be that preferential admissions programs will not, in fact, make a more equal society, because they may not have the effects their advocates believe they will. That strategic question should be at the center of debate about these programs. But we must not corrupt the debate by supposing that these programs are unfair even if they do work. We must take care not to use the Equal Protection Clause to cheat ourselves of equality.

ADDITIONAL READING

For contrasting legal views on affirmative action, see *City of Richmond v. J. A. Croson and Company*, Justice Sandra Day O'Connor writing in opposition to affirmative action and Justice Thurgood Marshall writing in support. A more recent case involving affirmative action is *Grutter v. Bollinger*, 2003. An excellent online source for Supreme Court cases is www.oyez.org.

Arguments in favor of affirmative action can be found in Bernard Boxill, *Blacks and Social Justice* (Totowa, N.J.: Rowman and Littlefield, 1984); Elizabeth Anderson, "Integration, Affirmative Action, and Strict Scrutiny," *NYU Law Review*, 77 (2002), 1,195–1,271; Gertrude Ezorsky, *Racism and Justice: The Case for Affirmative Action* (Ithaca, N.Y.: Cornell University Press, 1991); a particularly readable essay by Stanley Fish, "Reverse Racism, or How the Pot Got To Call the Kettle Black," *The Atlantic* (November 1993); Anne C. Minas, "How Reverse Discrimination Compensates Women," *Ethics*, 88 (1977); Cornel West, *Race Matters* (Boston: Beacon Press, 1993); and Diana Axelson, "With All Deliberate Delay: On Justifying Preferential Policies in Education and Employment," *Philosophical Forum* 9 (1977–1978), 264–288.

Opposing views are found in George Sher, "Reverse Discrimination, the Future, and the Past," *Ethics*, 90 (1979); Richard Posner, "The DeFunis Case and the Constitutionality of Preferential Treatment of Racial Minorities," in Gabriel Chin, editor, *Affirmative Action and the Constitution*, vol. 1 (New York: Garland, 1998); Shelby Steele, *The Content of our Character: A New Vision of Race in America* (New York: HarperPerennial, 1991); and Carl Cohen, *Naked Racial Preference* (Boston: Madison Books, 1995).

Some anthologies on the subject include W. T. Blackstone and R. Heslep, editors, *Social Justice and Preferential Treatment* (Athens: University of Georgia Press, 1976); Amy Gutmann and K. Anthony Appiah, *Color Conscious: The Political Morality of Race,* (Princeton, N.J.: Princeton University Press, 1996); Steven Cahn, editor, *Affirmative Action and the University* (Philadelphia: Temple University Press, 1993); and the particularly good collection edited by M. Cohen, T. Nagel, and T. Scanlon, *Equality and Preferential Treatment* (Princeton, N.J.: Princeton University Press, 1977).

A remarkably good online resource (provided by Elizabeth Anderson, University of Michigan) for examining the issue of affirmative action is: www-personal.umich.edu/~eandersn/biblio.htm. This site includes detailed descriptions of all the relevant literature, links to other sites, and a thorough and comprehensive review of all the important Supreme Court cases dealing with affirmative action.

CREDITS

✦ INDEX ✦